MANAGERIAL STATISTICS: A Unified Approach

CHRIS A. THEODORE
Boston University

Kent Publishing Company
Boston, Massachusetts
A Division of Wadsworth, Inc.

Kent Publishing Company
A Division of Wadsworth, Inc.

© 1982 by Wadsworth, Inc., Belmont, California 94002. All rights reserved. No part of this book may be reproduced, stored in a retrieval system, or transcribed, in any form, or by any means, electronic, mechanical, photocopying, recording, or otherwise, without the prior written permission of the publisher, Kent Publishing Company, Boston, Massachusetts 02116.

Printed in the United States of America

1 2 3 4 5 6 7 8 9 — 85 84 83 82 81

Library of Congress Cataloging in Publication Data

Theodore, Chris Athanasios.
   Managerial statistics.

   Bibliography: p.
   Includes index.
   1. Statistics. I. Title.
QA276.12.T48   519.5   81-14321
ISBN 0-534-01093-8   AACR2

**TO
ARTHUR,
SUZANNE,
AND
STUART**

CONTENTS

Preface		vii
INTRODUCTION		x
Chapter 1	**POPULATIONS AND DESCRIPTIVE STATISTICS**	**1**
	1 Populations and Frequency Distributions	2
	2 Summary Measures of Concentration	16
	3 Summary Measures of Dispersion	29
Chapter 2	**PROBABILITY CONCEPTS AND TOOLS**	**43**
	4 Sample Spaces and Events	43
	5 The Probability of an Event: The Addition Rule	54
	6 Probabilities: The Multiplication Rule	63
	7 Counting Techniques	74
Chapter 3	**PROBABILITY DISTRIBUTIONS: BINOMIAL AND POISSON DISTRIBUTIONS**	**83**
	8 Probability Distributions: Summary Measures	84
	9 The Binomial Distribution	94
	10 The Poisson Distribution	103
Chapter 4	**STATISTICAL INFERENCE: BASIC CONCEPTS AND TOOLS**	**113**
	11 Sampling Versus a Census	113
	12 Sampling Distributions	127
	13 The Normal Distribution	139

Chapter 5 SAMPLE DESIGN AND ESTIMATION **155**

    14 Sample Design 155
    15 Sample Selection: Estimating a Mean 170
    16 Estimating a Proportion 180

Chapter 6 HYPOTHESIS TESTING **189**

    17 Testing a Single Parameter 189
    18 Testing the Difference of Two Parameters 209

Chapter 7 CHI-SQUARE TESTS AND ANALYSIS OF VARIANCE **227**

    19 Chi-Square Tests 227
    20 Analysis of Variance 243

Chapter 8 REGRESSION AND CORRELATION ANALYSIS **257**

    21 Introduction to Regression and Correlation 258
    22 Simple Regression and Correlation 279
    23 Multiple Regression and Correlation 297

Chapter 9 NONPARAMETRIC STATISTICS **325**

    24 Rank-Sum Test for Two Independent Samples 327
    25 Signed-Rank Test for Matched Samples 332
    26 One-Factor Analysis of Variance by Ranks 338
    27 Rank Correlation 342

Chapter 10 TIME SERIES ANALYSIS AND INDEX NUMBERS **349**

    28 Secular Trend and Cyclical Fluctuations 352
    29 Seasonal Variations 373
    30 Index Numbers 389

Chapter 11 DECISION ANALYSIS **409**

    31 Basic Concepts 409
    32 Decision Tree Analysis 422
    33 The Value of Additional Information 436

SELECTED BIBLIOGRAPHY 448

APPENDIXES: STATISTICAL TABLES 451

A	2500 Random Digits	453
B	Cumulative Probabilities of the Binomial Distribution	454
C	Cumulative Probabilities of the Poisson Distribution	462
D	Areas for Standard Normal Distribution	466
E	t Distribution	467
F	Percent of Error e for a Given Statistic p and Sample Size n with 95 Percent Confidence	468
G	Chi-Square Distribution	469
H	F Distribution	470
I	Four-Place Common Logarithms	473

ANSWERS TO PROBLEMS MARKED WITH AN ASTERISK 477

INDEX 491

PREFACE

This volume introduces applied statistics from conceptual, pedagogical, and organizational viewpoints. A unified approach is followed in initiating the student to fundamental statistical concepts, models, and tools. Applications of these techniques are drawn from a wide range of real-world situations designed to serve the needs of students in management, education, and the sciences. The book lays the foundation for further work in statistics as well as for the effective use of statistics in quantitatively oriented courses of other disciplines. Organization of subject matter in small educational modules facilitates learning and allows flexibility in planning a course. No less important, the text does not require more than high school algebra.

What should be the character of a work in introductory statistics which systematically implements this unified approach and at the same time is an effective pedagogical instrument? This dual purpose guided me in designing and writing this volume.

The course begins with a brief introduction to frequency distributions and descriptive measures. This topic is followed by the elements of probability beginning with sample spaces, events, and probability rules. Discrete random variables, expected value and variance, and probability distributions are a logical sequence. This part of the course on probability performs two principal functions: it teaches the student to think probabilistically, and it lays the foundation for introducing statistical inference and decision theory.

Such an approach is a deliberate attempt to build conceptual and logical continuity. For example, formation of sampling distributions is closely related with sample spaces. Sampling from infinite and finite populations are systematically related to sampling with and without replacement. Treatment of the binomial and Poisson distributions, as models describing natural processes, paves the way for a better understanding of the normal distribution, as models describing sampling distributions. Decision trees are shown as logical extensions of tree diagrams. The contrast between objective and subjective interpretation of probability and the expected value as a decision criterion are better understood in the light of earlier topics on probability rules and expected value of a random variable.

This unified approach is reinforced with a rational sequence of subject matter. A few examples will illustrate this point. Mixing theory and applications, particularly in statistical inference, has been avoided as much as possible. Students are first introduced to the basic concepts which set the nature of the problem for collecting sample information. Next, they are exposed to the properties of sampling distributions and the normal distribution. Application of the theory follows the procedure of a practicing statistician: that is, sample design and selection *before* estimation and significance tests. Tools are introduced in a sequence which I have found pedagogically most effective. For example, estimation is discussed *before* tests of significance; this sequence is reversed in regression and correlation analysis; the normal distribution is introduced in a manner so that students do not get the false impression that the normal distribution is applicable exclusively to sampling distributions; Bayes's theorem appears as part of decision analysis rather than of probability laws.

These conceptual and topical arrangements are reflected in a new organizational format. The subject matter is presented in small learning modules, each treating a closely related set of concepts or a single model or method. Whenever possible, a motivating application of a technique to a real-world situation is an integral part of the text. Computational procedures in the text are deemphasized, as are problems requiring excessive calculations. The ubiquitous presence of pocket calculators made it unnecessary to include shortcut formulas for calculating summary measures such as the mean and standard deviation. Furthermore, the wide availability of computer programs is explicitly recognized: in addition to the traditional approach, students have the option to study regression and correlation analysis with computer printouts. Key formulas are boxed.

The problems of each module are stratified in three groups. The first consists principally of simple computational or conceptual exercises and problems designed to reinforce the student's comprehension of textual material. Most problems in the second group are designed to challenge the student's ability to apply the acquired knowledge to realistic situations similar to those illustrated in the text. For most sections a third group of problems is included in the Solutions Manual. This group contains horizon-expanding problems or minicases taken from journal articles or other published sources. Such problems further illustrate either successful or inappropriate applications of statistics to real-world situations.

The modular organization of subject matter allows for great flexibility in planning a course. Selective inclusion of modules may depend on the level of instruction as well as on the duration of a course or courses. First-group problems may be used as a study guide. Furthermore, the level of instruction may also be varied with the exclusion or inclusion of horizon-expanding problems and minicases from the Solutions Manual. Answers to most first-group and many second-group problems of each module are appended. The Manual contains detailed solutions to all problems.

Many individuals have contributed to the preparation of this volume. I am indebted to my present and former colleagues Paul D. Berger, John Buoncristiani, Joseph D. Blackburn, Stavros Frantzis, Samuel C. Hanna, Jerome D. Herniter, Greta Ljung, Donald G. McBrien, James P. Monahan, and Joseph Pliskin, for the valuable pedagogical and technical suggestions on portions or the whole manuscript; to the administration of our School of Management for encouragement and generous help; and to the following reviewers for their constructive criticism: Warren J. Boe, University of Iowa; Terry Dielman, Texas Christian University;

Preface

Allen D. Kartchner, Utah State University; Kathy Lewis-Corriher; Dennis W. McLeavey, University of Rhode Island; Richard L. Mills, University of New Hampshire; J. Burdeane Orris, Butler University; Lawrence E. Scheuerman, Nicholls State University; Panagiotis G. Stergianopoulos, Central Connecticut State College; and Richard Swanson, Bentley College. No less indebted am I to my graduate assistants Philip Atwood, Ann Connelly, Stephen J. Galiani, Will Keenan, Suzanne Knight, and Elizabeth S. Kurten for their help in editing and checking the computations of the text and of the Manual; and to Mary A. Byron, Kathy Collins, and Valerie A. Fenwick for their typing.

I am also grateful to the Literary Executor of the late Sir Ronald A. Fisher, F.R.S., to Dr. Frank Yates, F.R.S., and to Oliver & Boyd Ltd., Edinburgh, for permission to reprint Tables III and IV from their book *Statistical Tables for Biological, Agricultural, and Medical Research;* and to Holden-Day, Inc., for permission to use *Statistics: A Guide to the Unknown,* by editors J. M. Tanur, F. Mosteller, W. H. Kruskal, R. F. Link, R. S. Pieters, and G. R. Rising as the principal source for inspiring a considerable number of minicases. My indebtedness is also extended to other authors and publishers who generously granted permission to reprint tables or abridged versions of tables from their publications. Their permission is explicitly acknowledged at appropriate places.

Chris A. Theodore

INTRODUCTION

What Is Statistics?

The word *statistics* usually means numerical data. In this sense, statistics can represent information about any real-world situation or activity. For example, economic statistics are data on employment, production, earnings, prices, sales, and similar activities. Actuarial statistics consists of insurance claims for illness and death, automobile accidents, fire, theft, and other insurable risks. Social statistics include data on education, welfare, delinquency, crime, prisons, drug addiction, and the like. The list is long. An outstanding collection of statistics is in the *Statistical Abstract of the United States,* published annually by the U.S. Department of Commerce, Bureau of the Census.

In addition to numerical data, the word *statistics* has another, more specialized meaning. It refers to a subject, just as mathematics refers to a subject as well as to symbols, formulas, and theorems. That subject is a *collection of methods for gathering, analyzing, and drawing conclusions from data*. Recent developments in statistics place increasing emphasis on the use of statistical methods for decision making. In this respect, some statisticians prefer to recognize the subject of statistics as a *body of theory and methods which helps us make wise decisions under conditions of uncertainty*. It is in this sense that the term *statistics* is used in this book.

The Importance of Statistics

The subject of statistics pervades a wide variety of human activities. In the physical as well as social sciences, statistical applications range from the design of surveys and experiments to sophisticated techniques of data analysis and testing. Business and industry are engaged in the collection and publication of statistical information; statistical methods are also used extensively for planning and controlling operations and for decision making. Statistical applications include a wide range of activities: many manufacturers, for example, employ statistical methods for quality control and reliability testing of products and processes; a variety of firms rely on statistical techniques to conduct experiments, survey consumer plans, and forecast economic trends at the company, industry, and national levels.

The federal government and, to a lesser degree, state and local governments are large producers and users of statistical information. Some of the most massive undertakings such as the population census, the census of manufacturers, and the construction of economic indicators might not have been possible without federal financing. The same undertakings contributed greatly to the refinement of old and the development of new statistical methods. Both data and methods are being used increasingly for forecasting and for formulation of national objectives and policies.

Since World War II, the advent of electronic computers has given great impetus to the subject of statistics in at least two respects. First, existing statistical methods are being used more frequently and with increasing sophistication in practically every major field of human endeavor. Second, statistics either have

Introduction

provided the basis for or have stimulated the development of a new body of quantitative procedures and techniques for decision making. Part of this new body of tools has been the systematic employment of mathematical models as an approach to solving complex problems. These models consist of formulas or equations which express significant relationships among key variables relevant to the problem under study. Both developments have aided and improved decision making in the private as well as the public sector of our economy.

Thus, statistics is a nearly universally applied subject. And knowing the statistics in this book may well do more than improve our occupational performance. We may be able to evaluate better the findings of statistical investigations on such matters as product safety, health, and the environment. Learning proper applications as well as the limitations of statistical methods may help us become wiser citizens in an increasingly complex world.

Focus of Our Course

We begin with so-called *descriptive statistics;* the subject deals chiefly with summary calculations such as averages and with graphical displays. Consider, for example, a market feasibility study for building a shopping center. Our study may include several descriptive measures such as the average income and size of households which the shopping center may serve and the proportion of households owning a home or at least one automobile. Also, we may prepare graphs showing how households are distributed with respect to income, number of children, travel time to the shopping center, and other characteristics.

Would the use of descriptive statistics serve our market study adequately? Highly unlikely. Information about the thousands of potential customers may not be available. If available, the data may not be up to date or sufficiently detailed to serve our needs. In this as well as in many other statistical investigations, we must collect the data ourselves. In our case we must conduct a household survey. For economic and other reasons, to be explained later, we do not collect data from the thousands of households which represent the *statistical population* of our study. We may collect data only from a few hundred households which are called a *sample*. Therefore, at least part of our descriptive measures would be based on sample data. Our principal interest would be to use the sample measures in order to estimate the corresponding unknown population measures. For example, we may use the sample average income or the sample proportion of home-owning households to estimate the corresponding population average or proportion. Furthermore, we may need to *test* a number of assumptions about unknown population characteristics. We may test the assumption that the population average income is at least $15,000 on the basis of the sample average. Or we may use the sample proportion to test the assumption that no more than 50 percent of the household population has both parents working. Such estimation and testing procedures are basic methods of an important field of statistics called *statistical inference*.

The fact is that we need to know more than descriptive statistics in order to make full and reliable use of descriptive techniques; we must know the basics of statistical inference and the related elements of probability theory, a branch of mathematics. This is a very important point. The need to draw conclusions from

Introduction

descriptive sample measures may still be present even if our feasibility study for a shopping center were based entirely on published statistical data; in a majority of cases, published data from private as well as from public sources are likely to be obtained with sampling. In such an event, we would be unable to evaluate the reliability of sample data unless we know the basics of theory and practice related to sampling methods. Furthermore, failure to recognize that most available information is obtained from samples also carries a potential misinterpretation about the nature of statistical data; we may acquire a false sense of certainty about data which may be subject to variation because samples usually represent a small fraction of the parent population.

Therefore, after a brief introduction to descriptive statistics and elements of probability, we will devote considerable space to statistical inference. These subjects are followed with special topics. Some of these topics are extensions of the concepts and applications of the basic estimation and testing procedures of statistical inference and some are not. The last chapter of this volume covers a relatively new field of statistics called *statistical decision theory*. Essentially, decision making is central in the sense that this subject provides for a systematic and rational selection among uncertain consequences.

Chapter 1
POPULATIONS AND DESCRIPTIVE STATISTICS

In statistics, the term *population* has a special meaning. It refers to the *totality of observations of a specified characteristic we wish to study*. For example, if we are interested in the overtime work (characteristic) of production workers in a factory, then weekly overtime hours (observation) of all the workers may be our statistical population. In studying the profitability (charactertistic) of firms in a given industry, our statistical population may be the quarterly dollar profits (observation) of all the firms. In marketing a product, if the sex (characteristic) of potential consumers is important, then a male-female classification (observation) of all potential consumers is our statistical population. Since a statistical population includes the totality of observations in a given study, it is also called a *statistical universe*.

Although statistics deals primarily with decision making based on samples, we devote this chapter to statistical populations for a number of reasons. Populations rather than sample information focus our attention on planning our investigation systematically. We concentrate on whether or not we need such information rather than on the method used for gathering information. Failure to clearly define the scope of our investigation may lead to collecting data which might prove to be useless. Excluding treatment of sample data at this point is of no significance because descriptive techniques are equally applicable to populations as well as to samples. On the other hand, different symbols and other reasons justify introduction of required descriptive measures of sample data at the time we need such measures. Furthermore, this arrangement is consistent with the procedural steps which one may follow in carrying out a statistical investigation.

In this chapter, we deal with *cross-sectional* data, where observations are recorded at one point of time. For example, we may wish to know how production workers vary with respect to overtime work, or firms with respect to profits, or consumers with respect to food expenditures during a given time period. In Section 1 we show how to organize data into classes or frequency distributions and how to present the result graphically. In Section 2, we deal with averages or summary measures of concentration. Section 3 covers summary measures of dispersion which show the spread of data about an average. Frequency distributions and summary measures are two branches of descriptive statistics.

SECTION 1/ POPULATIONS AND FREQUENCY DISTRIBUTIONS

Our first task is to study the nature of statistical populations. The crucial question is: How can a statistical population be summarized and displayed graphically so it can reveal important patterns of variation? To this end, we show how a population may be organized into classes or groups called a *frequency distribution.* This is a table showing the number of observations which fall in each class or group. Then we focus on guidelines for constructing frequency distributions, their graphic display, and some special types of frequency distributions.

Statistical Populations

At the outset, it may be important to distinguish between observations of a characteristic and what may be called *elementary units* from which such observations can be obtained. For example, one problem may involve observations about the quality of a shipment of light bulbs. Whether a light bulb is good or defective is an observation of the characteristic quality. The collection of observations about all the bulbs in the shipment is a statistical population; the light bulbs themselves are referred to as the elementary units of the population.

Many studies, such as the light bulb shipment, may require analysis of a single statistical population. Single-characteristic studies present relatively simple yet realistic situations. They arise frequently in practice. In order to facilitate illustration of statistical techniques we shall usually limit our discussion to a single statistical population, remembering that the same techniques are applicable to multicharacteristic studies. The latter require analysis of several statistical populations observed from the same elementary units.

Example 1.1

Suppose we want to study the economic feasibility of building a shopping center. As part of the study, we may wish to obtain information about several characteristics of the thousands of households to be served by the center. From the same households, we can obtain an endless variety of statistical populations, one for each characteristic we wish to study. This procedure is illustrated in Fig. 1.1.

We have obtained a different statistical population for the size, sex of household head, and weekly earnings from the same elementary units, the households. Additional populations may be obtained for other household characteristics such as expenditures on food and other necessities, car ownership, home ownership, frequency of shopping, and many others which we think are relevant to the objectives of our study.

Statistical investigations may deal with very large populations. Bank deposits, company accounts, insurance policies of a firm, shipments of industrial parts,

Figure 1.1.
Obtaining several statistical populations from the same elementary units of households.

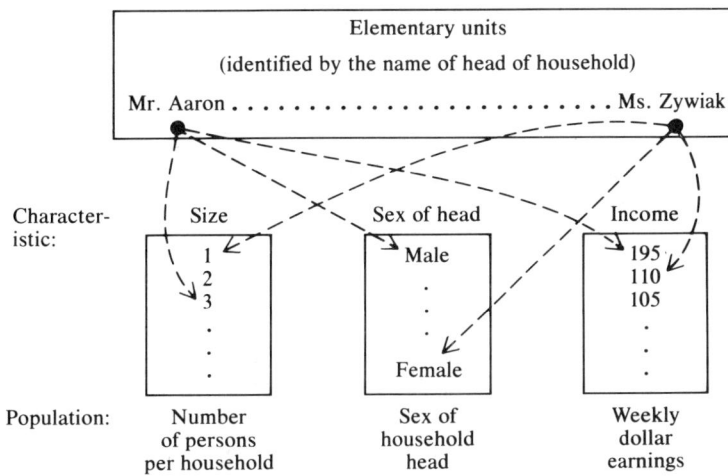

planted wheat acreage in a state, fish in a lake, residents of an area, employees of an organization, as well as any other collection of elementary units may generate one or more statistical populations. Depending on the nature and scope of our study, statistical populations may be *finite,* ranging from a few hundred to millions of observations, or *infinite,* that is, countless. In this connection, there is frequently no need to distinguish between the elementary units of a universe and the population of observations obtained from these units. In other words, it is frequently convenient to think of a population as the complete set of elementary units.

Example 1.2

One thousand Nerclo fasteners are shipped to a wholesaler of medical equipment. According to contract specifications, the lot shipment should contain no more than 5 percent defective fasteners. From the viewpoint of the wholesaler the statistical population is finite, consisting of the units in the shipped lot. From the viewpoint of the manufacturer—the lot producer—the population is infinite, consisting of all the Nerclo units the manufacturing process may produce. Both parties are interested in the same characteristic, namely product quality, and the same observation, namely the proportion of defective units. However, the wholesaler is concerned with the *proportion* of defective units *in the lot,* while the manufacturer is interested in the *proportion* of defective units from the *production process.*

The observations of a characteristic can be divided into two major classes: quantitative and qualitative. A *quantitative* population consists of observations which can be expressed numerically as height, weight, cost, income, etc. The values such as inches, pounds, and dollars which the observations may assume are called *numerical variables.*

Example 1.3

Table 1.1 shows a sample of elementary units whose characteristics can be expressed quantitatively. Note that the value of each numerical variable is a quantity such as hours, dollars, persons.

Table 1.1.
Illustration of Observations Representing Quantitative Populations

Elementary Unit	Characteristic of Interest	Unit of Numerical Variable
Household	Size	Persons
Worker	Weekly earnings	Dollars
Automobile	Weight	Pounds
Nerclo fasteners	Diameter	Millimeters
Battery	Lifetime	Hours
House	Age	Years
Farm	Size	Acres

A *qualitative* population, on the other hand, consists of observations which are expressed in nonnumerical terms or in terms of a qualitative aspect of their elementary units such as sex, marital status, product quality, etc. Terms such as *male–female* or *single–married* which may describe an elementary unit's characteristic are referred to as *attributes* or *categorical variables*.

Example 1.4

A sample of elementary units whose characteristics are expressed qualitatively is shown in Table 1.2. Note that, depending on the characteristic and other considerations, an elementary unit may be classified into more than two categories.

Table 1.2.
Illustration of Observations Representing Qualitative Populations

Elementary Unit	Characteristic of Interest	Attribute or Categorical Variable
Consumer	Marital status	Single, married, divorced, widowed
Light bulb	Quality	Good, defective
Household	Sex of head	Male, female
Firm	Legal status	Proprietorship, partnership, corporation
Apartment	Availability	Occupied, vacant
Employee	Opinion	Favorable, unfavorable, uncommitted
Legislator	Membership	Senate, House

In this chapter, we concentrate on quantitative populations for two major reasons. First, arithmetic operations can be performed on numerical variables. For example, we can calculate the average income of households in a study. Second, although other procedures must be employed for a qualitative population, categorical variables can always be encoded into numerical variables. For example, defective light bulbs can be denoted by 0 and nondefective ones by 1.

A numerical variable may be *discrete* or *continuous*. Definitionally, observations are considered discrete if their values change in jumps or steps. For example, daily finished output of an automobile assembly plant represents a discrete variable. Such an output must be reported in whole units, say 575 or 576 automobiles, but nothing in between these two integers.

By contrast, numerical variables are considered to be continuous if between any pair of measurements there is always the possibility of obtaining another, finer measurement. Time, for example, can be considered to be a continuous var-

Section 1 Populations and Frequency Distributions

iable since, at least in theory, time measurements can be infinitesimally small. So it is with weight and length. For most practical purposes, it is better to consider discreteness as a matter of degree; it depends on the precision of the measuring instrument as well as on the desired accuracy and nature of a statistical investigation. In statistical theory, on the other hand, the assumption is often made that a real-world discrete random variable is continuous in order to facilitate mathematical operations.

In sum, we have learned the following major points about statistical populations:

1. A statistical population is defined if we specify:
    a. A collection of elementary units;
    b. A characteristic of these units; and
    c. An appropriate numerical or categorical variable.
2. Depending on the nature and scope of a statistical investigation:
    a. We may consider a statistical population to be finite or infinite.
    b. We can specify several statistical populations from the same collection of elementary units where some populations represent numerical and others categorical variables.

Constructing a Frequency Distribution

As mentioned earlier, frequency distributions are one of the two important branches of descriptive statistics. Summarizing data into a frequency distribution is necessary because a statistical population is likely to consist of a long list of unorganized individual observations. Besides, frequency distributions form the basis of data analysis and facilitate the calculation of summary measures.

Example 1.5

The comptroller of Maloof Corporation, a small manufacturing firm, wishes to analyze the hourly wages of the 50 production workers in the plant. The individual values of the relevant statistical population are listed in Table 1.3.

The values in this table are referred to as *raw data* because they have not been organized or summarized. The size of the population is kept small for convenience. In reality, we are confronted with a large mass of raw data. How do we make sense out of this data base? We may be able to discover patterns in the variation

Table 1.3. Hourly Wages of 50 Production Workers of Maloof Corporation (Dollars)

5.10	5.65	6.55	7.60	8.20
7.90	6.25	5.75	7.75	5.60
6.25	5.25	5.40	5.60	5.75
5.20	5.60	5.80	7.15	7.65
7.30	5.85	5.25	8.95	6.40
6.80	6.25	7.10	6.55	5.40
6.45	5.95	6.75	7.20	6.20
5.80	5.75	5.75	5.75	5.65
6.95	6.10	6.30	7.25	6.10
5.50	8.25	6.70	6.60	6.35

Chapter 1 Populations and Descriptive Statistics

of the data if we construct a frequency distribution. As already explained, this is a table showing the number of observations which fall in each group or class of the data base. So let us see how we can construct such a frequency distribution.

Example 1.5 (continued)

We may group the raw data of Table 1.3 into eight classes, each 50¢ wide, beginning with $5.00 and ending with $9.00 hourly wages. (How we determine the number of classes and the width of each class will be discussed later.) Thus each hourly wage will fall into one of the classes $5.00 and under $5.50, $5.50 and under $6.00, etc. The eight classes are listed in increasing sequence in the first column of Table 1.4. Going down the list of the raw data, we place a tally mark next to the class within which each hourly wage falls. Also, we place a check mark next to the hourly wage in the list of the raw data which has been tallied in order to avoid double-counting. After the tally is completed, we determine the number of observations falling into each class by counting the tally marks and record each number under the last column of the table. The final result is a distribution showing the frequency with which hourly wages occur in each class of the data.

Table 1.4. Frequency Distribution of Hourly Wages for 50 Production Workers of Maloof Corporation

Hourly Wage (Dollars)	Tally	Workers (Number)
5.00 and under 5.50	⊞ /	6
5.50 and under 6.00	⊞ ⊞ ⊞	15
6.00 and under 6.50	⊞ ⊞	10
6.50 and under 7.00	⊞ //	7
7.00 and under 7.50	⊞	5
7.50 and under 8.00	////	4
8.00 and under 8.50	//	2
8.50 and under 9.00	/	1
		Total: 50

A frequency distribution reveals a pattern of data concentration and spread which are not discernible from the raw data. For example, from the distribution in Table 1.4, we are able to see at a glance how the data are clustered. The largest single group of production workers, 15 out of 50 or 30 percent, earns from $5.50 to under $6.00 per hour. Nearly two-thirds of the workers (31 out of 50) earn from $5.00 to under $6.50 per hour. Also, we can readily determine how the observations are spread. The range of hourly wages, the difference between the largest and the smallest values, is $4.00 = $9.00 − $5.00. But frequencies are not clustered around the middle of this range; they cluster near the lower one-third of the range. Furthermore, frequencies rise abruptly before and fall slowly after this clustering point.

Note that a frequency distribution can also be viewed as a grouping of the elementary units into classes of the numerical variable. The production workers, in our illustration, have been grouped into classes of hourly wages, referred to as *class intervals*. The values of the numerical variable which define the end points of each class interval are called *class limits*. The *width* of each class interval is the difference between the lower limits of two successive intervals. For example, the width of each class interval in Table 1.4 is $5.50 − $5.00 or 50¢.

A Few Guidelines for Constructing Frequency Distributions

We have shown that the raw data of a statistical population may concentrate within a segment of the data range. Furthermore, gaps may be present in which relatively few or no observations are available. And worse than this, there may be very few extremely large or extremely small values of the quantitative variable. Such irregularities are frequently present in a statistical population. How do we cope with such a data base? Although construction of a frequency distribution is largely a matter of good judgment, a number of guidelines may help us create order out of a confusing data base.

The *first* important difficulty focuses on the number and width of class intervals. Of course, class intervals with the same width are desirable because they facilitate comparison between classes. And they aid in the calculation of summary measures. If the data are suitable for constructing classes with the same width, one rule that may help us determine the width of class interval is

(1.1) $$\text{Interval width} = \frac{\text{largest value} - \text{smallest value}}{\text{number of class intervals}}$$

Example 1.6

In constructing a frequency distribution from the raw data in Table 1.3, we arbitrarily set eight equal class intervals. In fact, the largest and the smallest hourly wages of Maloof's production workers are $8.95 and $5.10, so by formula (1.1) the interval width is

$$\frac{\$8.95 - \$5.10}{8} \simeq \$.48*$$

In order to make our task easier, however, we used a width of 50¢ starting with $5.00 instead of $5.10 as the lower limit of the first class interval. The result is shown in Table 1.4.

The number and width of class intervals raise three major points:

1. There is no established rule indicating how many class intervals should be used. In practice, frequency distributions are constructed which contain as few as 5 to as many as 20 classes. Within this range, we want to construct a distribution with a relatively smooth change of class frequencies that will reveal an overall pattern of data variation. Having too many classes will unduly reduce the width of each class; the reverse is true with too few classes. For example, constructing a frequency distribution from the data in Table 1.3 using 4 or 16 equal class intervals may obscure any general pattern which the data may contain.

2. Widely spread data may require construction of a frequency distribution

*The symbol $\simeq$ means approximately equal to.

with unequal class intervals. Suppose the raw data in Table 1.3 contain also the following hourly wages: $9.60, $9.70, and $10.25. Their inclusion would require three additional equal class intervals: $9.00 and under $9.50, $9.50 and under $10.00, $10.00 and under $10.50, with zero, two, and one observations, respectively. One way of coping with this data irregularity is to widen the last class interval in Table 1.4 to $8.50 and under $10.50. Note that the width of this new class is a multiple of four units width of 50¢. This allows conversion of absolute frequencies in *frequencies per unit width*. The frequency per unit width is 4/4 or 1 since the new class contains four observations and four units width.

3. Unequal class intervals may not be a satisfactory solution to raw data containing extremely large or small values. Consider the construction of a distribution of households in the United States by annual income. Unequal class intervals may summarize most of the data range. The top group of households may require an *open-ended* class interval, that is, a class which specifies only the lower class limit. For example, the class interval may be stated as $100,000 or more. Sometimes the confidentiality of extreme values may require an open-ended class interval. For example, stating that the two largest firms have an inventory value of $10 million and under $11 million may be too revealing since it is likely to be known which firms are the largest in the industry. Confidentiality may be retained by stating an open-ended class interval of $10 million or more. Extremely small inventories, on the other hand, may require an open-ended class interval for the smallest firms.

The *second* important difficulty in constructing a frequency distribution relates to the sacrifice of detailed information. In computing certain statistical measures from a frequency distribution, the midpoint of each class interval, that is, the value located halfway between the two class limits, is assumed to represent the average value of the observations in that class. Therefore, special effort should be made to construct intervals with midpoints representing as close as possible the true class average. To the extent to which this is not achieved, detailed information is sacrificed for the sake of showing a general pattern of data variation.

Closely related to the above difficulty is the determination of class limits. Class intervals should always be mutually exclusive so that each observation falls into one and only one class. For example, if we state the class intervals in Table 1.4 as $5.00–$5.50, $5.50–$6.00, etc., it is not clear whether a wage of $5.50 falls into the first or the second class. On the other hand, the class intervals $5.00 and under $5.50, $5.50 and under $6.00, etc. leave no doubt that $5.50 falls into the second class. And the *midpoint* of each class interval is the average of the two lower limits of two successive class intervals. For example, the midpoint of class $5.00 and under $5.50 is ($5.00 + $5.50)/2 = $5.25.

In general, for achieving meaningful results, we must strike a balance between the number of class intervals, their width, and the clustering of observations at midpoints. Constructing several distributions with different numbers of classes, of unequal size if necessary, from the same data may prove to be a rewarding task. Comparing results, especially with graphs, we may be able to choose a distribution which we consider most suitable for statistical analysis.

Section 1 Populations and Frequency Distributions

Graphic Displays of Frequency Distributions

Graphs are effective ways of displaying the general pattern of data variation in a frequency distribution.

One method is to represent each class of a distribution with a rectangle or bar whose height corresponds to the frequency of the class. Such a graph is called a *histogram*.

Example 1.7

A histogram for the frequency distribution from Table 1.4 is shown in Fig. 1.2. Hourly wages are represented on the horizontal scale in terms of class intervals. The vertical axis represents the frequencies of the distribution. Since six workers earn $5.00 and under $5.50 per hour, the height of the first bar is 6. The bars touch in order to emphasize continuity on the horizontal scale.

Figure 1.2.
Histogram for the distribution of hourly wages for 50 production workers of Maloof Corporation.

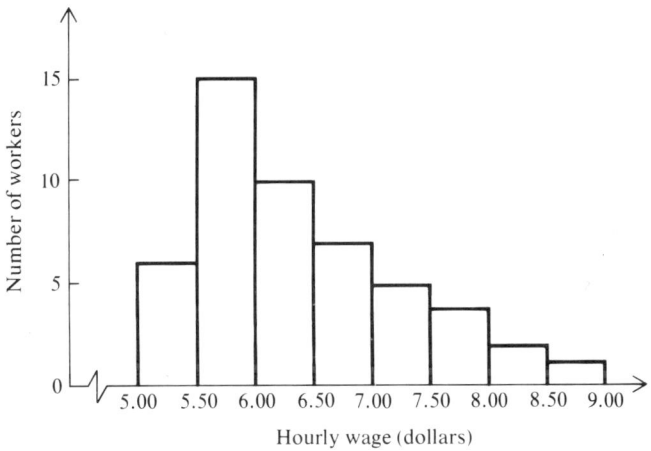

Displaying a frequency distribution of unequal class intervals with a histogram requires special care for classes larger than unit width. Earlier, we considered a modified frequency distribution of the distribution shown in Table 1.4 where the highest class interval was $8.50 and under $10.50. Since this class includes a multiple of four units width of 50¢, we converted the absolute frequencies into one frequency per unit width. We can display this change in the histogram in Fig. 1.2 by increasing the width of the rightmost bar 4 times while keeping its height unchanged. Thus, the area under the rightmost bar, its height (1) times the number of units of width (4), equals the total frequency (4) in the class interval. The result is that the *area* under *any* bar represents the frequency in each class interval.

An alternative method for portraying a frequency distribution graphically is the *frequency polygon*.

Example 1.8

A frequency polygon for the same frequency distribution from Table 1.4 is shown in Fig. 1.3. Note that the polygon is superimposed on the histogram

Figure 1.3.
Frequency polygon for the distribution of hourly wages for 50 production workers of Maloof Corporation.

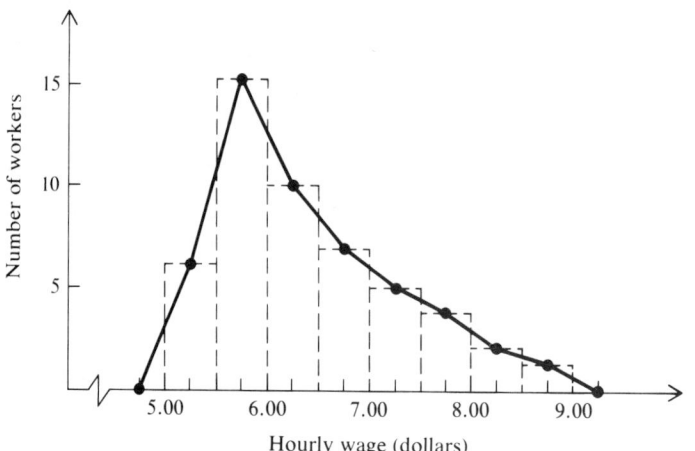

shown in Fig. 1.2 using the histogram's horizontal and vertical scales. Here, however, we place a dot representing the midpoint of each class at the height which corresponds to the frequency of that class. Then we connect these dots with line segments. In order to complete the graph, we draw line segments from the first dot and the last dot to the horizontal axis. These line segments touch the horizontal axis at points $4.75 and $9.25, representing half of the interval width below the lowest and above the highest class intervals. The graph is called a frequency polygon, which means a closed diagram with many sides.

Both graphic displays, the histogram and the frequency polygon, may depict the general pattern of data variation. Graphic comparison of such data variation, however, between two or more frequency distributions cannot be easily made by superimposing their corresponding histograms. Such a comparison can be visualized by superimposing their corresponding frequency polygons.

Frequency polygons are useful in another respect. They lead to a third method of displaying graphically frequency contributions, the *frequency curve*.

Example 1.9

Consider the frequency polygon in Fig. 1.3. The width of each class interval is 50¢. Let us assume that this population represents the hourly wages of millions of production workers. Suppose we increase gradually the number of classes and correspondingly reduce their width. The line segments of the frequency polygon would gradually approach more and more closely a smooth curve. As a limit to this process, the frequency polygon would take up the shape of a smooth frequency curve shown in Fig. 1.4. Note that the frequency curve is an idealization of a real-world or empirical frequency distribution which enables us to view hourly wages as a continuous rather than a discrete numerical variable.

Figure 1.4.
Frequency curve for the distribution of hourly wages for 50 production workers of Maloof Corporation.

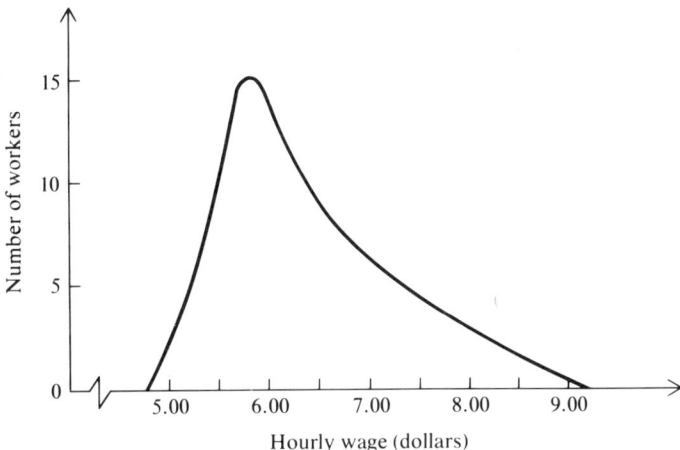

Such smooth frequency curves are referred to as *population models*. We shall see later that population models are important in understanding as well as properly applying statistical techniques: they permit us to classify empirical populations into categories or families with distinct characteristics and describe each family of population models with mathematically derived probability models.

Relative and Cumulative Frequency Distributions

A useful extension of an absolute frequency distribution is a *relative frequency distribution:* it shows the ratio of the number of observations falling into a given class to the total observations.

Example 1.10

A relative frequency distribution is shown in Table 1.5. It is obtained from the data given in Table 1.4. Each relative frequency represents the ratio of the number of observations in each class to the number of observations in the population.

Table 1.5. Relative Frequency Distribution of Hourly Wages for 50 Production Workers of Maloof Corporation

Hourly Wage (Dollars)	Relative Frequency
5.00 and under 5.50	$(6/50) = .12$
5.50 and under 6.00	$(15/50) = .30$
6.00 and under 6.50	$(10/50) = .20$
6.50 and under 7.00	$(7/50) = .14$
7.00 and under 7.50	$(5/50) = .10$
7.50 and under 8.00	$(4/50) = .08$
8.00 and under 8.50	$(2/50) = .04$
8.50 and under 9.00	$(1/50) = .02$
	Total: 1.00

Chapter 1 Populations and Descriptive Statistics

Relative frequencies can be a convenient basis for meaningful comparisons where absolute frequencies fail. For example, suppose we wish to make an industrywide comparison of Maloof production workers with respect to hourly wages. An absolute frequency distribution such as the one in Table 1.4 for the industry may include thousands of observations in each class interval. Stating, for example, that 6 Maloof production workers earn less than $5.50 per hour while the entire industry includes 5000 workers in the same class interval is not too revealing. However, we can convey a meaningful comparison if we state that 12 percent of Maloof production workers earn less than $5.50 while, say, only 7 percent of the workers in the entire industry fall into the same category.

Monthly retail sales of many items fluctuate considerably from season to season. If the same seasonal pattern persists, then the relative frequencies of monthly sales for a given month in two successive years may show the influence of growth factors. For this reason, economic analysts frequently compare the percent change of such time series as gross national product, unemployment, and stock prices over the month or quarter of the previous year.

Relative frequencies are also important in the analysis of categorical variables.

Example 1.11

The employees of Excell Inc., a textile firm, were asked the question "Are you in favor of or against mandatory overtime work?" The response is shown in Table 1.6. It can be seen that the relative frequency distribution reveals the weight of the response much more emphatically than the absolute frequency. Better than one-third of the respondents are strongly opposed to such a policy; while 56 percent of the respondents are against such a measure, only 20 percent are in favor.

Table 1.6. Absolute and Relative Frequency Distributions of the Response of Excell Inc. Employees to Mandatory Overtime Work

Response	Frequency Distribution	
	Absolute	Relative
Strongly in favor	141	.06
Moderately in favor	329	.14
Indifferent	564	.24
Moderately against	517	.22
Strongly against	799	.34
All responding employees:	2350	1.00

Relative frequency distributions of both numerical and categorical variables are particularly important in our discussion of probability.

Another useful extension of an absolute frequency distribution is a *cummulative frequency distribution:* it shows the sum of the frequencies of successively smaller or larger numbers of class intervals. In other words, an absolute frequency distribution gives rise to two cumulative frequency distributions: one on an "at least" and another on a "less than" basis. The following illustration shows construction of a cumulative frequency distribution on an "at least" basis.

Section 1 Populations and Frequency Distributions

Example 1.12 Although the relative frequency distribution in Table 1.5 shows clearly the pattern of data variation, the comptroller of Maloof Corporation wants to know the number and percent of production workers who earn at least a specified hourly wage. The information can be more easily obtained from Table 1.7. All 50 workers earn at least $5.00 per hour. The cumulative frequency for workers earning at least $5.50 per hour is found by subtracting the number of workers earning between $5.00 and under $5.50 per hour from the workers earning at least $5.00 per hour: 50 − 6 = 44. Thus, the cumulative frequency for a class interval represents the number of workers earning at least as much as the lower limit of that class.

Table 1.7. Cumulative Frequency Distributions of Hourly Wages for 50 Production Workers of Maloof Corporation

Hourly Wage (Dollars)	Number of Workers	Cumulative Frequency Distribution Absolute	Cumulative Frequency Distribution Relative
At least 5.00	6	50	(50/50) = 1.00
At least 5.50	15	(50 − 6) = 44	(44/50) = .88
At least 6.00	10	(44 − 15) = 29	(29/50) = .58
At least 6.50	7	(29 − 10) = 19	(19/50) = .38
At least 7.00	5	(19 − 7) = 12	(12/50) = .24
At least 7.50	4	(12 − 5) = 7	(7/50) = .14
At least 8.00	2	(7 − 4) = 3	(3/50) = .06
At least 8.50	1	(3 − 2) = 1	(1/50) = .02
At least 9.00	0	(1 − 1) = 0	(0/50) = .00
Total:	50		

Cumulative frequency distributions on an "at least" basis are helpful for reading probabilities from appended statistical tables. Cumulative distributions on a "less than" basis are discussed in the next section in connection with some summary measures.

PROBLEMS

Group One

1.1. For each collection of elementary units specify a characteristic of interest and the unit of a numerical variable.
- *(a) Employees of a firm
- (b) United States imports
- (c) Demand deposits of a bank
- (d) Dwelling units of a city
- (e) Motor vehicles of a state
- (f) Fish in a lake

1.2. For each collection of elementary units specify a characteristic of interest and an attribute or categorical variable.
- *(a) Voters
- (b) Insurance policies
- (c) Common stocks
- (d) Trees in a forest
- (e) United States wheat acreage
- (f) Gasoline

Answers to asterisked (*) problems are appended.

Chapter 1 Populations and Descriptive Statistics

1.3. The frequency distribution of cotton bales by weight in Southern County is as follows:

Weight (Pounds)	Bales (Thousands)	Weight (Pounds)	Bales (Thousands)
400 and under 420	10	480 and under 500	63
420 and under 440	20	500 and under 520	55
440 and under 460	45	520 and under 540	30
460 and under 480	60	540 and under 560	15

Sketch:
(a) A histogram
*(b) A frequency polygon
(c) A frequency curve

1.4. Linda Mink, the manager of a retail shop, follows the practice of preparing a frequency distribution of daily dollar sales. Suppose daily sales are as follows:

$52.22	32.65	43.25	54.63	48.86
69.99	28.75	51.75	47.32	37.75
35.95	50.60	59.99	56.80	25.52
44.96	60.95	38.42	45.61	65.72
55.90	58.10	41.23	55.05	46.72

*(a) Prepare a frequency distribution using five equal class intervals.
(b) Compute a cumulative frequency distribution on an "at least" basis.
(c) Linda considers a day profitable if 50 percent or more of sales bring in at least $50 each. Was the shop profitable during this day?

1.5 Is anything wrong with each of the designated class intervals?

(a)	(b)
20 and under 25	50 to 100
26 and under 30	100 to 150
etc.	etc.

1.6. Red-White Cab, Inc. operates a fleet of 20 taxi cabs. Herbert Osi, the manager of the company, wanted to study the gasoline consumption of the fleet. He collected the following data on miles per gallon for each cab during a given week.

18.8	21.0	20.3	22.2	19.6
19.2	18.1	22.4	19.8	21.5
20.3	20.9	21.9	20.0	20.9
21.5	19.2	20.1	21.6	22.9

*(a) Using five class intervals and "and under" upper class limits, construct a frequency distribution.
(b) How may the manager use the pattern of variation from this distribution in order to possibly reduce as well as control gasoline consumption?

1.7. Explain the following terms:
(a) Descriptive statistics
(b) Statistical population
(c) Frequency polygon
(d) Cumulative frequency distribution
(e) Open-ended class interval

Section 1 Populations and Frequency Distributions

      (f) Midpoint of a class interval   (k) Population model
      (g) Sample   (l) Cross-sectional data
      (h) Frequency curve   (m) Frequency per unit width
      (i) Frequency distribution   (n) Universe
      (j) Histogram

1.8. Distinguish between:
    (a) Statistical population and elementary units
    (b) Numerical and categorical variables
    (c) Class interval and interval width
    (d) Finite and infinite populations
    (e) Discrete and continuous numerical variables
    (f) Class limits and midpoint
    (g) Absolute and relative frequency distributions

Group Two

1.9. For each given elementary unit explain the type of statistical investigation which requires:
    (i) A finite population.
    (ii) An infinite population.
    *(a) A ball bearing   (c) An automobile
    (b) A cancer patient   (d) A drug addict

1.10. For each given statistical investigation specify:
    (i) The universe of elementary units.
    (ii) A population of a numerical variable.
    (iii) A population of a categorical variable.
    *(a) Absenteeism in a plant   (d) Racial integration in a school system
    (b) Fire accidents in a city   (e) Cotton production in a state
    (c) Stock market quotations

1.11. Consider the raw data in Table 1.3.
    (a) Construct a frequency distribution and a histogram using 4 equal class intervals.
    (b) Construct a frequency distribution and a histogram using 16 equal class intervals.
    (c) Compare these two histograms with the one given in Fig. 1.2. Which is more suitable for revealing a general pattern of data variation?

1.12. Consider the age distribution of residents in a city:

Age (Years)	Residents (Thousands)	Age (Years)	Residents (Thousands)
Under 10	15	40 and under 50	7
10 and under 20	20	50 and under 60	5
20 and under 30	17	60 and under 70	3
30 and under 40	12	70 and over	1

    *(a) Sketch a histogram.
    (b) Compute a relative frequency distribution.
    (c) Compute a cumulative *relative* frequency distribution on a "less than" basis.

(d) What general conclusions do these summarizing techniques suggest about the age of the city population?

1.13. Two cities of approximately equal population showed the following experience with street crimes per block during a year.

Crime Incidents	Blocks in City A	Crime Incidents	Blocks in City B
Under 10	50	Under 10	40
10 and under 20	80	10 and under 20	90
20 and under 30	150	20 and under 30	130
30 and under 50	90	30 and under 60	90

(a) Compare the two distributions by sketching a frequency polygon for each superimposed on the same diagram.
(b) Relatively speaking, which city appears to be better off? How may such an answer be qualified?

SECTION 2/ SUMMARY MEASURES OF CONCENTRATION

We have already demonstrated that frequency distributions can be useful in systematic organization of the raw data of a statistical population. For most purposes, however, the general pattern of data variation of a frequency distribution may not be adequate for making decisions. We need to develop summary measures of concentration or *central tendency;* they are single numbers such as the *proportion,* the *aggregate,* the *arithmetic mean,* the *median,* and the *mode,* which describe some properties of concentration of all observations. Since such measures are calculated from a population, they are called *parameters*.

The Proportion

We are already familiar with this measure in connection with the construction of a relative frequency distribution. Although the proportion is one of the most simple parameters, its role in statistical analysis and decision making is important enough to receive special attention.

The *proportion* is the ratio of the number of observations of special interest to the total number of observations in the population.

Example 2.1

A manufacturer purchases a lot of 5000 piston rings and finds 200 to be defective. The proportion of defective piston rings is $200/5000 = .04$ or 4 percent.

In general, the population proportion, denoted by π* (Greek lowercase *pi*), is defined as

$$\pi = \frac{\text{observations of interest}}{\text{total observations in the population}}$$

*Should not be confused with the constant $\pi = 3.14159$.

Section 2 Summary Measures of Concentration

Note that the interpretation of π depends on the property of the population we wish to study.

Example 2.1 (continued)

Suppose we are interested in the proportion of good rather than defective piston rings. If 200 piston rings are defective, then 4800 must be good; so the proportion of interest is $\pi = 4800/5000 = .96$ or 96 percent good piston rings.

In many problems an entire relative frequency distribution may be the basis of decision making since each proportion of the distribution is a property of the population we wish to study. The manager of a shoe store must decide on the proportion of the inventory which should be in different shoe sizes. An insurer who plans to set up a group life insurance program for the employees of a firm must consider, among other pieces of information, the proportion of employees who fall into each age class. A marketing strategy may require information about the market shares of competing brands, that is, the proportion of sales dollars consumers spend on each competing brand. Stock market analysts may make recommendations based on the proportion of stocks whose prices increased, decreased, or remained unchanged during a trading day.

In an equally great variety of situations, the proportion is a single summary measure for making all kinds of decisions. An employer may decide for or against a personnel policy on the basis of the proportion of employees who favor (or who do not favor) such a policy. A production manager may adjust a machine turning out an unusually high proportion of undersized or oversized items. A buyer may reject a shipment if it contains a higher than acceptable proportion of defective items. Approval of a new drug by the Food and Drug Administration depends on the proportion of certain chemical compounds in the product. In many elections for public office, the candidate who receives the largest proportion of votes (not necessarily the majority) is declared the winner.

It can be seen that the proportion is an important summary measure for quantitative populations; it is the only parameter available for qualitative populations. The proportion is one of the most important parameters in statistical inference.

The Arithmetic Mean and the Aggregate

The average known as the arithmetic mean, or simply the *mean,* is the most important of all parameters that measure central tendency of a quantitative population. Introducing the mean also provides the opportunity to introduce the necessary and important symbolism for other statistical measures.

As already explained briefly, the mean is the total of all values in a quantitative population divided by the population size.

Example 2.2

The weekly earnings of five employees in a retail store are as follows: $125, $190, $155, $210, and $420. These values may be treated as a population whose elementary units are the five employees of the store. Then the mean weekly earnings of this population is:

$$\frac{125 + 190 + 155 + 210 + 420}{5} = \$220$$

Note that in order to calculate the mean, we add the five weekly earnings and divide the total by 5, the number of employees.

At this point it is necessary to introduce some symbols. Symbolism allows us to generalize computational procedures and present them in compact form. Capital letter X is traditionally used to denote an observation. Subscripts 1, 2, 3, etc. are used to distinguish each possible observation. For example, we may use X_1 (read "X sub-1") for the first, X_2 for the second, X_3 for the third, X_4 for the fourth, and X_5 for the fifth observation of the retailer's population of weekly earnings. So the sum of the five observations is

$$X_1 + X_2 + X_3 + X_4 + X_5 = 125 + 190 + 155 + 210 + 420 = \$1100$$

Summing up a set of numbers is symbolized by letter Σ (capital Greek letter *sigma*). Symbol Σ is similar to such an operational symbol as $+$, which tells us to add. Also, we can let X_i (read "X sub-i") denote any ith observation of the population. So the previous summing operation can be denoted by

$$\sum_{i=1}^{5} X_i = \$1100$$

This expression means "summation of X sub-i from i equals 1 to i equals 5."

We may use letter N to denote a population of any size. Thus the operation of summing the values of a population of N size is

(2.1) $$X_1 + X_2 + \cdots + X_N = \sum_{i=1}^{N} X_i$$

where the dots between $+$ signs denote all the remaining observations between the second and the Nth.

It is important to realize that expression (2.1), the *total* of all observations, is a population parameter itself, called the *aggregate*. In many situations the aggregate is the key parameter of a statistical population. Companies need to know the total weekly payroll in order to determine their cash requirements. Total accounts receivable, total accounts payable, total cash on hand, and the total value of physical property are but a few of the aggregates needed for the preparation of financial statements. Investment analysts are interested in the total number of shares traded in a stock exchange. Market and economic analysts study, among other aggregates, total consumer purchases, total consumer credit, total value of inventory, total unemployment, and total gross national product in order to assess the state of our economy. In these and many other problems, attention is focused on some aggregate of a population.

If we divide the aggregate (2.1) by the population size N, we obtain the parameter *mean* μ (Greek lowercase *mu*):

(2.2) $$\mu = \frac{X_1 + X_2 + \cdots X_N}{N} = \frac{\sum_{i=1}^{N} X_i}{N}$$

Section 2 Summary Measures of Concentration

The last expression summarizes effectively the general procedure for calculating the mean from the raw data of a finite quantitative population of any size: we add all X_i values of the population to obtain the aggregate and divide this aggregate by the population size. The mean is also called the *arithmetic average* of numerical variables.

We may simplify formula (2.2) by dropping the subscript notation, so

(2.3) $$\mu = \frac{\Sigma X}{N}$$

Henceforth, with a few exceptions, we will use this simplified form of denoting a summing operation.

Formula (2.3) is suitable for calculating the exact value of the mean from the *raw* or *ungrouped* data of a population. This formula is especially appropriate when the population size is small or the data are available in a computer memory. Work is simplified if we calculate the mean from the grouped data of an available frequency distribution using the following method.

Example 2.3

Earlier, we showed how the comptroller of Maloof Corporation was able to study the pattern of hourly wages of the 50 production workers in the plant by means of a frequency distribution and graphic displays. In addition, the comptroller wants to know the total as well as the mean of weekly earnings. Calculation of these summary measures is shown in Table 2.1.

Table 2.1. Calculation of the Mean from Grouped Data: Weekly Earnings of 50 Production Workers of Maloof Corporation

Weekly Earnings[a] (Dollars)	Number of Workers f	Class Interval Midpoint m	fm
200 and under 220	6	210	1,260
220 and under 240	15	230	3,450
240 and under 260	10	250	2,500
260 and under 280	7	270	1,890
280 and under 300	5	290	1,450
300 and under 320	4	310	1,240
320 and under 340	2	330	660
340 and under 360	1	350	350
	50		12,800

$$\mu = \frac{\Sigma fm}{N} = \frac{12,800}{50} = \$256$$

[a]Obtained from Tables 1.3 and 1.4 by assuming a 40-hour work week times the hourly wage for each worker.

The frequency in each class f, number of workers, is multiplied by the corresponding midpoint value m. The sum of these products is $12,800. This is an approximation for the total weekly payroll for the production workers in the plant. This total is divided by the population size $N = 50$ to obtain the mean $256.

In general, for calculating the mean from the *grouped* data of a frequency distribution, formula (2.3) is modified to

(2.4)
$$\mu = \frac{\Sigma fm}{N}$$

where f = frequency of each class
m = midpoint or mid-value of each class interval
N = population size

It is important to realize that this method for calculating the mean usually results in some loss of accuracy. Unless each midpoint is a true average of the observations of the class it represents, formula (2.4) yields an *approximation* to the true mean. More frequently than not, the approximation is good. Furthermore, this method is the only procedure if data are available in no other form than in a frequency distribution.

Special attention should be paid to a frequency distribution where either the lowest or the highest or both class intervals are open-ended. Then the midpoint of such a class cannot be identified. For example, consider the earlier cited open-ended class of firms with inventory value of "$10 million or more." We would be unable to find the product fm for this class interval; we know f but not m (the mid-value of the open-ended interval). If the raw data are available, we should add the exact inventory value of each firm in this class; otherwise, the total value of the class must be estimated or obtained from other sources.

In averaging a set of observations which require weights, we need to compute a *weighted arithmetic mean*.

Example 2.4

The investment portfolio of a charitable institution consists of municipal, U.S. Treasury, and commercial bonds with interest rates and invested amounts shown in Table 2.2. What is the interest rate for the total investment? The question requires calculation of the weighted mean. Each interest rate is multiplied by the weight representing the amount invested in each

Table 2.2. Calculation of a Weighted Arithmetic Mean: Interest Rate for an Investment Portfolio of Three Bonds

Type of Bond	Interest Rate X	Invested Amount w	Interest Earned wX
Municipal	.06	$200,000	$12,000
U.S. Treasury	.07	300,000	21,000
Commercial	.08	500,000	40,000
		$1,000,000	$73,000

Weighted mean: $\mu_w = \dfrac{\Sigma wX}{\Sigma w} = \dfrac{\$73,000}{\$1,000,000} = .073 = 7.3\%$

Section 2 Summary Measures of Concentration

type of bond. In order to obtain the weighted mean interest rate of 7.3 percent, we divide the total interest of $73,000 earned by the total investment of $1,000,000.

Note that without the weights the average would be:

$$\mu = \frac{\Sigma X}{N} = \frac{.06 + .07 + .08}{3} = .07 = 7 \text{ percent}$$

according to formula (2.3). This is the interest rate *per type of bond*, an *unweighted arithmetic mean*. It disregards the different amounts invested in each type of bond; or, alternatively, it assumes that the same amount is invested in each type of bond.

In general, the weighted mean can be calculated from:

(2.5) $$\mu_w = \frac{\Sigma wX}{\Sigma w}$$

where μ_w = weighted arithmetic mean
X = value of each observation
w = weight of each observation

In words, we multiply each observation by its weight, sum the products, and divide this sum by the sum of the weights.

The Median and the Mode

Like the mean, the median is another important measure of central tendency of a quantitative population. For ungrouped data, the *median* is the middle value when all the observations are arranged in increasing sequence. For the weekly earnings of the five retail store employees, $125, $155, $190, $210, and $420, arranged in increasing sequence, the median is $190. Suppose $420 is eliminated because it represents the salary of the store owner. Then the population consists of four observations: $125, $155, $190, and $210. In this case, the median, denoted by Md, is the average of the two middle values:

$$\text{Md} = \frac{155 + 190}{2} = \$172.50$$

In short, the median is a *position* or *location* average: half the observations of a distribution are larger and half smaller than the median.

As in the case of the mean, finding the median from ungrouped data may be time-consuming because we must arrange all observation values in an increasing or decreasing order of magnitude. This task can be avoided if we calculate the median from grouped data. Furthermore, this procedure is the only method for calculating the median if data are available in no other form than in a frequency distribution. Finding the median from a frequency distribution requires application of the following formula:

(2.6) $$\text{Md} = L + \left(\frac{N/2 - F}{f}\right) W$$

where $L =$ lower limit of the median class
$N =$ population size
$F =$ cumulative frequency of classes preceding the median class
$f =$ frequency of the median class
$W =$ class interval width

Example 2.5

Let us consider again the weekly earnings of 50 production workers of Maloof Corporation. The frequency and the less-than cumulative frequency distributions are shown in Table 2.3. Calculation of the median involves two major steps:

Table 2.3. Calculation of the Median from Grouped Data: Weekly Earnings of 50 Production Workers of Maloof Corporation

Weekly Earnings (Dollars)	Number of Workers (Class Frequency)	Less-Than Cumulative Frequency
200 and under 220	6	6
220 and under 240	15	21
240 and under 260	10←	31←
260 and under 280	7	38
280 and under 300	5	43
300 and under 320	4	47
320 and under 340	2	49
340 and under 360	1	50
	50	

$$Md = L + \left(\frac{N/2 - F}{f}\right) W = 240 + \left(\frac{50/2 - 21}{10}\right) 20 = \$248$$

First, we locate the median class and its lower limit L. The cumulative frequency first exceeds $N/2 = 50/2 = 25$* for class "$240 and under $260," as the arrows indicate. This is the median class because 31 workers earn less than $260 but only 21 workers earn less than $240. The lower limit L is $240.

Second, we locate the value of the median within the median class interval. We assume that f, the 10 observations of the median class, are spread evenly over W, the $20 width of the median class. In other words, each observation is assumed to be one-tenth of $20 or $2 apart from another observation. In order to find the median value we must go inside the class interval by

$$\left(\frac{N/2 - F}{f}\right) W = \left(\frac{50/2 - 21}{10}\right) 20 = \$8$$

Adding this sum to the lower class limit $240, the median is

$$Md = 240 + 8 = \$248$$

according to formula (2.6).

*The midpoint is 25 rather than 25 + 1/2 because we assume that the middle value is interpolated over a continuous range of the median class.

Section 2 Summary Measures of Concentration

Note that the median from grouped data, like the mean, is an approximation. To the extent to which the median class frequencies are not evenly spread, the median may differ from its exact value obtainable from ungrouped data. Such an approximation, however, may prove satisfactory for most practical purposes.

The mode is the third important measure of central tendency of a quantitative population. The *mode* is most frequently occurring population value. Consider the price quotations of a stock: $10, $11, $12, $12, and $15. The mode is $12 because price $12 occurs most often.

Since the mode represents the most frequently occurring observation, its interpretation is analogous to what may be considered to be most "fashionable" in a given situation. Men and women dressed in current style are considered to be "in the mode" or "in fashion" although they may represent a small fraction of the general public. Like fashion, the mode may represent a minority value of all observations. The mode is a measure of *density*, that is, the value at which the concentration of observations is most dense. Primarily for this reason, identifying the mode requires a fairly large number of observations.

The mode is calculated from grouped data in a manner similar to that employed for determining the median. The formula commonly employed for determining the mode, denoted by Mo, is

$$(2.7) \qquad \text{Mo} = L + \left(\frac{d_1}{d_1 + d_2}\right) W$$

where L = lower limit of the modal class
d_1 = difference between the frequency of the modal and that of the preceding class
d_2 = difference between the frequency of the modal and that of the following class
W = class interval width

Example 2.6

The mode of weekly earnings for the 50 production workers of Maloof Corporation can be easily obtained from Table 2.3. The modal class interval is "220 and under 240," so the lower limit L is 220. The difference d_1 between the frequency of the modal and the preceding class is $9 = 15 - 6$; the difference d_2 between the frequency of the modal and the following class is $5 = 15 - 10$. Since the class interval width W is 20, the mode is

$$\text{Mo} = 220 + \left(\frac{9}{9 + 5}\right) 20 = \$232.86$$

according to formula (2.7).

Of course, the mode calculated from grouped data may not be the same as the mode obtainable from raw data. The reason is similar to that already explained in connection with calculating the median from grouped data.

The Mean, Median, and Mode Compared

So far we have concentrated on showing how to compute these three measures of central tendency. We now turn to a comparative discussion of these measures. In particular, we summarize their characteristics and limitations.

Chapter 1 Populations and Descriptive Statistics

The *mean,* unlike the other two measures of central tendency, has a number of mathematical properties. First, in many problems the mean may be used interchangeably with the aggregate. We have seen that the mean μ is defined as the aggregate ΣX divided by the total number of observations N. It follows that the aggregate ΣX equals $N\mu$, that is, the total times the mean. This indicates that we can find the aggregate if we know the mean and total number of observations.

Example 2.7

A case in point is the experience of a textile manufacturer during World War II. He learned that a war plane required an average of four parachutes and he heard that plans for 1940–41 provided for the production of 50,000 war planes. Multiplying these two numbers, he estimated that the demand would be for about 200,000 parachutes and adjusted his production plans accordingly.

Second, the mean is also additive. This means that the mean of two or more related frequency distributions can be added with proper weighting.

Example 2.8

Suppose the mean price of a group of 10 stocks is $20 and the mean price of another group of 15 stocks is $45. The mean price of all 25 stocks, by formula (2.5), is

$$\mu_w = \frac{\Sigma wX}{\Sigma w} = \frac{10(20) + 15(45)}{25} = \$35$$

The median and the mode of each related frequency distribution cannot be averaged to find the median or the mode of the 25 stocks. These measures must be obtained from the combined ungrouped data of the two sets of stock prices.

Third, the sum of the differences between each individual numerical observation of a population and the arithmetic mean equals zero.

Example 2.9

The mean of 2, 6, and 7 is 5. The differences from the mean are $2 - 5 = -3$, $6 - 5 = 1$, and $7 - 5 = 2$. Then the sum is

$$(-3) + (1) + (2) = 0$$

Because of its mathematical properties, the mean is used more extensively than any other measure of central tendency as the basis for the development of many statistical measures and techniques.

On the other hand, the mean has an important limitation; it is unduly influenced by extremely small or large values of a distribution.

Example 2.10

The mean weekly earnings of four retail store employees who earn $125, $155, $190, and $210 is

$$\frac{125 + 155 + 190 + 210}{4} = \$170$$

Earlier, we found that the mean jumps to $220 if the $420 earnings of the store owner are included in the distribution.

Note that the mean $220 is larger than the four values of the original distribution. Because of this limitation, the mean is not considered an appropriate measure of central tendency for a variable, such as household income, whose distribution may include a few very large or very small values.

Unlike the mean, the *median* is not seriously influenced by the presence of extreme values in a distribution.

Example 2.11

We found earlier that the median of four weekly earnings $125, $155, $190, and $210 is

$$\frac{155 + 190}{2} = \$172.50$$

The median increases to only $190 if the distribution includes the $420 earnings of the store owner.

Thus, the median rather than the mean is usually the basis for meaningful comparisons. This is especially true when the data include extremely large or extremely small values. For example, we may state that a person's income is above or below the median income of a town because the median is the middle value of the income distribution. Using the mean may be misleading since the town's income distribution may include a few very large incomes which would seriously influence the mean but not the median. The median and other location averages, which we introduce in the next section, are extensively used for rating individuals in college entrance examinations or employment tests.

Another interesting property of the median is that the sum of the absolute differences* between the median and the individual values *in a distribution* is a minimum.

Example 2.12

Consider numbers 1, 8, and 12. The median is 8. The absolute differences from the median are 7, 0, and 4. They total 11. This sum is a minimum. The absolute differences of 1, 8, and 12 from any value other than the median add up to more than 11. For example, the mean of the same numbers is

$$\frac{1 + 8 + 12}{3} = 7$$

The absolute differences from 7 are 6, 1, and 5, which add up to 12.

This property of the median has some practical applications. For example, a distributor may wish to minimize the total travel distance between a supply depot and several retail outlets located at different distances from a starting point along

---

*An absolute difference is one in which the algebraic sign, whether plus or minus, is ignored.

a highway. Total travel distance is minimized if the supply depot is located at a median distance from the starting point.

Since the *mode* is a measure where the observations of a distribution are most dense, adding or subtracting an extreme value does not change the mode. Thus this measure of central tendency is an appropriate measure in situations where decisions are made on the most common value of a distribution. Many retail stores expect to make a profit on policy based on a low markup and fast inventory turnover. To accomplish this objective they carry the most frequently demanded or modal-size merchandise. The mode is also meaningful as a measure of central tendency of distributions of categorical variables. In an election involving several candidates, the mode may determine the winner. Opinion polls focus on the most popular response to an issue. Nevertheless, the mode has fewer useful applications than either the mean or the median.

PROBLEMS

Group One

*2.1. Textron Electronics shipped the following number of minicomputers during each month of the last year:

$$9, 15, 6, 25, 8, 15, 12, 21, 15, 11, 17, 14$$

Calculate the mean, median, and mode. Explain the meaning of each measure.

*2.2. Somo and Gomo are two cities with 10,000 and 20,000 households, respectively. The mean annual income of households in Somo is $15,000 and in Gomo $25,000. Find the mean annual income of households in both cities.

2.3. Prospective buyers were asked: Do you plan to buy a new refrigerator within the next year? The response tabulated in two different ways was as follows:

Tabulation A		Tabulation B	
Response	Respondents	Response	Respondents
Yes	198	Yes	198
No	492	No	492
Don't know	960	*Total:*	690
Total:	1650		

Calculate the proportion of respondents who plan to buy a refrigerator for both tabulations. Interpret the result.

2.4. The editor of Torch Publishers considers two typesetters for printing the books of the company in the future. Five books from each typesetter contained the following errors:

$$\text{Right-Set: } 58, 10, 86, 46, 175$$
$$\text{Quick-Set: } 45, 165, 57, 223, 10$$

Answers to asterisked (*) problems are appended.

Section 2 Summary Measures of Concentration

Assuming that the two sets of books are comparable and that minimizing printing errors is the primary criterion, which typesetter should be chosen? Calculate the appropriate measure of central tendency.

2.5. At the end of a given month, the amount of credit extended to customers of a department store is distributed as follows:

Outstanding Credit (Dollars)	Number of Accounts
0 and under 100	60
100 and under 200	85
200 and under 300	45
300 and under 400	17
400 and under 500	10

*(a) Calculate the mean, mode, and median.
 (b) Pat Donovan, the comptroller of the store, plans to turn over collection of the total outstanding credit to a bank for a 5 percent fee. Approximately, what is the total fee Pat must pay the bank? How much net cash would Pat receive from the bank?

2.6. During a season, James Palmer's sawmill receives the following logs distributed by length:

Length (Feet)	Number of Logs
15 and under 20	252
20 and under 25	1567
25 and under 30	2381
30 and under 35	5896
35 and under 40	1443

(a) Calculate the mean, mode, and median.
(b) From experience Palmer knows that a linear foot of a log yields, on the average, 10 board feet of lumber. What is the approximate number of board feet which his sawmill will produce?

2.7. During the last fiscal year, a multinational, also called *transnational*, corporation realized the following percentages of return on sales:

Country	Return on Sales (Percentage)	Dollar Sales (Millions)
A	5	250
B	10	175
C	20	85

*(a) Calculate the unweighted mean percentage of return on sales.
*(b) Calculate the weighted mean percentage of return on sales.
(c) Explain the meaning of each average.

2.8. Explain the following terms:
(a) Summary measures
(b) Measures of central tendency
(c) Parameters

2.9. Briefly and in your own words explain the following measures:
(a) Mean   (d) Aggregate
(b) Proportion   (e) Weighted mean
(c) Median   (f) Mode

2.10. List the characteristics and limitations of the following measures of central tendency:
(a) Mean
(b) Median
(c) Mode

Group Two

2.11. Consider the daily dollar sales of Linda Mink's shop given in Problem 1.4.
*(a) Calculate the mean and the median from the given data.
(b) Prepare a frequency distribution using five equal class intervals and calculate the mean and the median from this distribution.
(c) Are the values obtained in (a) different from those obtained in (b)? Explain why.

2.12. In an investment course, the instructor presented to the class the purchasing of Lupon Industries common shares by two investors:

	Investor A				Investor B		
Quarter	Price	Shares	Cost	Quarter	Price	Shares	Cost
1	43	25	1075	1	43	23	989
2	35	25	875	2	35	29	1015
3	41	25	1025	3	41	24	984
4	38	25	950	4	38	26	988

Both investors purchased their shares at the same time during each quarter. Investor A, however, bought a constant number of 25 shares each quarter, while investor B spent a constant sum of $1000 each quarter, that is, as close to $1000 as prevailing stock price would allow.
(a) Calculate the mean cost per share for each investor.
(b) Which investor paid less per share? Explain why in terms of the weights involved in calculating the mean cost per share.

2.13. The management of Erb Farms considers limiting the five suppliers of fresh strawberries to those who ship better-than-average quality. Quality was measured in

Section 3 Summary Measures of Dispersion

terms of the percentage of one-pound baskets that contained substandard or spoiled strawberries. During the last 5 weeks this percentage was as follows:

		Suppliers		
A	B	C	D	E
20	12	6	7	22
15	26	16	17	6
10	8	24	16	25
14	14	10	25	17
26	30	14	10	25

Assuming that Erb Farms received the same number of baskets each week from each supplier:
*(a) Calculate the mean percentage of poor quality for each supplier.
 (b) Calculate the mean percentage of poor quality for all suppliers.
 (c) Assuming that limiting the suppliers would not create shortages, which suppliers should be retained? Why?

2.14. Which parameter measure, if any, do you think would be most appropriate for the following decision situations? Explain why.
*(a) Considering a distribution of depths in all parts of a lake, decide whether you would bet that you can walk safely across the lake bottom.
 (b) Decide whether to accept or reject a shipment of steel rods which must meet specified length and diameter requirements.
 (c) Determine the crime rate in five cities when the crime rate of each is given.
 (d) Find out whether your quiz grade lies in the upper half of all grades in the class.
 (e) Decide which dress sizes to order for a discount store with a high sales turnover.
 (f) Decide on a dividend distribution to common stockholders of a firm.

SECTION 3/ SUMMARY MEASURES OF DISPERSION

A measure of central tendency alone does not adequately summarize a statistical population. We can have a more meaningful numerical discription of an individual if we consider both the person's weight *and* height. Similarly, we can obtain a better numerical description of a distribution if we consider appropriate summary measures of central tendency *and* dispersion. *Parameter dispersion measures* express the degree to which observations scatter around a population center.

We introduce the notion of *dispersion* by showing how variation in observations affects the positional relationship of the mean, median, and mode of a distribution. Then we deal with two simple *distance* measures of dispersion: the *range*, largest less smallest values, and the *interquartile range*, 50 percent of the observations in the middle of a distribution. This topic is followed by two important measures of *average* dispersion: the *variance* and the *standard deviation*.

Dispersion, Concentration Measures, and Skewness

In the previous section, we explained that extreme values affect mostly the mean, less so the median, and hardly the mode. How does variation in general affect these measures of central tendency? Their comparative position can best be illustrated with frequency curves representing population models.

When a population has a bell-shaped symmetrical frequency curve, such as the one shown in Fig. 3.1(a), the three averages are equal in value. The vertical line marking the location of this common value on the X axis divides the distribution into two identical halves, one being the mirror image of the other. Such a bell-shaped symmetrical distribution is called a *normal distribution*. A population having a frequency curve which can be approximated by the normal distribution is said to be *normally distributed*. It is important to realize that many empirical or real-life populations are normal or normally distributed. Human physical and mental characteristics within a given race or nationality such as height, head size, brain weight, and intelligence (as measured by tests) are normally distributed. Populations from animals and plants such as the weight of dogs of a particular

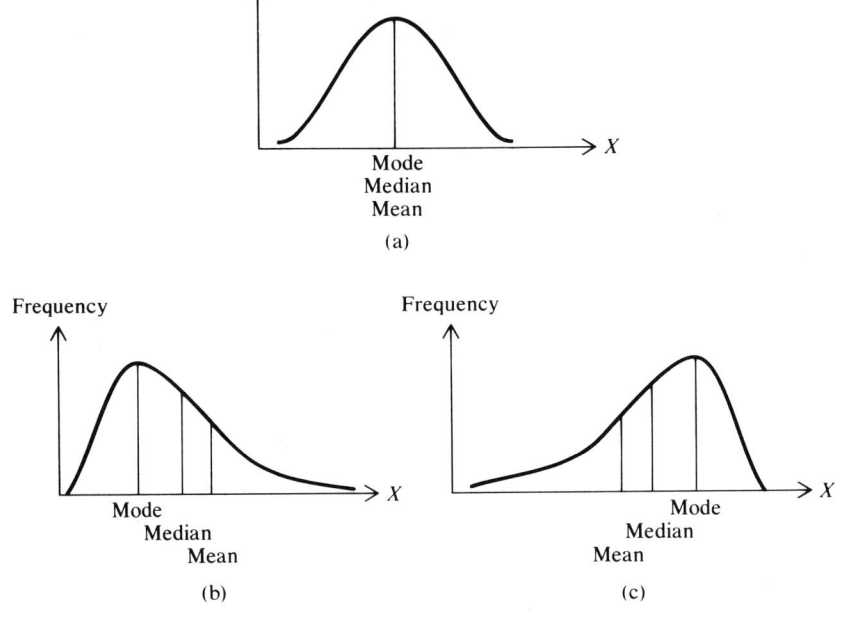

Figure 3.1. Positional comparison of mean, median, and mode (a) normal distribution; (b) positively skewed distribution; (c) negatively skewed distribution. (The letter X on the horizontal axis denotes values of a numerical variable.)

Section 3 Summary Measures of Dispersion

breed and the size and weight of oranges of any given variety are normally distributed. So are errors of scientific measurements such as velocity, force, and distance. Later we shall see that normal distributions play a very important role in statistical inference.

When a population contains some very large values, its frequency curve tails off to the right as shown in Fig. 3.1(b). The mean of such a rightwardly tailed population distribution is always larger than the median and the median larger than the mode. In other words, very large values pull the mean away from the mode in the direction of these large values. Such a distribution is said to be positively skewed because if we subtract the median from the mean, we get a *positive* difference.

Example 3.1   The distribution of weekly earnings of production workers analyzed earlier is positively skewed. We found that the mean is $256, the median $248, and the mode $232.86. The positive difference between the mean and the median is $8 = 256 − 248.

Sales and assets of corporations in many product lines or industries have positively skewed frequency distributions. A case in point is the distribution of sales of grocery outlets in the United States: in total numbers, there are a very few chain supermarkets with large sales compared to the number of independent small grocery stores. Another example is that individual incomes and wealth in the United States and other countries have positively skewed distributions.

A frequency distribution such as that shown in Fig. 3.1(c) is said to be negatively skewed. The long tail of the distribution lies on the left-hand side; the mean is smaller than the median and the median is smaller than the mode. If we subtract the median from the mean, we get a *negative* difference. Test scores of students admitted to college may have a negatively skewed distribution. The bulk of the admitted students fall close to the upper limit of SAT (Scholastic Aptitude Test) scores; the number of students fall off gradually for scores to the left of the upper limit. An epidemic of a communicable disease such as influenza generates a negatively skewed distribution of cases over time. Few persons are struck with the flu during the first days of the epidemic. Later on, the number of victims increases until the frequency curve reaches a peak before the epidemic tapers off rapidly.

The distributions in Fig. 3.1 are called *unimodal* because each of their frequency curves has a single peak (like a single-hump camel). Figure 3.2 shows the smooth frequency curves or population models of three other types of distributions.

The frequency curve in Fig. 3.2(a) may represent a large shipment of men's suits or women's dresses of different sizes where each size has the same number of units. Since the frequency is the same for every value of the numerical variable, the model of such a distribution is represented with a rectangle—hence the term *rectangular distribution;* it is also called a *uniform distribution* because frequencies are uniform throughout the values of the numerical variable. Note that a rectangular distribution is symmetrical with no modal value.

Figure 3.2.
Rectangular (a), exponential (b), and bimodal (c) population models. (The letter X on the horizontal axis denotes values of a numerical variable.)

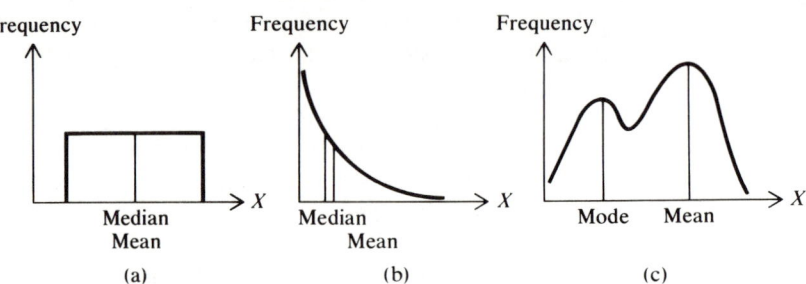

Some other distributions may take the form of the so-called *exponential distribution* shown in Fig. 3.2(b). Such a model may represent the age distribution of the United States population older than 65 years. The number of survivors decreases rapidly (exponentially) with the advance of age. An exponential distribution is slightly positively skewed, as illustrated by the small difference between the median and the mean values.

If the frequency curve of a distribution looks like a two-hump camel, as shown in Fig. 3.2(c), then the distribution is said to be *bimodal*. For example, a population of height measurements for the United States Army volunteers would yield a bimodal distribution; the smaller modal height would represent women and the larger modal height men. A distribution of weight measurements for the same volunteers would also be bimodal. A bimodal distribution is a clear indication that the data are not homogeneous with respect to the numerical variable they represent. Neither the mean nor the median are representative measures of central tendency because they are likely to fall in between the two modal values of the distribution. In addition, a bimodal distribution may or may not be skewed. Since sex is the "assignable cause" of the bimodal distribution of volunteer heights, the data may be organized into two distinct distributions, one for men and another for women. If there is no such basis for separating the data, statistical analysis of bimodal distributions should be handled very carefully.

In sum, a clear distinction should be made between skewness and dispersion. We have seen that the direction and degree of skewness may be expressed as a difference between the median and mean values of a distribution. More elaborate methods for measuring skewness are available but lie outside the scope of this volume. Dispersion, on the other hand, refers to the general spreading of observations from the population center regardless of the presence or absence of skewness. The presence of skewness is limited to nonsymmetrical distributions, while dispersion is present in nearly all forms* of frequency distributions. Skewness means lack of symmetry, while dispersion may be large or small, even if a distribution is symmetrical. Our exclusive concern here is to introduce general measures of dispersion.

---

*Except in the rare case where all observations have the same value and, therefore, the distribution has no dispersion.

Section 3 Summary Measures of Dispersion

Distance Measures of Dispersion

As mentioned earlier, the range and the interquartile range are two distance measures of dispersion we consider first.

The *range* is the simplest measure of dispersion; it is the difference between the largest and the smallest values in a population. We have already used the range to determine the width of class intervals for constructing a frequency distribution. Under certain conditions the range can be the basis for finding the approximate value of other population parameters. During a given trading day, the price of a stock may fluctuate within a very small range containing a large number of transactions. We can obtain an approximate value of the mean stock price by adding half the price range to the lowest transaction price.

The range is not free of important limitations. The measure is based on the two observations which are extremes rather than typical values of a population. Moreover, the range tells us nothing about how the observations are scattered within the range; are they clustered around a small segment of the range or are they spread out throughout the range?

On the other hand, the difference between the *third quartile* and the *first quartile*, called the *interquartile range*, ignores large and small values. The third quartile represents a value where three-fourths of the observations are smaller than such a measure; analogously, the first quartile is a value where one-fourth of the observations are smaller than such a measure. Hence, the difference between these two quartiles represents a range which contains 50 percent of the observations in the middle of a distribution. It is important to realize that the median is frequently referred to as the second quartile of a distribution, since two-fourths of the observations are smaller than the median.

Although calculation of quartiles from a frequency distribution is exactly analogous to the calculation of the median, quartile values can be easily approximated from a cumulative less-than relative frequency curve called an *ogive* (pronounced "ōjive").

Example 3.2

Such a curve for the weekly earnings of 50 Maloof Corporation production workers is shown in Fig. 3.3. The basic data for constructing this curve were obtained from the less-than cumulative frequency in Table 2.3. Each cumulative class frequency was expressed as a relative frequency. For example, the relative frequency for less than $220 earning is .12 or 6/50, for less than $240 earnings it is .42 or 21/50, and so on. These relative class frequencies appear as dots on the graph. For example, the bottom dot has coordinates (220, .12), that is, .12 of workers earned less than $220.

The ogive curve enables us to read off the horizontal axis the value of each quartile. We start from a point on the vertical axis representing a quartile. At the point where the broken line meets the ogive curve we draw a broken line perpendicular to the horizontal axis. Thus, the approximate value of a quartile represents a point where the broken line cuts the X axis. The values for the first, second (or median), and third quartiles are $226, $248 (calculated earlier), and $279, respectively. So the interquartile range is $53 = 279 − 226. The middle 50 percent of the workers earn between $226 and $279 per week.

Figure 3.3.
Cumulative "less than" relative frequency curve and interquartile range: weekly earnings of 50 production workers of Maloof Corporation. (Data from Table 2.3.)

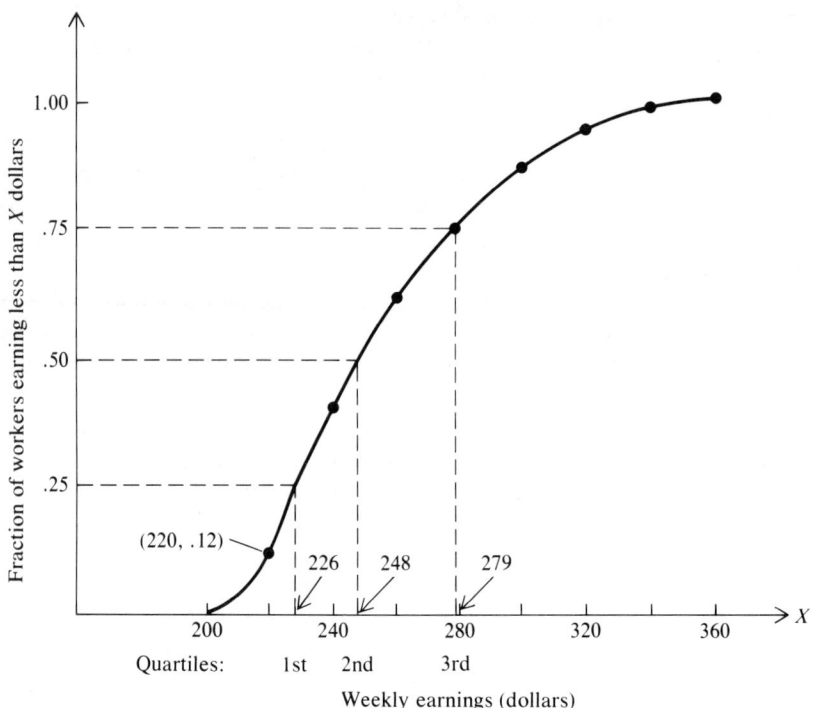

Again, the interquartile range, like the simple range, gives no information about how the middle 50 percent of the observations are scattered. Yet quartiles are useful measures, particularly as special cases of other general measures called *fractiles*. A fractile is a value where a certain proportion of observations are smaller than such measure. If a fractile is expressed as a percentage rather than as a proportion, it is called a *percentile*. Thus first quartile is also called the 25th percentile and the median the 50th percentile. Colleges use, among other criteria, an applicant's percentile in entrance examinations as part of the evaluation process for admission.

Average Measures of Dispersion

We have seen that the range represents the difference between the largest and the smallest population values. However, two or more populations may have the same range but quite different variability. We need to develop a formula which measures the variability of observations with respect to the distance of each observation from the population center as well as with respect to the frequency with which each observation occurs.

This is accomplished with measures of average dispersion. Such measures are based on the difference, called *deviation,* of each observation from the population's center. The most common deviation is the difference between an observation X and the population mean μ, that is, $X - \mu$. The sum of these deviations divided by the population size would be an average measure of dispersion. This

Section 3 Summary Measures of Dispersion

sum, however, is useless because it equals zero. Earlier, we saw that the sum of the deviation of 2, 6, and 7 from their mean 5 equals zero. Since we are interested in the magnitude rather than the sign of each deviation, we might avoid this difficulty by ignoring the minus signs or by squaring each deviation. The latter operation is the most mathematically tractable way for measuring variability. So the appropriate measure of average dispersion is to divide the sum of the squared deviations by the population size as follows:

$$\frac{(2-5)^2 + (6-5)^2 + (7-5)^2}{3} = \frac{9+1+4}{3} \simeq 4.67$$

In general, this measure, called *variance*, is denoted by σ^2 (Greek lowercase *sigma;* read "sigma squared") and is expressed by

(3.1) $$\sigma^2 = \frac{\Sigma(X-\mu)^2}{N}$$

where X = value of each observation
μ = population mean
N = population size

Formula (3.1) is appropriate for calculating the variance from ungrouped data.

Example 3.3. Calculation of the variance from the earnings of five retail store employees is illustrated in Table 3.1. Note that the sum of the deviations from the mean $220 equals zero, a desirable computational check. Each deviation from the mean is squared and the sum is divided by the population size 5. The value of the variance σ^2 is 10,850. This figure represents the mean of the squared deviations of each observation from the population mean.

Table 3.1.
Calculation of Variance from Ungrouped Data: Weekly Earnings of Employees in a Retail Store

Weekly Earnings X	Deviation from Mean $(X-\mu)$	Squared Deviation $(X-\mu)^2$
$ 125	$125 - 220 = -95	9,025
190	190 - 220 = -30	900
155	155 - 220 = -65	4,225
210	210 - 220 = -10	100
420	420 - 220 = +200	40,000
1100	0	54,250

$$\mu = \frac{\Sigma X}{N} = \frac{1,100}{5} = \$220 \qquad \sigma^2 = \frac{\Sigma(X-\mu)^2}{N} = \frac{54,250}{5} = 10,850$$

Chapter 1 Populations and Descriptive Statistics

Most real-world populations include a large number of observations. Calculation of the variance from such populations can be a time-consuming task. We can save time and effort by calculating the variance from the grouped data of a class frequency distribution. The appropriate formula is

(3.2) $$\sigma^2 = \frac{\Sigma f(m - \mu)^2}{N}$$

where f = frequency of each class
m = midpoint of each class interval

with all remaining symbols already explained.

Example 3.4

Table 3.2 illustrates calculation of the variance from a class frequency distribution. We first calculate the mean $256 as the sum of frequencies times midpoint values divided by the population size. (Also, see Table 2.1.) Then, we find the deviation $(m - \mu)$ of each midpoint from the mean.

Each squared deviation $(m - \mu)^2$ is multiplied by the corresponding frequency f. The sum of these products, 61,800, divided by the population size 50, yields a variance of 1236.

One important practical difficulty associated with the variance is its empirical interpretation. The observations and their variance are expressed in different units. While the observations in Table 3.2 are in dollars, the variance is in *squared* dollars! This is because we squared all dollar deviations in order to calculate the variance. In general, the variance represents squared units of a numerical variable, such as squared dollars, squared inches, and squared pounds. For practical statistical problems, we shall be working with the positive square root of the variance, the *standard deviation*. Since the square root of the variance eliminates the exponent, that is, $\sqrt{\sigma^2} = +\sigma$, the standard deviation for grouped data is the positive square root defined by

(3.3) $$\sigma = \sqrt{\frac{\Sigma f(m - \mu)^2}{N}}$$

The standard deviation for the weekly earnings of workers in Table 3.2 is obtained by taking the positive square root of the variance:

$$\sigma = \sqrt{1236} \simeq \$35.16$$

Note that the standard deviation is in dollar units. Unlike the variance, the standard deviation has a meaningful empirical interpretation because it is expressed in units of the numerical variable under study; the standard deviation is a practical summary measure of average dispersion. Both measures, however, contain the same information. The greater the variability of a population, the

Section 3 Summary Measures of Dispersion

Table 3.2.
Calculation of Variance from Grouped Data: Weekly Earnings of 50 Production Workers of Maloof Corporation

Weekly Earnings (Dollars)	Workers f	Class Midpoint m	fm	$(m - \mu)$	$(m - \mu)^2$	$f(m - \mu)^2$
200–220[a]	6	210	1,260	−46	2,116	12,696
220–240	15	230	3,450	−26	676	10,140
240–260	10	250	2,500	− 6	36	360
260–280	7	270	1,890	+14	196	1,372
280–300	5	290	1,450	+34	1,156	5,780
300–320	4	310	1,240	+54	2,916	11,664
320–340	2	330	660	+74	5,476	10,952
340–360	1	350	350	+94	8,836	8,836
	50		12,800			61,800

$$\mu = \frac{\Sigma fm}{N} = \frac{12,800}{50} = \$256^b \qquad \sigma^2 = \frac{\Sigma f(m - \mu)^2}{N} = \frac{61,800}{50} = 1236$$

[a]200–220 means 200 to under 220 throughout, as in Table 2.1.
[b]As in Table 2.1.

larger the values of both measures; by looking at the value of either σ or σ^2 we can tell whether variation is small or large, and we can always obtain the value of one when the value of the other measure is known.

The importance of the standard deviation in statistics, especially statistical inference, cannot be overemphasized. For example, normally distributed populations can be described in terms of their mean and standard deviation. In other words, we can construct a close approximation of the entire frequency distribution of a normal population if we know the population's mean and its standard deviation.

Furthermore, the standard deviation in conjunction with the mean can be used to indicate the percentage of observations of a normal population which fall within a specified range of values. The range of three standard deviations from either side of the mean, that is, the range $\mu \pm 3\sigma$, includes 99.7 percent of the observations of a normal population. Knowing the range of a normal population, we can approximate the value of the standard deviation if we divide the range by 6.

The standard deviation is an absolute measure of average dispersion. We can obtain a relative measure of dispersion if we express the standard deviation as a percentage of the arithmetic mean. The new measure, called *coefficient of relative variation*, or CRV for short, is defined as

$$(3.4) \qquad \text{CRV} = \frac{\sigma}{\mu}(100)$$

This measure is appropriate for making meaningful comparisons between populations whose observations are expressed in units of different magnitude or variability.

Example 3.5

The new measure for the weekly earnings in Table 3.2 is

$$\text{CRV} = \frac{35.16}{256}(100) = 13.7 \text{ percent}$$

Suppose we wish to compare the earnings of production workers with the earnings of Maloof Corporation executives. And suppose the mean and standard deviation of weekly earnings of the latter group are $850 and $70, respectively. A comparison of variability between the two populations in terms of standard deviations may be misleading. Comparison is meaningful if it is carried out in terms of coefficients of relative variation. The relative dispersion of executive earnings is

$$\text{CRV} = \frac{70}{850}(100) = 8.2 \text{ percent}$$

Therefore, the earnings of executives are relatively more uniform than the earnings of the production workers.

In sum, calculation of the standard deviation from grouped data* requires the following major steps:

1. To find the mean, multiply each frequency times the corresponding midpoint, sum the products, and divide the sum by the population size.
2. Subtract the mean from each midpoint value and square each deviation.
3. To find the variance, multiply each frequency times the corresponding squared deviation, sum the products, and divide the sum by the population size.
4. The standard deviation is the positive square root of the variance.

---

*Formula (3.2) for grouped data is all-inclusive; it reduces to formula (3.1) by letting each frequency f be equal to 1 and interpreting X as the value of an individual observation.

Section 3 Summary Measures of Dispersion

PROBLEMS

Group One

3.1. During the past year ALT Collaboratives, a research consulting firm, initiated the following number of research proposals per month:

10, 5, 15, 7, 8, 9, 12, 2, 4, 14, 16, 18

*(a) Calculate the range and the interquartile range.
*(b) Calculate the variance and standard deviation.
(c) How do these two sets of dispersion measures differ? Explain.

3.2. The frequency distribution of lifetimes for pocket calculator batteries is as follows:

Lifetime (Hours)	Number of Batteries
400 and under 500	269
500 and under 600	424
600 and under 700	152
700 and under 800	83
800 and under 900	47
900 and under 1000	25

*(a) Calculate the mean, median, and mode.
(b) Do these measures indicate that the distribution is positively or negatively skewed? Explain.
(c) Illustrate your answer to part (b) by indicating the position of these averages on a frequency curve of the distribution.

3.3 The Graduate Management Admission Test (GMAT) scores of students admitted to a graduate program in business administration are distributed as follows:

GMAT Scores	Number of Students
450 and under 500	12
500 and under 550	24
550 and under 600	28
600 and under 650	35
650 and under 700	62
700 and under 750	39

*(a) Calculate the mean, median, and mode.
(b) Do these measures indicate that the distribution is positively or negatively skewed? Explain.
(c) Illustrate your answer to part (b) by indicating the position of these averages on a frequency curve of the distribution.

Answers to asterisked (*) problems are appended.

3.4. For each indicated frequency distribution, calculate the variance and the standard deviation. Interpret the results.
   *(a) Problem 3.2
   (b) Problem 3.3
3.5. For each indicated frequency distribution, calculate the coefficient of relative variation and interpret the result.
   *(a) Problem 3.2
   (b) Problem 3.3
3.6. The placement director of your college tells you that the incomes of alumni 5 years after graduation are normally distributed with a range from $12,600 to $19,200.
   (a) What is the mean income of the group? Defend your answer.
   (b) Would the median and mode incomes of the group be equal to the mean income? Explain why or why not.
   (c) What is the standard deviation of this income distribution? Explain your answer.
3.7. Explain the following terms:
   (a) Normal distribution
   (b) Distance measures of dispersion
   (c) Negatively skewed distribution
   (d) Percentiles
   (e) Quartiles
   (f) Unimodal distribution
   (g) Exponential distribution
   (h) Average measure of dispersion
   (i) Positively skewed distribution
   (j) Bimodal distribution
   (k) Ogive curve
   (l) Fractiles
   (m) Deviation
   (n) Rectangular distribution
3.8. Briefly and in your own words explain the following measures:
   (a) Standard deviation
   (b) Range
   (c) Coefficient of relative variation
   (d) Interquartile range
   (e) Variance
   (f) Skewness

Group Two

3.9. The cumulative less-than relative frequency distribution of data in Problem 3.2 is

Lifetime	Frequency
Less than 500	.269
Less than 600	.693
Less than 700	.845
Less than 800	.928
Less than 900	.975
Less than 1000	1.000

   (a) Construct an ogive curve on coordinate paper.
   *(b) Approximate the median value, using the ogive curve, and verify the result by calculating the median with the formula.
   (c) Approximate the value of the interquartile range, using the ogive curve. Interpret the result.

Section 3 Summary Measures of Dispersion

3.10. The cumulative less-than relative frequency distribution of the GMAT scores in Problem 3.3 is

GMAT Score	Relative Frequency
Less than 500	.060
Less than 550	.180
Less than 600	.320
Less than 650	.495
Less than 700	.805
Less than 750	1.000

(a) Construct an ogive curve on coordinate paper.
*(b) Approximate the median value using the ogive curve and verify the result by calculating the median with the formula.
(c) Approximate the value of the interquartile range using the ogive curve and interpret the result.

3.11. At the end of a recruiting period, Joseph Kirby, U.S. Army noncommissioned officer, compiled the following distribution of recruits by weight.

Weight (Pounds)	Recruits	Weight (Pounds)	Recruits
95 and under 105	15	145 and under 155	81
105 and under 115	32	155 and under 165	133
115 and under 125	107	165 and under 175	74
125 and under 135	42	175 and under 185	41
135 and under 145	65	185 and under 195	10

*(a) Calculate the mean and median.
(b) Construct a frequency curve and indicate the location of these two measures.
(c) Are the mean and median appropriate measures of central tendency for this distribution? Explain why and make specific suggestions.

3.12. In Delmarve Manufacturing Corporation the mean daily output of machine knives was 437 units per production worker. The standard deviation was 58 units per worker. Management introduced a retraining program for all workers. After the termination of the program, the mean daily output increased to 493 units per worker and the standard deviation declined to 29 units.

(a) What effect are the above changes likely to have in the frequency distribution of output per worker? Assuming a unimodal, that is, single-peaked, distribution, describe this probable effect by sketching on a single diagram one frequency curve of the distribution before and one after the initiation of the program. Indicate the position of two means on the horizontal scale of the diagram.

(b) Which of the two distributions has greater variability? Calculate the appropriate measure for comparing variability.

3.13. Pamela Winig, the new assistant manager of DND Inc., a mail-order firm, wants to study the effectiveness of two procedures for filling mail orders. In order to control differences in performance which can be attributed to factors other than the procedures, she assigns at random one team of employees to each procedure and, after a few days, reverses the assigned procedures. The experiment yields the following measures:

	Procedure A	Procedure B
Mean number of filled orders per hour	352	375
Median number of filled orders per hour	384	343

(a) Which procedure may result in a larger number of filled orders? Explain why.

(b) Assuming that each of the two frequency distributions of filled orders per hour is unimodal, that is, with a single peak, what does the skewness of each distribution imply? Explain.

Chapter 2
PROBABILITY CONCEPTS AND TOOLS

Earlier, we explained that a sample is random if every elementary unit of the parent population has a chance of being selected with known frequency. Also, we pointed out that, in practice, we usually select a *single* random sample of a given number of elementary units in order to draw inferences from the parent population. For example, an assembly line turns out toasters and we know that, on the average, a certain percentage of them will be defective; then we can select a random sample of, say, two toasters from the assembly line and determine the probability that none, one, or both of them will be defective. Or consider a random sample of 50 households taken from a population of households in the area to be served by a proposed shopping center: we can calculate household income of the sample and determine the probability that such a sample mean may differ from an assumed value of the household population mean. Finding the probability of such random occurrences is one of the central problems of probability. In order to understand how such probabilities are determined, we introduce in the four sections of this chapter the necessary probability concepts and tools.

SECTION 4/ SAMPLE SPACES AND EVENTS

Our immediate purpose is to study the outcomes of all possible samples of a given size that can be randomly selected from a population. Consider again a random sample of two toasters from an assembly line; we may consider that none, one, or two defective toasters are the only possible outcomes. The collection of these distinct outcomes is called a *sample space*. The objects which specify these sample outcomes are referred to as the *elements* of a sample space. For example, numbers 0, 1, 2 corresponding to outcomes none, one, or two defective toasters would be the elements of the sample space for a random selection of two toasters.

Our first task, therefore, is to illustrate the formation of sample spaces and to distinguish between the different types of sample spaces. Then we pay special attention to events. We discuss the complement, intersection, and union of events, and joint versus disjoint events of a sample space.

Sample Spaces and Random Experiments

In probability and statistics, random experiments occupy a central position because they illustrate effectively important concepts. The term *random experiment* refers to procedures which result in the collection of observations related to phenomena that exhibit variation. For example, random selection of households from a population of households can be perceived as a random experiment; observations, say, about household income vary from household to household.

In statistics, an important experiment is selecting a random sample from a population. In most real-life sampling procedures a sample space from such an experiment contains a very large number of sample outcomes. The sample space of all possible sample means of 50 households from even a relatively small population of 20,000 households would contain an astronomical number of sample outcomes. Fortunately, however, we can illustrate our basic concepts just as effectively with random experiments involving sample spaces with a small number of outcomes.

Example 4.1

Consider the experiment of selecting at random a toaster as toasters come out of an assembly line. The selected toaster may be classified as good (G) or as defective (D). Prior to actual selection, however, we do not know whether the selected toaster will be good or defective. Hence, the sample space is

$$S_1 = \{G, D\}$$

read "S sub-1."

Observe that we use the capital letter S to denote the sample space and a numerical subscript for easy reference. The elements of the sample space are enclosed in braces: { }. Henceforth, we shall follow this notation.

Note that good and defective are the only possible outcomes of the sample space. If we select a toaster, one outcome must occur; the toaster can be either good or defective but not both. The experiment provides for the selection of one toaster. Such a selection is called a *trial*. Thus we can have an experiment consisting of two trials if it provides for the selection of two toasters, of three trials for selecting three toasters, and so on.

Example 4.2

Suppose we consider the experiment of randomly selecting two toasters from an assembly line. Unless there are reasons to believe otherwise, we may assume that the occurrence of a good (G) or a defective (D) toaster is random. The sample space is

$$S_2 = \{(G, G), (G, D), (D, G), (D, D)\}$$

Section 4 Sample Spaces and Events   **45**

The first element indicates that both toasters are good, the second element that the first toaster is good and the second defective, and so on. For every possibility in the first trial (selection) there are two possibilities in the second trial, and so there are $2 \times 2 = 4$ elements.

The elements of a sample space are *mutually exclusive*. This means that each element is separate and distinct from any other element; no two elements are identical. Also, the elements of a sample space are *collectively exhaustive*. This means that a sample space contains the totality of sample outcomes; it is an exhaustive list of all possible outcomes for a random experiment.

We speak of *a* rather than *the* sample space for a particular random experiment since there is more than one way to classify all possible sample outcomes of a random experiment. Hence, there is more than one suitable sample space for each random experiment.

Example 4.3

Consider again the random selection of two toasters from an assembly line. We may be interested in the *number* of defective toasters rather than whether a toaster is good or defective. Then the suitable sample space for the same experiment is

$$S_3 = \{0, 1, 2\}$$

where the numerals inside the braces denote the number of defective toasters in each sample outcome. Note that, although there are two elements in S_2 each containing one defective toaster, we list element 1 only once in S_3 in accordance with the definition of a sample space. In other words, sample outcomes with identical values are listed only once.

Suppose we are concerned only with whether the two toasters are alike (A)—that is, both good or both defective—and not alike (N)—that is, one good and the other defective. Then

$$S_4 = \{A, N\}$$

is still another sample space for the same experiment.

In short, *a sample space for a random experiment is a set containing all possible outcomes which may occur.* In particular:

1. The sample outcomes represent a set so that elements may be listed in any sequence while outcomes with identical values are listed only once.
2. The elements of a sample space are mutually exclusive and collectively exhaustive.
3. The number of sample spaces we can conceivably specify for a given experiment may be very large.
4. Sample spaces such as those already illustrated may actually be obtained. In real-life situations such as selecting a sample of 50 households from a population of 20,000 households, however, the elements of a sample space are not listed; we may simply imagine the outcomes from all possible samples, while

Sampling with and without Replacement

actual sampling usually involves selection of one and only one sample of 50 households.

If an elementary unit of a statistical population, say, of households, is allowed to be included in the sample more than once, sampling is said to be performed *with replacement*.

Example 4.4

In order to simplify work, let us assume that our statistical population consists only of three households, A, B, and C. Each letter name appears on a ball and the three balls are placed in an urn. Our random experiment consists of selecting a sample of two households by drawing two balls, one first and then a second after putting the first ball back into the urn.

We can illustrate formation of the sample space with a tree diagram. Selection of each ball represents a trial. Starting from a common point, we draw three lines for the three possibilities of the first trial, as shown in Fig. 4.1. For every possibility of the first trial, we draw three lines for the three possibilities of the second trial. The tree diagram is completed by recording each element in parentheses after each end point. Sampling is performed with replacement. And

$$S_5 = \{(A, A), (A, B), (A, C), (B, A), (B, B), (B, C), (C, A), (C, B), (C, C)\}$$

is a sample space for the experiment.

Observe that each of the two trials in this experiment includes three possibilities. Hence, there are nine sample outcomes: $3 \times 3 = 9$.

Figure 4.1.
Tree diagram for selecting two households from three households with replacement.

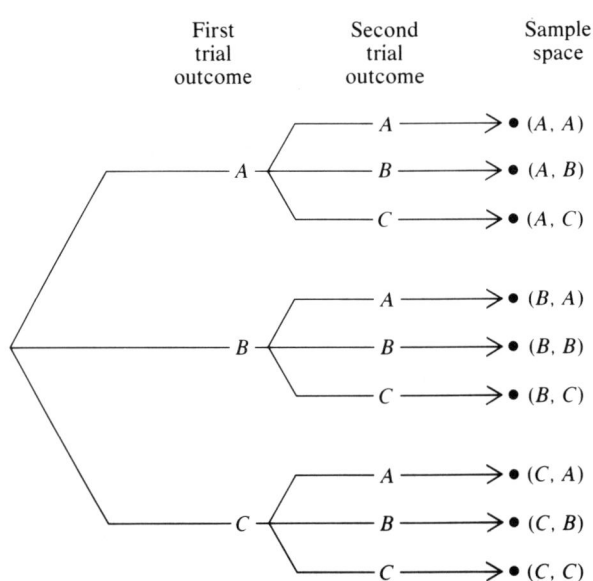

Section 4 Sample Spaces and Events

Also, note that for some random experiments, such as the sampling of the toaster assembly line, sampling with replacement is inherent in the assembling process. The sampled population is considered to be infinite, that is, countless. This is not so with the last random experiment where the population is finite, consisting of three households. Repeated selection of the same households is obtained by replacing the first ball before selecting the second ball. It is important to remember that sampling with replacement from a finite population is equivalent to sampling an infinite population.

On the other hand, an elementary unit of a statistical population may not be allowed to be included in a sample more than once. For example, in a consumer survey, we do not interview each household in the sample more than once. Second and subsequent sample selections of the same household are ignored. In such a case, sampling is said to be performed *without replacement*.

Example 4.5

Let us consider again sampling two households from a population of three households. This time, however, we do not put the first ball back into the urn before selecting the second ball.

There are three possibilities for the first trial; that is, we can select household A, B, or C. But the second trial includes only two possibilities because we do not replace the ball of the household which has been selected in the first trial. So there are only six elements: $3 \times 2 = 6$. Selection of two households without replacement is illustrated by a tree diagram in Fig. 4.2.

Figure 4.2.
Tree diagram for selecting two households from three households without replacement.

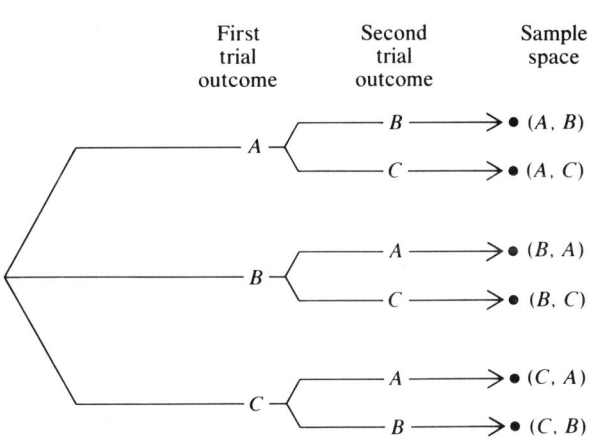

Observe that from each of the three lines for selecting the first household we draw two lines only because there are only two households left for the second selection. A sample space for this experiment is

$$S_6 = \{(A, B), (A, C), (B, A), (B, C), (C, A), (C, B)\}$$

as shown at the end points of the tree diagram.

The Complement, Intersection, and Union of Events

Each element of a sample space represents an *elementary event* which cannot be further divided into other events. For example, the element "Two good toasters" from sample space S_2 is an elementary event; so is the element "Households (A, B)" from sample spaces S_5 or S_6, specified earlier. By contrast, an event which contains two or more elements of a sample space is called a *compound event*. For example, "At least one defective toaster" is a compound event of sample space S_2 since it contains the elements (G, D), (D, G), and (D, D).

Elementary and compound events are related to three event types which are important for understanding probability laws as well as for calculating probabilities.

The *first* important type is the *complement* of an event.

Example 4.6

The production manager of Techtronics Ltd. takes periodically random samples of two transistors in order to check the quality of daily output. Each selected transistor is tested and classified as good (G) or defective (D). The relevant sample space is

$$S_2 = \{(G, G), (G, D), (D, G), (D, D)\}$$

the same as the sample space for the toaster experiment.

The production manager may be interested in finding the probability of event E:

$$E = \{(G, D), (D, G), (D, D)\}$$

defined as "At least one defective transistor." One way of finding the probability of event E is to add the probability of each of the three elementary events in E. Usually, however, it is easier to find this probability indirectly by calculating the probability of the complement of E, event *not-E*:

$$not\text{-}E = \{(G, G)\}$$

because it contains only one elementary event.

The relationship between event E and its complement *not-E* is portrayed in Fig. 4.3. The rectangle represents sample space S_2 and the circle event E. The shaded area outside the circle depicts the complement event *not-E*; it contains the elements of sample space S_2 which do not belong to event E.

Figure 4.3. Event E and its complement not-E.

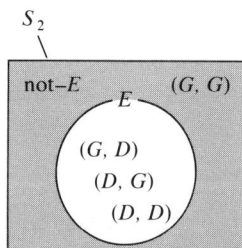

Section 4 Sample Spaces and Events

This classification of a sample space between events E and *not-E* has a wide range of applications. For example, the respondents of a survey are classified into male or female (not-male) and many of their responses into yes or no (not-yes) answers. Car buyers may be classified into those who preplanned or those who did not preplan their purchase; customers can be credit card holders or not credit card holders; companies use television or do not use television advertising, and so on.

A *second* important event category is the *intersection* of two events.

Example 4.7

A retailer considers three types of window displays for the holiday season: A, B, and C. The store, however, has only two display windows: a front and a side window. In how many ways can the three window displays be arranged if identical displays can occupy both windows?

We can perceive this situation as a random experiment of selecting two displays from three displays. Since identical displays can occupy both windows, sampling is with replacement. There are nine display arrangements because any of the three displays can occupy the front window as well as the side window. A sample space may be specified as

$$S_5 = \{(A, A), (A, B), (A, C), (B, A), (B, B), (B, C), (C, A), (C, B), (C, C)\}$$

Note that S_5 is the sample space obtained earlier for sampling two households from a population of three households with replacement.

Consider event

$$E = \{(A, A), (A, B), (A, C)\}$$

that is, "Display A occupies the front window," and event

$$F = \{(A, B), (B, B), (C, B)\}$$

that is, "Display B occupies the side window." The intersection of the two events is

$$E \text{ and } F = \{(A, B)\}$$

that is, "Display A occupies the front *and* display B occupies the side window." This is portrayed in Fig. 4.4. Again, the rectangle represents sample space S_5 and the circles events E and F. The intersection event $\{(A, B)\}$

Figure 4.4.
The intersection of events E and F.

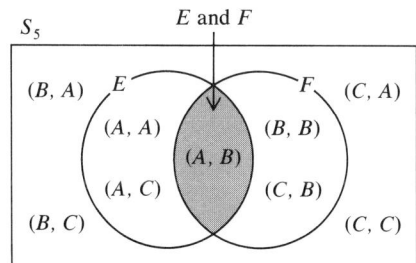

represents the shaded overlapping of the two circles; it is the event which contains the element common to both events E and F.

The *third* important event category is the *union* of two events.

Example 4.8

A distributor has two sales districts with such distinct characteristics that it is important which of the three salespersons A, B, and C is assigned to a particular district. In how many ways can the three salespersons be assigned to the two sales districts?

This problem can be perceived as a random experiment of selecting two persons from three persons. Sampling is without replacement because no salesperson can be assigned to more than one sales district. There are six assignments: any of the three salespersons can be assigned to the first district and any of the remaining two to the second district. The sample space is

$$S_6 = \{(A, B), (A, C), (B, A), (B, C), (C, A) (C, B)\}$$

Note that S_6 is the sample space obtained earlier for sampling two households from three households without replacement.

Then consider event

$$E = \{(A, B), (A, C)\}$$

that is, "Salesperson A is assigned to the first sales district," and event

$$F = \{(A, B), (C, B)\}$$

that is, "Salesperson B is assigned to the second sales district." The union of the two events is

$$E \text{ or } F = \{(A, B), (A, C), (C, B)\}$$

that is, "Salesperson A is assigned to the first *or* salesperson B is assigned to the second sales district."

The shaded area of the two circles in Fig. 4.5 portrays this union event. Note that event E or F contains the elements that belong to either event E or event F, or to both. However, the common elementary event (A, B) is listed once in accordance with the set definition.

Figure 4.5.
The union event E or F.

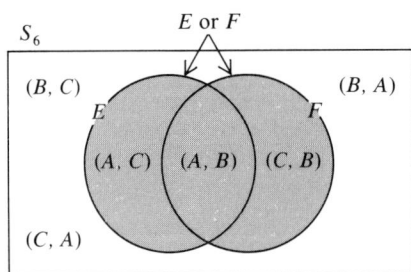

Section 4 Sample Spaces and Events

A great number of situations may be described in terms of the intersection or the union of two events. Furthermore, the same operations can be easily extended to situations which involve more than two events. For example, the production manager of Techtronics may be interested in the event that in a sample of three transistors the first is good, *and* the second is defective, *and* the third is defective; a car dealer may be concerned with persons who belong to a certain income bracket *or* are previous customers *or* live within a certain distance from the location of the dealership; and so on.

Joint and Disjoint Events

The intersection of two events in a sample space leads to another event category. Either the two events have at least one common element or they have none. Study of this category of events is important for determining probabilities.

If two events have at least one common element, they are called *joint* events. For example, event E and event F in Fig. 4.4 are joint because their intersection contains element (A, B) which is common to both events. The same holds true for event E and event F in Fig. 4.5. Element (A, B) is common to both events.

On the other hand, if two events have no common elements, they are called *disjoint* or *mutually exclusive*. For example, event E and its complement *not-E* shown in Fig. 4.3 are by definition disjoint. They are mutually exclusive because the occurrence of event E excludes the occurrence of event *not-E* and vice versa; their intersection contains no elements.

Again, a great number of situations may be described in terms of joint and disjoint events. For example, the respondents of a sample may be classified into male or female, smokers or nonsmokers. Each classification may be thought to represent disjoint events since a male respondent cannot be female and a smoker cannot be a nonsmoker. On the other hand, a cross-classification of respondents may be thought to constitute joint events, since being a male does not exclude being a smoker also; being a female does not exclude being a nonsmoker also; and so on. In addition, we can easily extend the discussion to joint and disjoint events involving more than two classifications.

PROBLEMS

Group One

4.1. Flashlight batteries are tested as they come out of a production line. They are classified as good (G), defective but restorable (D), or entirely rejected (R). Two batteries are randomly selected.
 *(a) Is the population of batteries which a production line may turn out infinite or finite? Explain why.
 (b) Specify a sample space for this random experiment.
 (c) Illustrate formation of this sample space with a tree diagram.
4.2. The president of International Disk Corporation wishes to send a three-member delegation to an international trade conference. Four salespersons, X, Y, Z, and

Answers to asterisked (*) problems are appended.

W, are considered as candidates. In order to be fair the president decides to select membership at random so that the first selected salesperson will be the chief of the delegation, the second the deputy, and the third in charge of trade displays.
*(a) Does this selection involve sampling with or without replacement? Explain.
(b) Illustrate formation of a sample space for this random experiment with a tree diagram.
(c) How many elements does the sample space contain? Explain in terms of trials and possibilities.

4.3. Three households consist of two, four, and six individuals.
*(a) Specify a sample space for the random experiment of selecting two households without replacement where each element represents the size of each selected household.
(b) Specify a sample space for the same random experiment where each element represents the total number of individuals.

4.4. The annual incomes of three households are $6000, $12,000, and $24,000. A random experiment consists of selecting the income of two households with replacement. For each of the following events, specify an appropriate sample space and list the elements contained in the event E.
*(a) "The income of the two households is $6000 and $24,000."
(b) "The total income of the two households is at least $30,000."
(c) "The average income of the two households is $15,000."

4.5. The accompanying diagram contains the sample space for rolling a die once where the numbers indicate the dots on each side. List the following events:

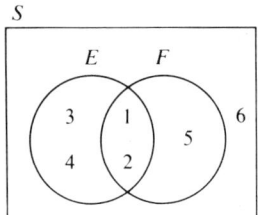

*(a) not-E (d) not-(E or F)
 (b) E or F (e) not-(E and F)
 (c) E and F (f) S and E

4.6. Distinguish between:
(a) Sample space and sample outcome
(b) Sampling with and without replacement
(c) Infinite and finite population
(d) Mutually exclusive and collectively exhaustive events.

4.7. Explain the following events:
(a) Compound   (e) Intersection
(b) Joint   (f) Disjoint
(c) Elementary   (g) Complement
(d) Union

Section 4 Sample Spaces and Events

Group Two

4.8. Four young physicians, X, Y, Z, and W, are considered for three internship positions at a hospital. List the elements of the following events:
*(a) "Physician X is selected."
(b) "Physicians X and Z are selected."
(c) "Physician X or Z is selected."

4.9. A child born from a healthy father and a hemophilia-carrying mother can be either a healthy boy (B), a healthy girl (G), a hemophilic boy (H), or a hemophilia-carrying girl (R). Suppose such a couple plans to have two children.
*(a) Is the statistical population of this random experiment infinite or finite? Explain why.
(b) Illustrate formation of a sample space for this random experiment with a tree diagram.

4.10. Again, consider a statistical population of three households A, B, C. Suppose household A has no children, household B has two children, and household C has four children.
(a) Specify a sample space S_1 for the random experiment of selecting two households with replacement where each element shows the number of children in each household.
(b) Specify a sample space S_2 for the same random experiment where each element shows the proportion of households with no children.
(c) List the elementary events of the two sample spaces S_1 and S_2 in separate columns. Then show with arrows the elementary events in S_1 that correspond to the elementary events in S_2. Discuss the relationship.

4.11. From a shipment of 100 radios, five are selected at random. Determine the number of all possible elements in a sample space for this random experiment if selection is:
*(a) With replacement
(b) Without replacement

4.12. The statistical population of households for studying the economic feasibility of a shopping center may be classified with respect to income and household size as follows:

	Persons in Household	
Income	Three or Fewer (F)	Four or More (M)
Above median (A)	A and F	A and M
Below median (B)	B and F	B and M

Indicate whether the following events are joint or disjoint. Are they also collectively exhaustive? Explain in terms of the intersection and the union of these events.
(a) A, B
(b) A, A and F
(c) A and F, B and M
(d) A and F, A and M, B and F, B and M

SECTION 5 / THE PROBABILITY OF AN EVENT: THE ADDITION RULE

With the ideas of a sample space and of an event now established, we are conceptually ready to introduce some basic rules and techniques for determining probabilities. Our task is facilitated by the fact that the union and the intersection of events are used for introducing two important probability rules: addition and multiplication, respectively; they occupy this and the next sections. The last section of this chapter introduces some counting techniques for determining probabilities.

In this section, we direct our attention first to answering a number of questions. To which real-world events shall we assign probabilities? Shall we assign probabilities to events such as the future demand for a product and the award of a business contract on the basis of historical data or even personal belief and hunches? Or shall we limit the assignment of probabilities to events from random sampling and real-life processes with coin-tossing characteristics? Then we illustrate determination of probabilities when the outcomes of a sample space are equally likely. This topic leads to the introduction of the addition probability rule for joint and disjoint events.

The Probability of Events

In speaking of the probability of an event, we generally mean a number between 0 and 1, which indicates the relative frequency with which such an event is likely to occur if the experiment in question is repeated a large number of times. We say that the probability of a coin falling heads is 1/2 because we believe that in a large number of tosses of a "fair" coin, half of them are likely to turn up heads. Although no one may quarrel with the above explanation of probability, there is an important empirical problem connected with the assignment of probabilities to events.

If the probability of an event means the relative frequency with which that event occurs in a large number of trials, then *to which real-world events shall we assign probability?* Questions of this nature touch upon matters of definition, interpretation, and use of probability which have occupied the minds of many statisticians, mathematicians, and philosophers interested in probability theory. Perhaps the fact that probabilists talk about at least five kinds of probability may give one an idea of the different approaches to the subject. But all approaches to probability revolve around two pivotal viewpoints, the objective and subjective.

Under the *objective* point of view, probability is applicable only to events which can be repeated a very large or infinite number of times under the same or nearly the same conditions. An objectivist talks about the probability of an event in connection with the tossing of a coin, the rolling of a die, or the manufacture of a mass-produced or processed item; an objectivist thinks of the probability of a good unit as a long-run ratio of the number of good units to the total large number of units produced by a machine. In sum, an objectivist assigns probabilities to events which can be repeated endlessly or nearly so, that is, to events where there is a long-run ratio in sight. Furthermore, probabilities are based on no other kind of evidence than that which can be verified by repeated trials.

Section 5 The Probability of an Event: The Addition Rule

Example 5.1

Consider the sales record of a retail item in Table 5.1; the relative frequency indicates the ratio of the number of days a certain number of units were sold to the total 100 sales days. Would an objectivist assign each relative frequency as the probability to the corresponding event? No, according to the objective viewpoint, because the above relative frequency does not represent long-run ratios. Would experience based on more than 100 days change an objectivist's position? No, for the fact remains that events are not likely to be repeated in the future under much the same conditions.

Table 5.1. Relative Frequency of Units Sold by a Retailer

Events: Units Sold	Days	Relative Frequency	Fraction of Occurrence
1	10	.10	10/100
2	18	.18	18/100
3	25	.25	25/100
4	27	.27	27/100
5	20	.20	20/100
	Total: 100	1.00	1.00

On the other hand, under the *subjective* viewpoint the probability of an event is a measure of personal belief about a particular situation; consequently, this school of thought is sometimes called *personalistic*. A case in point is the retailer's item in Table 5.1. A subjectivist would assign the historical relative frequencies as probabilities to the corresponding events in the belief that past sales reflect the retailer's hunches and expectations about future sales of the item. A personalist may assign probabilities to events connected with all the problems an objectivist would, and to many more. Since probability is a measure of subjective considerations, a personalist may assign probabilities to events even when historical data are extremely sparse or not available. In the absence of historical data, the retailer may assign a different relative weight to each sales volume and accept such weights as probabilities as long as the data reflect personal experience from the sale of similar items and hunches or expectations. Furthermore, on the same basis a subjectivist may apply probabilities even to unique events such as bidding on a contract, buying machinery, building a factory, or other similar events which by their nature may not be repeated frequently or at all.

Although the question about the kinds of events to which we may assign probabilities is important in probability theory, hereafter there will be little need to distinguish between objective and subjective probabilities. Whatever the justification, the probabilities of the events in a sample space must have *two* characteristics.

First, probabilities are numbers greater than or equal to zero. For example, the probability that demand for an item in Table 5.1 will be 2 units is .18 or a fraction 18/100; the numerator in this fraction cannot be negative. In symbols, the probability of event E must be

(5.1) $$P(E) \geq 0$$

Second, probabilities of all the outcomes must add up to one. For example, the sum of the numerators in each fraction in Table 5.1 cannot be greater than the denominator. Since the sample space includes all the outcomes of a random experiment, the sample space is a certain event with probability 1. In symbols,

(5.2) $$P(\text{sample space}) = 1$$

The event "1 to 5 units sold" in Table 5.1 is a certain event because it includes all sample outcomes of the random experiment.

Probabilities may be expressed in terms other than a fraction or a proportion. They may be expressed as percentages, as chances, or as odds. All such expressions can be easily translated into a fraction or a proportion. For example, we may say that there is a 50 percent probability that a fair coin will turn up heads. Dividing the percent by 100, we obtain the equivalent probability fraction 1/2 or proportion .50. Rather than talking in terms of probabilities, managers often talk about the chances or odds for an event. The statement "There is 1 chance in 10 that we will be awarded the contract" is equivalent to a probability 1/10 for such an event. Or consider the statement "The odds are 1 to 2 that Mr. J. C. Sims will make a sale." In order to express these odds in terms of a fraction, we add the two numbers, $1 + 2 = 3$, place the result in the denominator and the first number, 1, in the numerator, so the probability is 1/3. In general, the odds in favor of or for an event E are a to b if

(5.3) $$P(E) = \frac{a}{a + b}$$

In our illustration a is 1 and b is 2, so

$$P(E) = \frac{1}{1 + 2} = \frac{1}{3}$$

Conversely, if the probability of an event E is, say, .40, then we write

$$P(E) = \frac{4}{10} = \frac{4}{4 + 6}$$

Hence, a is 4 and b is 6, so the odds are 4 to 6 for event E.

Equally Likely Outcomes

We discuss first determination of the probability of an event when the sample outcomes are equally likely. The term *equally likely* or *equiprobable* refers to a random experiment where there is no reason to believe that every outcome of a sample space has other than equal probability of occurring.

Example 5.2

Earlier, we found that the sample space for selecting with replacement two households from three households A, B, and C is

$$S_5 = \{(A, A), (A, B), (A, C), (B, A), (B, B), (B, C), (C, A), (C, B), (C, C)\}$$

Section 5 The Probability of an Event: The Addition Rule

What is the probability of event

$$E = \{(A, A), (A, B), (A, C), (B, A), (C, A)\}$$

that is, "Household A is selected"?

Each element in S_5 is assigned $1/9$ probability because these elements correspond to sample outcomes which occur with equal probability. Since event E contains five of these equiprobable elements,

$$P(E) = 5(1/9) = 5/9$$

In general, when a random experiment results in a sample space S with equally likely outcomes, the probability of an event E is

(5.4) $$P(E) = \frac{\text{number of elements in } E}{\text{number of elements in } S}$$

In words, the probability of an event is the ratio of the number of elements in the event to the number of elements in the sample space.

Application of expression (5.4) may be illustrated more effectively as follows.

Example 5.3 The purchase of many consumer goods involves various degrees of preplanning. Items such as a pair of slacks or a suit may be the result of a few days or weeks of planning. Other, more expensive purchases such as an automobile or a house may require planning ahead for a year or more before actual buying takes place.

Numerous intensive studies have been conducted of consumer planning for the purchase of durable goods such as television sets, refrigerators, washing machines, stoves, and automobiles. In one such study, members of a randomly selected sample of 1000 individuals were asked whether they were planning to buy a new automobile in the next 12 months. A year later the same persons were interviewed again to find out whether they had actually made such a purchase. The response to both interviews is cross-tabulated in Table 5.2.

We can perform the following experiment. We may imagine an urn with 1000 balls in it, each bearing the proper letters denoting responses to

Table 5.2.
Response to Planning and Purchasing an Automobile (Hypothetical Data)

	First Interview		
Second Interview	Planners (A)	Nonplanners (B)	Row Totals
Buyers (B)	A and B (50)	C and B (150)	B (200)
Nonbuyers (D)	A and D (100)	C and D (700)	D (800)
Column totals:	A (150)	C (850)	S (1000)

both interviews as shown. There will be 50 balls with letters A and B for the respondents who planned to buy and actually bought a new automobile, 100 balls with letters A and D for the respondents who planned but did not buy one, and so on. The balls in the urn are thoroughly mixed, and one ball is drawn at random.

What is the probability of event A, that is, "A respondent plans to purchase an automobile"?

Since there are 150 planners out of a total of 1000 respondents and each respondent has equal probability of being selected, by expression (5.4)

$$P(A) = \frac{150}{1000} = .15$$

Note that if the outcomes of a sample space are equally likely, to find the probability of a compound event, we need not know *which* but only count *how many* elements are in the event. It must be evident that for sample spaces with a very large number of equiprobable outcomes we need effective techniques to find the probability of a compound event. Such techniques are discussed later.

The Addition Rule

What about events representing nonequiprobable outcomes? Expression (5.4) does not apply. In order to find the probability of such events, we must apply the *addition rule*. In its simplest form, the addition rule for any two events E and F is

(5.5) $\quad\boxed{P(E \text{ or } F) = P(E) + P(F) - P(E \text{ and } F)}$

The probability of the intersection event E and F is subtracted to avoid double-counting elements common to both E and F.

Example 5.4

Consider again the experiment of selecting a person at random from Table 5.2. What is the probability of event A or B, that is, "A respondent is a planner or a buyer"?

Earlier, we found that $P(A) = .15$ by application of expression (5.4). On the same basis, $P(B) = 200/1000 = .20$. Also, the two events are joint so $P(A \text{ and } B) = 50/1000 = .05$. Application of the addition rule (5.5) yields

$$\begin{aligned} P(A \text{ or } B) &= P(A) + P(B) - P(A \text{ and } B) \\ &= .15 + .20 - .05 \\ &= .30 \end{aligned}$$

When two events are disjoint or mutually exclusive, their intersection E and F has no elements. So $P(E \text{ and } F)$ is zero. This condition leads to the special expression of the addition rule:

(5.6) $\quad\boxed{P(E \text{ or } F) = P(E) + P(F)}$

Example 5.5

Earlier, we found that the sample space for assigning three salespersons A, B, and C to two districts is

$$S_6 = \{(A, B), (A, C), (B, A), (B, C), (C, A), (C, B)\}$$

Section 5 The Probability of an Event: The Addition Rule

Consider events
$$G = \{(A, B), (A, C)\}$$
that is, "Salesperson A is assigned to the first sales district," and
$$H = \{(B, A), (C, A)\}$$
that is, "Salesperson A is assigned to the second sales district." What is the probability of event G or H, that is, "Salesperson A is assigned to the first or the second district"?

The six sample outcomes in S_6 are equiprobable, so $P(G) = 2/6$ and $P(H) = 2/6$ by expression (5.4). Also, the two events are disjoint since the intersection event G and H has no elements in it. Application of rule (5.6) results in

$$\begin{aligned} P(G \text{ or } H) &= P(G) + P(H) \\ &= \frac{2}{6} + \frac{2}{6} \\ &= \frac{4}{6} \end{aligned}$$

The modified form (5.6) of the addition rule can be easily applied to situations where we wish to find the probability of more than two mutually exclusive events.

Example 5.6 Let us assume that the relative frequency in Example 5.1 represents the probabilities the retailer assigned to the elements of the sample space
$$S_7 = \{1, 2, 3, 4, 5\}$$
where the numbers represent units sold. What is the probability of the event "At least 2 units sold"?

Let E be the event "At least 2 units sold." Then
$$E = \{2\} \text{ or } \{3\} \text{ or } \{4\} \text{ or } \{5\}$$
that is, event E is the union of all elementary events 2 to 5, inclusive. Since the elementary events are mutually exclusive, by (5.6)

$$\begin{aligned} P(E) &= P(\{2\}) + P(\{3\}) + P(\{4\}) + P(\{5\}) \\ &= .18 + .25 + .27 + .20 \\ &= .90 \end{aligned}$$

We have seen that an event and its complement are mutually exclusive and collectively exhaustive. In other words, occurrence of the event excludes occurrence of its complement and vice versa; their union, furthermore, equals the sample space since they exhaust the list of elements in the sample space. It follows that for any event E and its complement *not-E* the addition rule yields

$$P(E \text{ or } not\text{-}E) = P(E) + P(not\text{-}E) = 1$$

Chapter 2 Probability Concepts and Tools

Subtracting $P(\text{not-}E)$ from the rightmost equality we obtain

(5.7)
$$P(E) = 1 - P(\text{not-}E)$$

Expression (5.7) may facilitate the determination of probabilities.

Example 5.6 (continued)

Note how we determined the probability of the event E: "At least 2 units sold." We added the probabilities of four elementary events in sample space S_7. We can find the probability of the same event much more easily by referring to the probability of the complement event. Since $P(\text{not-}E)$ is .10, application of (5.7) yields

$$P(E) = 1 - .10 = .90$$

as found previously.

PROBLEMS

Group One

5.1. From the objective point of view, to which of the following events would you assign and to which would you not assign probability? Defend your answer.
  (a) A card is drawn from a well-shuffled deck of 52 playing cards.
  (b) Of the 10,000 dealers representing an automobile manufacturer, 60 percent report monthly total sales of 50,000 units and 40 percent report 100,000 units.
  *(c) An agreement is negotiated for the merger of two firms.
  (d) A ball is drawn from an urn containing 100 balls of which 75 percent are black and 25 percent red.
  (e) Oil drilling is contemplated on a certain locality; previous oil drillings under similar prospects were 40 percent successful.
  (f) A light bulb is drawn from a large pile of light bulbs produced by a machine known to turn out .001 defective bulbs.

5.2. A cashier selects at random two coins from a register containing a penny (E), a nickel (N), a dime (D), and a quarter (Q). What is the probability that the sum of the two coins is less than 12¢ if sampling is:
  *(a) With replacement?
  (b) Without replacement?

5.3. Four salespersons X, Y, Z, and W are considered as candidates for a three-member delegation. The first selected salesperson will be the chief of the delegation, the second the deputy, and the third in charge of trade displays. What is the probability of the events:
  *(a) "Salesperson X is the chief of the delegation"?
  (b) "Salesperson X is the chief and Y the deputy of the delegation"?
  (c) "Either salesperson Z or salesperson Y is the chief of the delegation"?

5.4. Given the following odds for event E, find $P(E)$:
  *(a) 1 to 1   (d) 8 to 5
  (b) 2 to 1   (e) 20 to 1
  (c) 3 to 1   (f) 100 to 1

Answers to asterisked (*) problems are appended.

Section 5 The Probability of an Event: The Addition Rule

5.5. Given $P(E)$, find the odds for event E:
*(a) $P(E) = .50$
*(b) $P(E)$ is 10 percent
(c) $P(E) = 1/7$
(d) $P(E)$ is 1 percent
(e) $P(E) = .99$
(f) $P(E) = 4/5$

5.6. Consider Table 5.2 in the text. What is the probability of the event that the selected respondent represents:
*(a) "A planner and a nonplanner"?
(b) "A buyer or a nonbuyer"?
(c) "A nonplanner or a nonbuyer"?

5.7. Demand for a consumer product is as follows:

Units Demanded	Relative Frequency
5	.08
6	.10
7	.25
8	.30
9	.18
10	.09
	1.00

What is the probability that demand is:
*(a) 7 or 8 units?
(b) Less than 7 units?
(c) 9 or fewer units?

5.8. A sample space for tossing a coin twice is

$$S = \{(H, H), (H, T), (T, H), (T, T)\}$$

where H stands for heads and T for tails. Consider the elementary events

$$E_1 = \{(H, H)\}, \quad E_2 = \{(H, T)\},$$
$$E_3 = \{(T, H)\}, \text{ and } E_4 = \{(T, T)\}$$

Indicate whether each of the following assignments of probabilities to these elementary events is acceptable. Explain why.
*(a) $P(E_1) = 1/3, P(E_2 \text{ or } E_3) = 1/3, P(E_4) = 1/3$
(b) $P(E_4) = 1/3, P(E_2) = 1/2, P(E_1) = 1/2, P(E_3) = 0$
(c) $P(E_1) = 1/4, P(E_2) = 1/4, P(E_3) = 1/4, P(E_4) = 1/4$
(d) $P(E_2) = 1/2, P(E_1) = 1/6, P(E_3) = 1/8, P(E_4) = 1/5$

Group Two

5.9. Three households A, B, and C have annual incomes of $6000, $12,000, and $24,000, respectively. Two households are selected at random with replacement. What is the probability that the average income of the two households in the sample is:
*(a) $9000?
(b) $9000 or 12,000?
(c) More than $12,000?

5.10. Three households A, B, and C consist of 2, 4, and 6 individuals, respectively. Two

households are selected at random without replacement. What is the probability that the total number of individuals of the two households in the sample is:
*(a) 6 persons?
(b) 8 or 10 persons?
(c) No more than 8 persons?

5.11. A child born from a healthy father and a hemophilia-carrying mother can be either a healthy boy (B), a healthy girl, (G), a hemophilic boy (H), or an (unhealthy) hemophilia-carrying girl (R). Suppose such a couple plans to have two children. Assuming that outcomes are equiprobable, what is the probability that the couple gives birth to:
*(a) A healthy boy and a hemophilia-carrying girl?
(b) One healthy child and one unhealthy child?
(c) At least one hemophilic boy?

5.12. Three households A, B, and C have no children, two children, and four children, respectively. Two households are selected at random with replacement and the proportion of households with no children in each sample is recorded. What is the probability that this proportion is:
(a) Zero?
(b) Zero or .50?
(c) At least .50?

5.13. Consider the data of the survey of automobile buyers given in Table 5.2. Find
(a) $P(A$ and $D)$
(b) $P[(C$ and $B)$ or $(C$ and $D)]$
(c) $P[(A$ and $B)$ or $(C$ and $D)]$

5.14. A sample of 1000 adults are asked whether they regularly watch a certain weekly variety show on television. The following are their responses classified by age and education (data hypothetical):

Age	College	Watch Show	Response
Under 35	Yes	Yes	65
		No	85
	No	Yes	145
		No	105
35 or over	Yes	Yes	85
		No	115
	No	Yes	250
		No	150
		Total respondents:	1000

A ball is selected at random from an urn containing 1000 balls, one for each respondent of the survey. What is the probability that the chosen respondent is:
(a) Under 35 years old?
(b) College-educated?
(c) 35 years or older and watches the show?
(d) A regular viewer of the show?
(e) Not college-educated and watches the show?
(f) College-educated and watches the show?

SECTION 6 / PROBABILITIES: THE MULTIPLICATION RULE

We have seen that two or more events may occur *simultaneously*. In our illustration about automobile buyers a single trial, selection of one respondent, may generate the simultaneous occurrence of two events: the respondent is "A planner" and "A buyer." The probability of two events, "A planner and a buyer," occurring jointly, is called *joint* probability.

The probability of one event, say "A planner," without reference to the other event, "A buyer," is called *marginal* or *unconditional* probability; in other words, such an event does not refer to or is not conditioned by the occurrence of the other event. Finally, the probability of one event, "A buyer," on the condition that the other event, "A planner," has occurred is called *conditional probability*.

Two or more events may also occur in chronological order or *successively*, that is, be the result of two or more trials. The same survey of automobile buyers can be easily changed to illustrate two trials. Instead of selecting a ball from the urn representing respondents *after* the survey is completed, we may consider the survey *during* the time it is carried out. Then the result of the first interview could represent the first and of the second interview the second trial. We have already introduced several other cases which involve successively occurring events. For example, selection of two households from three households involves two trials. The result is occurrence of two successive events, one for each trial. The first household, for instance, may have an annual income of $6000 and the second an income of $12,000.

Whether two or more events occur simultaneously or successively the rules for determining their probabilities are the same. First we show how marginal, joint, and conditional probabilities are related. Then we discuss the multiplication rule which can be used for determining joint probabilities.

Marginal, Joint, and Conditional Probabilities

In order to introduce these probabilities, we consider two events which occur simultaneously, that is, in a single trial. Then determination of these probabilities from separate trials is a natural and effortless extension.

Example 6.1

In Table 5.2, we considered responses of 1000 individuals to planning and purchasing an automobile. The same data are reproduced in Table 6.1, the only difference being that the original frequencies are expressed as probabilities.

We found that the probability of the event "A respondent plans to purchase an automobile" is .15, since there are 150 planners out of a total 1000 respondents and each respondent has equal probability of being selected. Note that this probability does not refer to the other characteristic of the respondent, that is, whether or not the respondent has purchased an automobile. Since such a probability appears on the *margin* of Table 6.1, it is called a marginal probability.

Table 6.1.
Probability of Response to Planning and Purchasing an Automobile

Second Interview	First Interview		Marginal Probabilities
	Planners (A)	Nonplanners (C)	
Buyers (B)	P(A and B) = .05	P(C and B) = .15	P(B) = .20
Nonbuyers (D)	P(A and D) = .10	P(C and D) = .70	P(D) = .80
Marginal probabilities:	P(A) = .15	P(C) = .85	P(S) = 1.00

Note that Table 6.1 contains two sets of marginal probabilities. A selected respondent is classified as a planner or a nonplanner with marginal probabilities $P(A) = .15$ and $P(C) = .85$, respectively; the same respondent is also classified as a buyer or a nonbuyer with marginal probabilities $P(B) = .20$ and $P(D) = .80$, respectively. Also, observe that the sum of probabilities in each set is equal to one.

Classification of a respondent with respect to both characteristics gives rise to a joint probability. For example, the joint probability of the event "A respondent is a planner and a buyer" is .05, again determined by the fact that selection of respondents is equiprobable. Note that the marginal probability of the event "A respondent plans to purchase an automobile" is the sum of two joint probabilities:

$$P(A) = P(A \text{ and } B) + P(A \text{ and } D)$$
$$= .05 + .10$$
$$= .15$$

as found earlier. It is the sum of the joint probabilities which correspond to the event A. The other three marginal probabilities can be obtained by repeated application of the above procedure:

$$P(B) = P(A \text{ and } B) + P(C \text{ and } B) = .05 + .15 = .20$$
$$P(C) = P(C \text{ and } B) + P(C \text{ and } D) = .15 + .70 = .85$$
$$P(D) = P(A \text{ and } D) + P(C \text{ and } D) = .10 + .70 = .80$$

So far we have not broken new ground. Both marginal and joint probabilities were used earlier in connection with the addition rule. Here, we simply formalized their introduction. Now we are ready to proceed to a new and important topic in probability by introducing conditional probabilities.

Example 6.1 (continued)

Let us go back to Table 6.1. Supposing we are informed that the selected respondent is a planner, what is the probability that such a respondent is also a buyer?

This is the conditional probability $P(B|A)$, read "the conditional probability of B (buyer) given A (planner)." Knowing that the selected respon-

Section 6 Probabilities: The Multiplication Rule

dent is a planner reduces our sample space to the 150 planners out of 1000 respondents. Since each of the 150 planners has an equal probability of being selected and since only 50 of them are also buyers,

$$P(B|A) = \frac{P(A \text{ and } B)}{P(A)} = \frac{50}{150} = \frac{.05}{.15} = \frac{1}{3}$$

In general, for any two events E and F in a sample space S, the conditional probability $P(F|E)$, read "the conditional probability of F, given E," is

(6.1) $$P(F|E) = \frac{P(E \text{ and } F)}{P(E)} \quad \text{where } P(E) > 0$$

In other words, a conditional probability of two events is a ratio of their joint probability divided by the marginal probability of the event that has occurred. The condition in (6.1) that the probability of $P(E)$ must be positive is included in order to eliminate division by zero. Furthermore, the same definition (6.1) leads to

(6.2) $$P(E|F) = \frac{P(F \text{ and } E)}{P(F)} \quad \text{where } P(F) > 0$$

and where the probability of event F rather than of event E is given.

Example 6.2 Again, what is the probability of the event "A respondent has purchased an automobile, given that he or she planned such a purchase"?
Since $P(B \text{ and } A)$ is .05 and $P(B)$ is .20, by Eq. (6.2)

$$P(A|B) = \frac{P(B \text{ and } A)}{P(B)} = \frac{.05}{.20} = \frac{1}{4}$$

Managerial decision making may frequently involve conditional probabilities. For example, a car dealer may be interested in the probability that an automobile buyer is a planner in order to distinguish between prospective buyers who plan and those who do not plan to purchase a new automobile for more effective advertising. A bank investment officer may be interested in the probability that a home mortgage will be repaid given that the applicant has the ability to keep up with the monthly mortgage payments. A corporation executive may be concerned about the probability for a successful investment in new plant and equipment if demand for the product justifies expansion. The probability of a new food product being harmful to health, although it meets required health standards, may be of interest to the Food and Drug Administration. Also, conditional probabilities are quite common in everyday life. We wonder about the probability of rain if the weather forecast predicts such an event. And the probability of death depends on age, health, and numerous other factors related to a person's life.

Chapter 2 Probability Concepts and Tools

The Multiplication Rule

So far we have shown how to determine the conditional probability when the relevant joint and marginal probabilities are given. Many real-world problems require determination of a joint probability when the relevant marginal and conditional probabilities are given. Such a joint probability is obtained by applying the multiplication rule which follows directly from the definition of conditional probability.

Multiplying both sides of Eq. (6.1) by $P(E)$ and reversing their order, we obtain the multiplication rule

(6.3) $$\boxed{P(E \text{ and } F) = P(E) \, P(F|E)}$$

and, equivalently, from Eq. (6.2)

(6.4) $$\boxed{P(E \text{ and } F) = P(F) \, P(E|F)}$$

The joint probability $P(F \text{ and } E)$ equals $P(E \text{ and } F)$.

Example 6.3

We can illustrate the multiplication rule with the probabilities found in Example 6.1. What is the joint probability of the event "A respondent is a planner and a buyer"?

We know that $P(A)$ is .15 and $P(B|A)$ is 1/3. Applying Eq. (6.3), we have

$$\begin{aligned} P(A \text{ and } B) &= P(A) \, P(B|A) \\ &= .15 \times 1/3 \\ &= .05 \end{aligned}$$

The same joint probability can be obtained by applying Eq. (6.4). Since $P(B)$ is .20 and $P(A|B)$ is 1/4, we have

$$\begin{aligned} P(B \text{ and } A) &= P(B) \, P(A|B) \\ &= .20 \times 1/4 \\ &= .05 \end{aligned}$$

The multiplication rule (6.3) is equally applicable to two events which occur in chronological order or successively as the result of two trials. An effective way of showing application of the multiplication rule and its relation to marginal, conditional, and joint probabilities is by means of a tree diagram.

Example 6.4

Earlier, we considered a sample space for a random experiment of selecting two households from three households A, B, and C without replacement. A tree diagram for this experiment with the appropriate probabilities is shown in Fig. 6.1. Note that the first trial generates a set of marginal probabilities such as $P(A)$ and so on. Each is equal to 1/3 since we select a household from three households and the events are equally likely. The second trial is related to a set of conditional probabilities such as $P(B|A)$ and so on. Note

Figure 6.1.
Probabilities of selecting two households from three households without replacement.

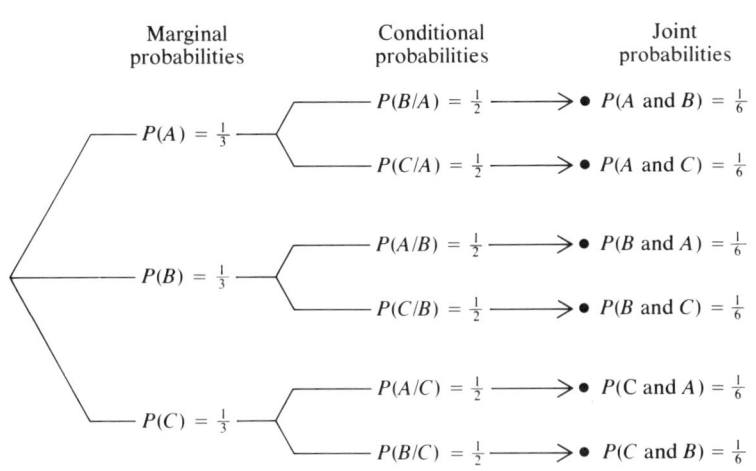

that a particular second-trial branch can be reached only by traversing a particular first-trial branch. Unlike marginal probabilities, however, each conditional probability is equal to 1/2 because of sampling without replacement. Multiplying marginal and conditional probabilities of each branch path, an application of the multiplication rule, we obtain the set of joint probabilities. For example,

$$P(A)\, P(B|A) = (1/3)(1/2) = P(A \text{ and } B) = 1/6$$

Multiplication rule (6.3) can easily be generalized to a rule for any three events E_1, E_2, and E_3:

(6.5) $P(E_1 \text{ and } E_2 \text{ and } E_3) = P(E_1)\, P(E_2|E_1)\, P(E_3|E_2 \text{ and } E_1)$

Example 6.5

A retailer of electrical appliances receives a shipment of 10 toasters, 2 of which are defective. Three toasters are selected at random without replacement. What is the probability of the first and the second toasters being good (G) and the third defective (D)?

The probability $P(G_1)$, that is, the first toaster is good, is 8/10 because 8 of the 10 toasters are good. The probability $P(G_2|G_1)$, that is, the second toaster is good, given that the first is good, is 7/9 since there are only 7 good toasters out of the remaining 9. And the probability $P(D_1|G_2 \text{ and } G_1)$, that is, a defective toaster is selected, given that the first 2 toasters are good, is 2/8 because there are 2 defective toasters out of the remaining 8. In sum and by rule (6.5), we have

$$P(G_1 \text{ and } G_2 \text{ and } D_1) = P(G_1)\, P(G_2|G_1)\, P(D_1|G_2 \text{ and } G_1)$$
$$= (8/10)(7/9)(2/8)$$
$$\simeq .156$$

Does it matter whether the defective toaster appears in any *specified* trial? No. The sequences (D_1, G_1, G_2) as well as (G_1, D_1, G_2) have the same probability as (G_1, G_2, D_1). Thus

$$P(D_1 \text{ and } G_1 \text{ and } G_2) = (2/10)(8/9)(7/8) \simeq .156$$

and

$$P(G_1 \text{ and } D_1 \text{ and } G_2) = (8/10)(2/9)(7/8) \simeq .156$$

as found earlier.

What is the probability that only one of the three toasters in the sample is defective?

Unlike the previous question, now we are interested in the probability that the defective toaster is selected in the first *or* the second *or* the third trial. This calls for application of the addition rule for mutually exclusive events, so

$$\begin{aligned}P(\text{one defective}) &= P(D_1 \text{ and } G_1 \text{ and } G_2) + P(G_1 \text{ and } D_1 \text{ and } G_2) \\ &\quad + P(G_1 \text{ and } G_2 \text{ and } D_1) \\ &\simeq .156 + .156 + .156 \\ &\simeq .468\end{aligned}$$

Analogously, multiplication rule (6.5) can be generalized to one for any n events $E_1, E_2, \ldots, E_n$:

(6.6) $P(E_1 \text{ and } E_2 \text{ and } \cdots \text{ and } E_n)$
$= P(E_1) \, P(E_2|E_1) \, P(E_3|E_2 \text{ and } E_1) \cdots P(E_n|E_{n-1} \text{ and } \cdots \text{ and } E_1)$

Statistically Dependent and Independent Events

Two or more events occurring simultaneously or successively can be either statistically dependent or independent.

In discussing conditional probabilities, we found that $P(B|A)$, that is, "A respondent is a buyer, given that automobile purchase involved preplanning," is 1/3 or about .33. We also found that $P(A|B)$ is 1/4 or .25. Note that in Table 6.1 the corresponding unconditional or marginal probabilities $P(B)$ and $P(A)$ are .20 and .15, respectively. Knowing that a respondent is a planner has increased the probability that such a respondent is a buyer; or, knowing that a respondent is a buyer, there is a greater probability than otherwise that such a respondent is a planner. In cases such as this, where the conditional probabilities are not equal to the corresponding marginal probabilities, the events are said to be *statistically dependent*.

Statistical dependence is equally applicable to successively occurring events. It arises in situations involving sampling without replacement. Consider Figure 6.1. Each marginal probability for selecting the first household is 1/3, less than the corresponding conditional probability 1/2 for selecting the second household. The same holds true in the sampling of three toasters in Example 6.5. Since sampling is without replacement, the probability of successive sample outcomes is

Section 6 Probabilities: The Multiplication Rule

affected by earlier sample outcomes. In both cases, conditional probabilities are not equal to the corresponding marginal probabilities.

If the conditional probabilities of two or more events are equal to their corresponding marginal probabilities, the events are said to be *statistically independent*. Any two events E and F are statistically independent if

(6.7) $$P(E|F) = P(E)$$

Then it is also true that

(6.7) $$P(F|E) = P(F)*$$

And the multiplication rule given in (6.3) and (6.4) is simplified to

(6.8) $$\boxed{P(E \text{ and } F) = P(E) P(F)}$$

This rule means that if two events are independent, their joint probability equals the product of their marginal probabilities. The way to find whether two events are independent is by applying either the definition for independence (6.7) or the special multiplication rule (6.8).

Example 6.6

Earlier, we explained that the events in Table 6.1 are dependent. This can be verified by the application of rule (6.8). For instance, from Table 6.1 we have

$$P(A \text{ and } B) = P(A) P(B)$$
$$.05 = (.15)(.20)$$
$$.05 \neq .03$$

Thus rule (6.8) does not hold. So events A and B are dependent. Repeated application of the same rule can verify that the other three pairs of joint events, A and D, C and B, and C and D, are also dependent.

Instead of the probabilities shown in Table 6.1, however, let us assume that we obtain the probabilities shown in Table 6.2. Now the four joint events are statistically independent. For instance, according to the special multiplication rule (6.8),

$$P(A \text{ and } B) = P(A) P(B)$$

Also, from Table 6.2, $P(A \text{ and } B) = .05$, $P(A) = .25$, and $P(B) = .20$. Hence, we have

$$.05 = (.25)(.20)$$
$$.05 = .05$$

---

*If several events are *collectively independent*, then every possible conditional probability for all combinations of events must equal the corresponding marginal probability. For example, events E_1, E_2, and E_3 are collectively independent if all the following conditions are satisfied:

$$P(E_1) = P(E_1|E_2) \qquad P(E_1) = P(E_1|E_2 \text{ and } E_3)$$
$$P(E_2) = P(E_2|E_3) \qquad P(E_2) = P(E_2|E_1 \text{ and } E_3)$$
$$P(E_3) = P(E_3|E_1) \qquad P(E_3) = P(E_3|E_1 \text{ and } E_2)$$

Table 6.2.
Probability of Response to Planning and Purchasing an Automobile

Second Interview	First Interview		Marginal Probabilities
	Planners (A)	Nonplanners (C)	
Buyers (B)	$P(A \text{ and } B) = .05$	$P(C \text{ and } B) = .15$	$P(B) = .20$
Nonbuyers (D)	$P(A \text{ and } D) = .20$	$P(C \text{ and } D) = .60$	$P(D) = .80$
Marginal probabilities:	$P(A) = .25$	$P(C) = .85$	$P(S) = 1.00$

So rule (6.8) holds and the two events are statistically independent. Repeated application of the same rule can verify that the other three joint events are also independent.

By analogy, two or more successively occurring events from sampling with replacement are also statistically independent. A case in point is the experiment of selecting two households from three households *with* replacement. A tree diagram demonstrating probabilities for such an experiment will be similar to the one in Figure 6.1, with one difference: for each marginal probability there will now be three conditional probabilities, each equal to 1/3. In other words, each conditional probability will be equal to the corresponding marginal or unconditional probability. So the events are independent.

Rule (6.8) can easily be generalized to a rule for n independent events E_1, $E_2, \ldots, E_n$:

(6.9) $\qquad P(E_1 \text{ and } E_2 \text{ and } \cdots \text{ and } E_n) = P(E_1) P(E_2) \cdots P(E_n)$

The following example illustrates application of rule (6.9) to the *average fraction defective* of a process. The term is used to denote the percentage of defective units a production process turns out in the long run.

Example 6.7

The fraction defective of an assembly line for toasters is 20 percent. (Of course, in a real-world situation such a fraction defective is much smaller.) Three toasters are randomly selected from the assembly line. What is the probability that the first and the second toasters are good (G) and the third defective (D)?

Unlike the earlier sampling from a shipment of 10 toasters, sampling from an assembly line is equivalent to sampling with replacement; an assembly line is considered to be capable of producing an infinite number of toasters; selecting a defective (good) toaster does not change the probability of selecting another defective (good) toaster. The .20 probability for selecting a defective toaster remains the same. Events are considered to be independent. By rule (6.9) we have

$$P(G_1 \text{ and } G_2 \text{ and } D_1) = P(G_1) P(G_2) P(D_1)$$
$$= (.80)(.80)(.20)$$
$$= .128$$

Section 6 Probabilities: The Multiplication Rule

What is the probability that one of the three toasters in the sample is defective?

Since a defective toaster can be selected in any of the three trials, and since the probability of being selected in a specified trial is the same, by the addition rule for mutually exclusive events

$$P(\text{any one defective}) = .128 + .128 + .128 = .384$$

In closing, it is worth summarizing a number of important points about statistically dependent or independent events because they are relevant to subsequent discussions:

1. *Sampling from a finite population is considered equivalent to sampling without replacement where successively occurring events are dependent.*
2. *Sampling from an infinite population is equivalent to sampling with replacement where successively occurring events are independent.*
3. *In determining whether two or more events are dependent or independent, we apply the multiplication rule for independent events.*
4. *Independent events should not be confused with mutually exclusive events.* In fact, *if two events with nonzero probabilities are independent, then they must be joint events.* Also, *if two events with nonzero probabilities are mutually exclusive, then they are dependent.*

PROBLEMS

Group One

6.1. Consider the data from the survey on planning and purchasing an automobile shown in Table 6.1.
  (a) Prepare a tree diagram starting with marginal probabilities for events "Planners" (A) or "Nonplanners" (C) and compute the conditional and joint probabilities.
  (b) Prepare a similar tree diagram starting with marginal probabilities for events "Buyers" (B) and "Nonbuyers" (D).
  *(c) How many different sets of marginal, conditional, and joint probabilities does the problem have where the sum of probabilities in each set equals one?

6.2. A random experiment consists of selecting two households from three households A, B, and C with replacement.
  (a) Prepare a tree diagram similar to the one shown in Figure 6.1.
  (b) Are the joint events from the two trials independent? Explain why or why not and support your explanation with the application of the multiplication rule.
  *(c) Consider the following events:

$$E = \{(A, B), (B, C), (C, A)\} \quad \text{and} \quad F = \{(A, A), (B, A), (C, B)\}$$

Are these two events independent? Explain.

Answers to asterisked (*) problems are appended.

6.3. A manufacturer of farm equipment inquired whether the dealers of the company were in favor of or against a new credit policy. The returned questionnaires showed the following response:

		Region			
Response		East (E)	West (W)	South (S)	Row Totals
For	(F)	105	250	305	660
Against	(A)	50	235	155	440
Column totals:		155	485	460	1100

What is the probability that a randomly selected questionnaire represents a dealer who is:
*(a) From the West and is in favor of the new credit policy?
(b) Against such a policy?
(c) For the new credit policy if it is known that the dealer is from the South?
(d) Are response and region independent events? Explain.

6.4. Three balls are drawn at random from an urn containing 1000 balls representing respondents with characteristics shown in Table 6.1. What is the probability that all three respondents are planners and buyers if sampling is:
*(a) With replacement?
(b) Without replacement?

6.5. The probability that a supermarket customer is a woman (W) and a smoker (K) is 40 percent, a woman 80 percent, and a smoker 50 percent.
*(a) Are the events W and K mutually exclusive? Explain.
(b) Are the same events independent? Explain.

6.6. A retailer has three television sets of make A, two of make B, and five of make C. If sales of different makes are random, what is the probability that in selling two television sets, both are of the same make?

6.7. The General Assembly of the United Nations debated the need for establishing international guidelines for the exploitation of natural resources in the oceans. The vote for such guidelines was as follows (data hypothetical):

		United Nations			
Vote		Industrial— "Free" (F)	"Communist Bloc" (C)	"Third World" (T)	Row Totals
Yes	(Y)	35	5	60	100
No	(N)	18	10	30	60
Abstained	(A)	7	15	20	40
Column totals:		60	30	110	200

Hypothetical data

Section 6 Probabilities: The Multiplication Rule 73

If a nation's vote is randomly selected, what is the probability that such a nation:
*(a) Belongs to the "Communist bloc" and is in favor of the need for guidelines for the exploitation of natural resources?
(b) Favors the need for guidelines?
(c) Favors the need for guidelines if it is known to belong to the "Third World" bloc?
(d) Are "Need for guidelines" and "Ideological" groupings of nations independent? Explain.
(e) If the two events in (d) are dependent, indicate how the voting pattern should be changed in order to make these two events independent.

6.8. Explain and illustrate the following terms:
(a) Dependent events   (e) Joint probability
(b) Conditional probability (f) Independent events
(c) Successive events   (g) Average fraction defective
(d) Marginal probability   (h) Simultaneous events

Group Two

6.9. Consider the following probabilities:
$P(E \text{ and not-}F) = 1/7$
$P(\text{not-}E \text{ and not-}F) = 2/5$
$P(E \text{ and } F) = 2/10$
*(a) Find $P(\text{not-}E \text{ and } F)$.
(b) Are events E, F independent?

6.10. The following probabilities are given:
$P(E) = .40;$ $P(F) = .50;$ $P(F/E) = .30$
(a) Find $P(E \text{ and } F)$.
(b) Are events E and F independent?
(c) Find $P(\text{not-}F/E)$.

6.11. The manager of Robert's Cleaning Company runs a weekly lottery for promotion. Each customer receives a ticket corresponding to a number in the lottery. During a particular week 100 tickets, numbered serially from 00 through 99, have been distributed. At the end of the week, a number is selected at random and the winner receives the equivalent of $25 worth of dry-cleaning service. What is the probability that:
*(a) The winning number is odd?
(b) The first digit of the winning number is odd and the second is even?
(c) The second digit is a 5 if the first digit of the winning number is a 7?

6.12. A person enters two singles tennis tournaments, A and B. The probability for winning A is .60 and for winning B is .40. However, if he wins tournament A, the probability for winning B is .50 because his opponent will be overly cautious. What is the probability that he wins at least one of the two tournaments?

6.13. A merchant of electrical appliances will accept a lot of 20 radios if a randomly selected sample of 3 contains no defectives. If a received lot contains 4 defective radios, what is the probability that the merchant will:
(a) Accept the lot?
(b) Reject the lot?

6.14. Three advertising agencies A, B, and C compete for the account of a cigarette manufacturer. The manager of agency A thinks that the chances of winning this account are equal to B's and twice as good as C's.

*(a) What is the probability of agency A's winning this account?
(b) Suppose the manager of agency A is informed that agency B has withdrawn from the competition. Given this information, what is the probability of agency A's winning this account?

SECTION 7/ COUNTING TECHNIQUES

In explaining the fundamentals of probability, we have intentionally restricted our illustrations to random experiments requiring sample spaces with a small number of elements. Finding all possible outcomes was a simple matter. It required no more than multiplying the small number of outcomes of one trial by the number of outcomes of another trial or by constructing a tree diagram. But our brief treatment of probability would be incomplete without lifting this restriction. In many problems already studied, the probability of an event could be most efficiently determined with counting techniques; still many other interesting and important problems cannot be easily solved without such techniques.

For accomplishing this task we briefly explain the multiplication principle, permutations, and combinations.

The Multiplication Principle

We have already illustrated how this principle can be applied to determine the number of elements in a sample space. For example, we have found that the sample space of randomly selecting three toasters from an assembly line and classifying them as good or as defective contains eight elements. Since each selection or trial includes two possibilities and since there are three trials, there are $2 \times 2 \times 2 = 2^3$ or eight elements. This, as well as other illustrations with tree diagrams, are simple applications of the multiplication principle.

What we need here is to express this principle in general terms. Suppose there is a job requiring two tasks (trials) such that for each of the N_1 different ways of doing task 1, there are N_2 ways of doing task 2. Then both tasks can be completed in $N_1 + N_1 + \cdots + N_1$ different ways, where there are N_2 terms in the sum. It follows from the definition of multiplication that the total number of ways of completing the whole job is the product $N_1 \times N_2$.

Example 7.1

Consider the random experiment for selecting two households from three households A, B, and C without replacements. The probability of selecting households A and B was found to be

$$P(A \text{ and } B) = P(A) P(B|A) = (1/3)(1/2) = 1/6$$

by application of the multiplication rule.

The same result can be obtained with the application of the multiplication principle. Since task N_1, selecting the first household, can be done in three ways and task N_2, selecting the second household, in two ways, the whole job can be done in $3 + 3 = 3 \times 2 = 6$ ways. Inasmuch as event (*A and B*) is one of the six joint events, its probability is $1/6$.

The multiplication principle can be generalized for experiments involving a sequence of any k tasks, where k is any positive integer. If the first of a sequence of k tasks can be performed in N_1 ways, the second in N_2 ways, and so forth for k tasks, then the total number of N ways for completing the whole job is determined by

(7.1) $$\boxed{N = N_1 \times N_2 \times \cdots \times N_k}$$

Example 7.2

For advertising a new product the management of ACME, an advertising agency, plans a nationwide contest. To enter the contest, a person must submit a three-letter word naming the new product. Repetition of letters is allowed, but the first and the third letters of the word must be consonants and the second a vowel. Although a person can enter the contest more than once, no person can qualify if the same word has already been submitted. A word will be selected at random from those submitted and the winner will receive a prize. The manufacturer of the new product felt that the contest would be an effective advertising device; however, the manufacturer reserved the right to decide whether the product would be named after the selected word.

What is the number of possible entries for the contest, and what is the probability of winning with one legal entry?

To complete the whole job of forming three-letter words, we must perform three tasks, so k is 3. The first and third letter positions (tasks 1 and 3) can be filled with any of the 21 consonants of the English alphabet. So N_1 and N_3 are each equal to 21, because repetitions of letters are allowed. For the same reason, the second letter position (task 2) can be filled with any of the 5 vowels. So N_2 is equal to 5. Thus, by formula (7.1),

$$N = 21 \times 5 \times 21 = 2205$$

is the number of possible entries for the contest. The probability of winning with one legal entry is $1/2205$.

The above application of the multiplication principle can be considered as a case involving a random experiment with replacement. The same problem can easily be converted into an experiment without replacement.

Factorials and Permutations

In arranging a number of objects in a line by the multiplication principle we take *order* into account.

Example 7.3

In a four-member board, the positions of the chairperson, treasurer, and secretary are determined by drawing at random from a box containing the letters *A*, *B*, *C*, and *D*. If letter *A* is drawn first, individual *A* becomes the chairperson; if letter C is drawn second, individual C becomes the treasurer, and so on. What is the probability that the board's composition will be (A, B, C, D)?

The chairperson's position can be occupied by any of the four board members; after the chairperson is chosen, the treasurer's position can be occupied by any of the three remaining board members; and so forth. Hence, by the multiplication principle (7.1) we have

$$N = 4 \times 3 \times 2 \times 1 = 24$$

possible arrangements of the board. Since positions are filled randomly, the probability is

$$P(A, B, C, D) = 1/24$$

In this illustration we had to arrange four objects into four positions without replacement. Suppose we wish to arrange n different objects into n positions without replacement. The first position can be filled in n ways since we can choose any one of the n objects. After the first position is occupied in any one of n ways, there remain $n - 1$ objects, any one of which can fill the second position. On the same basis, the third position can be filled in $n - 2$ ways, the fourth in $n - 3$ ways, the fifth in $n - 4$ ways, and so on. Finally, the nth position can be filled in $n - (n - 1)$ or 1 way. For any positive integer n, the product of the integers from n to 1 is denoted by $n!$ and is read "n factorial"; in symbols,

(7.2) $$n! = n \times (n - 1) \times (n - 2) \times \cdots \times 2 \times 1$$

Example 7.4

Consider the following factorial values:

$$1! = 1$$
$$2! = 2 \times 1 = 2$$
$$3! = 3 \times 2 \times 1 = 6$$
$$4! = 4 \times 3 \times 2 \times 1 = 24$$
$$\cdot$$
$$\cdot$$
$$\cdot$$
$$10! = 10 \times 9 \times \cdots \times 2 \times 1 = 3{,}628{,}800$$

The factorial of zero is defined as 1. This definition may appear strange at first. It makes sense, however, if we think of 0! as representing an arrangement of assigning zero objects to zero positions; this feat can be done in only one way. Furthermore, this definition enables us to be consistent with factorials for all nonnegative integers. Note that factorials increase in size very rapidly, making computations laborious.

Frequently, we may wish to arrange n different objects in r positions without replacement, where r is less than or equal to n.

Example 7.5

The manager of a department store has six displays and three display windows, each accommodating one display each day. The windows are situated

Section 7   Counting Techniques

in such a way that the order in which the displays are arranged is important. If the season lasts 40 days, does the manager have a sufficient number of display arrangements for the season?

The first display window can be filled in any six ways, the second in any five ways, and the third in any four ways. Therefore, by the multiplication principle (7.1),

$$N = 6 \times 5 \times 4 = 120$$

ways, more than a sufficient number of arrangements for the season.

Such arrangements of n objects in r positions without replacement, where r is less than or equal to n, are denoted by $_nP_r$ and called *permutations*. In symbols,

(7.3) $\quad _nP_r = n \times (n-1) \times (n-2) \times \cdots \times (n-r+1)$

since the rth position can be filled in $n - (r-1)$ or $n - r + 1$ ways.

Formula (7.3) leads to another convenient form. Multiplying (7.3) by $(n-r)!/(n-r)!$, we have

(7.4) $\quad _nP_r = \dfrac{n \times (n-1) \times (n-2) \times \cdots \times (n-r+1)(n-r)!}{(n-r)!}$

But the numerator of expression (7.4) is equivalent to $n!$, formula (7.2), since $(n-r)!$ is the factorial for the remaining $(n-r)$ of n objects. Hence, expression (7.4) can be written in the form

(7.5) $$\boxed{_nP_r = \dfrac{n!}{(n-r)!}}$$

read "the number of permutations of n objects taken r at a time." This is the standard formula for permutations.

Example 7.6   Encouraged by the success of the earlier contest, ACME plans to advertise the product with a half-hour television weekly show, "Name That Product." Each week five persons, preferably selected from those who participated in the contest, will be interviewed by a well-known comedian on television. During the interview 100 words of the possible 2205 will be selected and placed in an urn. Then each of the five television guests will draw at random a word from the urn with replacement. Any two or more players who draw the same word will win prizes. Among the things that ACME's management wanted to know in estimating the total cost of the show is the probability that at least two among the five guests will win.

Since drawings are with replacement and there are 100 words for each drawing, by the multiplication principle (7.1) the number of elements in the sample space is

$$N = 100 \times 100 \times 100 \times 100 \times 100 = 100^5$$

We wish to find event E, that is, "At least two among the five television guests draw the same word." In this problem, it is easier to find the probability of the complement event "No guest draws the same word," that is, $P(\text{not-}E)$. Event *not-E* contains all the permutations where $n = 100$ and $r = 5$. By formula (7.5), we have

$$_{100}P_5 = \frac{100!}{(100-5)!}$$
$$= \frac{100 \times 99 \times 98 \times 97 \times 96 \times 95!}{95!}$$
$$= 9{,}034{,}502{,}400$$

So the probability of the complement event is

$$P(\text{not-}E) = \frac{9{,}034{,}502{,}400}{100^5} = .90$$

And by the rule for complement events, we have

$$P(E) = 1 - P(\text{not-}E)$$
$$= 1 - .90$$
$$= .10$$

Combinations

Remember that in a permutation *order counts*. However, frequently we may be interested in a *selection* of r objects from n different objects, where r is less than or equal to n, *without* regard to their *order*. Such a selection is called a *combination* and is denoted by $_nC_r$.

The following example may help us understand the difference between a permutation and a combination.

Example 7.7

The bylaws of a nonprofit organization provide for the appointment of a three-member executive committee to carry out the everyday business of the institution. Four individuals A, B, C, and D are nominated for the committee.

Case 1. Suppose the bylaws provide that the positions of the chairperson, treasurer, and secretary in the committee are determined in that order by drawing three of the four nominees at random. What is the probability that the committee's composition is (A, B, C)?

Since *order* is important by formula (7.5), we have

$$_4P_3 = \frac{4!}{(4-3)!} = \frac{4 \times 3 \times 2 \times 1}{1!} = 24$$

The 24 permutations are listed in Table 7.1 in four groups. Since each of the 24 permutations is equally likely,

$$P(A, B, C) = 1/24$$

Case 2. Suppose the bylaws provide that the elected committee members decide among themselves who should assume the position of the chair-

Table 7.1. Permutations and Combinations of Four Individuals A, B, C, and D Taken Three at a Time

$_4P_3$	(A, B, C), (A, C, B) (B, A, C), (B, C, A) (C, A, B), (C, B, A)	(A, B, D), (A, D, B) (B, A, D), (B, D, A) (D, A, B), (D, B, A)	(A, C, D), (A, D, C) (C, A, D), (C, D, A) (D, A, C), (D, C, A)	(B, C, D), (B, D, C) (C, B, D), (C, D, B) (D, B, C), (D, C, B)
$_4C_3$	{A, B, C}	{A, B, D}	{A, C, D}	{B, C, D}

person, treasurer, and secretary. What is the probability that the composition of the committee is again A, B, and C?

In this case the order in which the committee members are drawn *does not count*. The question calls for combinations. Since order does not count, all six permutations of A, B, and C will form one combination, as shown in Table 7.1; each of the other three groups of six permutations will make up one combination. So there are four combinations and

$$P(\{A, B, C\}) = 1/4$$

Observe that each combination in Table 7.1 can be arranged in 3! ways or $3 \times 2 \times 1 = 6$ permutations. In order to find the total number of permutations we multiply the number of combinations by the number of permutations that can be arranged from the objects of each combination. In our example,

$$_4C_3 \times 3! = {}_4P_3 = \frac{4!}{(4-3)!} = 24$$

In general, the number of permutations of n objects, taken r at a time, is

$$_nC_r \times r! = {}_nP_r = \frac{n!}{(n-r)!}$$

where r is less than or equal to n. Multiplying this expression by $1/r!$, we have

(7.6)*
$$_nC_r = \frac{n!}{r!(n-r)!}$$

read "number of combinations of n objects, taken r at a time."

Example 7.7 (continued)

We can obtain the same number of combinations shown in Table 7.1 by applying formula (7.6). Since n is 4 and r is 3, we have

$$_4C_3 = \frac{4!}{3!(4-3)!} = \frac{4 \times 3 \times 2 \times 1}{3 \times 2 \times 1 \times 1!} = 4$$

*Formulas (7.5) and (7.6) are also applicable to problems when r equals n. In such cases, however, the permutations formula is equivalent to $n!$, that is, formula (7.2), since

$$_nP_n = \frac{n!}{(n-n)!} = \frac{n!}{0!} = n!$$

while the combinations formula is equal to 1 since

$$_nC_n = \frac{n!}{n!(n-n)!} = \frac{n!}{n!0!} = 1$$

Chapter 2 Probability Concepts and Tools

The difference between permutations and combinations must be clear now: when we speak of permutations we are concerned with "arrangements," so order counts; when we speak of combinations we are interested in "selections," and order does not count. Permutations are ordered r objects from n objects; combinations are r objects from n objects without order. For example, (A, B, C) and (C, B, A) are two arrangements that would represent two "different" committees if the order of appointments counts. Combination $\{A, B, C\}$ is a set representing one committee since order of appointments does not count. But how do we know whether a problem involves permutations or combinations? That depends on whether or not the nature of the problem indicates that order counts.

PROBLEMS

Group One

7.1. Evaluate:
  *(a) $_{10}P_3$ (c) $_3P_0$
  (b) $_{50}P_2$ (d) $_nP_0$

7.2. Evaluate:
  *(a) $_{10}C_3$ (c) $_eC_0$
  (b) $_{50}C_2$ (d) $_nC_0$

7.3. Suppose the rules of the contest planned by ACME's management in Example 7.2 provide that no consonant could be used more than once in forming a three-letter word. What is the probability of winning with one legal entry then?

7.4. Three salespersons are selected at random from a group of 10 salespersons, $A, B, \ldots, J$, to form a three-member trade delegation. What is the probability that:
  *(a) Salespersons A, B, and C are selected if A becomes the chief, B the deputy chief, and C the person in charge of displays?
  (b) Salespersons A, B, and C are selected if the president of the company reserves the right to appoint the chief and deputy chief among the selected salespersons?

7.5. A building contractor considers hiring 5 carpenters; 12 apply for the jobs. What is the probability that the contractor will select carpenters A, B, C, D, and E?

7.6. A state bureau of motor vehicles expects a registration of 5 million passenger vehicles. License plates can be made using two letters followed by a four-digit number.
  *(a) Does the bureau have enough license plates, if repetitions of letters and digit numbers are not allowed?
  (b) If repetitions are allowed and assuming equiprobable outcomes, what is the probability of getting number LT-5672 for your automobile?

*7.7. A bale of hay, a sheep, and a lion must be ferried by a small rowboat from one bank of a river to the other. However, the man in charge of the ferry service has a problem. The limited capacity of his boat permits the "safe" passage of not more than one of the above three items at a time, while for obvious reasons neither should the sheep be left alone with the bale of hay nor the lion alone with the sheep. List the pairs of items which can possibly be formed and devise a scheme which will allow the "safe" transport of the three items.

Answers to asterisked (*) problems are appended.

Section 7 Counting Techniques

7.8. Given the digits 1, 2, and 3, list the two-digit numbers which can be formed when repetitions are:
  *(a) Allowed
  (b) Not allowed
  (c) Not allowed and order does not count
  (d) Allowed but order does not count

7.9. How many words can be formed from the different letters of the word *business*, when the letters are:
  *(a) All taken together without repetitions?
  (b) Taken four at a time without repetitions?
  (c) Taken five at a time with repetitions?

Group Two

7.10. The manager of Quality Foods, a midwestern manufacturer, has decided to use three different sizes of boxes in marketing a new cold cereal. A single bright color will be used as background for each box size in order to maximize consumer's appeal for the product. Six different colors are considered.
  *(a) How many color arrangements can be formed if each color cannot be used more than once?
  (b) What is the probability that two states will receive boxes with identical colors?

7.11. The manager of Lakekatatina, an exclusive restaurant in a summer resort, plans 4 choices for an appetizer, 10 choices for the main course, 5 choices for dessert, and 6 choices for beverages.
  *(a) How many different complete dinners are possible if one choice in each category makes a complete dinner?
  (b) Suppose each customer represents an independent trial. What is the probability that three customers will ask for the same complete dinner? For three different dinners? At least two will ask for the same dinner?

7.12. Mario Grandiozo's Pizza Corner offers the following toppings for the plain cheese base of his delicious pizzas: anchovies, mushrooms, onions, peppers, and sausage.
  (a) How many different pizzas does he offer his customers?
  (b) Suppose each customer represents an independent trial. What is the probability that four customers will ask for the same pizza? For four different pizzas? At least two will ask for the same pizza?

7.13. An automobile dealer represents a manufacturer who produces five different models of cars. Two of the models are produced in four body styles: sedan, hardtop, convertible, and station wagon. Three of the models come as sedans and convertibles only. Each model is available in six colors.
  (a) How many distinguishable types of cars does the dealer have available?
  (b) If each customer represents an independent trial, what is the probability that three customers will buy identical cars? Different cars? At least two will buy identical cars?

7.14. Sometimes, one of the tasks of completing a job of permuting different objects from n objects must be performed in a special way. In such a case, it may be advisable to do this special task first. Suppose the manager of a department store in Example 7.5 wants to reserve the third window for two particular displays of the six prepared. If the season lasts 40 days, does the manager now have a sufficient number of display arrangements?

Chapter 3
PROBABILITY DISTRIBUTIONS: BINOMIAL AND POISSON DISTRIBUTIONS

In the ordinary course of business, managers make decisions under uncertain conditions. They rely on the future movements of key variables such as wages, prices, sales, and interest rates. They must decide whether and how much to manufacture from a wide variety of products whose demand is uncertain. They must choose the best marketing strategy from alternatives with uncertain profitability.

In statistics, such uncertain decision variables are usually called *random variables*. Informally, a random variable may be defined as a variable whose numerical values are determined by chance.* The values of a random variable and their probabilities form a *probability distribution*.

Probability distributions play an important role in traditional statistical investigations. We shall see later that probability distributions from sample spaces are the basis for inferring and testing the characteristics of statistical populations from sample evidence. Some special probability distributions are the basis for sophisticated applications of statistical inference.

Although applications of probability distributions appear throughout this volume, this chapter is limited to probability distributions of discrete random variables. First, we deal with the probability distribution of a discrete random variable in general. Then we introduce two important probability distributions, the *binomial* and the *Poisson*.

---

*Formally, a random variable is a function which assigns a number to each element of a sample space—for example, assigning "Number of defective toasters" to each outcome of a sample space for the experiment of randomly selecting two toasters from an assembly line.

SECTION 8 / PROBABILITY DISTRIBUTIONS: SUMMARY MEASURES

After illustrating formation and graphic representation of probability distributions in general, we focus on some of their summary measures: the mean, variance, and standard deviation.

The Probability Distribution of a Discrete Random Variable

Obviously, we can form a probability distribution from any of our earlier experiments.

Example 8.1

In selecting two households from a population of three households A, B, and C with replacement we can form the sample space

$$S_5 = \{(A, A), (A, B), (A, C), (B, A), (B, B), (B, C), (C, A), (C, B), (C, C)\}$$

Suppose households A, B, and C consist of two, four, and six individuals, respectively. The random variable is "Number of persons in sampled households." The probability distribution of this random variable is shown in Table 8.1 under the second and third columns. For element (A, A) we assign number 4 since household A consists of two persons and the sample contains two such households. For elements (A, B) or (B, A) we assign number 6 to each element since household A consists of two and household B of four persons, a total of six persons, and so on. The probability corresponding to each value of the random variable is determined in a straightforward manner. Since each sample outcome is equiprobable, the probability of each value of the random variable equals $1/9$ times the number of elements assigned such a value. For example, the probability for eight persons is $3/9$ since there are three elements each assigned a value of 8.

Table 8.1. Probability Distribution for Number of Persons in Sampled Households

Sampled Households	Number of Persons in Sampled Households x	Probability $P(X = x)$
(A, A)	4	1/9
$(A, B), (B, A)$	6	2/9
$(A, C), (C, A), (B, B)$	8	3/9
$(C, B), (B, C)$	10	2/9
(C, C)	12	1/9
		9/9

Following convention, we let capital letter X denote the random variable of a probability distribution. Lowercase letter x is used to denote any possible value assigned to the random variable. Symbol $P(X = x)$ denotes the probability that random variable X will take on a specified value x. For the probability distribution shown in Table 8.1, the values of the random variable are listed under column x and the corresponding probabilities under column $P(X = x)$. For example, $P(X = 4) = 1/9$, $P(X = 6) = 2/9$, and so on. Note that these probabilities add up to 1, since the values of the random variable represent mutually exclusive and collectively exhaustive elements of the sample space.

Example 8.1 (continued)

The graph of the probability distribution for the number of persons in sampled households is shown in Fig. 8.1. Note that the various values of the random variable X are displayed along the horizontal scale, with their probability on the vertical scale. The height of each vertical line originating from each value x depicts the probability of the corresponding event.

Figure 8.1.
Graph of probability distribution for number of persons in sampled households.

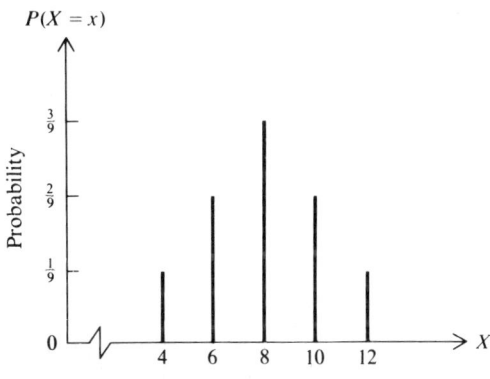

Example 8.2

Mercury Chemical Company produces a special volatile gas as a by-product of regular manufacturing. The sales manager thinks that the odds for weekly gas sales are as follows:

Gas Tanks Demanded	Odds
1	1 to 9
2	1 to 9
3	2 to 8
4	4 to 6
5	2 to 8

Earlier, we explained that the odds in favor of an event E are a to b if $P(E) = a/(a + b)$. Hence, the given odds correspond to the following probabilities:

$$P(X = 1) = 1/(1 + 9) = 1/10$$
$$P(X = 2) = 1/(1 + 9) = 1/10$$
$$P(X = 3) = 2/(2 + 8) = 2/10$$
$$P(X = 4) = 4/(4 + 6) = 4/10$$
$$P(X = 5) = 2/(2 + 8) = 2/10$$

The probability distribution of the random variable "Gas tanks demanded" is conveniently summarized in Table 8.2. Again, the probabilities of the distribution add up to 1.

Table 8.2. Probability Distribution for Number of Gas Tanks Demanded

Gas Tanks Demanded x	Probability $P(X = x)$
1	1/10
2	1/10
3	2/10
4	4/10
5	2/10
	10/10

The graph of this probability distribution is shown in Fig. 8.2.

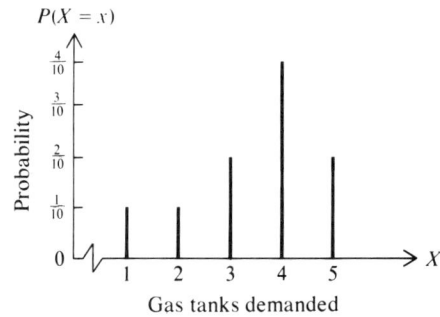

Figure 8.2. Graph of probability distribution for gas tanks demanded.

Note that the graph of a probability distribution vividly portrays the distribution's overall shape. The graph in Fig. 8.1 shows a symmetrical probability distribution. By contrast, the graph in Fig. 8.2 shows a nonsymmetrical probability distribution.

Section 8 Probability Distributions: Summary Measures

All told, when we speak of a probability distribution of a discrete random variable X whose probability value at x is $P(X = x)$, we should keep in mind the following:

1. We imply that we have taken three steps:
   (a) We have specified a sample space from a real or imaginary random experiment.
   (b) We have defined a random variable on such a space.
   (c) We have determined a probability corresponding to each possible value of the random variable.
2. The probability of every value of the random variable is either positive or zero. In symbols,

$$P(X = x) \geq 0 \quad \text{for all real values of } X$$

3. The sum of the probabilities assigned to the value of the random variable is equal to one. In symbols,

$$\Sigma P(X = x) = 1$$

Expected Value of a Random Variable

Earlier, we introduced the average or arithmetic mean for empirical frequency distributions. We can now introduce the corresponding average of a probability distribution. This measure is important because the mean of a random variable is used as a criterion for decision making under conditions of uncertainty.

Example 8.3

Suppose we are asked to play the following game with tossing a fair coin. If the tossed coin turns up "heads," we win $5; if the tossed coin turns up "tails," we lose $2. What is the fair price for playing the game?

The random variable is "The payoffs of the game." For a fair coin, we may be willing to assign $1/2$ probability to each of the values of the random variable so that

$$P(X = \$5) = 1/2 \quad \text{and} \quad P(X = -\$2) = 1/2$$

In other words, in the long run we win $5 in half and lose $2 in half the coin tosses. On the average, we expect to win

$$5(1/2) + (-2)(1/2) = \$1.50$$

per each coin toss. This average would be the fair price per coin toss. Paying this price would permit us to break even in the long run.

Computationally, the mean of the above random variable X is not different from the *weighted average* of an empirical frequency distribution. For instance, if a student receives 86 points in three quizzes and 91 points in two quizzes in a course, by an earlier formula (2.5) the weighted average grade will be

$$\mu_w = \frac{\Sigma wX}{\Sigma w} = \frac{86(3) + 91(2)}{3 + 2} = \frac{86(3/5) + 91(2/5)}{3/5 + 2/5} = 88 \text{ points}$$

Chapter 3 Probability Distributions: Binomial and Poisson Distributions

The only difference is that in a probability distribution the denominator is omitted since the weights are probabilities adding up to one.

In a probabilistic sense, however, the notion of the mean of a random variable differs from the notion of the average or arithmetic mean of an empirical frequency distribution. No random experiment is involved in the computation of an average such as the average grade in a course. When we speak of the mean of a random variable, we mean that if a real or an imaginary random experiment is performed a great number of times, then the long-run average is likely or expected to be close to the mean of the random variable defined on the sample space of the experiment. If we repeat the coin-tossing experiment many times, then, on the average, the fair price per toss is expected to be $1.50, the mean of the random variable as computed in the above example. Perhaps for this reason the mean of a random variable is called *mathematical expectation* or *expected value*.

Computation of the expected value for the coin-tossing game is conveniently summarized in Table 8.3. Obviously, calculation of expected value is similar to that for computing the mean μ of an empirical frequency distribution. The notational difference is important, however, because it denotes the different data base from which such a summary measure is obtained. Expected value $E(X)$ is the mean of a random variable. The arithmetic average μ is the mean of data which are not associated with a real or imaginary random experiment.

Table 8.3. Calculaton of the Expected Value for the Coin-tossing Game

Game Payoffs x	Probability $P(X = x)$	$xP(X = x)$
$5	1/2	$2.50
$2	1/2	−1.00
	1	$E(X) = $1.50

In general, let X be a discrete random variable that takes on the value x with probability $P(X = x)$. Then the mathematical expectation or *expected value* of X, denoted by $E(X)$, is defined by

(8.1) $$E(X) = \Sigma \, xP(X = x)$$

In words, we multiply each value of the random variable by its related probability and sum all the products.

Example 8.4

Jay & Sons is a supplier of oil-drilling equipment and parts. The company inventories KLM valves which are well known for their safety features. They effectively control the flow of oil from oil wells and they shut off in the

Section 8 Probability Distributions: Summary Measures

event of a fire. During the past year 10 percent of oil wells bought 1 valve, 25 percent 2 valves, and so on, as shown below:

KLM Valves Sold	Relative Frequency
1	.10
2	.25
3	.35
4	.30

Computing the expected value of sold KLM valves per well was part of the analysis to determine an optimal inventory policy.

Calculation of the expected value of KLM valves is shown in Table 8.4. During the past year, each oil well required, on the average, 2.85 KLM valves.

Table 8.4.
Calculation of the Expected Value of Demanded KLM Valves

KLM Valves Sold x	Probability $P(X = x)$	$xP(X = x)$
1	.10	.10
2	.25	.50
3	.35	1.05
4	.30	1.20
	1.00	$E(X) = 2.85$

In the above illustration the relative frequency from historical data is perceived as a probability distribution of the random variable "KLM valves sold." Other problems involve events that are likely to occur once in the future where the uncertainties of the situation are expressed in subjective probabilities.

Example 8.5

The management of Puritan, a company operating a chain of dairy bars, plans to build a new dairy bar in either of two locations. Management figures that the probability of the new unit being successful in location A is .75 and that, if it is successful, it will bring an annual profit of $4000. If it is not successful, however, management expects to lose $2000 a year. The probability of the unit succeeding in location B is only .50 with $7000 annual expected profit. If the unit in location B turns out to be a failure, the annual loss is expected to amount to $2300. Where should the company locate the new bar?

We may consider letters A and B to denote the random variable's profit or loss for the two locations, respectively. Calculation of the expected values of these random variables is shown in Table 8.5. Since $E(A)$ is greater than $E(B)$, management may maximize profit by building the new bar in location A.

Table 8.5. Calculation of Expected Values for Determining the Location of a New Dairy Bar

	Location A			Location B		
Profit or Loss a	Probability $P(A = a)$	$aP(A = a)$		Profit or Loss b	Probability $P(B = b)$	$bP(B = b)$
$4000	.75	$3000		$7000	.50	$3500
− 2000	.25	− 500		− 2300	.50	−1150
	1.00	$E(A) = \$2500$			1.00	$E(B) = \$2350$

Variance of a Random Variable

As in the case of expected value, the variance of a random variable is, computationally, analogous to the variance of an empirical frequency distribution. It is a measure of variability defined in terms of the extent to which a random variable varies about its expected value.

In general, let X be a discrete random variable that takes on the value x with probability $P(X = x)$. Then the variance of X, denoted by $V(X)$, is defined by

(8.2) $$V(X) = \Sigma\{[x - E(X)]^2 \, P(X = x)\}$$

Note that $V(X)$ is just the expected value of the squared deviations of a random variable. Thus, it is analogous to the population variance σ^2 in the same way the expected value $E(X)$ is analogous to the population mean μ.

Example 8.6

In addition to expected value, computation of variance was part of the analysis for determining an optimal inventory policy for KLM valves. The required calculations are shown in Table 8.6 with the probability distribu-

Table 8.6. Calculation of the Variance of Demanded KLM Valves

KLM Valves Demanded x	Probability $P(X = x)$	$x - E(X)$	$[x - E(X)]^2$	$[x - E(X)]^2[P(X = x)]$
1	.10	−1.85	3.4225	.342250
2	.25	− .85	.7225	.180625
3	.35	+ .15	.0225	.007875
4	.30	+1.15	1.3225	.396750
	1.00			$V(X) = .927500$

Section 8 Probability Distributions: Summary Measures

tion copied from Table 8.4. Deviations $x - E(X)$ are obtained by subtracting the expected value 2.85 from each value of the random variable. For example, when x is 1, $x - E(X)$ is equal to $1 - 2.85 = -1.85$. Then each deviation is squared and multiplied by the corresponding probability. For example, $(-1.85)^2$ is $3.4225 \times .10 = .342250$. The sum of these products is the variance .9275.

As explained earlier, the variance has no direct empirical meaning since it represents squares of the units of the random variable. In this case, $V(X)$ represents squares of valves. We can return to the original units by computing the standard deviation

(8.3) $$\boxed{SD(X) = \sqrt{V(X)}}$$

For our illustration,

$$SD(X) = \sqrt{.9275} \simeq .96 \text{ KLM valves}$$

The notational difference between the variance and the standard deviation of a random variable and the corresponding σ^2 and σ of an empirical frequency distribution is justified on grounds already explained in connection with expected value.

PROBLEMS

Group One

*8.1. Every year an organization conducts a lottery with an automobile costing $5200 as a prize. If 2000 lottery tickets are expected to be sold, what is a fair price for a ticket? Interpret the result.

*8.2. For every dollar a roulette player bets he wins $36 if he bets on a winning number. If the wheel has 37 numbers 0, 1, 2, ..., 36, is the game fair to the player?

8.3. Consider the random experiment shown in Table 8.1 about households. Let X be the random variable "Average number of persons per sampled household." How does this probability distribution differ from the given probability distribution?

8.4. An automobile dealer believes that for the forthcoming new models, sales of compact cars will be three times as large as sales of regular-size cars.
  *(a) If the average selling price of a compact car is $4200 and that of a regular car is $5800, what is the expected value of the dealer's receipts per sale?
  (b) If the dealer also believes that 5 percent of the people who visit the showroom will buy an automobile, what are the expected receipts per visitor? Interpret the result.

8.5. We have seen that the sample space for the number of defective toasters in a

Answers to asterisked (*) problems are appended.

random sample of two toasters from an assembly line is {0, 1, 2}. Suppose the probability of a defective toaster is .10.
*(a) Find the appropriate probability distribution for the random variable "Number of defective toasters."
(b) Present this probability distribution in a graph.

8.6. Nancy Woodworth, the new administration manager of Cable Associates, a research consulting company, wishes to establish a policy for charging the awarded research contracts the full cost of all research proposals prepared for bidding on contracts. She collected the following information:

Cost of Research Proposals	Relative Frequency
$1500	.15
2200	.25
3600	.40
4500	.20

(a) What is the expected cost per research proposal? Interpret the result.
(b) If only one out of four research proposals is awarded a research contract, how much should each awarded contract be charged on the average?

8.7. As a buyer of automobile parts and accessories, you consider purchasing battery X or battery Y. Earlier tests of several batteries have shown the following results:

Battery X		Battery Y	
Service Hours	Relative Frequency	Service Hours	Relative Frequency
5000	.20	5000	.15
6000	.20	6000	.20
7000	.20	7000	.30
8000	.20	8000	.20
9000	.20	9000	.15

For example, 20 percent of the tested X batteries gave 5000 hours of service, while only 15 percent of the tested Y batteries gave the same number of service hours.
*(a) Calculate the expected value and variance of service hours for each battery.
(b) Which battery should you purchase? Explain why.

8.8 Kram-A-Lex company considers marketing two new products. Depending on different demand circumstances, the odds for the realizable net profits are given below:

Product X		Product Y	
Profit	Odds	Profit	Odds
−$4,000	1 to 4	−$6,000	2 to 5
+ 5,000	2 to 3	+ 8,000	3 to 4
+10,000	2 to 3	+ 9,000	2 to 5

(a) Find the expected net profit for each product.
(b) If the company has funds for producing and marketing only one product, which product do you think should be marketed? Explain why.

Group Two

8.9. Three households A, B, and C have annual incomes of $6,000, $12,000, and $24,000, respectively. A sample of two households is selected at random without replacement. Let random variable $\bar{X}$ denote "Average annual income per household."
*(a) Find the probability distribution of this random variable.
(b) Find the expected value of the random variable and interpret the result.
(c) Calculate the variance and the standard deviation of the random variable.

8.10. The average fraction defective of an assembly line for transistors is 20 percent. Three transistors are selected at random.
*(a) Find the probability distribution of "Number of defective transistors."
(b) Present this probability distribution in a graph.
(c) Calculate the expected value, variance, and standard deviation of the random variable.

8.11 An insurance company charges a $3 premium for every $1000 of term insurance coverage. Joe Peletier carries a $40,000 term insurance policy with the company. If the mortality rate for Peletier's age group is .002 during a given year, what is the expected value of his policy to the insurance company? Interpret your answer.

8.12. In a lot of 10 items 3 are defective. A sample of 2 items is drawn at random. Let random variable X denote "Number of defective items." Find the probability distribution and calculate the expected value of the random variable when the sample is drawn:
(a) With replacement
(b) Without replacement

8.13. We have seen that Puritan's management (Example 8.5) should build its new plant in location A.
(a) Suppose the probability of success in location B is 5/8. Would this probability change management's decision?
(b) What is the probability of success for location B in order to make a matter of indifference the placing of the new dairy bar in either location?

SECTION 9 / THE BINOMIAL DISTRIBUTION

There are two important reasons for studying the binomial distribution. First, it represents a probability model of discrete random variables applicable to a wide variety of business as well as nonbusiness problems. For example, a production manager may be interested in what fraction of the output of a production line consists of good or defective units; a sales manager may be concerned about whether or not a reader of an advertisement will purchase the advertised product; a candidate for political office may want to know whether or not he or she is favored by the majority of voters. All these situations and many others involve processes with coin-tossing characteristics which can be analyzed with the binomial distribution. Second, the characteristics of the binomial distribution may help us better understand other random processes.

We begin with the process which gives rise to the binomial distribution. Then we focus our attention on the binomial distribution itself and illustrate the use of binomial distribution tables. Finally, we define and illustrate the application of the mean and variance of the binomial distribution.

Bernoulli Process

The random process which gives rise to the binomial distribution is frequently referred to as a *Bernoulli process** and the trials of the process as Bernoulli trials. Coin tossing, for example, is such a random process with each toss representing a trial. But let us consider a more practical illustration of the Bernoulli process.

Example 9.1

An automatic machine stamping out metal pieces for manufacturing uses is frequently cited as an illustration of a Bernoulli process. Each stamping of a metal piece may be considered to represent a trial of the process.

A random process such as metal stamping is considered to be a Bernoulli process if it meets the following conditions:

1. *Each trial represents a sample space with two outcomes referred to as "success" or "failure."* The stamped metal pieces can be classified as "good" representing a success and "defective" representing a failure. Which of the two outcomes is called a success and which a failure is completely arbitrary. What is important, however, is that once we specify one outcome as a success and the other as a failure, we must be consistent throughout the analysis of the problem.
2. *The probability of success remains constant from trial to trial.* We usually denote the probability of success with π (Greek lowercase *pi*) and the probability of the complement event, failure, with $(1 - \pi)$. Of course, the sum of two probabilities add up to 1, that is, $\pi + (1 - \pi) = 1$. In stamping metal

---

*Named after the Swiss mathematician James Bernoulli, 1654–1705.

pieces, the probability of a defective piece π may be .02 and of a good piece $1 - \pi = .98$ so that $.02 + .98 = 1$.
3. *Successive trial outcomes are independent.* The outcome in each trial is not affected by the outcome of preceding trials. The fact that a stamped piece turns up defective does not change the probability of a piece turning up defective in subsequent stamping trials.

Of course, these requirements describe an ideal experiment or a model. Real-life processes like the metal-stamping process may not meet these ideal conditions precisely. Real conditions, however, may be close enough to the model so that the process can be treated as a Bernoulli process.

Example 9.1 (continued)

Consider a production run of 1000 metal pieces stamped by the automatic machine with each piece being the outcome of a trial of the process. The production run may contain a percentage of defective pieces found by inspection or other means. Under normal production conditions we believe that this percentage or *average fraction defective* represents the probability of a defective metal piece on each trial. Yet the conditions of constancy of π and independence of trials may not be met exactly. During the production run, metal fatigue of the vital parts of the machine may set in, gradually increasing the number of defectives as production continues. Thus, π may not be quite the same for all 1000 trials. For all practical purposes, however, these deviations from the model may not make any appreciable difference, and the Bernoulli model can be used to study such a mechanical process.

Also, the Bernoulli model may be used advantageously to study real-world situations which by their nature may conform to the model less than automatic machines.

Example 9.2

The process of filling orders in a mail-order house may be one case in point. The task of filling a package with the requested merchandise ordered by a customer and addressing it correctly may be considered as a trial of the process, where success means that an order is improperly filled or addressed. Although π is less likely to be constant and the trials more dependent in this case than in the earlier case, the Bernoulli model may still be used to study the process.

In still other situations, the Bernoulli process may be used as a simulation device.

Example 9.3

The management of a newspaper with nationwide circulation considers a pocket-size book edition of last year's best articles which appeared in the magazine section of the Sunday issues of the newspaper. Think of the demand for the book as a Bernoulli process. Each reader who notices the advertisement about the book may be considered as a trial, and success may be defined as the reader who decides to purchase the book. Under certain conditions, simulation with the Bernoulli model may be used to determine

Chapter 3 Probability Distributions: Binomial and Poisson Distributions

the optimal survey sample size which should be taken to estimate the demand for the book.

In short, the Bernoulli model describes or simulates an enormous variety of processes related to business as well as to nonbusiness operations.

The Binomial Distribution

The probability distribution of a binomially distributed discrete random variable is obtained from the formula

(9.1) $$P(X = x | n, \pi) = \binom{n}{x} \pi^x (1 - \pi)^{n-x}$$

where n = number of Bernoulli trials
π = probability of success
x = number of successes
X = random variable representing the achieved number of successes
$x = 0, 1, \ldots, n$

Expression $P(X = x | n, \pi)$ reads "The binomial probability of x successes, given n and π." Expression $\binom{n}{x}$ reads "The number of combinations of n trials containing x successes"; it is defined as

(9.2) $$\binom{n}{x} = \frac{n!}{x!(n-x)!}$$

Formula (9.2) determines the number of elementary events with a given number of successes. Symbol $n!$, called *n-factorial*,* denotes the product of positive integers from 1 to n. Similarly, the symbols in the denominator represent the factorials of x successes and $n - x$ failures.

Example 9.3 (continued)

Suppose management believes that 2 out of 10 persons who read the advertisement about the pocket-size edition of articles purchase the book.

If 3 persons who read the advertisement are selected at random, what is the probability that none purchases the book? For $n = 3$ trials, $X = 0$ successes (purchases), and $\pi = 2/10 = .20$, according to formulas (9.1) and (9.2),

$$P(X = 0 | n = 3, \pi = .20) = \binom{3}{0}(.20)^0(.80)^3$$

$$= \frac{3 \times 2 \times 1}{0!3 \times 2 \times 1}(.20)^0(.80)^3$$

Factorial 0! is defined as 1 and, therefore, $\binom{3}{0} = 1$; in other words, there is only one elementary event (0, 0, 0) in the sample space with no successes

---

*For more detailed coverage of factorials and combinations the reader is referred to Section 7 on counting techniques.

Section 9 The Binomial Distribution

in three trials. For zero successes, we raise $\pi = .20$ to the zero power since $x = 0$ and $1 - \pi = 1 - .20 = .80$ to the third power since $n - x = 3 - 0 = 3$. The probability of no purchases is

$$P(X = 0 \mid n = 3, \pi = .20) = 1 \times 1 \times (.80)^3 = .512$$

since $\binom{3}{0} = 1$ and $(.20)^0 = 1$.

What is the probability that one of the three advertisement readers purchase the book? According to formulas (9.1) and (9.2),

$$P(X = 1 \mid n = 3, \pi = .20) = \binom{3}{1}(.20)^1(.80)^2$$
$$= \frac{3 \times 2 \times 1}{1!2 \times 1}(.20)^1(.80)^2$$

Note that $\binom{3}{1}$ equals 3; in other words, there are three elementary events (1, 0, 0), (0, 1, 0), (0, 0, 1) in the sample space with one success in the three trials. For one success, we raise π .20 to the first power since $X = 1$ and $1 - \pi = 1 - .20 = .80$ to the second power since $n - x = 3 - 1 = 2$. The probability of one purchase is

$$P(X = 1 \mid n = 3, \pi = .20) = 3 \times (.20)^1(.80)^2 = .384$$

The binomial distribution for none, one, two, or three purchases in three trials is shown in Table 9.1. The probability for two and three purchases

Table 9.1. Probability Distribution for Number of Books Purchased in a Sample of Three Advertisement Readers

Number of Purchases in Sample x	Probability $P(X = x) \mid n = 3, \pi = .20)$
0	$\binom{3}{0}(.20)^0(.80)^3 = .512$
1	$\binom{3}{1}(.20)^1(.80)^2 = .384$
2	$\binom{3}{2}(.20)^2(.80)^1 = .096$
3	$\binom{3}{3}(.20)^3(.80)^0 = \underline{.008}$
	1.000

was obtained by repeated application of formulas (9.1) and (9.2) as illustrated.

In sum, we would do well to keep in mind the following points about the binomial distribution (9.1).

1. The fact that the binomial distribution is a *probability distribution* can be easily proved. Since the probability of success π and the number of Bernoulli trials n are nonnegative numbers, the binomial probabilities cannot be negative. Furthermore, it can be proved mathematically that the sum of binomial probabilities for given n and π values must be equal to one.

2. The number of Bernoulli trials n and the probability of success π are called the *parameters* of the binomial distribution. Each pair of values of these parameters specifies a different probability distribution. So formula (9.1) specifies a family of probability distributions, one for each combination of values for n and π.

3. The binomial distribution is applicable to sampling from a finite population with replacement or, equivalently, to *sampling from an infinite population.* This can be easily seen from the underlying conditions of a Bernoulli process. As in the case of experiments with replacement, the probability of success remains constant from trial to trial. However, the binomial distribution may be used as a reasonable approximation to determine probabilities when sampling from a finite population without replacement. By convention, such an approximation is considered reasonable if the population is a least 20 times as large as the sample size and if the value of the probability of success π is not close to zero or to one. But what is considered a reasonable approximation may also depend on the objectives of a statistical investigation.

4. And a word of caution: the binomial distribution is a probability model applicable to a Bernoulli process with three underlying conditions. Real-life processes, however, may not meet these conditions precisely. Determining whether the model is a reasonable approximation of a real-life process requires a careful examination of the particular situation at hand. For example, metal fatigue of the machine-stamped metal pieces may change significantly the probability of defective pieces. Then conditions 2 and 3 of the Bernoulli process are violated. Before applying the binomial distribution, observations which can be attributed to such an assignable cause can be eliminated from the data. Suppose the pocket-size book of newspaper articles is sold together with other publications in a package deal. Then the independence condition 3 of the process is violated because sales of the book depend on the sales of the other publications in the package. Before applying the binomial distribution, independent sales can be segregated from package sales and the two sets of data may be treated separately. Another problem which statisticians encounter is establishing that a real-world process behaves like a Bernoulli process and therefore justifies application of the binomial model. Justification depends on whether a real-world frequency distribution is a reasonable approximation to an expected frequency distribution obtained from binomial probabilities. Later, we shall introduce a test that enables us to determine probabilistically how good such an approximation may be.

Section 9 The Binomial Distribution

Binomial Distribution Tables

When the number of Bernoulli trials is large, finding the probability of x successes by the binomial formula (9.1) is time-consuming. This is especially true in many applications of the binomial distribution when we would like to know the probability of at least x successes or at most x successes. It requires the laborious task of finding the probabilities of $x, x + 1, x + 2, \ldots, n$ successes and adding the results. Fortunately, extensive tables are available which contain the cumulative binomial distribution for a great number of n and π combinations. Such a cumulative binomial distribution for a small number of n and π values is given in Appendix B. For each specified pair of n and π values the uniquely determined cumulative binomial distribution for at least x successes is obtained by formula

$$(9.3) \qquad P(X \geqslant x \,|\, n, \pi) = \sum_{X=x}^{n} \binom{n}{x} \pi^x (1 - \pi)^{n-x}$$

Expression $P(X \geq x \,|\, n, \pi)$ reads "The binomial probability of at least x successes, given n and π." The summation sign Σ indicates that the desired probability is obtained by adding the probabilities for $x, x + 1, x + 2, \ldots, n$ successes.

Example 9.3 (continued)

Consider again the pocket-size book of newspaper articles. What is the probability that at least one of the three persons in the sample will purchase the book?

We wish to find $P(X \geqslant 1 \,|\, n = 3, \pi = .20)$. The probability is .488; it is read from Appendix B at row $x = 1$ for the binomial distribution $n = 3$ under column $\pi = .20$.

Since we shall make frequent use of cumulative binomial distributions, it is worthwhile demonstrating in greater detail how Appendix B can be utilized.

Example 9.4

Probabilities of the form

$$P(X \geqslant x \,|\, n, \pi)$$

can be read directly from Appendix B as already illustrated; other probabilities can be obtained indirectly. The following cases illustrate all possibilities:

(a) $P(X \geqslant 2 \,|\, n = 20, \pi = .05)$
This probability is .264; it is given at row $x = 2$ for the binomial distribution $n = 20$ and $\pi = .05$.

(b) $P(X > 2 \,|\, n = 20, \pi = .05)$
This probability is equivalent to

$$P(X \geqslant 3 \,|\, n = 20, \pi = .05) = .076$$

at row $x = 3$.

(c) $P(X < 2 \,|\, n = 20, \pi = .05)$

$$P(X < 2) = 1 - P(X \geqslant 2)$$
$$= 1 - .264$$
$$= .736$$

(d) $P(X \leq 2 | n = 20, \pi = .05)$

$$P(X \leq 2) = 1 - P(X \geq 3)$$
$$= 1 - .076$$
$$= .924$$

(e) $P(X = 2 | n = 20, \pi = .05)$

$$P(X = 2) = P(X \geq 2) - P(X \geq 3)$$
$$= .264 - .076$$
$$= .188$$

(f) $P(X \leq 2 | n = 5, \pi = .60)$

Even extensive binomial tables may not include values for π greater than .50. Thus, when π is greater than .50, the problem of finding probabilities from such tables must be rephrased in terms of $1 - \pi$:

$$P(X \leq 2 | n = 5, \pi = .60) = P[X \geq 3 | n = 5, (1 - \pi) = .40] = .317$$

It can be seen that Appendix B greatly reduces the effort of finding binomial probabilities; it should be used, whenever possible, instead of formulas (9.1) or (9.3).

Expected Value and Variance of Number of Successes

These two measurements can be easily derived from the corresponding definitions given in Section 8. Here, we shall merely illustrate their application.

For the random variable X denoting "Number of successes" in n Bernoulli trials its expected value is

(9.4) $$\boxed{E(X) = n\pi}$$

Example 9.5

Let us go back to the pocket-size book of newspaper articles. Again, management believes that 20 percent of persons who read an advertisement about the book will purchase it. If the advertisement is read by 2 million individuals, what is the expected sales volume?

Since $\pi = .20$ and $n = 2{,}000{,}000$, by (9.4),

$$E(X) = 2{,}000{,}000(.20) = 400{,}000 \text{ copies}$$

We interpret the average of a binomial distribution just as we interpret the expected value of any probability distribution. The long-run "Number of successes" from a very large number of Bernoulli trials is likely to be close to the expected value defined in formula (9.4). On the average, the "Number of successes" is expected to be equal to the number of trials n times the proportion π of such trials which represent "success."

Section 9 The Binomial Distribution

And the "Number of successes" is a random variable X with a variance defined as

(9.5)
$$V(X) = n\pi(1 - \pi)$$

and the standard deviation as

(9.6)
$$SD(X) = \sqrt{n\pi(1 - \pi)}$$

Example 9.5 (continued)

What are the variance and standard deviation of the sales volume for the pocket-size book of newspaper articles?
Since $\pi = .20$, $1 - \pi = (1 - .20) = .80$, and $n = 2{,}000{,}000$, by formula (9.5),

$$V(X) = 2{,}000{,}000(.20)(.80) = 320{,}000$$

and by formula (9.6), the positive square root of the variance is

$$SD(X) = \sqrt{320{,}000} \simeq 566 \text{ copies}$$

Again, the variance has no empirically meaningful interpretation; it represents square copies of the pocket-size book of newspaper articles. The standard deviation, on the other hand, represents number of copies and may have important practical applications. For example, for a sample of 2 million Bernoulli trials, the "Number of successes" will be normally distributed with mean 400,000 copies and a standard deviation 566 copies. This means that the management of the newspaper can be practically certain that sales will range within three standard deviations plus or minus from their expected value; in other words, sales will be within $400{,}000 \pm 3(566)$ or a range between 398,302 and 401,698 copies, if indeed $\pi = .20$ is true.

PROBLEMS

Group One

*9.1. Find the following binomial probabilities:
  (a) $P(X = 0 | n = 4, \pi = .01)$
  (b) $P(X \geq 2 | n = 6, \pi = .10)$
  (c) $P(X < 3 | n = 10, \pi = .20)$
  (d) $P(X \leq 3 | n = 9, \pi = .30)$
  (e) $P(X = 4 | n = 20, \pi = .45)$
  (f) $P(X < 15 | n = 50, \pi = .35)$

9.2. Find the binomial distribution when:
  *(a) $n = 6, \pi = .10$
  (b) $n = 9, \pi = .20$
  (c) $n = 11, \pi = .40$
  (d) $n = 20, \pi = .10$

Answers to asterisked (*) problems are appended.

Chapter 3 Probability Distributions: Binomial and Poisson Distributions

*9.3. Suppose a process of filling mail orders has a 20 percent average fraction defective. If eight filled mail orders are selected at random, what is the probability that none is defective?

9.4. If 10 persons who read the advertisement about the new pocket-size book of newspaper articles are selected at random and π is still .20, what is the probability that book sales will be:
  *(a) Exactly 4?   (d) Less than 4?
  (b) More than 4?   (e) Between 4 and 6 inclusive?
  (c) 4 or more?   (f) 4 or less?

9.5. Raymond Spinoza, the manager of a mail order house, selects 11 filled orders. Although he believes that the order-filling process performs as a Bernoulli, the average fraction defective varies from day to day and he does not know today's state of the process. What is the probability that the sample contains two or more incorrectly filled orders, given that the average fraction defective is:
  *(a) .01?   (d) .30?
  (b) .10?   (e) .40?
  (c) .20?   (f) .50?

*9.6. Maria Lopez sells life insurance for Providence Insurance Company. During a particular day she plans to visit nine prospective customers. On the average, the odds for selling a contract are 1 to 4. She also believes that sales are independent. What is the probability that she will:
  (a) Make no sales?
  (b) Sell less than two contracts?
  (c) Meet her daily quota of two sales?

9.7. Robert MacKay is in wildcat oil exploration business. For the next year he has enough venture capital to drill for 10 oil wells. He believes that the odds for an oil strike are 1 to 9. Assuming independence, what is the probability that he will:
  (a) Go broke?
  (b) Have one oil strike?
  (c) Have at least one oil strike?

9.8. The average fraction defective of a machine *in control* is .02. Debbie Connelly, the manager in charge of production, employs the following decision rule. Each hour five parts are selected at random from those produced by the machine during the hour; if more than one of the parts are found defective, the machine is stopped and reset; otherwise, the machine is considered to be in control and is permitted to continue producing parts without being reset. What is the probability that the machine is reset?

*9.9. An oil-heating company offers a discount if customers pay their bills within 10 days. Experience shows that about 25 percent of the 1000 customers take advantage of the discount. Assuming independence:
  (a) Find the expected number of customers who take advantage of the discount.
  (b) Find the expected number of customers within a range plus and minus three standard deviations from the expected value.
  (c) In a random sample of 50 customers, what is the probability that fewer than 10 will take advantage of the discount?

9.10. Patricia Woolworth is a stockbroker. She knows from experience that only 1 out of 10 telephone calls from her customers end in a stock transaction. Next year,

she expects about 3000 telephone calls from customers. Assuming that calls are independent:
(a) What is the expected number of stock transactions for the year?
(b) What is the expected number of transactions within a range plus and minus three standard deviations from the expected value?
(c) What is the probability that she will close less than 4 transactions if she expects 50 telephone calls next week?

Group Two

9.11. In a lot of 50 electronic components, 10 are defective. A sample of 4 components is drawn at random. What is the probability that the sample contains 0, 1, 2, 3, or 4 defective components:
(a) If sampling is with replacement?
*(b) If sampling is without replacement?
(c) Compare results.

9.12. Sketch the graph of the binomial distribution when $n = 10$ and $\pi = .50, .30,$ and .10. Discuss the shape of the distribution as π gets smaller than .50.

*9.13. John Shea is manager of the personal loans department in Downtown Bank, Ltd. He believes that personal loans may be considered a quasi-Bernoulli process where repayment of a loan represents a "success" and nonrepayment a "failure."
(a) If the probability of failure is .02, what is the expected number of failures in a set of 2000 loans due this month?
(b) After how many loans due does the expected number of failures reach 5 failures?

9.14. Tolaroid claims that 98 percent of their exposures for photoprints develop. Assuming independence, what is the probability that 19 or fewer photoprints will develop in a roll containing 20 exposures?

9.15. Contract bids for social research fail to secure a contract 85 percent of the time. Assuming independence, what is the probability that at least 40 of the 50 recent contract bids will fail to secure a contract?

SECTION 10/ THE POISSON DISTRIBUTION

Many decision problems involve random variables which cannot be studied with the binomial distribution. For example, blemishes in the surface of materials or arrivals of customers to a facility occur over a continuum of space or time. Such processes cannot be analyzed as a series of trials. Yet we need to study them, because knowing the probability distribution of such events has a wide variety of applications. For example, knowing the probability distribution of machine breakdowns may help management determine the number of repair personnel to be hired.

The probability of such discrete events is determined by the Poisson distribution.* As in the case of the binomial distribution, we first explain the corresponding Poisson process. Then we discuss the characteristics of the Poisson distribution and show how to find probabilities from Poisson distribution tables. Finally, we show how the Poisson distribution may be used as an approximation to the binomial distribution.

The Poisson Process

We have seen that the Bernoulli process consists of a series of independent trials where the probability of success is constant on each trial. As already stated, a Poisson process cannot be effectively handled as a series of independent Bernoulli trials.

Example 10.1

Consider a machine which insulates the surface of electric wire. Suppose we find that in the first 2000 feet of insulated wire the machine has produced 1000 pinhole defects, or .5 defect per foot. We wish to determine the probability that in the next 2 feet of insulated wire the machine will produce 0, 1, 2, ... defects, where the three dots mean all natural numbers to infinity.

Although the probability of a pinhole defect in the insulated surface may be constant from one surface point to another surface point, such points cannot be considered as trials. For all practical purposes the number of surface points cannot be identified or counted on a continuous surface. Hence, we are unable to assess the probability of the occurrence of a defect at a given point by considering the past fraction of defective points; neither can we apply the binomial distribution to determine the probability of having 0, 1, 2, ... defects in an interval of 2 feet of insulated wire, since such an interval is not a trial.

A process such as the above is called *Poisson* if it is considered to meet the following conditions:

1. The probability that two or more events, pinhole defects, occur in a very small subinterval, say 1/100 inch of wire, is so small that it may be considered to be zero.
2. The probability that exactly one event occurs in such a subinterval is very small and constant from subinterval to subinterval.
3. Occurrence of an event in a subinterval does not depend on where such subinterval is located.
4. Occurrence of an event in a subinterval does not depend on the occurrence of events in other nonoverlapping subintervals.

Note that the conditions of the Poisson process correspond to the conditions of the Bernoulli process where the requirement for independence is met by the third and fourth conditions. Like the Bernoulli process, the Poisson process is said to have *no memory*. Also, like the Bernoulli process, the conditions of the Poisson

---

*Named after the French mathematician Simeon Denis Poisson, 1781–1840, who discovered it.

Section 10 The Poisson Distribution

process describe a *model*. These conditions may not occur precisely in real-world situations.

Example 10.1 (continued)

We accept the proposition that the process of wire insulating can be regarded as Poisson, because we believe that the probability of occurrence of pinhole defects on the insulating surface remains constant and the events are independent. In reality, such conditions may not be precisely met. Yet we may accept the Poisson process as a satisfactory approximation for studying this real-life mechanical process.

Furthermore, as in the case of the Bernoulli model, we can use the Poisson process to study real-world processes which conform less to this model than do mechanical processes.

Example 10.2

Arrival of bank customers to teller booths is a case in point. The rate of such arrivals may vary according to the time of day as well as from day to day. Furthermore, arrivals may not always be independent. Yet the Poisson model may still be applied under carefully defined circumstances.

Last but not least, the Poisson process may be applied to simulate the demand for a product or a service.

Example 10.3

Arrival of oil tankers at a refinery is one common case illustrating application of the Poisson distribution. We can perceive ship arrivals as a Poisson process and simulate the process under varying average number of arrivals per day. Such analysis may be useful in determining whether or not to expand existing unloading facilities.

The Poisson model can be applied advantageously in studying a great variety of Poisson-like natural processes. Of particular significance is the application of the Poisson model to production management—in waiting lines, reliability of machines, and inventory control, for instance. In the sciences, applications can range from the study of microscopic organisms and pollution particles in the water or the air to the occurrence of urban crime.

The Poisson Distribution

The probability distribution of a Poisson-distributed discrete random variable is obtained from the formula

$$(10.1) \quad P(X = x \mid m) = \frac{m^x e^{-m}}{x!} \quad x = 1, 2, 3, \ldots \quad (m > 0)$$

where m = *average* number of occurrences for a specified number of unit measurements
e = 2.7183 ... (the base of Naperian or natural logarithms)
x = number of occurrences
X = random variable representing the achieved number of occurrences x
= 0, 1, 2, ... (to infinity)

Chapter 3 Probability Distributions: Binomial and Poisson Distributions

Expression $P(X = x|m)$ reads "The Poisson probability of x occurrences, given m." Average m is the product of the *mean rate* λ (Greek lowercase *lambda*), at which events occur *per unit* of measurement, and the *number of unit measurements t*.

Example 10.4

If a wire-insulating machine causes .5 pinhole defect per foot of insulated wire, what is the probability distribution of no defects in the next 2 feet of insulated wire?

Since λ is .5 and t is 2, m is (.5)(2) or 1. By formula (10.1) the probability of $x = 0$ defects is

$$P(X = 0 | m = 1) = \frac{1^0 e^{-1}}{0!} = e^{-1} = \frac{1}{2.7183} \simeq .368$$

since 1^0 equals 1 and the factorial 0! equals 1. Probabilities for larger numbers of defects are calculated in a similar manner by repeated application of formula (10.1):

In applying the Poisson distribution to real-world situations we should keep in mind the following points:

1. Like the binomial distribution, the Poisson distribution is a probability distribution.

2. Unlike the binomial distribution, the Poisson distribution has m, the average number of occurrences for a specified number of unit measurements, as a single parameter. So formula (10.1) specifies a family of probability distributions, one for each value of m.

3. A unique characteristic of the Poisson distribution is that parameter m is the expected value of a Poisson-distributed random variable, that is,

(10.2)
$$\boxed{E(X) = m}$$

4. Real random processes may not meet precisely the conditions of the Poisson process. Therefore, the Poisson model must be applied to empirical data with great care. For example, the mean rate λ of arrivals of bank customers to teller booths will be different at 9:00 A.M. than at 3:00 P.M.; it will be different on Fridays than on other workdays. Then condition 2 of the model is violated. We may be able to overcome such a difficulty by collecting data on customer arrivals for parts of a workday which appear to have the same value of λ and by applying a different Poisson distribution with the appropriate λ value to each set of data. Suppose milk deliveries to a supermarket are made on either Monday or Thursday between 9:00 A.M. and 10:00 A.M. If a delivery made on Monday excludes the need for a delivery on Thursday, the independence conditions 3 and 4 of the model are violated. Thursday deliveries depend on Monday deliveries and the reverse. How can we establish that a real-world process behaves like a Poisson process and therefore justifies application of the Poisson model? Such an application depends

Section 10 The Poisson Distribution

on whether a real-world frequency distribution is a reasonable approximation to an expected frequency distribution obtained from Poisson probabilities. A test, to be introduced later, enables us to determine probabilistically how good such an approximation may be.

Poisson Distribution Tables

For large values of parameter m, the task of determining the associated Poisson distribution is time-consuming. As in the case of the binomial distribution, the task becomes especially difficult when we wish to find the probability for at least x occurrences or at most x occurrences. For some range of m values the uniquely determined cumulative table of the Poisson distribution for at least x occurrences can be obtained from Appendix C.

Although the procedure for finding Poisson probabilities from this appendix is the same as the procedure for finding binomial probabilities, the following examples illustrate use of the appendix as well as applications of Poisson probabilities.

Example 10.5

We have already shown how to determine the probability of no pinhole defects in 2 feet of insulated wire when m is 1. The probability distribution is shown in Table 10.1. We can find the probabilities of this distribution from the cumulative probabilities which appear under column 1.0 in Appendix C. For zero defect,

$$P(X = 0 | m = 1) = 1 - P(X \geq 1 | m = 1)$$
$$= 1 - .632$$
$$= .368$$

For one defect,

$$P(X = 1 | m = 1) = P(X \geq 1) - P(X \geq 2)$$
$$= .632 - .264$$
$$= .368$$

and so on.

Table 10.1. Poisson Distribution of Pinhole Defects in 2 Feet of Insulated Wire When $m = 1$

Number of Defects x	Probability $P(X = x \mid m = 1)$
0	.368
1	.368
2	.184
3	.061
4	.015
5	.003
6 or more	.001

Note that the Poisson distribution sets no limit on the number of occurrences. The probability of any number of defects, even 100 or more, in 2 feet of wire is nonzero, although it must be very small indeed. For this reason probabilities are determined up to a certain number of defects, six in our case; beyond six, probabilities appear as zero if rounded to the nearest third decimal place.

Example 10.6

On Friday nights, when a store is open between 6:00 P.M. and 9:00 P.M., demand for an item has averaged 2 units per hour. Assuming that demand for the item is Poisson-distributed, what is the probability that the retailer will run out of stock next Friday night if the store's inventory has 7 units?

Since λ is 2 per hour and t is 3 hours, then m is $(2)(3) = 6$. The retailer will run out of stock if demand is 8 or more units. Hence

$$P(X \geq 8 | m = 6) = .256$$

which is read from Appendix C under column 6.0 and row 8.

Example 10.7

On Sundays, between 1:00 P.M. and 9:00 P.M., automobile arrivals for refueling at a gas station average 1 automobile per 7.5 minutes. Assuming that automobile arrivals are Poisson-distributed:

(a) What is the probability that 4 or fewer automobiles will arrive at the gas station during an hour on a Sunday afternoon?

The value of λ is 1 automobile per 7.5 minutes and t is 8, that is, $60 \div 7.5 = 8$. So m is $(1)(8)$ or 8 automobiles per hour. The probability is

$$P(X \leq 4 | m = 8) = 1 - P(X \geq 5 | m = 8)$$
$$= 1 - .90$$
$$= .10$$

(b) Happy Motoring Inc. owns 10 gas stations, each with the same mean rate of automobile arrivals on Sundays as the station in part (a). What is the probability that 4 or fewer automobiles will arrive at exactly 2 stations during an hour on a Sunday afternoon?

We may consider the probability of 4 or fewer automobiles at a given gas station as a Bernoulli trial and the 10 stations as trials. So π is .10 and n is 10. The probability, read from Appendix B, is

$$P(X = 2 | n = 10, \pi = .10) = P(X \geq 2) - P(X \geq 3)$$
$$= .264 - .070$$
$$= .194$$

Approximating Binomial Probabilities with Poisson Probabilities

Even the most extensive binomial probability tables contain a limited range of n and π parameter values. This is particularly true for a *large number* of n trials and a *small* π probability. In such a case, the Poisson distribution may be used as an approximation of the binomial probability. In order to approximate a binomial probability, we simply let $n\pi$ equal m and look up the value in Appendix C.

Example 10.8

Available information indicates that 2 out of 100 persons who read an advertisement will purchase the advertised product. Assuming that pur-

Section 10 The Poisson Distribution

chases are binomially distributed and a sample of 50 readers of the advertisement is drawn at random:

(a) What is the probability that at least 5 readers in the sample will purchase the product?

Since n is 50 and π is .02, from Appendix B of binomial tables we obtain

$$P(X \geq 5 \mid n = 50, \pi = .02) = .0032$$

The probability of the same event may be approximately determined from Appendix C of Poisson tables. The value m is 1, since $n\pi = 50(.02) = 1$, so

$$P(X \geq 5 \mid m = 1) = .0040$$

(b) What is the probability that between 2 and 4 sampled readers, inclusive, will purchase the product?

From Appendix B, the binomial probability is

$$P(2 \leq x \leq 4 \mid n = 50, \pi = .02) = P(X \geq 2) - P(X \geq 5)$$
$$= .2642 - .0032$$
$$= .261$$

The Poisson approximation from Appendix C is

$$P(2 \leq x \leq 4 \mid m = 1) = P(X \geq 2) - P(X \geq 5)$$
$$= .264 - .004$$
$$= .260$$

As a rule of thumb, a Poisson approximation may be considered reasonable when n is as small as 20 trials and π no larger than .03. However, use of the approximation depends on the accuracy desired by the statistical investigation at hand. And accuracy may vary depending on the event whose probability is to be determined, as the above case illustrates.

PROBLEMS

Group One

*10.1. Find the following Poisson probabilities:
    (a) $P(X = 0 \mid m = 1.9)$ (e) $P(1 \leq X \leq 3 \mid m = 5)$
    (b) $P(X < 2 \mid m = 2.6)$ (f) $P(2 < X < 6 \mid m = 7.5)$
    (c) $P(X \geq 4 \mid m = 4.8)$ (g) $P(X \leq 8 \mid m = 4.6)$
    (d) $P(X \leq 5 \mid m = 3.2)$ (h) $P(X > 6 \mid m = 8.5)$

10.2. Find the Poisson distribution and sketch its graph for $X \leq 8$ when:
    *(a) $m = 2$ (b) $m = 3$ (c) $m = 4$

10.3. Use the Poisson distribution to approximate the following binomial probabilities, then find the exact binomial probabilities:
    *(a) $P(X \geq 2 \mid n = 50, \pi = .01)$ (c) $P(1 \leq X \leq 2 \mid n = 50, \pi = .03)$
    (b) $P(X \geq 5 \mid n = 30, \pi = .10)$ (d) $P(X \geq 3 \mid n = 20, \pi = .05)$

Answers to asterisked (*) problems are appended.

Chapter 3 Probability Distributions: Binomial and Poisson Distributions

10.4. During peak air traffic hours, airplane arrivals at Jefferson Airport average .18 per minute. Assuming that airplane arrivals are Poisson-distributed, what is the probability that 2 or more airplanes will arrive during the next:
*(a) 5 minutes of peak traffic?
(b) 10 minutes of peak traffic?
(c) 20 minutes of peak traffic?

10.5. Leo Gordon, a publisher, knows from experience that even a carefully proofread textbook is likely to have 1 typographical error per 100 printed pages. Assuming that errors are Poisson-distributed, what is the probability that a 700-page text will:
*(a) Have at least 5 errors?
(b) Be error-free?

*10.6. During heavy pollution days the number of pollution particles in a city is Poisson-distributed with an average of 10 particles per cubic inch. Lucinda Moore, the director of the local office of the Federal Environmental Protection Agency, considers that pollution in the city is harmful to health if the air contains 15 or more particles per cubic inch. What is the probability that city pollution has reached this critical level?

10.7. On weekdays with no special events and during peak checkout hours, 11:00 A.M. to 1:00 P.M., the number of taxis arriving to pick up passengers at Grand Duchess Hotel average 4.5 taxis per hour. Assuming that taxi arrivals are considered a Poisson process:
*(a) What is the probability that 1 taxi will arrive during the 2-hour period?
(b) Suppose checking-out parties average 10 for the 2-hour period. Would the average number of taxi arrivals be sufficient to take care of this demand for taxi service?

10.8. The management of Midwest Mutual Insurance believes that monthly lapses of life insurance contracts are adequately described by a Poisson distribution. Contract lapses average .00005 per policy in force the previous month. If in a given month there are 100,000 policies in force:
(a) What is the probability that less than 5 policies will lapse next month?
(b) What is the probability that at least 10 policies will lapse during the next 2 months?

Group Two

10.9. Breakdowns of milling machines at National Steel Products Corporation average 4.5 during regular workday hours, 7:30 A.M. to 4:30 P.M. Management believes that, after a machine is operated for the first 100 hours, machine breakdowns are Poisson-distributed.
*(a) What is the probability that no breakdowns will occur during a given workday?
(b) Repairs take time, so a machine is not put back to production for 2 full days from the time it breaks down. How many machines should management keep ready to replace the broken-down machines in order to have more than 50 percent chance of preventing disruption in milling operations? (Assume the company operates at full capacity.)

10.10. The records of Friendly Airlines, Inc., show that fatal airplane accidents average 1×10^{-11} per passenger mile flown per year. If the company's fleet of airplanes expects to fly 1×10^{10} passenger miles next year:
(a) What is the probability that no fatal accidents will occur?
(b) If the airline insures for $100,000 per fatal accident, what is the expected amount of insurance payments to the victims?

Section 10 The Poisson Distribution

10.11. Millie Wolfburger, the principal of Monroe High, observes that on the average 2 percent of the class of 100 seniors are absent each day. Using Poisson approximation, what is the probability that at least 4 students will be absent:
   *(a) On next Monday?
   (b) During the next 5 days?

Chapter 4
STATISTICAL INFERENCE: BASIC CONCEPTS AND TOOLS

Most available statistical information is not obtained by collecting data from an entire statistical population. Instead, we may draw conclusions about the unknown characteristics of a population from the corresponding characteristics of a random sample. For example, we can use the mean income of a sample of households to estimate the mean income of a large household population. Also, on the basis of a sample, we can test a hypothesis such as that the market share of a brand cereal is no more than a given percentage. The theory and procedure which enable us to carry out such estimation and hypothesis testing constitute the important field of statistical inference.

This chapter introduces the basic concepts and tools of statistical inference. Our effort is centered around two major tasks. In Section 11, we discuss the advantages and limitations of various procedures for collecting statistical information. In Sections 12 and 13, we explain why and how statistical inference works; essentially, the task amounts to introducing the general theoretical apparatus of *statistical inference*.

SECTION 11/ SAMPLING VERSUS A CENSUS

We have defined a population as the totality of observations we wish to study. The procedure of counting or enumerating an entire population is called a *census*. If a census were always possible or advantageous, there would be no need to know most of the techniques in this volume. Unfortunately, taking a census is the exception rather than the rule; the most common practice for data collection is to take a sample. So it is important first to discuss the reasons for sampling. Next, we illustrate random sampling from a population. This topic is followed by the introduction of sample frequency distributions and sample summary measures; these subjects establish continuity with descriptive statistics discussed earlier. The section ends by drawing the distinction between random sampling error and procedural bias, that is, the nonrandom imperfections we may encounter in collecting statistical information.

Reasons for Using Samples

The importance of statistical inference cannot be fully appreciated unless we explain why sampling, rather than a census, is the preferred method of data collection. There are six main reasons which justify sampling: an infinite population, inaccessibility or unavailability of the entire population, destructiveness in measuring the elementary units, timeliness, accuracy, and economy.

In the first place, a statistical investigation of an *infinite* population can be carried out only with a sample.

Example 11.1

A manufacturer wishes to determine whether in a process turning out fuses the percentage of defective fuses does not exceed acceptable limits. However, any attempt to determine the percentage defective by taking a census of fuses is bound to fail. At any given point in time, a census would be only partially completed because the process can continuously manufacture new fuses. The population must be considered to be infinite in the sense that it is impossible to test *every* fuse the process is capable of producing. Sampling is unavoidable. Finding whether the process is in control can be accomplished with testing periodically a random sample of fuses.

Sampling of a population which is considered infinite is not limited to manufacturing processes. It extends to any man-made or natural process whose elementary units are impossible to observe within a reasonable time period.

Second, sampling is unavoidable because for many observations the elements of a statistical *population* are *inaccessible or no longer available*. This may be true even if the statistical population under study is considered finite. Economists must rely on available and incomplete records to study business fluctuations during colonial times. Archeologists must be content with studying ancient civilizations only from remains which were spared from the destructive forces of nature and human beings.

Third, even if a statistical universe is finite, sampling may be mandatory because *measurements destroy or weaken the elementary units* of the population.

Example 11.2

A wholesaler of light bulbs wishes to sell the available inventory with a guarantee of 2000 hours service life. If all light bulbs were tested in order to verify that they meet the guarantee requirements, no bulbs would be left to sell. Unless there were a device to determine the life of each bulb without burning it out, the wholesaler must limit the destructive test to a small and appropriately selected sample.

Fourth, one of the most important reasons for sampling rather than taking a census is the need for *timely reporting* of statistical information.

Section 11 Sampling Versus a Census

Example 11.3

Consider an opinion poll before a presidential election. Many eligible voters are undecided. Others may change their preference as the presidential campaign heats up. In order to predict voter preference reliably, surveys must be conducted as close to election time as possible; yet results must be reported prior to election time to have any value. Reliable and timely reporting is achieved with a highly controlled small sample (usually less than 3000) of eligible voters from the whole United States.

The federal government, state governments, and business organizations report periodically a wide variety of data on employment, output, inventory, sales, prices, and other indicators of economic activity at the national and state levels. Such data can be of little use for short-run forecasting and planning unless they are published as quickly as possible. Timeliness is one important reason why information must be obtained from a sample of elementary units.

Accuracy is a fifth reason why sampling may be preferable to a census. This is especially true with studies involving personal contacts with individuals to obtain the required information.

Example 11.4

Our Constitution requires a census of the United States population every 10 years. In the past, interviewing every household in the country required tens of thousands of interviewers. Training them was an enormous undertaking and offered opportunity for wide variations in the quality of interviewing. Introduction of sampling has increased the validity of census results. In the 1980 census, house-to-house enumeration was limited to less than 10 percent of the country. All other households received a mail-out-mail-back questionnaire. Follow-up procedures were used for those households which failed to mail back their questionnaires. This sample design required a much smaller group of interviewers. Both training and supervising a small group of well-qualified rather than thousands of less-qualified interviewers improved interviewing quality.

In general, accuracy becomes the overriding reason for sampling when measurements require a high degree of exactness and must be carried out with highly skilled personnel.

In most earlier illustrations, the underlying sixth reason for sampling is *economy*. More frequently than not, obtaining information from a sample is less costly than observing the entire population.

Example 11.5

In a survey of insurance experience of commercial fishing vessels, the sponsoring federal agency required random selection and personal interviewing of vessel owners. Many owners resided in isolated and remote parts of the country. Moreover, interviewing was time-consuming, sometimes requiring an interpreter. Locating and interviewing each vessel owner was so expensive that, if for no other reason, the survey could not have been carried out except with a sample.

Observe that economy as a reason for sampling refers primarily to variable cost, that is, cost per interviewed vessel owner. Other things being equal, the greater the variable cost, the more compelling the reason for sampling rather than taking a census.

Today, a very large portion of the statistical information published by both government and private sources is collected on a sample basis. Nevertheless, the importance of a census should not be unduly minimized. In the first place, the law may require a complete count. Notable cases are reporting on imports, registering ships and motor vehicles, and certifying the accounts of a firm. More important, a census may be necessary to collect information about a very small segment of a population. Even if our Constitution did not require a population census, we would still have needed one in order to obtain information about small towns and city neighborhoods. Finally, computers may increase the importance of census taking. Computer data files can hold very large statistical populations which can be reported on demand with extreme speed, perfect accuracy, and minimum cost. In a computerized society, a census may replace sampling in areas such as periodic reporting of data on economic activity. At the same time, a network of interconnected computer systems may augment the need for obtaining *additional* information with sampling.

In sum, sampling is the only alternative for obtaining information from infinite and inaccessible populations, or because of the self-destructive nature of measurements. If a choice exists between sampling and census, sampling is favored on grounds of timeliness, accuracy, and cost. In this connection, we shall speak later of optimal sample designs in terms of cost and statistical precision. Meanwhile, there is one important point to remember. Since most available data are sample-based, we cannot possibly evaluate properly most published statistical information unless we understand the basics of statistical inference.

The Frame and Random Sampling

We are now ready to show how to select a random sample. For this task we must prepare a list or specify other sources such as maps, directories, and so on from which all elementary units of a population may be identified. Such a physical list or the procedure which can account for all the units of a population is called a *frame*.

Any available source may be used to prepare a frame. Well-kept records may be utilized for preparing a frame in order to study the internal operations of both business and nonbusiness organizations. For extensive public surveys, telephone directories, automobile registrations, tax assessor's lists, city directories, lists of voters, customer lists, directories of professional and trade associations, and the like are being utilized for preparation of frames. Since these sources may not be adequate or reliable enough for most public surveys, geographical areas are being used in order to identify *clusters* of elementary units. In such a case, preparation of a frame may involve census enumeration districts, city blocks, standard metropolitan statistical areas (SMSAs), or county maps. Each selected geographical area becomes the basis for identifying or locating the elementary units of the study such as consumers, business establishments, dwelling units, and the like.

Section 11 Sampling Versus a Census

Initially, we may accept the idea that *random selection* occurs when we have no reason to believe that one elementary unit of a population is selected more frequently than another. In other words, each unit has equal probability of being chosen. Earlier random experiments involved random selection. However, the use of urns with balls or a physical lottery for actual sampling is cumbersome. Furthermore, these methods may introduce some selection bias because it is difficult to maintain randomness. For example, balls or capsules used in a lottery may not be thoroughly mixed before each selection.

A less cumbersome and more reliable method with which we can obtain a random sample is the use of random digits. Appendix A contains a table of random digits arranged in groups of five for selecting a random sample.

Example 11.6

In dealing with descriptive statistics we used as a population the hourly wages of 50 production workers of Maloof Corporation. For convenience the same population is reproduced in Table 11.1.

We may consider this table a frame from which we wish to select a random sample of hourly wages of 20 production workers. Ordinarily, hourly wages would be one of the unknown characteristics of production workers we wish to study. A frame would consist of worker names or other means, such as Social Security numbers, of identifying the elementary units of a population. Here, however, these qualifications are irrelevant because we wish to illustrate the procedure of selecting a random sample from a list of items.

First, we number serially each item (elementary unit) of the frame. Since the population size N is 50, we may assign serial numbers from 00 to 49 as shown in Table 11.1. Note that each item is assigned a unique number which consists of two digits, as many as the digits in the population size.

Table 11.1.
A Population of Hourly Wages of 50 Production Workers of Maloof Corporation[a]

Serial Number	Hourly Wage	Serial Number	Hourly Wage	Serial Number	Hourly Wage	Serial Number	Hourly Wage	Serial Number	Hourly Wage
00	$5.10	10	$5.65	20	$6.55	30	$7.60	40	$8.20
01	7.90	11	6.25	21	5.75	31	7.75	41	5.60
02	6.25	12	5.25	22	5.40	32	5.60	42	5.75
03	5.20	13	5.60	23	5.80	33	7.15	43	7.65
04	7.30	14	5.85	24	5.25	34	8.95	44	6.40
05	6.80	15	6.25	25	7.10	35	6.55	45	5.40
06	6.45	16	5.95	26	6.75	36	7.20	46	6.20
07	5.80	17	5.75	27	5.75	37	5.75	47	5.65
08	6.95	18	6.10	28	6.30	38	7.25	48	6.10
09	5.50	19	8.25	29	6.70	39	6.60	49	6.35

[a] Data (hypothetical) from Table 1.3.

Second, we point a pencil blindly on the page of random digits given in Appendix A in order to determine a starting point. Suppose the pencil point is nearest number 1021. Then our starting point is line 10, column 21. If several pages of random digits are available, a starting page may be randomly selected in a similar manner. In practice, statisticians begin from a point where the last sample selection has ended.

Finally, beginning with the starting point and proceeding across the page from left to right we read off groups of two-digit numbers. In our case, the first four two-digit numbers are 22, 10, 94, and 05. The third number 94, as well as any subsequent number larger than the highest number in our population, 49, are counted as blanks. If a previously selected number is drawn again, it is ignored. The important point is that each two-digit number has an equal probability of selection. We continue this procedure until we select a sample of 20 hourly wages, each marked with a circle in Table 11.1.

The above example illustrates selection of a *simple random sample* where each sample of given size, 20 in our illustration, has equal probability of being selected. Later, we shall discuss different types of random samples where selection of a given sample size may not be equiprobable. *Random samples,* also called *probability samples,* refer to any sample which has been selected with *known,* but not necessarily equal, probability.

In general, probability sampling usually involves four major steps:

1. The population of elementary units is clearly defined.
2. All elementary units are identified and a frame of such units is prepared or is made accessible.
3. A sample of elementary units is randomly selected from the frame with known probability.
4. The elementary units in the sample are located and information is collected from these units.

Sample Frequency Distributions: Statistics

The introduction here of sample frequency distributions and the sample mean, standard deviation, and proportion should not be considered a mere refresher course on descriptive statistics. These sample measures are extensively used in later topics. The symbols denoting sample measures are different from the symbols denoting parameters. No less significant, sample measures will help us better understand the all-important variation between a sample and the parent population, namely, random sampling error.

A sample frequency distribution is determined the same way as a population frequency distribution.

Example 11.7

Let us consider again the sample of 20 hourly wages shown in Table 11.1. We can find the weekly earnings of these workers, assuming a 40-hour workweek, by multiplying the hourly wage of each worker by 40. Using class interval widths of $20, we can form the sample frequency distribution shown in Table 11.2.

Table 11.2.
Frequency Distributions of a Population of 50 and a Sample of 20 Production Workers of Maloof Corporation by Weekly Earnings[a]

Weekly Earnings (Dollars)	Number of Workers		Relative Frequency	
	Population	Sample	Population	Sample
200 and under 220	6	2	.12	.10
220 and under 240	15	6	.30	.30
240 and under 260	10	4	.20	.20
260 and under 280	7	3	.14	.15
280 and under 300	5	1	.10	.05
300 and under 320	4	2	.08	.10
320 and under 340	2	1	.04	.05
340 and under 360	1	1	.02	.05
	$N = 50$	$n = 20$	$N = 1.00$	$n = 1.00$

[a] Population data from Table 2.1. Sample data calculated from Table 11.1 by assuming a 40-hour workweek.

In order to facilitate comparisons, the population distribution of 50 weekly earnings formed earlier is copied in Table 11.2. Both distributions are determined precisely in the manner already explained, but each summarizes a different data base. Furthermore, the sample distribution has a pattern of variation which is different from the population pattern. Consider the relative frequencies shown in Table 11.2. The relative frequency of the sample is identical to the relative frequency of the population only in the second and third class intervals with proportions .30 and .20, respectively. Discrepancies appear between the sample and population relative frequencies in all other six class intervals. These differences are shown graphically in Fig. 11.1. The crosshatched portion of each bar of the histogram repre-

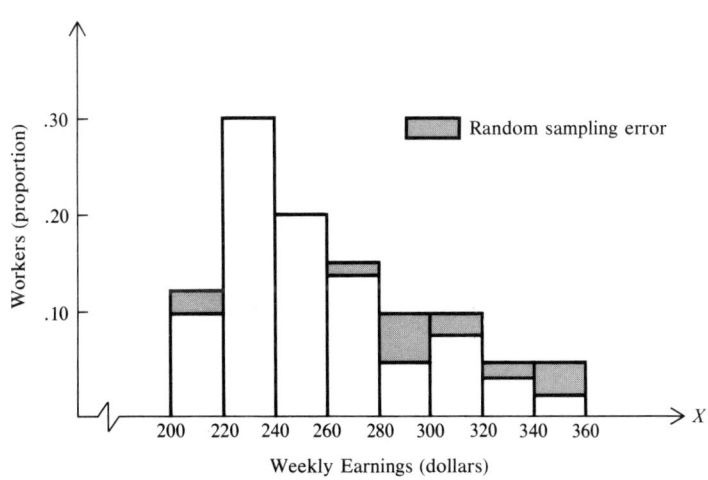

Figure 11.1. Histograms for the relative frequency distributions of a population of 50 and a sample of 20 production workers of Maloof Corporation by weekly earnings.

sents the difference between the sample and population relative frequencies. Earlier, we called these differences random sampling errors because they are caused by the random selection of the sample.

If the population were unknown, the pattern of variation in the sample may be used to draw conclusions about the characteristics of the population. For example, we may conclude correctly that 50 percent of the workers earn between $220 and under $260 per week. However, we may also be misled since the sample frequency is more positively skewed than the population frequency, indicating differences in summary measures. Drawing inferences from a sample about the unknown characteristics of the parent population requires calculation of sample summary measures. Such measures will help us better understand the nature of random sampling error.

At the beginning of this text, the term *statistics* was defined as the field of statistical techniques. The same term is also commonly used to denote data. Furthermore, *statistics* is given a third interpretation when used in statistical inference; it means summary measures obtained from sample data. What meaning the term is given depends on the context of the discussion.

Computationally, there is no significant difference between parameters and statistics. The formulas we used earlier to calculate each parameter can be also used to calculate the corresponding statistic. For reasons already explained we shall illustrate calculation of sample mean, standard deviation, and proportion.

The *sample mean,** denoted by $\bar{x}$, is the arithmetic mean of the observations in the sample:

(11.1)
$$\bar{x} = \frac{\Sigma fm}{n}$$

where f = frequency of each class
m = midpoint of each class
n = sample size

Example 11.8

Calculation of the sample mean from the sample frequency of weekly earnings of 20 production workers is shown in Table 11.3. As in the case of calculating a population mean, we multiply each class midpoint value by its corresponding class frequency, sum the products, and divide the sum $5,200 by the sample size 20. The sample mean $\bar{x}$ is $260.

Note that formula (11.1) is identical to the earlier formula for calculating a population mean. The only difference is that the numerator sum represents sample observations and the denominator sample size.

*For ungrouped data, the formula for the sample mean is $\bar{x} = \Sigma X/n$; it is analogous to formula (2.3) for the population mean.

Table 11.3.
Calculation of the Mean and Standard Deviation from Grouped Data: Weekly Earnings of a Sample of 20 Production Workers of Maloof Corporation

Weekly Earnings (Dollars)	Workers f	Class Midpoint m	fm	$(m - \bar{x})$	$(m - \bar{x})^2$	$f(m - \bar{x})^2$
200 and under 220	2	210	420	−50	2,500	5,000
220 and under 240	6	230	1,380	−30	900	5,400
240 and under 260	4	250	1,000	−10	100	400
260 and under 280	3	270	810	+10	100	300
280 and under 300	1	290	290	+30	900	900
300 and under 320	2	310	620	+50	2,500	5,000
320 and under 340	1	330	330	+70	4,900	4,900
340 and under 360	1	350	350	+90	8,100	8,100
	20		5,200			30,000

$$\bar{x} = \frac{\Sigma fm}{n} = \frac{5,200}{20} = \$260 \qquad s = \sqrt{\frac{\Sigma f(m - \bar{x})^2}{n - 1}} = \sqrt{\frac{30,000}{19}} = \$39.74$$

The same holds true for the *sample standard deviation,** denoted by s; it is the standard deviation of the observations in a sample:

(11.2)
$$s = \sqrt{\frac{\Sigma f(m - \bar{x})^2}{n - 1}}$$

where all symbols are already defined. Note that the denominator in formula (11.2) is $n - 1$ rather than the full sample size n. For reasons which will be explained later, using $n - 1$ for the denominator makes the value of s a better estimate of the parameter σ which is usually not known.

Example 11.8 (continued)

Calculation of the standard deviation from the same sample data is shown in Table 11.3. Each difference between a class midpoint and the sample mean is squared and multiplied by the corresponding class frequency; the products are added; the sum of the products, 30,000, is divided by 19, the sample size 20 less 1; the result is the sample variance. The positive square root of the variance yields the sample standard deviation of $39.74.

---

*For ungrouped data, the sample standard deviation is

$$s = \sqrt{\frac{\Sigma (X - \bar{x})^2}{n - 1}}$$

except for $n - 1$ in the denominator, this formula is analogous to the square root of formula (3.1) for the population variance.

Chapter 4 Statistical Inference: Basic Concepts and Tools

On a similar basis, the *sample proportion,* denoted by *p*, is defined as

(11.3) $$p = \frac{\text{observations of interest in sample}}{\text{total observations in the sample}}$$

Example 11.9

Suppose we are interested in the proportion of workers in the sample who earn less than $240 per week. Since there are eight workers with weekly earnings of interest,

$$p = \frac{8}{20} = .40$$

or 40 percent.

The proportion is the only summary measure available for categorical variables. For example, we may be interested in the proportion of production workers of Maloof Corporation who are in favor of or against certain management policies; the market share (proportion) of a brand item such as cereal, cosmetics, drugs, automobiles, appliances, and the like may be an important summary measure for making managerial decisions; election to public office is predicted on the proportion of a sample of voters who favor a candidate.

Note that statistics are denoted with letters of the Roman alphabet while parameters are designated by Greek letters. Each pair of symbols indicates the same summary measure from a different data base:

	Mean	Standard Deviation	Proportion
Parameter (population)	μ	σ	π
Statistic (sample)	$\bar{x}$	s	p

This symbolic distinction is very important in still another respect. From the viewpoint of classical statistical inference, parameters are fixed but unknown quantities; statistics, on the other hand, are known, since they are calculated from a sample, but subject to random error. Statistical inference consists of techniques designed to draw conclusions about unknown but fixed parameters from known statistics which are subject to random variation.

Random Sampling Error and Procedural Bias

Knowledge of statistics from random samples permits us now to explain more precisely the nature of random sampling error. We have seen that due to random error a statistic is likely to be different in value from the corresponding parameter. However, in addition to random error, numerical information from almost every

Section 11 Sampling Versus a Census

statistical study is likely to be subject to nonrandom "errors." For example, part of the difference between a sample mean and the *true* population mean in a real survey of workers of Maloof Corporation may arise from imperfections in the frame or poor sample selection; the method of interviewing workers may result in underreporting of earnings; or recording earnings as well as calculating and reporting the sample mean may involve clerical mistakes. Since such nonrandom "errors" arise from procedures employed in collecting statistical information, they are referred to as *procedural bias*.

In sum, the difference between a statistic and the true value of its parameter may consist of two types of "errors": random sampling error *and* procedural bias. This difference may be stated in equation form as follows:

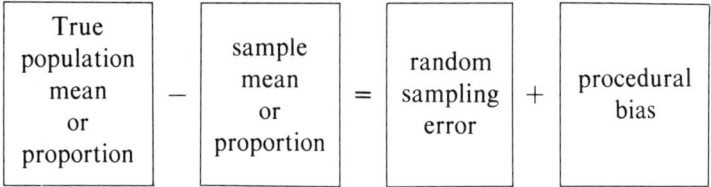

Due to random error, a statistic such as the mean from each possible random sample of the same size would differ from sample to sample in a sample space. Assuming absence of procedural bias, these sample means would tend to be distributed around the population mean. Small random errors, that is, small deviations of sample means from the population mean, would tend to occur more frequently than large random errors. These random errors are self-compensating. In other words, positive random errors would tend to offset negative random errors; in fact, for sufficiently large samples (what is considered a sufficiently large sample will be explained later) random errors would tend to be normally distributed (see Section 3).

Procedural bias consists of two major categories: sampling and nonsampling. *Sampling bias* arises from pitfalls and imperfections associated with sampling from an imperfect frame or from nonrandom selection. *Nonsampling bias* may occur in data collection procedures such as imperfect measuring instruments, nonresponse, clerical mistakes, and the like even when we take a census rather than a sample. In short, a census would eliminate random error and sampling bias. Nonsampling bias, however, may still be present. A faulty weight scale would yield biased weights of army recruits whether we sample or take a census of weights.

Unlike random errors, procedural biases tend to accumulate rather than compensate one another. An increase in sample size does not necessarily reduce bias. In fact, it may increase bias. Nor can bias be represented with probability models. Furthermore, while random error arises only from the chance selection of elementary units, the potential sources of both sampling and nonsampling bias are legion. Unfortunately, a survey of procedural bias lies outside the scope of this text. From now on, we shall be concerned exclusively with random sampling error.

PROBLEMS

Group One

11.1. Indicate the most important reasons why each of the following statistical investigations should be conducted by sampling rather than a census:
*(a) Rating a television show
(b) Testing steel coils for hardness
(c) Studying the rates of fattening yearling steers with two different diets
(d) Studying inventory policies of "neighborhood" food stores
(e) Forecasting employment opportunities for college graduates
(f) Determining whether or not air pollution over a city has reached a critical stage
(g) Determining the percentage of useful life remaining in the capital equipment of a telephone company

11.2. For each reason given below, describe a situation for which a sample would be more desirable than a census. Explain why.
(a) Timeliness   (d) Destructive observations
(b) Accuracy   (e) Inaccessibility
(c) Economy   (f) Infinite population

11.3. The management of a chain of department stores would like to determine the time floor managers spend on various tasks in supervising their department during normal workdays. What kind of frame would you recommend? Defend your answer?

11.4. Consider Example 11.6 where the first 4 two-digit random numbers were 22, 10, 94, and 05.
*(a) Write down the remaining 17 random numbers used for selecting the sample of 20 hourly wages.
(b) Verify that these random numbers correspond to the circled hourly wages shown in Table 11.1.

*11.5. Explain whether or not each of the following statements describes a satisfactory mechanism for random selection:
(a) Random selection is equivalent to hit-or-miss, haphazard, or aimless selection of elementary units from a frame.
(b) A sample representing a true cross section of a statistical population is equivalent to a randomly selected sample.
(c) The larger the sample size, the less important the random selection of elementary units from a frame.
(d) In the past, military draft lotteries consisted of putting into capsules slips of paper, each bearing the name of a young man eligible for the draft, placing the capsules into a bowl and mixing them, and allowing blindfolded dignitaries to draw capsules in a public ceremony. Such lotteries are satisfactory mechanisms for random selection of draftees.

11.6. We have found that the population of weekly earnings of production workers of Maloof Corporation has a mean $\mu = 256$, a standard deviation $\sigma = \$35.16$, and proportion π of workers earning less than $240 per week of .42. On the other

Answers to asterisked (*) problems are appended.

Section 11 Sampling Versus a Census

hand, the sample of 20 workers has a mean $\bar{x} = \$260$, a standard deviation $s = \$39.74$, and proportion p of workers earning less than \$240 per week of .40. Express random error as the difference between:

*(a) Sample mean and population mean
(b) Sample and population standard deviations
(c) Sample and population proportions of workers earning less than \$240 per week

11.7. Anthony Felcher, the comptroller of a large home appliances retailer, uses several methods for keeping an appropriate balance between cash outflow and cash inflow. One method consists of taking a random sample of 12 credit accounts. If the sample mean of outstanding credit exceeds \$200, he borrows money with a short-term note in order to ease a pending cash shortage. A random sample of 12 accounts shows the following outstanding credits to customers:

\$153.50	\$425.41	\$575.82
267.34	52.33	208.01
150.15	121.12	32.54
86.37	205.76	181.65

*(a) Find the sample mean.
(b) Should Anthony borrow money with a short-term note?
(c) Is it appropriate for Felcher to assume that the sample mean equals the unknown mean of all credit accounts? Explain why or why not.

11.8. Suzie Spitzer is a research analyst for a state crime commission. A random sample of 100 city blocks from two cities shows the following frequency of street crimes during a month:

City A		City B	
Crimes	Blocks	Crimes	Blocks
0	19	0	22
1	38	1	27
2	24	2	31
3	17	3	12
4	2	4	8

(a) Calculate the number of crimes per block in each city.
(b) Assuming definitions and all data collection procedures are the same in both cities, should Suzie conclude that the city with a higher crime rate per block is worse off than the other city as far as street crime is concerned?

11.9. Nautilus, Inc., a store of marine supplies and equipment, received a sample of 100 survival thermosuits. A frequency distribution of suits by number of blemishes is as follows:

Blemishes	Suits	Blemishes	Suits
0	32	4	9
1	20	5	5
2	20	6	3
3	9	7	2

*(a) Calculate the sample mean of blemishes per suit.
(b) Calculate the sample standard deviation.
(c) What is the proportion of suits with no blemishes?

11.10. Explain the following terms:
(a) Simple random sample
(b) Frame
(c) Random selection
(d) Statistics
(e) Statistical inference
(f) Random error
(g) Census
(h) Empirical distribution
(i) Probability sample
(j) Procedural bias

Group Two

11.11. Discuss the statement "There is no difference between random error and procedural bias as long as the latter is self-compensating, that is, bias contributing to the overestimation is offset by bias contributing to the underestimation of a parameter."

11.12. An advertiser takes a random sample of 40 households subscribing to the magazine *Pleasant Times*. Among other data, the sample yields the following distribution of households by the number of magazine readers:

Readers	Households	Readers	Households
1	6	4	6
2	11	5	5
3	8	6	4

*(a) Assuming that 1 million households subscribe to the magazine, calculate the total number of magazine readers.
(b) Is this readership total a parameter? Explain why or why not.

11.13. Carlton Bailey, a cotton broker, receives a shipment of 1000 cotton bales. In order to check the quality of the cotton, he selects a random sample of 100 cotton bales for testing. Frequency distributions for the population and the sample of cotton bales by weight are given below:

Weight (Pounds)	Population	Sample
400 and under 420	110	9
420 and under 440	228	19
440 and under 460	325	30
460 and under 480	226	27
480 and under 500	111	15

(a) Prepare a histogram of the population and sample relative frequency distributions and crosshatch the area in each bar which represents random error.

(b) Express random error as the difference between sample and population relative frequencies.

11.14. Consider the frequency distributions of cotton bales given in Problem 11.13:

*(a) Calculate the population and the sample mean. Express random error as the difference between the two measures.

(b) Calculate the population and the sample standard deviations. Express random error as the difference between the two measures.

SECTION 12/ SAMPLING DISTRIBUTIONS

In the preceding section, we advanced our knowledge in two major directions. On the one hand, we learned why and when we need to sample rather than to take a census, how to select a random sample, and how to calculate the sample mean, standard deviation, and proportion. On the other hand, we distinguished between random sampling error and procedural bias.

In statistical inference, one objective is to estimate a population parameter such as the mean μ or proportion π. In practice, we usually select one random sample of size n, calculate the sample mean $\bar{x}$ and proportion p, and employ these statistics to estimate the corresponding unknown parameters. During the planning stage of a statistical study, however, sampling a population can be perceived as an imaginary random experiment. Before we collect information, we can speak of $\bar{X}$ and P, the corresponding random variables of the sample mean $\bar{x}$ and proportion p, only in terms of probability; in other words, we are concerned with the probability with which the varying values of a random variable will occur in order to determine the accuracy of sampling error. Thus the probability distributions of $\bar{X}$ and P are very important for subsequent discussions. They are called *sampling distributions.* This term distinguishes them from probability distributions of other random variables which are not connected with sampling procedures.

First, we introduce sampling distributions of the mean and the proportion as well as their summary measures. Next we pay attention to two properties of these sampling distributions. Finally, we illustrate the effect of sample size on the shape of a sampling distribution.

Sampling Distribution of the Mean and the Proportion

A sampling distribution is determined in much the same way as a probability distribution for any other random variable. In order to simplify numerical work, we shall base our illustrations on very small population and sample sizes. The procedure, however, is the same irrespective of the number of observations which we may encounter in a real-world situation.

Example 12.1

A consortium of retailers wants to determine the economic feasibility of building a shopping center in a certain location. In addition to published information about the area, there is need to conduct a survey of the households which might be potential shoppers. The purpose of the survey is to collect information about several socioeconomic and shopping characteristics of potential customers such as age, sex, income, occupation, and especially present expediture and shopping patterns. We are part of the team which will plan and conduct the survey.

A frame of three household names appear in Table 12.1. A key numerical variable which will be associated or cross-tabulated with other numerical and categorical variables is income. Calculations in the table show that the average income μ is \$16,000 and the standard deviation σ is \$9092.

Table 12.1. Hypothetical Population of Three Household Incomes

Household Name	Annual Income (Thousands of Dollars) X	Households with $28,000 Income
Aaron	6	0
Sullivan	14	0
Zywiak	28	1

$$\mu = \frac{6 + 14 + 28}{3} = 16 \qquad \pi = \frac{1}{3}$$

$$\sigma = \sqrt{\frac{(6-16)^2 + (14-16)^2 + (28-16)^2}{3}} \simeq 9.092$$

Another key numerical variable is the proportion of households with income of \$28,000. The first two households are assigned a zero because they do not earn this sum; the third household earning this amount is assigned a 1. So the population proportion π is 1/3.

Section 12 Sampling Distributions

Key numerical variables such as income and proportion in our illustration are frequently called *decision parameters*. In a real sampling study, decision parameters are the basis for preparing sampling plans and for analyzing the collected data.

We have defined simple random sampling as the procedure whereby each one of all possible samples of a given size has equal probability of being chosen. This type of probability sampling is not always used in practice.

At this point, however, a simple random sample is necessary: it is important in the theory of statistical inference, and its simplicity illustrates effectively the fundamentals of this theory. It can be used as a first approximation for types of random samples which are widely used in practice.

Also, in order to simplify matters we shall form sampling distributions involving sampling with replacement. Later, we shall introduce sampling without replacement.

Finally, it is important to realize that the parameter summary measures are usually unknown in practice. Here, we assume they are known in order to introduce the mechanism upon which statistical inference is based.

Example 12.2

Suppose we decide to select a simple random sample of two households with replacement. The nine possible samples of our sample space are listed in the first column in Table 12.2. Since we are interested in the average annual income and the proportion of households earning $28,000, our random variables are denoted by $\bar{X}$ and P, respectively. We can easily calculate a particular value of each random variable from each sample. For example, the mean for the first sample (A, A) is

$$\bar{x}_1 = \frac{6 + 6}{2} = \$6 \; (\times 1000)$$

and the proportion is

$$p_1 = \frac{0 + 0}{2} = 0$$

Table 12.2. All Possible Sample Outcomes for Randomly Selecting Two Household Incomes from Three Household Incomes with Replacement

Households in Sample[a]	Annual Income (Thousands of Dollars)	Sample Mean (Thousands of Dollars) $\bar{X}$	Sample Proportion P
(A, A)	(6, 6)	6	0
(A, S)	(6, 14)	10	0
(A, Z)	(6, 28)	17	1/2
(S, A)	(14, 6)	10	0
(S, S)	(14, 14)	14	0
(S, Z)	(14, 28)	21	1/2
(Z, A)	(28, 6)	17	1/2
(Z, S)	(28, 14)	21	1/2
(Z, Z)	(28, 28)	28	1

[a] A stands for Aaron's, S for Sullivan's, and Z for Zywiak's household.

Chapter 4 Statistical Inference: Basic Concepts and Tools

The mean for the third sample (A, Z) is

$$\bar{x}_3 = \frac{6 + 28}{2} = \$17 \ (\times 1000)$$

while the proportion is

$$p_3 = \frac{0 + 1}{2} = 1/2$$

The nine values for each random variable are listed in the last two columns of the table.

Note that we use capital letters to denote the random variable of a statistic and lowercase letters to denote a specific value of such a statistic.

Using the sample outcomes shown in Table 12.2, we can determine the sampling distribution of the mean and calculate its summary measures.*

Example 12.3

The probability that a sample will yield a given value of a statistic is equal to the relative number of times such value will possibly occur. For instance, from Table 12.2 we can see that the sample mean 6 ($6000) occurs in one out of nine possible sample outcomes, so the probability of $\bar{x}_1 = 6$ is $1/9$. Sample mean 10 ($10,000) occurs twice, so the probability of $\bar{x}_2 = 10$ is $2/9$. In this manner, we obtain the sampling distribution of the sample mean shown in Table 12.3. The expected value of this probability distribution $E(\bar{X})$ is $16,000, and its standard deviation $SD(\bar{X})$ is $6429.

Table 12.3.
Sampling Distribution of the Mean for Randomly Selecting Two Household Incomes from Three Household Incomes with Replacement; Calculation of $E(\bar{X})$ and $SD(\bar{X})$ (Income in Thousands of Dollars)

$\bar{X} = \bar{x}$	$P(\bar{X} = \bar{x})$	$\bar{x}P(\bar{X} = \bar{x})$	$\bar{x} - E(\bar{X})$	$[\bar{x} - E(\bar{X})]^2$	$[\bar{x} - E(\bar{X})]^2 P(\bar{X} = \bar{x})$
6	1/9	6/9	−10	100	100/9
10	2/9	20/9	− 6	36	72/9
14	1/9	14/9	− 2	4	4/9
17	2/9	34/9	+ 1	1	2/9
21	2/9	42/9	+ 5	25	50/9
28	1/9	28/9	+12	144	144/9
	1		0		41.333
		$E(\bar{X}) = 16$	$SD(\bar{X}) = \sqrt{41,333} \simeq 6.429$		

These two summary measures are so important as to deserve a careful interpretation. The expected value $E(\bar{X})$ is the average of all possible sample means. Its value of $16,000 is equal to the true value of the parameter μ we calculated in Table 12.1. Since each sample mean occurs at random, the difference of each sample mean from $E(\bar{X})$ represents a random-error value. Then it follows that

---

*At this point, you may wish to conduct a quick review of Section 8.

Section 12 Sampling Distributions

the standard deviation SD($\bar{X}$) measures random error. In statistical inference, the standard deviation of a sampling distribution of a statistic such as SD(X) is called *standard error*.

Let us now see how we can determine a sampling distribution of the proportion and calculate its summary measures.

Example 12.4

The sampling distribution of the proportion of households earning $28,000 can be determined from Table 12.2. Since four of the nine sample outcomes have zero proportion, the probability of $p = 0$ is 4/9; the probability for $p = 1/2$ is 4/9; and the probability for $p = 1$ is 1/9. The sampling distribution is shown in the first two columns in Table 12.4; its expected value $E(P)$ is 1/3; and its standard deviation or standard error SD(P) is 1/3.

Table 12.4.
Sampling Distribution of the Proportion for Randomly Selecting Two Household Incomes from Three Household Incomes with Replacement

Again, as in the case of the sample mean, the expected value $E(P)$ is the average of all sample proportions. Its value of 1/3 is equal to the true value of the parameter proportion π we calculated in Table 12.1. The difference of each sample proportion from $E(P)$ represents a random-error value.

$P = p$	$P(P = p)$	$pP(P = p)$	$p - E(P)$	$[p - E(P)]^2$	$[p - E(P)]^2 P(P = p)$
0	4/9	0	$-1/3$	1/9	4/81
1/2	4/9	2/9	$+1/6$	1/36	1/81
1	1/9	1/9	$+2/3$	4/9	4/81
	1				1/9
		$E(P) = 1/3$			$SD(P) = \sqrt{1/9} = 1/3$

Where $\pi = 1/3$;
Calculation of $E(P)$ and SD(P)

Before proceeding with the two properties of these sampling distributions, let us summarize a number of qualifying observations:

1. In our illustrative case, we reduced the population and the sample to the smallest possible size in order to avoid unnecessary computational work; we shall continue doing so whenever appropriate. In practice, both population and sample sizes are likely to be large.

2. We have illustrated the process for forming a sampling distribution of a statistic from a finite population with replacement. With a qualification to be introduced later, the same procedure applies also to sampling a finite population without replacement.

3. We must realize that the process for forming a sampling distribution of a statistic such as the mean involves three types of distributions as visualized graphically in Fig. 12.1: (a) a *population distribution* representing the sampled population; (b) *sample distributions*, one for each of k possible samples of size n; and (c) a *sampling distribution* of all sample means. In practice, the mean and other parameters of the population are not known and we usually take a single sample of size n because of cost and other reasons. Here, we *assume* that the

Figure 12.1.
Formation of a sampling distribution of the mean: all possible random samples of size n from a population of size N: (a) population frequency distribution of size N; (b) sample distributions from k samples; (c) sampling distribution of mean from all k possible samples of size n.

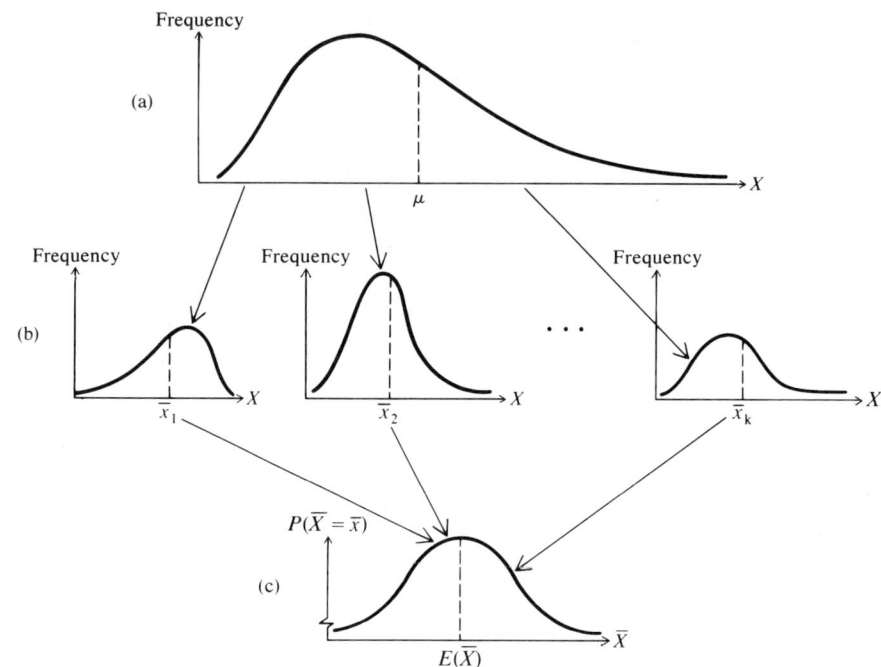

parameters are known and we are interested in all possible samples of size *n* because we are interested in understanding how the theory itself works.

4. In forming the sampling distribution of a statistic we had to specify: (a) the *particular statistic*, the mean or proportion; (b) the specific *population* of observations, annual household income; (c) the *sample size n*; and (d) the *method of sample selection*, simple random sampling. Thus we can speak of a given sampling distribution only by specifying *all* four conditions. We have already seen in the two examples that we were able to obtain two different sampling distributions by changing only one of the four conditions, the statistic. So any change in one or more of the four conditions uniquely determines a new sampling distribution.

5. Depending on the specified statistic, sampling distributions may take a variety of forms. These forms may be described or approximated by one of several probability models developed by mathematical statisticians, such as the binomial and the normal. It is important to know that these two probability models do not describe the random variability of all statistics.

Expected Value of Sample Mean or Proportion

In our shopping center survey $E(\bar{X})$ is $16,000 as shown in Table 12.3; this expected value equals the parameter μ we calculated in Table 12.1. This equality is not sheer coincidence; it is based on a relation which is true for any sampling distribution of the mean. In general,

(12.1) $$E(\bar{X}) = \mu$$

Section 12 Sampling Distributions

Expression (12.1) says that the average value of all possible sample means is always equal to the population mean.

The same relation holds true about a sample proportion. In our survey example we found that $E(P)$ is $1/3$ in Table 12.4 which is equal to parameter π calculated in Table 12.1. In general,

(12.2) $$E(P) = \pi$$

Expressions (12.1) and (12.2) represent the *first* property of sampling distributions: *the expected value of a sampling distribution of the mean or the proportion equals the corresponding population mean or proportion.*

From the practical standpoint, what does this property mean? In practice, we take a single sample of size n and obtain its mean $\bar{x}$ or desired proportion p. This specific sample mean or proportion is called a *point estimate* of the corresponding unknown parameter μ or π. The difference $\bar{x} - \mu$ or $p - \pi$ is a value of the random error. This random error is self-compensating, that is, the algebraic sum of all its possible values equals zero.

We can generalize this property of the expected value of a statistic as follows: Let θ (Greek letter *theta*) denote μ, π, or another parameter and $\hat{\theta}$ (read "theta-hat") denote a sample statistic such as the mean or proportion. Then expressions (12.1) and (12.2) may be stated symbolically as

(12.3) $$E(\hat{\theta}) = \theta$$

Condition (12.3) is associated with concepts which are important in the preparation of a sample design for our shopping center survey.

1. Sample statistic $\hat{\theta}$, which will be used to estimate parameter θ, is called an *estimator*. This term should not be confused with the term *point estimate*. The term *point estimate* refers to a *specific numerical value,* while the term *estimator* refers to the *method* of estimation. For instance, the numerical value of the sample mean $6000 in Example 12.2 is a *point estimate* of the population mean $16,000 in Example 12.1. On the other hand, the statistic $\bar{x}$ used as a means of estimating the population mean μ is referred to as an *estimator*.
2. If condition (12.3) is met, then $E(\hat{\theta}) - \theta = 0$, and $\hat{\theta}$ is said to be an *unbiased estimator*. Since the mean and the proportion meet condition (12.3), both are unbiased estimators.

The Standard Error of Sample Mean or Proportion

In Table 12.3 we found that the standard error of sample mean $SD(\bar{X})$ is $6429 as calculated directly from the sampling distribution. Because $SD(\bar{X})$ is a very important measure, it is denoted by the special symbol $\sigma_{\bar{x}}$ (read "sigma sub-X-bar") and defined as

(12.4) $$\sigma_{\bar{x}} = \frac{\sigma}{\sqrt{n}}$$

Chapter 4 Statistical Inference: Basic Concepts and Tools

If the sample size n is 1, then $\sigma_{\bar{x}}$ equals σ; however, $\sigma_{\bar{x}}$ will be smaller than σ when the sample size exceeds 1 observation. This makes sense since sample means are more alike than individual sample observations. So the curve of a sampling distribution will become increasingly narrower and more peaked than the curve of the sampled population as the sample size gets larger and larger.

The important point is that with formula (12.4) we can calculate the standard error of sample mean from the population standard deviation rather than from the sampling distribution itself.

Example 12.5

In Table 12.1 we found that σ is \$9092. Since n is 2, by formula (12.4) we have

$$\sigma_{\bar{x}} = \frac{9092}{\sqrt{2}} = \$6429$$

Note that standard error of sample mean $\sigma_{\bar{x}}$ is the standard deviation of the sampling distribution of the mean; it should not be confused with σ, the population standard deviation.

Analogously, in Table 12.4 we found that SD(P) is 1/3 as calculated directly from the sampling distribution of the proportion. This standard error is also denoted by the special symbol σ_P (read "sigma sub-P") defined as

(12.5)
$$\boxed{\sigma_P = \sqrt{\frac{\pi(1-\pi)}{n}}}$$

So σ_P can be calculated from the population proportion π rather than from the sampling distribution.

Example 12.6

We know that π, the proportion of households earning \$28,000, is 1/3. By formula (12.5) we have

$$\sigma_P = \sqrt{\frac{(1/3)(1-1/3)}{2}} = \frac{1}{3}$$

Again, bear in mind that the standard error of sample proportion σ_P is the standard deviation of the sampling distribution of the proportion.

Formulas (12.4) and (12.5) represent the *second* property of sampling distributions. What is the practical significance of this property?

1. We can calculate the standard error $\sigma_{\bar{x}}$ or σ_P directly from a known population standard deviation σ or population proportion π; we do not need to calculate these measures by forming the appropriate sampling distributions. This is an advantage of great significance.

2. The standard error measures sample variability: it measures (inversely) what statisticians call the *precision* of a statistic, that is, how close a statistic is

Section 12 Sampling Distributions

likely to be to its corresponding parameter. In Example 12.5, we found that $\sigma_{\bar{X}}$ is $6429. This value measures how close any of the nine sample means of the sampling distribution is likely to be to the parameter value of $\mu = \$16,000$. The smaller the standard error, the greater the precision. Thus precision depends on the size of the numerator σ or π and the denominator n of formulas (12.4) and (12.5).

3. The standard error $\sigma_{\bar{X}}$ or σ_P varies directly with the corresponding parameter σ or π: for a given sample size n, the greater the value of σ or the closer π is to .50, the greater the standard error and the smaller the precision of a statistic.

4. The standard error $\sigma_{\bar{X}}$ or σ_P varies inversely with the square root of the sample size. This means that a mean or a proportion from a large sample should be more precise in estimating the corresponding parameter than the same statistic from a small sample. When a sample is large, the values of the random variable $\bar{X}$ or P will tend to cluster closer to their expected value $E(\bar{X})$ or $E(P)$. In other words, for a given σ or π, the standard error $\sigma_{\bar{X}}$ or σ_P will tend to get smaller and smaller for larger and larger samples. Precision, however, increases at a diminishing rate: In Example 12.5, we found that precision as measured by the standard error $\sigma_{\bar{X}}$ was $6429 when the sample size n was 2; a *fourfold* increase of n to 8 would reduce standard error to $3214.50 or increase precision by a factor of 2 since $\sqrt{4} = 2$; a *ninefold* increase of n to 18 would reduce standard error to $2143 or increase precision by a factor of 3 since $\sqrt{9} = 3$.

5. Formulas (12.4) and (12.5) are valid whether the sampled population is normal or skewed. This is on the condition that the population variance is finite, which is the case in practical situations.

The Central Limit Theorem

The effect of sample size is not limited to the magnitude of standard error. As the sample size increases the sampling distribution of the sample mean tends to be normally distributed even when the sampled population is skewed. This result is called *central limit theorem*.

Example 12.7

Table 12.5 shows the relative frequency population distribution for the number of college degrees held by researchers at Biomedical Laboratories Ltd.

Table 12.5. Number of Degrees Held by Researchers at Biomedical Laboratories Ltd.

Number of College Degrees X	Proportion of Researchers f	fx	$(X - \mu)^2$	$f(X - \mu)^2$
1	.4	.4	1	.4
2	.3	.6	0	0
3	.2	.6	1	.2
4	.1	.4	4	.4
		$\mu = 2.0$		$\sigma = 1.0$

Calculations in the table show that the population mean μ is 2 college degrees and the standard deviation σ is 1 college degree.

The effect of increasing sample size on the sampling distribution of the sample mean is shown in Fig. 12.2. If $n = 1$, the graph of the sampling distribution is identical to the graph of the population distribution in Table 12.5; it is positively skewed. The expected value of the sampling distribution $E(\bar{X})$ equals 2, the population mean μ; and the standard error $\sigma_{\bar{x}}$ equals 1, the population standard deviation σ, since $\sigma_{\bar{x}} = \sigma/\sqrt{n} = 1/\sqrt{1} = 1$.

Note that as n increases, the sampling distribution of the mean tends to be normally distributed even though the sampled population is skewed. This effect is quite evident with a sample size as small as 4 observations.

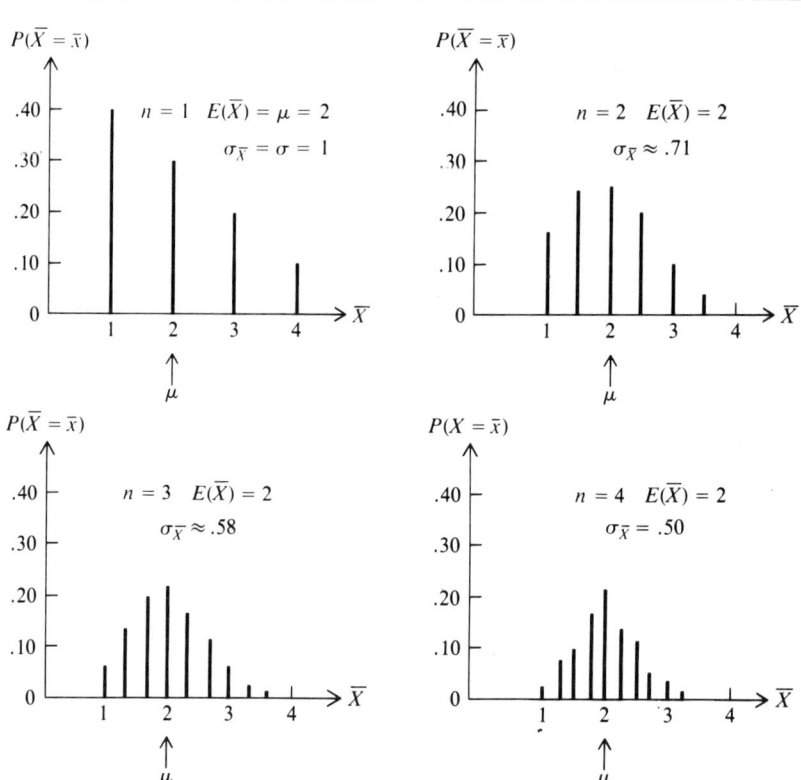

Figure 12.2. Effect of increasing sample size on the sampling distribution of the sample mean. All possible random samples of $n = 1$, 2, 3, and 4 with replacement.

In addition, the expected value $E(\bar{X})$ in Fig. 12.2 equals the population mean $\mu = 2$ irrespective of sample size. Also, note how the standard error $\sigma_{\bar{x}}$ is inversely related to the square root of the sample size. When n increases fourfold, from 1 to 4, the standard error decreases to .50; so the precision of the sample mean doubles. Thus, Fig. 12.2 illustrates the central limit theorem as well as the two properties of sampling distributions.

In general, the central limit theorem states that *as the sample size increases*

Section 12 Sampling Distributions

without limit, a sampling distribution of the mean* approaches a normal distribution almost regardless of the shape of the sampled population distribution. The theorem may sound intuitively understandable if the sampled population itself is normal. It is important to remember that the theorem is equally applicable to nonnormal population distributions, such as bell-shaped but skewed, bimodal, rectangular, exponential, and U-shaped; it is also true for discrete as well as continuous random variables as long as the sample size is sufficiently large. How large a sample is considered to be sufficient depends on the shape of a particular distribution.

The central limit theorem lies at the foundation of the statistical inference apparatus. For sufficiently large samples, it enables us to represent a sampling distribution of a statistic with the normal probability model, which we introduce next. In turn, this model enables us to infer population measures without knowing anything more about such population than *its standard deviation σ and what we can obtain from a sample.*

PROBLEMS

Group One

12.1. The monthly salaries, in thousands of dollars, of four top executives of Technoco Oil Corporation are 90, 120, 80, and 70. Two salaries are selected at random with replacement.
  (a) List all possible samples, calculate the mean of each sample, and specify an appropriate sample space.
  *(b) Form a sampling distribution of the mean.
  (c) Calculate the expected value from this sampling distribution.
  (d) Should this expected value equal the population mean μ? Explain.

12.2. A child born from a healthy father and a hemophilia-carrying mother can be either a healthy boy (B), a healthy girl (G), a hemophilic boy (H), or a hemophilia-carrying girl (R). Assume that the probability π of a hemophilia-carrying girl is .25 and such a couple plans to have two children.
  (a) List all possible sample outcomes, calculate the proportion of hemophilia-carrying girls in each sample, and specify an appropriate sample space of sample proportions.
  *(b) Form a sampling distribution of the proportion.
  (c) Calculate the expected value from this sampling distribution.
  (d) Should this expected value equal the population proportion π? Explain.

12.3. One of the variables of interest in our shopping center survey might be the number of automobiles owned by each household. Suppose Aaron does not own an automobile, Sullivan owns one, and Zywiak owns two.
  *(a) Calculate the parameter mean and standard deviation according to procedures shown in Table 12.1.

---

*The proof of the central limit theorem is based on the sampling distribution of the mean. However, we may easily establish that the theorem applies to the sampling distribution of the proportion as well.
Answers to asterisked (*) problems are appended.

(b) Form the sampling distribution of the mean for a random sample of two households drawn with replacement.
(c) Calculate the expected value and standard error of this sampling distribution according to procedures shown in Table 12.3.
(d) On the basis of your calculations in parts (a) and (c), verify the two properties of a sampling distribution.

12.4. Consider the proportion of households owning one or two automobiles in the population of three households given in Problem 3.
*(a) Calculate the parameter proportion as shown in Table 12.1.
(b) Form the sampling distribution of the proportion for a random sample of two households selected with replacement.
(c) Calculate the expected value and standard error of this sampling distribution according to procedures shown in Table 12.4.
(d) On the basis of your calculations in parts (a) and (c), verify the two properties of this sampling distribution.

12.5. George Masden is in charge of quality control at Continental Dairy Company, a distributor of milk and other dairy products. One of the rules he established concerns the maintenance of uniformity in the net weight of 1-quart milk cartons. George selects a random sample of 5 cartons; if the net weight of a carton is short by more than 1/4 ounce of milk, it is rejected as underfilled; otherwise, a carton is accepted. Assume that filling milk containers is a Bernoulli process underfilling 20 percent of the cartons.
*(a) Form the sampling distribution of the proportion of rejected cartons.
(b) Calculate the expected number of the proportion of rejected cartons from this sampling distribution.
(c) Should this expected value equal the average proportion π of the process? Explain.

12.6. Rita Dobrinsky is a researcher for a marketing research firm. She is preparing a research design for a survey for a client pharmaceutical company. The purpose of the survey is to collect up-to-date information about potential consumers of Dalium, a nonprescription drug. Presently, the company's market share for this product is 15 percent and Rita is considering a sample size of 100 potential consumers. Find the standard error of sample proportion.

12.7. How can there be a sampling distribution of the mean when in practice we select a single sample? Explain the process of forming a sampling distribution, its properties, and its significance in statistical inference.

12.8. If the random variable of a statistic is an unbiased estimator, does this mean that a point estimate always equals the corresponding parameter? Explain.

12.9. Use the sampling distributions of the mean and the proportion given in Tables 12.3 and 12.4. respectively, to illustrate the difference between:
(a) μ, $E(\bar{X})$, and $\bar{x}$
(b) p, π, and $E(P)$

12.10. Explain:
(a) Unbiased estimator
(b) Precision
(c) Sample distribution
(d) Decision parameter
(e) Point estimate
(f) Standard error
(g) Sampling distribution
(h) Central limit theorem

Group Two

12.11. Herb's Haberdashery has five employees with the following weekly salaries: $400, $500, $400, $600, $600.

Section 13 The Normal Distribution

- *(a) Form a sampling distribution of the mean for each sample size of 1, 2, 3, and 4 employees drawn with replacement.
- (b) Calculate the expected value and standard error from each sampling distribution.
- (c) Sketch a graph of each sampling distribution.
- (d) Discuss results in terms of the two properties of sampling distributions and the central limit theorem.

12.12. In an introductory statistics course the relative frequency distribution of grades on a 100-point scale were as follows:

Grade	70	80	90
Relative Frequency	.60	.30	.10

- (a) Form a sampling distribution of the mean for each sample size of 1, 2, 3, and 4 students drawn with replacement.
- *(b) Calculate the expected value and standard error of each sampling distribution.
- (c) Sketch a graph of each sampling distribution.
- (d) Discuss results in terms of the two properties of sampling distributions and the central limit theorem.

12.13. The average fraction defective of a Bernoulli process is 20 percent.
- (a) Form a sampling distribution of proportion for a sample size of 10, 20, and 30 observations.
- *(b) Calculate the expected value and standard error of the proportion of each sampling distribution.
- (c) Sketch a histogram of each sampling distribution.
- (d) Discuss results in terms of the two properties of sampling distributions and the central limit theorem.

SECTION 13 / THE NORMAL DISTRIBUTION

In discussing summary measures of dispersion (see Section 3), we mentioned that many real-life populations turn out to have roughly normal frequency distributions. Besides, there is another, more fundamental reason why the normal distribution deserves our attention: it occupies a pivotal position in statistical inference. The properties of a sampling distribution of a statistic and the central limit theorem allow us to use the normal distribution for determining the probability of various sample outcomes. Moreover, using the normal distribution, we can draw conclusions about unknown population measures such as the mean and proportion from corresponding sample measures.

After introducing the characteristics of the normal distribution as a probability model, we show how to find areas under the normal curve. Then we illustrate how to approximate sampling distributions with the normal distribution.

Characteristics of the Normal Distribution

You may recall that the normal distribution has several interesting features. For convenience we reproduce such a distribution in Fig. 13.1. Note that the curve is bell-shaped and single-peaked or unimodal; it is symmetrical so that one-half the curve is a mirror-image of the other half. The line which divides the curve into two identical halves marks the location for the mean, median, and mode which have the same value. The tails extend indefinitely in both directions, approaching but never quite touching the horizontal axis. The vertical scale represents relative rather than absolute frequencies. Thus the curve portrays a normal probability distribution which is a model like the binomial and Poisson probability models.

A population whose distribution can be approximated by the shape of the normal distribution is said to be *normally distributed*. Also, a variable representing the value of an elementary unit selected randomly from a normally distributed population is said to be normally distributed. Such a normal distribution is specified by only two parameters: the mean μ and the standard deviation σ.* However, no matter what the values of these parameters may be, the total area under the curve of the normal distribution is always equal to one. Like the binomial distribution, there is a large number of normal distributions, one for each combination of the parameters μ and σ. Once these values are specified, they uniquely determine a particular normal distribution.

Example 13.1

Electric Corporation manufactures five types of fuses. Fred Drost, the production manager, has made extensive measurements of the service life of each type of fuse. These measurements showed that a histogram for the distribution of service days of each fuse is nearly bell-shaped and symmetrical. So Fred believes that the manufacturing process turns out fuses whose service life is normally distributed. Figure 13.2 shows the curves for these five normally distributed populations.

Figure 13.1. Frequency curve for the normal distribution.

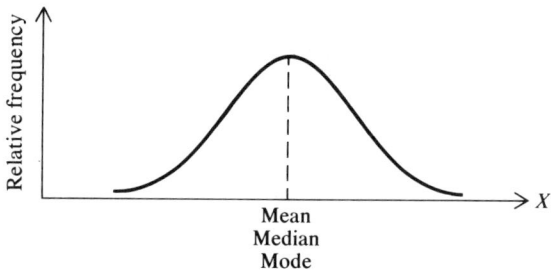

*The function defining the height of the normal curve in Fig. 13.1 is

$$f(x) = \frac{1}{\sigma\sqrt{2\pi}} e^{-1/2 \left[\frac{x-\mu}{\sigma}\right]^2}$$

where π and e are constants approximately equal to 3.141 and 2.7183, respectively; π is the ratio of the circumference to the diameter of a circle; and e is the base of natural logarithms. We denote the function by $f(x)$ in order to indicate that the normal distribution is continuous. The normal distribution is also called Gaussian distribution, named after the mathematician and astronomer Karl Gauss (1777–1855).

Section 13 The Normal Distribution

Figure 13.2.
Normal distributions for the service life of five different electrical fuses.

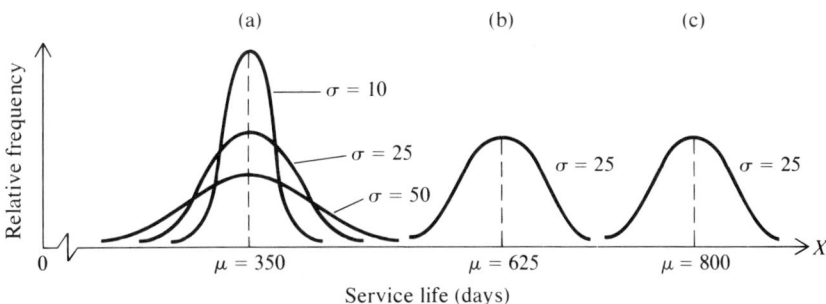

Three distributions in parts (a), (b), and (c) of the diagram have the same standard deviation of 25 days but different means: 350, 625, and 800 service days. Figure 13.2(a) shows three normal distributions having the same mean of 350 days but different standard deviations: 10, 25, and 50 service days. Thus, all three are sketched at the same point on the common scale of variable X. Their peakedness, however, is different: the distribution with the largest standard deviation of 50 days is wide with a flat peak; the distribution with the smallest standard deviation of 10 days is narrow with a pronounced peak.

Unlike a discrete distribution such as the binomial distribution, the normal distribution is continuous. This characteristic makes a great deal of difference in determining probabilities.

Example 13.2

A histogram for the relative frequency distribution of the service life of electric fuses from the manufacturing process at Electric Corporation is shown in Fig. 13.3. The corresponding normal distribution from Fig. 13.2(c) is superimposed on the histogram.

Suppose the histogram represents a discrete distribution where the variable X, service life of fuses, is quoted in 5-day units. Then the probability

Figure 13.3.
Service life of electric fuses; approximation of a histogram by a continuous curve.

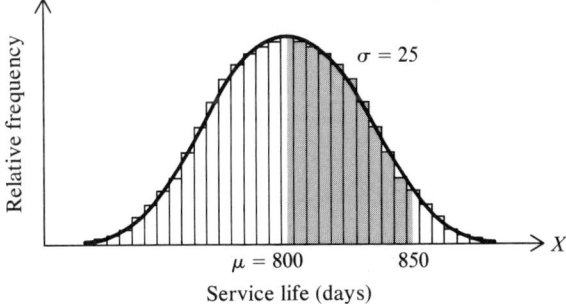

(relative frequency) for fuses with life of, say, 800 days is the height (ordinate) of the bar at $x = 800$. Let us now interpret the 5-day units not as discrete values but rather as midpoints of classes with 5-day intervals. So the lower limit of each class is $2\frac{1}{2}$ days less and the upper limit $2\frac{1}{2}$ days more than each midpoint value. Then the probability (relative frequency) of each class is represented by the area of each bar. For example, the probability that the service life of fuses is between 797.5 and 802.5 days is the area of the bar at $x = 800$. In such a case, the area under the superimposed smooth curve of the normal distribution bounded by the vertical lines at $x = 797.5$ and $x = 802.5$ days is approximately equal to the area of the bar at midpoint $x = 800$ days.

We can make this approximation as close as we wish by reducing the width of each class interval from 5 days to 1 day, 1 hour, 1 minute, and so on. The refined histogram with bars increasingly narrower will practically coincide with the superimposed smooth curve of the normal distribution; and the discrete variable, service life time, will be considered to be continuous with infinite values. The total area of the bars in the histogram representing the probability distribution of a discrete variable is equal to one; and the total area under the smooth curve representing the probability distribution of a continuous variable will be also equal to one. However, in the discrete case, we can determine the probability that the variable takes on a *specific* value such as 800 days. In the continuous case, we cannot determine the probability at point $x = 800$ because there is an infinite number of values of the variable at such a point. So the probability of any one of these values must be considered zero. Therefore, in the continuous case, probabilities can be interpreted graphically only in terms of areas between two values of the variable. For example, the probability for the fuses having a service life between 800 and 850 days is the shaded area under the smooth curve in Fig. 13.3.

Note that a little more than two-thirds, 68.3 percent, of the observations in *any* normal distribution are within one standard deviation of the mean.

Areas for one, two, and three standard deviations are shown in Table 13.1. About 95 percent of all observations are within two and nearly all observations within three standard deviations of the mean. So, although the values of a normally distributed variable may range from minus infinity to plus infinity, only 3 out of every 1000 observations lie beyond three standard deviations.

Table 13.1. Areas Under the Curve of a Normal Distribution for Specified Standard Deviation Units	Interval Between X Values	Area Percent
	$\mu \pm \sigma$	68.3
	$\mu \pm 2\sigma$	95.5
	$\mu \pm 3\sigma$	99.7

Section 13 The Normal Distribution

Assuming that a variable is normally distributed, we can use Table 13.1 to find quickly the proportion of observations which lie within a given range of the variable.

Example 13.3

Radio Mack is a retailer of electrical supplies and products with stores located in several regions of the United States. Peter Mansfield, Mack's manager in charge of purchases, considers negotiating a contract to buy electrical fuses from Electric Corporation; he considers the distribution shown in Fig. 13.2(c) with mean 800 days and standard deviation 25 days. Suppose Peter wishes to purchase 10,000 fuses. Using Table 13.1, he finds the following number of fuses for a given range of service days:

Service Life (Days)	Number of Fuses
775 to 825	6830
750 to 850	9550
725 to 875	9970

For example, the range $\mu \pm \sigma$ is 800 ± 25 or 775 to 825. Since this range includes 68.3 percent of the fuses, there are $.683 \times 10,000$ or 6830 fuses within the range.

Summarizing our major findings about the normal distribution:

1. The curve of a normal distribution is unimodal, bell-shaped, and symmetrical: the curve's tails extend indefinitely in both directions, approaching but never touching the horizontal axis.
2. The normal distribution model represents a family of distributions: each can be uniquely determined when the values of its parameters, mean μ and standard deviation σ, are specified.
3. The normal distribution is continuous: the probability of an event can be interpreted graphically only in terms of an area between two values.
4. About 68 percent of the observations in any normal distribution are within one, 95 percent are within two, and only 3 out of every 1000 observations lie beyond three standard deviations from the mean.

Finding Areas Under the Normal Curve

Finding the probability of an event from a given normal distribution would ordinarily require extensive tables. Fortunately, the above-mentioned characteristics of the distribution simplify this task.

We already know that the relative frequency (probability) of an event is expressed as an area under the normal curve. We can go one step further and express the difference between the value of the variable and its mean in terms of standard deviation units.

Example 13.4

Consider again Peter Mansfield's contemplated purchase of fuses. The normal curve of the involved population distribution is reproduced in greater detail in Fig. 13.4.

What is the proportion of fuses with a service life between the mean 800 days and 850 days?

Since μ is 800 days, the distance between $X = 850$ and $\mu = 800$ is 50 days; inasmuch as σ is 25 days, a fuse with 850 service days is 50/25 or +2 standard deviations above the mean. According to Table 13.1, 2σ above the mean μ is half of 95.5 percent of the area under the curve. Hence, the area of the shaded portion of the graph is $.955/2 = .4772$. Therefore, 47.72 percent of 4772 fuses have a service life between 800 and 850 days.

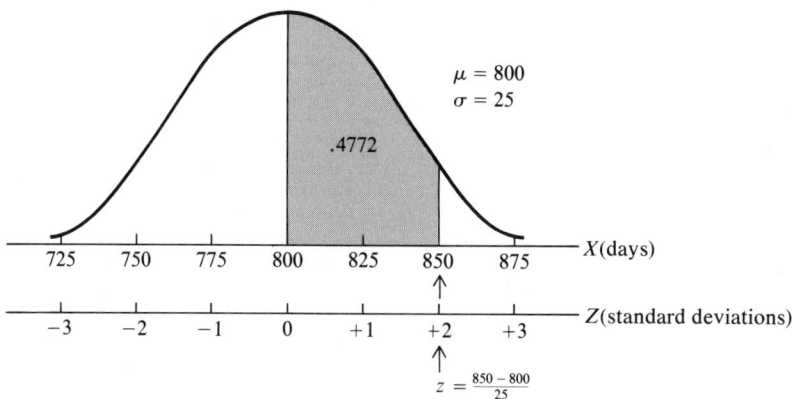

Figure 13.4. Finding the area under a normal curve.

Note that, in order to find the area under a normal curve, we changed the X scale to a Z scale; scale X represents a variable measured in physical units, days in this case; scale Z represents a variable measured in standard deviation units. Furthermore, this variable change, called *z transformation*, equates the value of the mean μ of a normal distribution to zero. Thus, the z transformation expresses the variability of any normally distributed variable X in terms of units of its own standard deviation. In general, the Z variable is defined as

(13.1) $$Z = \frac{X - \mu}{\sigma}$$

the difference between a given value of a variable X and its mean μ, divided by its own standard deviation σ. Understandably, it is called the *standard normal deviate* or, in short, the *Z deviate*. Consistent with earlier notation we use capital letter Z to denote the standard deviate of a variable and lower case z to indicate a specific value or values of such a deviate.

What is the significance of the z transformation? First, this transformation expresses *any* normally distributed variable representing time, weight, length, dollars, and so on as a single variable, the Z deviate. For this reason, the normal distribution of the Z deviate is called the *standard normal distribution*. Because there is one and only one such distribution, it is more frequently called the *normal curve*. The relationship between normal distributions and the normal curve is portrayed in Fig. 13.5. The three normal distributions may represent three of the five population distributions of fuses shown in Fig. 13.2. Observe that, in addition to changing the horizontal X scale, the z transformation sometimes decreases and sometimes increases the peakedness of a normal distribution.

Second, since the Z deviate is unique, a *single* table of areas is sufficient to determine the area for any value of a normally distributed variable. Such a table appears in Appendix D. Numbers in the body of the table represent areas under the right-hand half of the curve, that is, between zero and positive Z values. Because of symmetry, areas under the left-hand half of the curve, that is, between zero and negative Z values, are read from the same table by ignoring the negative sign. Also, it does not matter whether the Z variable is expressed in terms of a "strict" inequality ($<$), indicating "less than," or a weak inequality ($\leq$), indicating "less than or equal to." This is because the normal distribution is continuous and the area at any specific point on the Z scale is zero. In fact, stating that the area .4772 found in Example 13.3 corresponds to $z = +2$ would be incorrect. The correct statement is that area .4772 corresponds to interval $0 \leq z \leq +2$ on the Z scale. We shall follow convention and use weak inequalities throughout the text.

We have already shown how to find the area between the mean and a value of a normally distributed variable above the mean. This is the area which can be read directly from the table of areas in Appendix D. For $0 \leq z \leq +2$ the area under column .00 of the table is .4772, as found earlier. This table, however, can

Figure 13.5.
Linear transformation of normal distributions to the normal curve: an illustration.

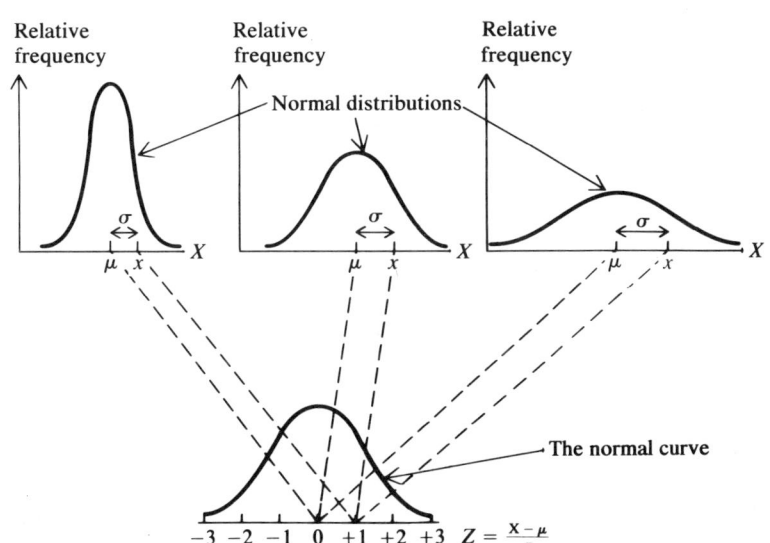

146   Chapter 4 Statistical Inference: Basic Concepts and Tools

be used to find the area under the normal curve for any value of a normally distributed variable. Because finding areas is very important in later topics, we illustrate representative possibilities.

Example 13.5

Let us consider again the shipment of 10,000 electrical fuses which Peter Mansfield received from a manufacturer. Now, Peter can use Appendix D to find the proportion (area) of fuses in the shipment having any given range of service days. Representative cases are portrayed in Fig. 13.6.

What is the proportion (area) of fuses in the shipment with the following service lives?

(a) *Less than or equal to 850 days*

We have already found that the area for $0 \leq z \leq +2$ is .4772. For a

Figure 13.6. Areas under the normal curve for representative values of $\bar{X}$, service days, of fuses in shipment: $\mu = 800$ days and $\sigma = 25$ days.

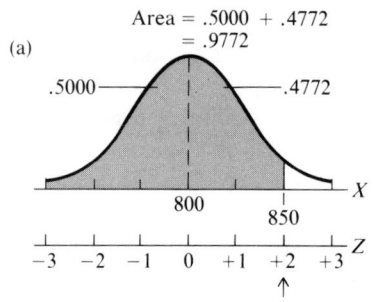
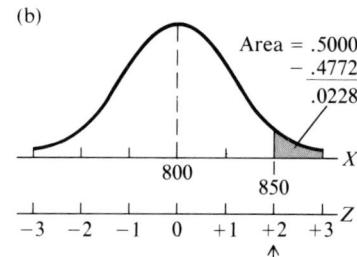
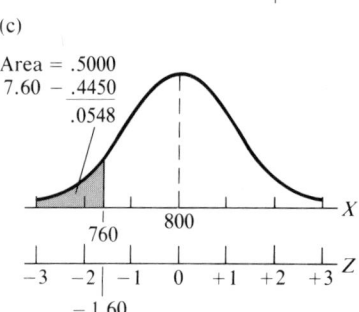
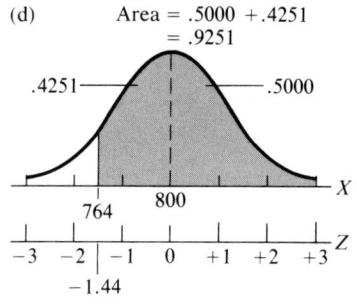
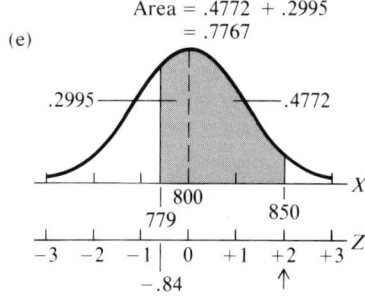
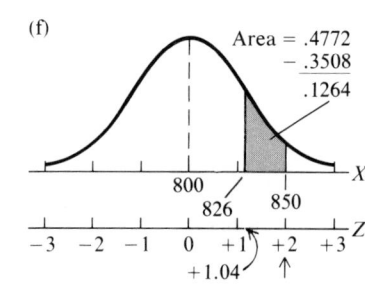

Section 13 The Normal Distribution

$z \leq 0$ the area is the entire left-hand half of the curve equal to .5000. So the total area is .5000 + .4772 = .9772 as shown in Fig. 13.6(a).

(b) *At least 850 days*

The area cannot be read directly from Appendix D. We must obtain the area between 800 and 850 days first and subtract that area from the right-hand half of the curve. We already know that $z = (850 - 800)/25 = +2$; so the area for $0 \leq z \leq +2$ is .4772; and the area for $z \geq +2$ is .5000 − .4772 = .0228. See Figure 13.6(b).

(c) *Less than or equal to 760 days*

The z value for interval $(760 - 800)/25$ is -1.60. Ignoring the negative sign, the area for $0 \leq z \leq 1.60$ from Appendix D is .4452; so the area for $z \leq -1.60$ is .5000 − .4452 = .0548 as shown in Fig. 13.6(c).

(d) *At least 764 days*

The z value for interval $(764 - 800)/25$ is -1.44. From Appendix D we find that the area for $0 \leq z \leq 1.44$ is .4251; so the area for $z \geq -1.44$ is .5000 + .4251 = .9251 shown in Fig. 13.6(d).

(e) *Between 779 and 850 days*

For interval $(800 - 850)/25$ the z value is $+2$, and we already know that for $0 \leq z \leq +2$ the area is .4772. The z value for interval $(779 - 800)/25$ is $-.84$; so the area for $0 \leq z \leq .84$ is .2995, and the total area is .4772 + .2995 = .7767 as shown in Fig. 13.6(e).

(f) *Between 826 and 850 days*

We already know that for $(800 - 850)/25$, the z value is $+2$, and for $0 \leq z \leq +2$ the area is .4772. For a z value $(826 - 800)/25 = +1.04$, the area for $0 \leq z \leq +1.04$ is .3508; so the area of our interest is .4772 − .3508 = .1264.* See Fig. 13.6(f).

So far, we have dealt with problems which required finding the area under the normal curve for a given interval of a variable. Frequently, it is desirable to find a given percentile value of a normally distributed population. Finding such a value requires that we reverse the earlier procedure of finding z; we calculate the corresponding population value with the following expression:

(13.2) $$X = \mu + z\sigma$$

Symbol X represents the value for a given percentile of a normally distributed population. Of course, below the 50th percentile we use the left-hand side tail of the normal curve with a negative z value.

Example 13.6

Hans and Gradle Steptoe are applying for salesperson's positions at Auto-Parts International Ltd. As part of their evaluation they must take a special

---

*Until you internalize the process of finding areas under the normal curve, it may be desirable to visualize the area sought with a diagram before looking up the answer from Appendix D.

test. They discover that the company evaluates applicants using the normal curve on a 100-point scale with 80 points as the mean and 6 points as the standard deviation of the distribution.

Rumors have it that the company will follow the same grading policy for this year's applicants. Hans and Gradle are anxious to know the minimum grade points they must earn in order to be included among the top 5 percent of this year's applicants.

First, we must determine the z value. Appendix D shows half the area under the normal curve. So we are interested only in the 45 percent upper half of the normal curve. The value of z which corresponds to .4500 area above the mean 80 grade points is 1.65. Interpolation is ignored.

Second, substitution for $\mu = 80$, $\sigma = 6$, $z = 1.65$ in formula (13.2) yields

$$X = 80 + 1.65(6) = 90 \text{ grade points}$$

Hans and Gradle must earn at least 90 points in order to be included among the top 5 percent of this year's applicants.

With the table of areas in Appendix D we can handle two types of problems:

1. We may wish to find the area under the normal curve for a given interval of a normally distributed variable. For this problem, we determine the value of the z deviate and look up the corresponding area from the body of the table.
2. Or we may wish to find a given percentile value of a normally distributed population. In this case, we reverse the procedure. We find the area in the body of the table and look up the corresponding value of the z deviate from the left-hand column of the table.

The Normal Curve As An Approximation to Sampling Distributions

So far, we have applied the normal curve to population distributions. We are now ready to show how and under what conditions the normal curve can be applied to a sampling distribution.

We have already seen that, according to the central limit theorem, a sampling distribution of mean or proportion tends to become normal as the sample increases almost regardless of the shape of the sampled population. According to formula (13.1), the random variable of a statistic may be transformed into the standard normal random variable by formula

(13.3) $$Z = \frac{\text{statistic} - \text{expected value}}{\text{standard error}}$$

Note that the statistic may be the value of a random variable for the mean $\bar{X}$ or proportion P of a given sample; and the expected value and standard error may be the mean and standard deviation of their respective sampling distributions.

Using formula (13.3) to find probabilities is not different from using formula (13.1) to find areas under the normal curve. However, there is an important rea-

Section 13 The Normal Distribution

son for showing how the procedure applies to sampling distributions. Later, we shall use the normal curve for statistical inference, estimating and testing of unknown parameters in particular. Therefore, it is important to know the conditions under which such a procedure is appropriate.

If the critical decision parameter in the preparation of a sampling plan is the sample mean, then we may define formula (13.3) as

(13.4) $$Z = \frac{\bar{X} - \mu}{\sigma_{\bar{X}}}$$

since $E(\bar{X}) = \mu$, and use the table of areas accordingly.

Example 13.7

Let us assume that the population of households for our shopping center survey is very large with a mean $\mu = \$16{,}000$ and a standard deviation $\sigma = \$9092$. What is the probability that a random sample of 100 households will have a sample mean between \$15,000 and \$18,000?

Treating $\bar{X}$ as an approximately normal random variable and on the basis of formula (13.4) and Appendix D,

$$P(15{,}000 \leq \bar{X} \leq 18{,}000) = P\left(\frac{15{,}000 - 16{,}000}{9092/\sqrt{100}} \leq \frac{\bar{X} - \mu}{\sigma_{\bar{X}}} \leq \frac{18{,}000 - 16{,}000}{9092/\sqrt{100}}\right)$$
$$= P(-1.10 \leq z \leq +2.20)$$
$$= .3643 + .4861$$
$$= .8504$$

If the decision parameter in the preparation of a sampling plan is a proportion, then we may define formula (13.3) as

(13.5) $$Z = \frac{P - \pi}{\sigma_P}$$

since $E(P) = \pi$, and use the table of areas accordingly.

Example 13.8

Let us consider again a very large population of households for our shopping center survey. The proportion π of households with \$28,000 income is .33. Suppose we take a random sample of 50 observations. What is the probability that at least 40 percent of the 50 households in the sample earn \$28,000?

Since $\pi = .33$ and $n = 50$, the standard error by formula (12.5) is

$$\sigma_P = \sqrt{\frac{\pi(1-\pi)}{n}} = \sqrt{\frac{(.33)(1-.33)}{50}} \simeq .0665$$

Treating P as an approximately normal random variable and on the basis of formula (13.5) and Appendix D,

$$P(P \geq .40) = P\left(\frac{P - \pi}{\sigma_P} \geq \frac{.40 - .33}{.0665}\right)$$
$$= P(z \geq +1.05)$$
$$= .5000 - .3531$$
$$= .1469$$

It is important to realize that for determining the probability of the above sample event we used the continuous normal distribution. But the normal curve is an approximation to the sampling distribution which is a *discrete* binomial distribution. The question is how good is the normal approximation to the exact binomial probability?

Example 13.8 (continued)

From Appendix B the exact binomial probability is

$$P\left(P \geq \frac{20}{50} = .40 \mid n = 50, \pi = .33\right) = .1826$$

This is a difference of .0357 between the exact binomial and the approximate normal probabilities.

Most of this discrepancy can be attributed to the fact that the normal probability is continuous. This means that the probability of each event is determined from the middle point of each bar of a histogram. The binomial probability for the same event, on the other hand, begins from the *left-hand* side, encompassing the entire bar of the histogram. The discrepancy can be corrected with the so-called *continuity correction*. For the normal approximation, the continuity correction is $1/2n$, where n is the sample size.

Example 13.8 (continued)

The corrected left-hand line of the sample proportion P is

$$.40 - \frac{1}{2n} = .40 - \frac{1}{2(50)} = .39$$

and the normal probability corrected for continuity is

$$P(P \geq .39) = P\left(\frac{P - \pi}{\sigma_P} \geq \frac{.39 - .33}{.0665}\right)$$
$$= P(z \geq +.90)$$
$$= .5000 - .3159$$
$$= .1841$$

a difference of only .0015 from the exact binomial probability.

Of course, whether we subtract or add the continuity correction depends on the event whose probability we wish to determine. For example, suppose we wish to find the probability that more than 40 percent of the households in the sample earn $28,000. Then the corrected P value should be $.40 + 1/2(50) = .41$.

Section 13 The Normal Distribution

Although the need for continuity correction is always present, this adjustment becomes increasingly small as the sample increases. It may be ignored for sufficiently large samples. Whether a sample is considered sufficiently large depends on the desired accuracy. For a given sample size, however, the continuity correction may be more desirable when we wish to approximate the probability of a single term rather than of several terms of the binomial distribution. Here, we follow the policy of ignoring the continuity correction unless the need for such a correction is stated.

What is the significance of the normal approximation? We have introduced a magnificent tool for measuring sample variability, that is, the random error of a statistic. This can be done *without the need to form a sampling distribution of that statistic*. Nevertheless, at this point, it is imperative to remember the following qualifications about the normal approximation:

1. So far, we have illustrated approximation of the normal distribution to sampling distributions from samples drawn with replacement. This is equivalent to sampling from an infinite population.

2. The key measure for statistical inference is the standard error of estimate. We have seen that we can calculate this measure from σ, the population standard deviation. The use of the normal distribution assumes that *we know the standard deviation of the population to be sampled*.

3. Also, the normal approximation is satisfactory if the sample is sufficiently large. If the population is normal, a sample of any size would yield a normal sampling distribution. A sampling distribution from a skewed population, however, requires a large sample in order to approach the normal curve. By convention, statisticians feel that the normal distribution can be safely applied to most situations involving *a sample of 30 or more observations*. Later, we shall introduce more detailed guidelines specifying the minimal sample size necessary for a good normal approximation to populations with varying degree of skewness.

These qualifications raise an important question: How do we cope with situations where sampling is carried out without replacement, the standard deviation of the population to be sampled is not known with certainty, and the sample size is less than 30 observations? The answer requires that we introduce some refinements to the normal distribution model. We introduce these refinements as we apply our acquired knowledge to practical problems.

PROBLEMS

Group One

13.1. Peter Mansfield, the purchasing manager of Radio Mack, receives a shipment of 5000 special flashlight batteries. The service life of these batteries is normally distributed with a mean of 625 hours and a standard deviation of 25 hours. Peter wants to know the proportion of batteries which the shipment includes for each of the following intervals. Find and illustrate your answer by sketching the appropriate area under the normal curve along both the X and the Z horizontal scales

*(a) No more than 576 hours
(b) Between 576 and 674 hours
(c) At least 689.5 hours
(d) Between 560.5 and 689.5 hours
(e) Between 560.5 and 576 hours
(f) No more than 576 and at least 674 hours
(g) Less than 560.5 and at least 689.5 hours

13.2. Martha Waldron is vice-president in charge of tellers at the Peacock National Bank. Available data indicate that the time required for a teller to serve a customer is normally distributed with a mean of 50 seconds and a standard deviation of 6 seconds. Martha believes that such a distribution is applicable in the future. What percentage of customers will require service lasting:
  *(a) No more than 38.24 seconds?
  (b) Between 38.24 and 61.76 seconds?
  (c) At least 65.48 seconds?
  (d) Between 34.52 and 65.48 seconds?
  (e) Between 34.52 and 38.24 seconds?
  (f) No more than 38.24 and at least 61.76 seconds?
  (g) Less than 34.52 and at least 65.48 seconds?

13.3. Vista Travel Inc., an agency issuing travelers checks, has a daily float of funds which is normally distributed with mean and standard deviation of $16 and $2 million, respectively. (*Float,* the cash which the agency holds between the time a customer pays cash for checks to the time the checks are cashed, is a considerable source of revenue to the agency since it is invested in short-term securities.) Assuming past experience will continue in the next 365 days, how many days would the float be:
  (a) More than $19.3 million?
  (b) Less than $11.34 million?

*13.4. Zolota and White, Inc., is a shipyard specializing in the construction of yachts. Management wants to design the main cabin of a new type of yacht so that 95 percent of the persons standing inside the cabin will have at least 10 inches clearance. Assuming that heights of persons are normally distributed, with a mean of 68 inches and standard deviation of 3 inches, how high should the cabin be made?

13.5. The daily effluent of pollutants dumped into Penomstock River by Nawhak Textiles Inc. is normally distributed with a mean of 100,000 gallons and a standard deviation of 10,000 gallons. The state Environmental Control Board considers it a violation of established standards if the company's daily effluent exceeds 123,000 gallons. Assuming past experience is likely to continue for the next 365 days, what is the number of days during which the company can be expected to violate pollution standards?

13.6. Yellow Sox, a team of baseball players, have batting averages which are normally distributed with a mean of .250 and a standard deviation of .048. Assuming this experience is likely to repeat itself during the current baseball season, what is the highest batting average which 1 out of 25 team players is likely to achieve?

Answers to asterisked (*) problems are appended.

Section 13 The Normal Distribution

13.7. Vincent Moscat is comptroller of Jetty Oil Company. From experience he knows that the accounts receivable of the firm are normally distributed with a mean of $500 and a standard deviation of $50.
  *(a) What is the proportion of accounts receivable with at least $600?
  (b) Suppose a simple random sample of 25 accounts is taken. What is the probability that the sample mean will be at least $520?
  (c) What is the difference between your answers to part (a) and (b) of the problem?
  (d) Does it matter that the sample size is less than 30 accounts receivable?

13.8. Kelsey Perkins, the administrative assistant to a congressman, knows that 30 percent of the eligible voters in a suburban town of the congressional district are independent, that is, they have not declared their political affiliation with any political party. In order to assess voter preference for the forthcoming elections, Kelsey plans to take a simple random sample of 50 eligible voters in the town. (At the present time we may assume sampling with replacement, an assumption which we shall drop later.)
  *(a) What is the exact binomial probability that the sample will contain at least 40 percent independent voters?
  (b) Find the probability of the same event using the normal curve.
  (c) Find the normal probability of the same event with continuity correction.

13.9. Distinguish between:
  (a) Normal distributions and the normal curve
  (b) Discrete and continuous probability distributions
  (c) Normally distributed random variables and the standard normal deviate
  (d) Standard error and population standard deviation

13.10. Explain:
  (a) Standard normal distribution   (d) The normal curve
  (b) Standard normal deviate   (e) z Transformation
  (c) Continuity correction   (f) Z Deviate

Group Two

13.11. Sally Benson is in charge of the public relations office for the state governor. It is known that 30 percent of adults in the state are against building atomic power plants. Although Sally knows that the 50 persons attending a debate on the pros and cons of atomic energy may not represent a random sample of adults, she may assume that they do in order to get a rough idea of attendance by persons who may oppose atomic energy.
  *(a) What is the exact binomial probability that at least 15 persons at the debate will be against atomic energy?
  (b) Compare it with the normal probability.
  (c) Find the normal probability with continuity correction.

13.12. The management of Thorndike and Thorndike Co., a mail-order house, has established the policy that 98 percent of the orders during a regular workday must be properly filled. To implement this policy, a simple random sample of 100 orders is selected from each daily output. If the sample shows that less than 5 percent of the orders are not properly filled, the daily output is not inspected; otherwise, inspection takes place. What is the probability that an inspection is necessary? (Adjust for continuity)

Chapter 4 Statistical Inference: Basic Concepts and Tools

13.13. A process for manufacturing transistors has a 10 percent fraction defective. The process is considered to be in control if 108 or fewer transistors in a sample of 900 are found defective; otherwise, the process is adjusted. What is the probability that the process will need adjusting if the average fraction defective:
  *(a) Remains at 10 percent?
  (b) Shifts to 12 percent?
  (c) Shifts to 14 percent?

13.14. On the average, 10 percent of the patients entering a hospital need 1 pint of blood plasma. During an ordinary day about 400 patients enter a hospital. What is the minimum stock of blood plasma which the hospital must carry in order to avoid the risk of running out of stock with probability:
  (a) 5 percent?
  (b) 1 percent?
  (c) .1 percent?

Chapter 5
SAMPLE DESIGN AND ESTIMATION

The foundation of statistical inference largely rests on the normal distribution. With the normal curve we were able to answer the question: What is the probability that a statistic such as the mean varies within a range of certain values from its population mean? For example, with $\mu = \$16,000$ and $\sigma = \$9092$ we found that the probability is .85 for a random sample of 100 households to have a mean income between $15,000 and $18,000 (Example 13.7).

But this is theory. In practice, a crucial question we wish to answer is: What is the confidence that a certain range of income values, based on a single sample mean, includes the unknown population mean? For example, we may take a simple random sample of 100 households and find that the sample mean is $16,500. Then we may construct an interval, that is, a range of income values, which may include the unknown population mean with a stated degree of confidence. The sample mean is called a *point estimate* of the population mean and the range of income values a *confidence interval estimate*.

How such estimates are obtained and what they mean is the central theme of this chapter. First, in Section 14, we discuss some preparatory work necessary for carrying out estimation. Then we apply our acquired knowledge to estimating population means (Section 15) and proportions (Section 16). We limit our presentation to simple random samples. More elaborate sampling procedures and estimation of other parameters introduce no new principles.

SECTION 14 / SAMPLE DESIGN

How do we go about applying the principles of statistical inference to estimating unknown parameters? The initial effort consists of plans which statisticians frequently call a *sample design*. Under this topic we consider criteria for choosing a suitable estimator, explaining estimation error and risk, determining sample size, and preparing an optimal sample design.

Criteria for Choosing Estimators

We have already explained that the use of a statistic as a means of estimating a parameter is called an estimator. Careful selection of an estimator is necessary for serving our study objectives and for determining sample size.

Chapter 5 Sample Design and Estimation

Which statistic is most suitable for estimating our decision parameter or parameters? Frequently, several statistics can be used as estimators alternatively. For example, we could use the sample mean or median to estimate the population mean. In order to determine which sample measure is most suitable, we may employ three principal criteria: unbiasedness, consistency, and efficiency.

Unbiasedness. We have already established that an estimator $\hat{\theta}$ is unbiased (Eq. 12.3) if its expected value $E(\hat{\theta})$ equals its parameter θ; that is,

$$(14.1) \qquad E(\hat{\theta}) = \theta$$

And we have already shown that the sample mean and proportion are unbiased estimators of their parameters. The value of a sample mean or proportion may vary from sample to sample due to random error; on the average, however, these statistics would correctly estimate their parameters. In other words, positive and negative random error values would cancel each other, leaving zero difference between the expected value of the statistic and the parameter.

Also, the expected value of the sample variance s^2, with $n - 1$ as divisor, is an unbiased estimator of the population variance σ^2. According to (14.1),

$$(14.2) \qquad E(s^2) = E\left[\frac{\Sigma f(m - \bar{x})^2}{n - 1}\right] = \sigma^2$$

This mathematical statement explains why the sample standard deviation s, with $n - 1$ as divisor, is a better (Eq. 11.2), although a biased, estimator of the population standard deviation. In other words, condition (14.1) holds for the sample variance s^2 but not for sample standard deviation s. This type of bias has nothing to do with procedural bias; an estimator can be biased even when procedural bias is absent.

The condition of unbiasedness tells us that, on the average, there will be zero random error between an estimator and the parameter being estimated. This, however, may be of little practical use; it does not tell us how closely an estimator is likely to approach its parameter. In fact, the random error of a given value of a statistic may be large. Therefore, we cannot determine which of two or more unbiased estimators should be preferred. We need additional criteria which indicate the closeness of an estimator to its parameter.

Consistency. An unbiased estimator is *consistent* if its value gets closer and closer to the true parameter as the sample size n gets larger. The sample mean $\bar{x}$ is a consistent estimator of the population μ. This can be seen from the standard error formula (12.4) which we reproduce here for convenience:

$$(14.3) \qquad \sigma_{\bar{x}} = \frac{\sigma}{\sqrt{n}}$$

As discussed earlier, standard error $\sigma_{\bar{x}}$ which measures sample variability of $\overline{X}$, becomes smaller as n gets larger. In other words, for a given standard deviation

σ, statistical precision increases *consistently*. The effect of an increasing sample size on the shape of the curve of a sampling distribution can be easily visualized. As *n* gets larger and larger, the base of such a curve shrinks while its peakedness increases, approaching a widthless line. On similar grounds, the sample proportion *P* is a consistent estimator of parameter π.

Efficiency. For a given sample size, the random variable of one statistic is a more *efficient estimator* than another if its standard error is smaller. We can illustrate efficiency by comparing the sample mean and sample median. If a population is normal, the population mean and median have the same value. In estimating μ, we may use either the sample mean or the sample median, for both are unbiased and consistent estimators. The standard error of the sample median, however, is 1.2533 times larger than the standard error of the sample mean. This means that the sample median is $(1.2533)^2 \simeq 1.57$ or 57 percent less efficient than a sample mean. In order to obtain a given degree of precision, we would need a sample size 57 percent larger if we use the sample median rather than the sample mean to estimate the population mean.

The sample mean and proportion may be considered all-purpose estimators. They are used as the "best" point estimates of the corresponding parameters in many statistical applications; they are suitable estimators for preparing simple random sample designs; they can be used for preparing more sophisticated sample designs as well. Yet we should keep in mind that neither the sample mean nor the sample proportion are the most preferred estimators under all circumstances.

Estimation Error and Risk

How does one decide how large a sample to select in a given sampling study? This question requires an understanding of the procedure in confidence interval estimation. This procedure is based on the concept of the sampling distribution which explains the rationale of interval estimation.

Let us consider again our household survey for determining the economic feasibility of a shopping center (Example 12.1). Suppose we wish to estimate the mean income μ of the households to be served by the center. We may also assume a very large statistical population with a known standard deviation σ. In order to estimate μ, our decision parameter, we wish to establish an interval with a lower endpoint *a* and an upper endpoint *b* containing μ such that

(14.4) $$a \leqslant \mu \leqslant b$$

We plan to use the sample mean as an estimator to accomplish this objective. Usually, we choose the endpoint values *a* and *b* so that the interval is centered at the specific value of the sample mean $\bar{x}$ we would actually obtain from our sample. In addition, we wish to assign to the interval a measure of reliability, say .99, for estimating μ.

For a sufficiently large sample, say 100 households, the sampling distribution of sample means will be normally distributed with mean $E(\bar{X}) = \mu$ and standard error $\sigma_{\bar{x}} = \sigma/\sqrt{n}$. We already know how to make probability statements about the range of values which the random variable $\bar{X}$ of sample means can assume. In our case, 99 percent of all possible sample means would lie within 2.58 standard

Chapter 5 Sample Design and Estimation

error units of the mean μ or between $\mu - 2.58\,\sigma_{\bar{x}}$ and $\mu + 2.58\sigma_{\bar{x}}$. Formally, the probability statement is

(14.5) $$P(\mu - 2.58\sigma_{\bar{x}} \leq \bar{X} \leq \mu + 2.58\sigma_{\bar{x}}) = .99$$

as portrayed in Fig. 14.1. The z value of 2.58 is read from Appendix D; it represents half of .99 or .495 of the area under the normal curve. This is according to the theory we learned in the last two sections.

In applying this theory to the construction of an actual confidence interval, we take only a single sample of size n, 100 households in our case. We are interested in the *confidence* that such an interval includes the population mean μ as follows:

(14.6) $$\bar{x} - 2.58\,\sigma_{\bar{x}} \leq \mu \leq \bar{x} + 2.58\sigma_{\bar{x}}$$

where the term to the left of μ defines endpoint a and the term to the right of μ endpoint b in expression (14.4).

What does such an interval estimate mean? Suppose the first sample of 100 households yields a mean $\bar{x}_1$. The position of $\bar{x}_1$, shown on the horizontal axis of the graph in Fig. 14.1, indicates that $\bar{x}_1$ is to the right of μ but at a distance less than $2.58\sigma_{\bar{x}}$ from μ. We construct an interval estimate such as (14.6) shown immediately below the graph. Note the interval includes μ since $\bar{x}_1$ is at a distance

Figure 14.1.
Sampling distribution of $\bar{X}$ and possible confidence interval estimates.

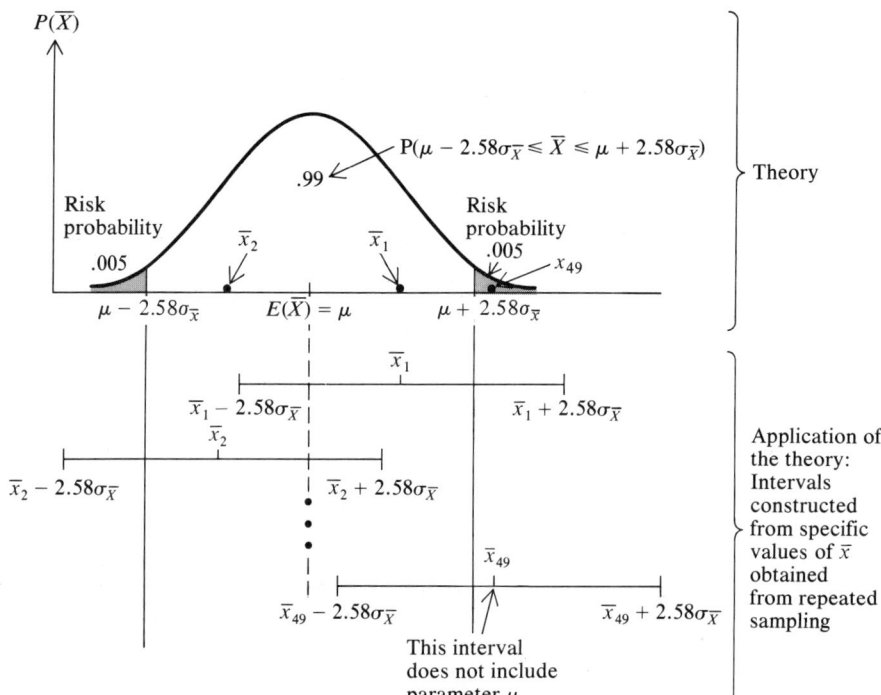

less than $2.58\sigma_{\bar{x}}$ from μ. A second sample of 100 households yields a mean $\bar{x}_2$ with its position shown on the horizontal axis of the graph. Again the interval based on $\bar{x}_2$ contains μ since $\bar{x}_2$ is to the left of μ but at a distance less than $2.58\sigma_{\bar{x}}$ from μ. We may repeat construction of intervals until the 49th sample of 100 households yields a mean $\bar{x}_{49}$. The position of $\bar{x}_{49}$ on the horizontal axis of the graph indicates that $\bar{x}_{49}$ lies to the right of μ but at a distance greater than $2.58\sigma_{\bar{x}}$ from μ. Note that this interval does not contain μ since $\bar{x}_{49}$ is at a distance greater than $2.58\sigma_{\bar{x}}$ from μ. Suppose we repeat the above procedure of interval construction a large number of times. We can assert that 99 percent of such intervals include the population mean μ since 99 percent of samples means fall within $\pm 2.58\sigma_{\bar{x}}$ of μ.

The meaning of expression (14.6) and its relation to expression (14.5) must be clear by now. In both expressions, the sample mean is a random variable while the population mean is a constant. Expression (14.5), however, is a probability statement because it refers to the sampling distribution of all possible values of the random variable $\bar{X}$ of sample means. Expression (14.6), on the other hand, is not a probability statement. In applying the theory to a particular situation, we usually take a single sample of a given size, 100 households in our case; we calculate the mean of that sample; and we construct an interval such as (14.6). This interval itself is referred to as a *confidence interval*. Expression (14.6) means that if repeated simple random samples each of 100 households were drawn from the population of households and interval (14.6) were constructed from each sample, then 99 percent of these intervals would contain the population mean; 1 out of every 100, the 49th in our illustration, with a range too far to the right or too far to the left of μ, would not include the population mean. The 99 percent figure, expressed in terms of z value, is called the *degree of confidence*.

The first step in estimation is the task of determining the desired sample size. In this connection, we must specify the width of the interval we wish to construct. In our illustration, the width of the interval was set at $\pm 2.58\sigma_{\bar{x}}$ for a 99 percent degree of confidence. In general, the width of an interval is called the *tolerable error*, denoted by e and defined as*

$$(14.7) \qquad e = z\sigma_{\bar{x}}$$

The value of e represents the maximum error a decision maker is willing to tolerate in estimating parameter μ. The difference of the degree of confidence from 1 represents the risk of committing an error equal to or greater than e. Thus for a 99 percent degree of confidence the risk is $.01 = 1 - .99$ shown as shaded areas in the two tails of the graph in Fig. 14.1. This means that there is a 1 percent risk that the interval to be constructed will not include parameter μ. Different risk levels and the corresponding z values are shown in Table 14.1. They represent conventional risk levels frequently used by practicing statisticians.

In sum, the first step in determining the required sample size is to specify

---

*In this and other formulas to be introduced later the lowercase letter z is justified because, in applying theory to a practical estimation or testing problem, we speak of a specific value of the random variable Z.

Table 14.1.
Risk Levels of Exceeding Specified Errors and Their z Values

Risk	z Value
.15	1.44
.10	1.64
.05	1.96
.01	2.58
.003	2.97

two items: (1) the tolerable error, which determines the width of the desired confidence interval; and (2) the degree of confidence, which determines the risk that the interval will not include the parameter being estimated.

Example 14.1

In order to increase accuracy, the National Physical Laboratory in Britain takes the average of several atomic clocks as an estimate of the true Universal Mean Time (UMT). UMT is extensively used in many fields, especially in international business transactions. Since 1955, when the first atomic timepiece was put into service, the laboratory increased the number of atomic clocks; so their average time estimates the true UMT within 3 microseconds* faster or slower per year with 99 percent degree of confidence. How many clocks would the laboratory need to obtain the specified precision in estimating the true UMT?

In order to answer this question, we may first concentrate on error e and its risk. It is clear that the tolerable error is 3 microseconds. Since the degree of confidence is .99, the risk that the confidence interval will not include the true UMT is $.01 = 1 - .99$. According to Table 14.1, this risk corresponds to a z value of 2.58

Sample Size for an Infinite Population

Let us see now how this information about tolerable error and its risk can help us determine sample size. We know that the standard error of $\bar{X}$ is defined as

$$\sigma_{\bar{X}} = \frac{\sigma}{\sqrt{n}}$$

So we may write the tolerable error (14.7) as

$$e = z \frac{\sigma}{\sqrt{n}}$$

and solve this expression for the sample size as follows:

$$\sqrt{n} = \frac{z\sigma}{e}$$

(14.8)
$$\boxed{n = \frac{z^2 \sigma^2}{e^2}}$$

*A microsecond is one-millionth of a second.

We are already familiar with error e and its risk. We need to concentrate on the third element of formula (14.8), the population variance σ^2. However, we are faced with a dilemma: we must have prior knowledge of the variance of a population we are supposed to study! And frequently, we do not know the population variance.

Fortunately, we need to know, not the exact value, but only an approximate value of σ^2. Several methods are available for obtaining such a rough estimate. For example, an estimate of the variance may be obtained from prior studies of the same elementary units. Government agencies conduct periodic surveys on employment, production, wages, sales, and so forth. Assuming the variance of such a statistical universe is not erratic or unusually unstable, it provides a satisfactory base for estimating σ^2. If past information is not available, a rough estimate of the variance may be obtained from knowing the range of a population distribution. For example, suppose the difference between the highest and the lowest value in a distribution of service life of electrical fuses is 150 days. Assuming the population is approximately normal, nearly all observations will be within six standard deviations, three on each side of the mean. And a reasonably good estimate of σ is 150/6 or 25 service days. Finally, a small pilot study may yield the desired information. In such a case, however, the divisor of the range varies with the size of the sample as shown in Table 14.2

Example 14.1 (continued)

The first five atomic timepieces the laboratory introduced showed a range of 20 microseconds per year. According to Table 14.2, the standard deviation is about 20/2 or 10 microseconds. Now we are ready to determine the number of atomic clocks needed to obtain an error of 3 microseconds with 99 percent degree of confidence using formula (14.8).

Since e is set at 3 microseconds and z at 2.58, and σ is approximately 10 microseconds, the laboratory would need

$$n = \frac{(2.58)^2(10)^2}{(3)^2}$$
$$= 74 \text{ atomic timepieces}$$

to obtain the specified degree of precision in estimating the true UMT.

Table 14.2. Relationship Between Sample Size and Range Divisor for a Rough Estimate of Standard Deviation From a Pilot Study

If n Nearly This Size:	Divide Range by:
5	2
10	3
25	4
100	5

Source: George W. Snedecor and William G. Cochran, *Statistical Methods* 6th ed. (Ames: Iowa State University Press, 1967). © 1967 by The Iowa State University Press. Reprinted by permission.

Chapter 5 Sample Design and Estimation

The formula for determining the required sample size when a proportion π is the decision parameter may be derived in a manner similar to that employed for the mean. The tolerable error (14.7) for a proportion can be expressed as

$$e = z\sigma_P$$

We know that the standard error of the sampling distribution of P is defined as (Eq. 12.5)

$$\sigma_P = \sqrt{\frac{\pi(1-\pi)}{n}}$$

So we may write the tolerable error as

$$e = \frac{z\sqrt{\pi(1-\pi)}}{\sqrt{n}}$$

and solve this expression for the sample size n as follows:

$$\sqrt{n} = \frac{z\sqrt{\pi(1-\pi)}}{e}$$

(14.9)
$$n = \frac{z^2\pi(1-\pi)}{e^2}$$

Again we are faced with the dilemma for determining the population proportion π. We must have some advance knowledge of π, precisely the parameter our sample is supposed to estimate! The approximate value of π may be based on prior experience.

Example 14.2

Highway safety regulations require that trucks do not exceed a specified maximum gross weight while using state highways. Traffic regulations such as this are aimed at reducing wear and tear of the highways and at minimizing accidents. At the same time, they affect the cost of transporting goods by truck. In order to estimate the proportion of overloaded trucks, the chief of the State Highway Patrol plans to select a sample of trucks for inspection during a month. (At this point, we are not concerned about how a simple random sample of trucks can be selected from the state highways.) Trucks will be stopped on the highway and weighed on the spot by a portable balance. The chief believes that about 10 to 20 percent of the trucks on the state highways are overloaded. How many trucks should be inspected for estimating the true proportion of overloaded trucks with .03 error and 95 percent degree of confidence?

Since the error e is set at .03 and the confidence factor z at 1.96, and π is believed to be no more than .20, by formula (14.9) we have

$$n = \frac{(1.96)^2(.20)(.80)}{(.03)^2}$$
$$= 683 \text{ trucks}$$

Section 14 Sample Design

It is important to realize that in determining sample size we set π at .20, the highest value of the given range. Otherwise, if we set π at less than .20, say .15, and in fact the true π is .20, the sample size would not be large enough to secure the desired tolerable error and risk. Setting π at .20 secures the desired precision irrespective of the true value of π within the specified range.

If we have no way of knowing the approximate value of π, we may assume that the population to be sampled has the largest variability with π equal to .50. Then factor $\pi(1 - \pi)$ in formula (14.9) would be as large as possible, requiring the largest sample size for a desired degree of precision. Of course, we must realize that, if true π is less than .50 and we set π at .50, we run the risk of requiring a sample far larger and costlier than necessary to obtain the desired degree of precision.

Sample Size for a Finite Population

Sampling from a finite population is ordinarily done without replacement. If a household is selected in the sample more than once, second or subsequent selections are ignored since each elementary unit is interviewed only once. In such a case, sample observations are dependent and dependence reduces standard error. Since standard error is part of the formula for determining sample size, dependence in turn reduces somewhat the required sample size for the same precision.

Moreover, a statistical investigation may require estimation of several parameters. Estimating the Universal Mean Time and the proportion of overloaded trucks were single-parameter surveys. An opinion poll survey, on the other hand, may require estimation of several parameters; in addition to the percentage of voters favoring a given candidate, we may be interested in estimating the response to several aspects and issues of the campaign. Frequently, it is not obvious which measure is most important and selection of a decision parameter may present difficulties. Let us now see how we can cope with these two complications.

In sampling from a finite population without replacement, the standard error of estimate $\sigma_{\bar{x}}$ or σ_P is reduced by the so-called *finite population correction* or fpc:

$$(14.10) \qquad \text{fpc} = \sqrt{\frac{N - n}{N - 1}}$$

where N = population size
n = sample size

In order to determine the sample size for a mean, we begin with error e:

$$e = z\sigma_{\bar{x}}$$

but now the standard error must be found from

$$\sigma_{\bar{x}} = \frac{\sigma}{\sqrt{n}} \sqrt{\frac{N - n}{N - 1}}$$

If we solve

$$e = z \frac{\sigma}{\sqrt{n}} \sqrt{\frac{N - n}{N - 1}}$$

Chapter 5 Sample Design and Estimation

for n, we obtain

(14.11)
$$n = \frac{z^2\sigma^2 N}{(N-1)e^2 + z^2\sigma^2}$$

Example 14.3

In our household survey for a shopping center, we may recall that average household income was considered as a decision parameter; income measures purchasing power and can be cross-tabulated with several numerical and categorical variables such as age, sex, occupation, and spending and shopping habits.

In order to estimate average household income (no longer assumed to be known) and other variables, we plan to select a sample with a $1000 tolerable error and 99 degree of confidence. For illustrative purposes, let us assume that the population consists of 5000 households only. Available census data indicate that the population standard deviation is about $9000. What is the sample size for securing the desired degree of precision?

Substituting 2.58 for z, 9000 for σ, 5000 for N, and 1000 for e in formula (14.11) we find

$$n = \frac{(2.58)^2(9000)^2(5000)}{(5000-1)(1000)^2 + (2.58)^2(9000)^2}$$
$$= 487 \text{ households}$$

For an infinite or very large population the sample size by formula (14.8) is 539 households; the reduction of sample size to 487 is the effect of the fpc.

Frequently, we may prefer to use a proportion rather than a mean as our decision parameter for two principal reasons. First, we have already seen that setting π at .50 guarantees that the sample size will be large enough to secure the desired degree of precision. Second, a proportion is applicable to numerical as well as to categorical variables.

In a similar manner we can obtain the sample size formula for π for sampling without replacement:

(14.12)
$$n = \frac{z^2\pi(1-\pi)N}{(N-1)e^2 + z^2\pi(1-\pi)}$$

Note that this formula is analogous to (14.11) with the only difference that $\pi(1-\pi)$ has replaced σ^2.

Example 14.4

Tend is a new allergy-free detergent introduced recently by Alpha Inc., a manufacturer of toiletry products. Tend has been marketed in a middle-size town considered to be "typical" in many respects of the United States market. The product had considerable consumer appeal because its allergy-free feature was considered environmentally sound. Encouraged by initial mar-

Section 14 Sample Design

ket response, management plans an advertising campaign for introducing Tend nationally. In preparation of this campaign Alpha Inc. wants to collect information about the present users of Tend. In particular, household size, income, occupation, frequency of use, and especially reasons for switching to Tend would be valuable data for planning the advertising campaign.

Through coupon purchases, a population of 4000 regular users of Tend were identified. Management felt that a 5 percent error and a 95 degree of confidence would adequately serve the purpose of the study. What is the required sample size?

Since there is no clear indication which measure should be a decision parameter, we may select π to represent the proportion of users who prefer Tend because of its allergy-free feature and set it at $\pi = .50$; error e is set at .05, and the confidence factor z is 1.96. Substitution in formula (14.12) yields

$$n = \frac{(1.96)^2(.50)(.50)(4000)}{(4000-1)(.05)^2 + (1.96)^2(.50)(.50)}$$
$$= 351 \text{ regular users of Tend}$$

At this point, it is desirable to summarize the importance of fpc, (Eq. 14.10) in relation to changes in the sizes of population and sample.

1. When n is one, fpc is equal to one and the standard error $\sigma_{\bar{x}}$ or σ_P is the same whether we sample with or without replacement.
2. When n is equal to N, fpc is zero, so the standard error is also zero. This makes sense. When the sample includes the entire population, there is no random error; the sample mean or proportion is equal to its respective parameter.
3. For n greater than one but less than N, fpc is always smaller than one. This means that, for a given n, the standard error is smaller in sampling without replacement than in sampling with replacement. For this reason, fpc is also called the *reduction factor*. The reduction is insignificant for large populations. By convention, statisticians ignore fpc when the percentage of sample to population, called *sample fraction*, is less than or equal to 5 percent.
4. Using a 5 percent sample fraction (or any percentage for that matter) to determine sample size is *wrong*. The size of a sample is determined on the basis of the tolerable error and the desired degree of confidence.

Optimal Sample Designs

So far statistical precision has been the sole criterion for determining sample size. We conveniently ignored unit sampling costs as well as the requirements for data analysis. The importance of these constraints may vary depending on circumstances; nevertheless, they must be taken into consideration in the preparation of a sample design. Furthermore, simple random sampling assumes that the population to be sampled is fairly homogeneous. Skewed populations or lack of a suitable frame require more sophisticated than simple random sample designs.

In many problems, statistical precision may be the predominant, if not the exclusive, criterion for determining sample size. In estimating, for example, the fraction of defective batteries in a shipment, statistical precision may be the sole criterion for determining sample size; once the sample size is determined, no revision of its size may be necessary; sampling costs may be insignificant and data analysis requirements minimal. In other problems, however, available funds become an important constraint on sample size. Then, initially, we are not concerned about determining the sample size which secures a given degree of precision; we are interested in how much precision we can buy from a sample we can afford.

Example 14.5

Suppose the laboratory in Example 14.1 cannot afford 74 atomic timepieces necessary to achieve the stated error of 3 microseconds. Appropriations provide for the installation of only 25 atomic clocks. Assuming we wish the same degree of confidence, what is the error for estimating the true UMT?

Tolerable error has been defined as

$$e = z \frac{\sigma}{\sqrt{n}}$$

Since z is 2.58, σ is about 10, and n is set at 25,

$$e = 2.58 \frac{10}{\sqrt{25}}$$
$$= 5.16 \text{ microseconds}$$

Of course, this increase in error may be reduced if the laboratory is willing to assume a risk higher than the initial .01. Suppose a risk of .05 is acceptable. Then the confidence factor z is 1.96 and

$$e = 1.96 \frac{10}{\sqrt{25}}$$
$$= 3.92 \text{ microseconds}$$

While financial resources may impose an upper limit, requirements for the analysis of the collected data may place a lower limit on sample size. This constraint may rise from the need to cross-tabulate two or more variables of a subsample.

Example 14.6

In the survey for a shopping center we may need to analyze monthly dollar expenditures on apparel by household income and size. Households may be classified into 5 income and 3 size groups which requires a 5 × 3 table of 15 subgroups or categories. A sample of 487 households may be a sufficient data base. Suppose, however, we wish to do the same analysis for households headed by a single parent and there are only 50 of them in the sample. Analysis of a subsample of this size may be an inadequate data base for meaningful results. Statistical error may also increase to an unacceptable level since estimation must be based on the 50 observations.

Statisticians strive to obtain an *optimal sample design* which maximizes statistical precision within the limits of available resources and analytical objectives. To this end, they have developed more sophisticated than simple random sample designs. We can briefly explain only two of them: *stratified sampling* and *cluster sampling*.

In *stratified sampling,* the population is classified into mutually exclusive subgroups, or *strata,* and an independent simple random sample is drawn from each stratum. Then measures such as the means or proportions from these samples are combined to yield an overall estimate of the corresponding parameter. For example, for estimating consumer expenditures on durable goods we may classify the household population into a number of strata by size and income. Then we take a simple random sample mean of expenditures from each stratum, weight each mean by the proportion of the household population in each stratum, and use the weighted average of expenditures as an estimate of the parameter mean.

A stratified sample design is generally suitable in situations involving a heterogeneous population. Its principal advantage is that it increases statistical precision by controlling the population variance. For example, household expenditures on durable goods may vary considerably with respect to the stratifying variable of size and income. To the extent size and income are related to household expenditures, stratification reduces expenditure variance by classifying the population into homogeneous strata. The result is a weighted average of expenditures with precision greater than the precision of an average from a simple random sample of the same size. Of course, stratification is only possible if the frame contains information about household size and income.

Cluster sampling, on the other hand, is generally appropriate in situations where the elementary units of the population are geographically dispersed and a suitable frame is not available. The principal if not exclusive advantage of a cluster sample design is that it reduces survey costs. In estimating next season's crop of winter wheat, we may designate counties as clusters of farm units and select a simple random sample of counties. Then we either take a census of farm units of sampled counties or prepare a frame of farm units of sampled counties and draw a simple random sample of farm units from each frame. Survey costs are substantially less than in a simple random sample because cluster sampling limits preparation of a frame and field work expenses to the sampled counties. Cost gains, however, must be viewed in the light of potential sampling bias since nonsampled counties may be different in some important respects from sampled counties.

One way statisticians are able to control such a sampling bias is with stratification of clusters. For example, in estimating next season's crop of winter wheat we may stratify counties (clusters) into homogeneous strata (groups). Then we may take a simple random sample of counties from each stratum and prepare a frame of farm units growing winter wheat in each sampled county. The final sampling stage may involve a simple random sample of farm units growing winter wheat from each frame. Frequently, farm units may vary widely in size. Then we may stratify further the farm units growing winter wheat in each frame by size and take a stratified random sample from each frame. These are two of the ways nationwide surveys in industry and agriculture may combine stratified and cluster sampling techniques.

Chapter 5 Sample Design and Estimation

As pointed out earlier, such complex sample designs introduce no new principles of statistical estimation. However, estimation formulas and computational procedures are more complicated than in simple random sampling. And the task of preparing an optimal sample design is not easy.

PROBLEMS

Group One

14.1. For each situation, indicate whether you consider the mean or proportion an appropriate estimator for determining sample size. Defend your answer.
*(a) An opinion poll for forecasting the election of a political candidate in a two-way contest
*(b) A survey to collect information about the extent and composition of a magazine's readership when the standard deviation of the estimator is approximately known
(c) A public opinion poll on whether the president of the United States is handling our foreign policy satisfactorily when the standard deviation of the estimator cannot be known
(d) A survey to determine the extent of malnutrition among children in an underprivileged community with the standard deviation known approximately

14.2. A statistics instructor selects a simple random sample of 5 students from a class of 50. The mean height of the students in the sample is 68 inches. The instructor also asks one of the students to take a sample of 5 students who happen to enter the class session late. The mean height of the students in this sample is 69 inches. Both averages are point estimates of the parameter mean height of 50 students in the class. A later census of the class yields a population mean of 70 inches. Should we conclude that the sample mean of the sample the student selected is a better estimator of the population mean than the mean of the simple random sample? Explain why or why not.

*14.3. A sample of 10 chief executives in a given industry includes the following salaries in thousands of dollars:

| 75 | 120 | 95 | 115 | 132 |
| 92 | 133 | 87 | 102 | 99 |

Calculate the value of the estimator for the population's:
(a) Mean salary
(b) Standard deviation of salaries
(c) Proportion of salaries in excess of $100,000.

14.4. For a given degree of confidence, we can always decrease the tolerable error by increasing sample size. Why, then, can we not always specify the desired error and then draw the specified sample size?

*14.5. In what ways can we decrease the width of a confidence interval for estimating μ on the basis of the sample mean $\bar{x}$?

14.6. In each of the following situations, would you recommend a simple random, stratified, or cluster sample? Defend your answer.

Answers to asterisked (*) problems are appended.

Section 14 Sample Design   **169**

*(a) An estimate of the monthly average balance of "Now" checking accounts in a savings bank
(b) An estimate of the proportion of production workers in a factory who are in favor of the present management policy on overtime work
(c) A survey to estimate the number of vacant apartments in a city of 1 million inhabitants
(d) An estimate of the inventory of a department store
(e) An estimate of the fraction defective in a shipment of metal fasteners

*14.7. Vernon Westcott checks the quality of each shipment of supplies to Jenkins Memorial Hospital by inspecting 10 percent of the items, regardless of the size of each shipment. Do you think this is a sound sampling policy? Defend your answer.

14.8. Explain in your own words the condition under which an estimator is:
(a) Unbiased
(b) Consistent
(c) Efficient

14.9. Distinguish between:
(a) Confidence interval and degree of confidence
(b) Point estimate and interval estimate
(c) Stratified and cluster sampling

14.10. Identify the following terms:
(a) Sample fraction   (e) Confidence factor
(b) Optimal sample design   (f) Finite population correction
(c) Reduction factor   (g) Tolerable error
(d) Risk

Group Two

*14.11. Melany Curtis is manager of WBYH radio station. Melany wants to estimate the proportion of adult women who listen to a radio program, "Women Today." There is no way of knowing in advance the approximate value of the proportion. What is the required sample size of a 3 percent error and an 85 percent degree of confidence?

14.12. The management of MacCallum Farm Supplies wants to estimate the proportion of wheat seeds that fail to germinate in a standard test. Past experience in testing other seeds has shown that failures are not likely to exceed 10 percent. MacCallum is willing to run a 1 percent risk that the sample evidence would not exceed an error of 2 percentage points.
*(a) What is the required sample size?
(b) What is the required sample size for sampling a bag containing 10,000 uniformly mixed wheat seeds?

14.13. Orbis, a food processor, wishes to collect information about rice consumption. The decision parameter is the average monthly frequency (by households) of serving rice dishes. A tolerable error of .10 servings with a 10 percent risk for exceeding this error is considered sufficient. The standard deviation is roughly 2 servings per month.
*(a) How many households should be sampled for securing the required degree of precision?
(b) Would the fact that the population consists of 200,000 households change the sample size significantly? Explain why or why not.

(c) What additional information on rice consumption do you think the wholesaler would like to collect from the sampled households? List no more than six variables you consider important.

14.14. Shirley Shobeck plans to study the members of a professional organization, particularly the professional specialties. Although there are 200,000 members in the organization, some specialties may include as few as 100 individuals. Barry Wiles, Shirley's classmate, advises her to take a 5 percent simple random sample of the entire membership because of the analytical needs of the study.
(a) Do you agree with this advice? Explain why or why not.
(b) Would you recommend a simple random or a stratified random sample? Defend your answer.

14.15. Herrman Brothers, Inc., a men's clothing manufacturer, receives an order to make a special ceremonial shirt for each of the 1 million members of a fraternal organization. On large orders such as this one, it is a common practice to base production on measurements from a sample rather than from each member. The neck perimeter is considered the decision parameter; it usually requires a 99.7 percent degree of confidence with a tolerable error of only .01 inch. The population is approximately normally distributed with a 3-inch range in neck perimeter, from 15 to 17 inches inclusive.
(a) Find the required sample size.
(b) Suppose the organization has only 100,000 members. What should the sample size be then?
(c) Find the sample size if the tolerable error is changed from .01 to .10 inch.
(d) What conclusions can you reach from the answers about sample size?

14.16. Heritage Foods, Inc., plans to conduct a survey about household food expenditures in a large city. The average annual household food expenditure is considered to be the decision parameter. A sample of 25 households discloses a range of $2000 expenses on food.
(a) What is the required sample size for a $10 tolerable error and 5 percent risk?
(b) What is the tolerable error if management can afford a sample on 1000 households only and insists on the same 5 percent risk?
(c) What is the risk associated with a sample of 1000 households if management does not wish to change the initial $10 error?

SECTION 15/ SAMPLE SELECTION; ESTIMATING A MEAN

Suppose we have determined the sample size of our study on the basis of the stated criteria for an optimal sample design. Now it is time to revisit sample selection in order to discuss some complications in the selection process. This section is devoted to the estimation procedure, that is, the construction of confidence interval estimates. In particular, we discuss estimation of a mean with large as well as with small samples. Estimation of a proportion is handled in the next section.

Sample Selection Revisited

Earlier, we illustrated how to select a random or probability sample from a complete frame. At that time, our main objective was to illustrate random selection in order to draw a clear distinction between random error and procedural bias. Here, we discuss complications in the sampling procedure and systematic sampling.

Sample drawing requires some method of uniquely identifying each elementary unit in a frame. Occasionally, this is not a problem since the units to be sampled may be already prenumbered. Then sample selection is greatly simplified because the time-consuming task of assigning serial numbers to the elementary units of the frame is eliminated.

Frequently, however, the elementary units of a population are not prenumbered. Even if they are prenumbered, random selection of a large sample is time-consuming. Under certain conditions *systematic sampling* offers a time-saving and flexible alternative to simple random sampling. The method consists of selecting every kth elementary unit from the frame, where k is the ratio of population size N to sample size n, that is, $k = N/n$. Usually, systematic sampling begins with a random start, that is, we select the starting unit at random from the first k units and then we select every kth unit.

Example 15.1

The student government of a college plans to collect information about the views of students on certain current issues affecting campus life; a list (frame) consisting of 1875 student names is readily available from the registrar's office; a sample of 125 students is considered sufficient for the objectives of the study. We may assign serial numbers to the names in the list and take a simple random sample. Or we may avoid assigning serial numbers by drawing a systematic sample with a random start. Since k is equal to $1875/125 = 15$, we select at random the first unit from the first 15 names of the list. Suppose the 3rd name is selected. Then the 3rd, 18th, 33rd, and so forth names of the list would be included in the sample.

Systematic sampling may yield results similar to those obtained from simple random sampling. In the above illustration, selection of 125 student names is equiprobable with a probability $125/1875$ or $1/15$, which is an underlying requirement of simple random sampling. But the method should be used with caution to avoid complications and possible procedural bias.

First, systematic sampling requires more careful screening of the frame than simple random sampling. For example, in simple random sampling ineligible or duplicate elementary units may be treated as blanks without affecting sample size or equiprobable selection. This is not so with systematic sampling.

If the frame contains a given proportion of ineligible elementary units, systematic selection will yield a sample proportionately smaller than the required size. The shortfall may be corrected by adjusting the k selection interval.

Example 15.2

Consider Example 15.1. Suppose only 3/4 of the students in the list of 1875 are presently enrolled in courses. The remaining students are away on field work assignments and cannot be reached in time for the survey. A k interval of 15 will yield a sample 1/4 smaller than the required sample of 125 student names. Substitution of available for unavailable students is *not* appropriate. Instead, the sampling k interval is adjusted to

$$k = \frac{3}{4} \times 15 = \frac{45}{4}$$

From the first 45 names in the list we select 4 at random, use them as starting points, and take every 45th unit thereafter. Suppose we select randomly the 3rd, 10th, 25th, and 40th units. Then the sample consists of the starting units and the 48th, 55th, 70th, 85th, and so forth units of the list.

Also, the presence of duplicate units may destroy equiprobable selection. Special techniques may be used to cope with the bias arising from duplicate units. The simplest method is the removal of all duplicate units from the list before sampling.

Second, systematic sampling is akin to simple random sampling on the condition that the units in the frame occur in a random fashion. A Bernoulli or a Poisson process ideally meets the random-order condition. For most practical purposes, even units arranged in a particular sequence may be considered to form a reasonably appropriate frame as long as the sequence is not correlated with the unit characteristic under study. For example, in using an alphabetical list of telephone subscribers to study their vacation patterns, it may be reasonable to assume that alphabetical order is unrelated to vacation patterns.

The presence of a trend related to studied characteristics violates the random-order condition. For example, suppose the telephone subscribers are arranged in order from the highest to lowest income. Since income may be related to vacation patterns, systematic sampling may yield results similar to those obtained from proportionate stratified sampling.

Systematic sampling may prove to be particularly inappropriate if the population contains a periodic or cyclical pattern. Every 10th card in the card files of production workers in a factory may represent a foreman. A housing development may contain, at regular intervals, corner houses with market value higher than the value of a typical house. The last name of persons of various ethnic or national origin may create distinct periodic patterns in an alphabetical list. In all these cases and many more, systematic sampling of intervals coinciding with existing periodicity would certainly yield biased results. The risk of procedural bias is particularly serious since the sample itself may give no sign that periodicity is present. Thus, before sampling systematically, we must make sure that (1) the population to be sampled does not contain periodic patterns; and (2) the sampling interval is not a multiple or submultiple of the period. In case of doubt and as an added protection, instead of a random start we may select at random from each k sampling interval, that is, a *systematic random sample.*

Estimation with Large Samples

Statistical estimation is part of the analysis stage in planning and executing a sampling study. Intermediate steps between sample drawing and estimation such as field work and data processing are related to problems of procedural bias rather

Section 15 Sample Selection; Estimating a Mean

than statistical error. Let us assume that such steps have been carried out successfully and the sample information has been collected. Thus we can focus on the subject at hand, namely, statistical inference.

Recall that we have already utilized elements of statistical estimation in Section 14. But the purpose was not estimation; the error and risk of a hypothetical interval estimate were used *prior to sampling* and with approximately known population standard deviation for the sole purpose of determining sample size. We are now considering construction of actual interval estimates based *entirely on sample information*.

Also, we have already discussed point estimation in connection with the selection of "good" estimators. We pointed out that the sample mean and proportion may be considered the "best" point estimates of the corresponding parameters. Here, we shall deal with the construction of an actual interval estimate for the mean of a finite population.

We have already explained the rationale of interval estimation. Now, we wish to construct a confidence interval for estimating an unknown population mean μ on the basis of sample information. Such an interval may be defined as*

(15.1) $$\bar{x} \pm z s_{\bar{x}}$$

where $\bar{x}$ = sample mean
z = standard normal deviate representing degree of confidence
$s_{\bar{x}}$ = an estimate of standard error $\sigma_{\bar{x}}$ defined as

(15.2) $$s_{\bar{x}} = \frac{s}{\sqrt{n}}$$

When the sample fraction n/N is greater than 5 percent, $s_{\bar{x}}$ in (15.2) is multiplied by the fpc $\sqrt{(N-n)/(N-1)}$.

Example 15.3

In our household survey for a shopping center, we found that we need a sample of 487 households from a population of 5000 households to obtain the required precision (Example 14.3). Suppose the sample results are $\bar{x} = \$16,500$ and $s = \$8500$.

---

*In order to simplify notation, formula (15.1) has replaced the cumbersome form

$$\bar{x} - z s_{\bar{x}} \leq \mu \leq \bar{x} + z s_{\bar{x}}$$

This form is a generalization of expression (14.6) for any z value and when the population standard deviation σ is not known.

According to formula (15.2),

$$s_{\bar{x}} = \frac{8500}{\sqrt{487}} \sqrt{\frac{5000 - 487}{5000 - 1}}$$

$$= \$366$$

The fpc is included because the sample fraction 487/5000 is greater than 5 percent. Since the value of z reflects the risk we are willing to tolerate as decision makers, its value used for determining sample size may remain the same for constructing an actual interval estimate. We set a degree of confidence of 99 percent, so z is 2.58; and, by formula (15.1), the interval for the population mean μ is

$$16{,}500 \pm 2.58(366) = \$15{,}556 \text{ to } \$17{,}444$$

This interval may include the mean income of all 5000 households with 99 percent confidence.

What does this confidence interval mean? Suppose we repeat the above sampling procedure a large number of times and with each sample we construct an interval similar to the one shown in the example. Then 99 out of every 100 such intervals may include, on the average, the unknown true value of the population mean; only 1 out of every 100 such intervals may fail to include the population mean.

The standard error $s_{\bar{x}}$ was reduced by the fpc. This reduction factor is ignored in calculating $s_{\bar{x}}$ if the sample fraction n/N is less than 5 percent or if the population is infinite.

Example 15.4

Juddy Kidd is a new supervisor of Lopes Shoes Inc., which employs several salespersons. As part of evaluating a salesperson's performance, Juddy wants to construct an interval estimate of the average time required to service a customer. This interval for all salespersons may be used as a standard of comparison with the average time which a particular employee takes to service a customer.

Suppose a random sample of 100 observations results in an average of 15 minutes and a standard deviation of 4 minutes service time. An interval estimate with a 90 percent degree of confidence was considered sufficient for serving the stated objective.

The statistical population is infinite because management wishes to estimate the average service time of a process. So we ignore the fpc. Since s is 4 minutes and n is 100, the standard error of estimate by formula (15.2) is

$$s_{\bar{x}} = \frac{4}{\sqrt{100}} = .4 \text{ minute}$$

For 90 percent degree of confidence, the value of the z deviate is 1.65; it corresponds to half the 90 percent degree of confidence or exactly .4505 of the area under the normal curve in Appendix D. The sample mean $\bar{x}$ is

Section 15 Sample Selection; Estimating a Mean

15 minutes. This is a point estimate of the unknown parameter μ. So the desired interval estimate for the population μ by formula (15.1) is

$$15 \pm 1.65(.4) = 14.34 \text{ to } 15.66 \text{ minutes}$$

Juddy can be 90 percent confident that this interval may include the true average time of serving a customer.

It is important to realize that the standard error $s_{\bar{x}}$ is a point estimate of $\sigma_{\bar{x}}$ and hence it has a random error of its own. When σ must be estimated from statistic s, the normal distribution yields approximate confidence intervals.

For most practical purposes, however, the normal distribution is a reasonable approximation when the sample size is equal to or greater than 30 observations. The theoretically appropriate model is another distribution which we introduce next.

Estimation with Small Samples: the *t* Distribution

The normal Z deviate (Eq. 13.4) is based on a single random variable, the sample mean $\bar{x}$, and a constant, its *known* standard deviation σ. When the population standard deviation σ is not known, construction of a confidence interval involves *two random variables,* the sample mean $\bar{X}$ *and* the sample standard deviation s. So ratio $\bar{X}/s_{\bar{x}}$ represents a new random variable called *t statistic;* it is defined as

$$(15.3) \qquad \boxed{t = \frac{\bar{X} - \mu}{s_{\bar{x}}}}$$

and it requires the use of another probability model, the *t distribution*. Note the analogy between the Z deviate and the t statistic. Both express the values of a sample mean in standard deviation units of its error. Nevertheless, there are important differences between these two standard random variables and their corresponding probability models:

1. The Z deviate represents a ratio of a single random variable $\bar{X}$ and a constant $\sigma_{\bar{x}}$, the value of mean $\bar{X}$ is calculated from the drawn sample, while $\sigma_{\bar{x}}$ is obtained from σ, which is assumed to be known. The t statistic, on the other hand, represents a ratio of two random variables $\bar{X}$ and $s_{\bar{x}}$, both calculated from the selected sample.
2. Unlike the normal distribution, the t distribution assumes that a sample is obtained from a normally distributed population. In practice, however, the t distribution may be used for a sample obtained from a population which is not highly skewed.
3. When σ is not known, the t distribution is the theoretically correct model for constructing a confidence interval irrespective of sample size. In practice the use of this model is limited to a sample of fewer than 30 observations. For larger samples, the normal distribution is used as a reasonable approximation to the t distribution. So a sample size of 30 observations is a conventional line of demarcation separating the use of the t distribution from the use of the normal distribution.

4. Until this point, we denoted random variables with capital letters: X, X, P, Z, and S. The t distribution signals a break in this notation.

The probability distribution of the t statistic* is specified by a single parameter: the *number of degrees of freedom* $n - 1$, abbreviated to df. From the mathematical standpoint the number of degrees of freedom is the parameter whose value specifies a particular t distribution. But what is the explanation that df equals $n - 1$? In defining the t statistic in formula (15.3), we used $n - 1$ as divisor to calculate the sample standard deviation s. So $n - 1$ may be interpreted to represent the number of deviations of n observations from their sample mean $\bar{x}$ which can be independently determined in calculating s. The nth deviation is not independent, that is, not freely determined; it is determined by the condition that the sum of the n deviations must equal zero.

It is important to realize that while there is one standard normal distribution, the normal curve, the t distribution model specifies one distribution for each value of the parameter df. The graphs of three such t distributions are shown in Fig. 15.1.

Note that each t distribution is continuous, unimodal, bell-shaped, and symmetrical. However, for a small sample size, the standard deviation of a t distribution is considerably greater than the standard deviation of the normal distribution. For example, when df $= 1$, that is, when the sample size is 2, the graph of the t distribution is spread out with considerably more area under both tails than the normal curve. The greater standard deviation is justified because the use of the random variable s rather than the known constant σ introduces a degree of uncertainty not present in the normal distribution. Furthermore, for a small n the divisor $n - 1$ for calculating s becomes significantly small, which increases the standard error $s_{\bar{x}}$. As the sample size n increases, the standard deviation of the t distribution approaches the standard deviation of the normal distribution. It can be proved that as df approaches infinity as a limit, that is, df $\to \infty$, the t distribution and the normal curve are identical, as shown in Fig. 15.1.

Since there is a different t distribution for each sample size, each distribution

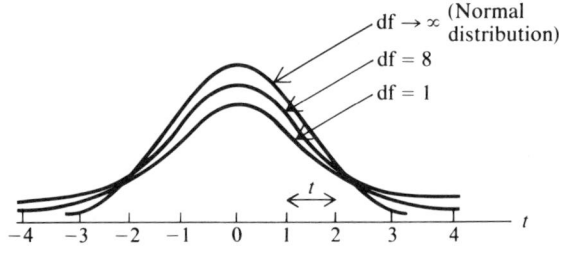

Figure 15.1.
Comparison of the t distribution for df $=$ 1 and df $=$ 8 and the normal distribution.

*The t distribution is also known as *Student's t distribution*. The term originated from the early work on the subject carried out by W. S. Gossett while an employee of Guinness Brewery in Dublin, Ireland. The management prohibited publication of research findings under an employee's name, so Gossett published his exciting discovery under the pseudonym of "Student."

Section 15 Sample Selection; Estimating a Mean

requires a separate table of areas similar to the one for the normal curve. In order to obtain compactness while serving our purpose, only a selected number of t values and their corresponding proportion of area (probability) for different t distributions are shown in Appendix E. The first and the last columns contain the number of degrees of freedom so that each row represents the t values of a different t distribution. Subsequent column headings show the proportion of area (probability) under the right-hand tail of the curve which falls beyond the specified t value in each distribution. Consider a sample size of 11 observations: df is $11 - 1$ or 10, so row 10 contains our t distribution. For an area of .01 under the right tail of the curve, the value of the t statistic is $+2.764$. In other words, in a t distribution with 10 degrees of freedom the probability is .01 that t is greater than $+2.764$.

As in the case of the normal curve, we can use Appendix E to construct a confidence interval for an unknown population mean μ defined as

(15.4) $$\boxed{\bar{x} \pm ts_{\bar{x}}}$$

Example 15.5

Let us consider again the case of the National Physical Laboratory in Britain using atomic clocks to estimate the true Universal Mean Time (UMT). Suppose appropriations allow the installation of only 25 atomic timepieces. During the last second of an hour, the 25 atomic clocks show an average of 1,000,002 microseconds and a standard deviation of 6 microseconds. Again we may wish to construct a confidence interval with 99 percent degree of confidence, exactly the confidence used to determine the original sample size (Example 14.1).

Since the sample is less than 30 observations and assuming a normal population, we use the t distribution. For $n = 25$, df is $24 = 25 - 1$. The risk is .005. We obtain this value by subtracting the 99 percent degree of confidence from 1 and dividing the difference by 2, that is, $(1 - .99)/2 = .005$, because we are interested in both tails of the t distribution. For 24 degrees of freedom and .005 risk on each tail the value of t from Appendix E is $+2.797$.

Since we deal with an infinite population, we ignore the fpc in formula (15.2) and $s_{\bar{x}} = 6/\sqrt{25} = 1.2$ microseconds.

Substitution of these statistics in formula (15.4) yields an interval estimate for the population mean μ of

$$1{,}000{,}002 \pm 2.797(1.2) = 999{,}998.64 \text{ to } 1{,}000{,}005.36 \text{ microseconds}$$

This interval will include the true UMT with 99 percent confidence. The t distribution makes it possible to construct confidence intervals when the size of the obtainable sample is severely limited for a number of reasons. The cost of constructing a large sample of atomic clocks may be prohibitive; the rate of manufacturing oil tankers may be too slow for collecting a large sample; the self-destructive nature of space missiles limits the size of trial run samples; rare phenomena such as major volcano erruptions or nuclear reactor accidents represent small samples. Many experiments with people and animals in food processing, pharmacology, medicine, psychology, and education are carried out with small samples.

A Few Salient Points

In interpreting an interval estimate we should keep in mind the following:

1. The sample mean $\bar{x}$ is a point estimate of the population mean μ.
2. The value of the unknown population mean does not vary. According to our theory, the population mean is considered to be a constant, a fixed quantity which does not vary. It is the interval estimate which varies; it is based on the sample mean which is one of the possible values of the random variable $\bar{X}$; as such the sample mean and its interval estimate are subject to random sample variation.
3. But once a sample is taken, the sample mean calculated, and an interval estimate constructed, this interval is no longer subject to random variation. Hence, such an interval is not a probability statement; it is referred to as a *confidence interval* and the confidence area under the normal curve as the *degree of confidence* assigned to the interval. The lower and upper values of a confidence interval are called *lower limit* and *upper limit*, respectively.
4. A statement such as "The population mean will fall in the interval 95 percent of the time" incorrectly interprets the meaning of an interval estimate; such a statement implies that the population mean varies rather than the interval. A correct interpretation would require a statement such as "We are 95 percent confident that the interval will include the true population mean."
5. The interpretation of an interval estimate for the population mean we presented here applies to estimating the population proportion as well as other parameters.

PROBLEMS

Group One

15.1. Consider drawing a sample of 10 numbers from integers 001 to 100.
  *(a) List the 10 sampled numbers beginning with a number 007 as a random start and selecting every 10th number thereafter.
  *(b) In addition to random number 007, draw a systematic random sample for the 9 remaining elementary units. Use random number 2026 to locate a random start in Appendix A and read the required random numbers for each k sampling interval.
  (c) Discuss the results of the two systematic samples with respect to possible complications and procedural bias in systematic sampling.
15.2. In a frame of 2000 elementary units, 1/3 of them are considered unsuitable for the purpose of a study. Suppose you are asked to select a systematic sample of 100 units without discarding the unsuitable units.

Answers to asterisked (*) problems are appended.

Section 15 Sample Selection; Estimating a Mean

    *(a) Determine the interval which may secure the required sample size.
    (b) Illustrate how such a systematic sample may be drawn.

*15.3. What happens if a population size N is not an integral multiple of interval k? One method of selecting a systematic sample is to consider the population list to be circular, choose a random start from 1 to N, and add an integral interval k nearest to ratio N/n until a sample of n units are selected, going to the end of the list and continuing from the beginning. Use this method to draw a systematic sample of 10 units when the population N is 82 units. Assume that the 50th unit in the list is your random start.

15.4. Find the value of the t statistic for each of the following sets of sample size and degree of confidence:
  *(a) $n = 11$, 95 percent   (c) $n = 7$, 80 percent
  (b) $n = 15$, 98 percent   (d) $n = 21$, 90 percent

15.5. For each sample size n, find the probability of each specified value of the t statistic:
  *(a) $n = 16$, $t \geq +2.602$ (c) $n = 26$, $t \geq +1.708$
  (b) $n = 16$, $t \leq -2.602$ (d) $n = 26$, $-1.708 \geq t \geq +1.708$

15.6. Discuss in your own words important differences between the Z deviate and the t statistic.

15.7. Distinguish between:
  (a) Systematic sampling and systematic random sampling
  (b) Standard errors $\sigma_{\bar{x}}$ and $s_{\bar{x}}$
  (c) Confidence interval and degree of confidence.
  (d) Upper limit and lower limit of confidence.

15.8. The student government in Mendlay College takes a survey using a simple random sample of 100 students. From their response a 95 percent confidence interval of average income between $650 and $700 is constructed as an interval estimate of mean income for all the students in the college. Which of the following statements interprets correctly the meaning of this confidence interval?
  (a) Ninety-five percent of all the college students have an income between $650 and $700.
  (b) Of all possible sample means obtained from samples drawn from the same student population, 95 percent of such means will fall in the stated interval.
  (c) The population mean will fall in the interval 95 percent of the time.
  (d) Ninety-five percent of intervals constructed from all possible simple random samples of size 100 drawn from the same population will contain the population mean.

15.9. Explain the statement "Interval estimation enables us to be precise, yet vague."

15.10. A confidence interval estimate can be either correct or wrong. Explain how chance enters the construction of such a statement.

Group Two

15.11. Eaton Aircraft, Inc., a manufacturer of aircraft parts, wants to estimate the average shearing strength of a certain type of weld. Since the test is self-destructive, testing is limited to a sample of 20 welds. The sample yields a mean strength of 800 pounds and a standard deviation of 30 pounds. Construct a 95 percent confidence interval of the mean shearing strength of weldings.

15.12. Orbis, a food processor, wishes to estimate the average monthly frequency of serving rice dishes by households. A sample of 400 households yields an average monthly frequency of 8 servings, with a standard deviation of 1.9 servings per household.

*(a) Construct a 90 percent confidence interval estimate of monthly servings.

(b) If the sample design was based on a population standard deviation of 2 servings per month, has the planned statistical precision, as measured by the standard error of estimate, been achieved?

15.13. Herman Brothers Inc., a men's clothing manufacturer, receives an order to make a special ceremonial shirt for each of the 1 million members of a fraternal organization. Since the neck perimeter is considered the decision parameter, management decides to base manufacturing of the shirt on the average neck perimeter of a random sample of 225 members. The sample yields an average perimeter of 15.5 inches, with a standard deviation of .4 inch.

*(a) Construct a 99.7 percent confidence interval estimate for the average neck perimeter of all the members.

(b) Suppose the parameter mean neck perimeter is 16 inches. Interpret the interval you have constructed.

15.14. Heritage Foods, Inc. takes a sample of 900 households from a large city. The sample yields an average annual food expenditure of $3000 per household with a standard deviation of $400.

(a) Construct a 95 percent confidence interval estimate of the average household expenditure for food in the city.

(b) Construct a 95 percent confidence interval for the same estimate assuming a population of 4500 households.

15.15. An actuary at Freedom Mutual Insurance Company wishes to estimate the average dollar value of claims arising from fire in tenement housing in a city. Last year there were 16 claims averaging $45,572 each with a $12,356 standard deviation. Assuming the sample is random:

(a) Construct a 90 percent confidence interval estimate of the average dollar value per claim.

(b) What assumption should you make about the shape of the population for this estimate? Explain in detail.

SECTION 16 / ESTIMATING A PROPORTION

Estimating a proportion is analogous to estimating a mean both with respect to interval construction and interpretation. Yet the subject deserves separate treatment. A proportion applies to variables as well as to attributes; and unless the sample size is large, an exact confidence interval of a proportion is not symmetrical around its point estimate except when $\pi = .50$.

For this reason we first discuss interval estimation from large samples where application of the normal distribution is a satisfactory approximation. Then we concentrate on the construction of nonsymmetrical confidence intervals.

Section 16 Estimating a Proportion

Estimation with Large Samples

The confidence interval estimate of an unknown population proportion π is analogous to the interval of a mean (Eq. 15.1); it is defined as

(16.1)
$$p \pm zs_p$$

where p = sample proportion
z = standard normal deviate representing degree of confidence
s_p = an estimate of standard error σ_P defined as

(16.2)
$$s_p = \sqrt{\frac{p(1-p)}{n}}$$

multiplied by the fpc $\sqrt{(N-n)/(N-1)}$ when the sample fraction n/N is greater than 5 percent.

Example 16.1

The management of Alpha Inc., a manufacturer of toiletry products, decides to survey a sample of 351 out of 4000 regular users of Tend, a new allergy-free detergent. The sample shows that 60 percent of respondents like Tend because of its allergy-free feature. Construct a 95 percent confidence interval to estimate the population proportion.

Substitution of $p = .60$, $N = 4000$, and $n = 351$ in formula (16.2) yields

$$s_p = \sqrt{\frac{(.60)(1-.60)}{351}} \sqrt{\frac{4000-351}{4000-1}}$$
$$= .025$$

Note that the value of s_p is multiplied by the fpc because the sample fraction 351/4000 is greater than 5 percent. For 95 percent degree of confidence, z is 1.96 and, by formula (16.1), the interval for the population proportion π is

$$.60 \pm 1.96(.025) = .551 \text{ to } .649$$

So we are 95 percent confident that between 55.1 and 64.9 percent of all the 4000 users of Tend prefer the product because of its allergy-free feature.

In cases where the population is infinite or the sample fraction n/N is less than 5 percent, the fpc is ignored. So estimating a proportion is analogous to estimating a mean in many respects except one. A confidence interval of a proportion is not symmetrical around its point estimate except when $\pi = .50$. But lack of symmetry decreases as sample size increases. For large samples such as the one in our illustration, lack of symmetry is negligible so that a symmetrical interval with the normal curve is a good approximation to the true nonsymmetrical interval.

What is the smallest sample size necessary to construct a symmetrical inter-

Table 16.1
Minimum Sample Size for Using the Normal Approximation to Construct Symmetrical Intervals

If π Equals This Value:	Normal Approximation If n Equals at Least:
.50	30
.40 or .60	50
.30 or .70	80
.20 or .80	200
.10 or .90	600
.05 or .95	1400

Source: W. G. Cochran, *Sampling Techniques* (New York: John Wiley & Sons, 1953), p. 41. Reprinted by permission.

val using the normal approximation? Table 16.1 shows such sample sizes for certain values of parameter π. Note two important points. First as π, or its complement $1 - \pi$, moves away from .50, indicating an increasingly skewed distribution, this minimal sample size increases. Second, if π is .50, the case of interval estimation for a proportion is analogous to that for the mean of a normally distributed population with n equal to or greater than 30, the conventional line of demarcation between small and large samples.

For constructing confidence intervals quickly, statisticians have prepared tables which indicate the percent error for a given value of p, a sample size n, and a specified degree of confidence. One such table for some values of p and n and 95 percent confidence is shown in Appendix F.

Example 16.1 (continued)

For the allergy-free detergent Tend the same confidence interval can be obtained from Appendix F. Since the complement of $p = .60$ is $.40 = 1 - .60$, we look under column .40 and row n equal to 350. The error e is .051. Because the sample fraction is $351/4000 = .088$ or greater than 5 percent, we reduce the error by the fpc:

$$e = .051 \sqrt{\frac{4000 - 351}{4000 - 1}} \simeq .049$$

The interval for the population proportion π is

$$.60 \pm .049 = .551 \text{ to } .649$$

as found earlier.

Tables such as the one in Appendix F are a great convenience because many sampling studies require construction of several confidence intervals for different values of p as well as n. In addition, the same table can be used to find the approximate sample size for a simple random sample without the use of formulas.

Section 16 Estimating a Proportion

Example 16.2

In estimating the proportion of overloaded trucks (Example 14.2), we found that the chief of State Highway Patrol needed to inspect 683 trucks. This sample was determined on the basis of a 3 percent error, an assumed .20 proportion π, and a 95 percent degree of confidence. Under column p equal to .20 in Appendix F we locate the error of 3 percent, and read the sample size from the leftmost column; it is 700, which is close to 683 trucks found earlier by formula.

Estimation with Nonsymmetrical Confidence Intervals

For greater accuracy or for samples smaller than the sizes specified in Table 16.1, the normal curve may not be considered a satisfactory approximation for constructing confidence intervals. One method for determining accurate confidence intervals is by means of a chart such as the one in Fig. 16.1. Observe that for each sample size there are two curves, one for the upper limit and another for the lower limit of confidence. The two curves of a given sample size specify a band which

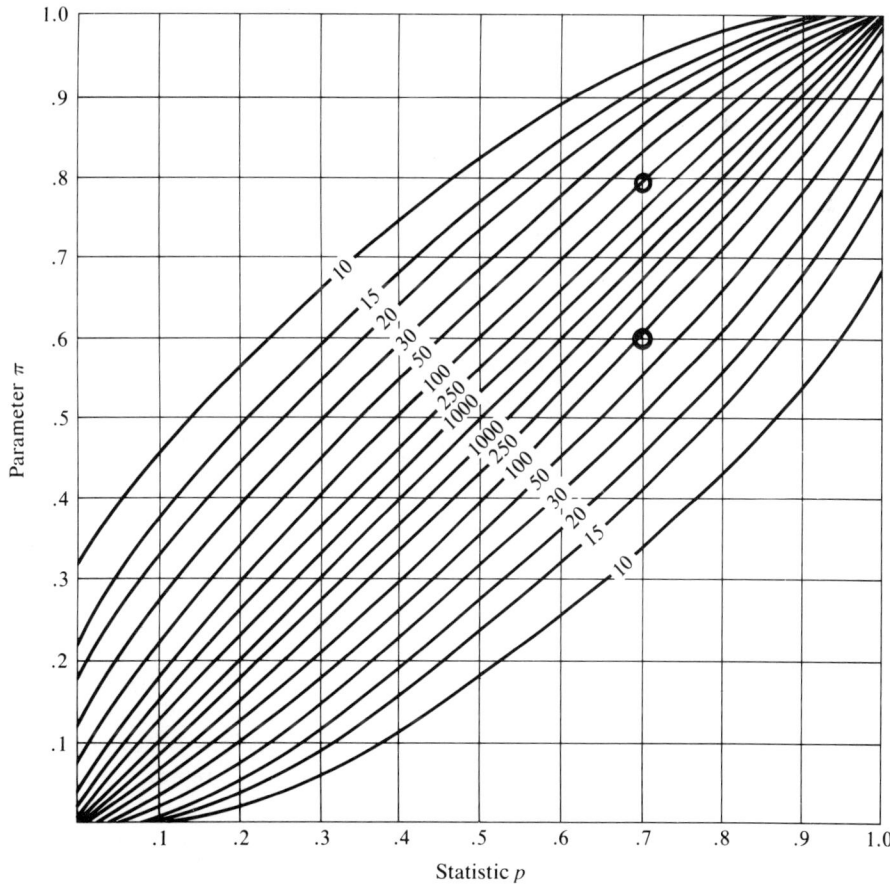

Figure 16.1. Ninety-five percent nonsymmetrical confidence intervals for selected sample sizes. *Source:* C. J. Clopper and E. S. Pearson, "The Use of Confidence or Fiducial Limits in the Case of the Binomial," *Biometrika*, vol. 26 (1934), p. 410. Reprinted by permission.

184   Chapter 5   Sample Design and Estimation

represents a 95 percent confidence interval on the vertical scale of the chart. Also, note that the lower limit of each confidence band converges to zero while the upper limit does not. This is consistent with common sense. If, for instance, there are no clam diggers in the United States, that is, if $\pi = 0$, then any sample statistic p must be zero since no sample of individuals can include clam diggers. On the other hand, if a sample of individuals does not include clam diggers, that is, if $p = 0$, then we cannot necessarily infer that the United States has no clam diggers, that is, that π is also zero. For a given statistic p, the larger the sample is, the narrower the band or interval. Charts for 99 percent, as well as for other degrees of confidence, can easily be constructed.

The following comparison between approximate symmetrical and exact non-symmetrical confidence intervals make the point clearer.

Example 16.3

National Mills, a manufacturer of cereals, wants to determine the proportion of children favoring Trick or Treat, the company's leading cold cereal, over a similar product of a major competitor. A sample of 100 children is randomly selected. Each child is given three boxes of Trick or Treat designated as Brand X and three boxes of the competing cereal designated as Brand Y; otherwise all six boxes are identical in appearance. Half of the sample is randomly assigned to start with Brand X and the other half with Brand Y. Parents are asked to alternate the remaining boxes of the two brands and serve the cereals for a period not to exceed 3 months. Also, they are asked to rate the children's reactions to each brand on a scale of 1 to 10. The brand with the highest score would be considered the preferred product. Seventy percent of the children in the sample rate brand X as the preferred product. Management wants to construct a 95 percent confidence interval for the proportion of the child population which prefer Trick or Treat.

We can find the approximate symmetrical interval from Appendix F. The sample proportion .70 is larger than .50 and therefore it is not shown in the appended table. We can obtain the same error from the proportion, .30, of the complementary event. This is .09, which is located at the intersection of column .30 and sample size 100. So the approximate confidence interval for the population proportion π is

$$.70 \pm .09 = .61 \text{ to } .79$$

We are 95 percent confident that between 61 to 79 percent of the child population prefer Trick or Treat.

The exact nonsymmetrical confidence interval is read from Fig. 16.1. We first locate the points (small circles) where the vertical line originating from p equal to .70 on the horizontal scale cuts the two curves for n equal to 100. Then through each point we draw an imaginary line perpendicular to the vertical scale. The limits, representing the intersection of these lines with the vertical scale, are approximately .60 and .78; so the interval for the population proportion π is .60 to .78. Between 60 to 78 percent of the children in the population prefer Trick or Treat.

Section 16 Estimating a Proportion

The difference between the above two estimates is not too large because the sample size of 100 is greater than the minimal required size of 80 for a normal approximation shown in Table 16.1 for p equal to .70. But consider the following case.

Example 16.4

MCA is a manufacturer of television sets. To maintain product quality a sample of television tubes is checked with a test. Because the test is destructive, only a random sample of 20 tubes from a weekly output of 10,000 tubes is checked in order to keep sampling costs low. In a random sample of 20 tubes, 6 are found substandard. Construct a 95 percent confidence interval.

The fraction of defective tubes p is 6/20 or .30. (The fraction defective has been set unrealistically high to illustrate the point. In the real world a fraction defective is usually very small.) The exact nonsymmetrical confidence interval for the population proportion π from Fig. 16.1 is .12 to .56. The output of the week may contain between 12 percent to 56 percent substandard tubes with a 95 percent confidence. The interval is quite nonsymmetrical. The lower value of the interval is only .18 (.30 − .12) points below while the upper value is .26 (.56 − .30) points above $p = .30$, the point estimate.

It is important to realize that the line of demarcation between the use of an approximate symmetrical and an exact nonsymmetrical confidence interval is arbitrary. Which estimate should be used depends on the desired accuracy and the objectives of the study.

PROBLEMS

Group One

16.1. For each given value of statistic p, sample size n, and population N, construct a 95 percent symmetrical confidence interval using formula (16.1). Verify the result using Appendix F.
  *(a) $p = .20$, $n = 500$, and N very large
  *(b) $p = .30$, $n = 900$, and $N = 6000$
  (c) $p = .75$, $n = 200$, and N very large
  (d) $p = .60$, $n = 600$, and $N = 4000$

16.2. Use Appendix F to determine the approximate sample size for each specified value of π, error e, a very large population, and an interval with 95 percent degree of confidence:
  *(a) $\pi = .45$ and $e = 6.2$ percent   (c) $\pi = .35$ and $e = 3.4$ percent
  (b) $\pi = .65$ and $e = 4$ percent   (d) $\pi = .15$ and $e = 2.4$ percent

16.3. For each given value of statistic p, sample size n, and a very large population N, construct a 95 percent symmetrical confidence interval using formula (16.1).

Answers to asterisked (*) problems are appended.

Chapter 5 Sample Design and Estimation

Find the corresponding nonsymmetrical interval from Fig. 16.1 and compare results.
*(a) $p = .20$ and $n = 50$ (c) $p = .20$ and $n = 250$
(b) $p = .20$ and $n = 100$ (d) $p = .20$ and $n = 1000$

*16.4. A simple random sample of 100 university students includes no radicals. What interval estimate of the proportion of radicals in the student population of the university would you make with 95 percent degree of confidence? Use Fig. 16.1.

16.5. An army inspector finds no defective inner soles in a simple random sample of 30 inner soles. What interval estimate of the proportion of good inner soles in a large shipment should he make with 95 percent degree of confidence? Use Figure 16.1.

16.6. Distinguish between symmetrical and nonsymmetrical confidence intervals.

Group Two

*16.7. Two out of 10 Hawk missiles fail to place their payload of experimental instruments in a designated orbit. Construct a 95 percent confidence interval of the proportion of failing Hawk missiles. Use Fig. 16.1.

*16.8. One of the questions asked in a nationwide survey was: "Do you think it is in the best interest of our country to abolish political contributions larger than $50?" Seventy percent of a random sample of 2000 eligible voters answered yes. Construct a 95 percent confidence interval of voters who favor such a measure. Use Appendix F.

*16.9. A time study is conducted to determine the proportion of time an automobile assembly worker spends in unproductive activities during regular working hours. At a randomly selected instance an assembly worker is observed to determine if the worker is engaged in unproductive activity. During regular working hours of a month, 4000 random observations show that an assembly worker was engaged in unproductive activity 5 percent of the time. Construct a 95 percent confidence interval of the proportion spent on unproductive activity. Use Appendix F.

16.10. Dalton Integrated Circuits, Inc., receives a shipment of 1000 circuit assemblies. In a random sample of 100 circuit assemblies, 30 are found to be defective. Construct a 95 percent confidence interval of the fraction defective in the shipment. Use Appendix F.

16.11. Melany Curtis, manager of WBYH radio station, takes a random sample of 530 adult women in order to estimate, among other variables, the proportion who listen to the "Women Today" radio program. Thirty percent of the respondents said that they listen to the program at least once each week.
  (a) Construct an 85 percent confidence interval of the proportion of adult women who listen to the program.
  (b) Suppose error e for determining sample size was set at 4 percent. Was such an error achieved?

16.12. Hugh MacCullum II, the manager of MacCullum Farm Supplies, takes a random sample of 1000 wheat seeds which have been especially processed for distribution to farmers during the sowing season. A standard test shows that 9 percent of the seeds in the sample failed to germinate.
  (a) Construct a 95 percent confidence interval of the proportion of failing seeds in the process.
  (b) Suppose the sample was taken from a shipment containing 10,000 uniformly mixed wheat seeds. Construct a 95 percent confidence interval of the proportion of failing seeds in the shipment.

Section 16 Estimating a Proportion

16.13. A survey of 650 eligible voters in a town shows that 53 percent of the sampled residents favor candidate A for mayor.
   (a) Construct a 99 percent confidence interval of the proportion of voters who favor candidate A.
   (b) If this is a two-candidate contest and the one with more than 50 percent of the votes wins the race, is it certain that candidate A would win?

Chapter 6
HYPOTHESIS TESTING

In the preceding chapter we introduced *estimation* procedures. We now turn to *testing* procedures, the second branch of statistical inference. In testing, the sample evidence is the basis for deciding between two or more prestated alternatives. Although multiaction testing problems often arise in business, we concentrate on situations in which a decision maker has only two alternatives from which to choose.

These alternatives are formulated as two complementary assumptions about the true value of a decision parameter. For example, the mean household income of a shopping area will either be or not be $20,000; the allergy-free detergent Tend will either be or not be preferred by 30 percent of potential users; a process or a shipment of parts will either have more than 5 percent or have not more than 5 percent defective parts; a new training program will either raise labor productivity by at least 5 units per hour or it will not. These complementary assumptions are called *hypotheses*.

The procedure for formulating these hypotheses and using sample evidence to decide which should be "accepted" is called a *hypothesis test* or a *significance test*. Thus in hypothesis testing, unlike in estimating, we *assume* certain values of the decision parameter before sampling and decide on their validity on the basis of sample evidence.

In the first section of this chapter, we deal with procedures for testing a single population mean or proportion. The second section covers procedures for testing the difference of two population means or proportions.

SECTION 17 / TESTING A SINGLE PARAMETER

First, we introduce the basic concepts and the testing procedure with a case. Second, we summarize the testing procedure for different types of testing problems. Third, we elaborate on the two types of risks involved in testing. Finally, we show how to determine the sample size which controls both risks at prespecified levels.

Chapter 6 Hypothesis Testing

Basic Concepts

We focus on a case for introducing the general structure of a hypothesis-testing problem and the required terminology. This introductory material facilitates a systematic presentation of the subject for the entire chapter.

Example 17.1

Paxwell House Inc. markets roasted ground coffee in vacuum-sealed cans of 16 ounces net weight. Management cannot be positive that each can will contain exactly 16 ounces of coffee. Although the net weight may be 16 ounces on the average, the weight of each can may vary from this average because of random as well as assignable nonrandom factors affecting the coffee-canning process. Managements's goal is to see that the process mean μ remains at 16 ounces net weight of coffee.

We may make two complementary assumptions about the natural state of the canning process. We may assume that the process is in control, that is, the process mean μ is indeed 16 ounces of ground coffee. This is called the *null hypothesis* and is denoted by H_0. Or we may assume that the process is out of control, that is, mean μ is other than 16 ounces of ground coffee. This is called the *alternative hypotheses* and is denoted by H_1. The null and the alternative hypotheses about the natural state of the canning process are shown in Table 17.1.

On the basis of sample evidence, we may consider two alternative decisions. We may leave the canning process alone or take remedial action. Either course of action may lead to a correct decision. We may leave the process alone when the null hypothesis is true, that is, μ is 16 ounces. Or we may take remedial action when the alternative hypothesis is true, that is, μ is not 16 ounces.

However, the same two courses of action may also lead to an incorrect decision. We may leave the process alone when the null hypothesis is false, that is, μ is not 16 ounces. This incorrect decision of *accepting a false null hypothesis* is called *Type II error*. Or we may take remedial action when the null hypothesis is true, that is, μ is 16 ounces. This incorrect decision of *rejecting a true null hypothesis* is called *Type I error*. The probabilities for Type I and Type II errors are called *error probabilities* α (Greek letter *alpha*) and β (Greek letter *beta*), respectively, or α risk and β risk.

Example 17.1 (continued)

Paxwell's management is most anxious to avoid committing Type I error, that is, taking remedial action when the process is indeed in control: workers remain idle while the process is studied in order to discover the cause of

Table 17.1. States of Nature and Decision Alternatives in a Hypothesis-Testing Procedure

Decision Alternative	State of Nature	
	H_0: μ = 16 ounces	H_1: $\mu \neq$ 16 ounces
Accept H_0 (Leave process alone)	Correct decision $1 - \alpha$ = .99	Incorrect decision Type II: β = .05
Reject H_0 (Take remedial action)	Incorrect decision Type I: α = .01	Correct decision $1 - \beta$ = .95

excessive variability in the net weight of cans; stopping the process may create serious delays in delivery schedules; roasted coffee may lose its aroma and taste unless it is vacuum-canned immediately after it is roasted and ground. Such consequences are considered to be so serious that management sets error probability α as low as .01. This means that, on the average, in only 1 out of every 100 random samples of size n shall we erroneously stop the process and take remedial action; in 99 out of every 100 random samples we shall infer correctly that the process is indeed in control. On the other hand, committing Type II error, that is, leaving the process alone although it needs remedial action, may not be considered as serious: management may be willing to assume the cost of some excessively overfilled cans; consumer complaints about some excessively underfilled cans can be resolved at the retailer's level. Therefore, management is willing to set error probability β at .05. In other words, on the average, in 5 out of every 100 random samples of size n we shall fail to correct a process out of control; in 95 out of every 100 random samples we shall infer correctly that the process is indeed out of control and take remedial action.

Note that the two types of errors are opposites; when one occurs the other cannot occur. Occurrence of an error always depends on the existence of a particular state of nature: Type I error can occur *only if* the process mean μ is indeed 16 ounces, that is, if the null hypothesis is true; Type II error can occur *only if* the process mean μ is not 16 ounces, that is, if the null hypothesis is false. By convention, statisticians recognize as Type I error the error which the decision maker is most eager to avoid. Thus, stopping the canning process when it is in control represents Type I error because this is the wrong decision management is most eager to avoid.

The Hypothesis-Testing Procedure

Three major steps are required in carrying out a significance test: formulating the null and the alternative hypotheses, establishing a decision rule, and applying the decision rule to sample data. We may use our Paxwell House case to illustrate the testing procedure.

Example 17.1 (continued)

We can readily formulate the null and the alternative hypotheses from Table 17.1. Our assumptions about the natural state of the canning process are that either μ equals 16 ounces or it does not equal 16 ounces. Our hypotheses are

$$H_0: \mu = 16 \text{ ounces}$$
$$H_1: \mu \neq 16 \text{ ounces}$$

where μ denotes the mean net weight of roasted coffee per can when the canning process is in control. Sign $\neq$ denotes inequality.

Hypothesis testing is based on the *decision rule* we wish to establish. Such a rule partitions the sampling distribution of a statistic into two mutually exclusive regions of accepting or rejecting a null hypothesis; it is a guide which enables us

Chapter 6 Hypothesis Testing

to translate the sample result into action: to accept or to reject the null hypothesis shown in Table 17.1.

Example 17.1 (continued)

The decision parameter in our case is the mean μ of the canning process. For a sufficiently large sample and according to the central limit theorem, the sampling distribution of the random variable $\bar{X}$ of sample means will be normally distributed, as shown in Fig. 17.1. The region for accepting the null hypothesis is related to the interval within which the values of the random variable $\bar{X}$ fall with the desired .99 probability. The regions shown as shaded tails of the curve depict the error probability α of .01 which management is willing to assume. Since management is interested in excessively overfilled as well as excessively underfilled cans, half the error probability appears in each tail of the curve. The mean values of $\bar{x}_1^*$ and $\bar{x}_2^*$ set the limits on the magnitude of sample variability that management feels is consistent with accepting the null hypothesis.

Figure 17.1. Two-tailed test; sampling distribution of the mean with regions for accepting or rejecting a null hypothesis.

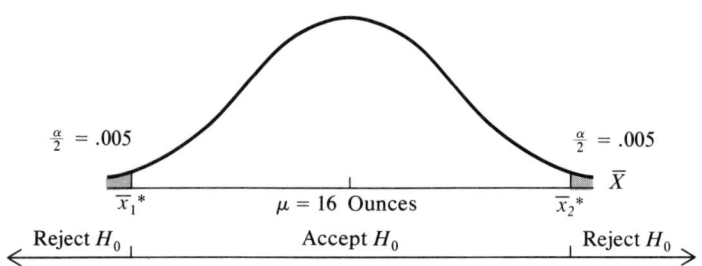

This procedure is called the *two-tailed* or *two-sided* test because the null hypothesis requires both tails of the normal distribution. The mean values $\bar{x}_1^*$ and $\bar{x}_2^*$ in Fig. 17.1 which separate the acceptance and rejection regions are commonly referred to as *critical values*. They are defined as*

(17.1)
$$\bar{x}_1^* = \mu - z_c \sigma_{\bar{x}}$$
$$\bar{x}_2^* = \mu + z_c \sigma_{\bar{x}}$$

where the standard error (Eq. 12.4) is

(17.2)
$$\sigma_{\bar{x}} = \frac{\sigma}{\sqrt{n}}$$

and z_c is the *critical value* of the Z deviate which corresponds to error probability α. For an observed sample mean $\bar{x}$, the decision rule may be expressed as follows:†

(17.3)
If $\bar{x}_1^* \leq \bar{x} \leq \bar{x}_2^*$, accept H_0
If $\bar{x} < \bar{x}_1^*$ or $\bar{x} > \bar{x}_2^*$, reject H_0

---
*Generalization of expression (14.6) for any z value and a known population standard deviation σ.
†We follow convention and include the equality sign ($\leq$) in the acceptance alternative of the decision rule. However, the convention is of little importance. Since the normal distribution is continuous, it is a matter of indifference whether the equality sign appears in either alternative of the decision rule.

Example 17.1 (continued)

For half the region of rejection, the error probability is $\alpha/2 = .01/2 = .005$ and the corresponding critical value z_c, obtained from Appendix D, is ± 2.58. (A plus-or-minus sign is required because we have a two-tailed test.) Let us assume that the sample size n is 100. It is known that the population standard deviation of the canning process σ is 2.0 ounces. Hence, by formula (17.2), the standard error is

$$\sigma_{\bar{x}} = \frac{2.0}{\sqrt{100}} = .20 \text{ ounce}$$

Substituting for $z_c = 2.58$, $\sigma_{\bar{x}} = .20$, and $\mu = 16$ in formula (17.1), we obtain the critical values:

$$\bar{x}_1^* = 16 - 2.58(.20) = 15.48 \text{ ounces}$$
$$\bar{x}_2^* = 16 + 2.58(.20) = 16.52 \text{ ounces}$$

According to (17.3), the decision rule is

If $15.48 \leq \bar{x} \leq 16.52$, accept H_0 (leave process alone)
If $\bar{x} < 15.48$ or $\bar{x} > 16.52$, reject H_0 (take remedial action)

In words, if the sample mean of 100 randomly selected cans is between 15.48 and 16.52 ounces, do not reject the null hypothesis and leave process alone; if the sample mean is less than 15.48 ounces or more than 16.52 ounces, reject the null hypothesis and take remedial action.

This decision rule and its application to sample evidence are portrayed in Fig. 17.2. The critical values outline the .99 region of accepting the null hypothesis in terms of the sample mean as well as z values. Other numbers in the diagram will be explained shortly.

Suppose a random sample of 100 cans yields a sample mean $\bar{x}$ of 15.80 ounces. Since the sample mean falls within the acceptance region, the null hypothesis is not rejected. We conclude that the process is in control; management should leave the process alone.

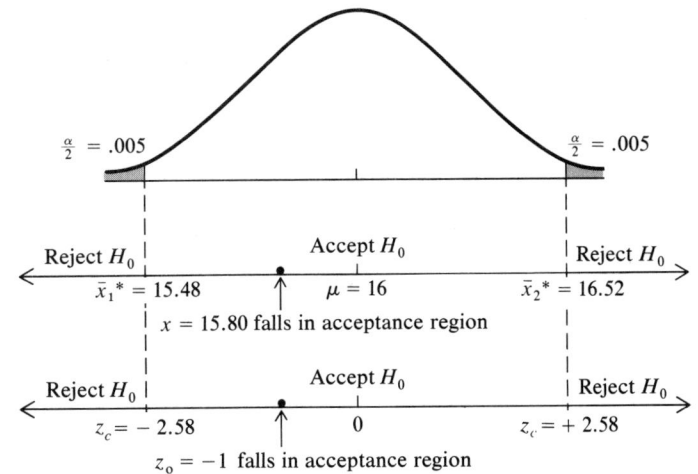

Figure 17.2. Two-tailed test; sampling distribution of the mean with regions for accepting or rejecting a null hypothesis.

Chapter 6 Hypothesis Testing

In other words, any variation of the sample mean $\bar{x}$ from μ that falls in the acceptance region is an event which we are willing to accept as occurring by chance alone. Such variation is consistent with the null hypothesis. The difference between the sample and the hypothesized parameter mean is attributed to random error. Hence, we do not reject the null hypothesis. Note that we either reject or not reject the null hypothesis. We cannot say that we accept the null hypothesis in the sense that we cannot really prove that the hypothesized parameter is exactly equal to the true parameter. Statisticians use the term *accept* the null hypothesis in order to avoid the awkwardness of a double negative. We shall follow convention and use the term *accept* while in fact we mean *not reject* the null hypothesis.

In statistical terminology, accepting a null hypothesis means that the sample statistic does not differ significantly from the assumed parameter. The test result is *not statistically significant*. If the sample mean in the Paxwell case were a value such as 15 ounces, it would have fallen in the rejection region in Fig. 17.2; we would have rejected the null hypothesis; we would have accepted the alternative hypothesis and concluded that the process is not in control. Such a conclusion would have been reached because a sample mean of 15 ounces or less occurs with a frequency of less than .01; this is less than Paxwell's management is willing to attribute to sample variability *if* the true parameter mean were 16 ounces. The sample statistic is inconsistent with the null hypothesis because it differs significantly from the hypothesized parameter: the test result is *statistically significant*. Type I error probability α is called the *level of significance*.

Instead of the critical values $\bar{x}_1^*$ and $\bar{x}_2^*$, the same testing procedure may be carried out in terms of z values with decision rule:

(17.4)
$$\text{If } -z_c \leq z_o \leq +z_c, \text{ accept } H_0$$
$$\text{If } z_o < -z_c \text{ or } z_o > +z_c, \text{ reject } H_0$$

Value z_o represents an *observed value* obtained from the sample data; it is defined as*

(17.5)
$$z_o = \frac{\bar{x} - \mu}{\sigma/\sqrt{n}}$$

where σ is known and n is sufficiently large (say, $n \geq 30$) to justify the use of the normal distribution.

Example 17.1 (continued)

Earlier, we found that the critical values $z_c = \pm 2.58$ correspond to .01 significance level. According to (17.4), the decision rule is

If $-2.58 \leq z_o \leq +2.58$, accept H_0 (leave process alone)
If $z_o < -2.58$ or $z_o > +2.58$, reject H_0 (take remedial action)

---

*Formula (13.4), where z_o and $\bar{x}$ are observed sample values of the corresponding random variables.

Substituting for a sample mean $\bar{x} = 15.80$ ounces and a known $\sigma = 2.0$ ounces in (17.5), we obtain

$$z_o = \frac{15.80 - 16}{2.0/\sqrt{100}} = -1$$

We accept the null hypothesis because the observed $z_o = -1$ falls in the acceptance region as shown in Fig. 17.2. The process is in control, as we concluded earlier. Management should leave the process alone.

It is important to realize that a confidence interval is the basis for testing *any* hypothesis. Consequently, we first discussed a two-tailed test in terms of critical values $\bar{x}_1^*$ and $\bar{x}_2^*$. This testing procedure established conceptual and logical continuity with statistical estimation. However, decision rule (17.3) cannot be constructed unless we know σ. On the other hand, decision rule (17.4) can, since its construction does not require the use of σ. Because rule (17.4) is less restrictive than rule (17.3), from now on we shall carry out tests for a mean in terms of z values.

One-Tailed Tests for a Mean

In Example 17.1 the management of Paxwell House is interested in whether or not the mean weight of the canning process remains at 16 ounces; excessively overfilled cans are as important as excessively underfilled ones. In other words, in problems of this kind we wish to know whether or not the hypothesized value of the tested parameter has *changed irrespective of the direction of change.* As mentioned earlier, problems such as the one in Example 17.1 give rise to *two-tailed* or *two-sided* tests.

In another type of problem, we may wish to know whether or not the tested parameter is *less than* or *more than* its hypothesized value. In other words, we are interested in the *direction the value of the tested parameter may have changed.* This type of problem gives rise to *one-tailed* or *one-sided* testing procedure.

Example 17.2

Paxwell House receives a very large order for roasted ground coffee from Continental Stores, a chain of supermarkets. In preparing the shipment Paxwell's production manager is most anxious to avoid the risk of holding the shipment while the mean net weight of coffee is at least 16 ounces. This problem requires a one-tailed test. The null hypothesis is "The shipment contains cans with a true mean of at least 16 ounces"; the alternative hypothesis is "The true mean is less than 16 ounces." Formally, the two hypotheses may be expressed as follows:

$$H_0: \mu \geq 16 \text{ ounces}$$
$$H_1: \mu < 16 \text{ ounces}$$

Suppose Paxwell's production manager is willing to assume a risk of 1 percent for rejecting the shipment with a true mean of at least 16 ounces. The two regions for accepting and rejecting the null hypothesis are portrayed in Fig. 17.3. For an α risk .01, the critical value z_c is -2.33, obtained

Figure 17.3.
Lower-tailed test; sampling distribution of the mean with regions for accepting or rejecting a null hypothesis.

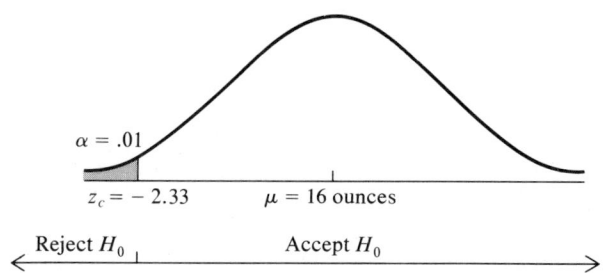

from Appendix D. (The minus sign is required because the rejection region represents the lower tail of the normal curve.)

In terms of z values the decision rule is

If $z_o \geq -2.33$, accept H_0 (ship order to Continental)
If $z_o < -2.33$, reject H_0 (hold order to Continental)

Since the rejection region represents the lower tail of the normal curve, the procedure is called a *lower-tailed* test. In general, for lower-tailed tests decision rule (17.4) is modified to

(17.6)
$$\boxed{\begin{array}{l} \text{If } z_o \geq -z_c, \text{ accept } H_0 \\ \text{If } z_o < -z_c, \text{ reject } H_0 \end{array}}$$

This analysis illustrates acceptance sampling which is widely used in practice. In cases such as this Type I error probability α is referred to as the *producer's risk;* Paxwell House, the producer, runs the risk of rejecting a good shipment. Type II error probability β is called the *consumer's risk;* Continental Stores, the consumer, runs the risk of receiving a bad shipment of excessively underfilled cans.

If the rejection region of a one-tailed test represents the upper tail of the normal curve, the procedure is called an *upper-tailed* test. By analogy to (17.6), the decision rule for such a test is

(17.7)
$$\boxed{\begin{array}{l} \text{If } z_o \leq z_c, \text{ accept } H_0 \\ \text{If } z_o > z_c, \text{ reject } H_0 \end{array}}$$

Example 17.3

The analysis in Example 17.2 was carried out from the viewpoint of the producer. Analysis of the same acceptance problem from the viewpoint of the consumer, Continental Stores, requires reversal of error probabilities α and β. Since Continental Stores is most eager to avoid receiving excessively

Section 17 Testing a Single Parameter

underfilled cans, the null hypothesis is "The shipment contains cans with a true mean equal to or less than 16 ounces of coffee"; the alternative hypothesis is that "The true mean is more than 16 ounces." Formally,

$$H_0: \mu \leq 16 \text{ ounces}$$
$$H_1: \mu > 16 \text{ ounces}$$

Now the error probability α is to reject a true null hypothesis and receive a bad shipment with excessively underfilled cans. Error probability β is to accept a false null hypothesis and refuse a good shipment. For the same .01 significance level, z_c is $+2.33$, obtained from Appendix D. (The plus sign is required because we deal with an upper-tailed test.) The acceptance and rejection regions of the test are shown in Fig. 17.4. According to (17.7), the decision rule is

If $z_o \leq +2.33$, accept H_0 (refuse shipment)
If $z_o > +2.33$, reject H_0 (receive shipment)

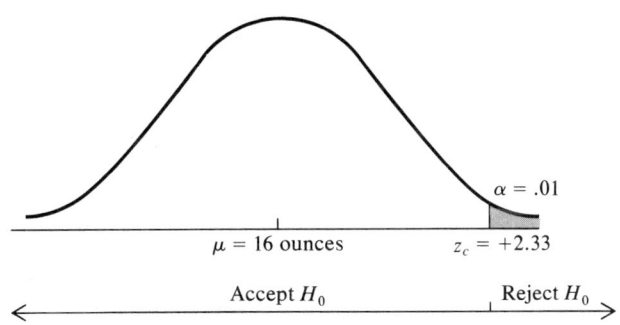

Figure 17.4. Upper-tailed test; sampling distribution of the mean with regions for accepting or rejecting a null hypothesis.

We may leave application of the decision rules for one-tailed tests involving the mean as exercises and concentrate on testing for a proportion.

Testing for a Proportion

The above testing procedure for a mean can be easily adapted to tests when the decision parameter is the proportion π. By analogy to (17.1) the critical values for a proportion are defined as

(17.8)
$$p_1^* = \pi - z\sigma_P$$
$$p_2^* = \pi + z\sigma_P$$

where the standard error is (Eq. 12.5)

(17.9)
$$\sigma_P = \sqrt{\frac{\pi(1-\pi)}{n}}$$

Chapter 6 Hypothesis Testing

The testing procedure can also be carried out in terms of z values with decision rules (17.4), (17.6), and (17.7) where

(17.10)
$$z_o = \frac{p - \pi}{\sqrt{\pi(1 - \pi)/n}}$$

with standard error (17.9) in the denominator.

We illustrate application of these formulas with an upper-tailed test.

Example 17.4

Holiday Mark, a firm specializing in greeting cards, plans to advertise for the coming holiday season with a 2-hour television spectacular. From past experience, such a show is considered to be effective in generating additional sales if it attracts at least 20 percent of the TV audience in the country. Management is most eager to avoid sponsoring an ineffective show.

This is an upper-tailed test because the show is ineffective if no more than 20 percent of the TV audience watches the performance; the incorrect decision, which management is most eager to avoid, is to sponsor an ineffective show. The null and the alternative hypotheses are

$$H_0: \pi \leq .20 \text{ viewers}$$
$$H_1: \pi > .20 \text{ viewers}$$

Management wishes to test the null hypothesis at 5 percent level of significance. The critical z_c value, obtained from Appendix D, is $+1.64$. (The plus sign is required because we have an upper-tailed test.)

The show is tried in a small geographical area representing a cross section of the potential audience in the country. Let us assume that management considers taking a simple random sample of 400 households in order to estimate the percentage of TV viewers who watched the show. Since the population proportion is .20, by formula (17.9) the standard error is

$$\sigma_P = \sqrt{\frac{(.20)(.80)}{400}} = .02$$

Substitution of $\pi = .20$, $z = +1.64$, and $\sigma_P = .02$ in (17.8) yields the upper-tail critical value

$$p_2^* = .20 + 1.64(.02) \simeq .233$$

The acceptance and rejection regions of the test in both critical p and z values are portrayed in Fig. 17.5.

In terms of an observed sample proportion p, the decision rule* is

If $p \leq .233$, accept H_0 (show ineffective; do not sponsor show)
If $p > .233$, reject H_0 (show effective; sponsor show)

---

*From formula (17.7) by substituting p for z_o.

Figure 17.5.
Upper-tailed test; sampling distribution of the proportion with regions for accepting or rejecting a null hypothesis.

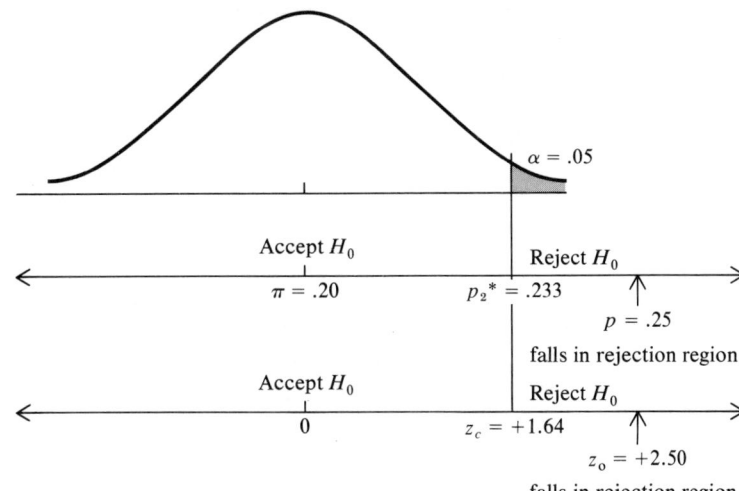

In words, if the sample proportion p of viewers watching the show is less than or equal to .233, accept the null hypothesis that $\pi \leq .20$; conclude that the show is ineffective and may not be sponsored. If the sample proportion p is larger than .233, reject the null hypothesis that $\pi \leq .20$; conclude that the show is effective and may be sponsored.

Suppose the sample of 400 households indicates that 25 percent of the TV viewers watched the show. Since the sample proportion falls in the rejection region as shown in Fig. 17.5, management may sponsor the show.

The alternative decision rule (17.7) is

If $z_o \leq +1.64$, accept H_0 (show ineffective; do not sponsor show)
If $z_o > +1.64$, reject H_0 (show effective; sponsor show)

We may assume a very large statistical population and ignore the fpc (finite population correction). Substituting for $\pi = .20$, $p = .25$, and $n = 400$ in formula (17.10), we obtain

$$z_o = \frac{.25 - .20}{\sqrt{(.20)(.80)/400}} = +2.50$$

The null hypothesis is again rejected, as shown in Fig. 17.5, because the z_o value falls in the rejection region.

A Few Important Points

Now we are ready to summarize the testing procedure and discuss a number of additional considerations.

I. The procedure for hypothesis testing requires three major steps:

1. *Formulate a null hypothesis and its alternative.* The null hypothesis is stated in such a way that Type I error probability can be controlled.

2. *Establish a decision rule.* The rule partitions the sampling distribution of the test statistic into regions for accepting or rejecting the null hypothesis. The partition is determined on the basis of the direction of the hypothesized parameter (two-sided or one-sided test) and the desired level of significance.
3. *Decide to accept or reject the null hypothesis by applying the decision rule to the collected sample data.* We either accept (that is, we do not reject) or reject the null hypothesis; rejection of the null hypothesis implies acceptance of the alternative hypothesis.

II. In all our illustrations for testing a mean, we assumed that the population standard deviation σ is known. If σ is unknown, we use the sample standard deviation s to estimate σ. So instead of computing $\sigma_{\bar{x}} = \sigma/\sqrt{n}$, we calculate an estimated standard deviation of the mean $s_{\bar{x}} = s/\sqrt{n}$. In such a case, we construct decision rules (17.4), (17.6), or (17.7) because rule (17.3) cannot be used before a sample is taken unless we know σ. Of course, if σ is unknown and s is used instead, the appropriate distribution for testing is the t distribution irrespective of sample size. In hypothesis testing, however, as in interval estimation, the distinction between large and small samples becomes important:

1. For sufficiently large samples, usually 30 or more observations, the normal distribution is used as an acceptable approximation to the t distribution. In all other respects the testing procedure is carried out in terms of z values as already illustrated.
2. If the sample is small, usually less than 30 observations, we assume that the statistical population is normal and use the t distribution.* Then the testing procedure is carried out in terms of t rather than z values. In all other respects the procedure is the same as already explained.
3. If the sample is small and the statistical population is considered to be quite skewed, other tests, called nonparametric, may be employed.

III. In all our illustrations, no fpc (finite population correction) was used because the population was infinite or we assumed a very large finite population. If the sample fraction n/N is large, usually larger than 5 percent, the standard error $\sigma_{\bar{x}}$, $s_{\bar{x}}$ or σ_P should be multiplied by the fpc $\sqrt{(N-n)/(N-1)}$.

IV. The proper use of confidence intervals and hypothesis tests is closely associated with our research objectives. Confidence intervals are appropriate when no hypotheses are formulated in advance of a statistical investigation. Application of significance tests, on the other hand, requires that clear-cut hypotheses be formulated *prior* to data collection. In fact, the formulated hypotheses become the basis for preparing an optimal sample design. Confidence intervals may be used, of course, for a fuller interpretation of the test results.

V. Frequently, hypotheses are formulated from and tested by the same data. This practice may not prove to be a mere procedural mistake. The number of possible measurements which can be computed from the data of a study of even a moderate size is quite large. The probability is quite high that some of these measurements may yield statistically significant results by chance rather than by

---

*For most practical purposes this assumption is not too restrictive because the t distribution is fairly insensitive to the normality condition.

Section 17 Testing a Single Parameter

prior design. And it is quite likely that such analysis may be the source of seriously misleading results unless the available data are used to formulate hypotheses and a new set of data is collected for testing these hypotheses.

VI. Error probabilities α and β are inversely related for a given sample size, if α is decreased, β is increased, and vice versa. The only way to reduce both risks is to increase the sample size. In our illustrations construction of the decision rule for testing was based on controlling only the α risk. How to measure and control the β risk is discussed next.

The Power Curve; Controlling α and β Risks*

So far our testing procedures have focused on controlling Type I error probability α. The immediate question is: How do we handle Type II error probability β? First, we show how to measure and study the behavior of probability β. Second, we illustrate how to determine the sample size and decision rule which control both α and β risks at predetermined levels.

According to Table 17.1, if we reject the null hypothesis, we are led to accepting the alternative hypothesis H_1 that the process mean μ is not 16 ounces. However, this conclusion opens a Pandora's box. Usually, we have no prior knowledge how far the process mean is from 16 ounces. Thus the alternative hypothesis is a *composite* hypothesis containing a whole range of values with one of β probability for every assumed value of μ.

The procedure for determining β probabilities is the same whether the test is two-sided or one-sided as well as whether the parameter is the mean or a proportion. We illustrate this procedure with a two-sided test for the mean. We may use μ_0 to denote the mean of the null hypothesis and μ_1 the mean of the alternative hypothesis.

Example 17.5

Consider again the test for the canning process of Paxwell House we carried out earlier (Example 17.1). With minor changes, the decision rule for the test is portrayed in Fig. 17.6(a). The shaded region under the normal curve represents probability $(1 - \alpha) = .99$ for correctly accepting a true null hypothesis, as shown in Fig. 17.2.

If management accepts a true null hypothesis, β probability does not occur because this would be a correct decision. However, β probability occurs if H_0 is false and H_1 is true. Suppose the true mean μ_1 is 16.32 ounces. Then the sampling distribution of the mean will move closer to the upper critical value $\bar{x}_2^* = 16.52$ ounces, as shown in Fig. 17.6(b). The shaded region of the normal curve represents the probability for accepting a false null hypothesis. For $\mu_1 = 16.32$, $\bar{x}_2^* = 16.52$, and $\sigma_{\bar{x}} = .20$ ounce, the value of β probability is calculated as follows:†

$$\beta = P\left(z_2 \leqslant \frac{\bar{x}_2^* - \mu_1}{\sigma_{\bar{x}}} \leqslant \frac{16.52 - 16.32}{.20} \right)$$

$$= P(z_2 \leqslant +1) = .5000 + .3413 \simeq .84$$

---

*This subsection may be omitted without loss of continuity in subject matter.
†For a μ_1 value very close to μ_0 (say 16.02 ounces), it is necessary to calculate the β values for both upper and lower acceptance limits. This was not necessary for $\mu_1 = 16.32$ because the left-tail value is very close to .5000.

Figure 17.6.
Two-sided test for Paxwell House canning process. Error probabilities β for various values of μ_1 given that $\mu_0 = 16$ ounces, $\sigma = 2$ ounces, $\alpha = .01$, and $n = 100$.

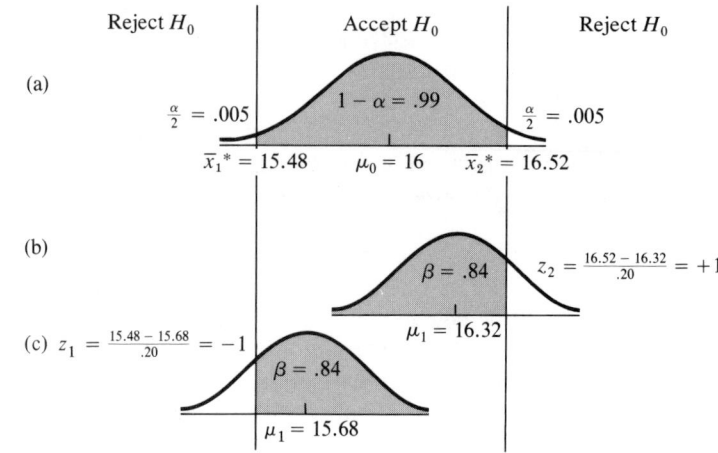

Note that this probability consists of the entire left-half region of the normal curve plus region .3413 between $\mu_1 = 16.32$ and $\bar{x}_2^* = 16.52$ ounces. On the other hand, suppose the true mean μ_1 is 15.68. Then the sampling distribution of the mean will move closer to the lower critical value $\bar{x}_1^* = 15.48$ ounces as shown in Fig. 17.6(c); but the β value will be the same .84 as in Fig. 17.6(b) because of symmetry.

In this manner, we can obtain a β value for each particular value of μ_1 greater than or less than $\mu_0 = 16$ ounces. A smooth solid-line curve connecting the complementary probability of β, that is, $1 - \beta$, for each value of μ_1 for our Paxwell House case is shown in Fig. 17.7. Such a curve is called a *power curve* or a *power*

Figure 17.7.
Power curve for the two-sided test of the Paxwell House canning process.

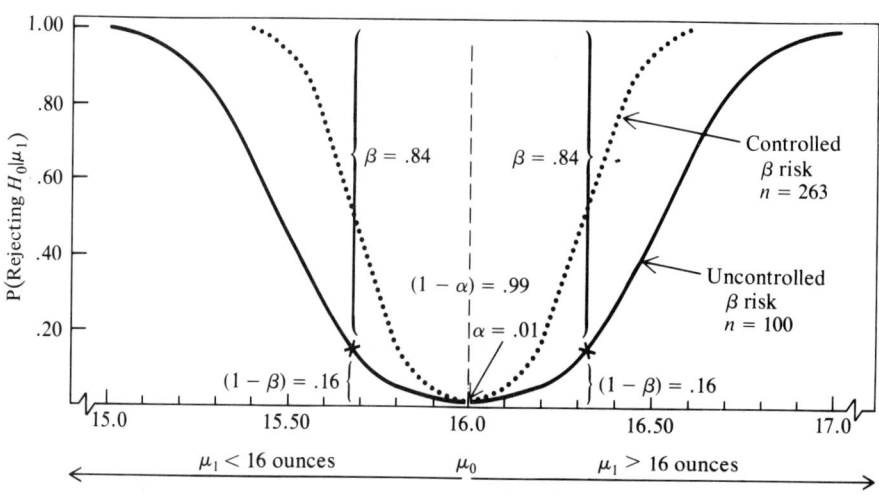

function. Note that the power curve with a solid line represents an uncontrolled β risk when $n = 100$. The power curve with a dotted line will be explained shortly.

The height of the coordinate at $\mu_0 = 16$ ounces represents probability $\alpha = .01$ and $1 - \alpha = .99$. For a given value of μ_1 the height of the coordinate below the curve represents probability $(1 - \beta)$ of correctly rejecting a false null hypothesis—in symbols, $P(\text{Rejecting } H_0 | \mu_1)$. The closer a value of μ_1 is to μ_0 the smaller the probability $(1 - \beta)$ of correctly rejecting a false null hypothesis and the larger the β risk of erroneously accepting a false null hypothesis. For example, suppose the true mean μ_1 is 16.32 or 15.68 ounces; the probability $(1 - \beta)$ for management to take the correct action of adjusting the process is only .16; however, the β risk for failing to adjust the process when out of control is .84. In short, probability $(1 - \beta)$ is smaller than .50 for values of μ_1 which lie between μ_0 and the critical acceptance values $\bar{x}_1^* = 15.48$ and $\bar{x}_2^* = 16.52$ ounces. The question is: Does the test discriminate satisfactorily for μ_1 values close to the null hypothesis mean μ_0?

We may be able to answer this question by analyzing the consequences of a statistical decision with a power curve.* For example, the management of Paxwell House may feel comfortable with the high β probabilities of the test and proceed with the testing in a manner already explained. However, management may feel that the power of the test is too low because $(1 - \beta)$ probabilities are low; in other words, the β risk may be unacceptable to management. Then we may use the power curve to examine what happens to β values if we follow two options. First, we may change probability α. However, for a fixed sample size, probabilities α and β are inversely related; in order to decrease β and hence increase the power of the test we must increase the α probability. In order to reduce both α and β probabilities we must follow the second option: increase the sample size.

In this connection, we may consider a new sample design and decision rule based on prespecified α and β risks at desirable levels. For a two-sided test for the mean the sample size is determined by

(17.11)
$$n = \frac{(z_{\alpha/2} + z_\beta)^2 \sigma^2}{(\mu_1 - \mu_0)^2}$$

The same formula is suitable for a one-sided test if we use z_α instead of $z_{\alpha/2}$.

Example 17.6

Consider again the Paxwell House canning process (Example 17.1). For $\alpha/2 = .01/2 = .005$, the z value is 2.58; the corresponding z value for $\beta = .05$ is 1.64, obtained from Appendix D. The standard deviation σ is 2 and $\mu_0 = 16$ ounces. Management wishes that $\mu_1 = 16.52$ ounces, equal to the critical value $\bar{x}_2^*$. Substitution of these values in formula (17.11) yields

$$n = \frac{(2.58 + 1.64)^2 (2)^2}{(16.52 - 16)^2} \simeq 263 \text{ cans}$$

*In industrial quality control, it is customary to use the so-called *operating characteristics curve* or the *OC curve*, for short. The OC curve is the complement of the power curve where the height of the coordinates under the curve represent the β risk for each value of μ_1.

This is the required sample size for protecting Paxwell's management against both wrong decisions with probabilities $\alpha = .01$ and $\beta = .05$.

Substituting in formula (17.1), we obtain the new critical values

$$\bar{x}_1^* = 16 - 2.58 \frac{2}{\sqrt{263}} = 15.68 \text{ ounces}$$

$$\bar{x}_2^* = 16 + 2.58 \frac{2}{\sqrt{263}} = 16.32 \text{ ounces}$$

The decision rule for the test with an observed sample mean $\bar{x}$ is

If $15.68 \leq \bar{x} \leq 16.32$, accept H_0 (leave process alone)
If $\bar{x} < 15.68$ or $\bar{x} > 16.32$, reject H_0 (take remedial action)

Suppose from a random sample of 263 cans we find that the observed sample mean $\bar{x}$ is 15.60 ounces. Since this value is less than the critical value $\bar{x}_1^* = 15.68$ ounces, we reject the null hypothesis. The canning process is out of control and should be adjusted.

What has the new decision rule accomplished? The power curve for this rule is the dotted line in Fig. 17.7. Under the initial decision rule only the α risk was prespecified at a .01 significance level with values $\bar{x}_1^* = 15.48$ and $\bar{x}_2^* = 16.52$ ounces. In other words, we controlled only the producer's risk. The consumer's risk was left uncontrolled with β probability .84 if $\mu_1 = 16.32$ or $\mu_1 = 15.68$ (Fig. 17.6(b) and (c)). We considered this β risk level unacceptable, prespecified its value at .05, and established a new decision rule with critical values $\bar{x}_1^* = 15.68$ and $\bar{x}_2^* = 16.32$ ounces. Now at $\mu_1 = 16.32$ or $\mu_1 = 15.68$ the power of the test, $(1 - \beta)$ probability, increased from .16 to .50. However, in order to increase the power of the test we had to increase the sample size from 100 to 263 observations.

From the conceptual and procedural standpoints, testing with a proportion while controlling both risks is analogous to testing with the mean. The formula for determining the required sample size for one-sided test is

(17.12) $$n = \left[\frac{z_\alpha \sqrt{\pi_0(1 - \pi_0)} + z_\beta \sqrt{\pi_1(1 - \pi_1)}}{\pi_0 - \pi_1} \right]^2$$

where π_0 is the proportion for the null hypothesis and π_1 the proportion for the alternative hypothesis. The same formula can be used for determining the sample size of a two-tailed test if z_α is changed to $z_{\alpha/2}$.

Example 17.7

In the Holiday Mark case (Example 17.4) management was considering whether or not to sponsor a 2-hour television spectacular for the coming holiday season. This time, however, attention is focused on two rather than one value of the proportion of the audience the show may attract: proportion $\pi_0 = .16$ at which the show is considered ineffective and would not be sponsored; and $\pi_1 = .20$ at which the show is considered effective and would be sponsored. Management is willing to take a .05 chance (α probability) of sponsoring an ineffective show and .10 chance (β probability) of failing to sponsor an effective show.

For $\alpha = .05$ the value z_α is 1.64 and for $\beta = .10$ the value z_β is 1.28, read from Appendix D. Substitution of given values in (17.12) yields

$$n = \left[\frac{1.64 \sqrt{(.16)(.84)} + 1.28 \sqrt{(.20)(.80)}}{.16 - .20} \right]^2$$
$$= 775$$

Substitution of $\pi_0 = .16$, $z_\alpha = 1.64$, and $n = 775$ in formula (17.8) yields the upper-tail critical value

$$p_2^* = .16 + 1.64 \sqrt{\frac{(.16)(.84)}{775}}$$
$$\simeq .182$$

and the decision rule is

If $p \leq .182$, accept H_0 (show ineffective; do not sponsor show)
If $p > .182$, reject H_0 (show effective; sponsor show)

Suppose 19 percent of a random sample of 775 TV viewers watched the show. We reject the null hypothesis because the observed p of .19 is greater than the critical proportion .182. Holiday's management may sponsor the show.

Sampling unit costs and other factors being equal, which decision parameter, the mean or the proportion, should be preferred? In general, the mean provides more information than the proportion. For the same sample size and a fixed α probability, a decision rule based on the mean should provide a lower β probability than a rule based on a proportion; a mean test can be shown to be more powerful than a proportion test.

PROBLEMS

Group One

17.1. What does the statement "The test result is statistically significant" mean? Explain carefully.
17.2. Does accepting or rejecting the null hypothesis prove that the hypothesis is true or false? Discuss.
17.3. If a sample statistic is inconsistent with a hypothesis, does such sample evidence lead to the rejection or acceptance of that hypothesis? Explain.
17.4. For each statement, indicate whether you agree or disagree. Explain why.
   *(a) As soon as we have decided on a test, we know whether Type I or Type II error may have occurred.

Answers to asterisked (*) problems are appended.

(b) Since decreasing Type I error increases Type II error and vice versa, it is impossible to reduce both errors.
(c) A test should be designed to control Type I error because it is more important than controlling Type II error.
(d) A Type I error occurs when we reject a true null hypothesis, and Type II error occurs when we accept a false null hypothesis.

17.5. For each null hypothesis, construct a table, such as Table 17.1, and indicate which of the four statements represent Type I error, Type II error, or a correct decision:
*(a) H_0: New drug is not effective
 (1) Do not market new drug when effective.
 (2) Market new drug when effective.
 (3) Do not market new drug when ineffective.
 (4) Market new drug when ineffective.
(b) H_0: New training program is not better than old one
 (1) Retain old program when new program is better.
 (2) Introduce new program when new program is not better.
 (3) Retain old program when new program is not better.
 (4) Introduce new program when new program is better.
(c) H_0: Shipment of batteries is of bad quality
 (1) Do not send a bad shipment.
 (2) Do not send a good shipment.
 (3) Send a good shipment.
 (4) Send a bad shipment.
(d) H_0: Production lot of TV tubes is of good quality
 (1) Do not ship a bad lot.
 (2) Ship a bad lot.
 (3) Do not ship a good lot.
 (4) Ship a good lot.

17.6. For each specified level of significance α, observed z_o value, and indicated lower-tailed or upper-tailed test, decide whether you would accept or reject the null hypothesis. Portray your decision with an appropriate diagram.
*(a) $\alpha = .05$, $z_o = +1.2$, lower (c) $\alpha = .10$, $z_o = -2.33$, lower
(b) $\alpha = .01$, $z_o = +1.85$, upper (d) $\alpha = .001$, $z_o = +3.85$, upper

17.7. For each specified level of significance α, sample size n, observed value t_o, and indicated lower-tailed or upper-tailed test, decide whether you would accept or reject the null hypothesis. Portray your decision with an appropriate diagram.
*(a) $\alpha = .01$, $n = 16$, $t_o = +3.52$, upper
(b) $\alpha = .005$, $n = 20$, $t_o = +1.95$, lower
(c) $\alpha = .10$, $n = 25$, $t_o = +1.20$, upper
(d) $\alpha = .15$, $n = 9$, $t_o = -1.26$, lower

17.8 Explain the following terms:
(a) Power curve or power function (e) Decision rule
(b) Level of significance (f) Significance test
(c) Critical values (g) Composite hypothesis
(d) Hypothesis test (h) Operating characteristics curve

17.9. Distinguish between:
(a) One-tailed and two-tailed tests
(b) Type I and Type II errors
(c) Null hypothesis and alternative hypothesis

(d) α risk and β risk
(e) Estimating and testing procedures
(f) Upper-tailed and lower-tailed tests
(g) Producer's risk and consumer's risk

Group Two

17.10. For each specified set of hypotheses, parameter σ, level of significance, sample size, and observed statistic obtained from a large population, answer the following:
  (i) Indicate whether the procedure requires a two-sided or one-sided (lower-tailed or upper-tailed) test.
  (ii) Calculate the critical $\bar{x}^*$ value(s).
  (iii) On the basis of the observed $\bar{x}$ value, decide whether you should accept or reject the null hypothesis. Explain why.
  (iv) Verify your decision in terms of z values.
  *(a) $H_0: \mu = 50$; $H_1: \mu \neq 50$; $\sigma = 5$; $\alpha = .01$; $n = 100$; $\bar{x} = 48.50$
  (b) $H_0: \mu \geq 25$; $H_1: \mu < 25$; $\sigma = 6$; $\alpha = .001$; $n = 900$; $\bar{x} = 24.50$
  (c) $H_0: \mu \leq .9$; $H_1: \mu > .9$; $\sigma = .3$; $\alpha = .05$; $n = 36$; $\bar{x} = 1.0$

17.11. For each specified set of hypotheses, parameter π, level of significance, sample size, and observed statistic obtained from a large population, answer the following:
  (i) Indicate whether the test is lower-tailed or upper-tailed.
  (ii) Calculate the critical p^* value.
  (iii) On the basis of the observed p value, decide whether you should accept or reject the null hypothesis. Explain why.
  (iv) Verify your decision in terms of z values.
  *(a) $H_0: \pi \leq .30$; $H_1: \pi > .30$; $\alpha = .01$; $n = 625$; $p = .35$
  (b) $H_0: \pi \geq .80$; $H_1: \pi < .80$; $\alpha = .05$; $n = 121$; $p = .76$

17.12. Ideal Inc., a manufacturer of cosmetics, would place special ads for a new face cream if 25 percent or less of potential customers definitely favor the product. The alternative hypothesis is not to place special ads if more than 25 percent of the customers definitely favor the product.
  *(a) Formulate the appropriate hypotheses and establish a decision rule for a 1 percent significance level in terms of z values.
  (b) In a panel of 150 potential customers, 51 are definitely in favor of the new face cream. Should Ideal place special ads for the new product?
  (c) To what kind of risk may the test result lead? Explain carefully.

17.13. The alumni association of Danford Business School claims that at least 30 percent of the graduates switch jobs within 3 years after graduation.
  *(a) Formulate the appropriate hypotheses and establish a decision rule for a 5 percent significance level in terms of z values.
  (b) From a total of 1000 alumni who graduated 4 to 7 years ago a sample of 200 is taken at random. The sample shows that 52 alumni switched jobs within 3 years after they graduated. Is the alumni association correct?

17.14. Consumer's Advocate, a nonprofit organization, claims that Zambell's vegetable beef soup cans contain less than the required 50 chunks of beef per can. A sample of 225 cans from a large shipment produces an average of 51 and a standard deviation of 5 chunks of beef. Does the sample evidence support this claim or the alternative hypothesis that each can contains at least 50 chunks of beef? Test at 1 percent significance level.

(a) Formulate the appropriate hypotheses and the decision rule in terms of z values. Interpret the test result.
(b) Portray testing graphically.

17.15. A spokesperson for the Council of Economic Advisors to the president of the United States claims that, during the last year, increases in the hourly wage rate of production workers kept within the guidelines of 7 percent or less necessary to combat inflation. The hourly wage rate stood at $7.00 at the beginning of last year. The next year Vincent Scallisi and Jane Wixen, economists at Chemical Trust Company, took a well-designed sample of 400 industrial companies. The sample yielded a $7.54 average hourly wage rate and a 40¢ standard deviation. Does the sample support the spokesperson's claim at .001 significance level? Show all steps and carry out testing in terms of z values.

17.16. The management of Howard Thompson plans to replace its maple walnut ice cream with a new, less costly Brazil nut ice cream. For test-marketing the new product the company's restaurants in a representative metropolitan area are directed to withdraw the maple walnut and serve the Brazil nut ice cream for 21 consecutive days. Historically, daily demand for maple walnut ice cream in the same restaurants and during the same period of days averaged 10,000 gallons. Management will not make the switch if daily demand for Brazil nut ice cream is less than this historical average. The alternative hypothesis is to make the change if daily demand for the new ice cream exceeds the historical average.
(a) Formulate the appropriate hypotheses and establish a decision rule for a .005 significance level in terms of t values.
(b) During the 21 days of the market trial, daily demand for Brazil nut ice cream averaged 10,150 gallons with 200 gallons standard deviation. Should management switch to selling Brazil nut ice cream?
(c) What kind of risk does management assume with the test result? Explain carefully.

17.17. Suppose the true process average weight of a coffee can in Example 17.5 is $\mu_1 = 16.02$ ounces. Verify that the value of the β probability is about .9903.

17.18. Consider Example 17.2. The management of Paxwell House set the α probability (producer's risk) at .01 significance level. Suppose management wishes to set β probability (consumer's risk) at .10 and $\mu_1 = 15.48$ ounces, equal to critical value $\bar{x}_1^*$ determined in Example 17.1.
(a) Find the required sample size which controls both above-specified risks.
(b) Suppose a sample of the size you found in (a) yields a mean $\bar{x} = 15.70$ ounces and standard deviation $s = 2.1$ ounces. Should management ship the order to Continental?
(c) New government regulations impose such tight quality standards that Paxwell's management is forced to lower β risk to .01. Find the required sample size.
(d) Suppose the new sample in (c) yields the same mean and standard deviation as in (b). What action does the new sample suggest? How may such an action affect manufacturing costs?

17.19. Historical records show that, on the average, 70 percent of the customers of Dexall's, a chain of drug stores, pay their bills on time. Camilia Higgins, the new assistant comptroller, observes that if the percentage stays within 10 percentage points above or below the historical average during the first 10 days of each month, the comptroller can meet ordinary end-of-month cash requirements. Otherwise, the comptroller must either borrow extra money or invest the excess cash in short-term securities. However, erroneously borrowing more or investing more

than necessary is costly. Camilia believes that determining the percentage of paid accounts with a random sample taken during the first 10 days of each month could protect management against both wrong decisions. The comptroller feels that each risk should be set at .05 error probability.
(a) Is this an upper-tailed, lower-tailed, or two-sided test? Formulate the null hypothesis and its alternative.
(b) Explain Type I and Type II errors.
(c) Determine the required sample of customer accounts. (Assume a large statistical population.)
(d) Establish the appropriate decision rule in terms of critical p^* value(s).

SECTION 18/ TESTING THE DIFFERENCE OF TWO PARAMETERS

Testing the difference of two population means or proportions is important in at least two respects. Often, such methods and procedures represent *comparative experiments* where observations are created by the statistical study itself. For example, contrast testing the coffee-canning process of Paxwell House with a palatability test of a new food product. In the case of the canning process, observations are available and would be available whether or not we study the process. In the food manufacturer case, however, the individuals in each sample must be subjected to tasting each food product in order to determine whether or not the new product is superior. Observations are created by the study itself, which introduces the experimental stimulus, tasting the products. In addition, such comparative experiments are forerunners of more sophisticated tests, which are introduced later.

As in the case of a single sample, inferences from two samples may take the form of an estimate or a test. Since in most cases a testing problem can easily be reformulated into an interval estimation problem, we focus on hypothesis testing. First, we relate the present topic to known theory of statistical inference. Then we introduce a select number of testing procedures for two means and two proportions based on two independent samples. Finally, we introduce matched sampling for means and draw the distinction between independent and matched samples. Throughout the section we assume familiarity with already-explained procedures for formulating the appropriate null and alternative hypotheses, and so we concentrate on unknown procedural aspects.

Confidence Intervals for the Difference in Two Population Means

To establish logical continuity, let us review the basics of statistical inference and construct an interval estimate of the difference in two population means. The difference, denoted by D, is a new parameter defined as

(18.1) $$D = \mu_A - \mu_B$$

where μ_A = mean of population A
μ_B = mean of population B

Example 18.1

Alpine Products is a manufacturer of ropes and other equipment for mountain climbing. The research and development department of the company has invented a new method for processing nylon rope. The new processing method A and the old method B are comparable with respect to production cost and other characteristics except possibly breaking strength, the pounds of weight a rope can lift before breaking.

Rope manufactured with the new method A represents a population with an unknown mean breaking strength μ_A and standard deviation σ_A. The rope population from the old method B has an unknown mean breaking strength μ_B and standard deviation σ_B. Of course, the breaking strength within each rope population may vary slightly from one processing batch to the next because of random and uncontrollable causes. Management's concern is the uncertainty about the difference D between the unknown averages μ_A and μ_B. We need to estimate this difference.

We may conduct the following experiment: select a random sample of n_A pieces of rope of given length from method A and n_B pieces from method B, subject each piece to a weight-lifting test, record its breaking weight, and calculate the mean breaking weight $\bar{x}_A$ and $\bar{x}_B$ from each sample. Then we can use the statistic defined as

(18.2) $$d = \bar{x}_A - \bar{x}_B$$

to estimate the unknown parameter D. Before illustrating the experimental results with a numerical example, let us trace briefly important elements of the underlying theory.

The two random samples are independent since the probabilities of selecting elementary units in one sample do not affect the probabilities of selecting units in the other sample. The difference d of two sample means from all possible samples of size n_A and n_B will form a sampling distribution of statistic d. This is the manner with which we were able to form earlier a sampling distribution of the mean from all possible samples of size n. And the properties of the sampling distribution of statistic d are analogous to the properties of the sampling distribution of the mean. In particular:

1. Statistic d is an *unbiased estimator* of parameter D. In symbols,

(18.3) $$E(d) = D$$

2. The *standard error* of statistic d is*

(18.4) $$\sigma_d = \sqrt{\frac{\sigma_A^2}{n_A} + \frac{\sigma_B^2}{n_B}}$$

---

*If we assume that σ_A^2 and σ_B^2 are equal, we may replace their common value with σ^2 and simplify formula (18.4) to

$$\sigma_d = \sigma \sqrt{\frac{1}{n_A} + \frac{1}{n_B}}$$

Sample size n_A and n_B need not be equal. However, when experimental conditions do not dictate an unequal sample size, σ_d is minimized when factor $\sqrt{1/n_A + 1/n_B}$ has its lowest value. If the sum of the two sample sizes is held constant, this lowest value occurs when n_A and n_B are equal.

Section 18 Testing the Difference of Two Parameters

3. According to the central limit theorem, the sampling distribution of statistic d approaches the normal distribution as both samples n_A and n_B become large.

The qualifications for applying the normal distribution to the mean are equally applicable to the difference of two means. Usually, when μ_A and μ_B are unknown, their respective standard deviations σ_A and σ_B will also be unknown. We may estimate these parameters using the corresponding sample standard deviations s_A and s_B. For sufficiently large samples (each of 30 or more observations), we may obtain an estimate of σ_d in (18.4) with

$$(18.5) \qquad s_d = \sqrt{\frac{s_A^2}{n_A} + \frac{s_B^2}{n_B}}$$

Example 18.1 (continued)

We assume that sample fractions are too small or the populations are infinite so there is no need for an fpc (finite population correction). Under the above qualifications, an interval estimate of D is defined as

$$(18.6) \qquad d \pm z s_d$$

Suppose we randomly select one sample of 100 pieces of rope from each rope population and obtain the following results:

New Method A	Old Method B
n_A = 100 pieces of rope	n_B = 100 pieces of rope
$\bar{x}_A$ = 2000 pounds	$\bar{x}_B$ = 1990 pounds
s_A = 47 pounds	s_B = 45 pounds

We wish to construct an interval estimate of D with 99 percent degree of confidence. For this confidence the value of z from Appendix D is 2.58. According to formula (18.5) an estimate of the standard error is

$$s_d = \sqrt{\frac{(47)^2}{100} + \frac{(45)^2}{100}}$$

$$= 6.51 \text{ pounds}$$

Since d is equal to 10 pounds (2000 − 1990), from expression (18.6) we have an interval estimate of parameter D of

$$10 \pm 2.58(6.51) = -6.80 \text{ to } +26.80 \text{ pounds}$$

The difference in the mean breaking strength between the two methods is estimated to be between −6.80 and 26.80 pounds. The fact that these limits are of opposite algebraic sign leads to the following interpretation. The lower limit −6.80 indicates that method B may be better and the inferiority in the average breaking strength in using method A might be 6.80 pounds; the upper limit +26.80, on the other hand, indicates that method A may be better and the superiority in the average breaking strength in using method A might be 26.80 pounds.

We are 99 percent confident that this interval will include the true difference D. Since the limits of the interval are of opposite algebraic sign, this estimate does

Chapter 6 Hypothesis Testing

not clearly indicate a significant difference between the breaking strength of the two methods.

Testing Two Means: Large Samples

Instead of estimating the difference between two population means (or two proportions) we may wish to test the hypothesis that the mean of population A differs significantly from the mean of population B. In the Alpine Products case management may not be primarily concerned about the uncertain value of the mean difference D; management's principal interest may be in whether method A manufactures nylon rope with a significantly higher breaking strength, and therefore of superior quality, than processing method B. A personnel director may introduce a new program for training employees because it is found to be more effective than an old program. A pharmaceutical company may compare hundreds of chemical compounds in order to determine which are most effective anticancer agents.

Formulation of appropriate hypotheses and testing procedures for testing two means are analogous to those already introduced for testing a single mean. The null hypothesis may be expressed in terms of parameter $D \, (= \mu_A - \mu_B)$ and take any one of the following forms:

$$H_0: \mu_A \leqslant \mu_B \text{ (upper-tailed test)}$$
$$H_0: \mu_A \geqslant \mu_B \text{ (lower-tailed test)}$$
$$H_0: \mu_A = \mu_B \text{ (two-tailed test)}$$

We will concentrate on one-tailed tests and consider problems with large as well as small samples.

When large samples are used (n_A and n_B each consist of 30 or more observations), we already know that statistic $d = \bar{x}_A - \bar{x}_B$ is normally distributed with a mean $D = \mu_A - \mu_B$ and standard deviation σ_d. Testing may be carried out in terms of the Z deviate with an observed value defined as

(18.7)
$$z_o = \frac{\bar{x}_A - \bar{x}_B}{\sqrt{\dfrac{s_A^2}{n_A} + \dfrac{s_B^2}{n_B}}}$$

where the numerator is statistic d defined in (18.2) and the denominator is s_d, an estimate of σ_d, defined in (18.5). For large samples we do not need to assume that the population standard deviations σ_A and σ_B are equal.

Example 18.1 (continued)

Should new method A for processing nylon rope replace old method B? Management wishes to use the null hypothesis that method A is no better than method B and therefore method B should be kept. The null hypothesis and its alternative are:

$$H_0: \mu_A \leqslant \mu_B$$
$$H_1: \mu_A > \mu_B$$

This is an upper-tailed test where extremely positive values of statistic d will refute the null hypothesis. Note that rejecting the null hypothesis will result in introducing new method *A*. Such a decision may be incorrect, leading to Type I error, if new method *A* is indeed no better than old method *B*. Management wishes to avoid committing such an error with a .01 α probability.

For a one-tailed test and 1 percent significance level, the critical value z_c from Appendix D is $+2.33$. So the decision rule is

If $z_o \leq +2.33$, accept H_0 (keep old method *B*)
If $z_o > +2.33$, reject H_0 (introduce new method *A*)

From the sample data we have found that statistic d is 10 pounds and the standard error s_d is 6.51 pounds. Substitution in formula (18.7) yields an observed value

$$z_o = \frac{10}{6.51} = +1.54$$

The null hypothesis is accepted because the z_o value falls in the acceptance region of the normal curve. There is not enough evidence to conclude that method *A* for processing nylon rope is significantly superior to method *B* with respect to breaking strength. Management may keep old method *B*.

In comparative experiments, a design with two independent samples may be appropriate when the nature of the study permits measurement of the elementary units only *after* the "experimental stimulus" has been introduced. In the Alpine Products case, it is impossible to compare the same nylon rope processed by both methods. Observations from the rope population of the old method *B* may be referred to as the *control sample*. The new method *A* may be considered to represent the experimental stimulus so that observations from the rope population of method *A* constitute the *experimental sample*. Such a design is sometimes called *after-only* with two independent samples, one control and one experimental.

Frequently, researchers make the control sample larger than the experimental in order to obtain a more precise estimate of the control population mean. This is especially desirable if the mean of the control sample is used repeatedly for comparing it with the mean of several experimental samples. Also, a smaller experimental than control sample may be necessary because subjecting each elementary unit to the experimental stimulus may be too costly, or for other reasons.

Testing Two Means: Small Samples

Experimental and other conditions may require the use of small samples, that is, when both n_A and n_B are smaller than 30. Then we must use the *t* instead of the normal distribution. The principles of statistical inference and the testing procedures we have already expounded are equally applicable in using the *t* distribution with only one important qualification: the *t* distribution requires that the two *populations have the same standard deviation and that both be normally distributed*. So in testing two means with small samples we must assume that $\sigma_A = \sigma_B = \sigma$. This means that both s_A and s_B are estimates of σ. We may obtain a better estimate of σ by taking the square root of the weighted average of the sample variances. This estimate of σ is defined as

(18.8) $$s = \sqrt{\frac{(n_A - 1)s_A^2 + (n_B - 1)s_B^2}{n_A + n_B - 2}}$$

Chapter 6 Hypothesis Testing

Then the estimated standard error of d is

(8.9) $$s_d = \sqrt{\frac{(n_A - 1)s_A^2 + (n_B - 1)s_B^2}{n_A + n_B - 2}} \sqrt{\frac{1}{n_A} + \frac{1}{n_B}}$$

The ratio $(\bar{x}_A - \bar{x}_B)/s_d$ is distributed according to the t distribution with value

(18.10) $$t_o = \frac{\bar{x}_A - \bar{x}_B}{\sqrt{\frac{(n_A - 1)s_A^2 + (n_B - 1)s_B^2}{n_A + n_B - 2}} \sqrt{\frac{1}{n_A} + \frac{1}{n_B}}}$$

Example 18.2

Hope Enterprises is a large cattle-raising company. Young steers are purchased from farmers and placed in big feedlots. After reaching a certain weight, the steers are sold to packing houses. The company is able to make handsome profits because management is constantly experimenting with new animal feed. Experimentation is done in cooperation with McDonald Brothers, a manufacturer of animal feed. The latest experiment involves testing C2, a new feed rich in protein concentrates. Management wishes to find out whether C2 helps cattle gain more weight than ordinary feed within a given feeding period.

A random sample of 10 steers are fed C2 while the control random sample n_B of 15 steers receive the ordinary feed. All other feeding and living conditions are the same for both groups of cattle. At the end of the feeding period the weight each steer has gained is measured and each sample average gain in weight is calculated. Suppose management wants to test the mean gain in weight at 5 percent significance level. This is the risk of erroneously concluding that the new C2 feed is superior to the ordinary feed. The sample data are as follows:

C2 Animal Feed	Ordinary Feed
n_A = 10 steers	n_B = 15 steers
$\bar{x}_A$ = 705 pounds	$\bar{x}_B$ = 620 pounds
s_A = 85 pounds	s_B = 90 pounds

Is C2 a superior animal feed?

The null hypothesis is that C2 is no better than the ordinary feed—in

Section 18 Testing the Difference of Two Parameters

other words, that the mean gain in weight μ_A is less than or equal to the mean gain in weight μ_B. The null hypothesis and its alternative are

$$H_0: \mu_A \leq \mu_B$$
$$H_1: \mu_A > \mu_B$$

This is an upper-tailed test where extreme positive $d = \bar{x}_A - \bar{x}_B$ values will refute the null hypothesis.

Since the significance level is 5 percent and there are $n_A + n_B - 2 = 10 + 15 - 2 = 23$ degrees of freedom,* the critical t_c value is $+1.714$; it is obtained from Appendix E. The decision rule is:

If $t_o \leq +1.714$, accept H_0 (keep ordinary feed)
If $t_o > +1.714$, reject H_0 (switch to new C2 feed)

Substitution of the sample data in formula (18.10) yields an observed statistic

$$t_o = \frac{705 - 620}{\sqrt{\frac{9(85)^2 + 14(90)^2}{23}} \sqrt{\frac{1}{10} + \frac{1}{15}}}$$

$$= +2.36$$

The null hypothesis is rejected because the observed t_o value falls in the rejection tail of the t distribution. Management may switch to new C2 feed. The risk, however, is 5 percent that C2 may not be superior to the ordinary feed.

Testing Two Proportions

We have seen that the proportion is an important general measure; it is the only parameter measure of qualitative populations, that is, populations of categorical variables such as sex, marital status, defective parts, preferences, and opinions. So testing two parameter proportions is as important as testing two parameter means. For example, a production manager may wish to know whether or not the proportion of defective parts differs between two machines or processes; a personnel director may be interested in whether or not a larger proportion of employees favors the new over the old vacation policy; opinion-polling "contests" are carried out in terms of the proportion of constituents favoring various candidates for political office.

The normal distribution is equally applicable to testing the difference between two proportions when the samples are large. The refinements for applying the normal distribution to a single proportion are largely applicable to the difference between two proportions. The testing procedure is analogous to the procedure for testing two means. Only the formulas are different.

---

*In this two-sample case, we use each of the sample variances in formula (18.8) to obtain a pooled estimate of the population variance. So the combined sample is $n_A + n_B$; it must be reduced by 2 because 1 degree of freedom is lost in calculating each sample variance.

Chapter 6 Hypothesis Testing

The difference between two population proportions π_A and π_B is

(18.11) $$D = \pi_A - \pi_B$$

This is our decision parameter for which we may formulate the following null hypotheses:

$$H_0: \pi_A \leq \pi_B \text{ (upper-tailed test)}$$
$$H_0: \pi_A \geq \pi_B \text{ (lower-tailed test)}$$
$$H_0: \pi_A = \pi_B \text{ (two-tailed test)}$$

The test statistic is defined as

(18.12) $$d = p_A - p_B$$

the difference representing a point estimate of D. For large samples, d is normally distributed with a sampling distribution having an expected value equal to D and standard error of the difference between two proportions

(18.13) $$\sigma_d = \sqrt{\frac{\pi_A(1 - \pi_A)}{n_A} + \frac{\pi_B(1 - \pi_B)}{n_B}}$$

Here, we assume that π_A is equal to π_B for any of the above null hypotheses. Then difference D is equal to zero ($\pi_A - \pi_B = 0$) and the sample proportions may be treated as if they originate from the same population. For an estimate of either π_A or π_B, the sample proportions may be combined into a weighted average

(18.14) $$\bar{p} = \frac{n_A p_A + n_B p_B}{n_A + n_B}$$

The average $\bar{p}$ is the best estimate of the common π. Then an estimate of standard error σ_d is

(18.15) $$s_d = \sqrt{\bar{p}(1 - \bar{p})\left(\frac{1}{n_A} + \frac{1}{n_B}\right)}$$

Finally, using formulas (18.12) and (18.15), the z value is defined as

(18.16) $$z_o = \frac{p_A - p_B}{\sqrt{\bar{p}(1 - \bar{p})\left(\frac{1}{n_A} + \frac{1}{n_B}\right)}}$$

Example 18.3   Tree Farms is a company with extensive holdings of fruit trees. The company has been spraying palathion, a chemical pesticide, to combat aphid infestation of orange trees. Pettina Sacks, the newly appointed agronomist for the company, believes that aphid infestation can be controlled more effectively with ladybugs, a natural predator of aphids and other soft-shell

Section 18 Testing the Difference of Two Parameters

insects. Besides, unlike chemical pesticides, a natural predator does not pollute the environment.

In a randomly selected grove of 1000 trees inundated with ladybugs 108 trees were damaged, while 256 trees were damaged in a grove of 1600 trees sprayed with palathion. Is natural control more effective than chemical control of aphids?

Pettina's null hypothesis is that ladybugs are no better than palathion pesticide; so the proportion of damaged trees treated with ladybugs, π_A, is at least as high as the proportion sprayed with palathion, π_B. In symbols,

$$H_0: \pi_A \geq \pi_B$$
$$H_1: \pi_A < \pi_B$$

This is a lower-tailed test where the null hypothesis will be refuted with extreme negative values of statistic $d = p_A - p_B$.

Pettina, wanting to be almost positive about the effectiveness of ladybugs, sets the significance level at .001. The critical z_c value which corresponds to this significance level is -3.08, obtained from Appendix D. And the decision rule may be formulated as follows:

If $z_o \geq -3.08$, accept H_0 (ladybugs not effective; stay with palathion)
If $z_o < -3.08$, reject H_0 (ladybugs effective; use ladybugs)

According to the available sample data,

$$\bar{p} = \frac{108 + 256}{1000 + 1600} = .14$$

by formula (18.14). Since $p_A = 108/100 = .108$ and $p_B = 256/1600 = .160$, substitution in (18.16) yields

$$z_o = \frac{.108 - .160}{\sqrt{(.14)(.86)(1/1000 + 1/1600)}}$$
$$= -3.72$$

Pettina should reject the null hypothesis because the observed z_o value falls in the rejection region; ladybugs may be used to control aphid infestation.

Note that costs are not an integral part of the procedure. For example, assuming ladybugs are indeed effective but are more expensive than palathion, such costs may offset the gains from more effective pest control. If these costs more than offset anticipated gains and environmental regulations prohibit application of chemical pesticides, use of ladybugs may result in higher production costs. Since higher costs are likely to be passed on to consumers, the net result may be a tradeoff between higher cost of living and an improved environment.

Matched Samples

So far we have dealt with designs of two independent random samples. In this type of sample design reduction of the effect which extraneous factors may have on a test result is accomplished through random and independent selections of elementary units for each sample. For example, a pharmaceutical firm wishes to study the effectiveness of a new drug in treating arteriosclerosis, that is, hardening of the arteries. Suppose the experimental sample which receives the drug treatment happens to include much younger and healthier individuals than the control sample which receives no drug treatment. Then, to the extent to which such characteristics may retard the occurrence of arteriosclerosis, the test result may be obscured. Such extraneous factors may influence the test result. One method of reducing such extraneous influences is random and independent sample selection. Large random samples would even out the differences of extraneous factors between the two samples so that the test result may be attributed to the effectiveness of the new drug.

Another method of reducing the effect of extraneous factors is the use of *matched-pairs* samples. Elementary units are matched with respect to characteristics which may influence the effect under study. For example, in the evaluation of the drug for arteriosclerosis, participants may be paired with respect to sex, age, weight, height, build, health history, and other physiological characteristics which are thought to be associated with the onset of the disease. Prior to experimentation, the individuals of each matched pair are randomly assigned one to the experimental and the other to the control sample. Matched-pairs samples, therefore, attempt to directly control extraneous influences so that the test result may be explained in terms of sample difference.

Matched-pairs samples should be distinguished from *matched-observations* samples in which a pair of observations are obtained from the same elementary unit. For example, consider a test for evaluating the effectiveness of a catalytic converter on automobile engines. Instead of selecting two independent random samples, we may use a single random sample of engines and measure the sulfur dioxide emissions level from each engine before and after installing the catalytic converter. In contrast to after-only experiments with matched-pairs samples, matched-observations samples involve a *before-and-after* experiment with a single random sample of elementary units.

The theory and the testing procedure for means with independent samples is applicable for means with matched samples, but the test statistic requires careful explaining. We focus on a problem where matched-observations sampling is feasible although the same test statistic can be used for testing with matched-pairs samples.

For the mean, the test statistic, denoted by $\bar{d}$, represents the average of the difference between measurement x_1 taken from each elementary unit before and measurement x_2 taken after the introduction of the experimental stimulus. This average is defined as

(18.17) $$\bar{d} = \frac{\Sigma d}{n}$$

where $d = x_2 - x_1$ for each elementary unit
n = sample size (number of differences)

Section 18 Testing the Difference of Two Parameters

The sample distribution of d differences has a standard deviation

$$(18.18) \qquad s_d = \sqrt{\frac{\Sigma(d - \bar{d})^2}{n - 1}}$$

Example 18.4

Richard Maytag, the production manager of General Autos Company, wishes to evaluate the effectiveness of X1 catalytic converter (X1-CC) in controlling exhaust emissions of automobile engines. Richard selects a random sample of 10 engines. The sulfur dioxide emissions level in ppm (parts per million) of each engine is measured before and after the installation of an X1-CC. These measures together with the calculation of average difference $\bar{d}$ and standard deviation s_d are conveniently summarized in Table 18.1. Note that the computational steps are the ones we have introduced earlier (Table 11.3).

Table 18.1. Sulfur Dioxide Emissions Level Before and After Installation of X1-CC to a Random Sample of 10 Automobile Engines (ppm)

Engine Number	Before x_1	After x_2	Difference $d = x_2 - x_1$	$d - \bar{d}$	$(d - \bar{d})^2$
1	60	51	−9	−4	16
2	58	56	−2	+3	9
3	63	63	−0	+5	25
4	57	52	−5	0	0
5	61	55	−6	−1	1
6	64	57	−7	−2	4
7	65	63	−2	+3	9
8	58	49	−9	−4	16
9	62	58	−4	+1	1
10	60	54	−6	−1	1
			−50	0	82

$$\bar{d} = \frac{\Sigma d}{n} = \frac{-50}{10} = -5; \quad s_d = \sqrt{\frac{\Sigma(d - \bar{d})^2}{n - 1}} = \sqrt{\frac{82}{9}} = 3.02$$

In this case, it would be inappropriate to run a t test for determining whether there is a significant difference between the mean of x_1 values and the mean of x_2 values. These pairs of observations are not independent; the level of sulfur dioxide emissions after is not independent of the level of emissions before installing X1-CC; each difference, $d = x_2 - x_1$, represents two observations from the same engine. And it is assumed that subtracting x_1 from x_2 emissions level removes the effect of all factors except that of X1-CC.

**Example 18.4
(continued)**

Richard Maytag is anxious to avoid the costly mistake of installing an ineffective X1-CC on all automobiles of the company next year. Hence, his null hypothesis is that there is no difference between the population mean level of sulfur dioxide emissions before and after the installation of X1-CC. The alternative hypothesis is that the mean level of emissions is less after than before the installation of X1-CC. In brief, the null and the alternative hypotheses are

$$H_0: \mu_2 - \mu_1 = 0$$
$$H_1: \mu_2 - \mu_1 < 0$$

where μ_2 is the mean level of emissions after and μ_1 before the installation of X1-CC.

According to this null hypothesis, there is a population of differences d in the emissions level before and after X1-CC is installed, where the mean of these differences is zero. The objective of the test is to determine whether a simple random sample of differences d comes from this population. For such a test, we calculate the mean $\bar{d}$ of the sample differences and test whether such a sample mean differs significantly from zero.

An estimate of the standard error of the sampling distribution of $\bar{d}$ is defined as

(18.19) $$s_{\bar{d}} = \frac{s_d}{\sqrt{n}}$$

where s_d is the standard deviation of sample differences defined in (18.18) and n is the sample size (number of differences). Assuming a normally distributed population of differences, the ratio $(\bar{d} - 0)/s_{\bar{d}}$ is distributed according to the t distribution with an observed value

(18.20) $$\boxed{t_o = \frac{\bar{d}}{s_d/\sqrt{n}}}$$

The zero in the numerator of the ratio is ignored and the denominator is the standard error defined in (18.19).

**Example 18.4
(continued)**

The formulated hypotheses indicate that this is a lower-tailed test where extreme negative values of the mean difference $\bar{d}$ will refute the null hypothesis. Richard wishes to test his null hypothesis at .005 significance level. The number of degrees of freedom is $n - 1$, where n is the number of d values. Since $n = 10$, the number of degrees of freedom (df) is $10 - 1 = 9$. The critical value t_o for .005 and 9 df is -3.25. The decision rule is

If $t_o \geq -3.25$, accept H_0 (X1-CC ineffective, do not install)
If $t_o < -3.25$, reject H_0 (X1-CC effective; install)

Section 18 Testing the Difference of Two Parameters

Substitution of the computed values $\bar{d}$ and s_d from Table 18.1 in formula (18.20) yields

$$t_o = \frac{-5}{3.02/\sqrt{10}} = -5.23$$

As earlier, the null hypothesis is rejected because the observed t_o value falls into the rejection tail of the t distribution. X1-CC may effectively lower the sulfur dioxide emissions level of the tested type of automobile engines.

Before closing our discussion of two-parameter testing, let us briefly compare designs with matched and independent samples. Often and wherever matched sampling is feasible, it may require a much smaller sample size than independent sampling to obtain the same statistical precision. Matched samples have a distinct cost advantage over independent samples in studies where matching is relatively easy and feasible and experimentation requires monitoring of elementary units over a long period of time. Such designs are preferred in biological, pharmaceutical, and medical research when the cost of matching is small compared to the total experimental expense. On the other hand, independent samples may be preferred because matching is too costly; matching may require the availability of a large data base for each elementary unit. In addition, for problems requiring an after-only experiment matched-observations sampling is not feasible and matched-pairs sampling may be nearly impossible to accomplish.

Some persons may consider comparative experiments the exclusive province of scientific research. Chemical, pharmaceutical, and oil companies, to be sure, are engaged in laboratory experiments. Such companies, however, as well as others in agriculture, manufacturing, and service industries also have interest in experiments on production processes, training programs, marketing, advertising, and other business operations. Comparative experiments are also used in the social sciences. At any rate, a manager with some knowledge of comparative experiments may be able to identify appropriate applications of these techniques, to communicate with experts in the field, and evaluate a statistician's recommendations.

PROBLEMS

Group One

18.1. For each significance test carried out in the indicated example, portray the test graphically.
  *(a) Example 18.1   (c) Example 18.3
  (b) Example 18.2   (d) Example 18.4

18.2. For each significance test in the indicated example, carry out the testing procedure in terms of the critical value defined as $d^* = 0 \pm z_c s_d$,
  (i) computing its value;
  (ii) formulating the decision rule; and
  (iii) applying the decision rule:
  *(a) Example 18.1   (c) Example 18.3
  (b) Example 18.2   (d) Example 18.4

Answers to asterisked (*) problems are appended.

Chapter 6 Hypothesis Testing

18.3. Distinguish between:
  (a) Matched-pairs and matched-observations sampling
  (b) After-only and before-and-after experiments
  (c) Control and experimental samples
  (d) Independent and matched sampling
18.4. Compare the advantages and disadvantages of independent and matched sampling.

Group Two

18.5. Pettina Sacks, the agronomist of Tree Farms, did not feel comfortable with the test result (Example 18.3). A careful evaluation of field work disclosed that the field workers, in spite of written instructions, showed wide variations in classifying trees as damaged by aphids. So the observed difference in the proportion of damaged trees may have been the result, at least partially, of misclassification rather than of pest control methods. Fortunately, the company kept records on the number of marketable oranges collected from each tree. Pettina felt that carrying out a test in terms of the difference in the average number of marketable oranges per tree would eliminate possible bias from misclassification. The sample data are as follows:

Ladybug Control	Palathion Control
n_A = 1000 trees	n_B = 1600 trees
$\bar{x}_A$ = 1050 oranges	$\bar{x}_B$ = 1015 oranges
s_A = 152 oranges	s_B = 150 oranges

  *(a) Formulate the null and the alternative hypotheses.
  (b) State the decision rule at .001 significance level.
  (c) Does this test support the earlier test result?
18.6. Automatic screw machines at Metal Fasteners Company produce an equal number of bushings and shafts. Assembly takes place by randomly fitting a bushing over a shaft. Clearance is the difference between the diameter of a bushing and the diameter of a shaft. The two machines are in control if the mean diameter μ_B of bushings less μ_S of shafts is .0015 inch; otherwise, the machines are out of control, turning out bushings and shafts with unacceptable clearance. Perry Tifft, the production manager, is most eager to avoid erroneously adjusting the machines, a time-consuming and costly operation, with .00006 error probability α. Random samples yield the following data:

n_B = 100 bushings	n_S = 100 shafts
$\bar{x}_B$ = 2.002 inches	$\bar{x}_S$ = 2.000 inches
s_B = .002 inch	s_S = .001 inch

Section 18 Testing the Difference of Two Parameters

*(a) Formulate the null hypothesis and its alternative.
(b) State the decision rule in terms of critical clearance d^* values defined as $0 \pm z_c s_d$.
(c) Is the clearance good or bad at .00006 significance level? In other words, are the machines in control?

18.7. In order to double-check the test result for the new animal feed (Example 18.2), the management of Hope Enterprises decides to experiment with matched-pairs samples. Nine twin pairs of steers were randomly selected and one of each twin pair was randomly assigned to the experimental and the other to the control sample. The sample data are as follows:

	Gain in Weight (Pounds)	
Twin Steers No.	C2 Feed n_A	Ordinary Feed n_B
1	710	650
2	695	600
3	630	550
4	660	620
5	880	800
6	845	755
7	750	695
8	740	730
9	690	660

*(a) Calculate the average and standard deviation of the differences.
(b) Formulate the appropriate decision rule for a .005 level of significance.
(c) Should management switch to the new C2 feed?

18.8. Rick Cole, personnel director of Star Consolidated Company, considers two retirement programs for the employees of the company. Premium contributions to each program are the same, but program A has some attractive features about monetary benefits while program B is superior with respect to fringe benefits. Rick had no prior information as to which program may be preferred.
*(a) Formulate the null hypothesis and its alternative. Is the test two-sided, lower-tailed, or upper-tailed? Explain why.
(b) State the appropriate decision rule for 5 percent significance level.
(c) Two samples of employees are shown the provisions of the existing program, while each new program is shown to one of the samples. In a sample of 200 employees 160 prefer program A to the existing program, and in a sample of 300 employees 210 prefer program B to the existing program. What is your recommendation?

18.9. Panels of tasters are used for evaluating the palatability of a new food product H. Individuals recruited from local churches and club groups are randomly assigned to two samples of 50 persons each, half male and half female. After tasting product H in liquid form, each person of the first sample is asked to rate the product on a 7-point pictorial scale ranging from $+3$ to -3. The persons in the second sample are asked to rate a competing product C on the same scale. The average score and variance for each sample are as follows:

Product H	Product C
$\bar{x}_H = 1.18$	$\bar{x}_C = .22$
$s_H^2 = 1.40$	$s_C^2 = 1.465$

*(a) Formulate the null and the alternative hypotheses.
(b) State the decision rule at 1 percent significance level.
(c) Was the palatability of the new product H significantly superior to that of competing product C?

Source: L. Street and M. B. Carroll, "Preliminary Evaluation of a New Food Product," in J. M. Tanur, F. Mosteller, et al., eds., *Statistics: A Guide to the Unknown* (San Francisco: Holden-Day, 1972), pp. 220–28.

18.10. An interesting after-only experimental design is the *placebo control approach* of two independent samples which medical statisticians employed in order to test the effectiveness of the Salk poliomyelitis vaccine. Children between the ages of 5 and 9 years were randomly assigned to two independent samples. Each sample included about 200,000 children. Subjects in the experimental sample A were inoculated with the Salk vaccine; children in the control sample B were inoculated only with an ineffective salt solution. In order to eliminate observer bias, the experiment was *double-blind;* that is, neither the children nor the evaluating diagnosticians knew whether each child was given the Salk vaccine or a placebo injection. The proportion of children struck by polio was .00041 for the experimental and .00081 for the control sample. On the basis of these sample results, was the Salk vaccine effective? Test at .001 significance level.

*(a) Formulate the null and the alternative hypothesis. Is the test two-sided, lower-tailed, or upper-tailed? Explain why.
(b) State the decision rule.
(c) Apply the decision rule and explain the test result.
(d) The actual polio vaccine experiment, which took place during 1954, was more elaborate than the problem suggests. Ethical and other considerations required another experimental design (see next problem) in addition to the placebo approach. The whole study involved over 1.8 million children. For details see P. Meier, "The Biggest Health Experiment Ever: The 1954 Field Trial of the Salk Poliomyelitis Vaccine," in Tanur et al., *Statistics,* pp. 2–13.

18.11. In addition to the placebo control approach (see Problem 18.10), research in the Salk vaccine experiment used the *observed control approach* of two independent samples. In a given geographical area, the *treated* sample A consisted of all second-graders and the *control* sample B of all children in the first and third grades. Although polio incidence was expected to vary somewhat with age, it was considered reasonable that the average of the first and third grades would be a sufficient control for the second grade. Participation was voluntary and physicians

Section 18 Testing the Difference of Two Parameters

were aware of the fact that only second-graders were vaccinated. The sample data were as follows:

	Sample (Approx.)	Polio Cases
Treated	222,000	76
Control	725,000	439

(a) Assuming that voluntary participation yielded random samples, was the polio vaccine effective at .001 significance level?

(b) How does the reliability of this approach compare with the placebo control approach?

(c) Why did not the researchers follow the *vital statistics* approach, that is, inoculating all children of susceptible ages in the United States and then observing the effect of the vaccine on the rate of polio incidence? For a discussion of the pros and cons of all three approaches, read the article cited in Problem 18.10.

18.12. In a sex discrimination court case the dean of the college disclaimed entertaining any sex bias: of a total of 101 male nontenured faculty applicants for tenure, 12 were denied reappointment, while for female applicants the score was 6 out of 43.

(a) Is the dean's disclaimer justified statistically? Answer in terms of the probability value of the observed z_o value.

(b) Should the judge consider the data as sufficient evidence to accept or reject the dean's disclaimer?

Chapter 7
CHI-SQUARE TESTS AND ANALYSIS OF VARIANCE

Frequently, problems may require a comparison of several population proportions. Such a comparison is particularly important because a proportion is the only measure for categorical or qualitative variables. For example, we may wish to determine whether the binomial distribution is a close enough approximation to a sample frequency distribution of, say, family cereal servings per week; establishing that the frequency of servings is binomially distributed would justify application of the Bernoulli model for planning a marketing strategy. Comparisons such as this are accomplished with *chi-square tests,* which occupy the first section of this chapter.

Still other problems may require a comparison of several population means. An experimental agricultural station may compare the mean yield of a crop after application of different fertilizer quantities in order to determine the most productive dosage. An advertising agency may compare the sales of different advertising displays in order to find the most sales-effective display. A detergent manufacturer may determine the effectiveness of a new liquid cleanser by comparing the removal of stains at different levels of water hardness. Problems such as these where we wish to compare several means are handled in the second section of this chapter with a technique called *analysis of variance*.

SECTION 19/ CHI-SQUARE TESTS

Does a set of observed frequencies differ significantly from a set of theoretical or expected frequencies? A chi-square test which is designed to answer such a question is called a *goodness-of-fit test.* In other situations, we may wish to test whether or not two variables are independent. For example, is magazine readership related to personality characteristics of readers such as achievement orientation vs. non–achievement orientation? We may hypothesize that the observed frequencies of magazine readership are independent of such personality traits. Rejecting the hypothesis and establishing dependence may help us select the appropriate magazine for a more effective advertising campaign. This type of chi-square testing is called a *test of independence* or a *contingency test*.

These two types of chi-square tests are considered after we introduce the chi-square probability distribution.

The Chi-Square Distribution

For large sample sizes the sampling distribution of chi-square can be closely approximated by the chi-square probability distribution. This approximation is analogous to the normal distribution for the Z statistic and the t distribution for the t statistic. Here, we use an illustration to introduce the chi-square statistic and its distribution.

Example 19.1

Bacchus Inc., a wine-making firm, wishes to determine which of four white table wines is preferred by consumers. Samples of the four wines are contained in a set of small identical glasses designated A, B, C, and D. A panel of 200 regular wine drinkers is randomly selected and each panel member drinks from a set of the four glasses in a randomly determined order. The preferences of the panel members are shown in Table 19.1.

Table 19.1.
White Wine Preferences by a Panel of 200 Tasters

Type of Wine		Number of Tasters
Mountain	(A)	64
Garten	(B)	38
Rhine	(C)	35
Chablis	(D)	63
		200

Are the preferences of the panel members true preferences of the consumer population or are the tasters drawn from a consumer population with no difference in their preference? If all consumers have no differences in their preference, then their proportions π who prefer each of the four wines are equal to 25 percent. The null and the alternative hypotheses may be formulated as follows (where each subscript letter denotes a given wine).

$H_0: \pi_A = \pi_B = \pi_C = \pi_D$ (no difference in preference)
H_1: The π values are not all equal (preferences are different)

If the null hypothesis that consumers equally prefer each of the four wines is true, the *expected* number of the 200 wine tasters in the sample who would prefer each wine would be $50 = .25 \times 200$. The chi-square statistic, denoted by χ^2, measures the difference between the observed number of tasters in the sample who prefer each of the four wines shown in Table 19.1 and the expected number

Section 19 Chi-Square Tests

of 50 tasters who would have preferred each wine *if* the null hypothesis is true. The value of χ^2 is calculated by

(19.1)
$$\chi^2 = \Sigma \frac{(f_o - f_e)^2}{f_e}$$

where f_o = observed frequency in a class
f_e = expected frequency in the same class if the null hypothesis is true

Example 19.1 (continued)

The steps for calculating the χ^2 value for our wine preference problem are shown in Table 19.2. The observed frequency f_o for each type of wine is obtained from Table 19.1. The theoretical or expected frequencies f_e represent the hypothesis that the proportion of consumers in the population who definitely prefer each of the four wines is the same. Note that the algebraic sum of the differences $\Sigma (f_o - f_e)$ in column 4 is equal to zero, as it must always be. These differences are squared, divided by the corresponding expected frequency, and summed, as required by formula (19.1), to obtain the observed chi-square value, denoted by χ_o^2, equal to 14.68.

Table 19.2. Calculation of χ^2 Statistic for Wine Preference

Type of Wine (1)	Observed Preference f_o (2)	Expected Preference f_e (3)	$f_o - f_e$ (4)	$(f_o - f_e)^2$ (5)	$\frac{(f_o - f_e)^2}{f_e}$ (6)
Mountain	64	50	+14	196	3.92
Garten	38	50	−12	144	2.88
Rhine	35	50	−15	225	4.50
Chablis	63	50	+13	169	3.38
	200	200	0		14.68

$$\chi_o^2 = \Sigma \frac{(f_o - f_e)^2}{f_e} = 14.68$$

Does the observed chi-square value indicate a significant difference between observed and expected frequencies for rejecting the null hypothesis and concluding that consumers preferences are different? Before answering this question we must discuss the characteristics of the probability model upon which the decision procedure is based. The chi-square distribution has the number of df (degrees of freedom) as its only parameter.* Like the t distribution, χ^2 is a continuous random

---

*The chi-square distribution is defined by the function

$$P(\chi^2) = c(\chi^2)^{(\nu/2)-1} e^{-\chi^2/2}$$

where ν = number of degrees of freedom (Greek letter *nu*)
c = a constant depending on ν (df)
e = 2.718 ...

variable with a uniquely determined distribution for each value of df. Beyond these general similarities, there are important differences.

First, unlike the *t* distribution, the chi-square distribution is skewed to the right, as shown in Fig. 19.1. Note that as the degrees of freedom increase, the chi-square distribution becomes bell-shaped and symmetrical. In fact, for a sufficiently large number of degrees of freedom the chi-square distribution can be approximated by the normal distribution.

Second, the number of degrees of freedom is not determined from the sample size *n* but from the number of *k* classes to which expected frequencies are grouped. In Example 19.1, *k* equals 4 since expected frequencies are grouped into four classes, one for each type of wine. Furthermore, we shall see that determination of the number of degrees of freedom in each case depends on the method employed in obtaining expected frequencies.

Third, the value of the random variable χ^2 is always greater than or equal to zero. For a given df, the greater the value of χ^2, the smaller the probability (tail area) which corresponds to that value. Since there is a different chi-square distribution for each degree of freedom, each distribution requires a separate table of areas. Compactness is obtained with a table shown in Appendix G. For each degree of freedom there is a separate chi-square distribution shown in a row of the table; each row contains only selected χ^2 values which correspond to the area in the right-hand tail of the distribution. Consider the chi-square distribution with 5 degrees of freedom. The probability for a χ^2 value greater than 15.09 is .01. It is the shaded area in the right-hand tail of the curve.

The general characteristics of the chi-square distribution, especially the determination of the number of degrees of freedom, are discussed in greater detail later in our coverage of chi-square test procedures.

Example 19.1 (continued)

Suppose we wish to test our wine preference hypothesis at 1 percent level of significance. Since there are *four* classes (Table 19.2), *k* equals 4. The number of degrees of freedom is obtained by reducing the number of classes *k* by 1. Hence, df is 4 − 1, or 3. The reason for subtracting 1 from *k* is because we forced the total expected frequencies to be equal to the total observed frequencies, that is, $\Sigma f_e = \Sigma f_o$. Once the total expected frequen-

Figure 19.1.
Graphs of χ^2 distributions for df equal to 1, 5, and 10.

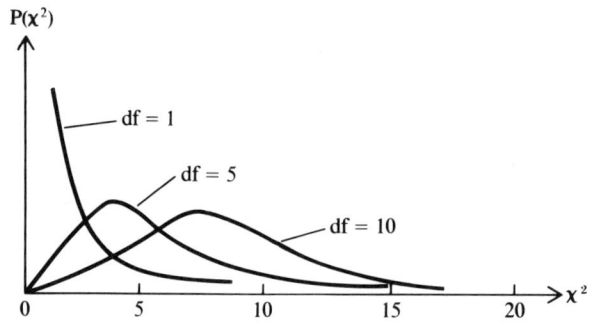

cies are fixed, only three f_e values are freely assignable to the classes. The f_e value for the fourth class is determined residually, that is, as the difference between the sum of frequencies of the three classes and the fixed sample size of 200. From Appendix G we find that for df = 3 and under the column heading .010 the critical value of chi-square, denoted by χ_c^2, is 11.35.

Our decision rule is

If $\chi_o^2 \leq 11.35$, accept H_0 (no difference in preference)
If $\chi_o^2 > 11.35$, reject H_0 (preferences are different)

Since the observed χ_o^2 of 14.68, calculated in Table 19.2, is greater than the critical χ_c^2 of 11.35, we reject the null hypothesis. The difference between observed and expected preferences cannot be attributed to chance alone. Indeed, consumers may prefer mountain and chablis over garten and Rhine white wines.

Instead of testing a hypothesis at a prespecified level of significance, researchers frequently prefer to state only the probability which corresponds to the observed chi-square value. It is left for the reader to decide whether or not the difference between observed and expected frequencies is significant. Since the observed χ_o^2 value in our example is 14.68 and df = 3, from Appendix G we can see that the probability of a χ^2 value larger than 14.68 is less than .005.

Goodness-of-Fit Tests

We have seen that statistical analysis of real-world problems frequently requires application of a probability model. For example, estimation of a population mean is based on the application of the t distribution or the normal distribution. Data from business and social and physical sciences may be studied by applying the binomial, Poisson, or other probability distributions. These applications are based on the assumption that the observed data conform to the conditions underlying the applied model.

But the observed data rarely conform precisely to the conditions of a probability model. Conformity of the observed data to the conditions of the model may be validated with a chi-square test. Since it measures how well the observed frequencies fit the expected frequencies of the chosen model, such a test is called a *goodness-of-fit test*.

In fact, testing of the wine preference hypothesis may be considered a goodness-of-fit test where expected frequencies represent an equiprobable or uniform probability model. Our null hypothesis was that there is a good fit between the model and the observed data. By rejecting the null hypothesis we concluded that the observed and expected frequencies were a poor fit; there are significant differences in wine preference among consumers. Another illustration will give us the opportunity to introduce some refinements in the application of the chi-square distribution.

Example 19.2

The management of Continental Foods, Inc., a midwestern firm, wishes to study some marketing aspects of the company's cold cereals. A sample of 200 families are asked how many days each week the firm's cold cereals were served for breakfast. The sample data are shown in Table 19.3, columns 1 and 2. One of the initial hypotheses is that the number of weekly servings is binomially distributed. Validating this hypothesis is important for planning a marketing strategy for cold cereals.

Testing the hypothesis requires the derivation of the expected binomial frequencies. The procedure is shown in Table 19.3. First, we multiply the number of serving days in column 1 by the number of families in column 2 to find the total number of times cold cereals were served by all the families in the sample, as shown in column 3. Second, we calculate the proportion of servings out of a total possible times cold cereals could have been served each week. Since the sampled families served collectively 400 servings and the total possible could have been 1000 = (200)(5) servings, the proportion p is

$$p = \frac{400}{1000} = .40$$

Third, the binomial probabilities for $n = 5$ and $\pi = .40$, shown in column 4, are obtained from Appendix B. Finally, we multiply these probabilities times the sample size 200 to find the expected frequencies in column 5.

Table 19.3.
Expected or Theoretical Distribution of 200 Families Served Cold Cereals Each Week Assuming a Binomial Distribution

Days Cold Cereals Served (1)	Observed Number of Families (2)	Servings Col. 1 × Col. 2 (3)	Probability $n = 5, \pi = .40$ (4)	Expected Frequency Col. 4 × 200 (5)
0	15	0	.0778	15.6
1	59	59	.2592	51.8
2	57	114	.3456	69.1
3	54	162	.2304	46.1
4	10	40	.0768	15.4
5 or more	5	25	.0102	2.0
	200	400	1.0000	200.0

The fact that the bottom class in Table 19.3 contains only 2 occurrences raises an important question. We explained that the chi-square function represents the distribution of a *continuous* random variable. But the χ^2 values are calculated with formula (19.1). They are the values of a discrete random variable since the number of possible combinations of f_e values are finite, yielding a finite number of computed χ^2 values. Therefore, the calculated χ^2 values are only approximations of the continuous chi-square distribution. This approximation is adequate for sufficiently large class frequencies. As a rule, if a class contains 5 or more *expected* frequencies, the approximation is considered adequate for most practical problems. Otherwise, contiguous classes are merged and their frequencies are grouped together.

Example 19.2 (continued)

The basic data from columns 1, 2, and 5 of Table 19.3 are reproduced in Table 19.4. Observe that the expected frequencies 15.4 and 2.0 of the bottom two classes from Table 19.3 are added and their sum equals 17.4.

Table 19.4. Calculation of χ^2 Statistic for the Cold Cereals Problem

Days Cold Cereal Served	f_o	f_e	$f_o - f_e$	$(f_o - f_e)^2$	$\dfrac{(f_o - f_e)^2}{f_e}$
0	15	15.6	− .6	.36	.02
1	59	51.8	+ 7.2	51.84	1.00
2	57	69.1	−12.1	146.41	2.12
3	54	46.1	+ 7.9	62.41	1.35
4 or 5	15	17.4	− 2.4	5.76	.33
	200	200.0	= 0		4.82

$$\chi_o^2 = \Sigma \frac{(f_o - f_e)^2}{f_e} = 4.82$$

After this adjustment, we may determine the number of degrees of freedom. This is necessary in order to apply the appropriate chi-square distribution for testing our hypothesis. In the wine preference problem (Example 19.1) we found that the appropriate chi-square distribution had 3 degrees of freedom. We determined this number by subtracting 1 from k classes, where k was 4. The reason for subtracting 1 is because we forced the total expected frequencies to be equal to the total observed frequencies. The degrees of freedom were not reduced further because we imposed no additional restrictions in the calculation of the expected frequencies. Otherwise, the degrees of freedom are further reduced by 1 for every additional restriction. If determination of expected frequencies requires that m parameters be replaced with estimates, we impose m additional restrictions. In general, the number of degrees of freedom is

(19.2) $$\boxed{df = k - 1 - m}$$

where k = number of classes
  1 = the initial reduction because of the restriction that the sum of the expected must equal the sum of the observed frequencies, that is, $\Sigma f_e = \Sigma f_o$.
  m = the number of parameters estimated by the sample

Example 19.2 (continued)

For our cold cereals problem, (Table 19.4) k is 5. Since we used statistic p to estimate parameter π of the binomial distribution, m is 1. Therefore, by formula (19.2) the number of degrees of freedom is df = 3 = 5 − 1 − 1. Suppose we wish to test our hypothesis that the number of weekly servings of cold cereals is binomially distributed at a 5 percent level of significance.

For 3 degrees of freedom the table in Appendix G shows that the critical χ_c^2 value is 7.81 at $\alpha = .05$. The decision rule is

If $\chi_o^2 \leq 7.81$, accept H_0 (binomial is a good fit)
If $\chi_o^2 > 7.81$, reject H_0 (binomial is not a good fit)

The basic calculations are shown in Table 19.4. Since the χ_o^2 value of 4.82 is less than the χ_c^2 value of 7.81, we accept the null hypothesis. Alternatively, we may argue that the probability value of $\chi_o^2 = 4.82$ is approximately .17 (obtained by interpolation). Thus, the null hypothesis is not rejected at the .05 level. We reach the conclusion that the number of days the cold cereals of the firm were served each week may be binomially distributed.

Of course, the nature of conclusions reached with hypothesis-testing procedures should not be forgotten. This example, however, raises one additional, subtle technical point. The same sample evidence was utilized for establishing and for testing the null hypothesis. This departure from classical hypothesis-testing procedures, requiring hypothesis formulation not based on the same sample evidence, used to test the hypothesis may not be too serious in this case. But it reduces the number of degrees of freedom by 1. If the parameter π of the binomial distribution were known, then the hypothesis would have been tested with a chi-square distribution having 4 degrees of freedom. In our case, this would have strengthened acceptance of the null hypothesis. On the other hand, had our sample supported rejection of our null hypothesis, the same adjustment in degrees of freedom may have reversed our conclusion. In borderline cases, it would be better to suspend judgment and check the results with other independent sources.

Goodness-of-fit tests may be applied to solving practical problems. For example, since we have shown that cold cereal servings may be binomially distributed, we may employ the binomial distribution in order to determine an appropriate marketing strategy for cold cereals. Or if we show that arrivals of cargo ships at a dock are Poisson-distributed, we may simulate such arrivals, using the appropriate Poisson distribution, in order to determine the need for new docking facilities. In general, establishing that observed data are distributed like a binomial, Poisson, normal, or any other probability model may become the basis for further analysis and solution of a problem.

Contingency Tests

The null hypothesis in a contingency test is not based on a probability model but on the probability rule for independent events. For this reason, it is also called a test of independence. The following simple example illustrates the testing procedure.

Example 19.3

Advertisers select media so that the brand image of the advertised product may have the greatest influence on potential customers. Selection requires, among other matters, knowledge of the personality characteristics of readers. One hundred male readers of two magazines were given 15 tests designed to measure their personality traits. The results of one test measur-

Table 19.5.
Sample of 100
Readers Classified by
Magazine Read and
Achievement
Orientation

Orientation		Magazine A	Magazine B	Total
Achievement	(C)	12	28	40
Nonachievement	(D)	30	30	60
Totals:		42	58	100

ing whether or not the respondents are achievement-oriented appear in Table 19.5. Are the readers of the magazine significantly different with respect to this trait? In other words, advertisers wish to know whether or not the preference for the two magazines is independent of this personality trait of the readers. If the two events are dependent, then advertisers may select the magazine with personality characteristics of readers which are likely to have maximum impact on potential sales.

In contingency tests, the null hypothesis is that events are independent. And expected frequencies are calculated by assuming that the null hypothesis is true.

Example 19.3 (continued)

In our case the null and the alternative hypotheses would be

H_0: Magazine readership is *independent* of achievement orientation

H_1: Magazine readership is *dependent* on achievement orientation

According to Table 19.5 and the probability rule (6.8) for independent events

$$P(A \text{ and } C) = P(A) \, P(C)$$

In other words, the probability of the joint event *A and C*, readers of magazine *A* who are achievement-oriented *C*, is equal to the product of the marginal probabilities for these events. In numbers,

$$P(A \text{ and } C) = \frac{42}{100} \times \frac{40}{100} = .1680$$

Multiplying this joint probability by the sample size 100, we find that the expected frequency is 16.8. This calculation may be simplified with the following formula:

(19.3) $$f_e = \frac{\text{column total} \times \text{row total}}{\text{grand total}}$$

Thus, the expected frequency for the same joint event *A and C* is, by formula (19.3),

$$f_e = \frac{(42)(40)}{100} = 16.80$$

In the same manner we may obtain the expected frequencies of the other joint events as follows:

Joint Event	Formula (19.3)		Frequency f_e
A and D	(42)(60)/100	=	25.20
B and C	(58)(40)/100	=	23.20
B and D	(58)(60)/100	=	34.80

These expected frequencies are summarized in Table 19.6.

Table 19.6. Expected Frequencies for 100 Readers Classified by Magazine Read and Achievement Orientation

Orientation		Magazine A	Magazine B	Total
Achievement	(C)	16.80	23.20	40.00
Nonachievement	(D)	25.20	34.80	60.00
Totals:		42.00	58.00	100.00

The observed chi-square value is calculated from the data of Tables 19.5 and 19.6 in the usual manner as shown in Table 19.7.

Table 19.7. Calculation of the χ^2 Statistic for Achievement Orientation of Magazine Readers

Joint Events	f_o	f_e	$f_o - f_e$	$(f_o - f_e)^2$	$\dfrac{(f_o - f_e)^2}{f_e}$
A and C	13	16.8	−4.8	23.04	1.37
A and D	30	25.2	+4.8	23.04	.91
B and C	28	23.2	+4.8	23.04	.99
B and D	30	34.8	−4.8	23.04	.66
	100	100.0	0		3.93

$$\chi_o^2 = \Sigma \frac{(f_o - f_e)^2}{f_e} = 3.93$$

This value measures how far the observed frequencies are from the frequencies obtainable if the joint events were independent. Testing requires determination of the number of degrees of freedom and the desired χ_c^2 values. A table such as Table 19.5 is called a *two-by-two* (also denoted by 2 × 2) *contingency table*. In general, a table with r rows and k columns is called an *r-by-k* ($r \times k$) contingency table. The product of rows and columns determines the number of cells in a contingency

Section 19 Chi-Square Tests

table. Thus, a 2 × 2 table has 4 cells, a 2 × 3 has 6 cells, a 3 × 3 has 9 cells, and so forth. In a contingency table with r rows and k columns, the number of degrees of freedom is

(19.4)
$$df = (r - 1)(k - 1)$$

Example 19.3 (continued)

Our problem has 1 degree of freedom since by (19.4) $df=(2-1)(2-1)=1$. The reason is that as soon as one of the expected frequencies is determined, the frequencies of the other three joint events or cells can be determined residually from the fixed marginal totals of Table 19.5. We found that the joint event A and C has an expected frequency of 16.8 by applying the product rule for independent events. Then the joint event A and D has an expected frequency of 25.2 since 42 (all magazine A readers) less 16.8 is equal to 25.2; the relative frequency of event B and C is 23.2 = 40 − 16.8 and of event B and D is 34.8 = 60 − 25.2 as shown in Table 19.6.

Suppose we wish to test the independence hypothesis at a 5 percent level of significance. From Appendix G and for 1 degree of freedom we find that χ_c^2 is 3.84. Our decision rule is

If $\chi_o^2 \leq 3.84$, accept H_0 (magazine readership is *independent* of achievement orientation)
If $\chi_o^2 > 3.84$, reject H_0 (magazine readership is *dependent* of achievement orientation)

Since $\chi_o^2 = 3.93$, shown in Table 19.7, is greater than 3.84, we reject the null hypothesis. We conclude that the events of the case may be dependent. Magazine preference and the achievement orientation of readers may be related.

But χ_o^2 is only 3.93, very close the the critical χ_c^2 value of 3.84. Had we set the level of significance at 1 percent, we would have accepted the null hypothesis and concluded that magazine preference and the personality trait of readers may not be related. Furthermore, for 2 × 2 contingency tables it may be necessary to adjust the χ_o^2 value with a correction for continuity. For this correction, formula (19.1) is modified to

(19.5)
$$\chi_o^2 = \Sigma \frac{(|f_o - f_e| - 1/2)^2}{f_e}$$

The continuity correction is introduced because we use a theoretical continuous distribution to test discrete data. In other words, the computed χ_o^2 value does not correspond exactly with probabilities read from Appendix G.

Example 19.3 (continued)

Applying this correction, the original value χ_o^2 of 3.93 in Table 19.7 is reduced to 3.16. At this χ_o^2 value and 5 percent level of significance the null hypothesis is accepted. Events are independent. We conclude that the relationship between magazine preference and achievement orientation of readers may not be significant.

If the test results are inconclusive, as in this case, it may be wise to suspend judgment. We may double-check the test results with data from other independent sources or, if possible, increase the sample size.

The continuity correction reduces the χ_o^2 value, thus adjusting for bias toward rejecting the null hypothesis too often. When the absolute difference $|f_o - f_e|$ in a particular cell is less than $1/2$, such correction should be omitted. In large samples, the continuity correction has little effect on the χ^2 value. But it may as well be part of the computational routine since it can be easily calculated. In all other respects the test procedure for contingency tables larger than 2×2 is identical to the one already described.

Summary and Comments

Chi-square testing is an extension or generalization of techniques for testing equality of two proportions. Both the goodness-of-fit and contingency testing procedures involve the following sequence of steps:

1. We formulate the null and the alternative hypotheses and determine the level of significance for rejecting the null hypothesis.
2. We draw a random sample of observations from the population under study.
3. We establish a decision rule on the basis of a critical chi-square value χ_c^2.
4. We derive a set of expected, or theoretical, frequencies under the assumption that the null hypothesis is true. For a goodness-of-fit test, such observations are obtained from a probability distribution model which is assumed to be applicable to the statistical population under study. For a contingency test, the observations are obtained under the assumption that events are independent.
5. We calculate the observed chi-square value, χ_o^2, which measures differences between observed and expected frequencies.
6. We reject the null hypothesis if the observed χ_o^2 value is greater than the critical χ_c^2 value. This means that the aggregate of differences between observed and expected frequencies is too great to be attributed to chance alone at the specified significance level.

Interpretation of statistical results is subject to a number of limitations especially related to chi-square tests:

1. We have seen that the null hypothesis is rejected if the χ_o^2 value is large enough. The question is whether we should also reject the null hypothesis for χ_o^2 values too close to zero. Of course, very close agreement between observed and expected frequencies should be examined carefully. But instead of rejecting the null hypothesis as "too good to be true," it might be desirable and certainly wise to double-check data reliability. We may discover that we should reject the data, because of errors in data measurement or collection, rather than the null hypothesis.
2. Since the sample size is fixed in advance, we are able to control only the value of error probability α for rejecting a true null hypothesis. The β risk for

accepting a false null hypothesis may be large. However, finding β probabilities is a task that lies outside the scope of this text. The β risk can be reduced by increasing the level of significance, that is, probability α. Furthermore, in the case of goodness-of-fit tests we may compare the observed data with expected frequencies from more than one probability model and select the model with the smallest χ_o^2 value. Of course, the larger the sample, the greater the protection against β risk.

3. Rejecting the null hypothesis in a contingency test leads to the conclusion that the classifying characteristics are related. In our example, we concluded that magazine preference is related to the achievement-orientation trait of readers. But this association is between categorical variables. It is qualitative and not quantitative in nature. It is not a method for estimating the values of one numerical variable from the known values of another numerical variable or variables. This is possible with regression analysis, which is covered in the next chapter.

PROBLEMS

Group One

19.1. Find the value of the chi-square for each set of level of significance α and number of degrees of freedom.

   *(a) $\alpha = .01$, df $= 5$ (d) $\alpha = .025$, df $= 29$

   (b) $\alpha = .10$, df $= 3$ (e) $\alpha = .005$, df $= 16$

   (c) $\alpha = .05$, df $= 10$ (f) $\alpha = .75$, df $= 7$

*19.2. A random sample of 300 farms was selected for an agricultural experiment. Since only 160 farms completed the experiment, the question was raised as to whether or not the initial and the recovered samples vary significantly with respect to certain characteristics relevant to the study. Chi-square tests yield the following results:

Basis for Comparison	Degrees of Freedom	Observed Chi-Square	Critical Chi-Square for $\alpha = .05$
A. Age of farm operator	5	6.25	11.07
B. Total acreage per farm	11	25.36	19.68
C. Type of farm	6	8.57	12.59
D. Level of farm income	4	6.84	9.49

For what comparisons do the samples vary significantly? Explain.

19.3. Arrow Advertising Agency wishes to determine whether a reader's preference for magazine A, B, or C is independent of his or her personality characteristics, given below in (a), (b), and (c). For each personality characteristic, the given level of significance α, and observed χ_o^2 value:

   (i) Formulate the null and alternative hypotheses.

   (ii) Determine the number of degrees of freedom.

Answers to asterisked (*) problems are appended.

(iii) Find the critical χ_c^2 value and establish the appropriate decision rule.
(iv) Conclude whether the null hypothesis of independence should be accepted or rejected and explain the meaning of your conclusion.
*(a) Compliance vs. noncompliance to authority; $\alpha = .01$ and $\chi_o^2 = 5.36$
(b) Degree of aggression as measured on an integer scale from 1 to 3; $\alpha = .05$ and $\chi_o^2 = 15.72$
(c) Degree of self-esteem as measured on an integer scale from 1 to 5; $\alpha = .005$ and $\chi_o^2 = 25.65$

19.4. Random samples of various sizes have been selected for each of the contingency test situations in (a), (b), (c), and (d). For the stated level of significance α and the observed χ_o^2 value:
(i) Determine the number of degrees of freedom.
(ii) Find the critical value χ_c^2 and establish the appropriate decision rule.
(iii) Conclude whether the null hypothesis of independence should be accepted or rejected and explain the meaning of your conclusion.
*(a) Medical practice (general practitioner, internist, gynecologist, all other) vs. knowledge and use of formula Y (not heard of, heard of but not used, heard of and used) for $\alpha = .01$ and $\chi_o^2 = 11.13$
(b) Product (A, B, and C) vs. degree of satisfaction (satisfied, moderately satisfied, dissatisfied, don't know) for $\alpha = .05$ and $\chi_o^2 = 18.22$
(c) Smokers (filter, nonfilter) vs. residence in the United States (East, Central, South, West) for $\alpha = .005$ and $\chi_o^2 = 19.33$
(d) Political affiliation (Democratic, Republican, independent, don't know) vs. U.S. government policies on energy (strongly approve, approve, disapprove, strongly disapprove, don't know) for $\alpha = .10$ and $\chi_o^2 = 27.41$

19.5 We have seen that the continuity correction reversed the test results in Example 19.3. One way of resolving the inconclusive results would be to increase the sample size. Suppose there is a proportional increase of the sample shown in Table 19.5 to 1000.
*(a) Are magazine readership and achievement orientation of readers related significantly? Test at 5 percent level of significance.
(b) What is the effect of continuity correction?

19.6. Suppose the proportion π of days serving cold cereals in Example 19.2 is known to be .45.
*(a) Carry out a chi-square test at 1 percent level of significance.
(b) Is it appropriate to conclude that the observed data are not binomially distributed?

19.7. Identify and explain the following terms:
(a) Chi-square distribution
(b) Correction for continuity
(c) Contingency table
(d) Degrees of freedom
(e) Contingency test
(f) Goodness-of-fit test

Group Two

*19.8. George Higgins, the production manager of a firm manufacturing metal components for engines, claims that an automatic machine operates at 10 percent average fraction defective. This means, on the average, 10 percent of the metal pieces the machine stamps out are expected to be defective. In order to evaluate the machine's performance Clara Boyd, the quality control engineer, instructs the machine operator to take, at regular intervals, a random sample of 7 pieces and record the number of defective pieces in each sample. The record shows the following:

Number of defective pieces	0	1	2	3	4	5	6	7
Number of 7-piece samples	411	395	154	30	6	2	1	1

On the basis of this data, the quality control engineer claims that the average fraction defective of the machine is 12 percent. Which individual is correct? Test at 5 percent significance level.

19.9. The manager of Burger Queen, a chain of quick-service restaurants, wishes to determine the palatability of a new product. Therefore, the marketing department of the firm designs an experiment. The new product and a competing product, each in liquid and solid forms, are placed in four identical containers designated A, B, C, and D. One hundred randomly selected individuals are assigned the four containers in a randomly determined sequence. They are asked to taste each product and indicate which they most prefer. The results are as follows:

Product	A	B	C	D
Individuals	18	32	17	33

(a) Formulate the null and the alternative hypotheses.
*(b) Are the observed differences in product preference significant? Test at 5 and 1 percent levels of significance.
(c) If B and D contain the new product in liquid and solid forms, respectively, what conclusion does the chi-square test suggest?

19.10. Supreme Stores Inc. markets bread and other bakery products through company-owned A stores as well as franchised-type B stores. While type A stores are managed by employees of the company, type B are independently owned and managed as dealerships. The company wants to know if the two types of stores cater to two distinctly different customer markets. The information is valuable for nationwide advertising. A survey was taken of 200 credit-card customers who were asked, among other questions, the principal reason for preferring one or the other type of store. The response was as follows:

	Customer Preference	
Principal Reason	Store A	Store B
Location	27	13
Staff appearance	60	30
Quality of service	33	37
Totals:	120	80

(a) Formulate the null and alternative hypotheses.
(b) Establish the appropriate decision rule at 1 percent level of significance.
*(c) Is type of store related to the reasons of customer preference?

19.11* Timothy Neiman, operations manager of Fairbank Transportation Authority (FTA), commissions a survey designed to study automobile traffic at an FTA toll bridge. For several typical traffic days and for the period between 7:00 A.M. and 9:00 P.M., automobile arrivals at toll booths are counted during randomly selected 1-minute intervals. The obtained data are as follows:

Number of car arrivals	0	1	2	3	4	5	6	7	8 or more
Number of time intervals	130	283	265	190	82	32	10	6	2

(a) Are automobile arrivals at the toll booths Poisson-distributed? Test at 5 percent level of significance.
(b) Suppose they are Poisson-distributed. How may Timothy use this information?

19.12. Does the quality of the legal counsel have a significant effect in the outcome of criminal trials? To find out, a sample of 2790 jury trials was studied. After each trial the presiding judge told the researchers in confidence how he or she would have decided the case had the case been tried without a jury. The judge's private decision was considered the basis for comparing quality of counsel under the assumption that the skill of the counsel is likely to affect the judge far less than the jury.

Class	Defense Counsel Superior	Abilities Equal	Prosecutor Superior
Jury acquitted and judge would have acquitted	63	402	65
Jury convicted and judge would have convicted	194	1739	327
Totals:	257	2141	392

What is your answer to the question about the quality of the counsel? Test at 5 percent level of significance.

*Requires knowledge of Section 10.

For an analysis of the findings see H. Zeisel and H. Kalven, Jr., "Parking Tickets and Missing Women: Statistics and the Law," in Tanur et al., *Statistics,* pp. 109–10.

SECTION 20 / ANALYSIS OF VARIANCE

While the chi-square test is an extension of techniques for testing two proportions, analysis of variance is an extension of techniques for testing two means. We introduce the simplest form of the method, namely, one-factor analysis of variance. Together with the computational steps, we explain the rationale of the test, introduce the F distribution, and illustrate the testing procedure.

Introduction

Analysis of variance, frequently referred to as ANOVA, is designed to answer the following question: If we are considering data from more than two samples, are these samples drawn from populations having identical means? Thus, testing is based on the null hypothesis that all population means are equal, and we wish to determine whether the observed differences among the sample means justify acceptance or rejection of the null hypothesis. Although the purpose of the test is to determine whether or not the sample means differ significantly, actual analysis is carried out in terms of sample variance, as the name of the test indicates. The reason for this will soon become obvious.

Example 20.1

Donaldson Associates, an advertising agency, wishes to test the sales effectiveness of two advertising displays with different campaign themes. The experiment includes three advertising methods or *treatments*. Two consist of special advertising displays. The third method represents an "ordinary" treatment with no special display or other promotional effort; it provides the

Table 20.1.
Sales (Units per 1000 Customers) by Advertising Method for Donaldson Associates Problem

Sampled Store Row i	Advertising Method—Treatment		
	$j = 1$	2	3
1	20	23	17
2	24	26	19
3	18	22	17
4	22	25	19
Total:	84	96	72
Mean $\bar{X}_j =$	21	24	18
Grand mean $\bar{\bar{X}} =$	$\dfrac{20 + 24 + \cdots + 19}{12} = 21$		

basis for comparing the other two methods. Four retail stores are randomly assigned to each of the three treatments, making a total of 12 stores. The experimentation period lasting 4 weeks yields the sales data shown in Table 20.1.

Columns 1, 2, and 3 denote the two displays and the "ordinary" treatment, respectively. Each of the 12 entries in the table represents the number of units sold per 1000 customers during a 4-week period in a given store.

At this point, we need to introduce some basic notation which will facilitate subsequent computational work. The position of each observation, such as in Table 20.1, may be indicated with two subscripts: the row subscript i and the column subscript j. In Table 20.1, i takes on the values 1, 2, 3, or 4, each denoting a sample, and j takes on the values 1, 2, and 3, each denoting an advertising method or treatment. For example, the value X_{12} is 23, representing the first sample, row 1, from the second advertising method, column 2. In general, X_{ij} represents the value of an observation, where i denotes the row number and j the column number.*

Example 20.2

In our illustration we deliberately used a small sample of stores in order to explain the method with a minimum of computational work. In actual practice large samples would be necessary to yield reliable results. But the procedure is equally applicable to problems of any sample size. Dividing the column totals in Table 20.1 by 4, the sample size per treatment, we obtain the column $\bar{X}_j$ mean values as follows:

$$\bar{X}_1 = \frac{84}{4} = 21, \qquad \bar{X}_2 = \frac{96}{4} = 24, \qquad \bar{X}_3 = \frac{72}{4} = 18$$

The grand mean, denoted by $\bar{\bar{X}}$ (and read "X double-bar"), is obtained as illustrated in Table 20.1 by dividing the sum of all observations by 12.

Observations are classified with respect to one factor, advertising method in our case. This is the experimental factor or experimental stimulus (treatment). We wish to determine whether or not this experimental factor has had any significant effect on a variable, sales volume in our illustration.

If the advertising displays have had no significant effect on sales, then we may assume that the observed data are obtained from three populations with identical means. This is our null hypothesis. The null and the alternative hypotheses may be expressed formally as follows:

$H_0: \mu_1 = \mu_2 = \mu_3$ (displays do not affect sales)
H_1:All μ_j values are not equal (displays affect sales) $(j = 1, 2, 3)$

---

*Following tradition and contrary to earlier sample notation, we use capital letter X (in X_{ij}) to denote sample observations.

Section 20 Analysis of Variance

The null hypothesis is based on the assumptions that the three populations are normally distributed and have identical variances.

Decomposition of Total Variation

Testing the null and the alternative hypotheses is based on the decomposition of total sample variation into variation between treatments and within treatments. The term *variation* in statistics refers to the sum of squared deviations of a set of observations from their mean. The term is simplified to *sum of squares*. The general relationship of the three types of variation is

(20.1) Total variation = between-treatments + within-treatments

We take up each variation in turn.
Total variation is defined as

(20.2) $$SS_t = \sum_{j=1}^{k} \sum_{i=1}^{r} (X_{ij} - \bar{\bar{X}})^2$$

where SS_t = total sum of squares
X_{ij} = observed value in the ith row and jth column
$\bar{\bar{X}}$ = the grand mean

The summation signs mean that the squared difference between each observed value and the grand mean are first summed over all observations within each treatment and next summed over all treatments. Computation of the SS_t value is not necessary for testing because it is the sum of the other two types of variation. At any rate, its calculation can be used as a check. We need only to know that total variation measures the deviation of all observed values from the grand mean.

The between-treatment variation is in fact variation among treatments (columns). But convention dictates the term *between*.
It is defined as

(20.3) $$SS_b = \sum_{j=1}^{k} r_j (\bar{X}_j - \bar{\bar{X}})^2$$

where SS_b = between-treatment sum of squares
r_j = number of rows or sample size for calculating the mean of the jth column (treatment)
$\bar{X}_j$ = mean of the jth column (treatment)
$\bar{\bar{X}}$ = grand mean

Example 20.3

For the data in Table 20.1 and by formula (20.3), we have
$$SS_b = r_1(\bar{X}_1 - \bar{\bar{X}})^2 + r_2(\bar{X}_2 - \bar{\bar{X}})^2 + r_3(\bar{X}_3 - \bar{\bar{X}})^2$$
$$= 4(21 - 21)^2 + 4(24 - 21)^2 + 4(18 - 21)^2$$
$$= 72$$

Chapter 7 Chi-Square Tests and Analysis of Variance

In general, calculation of the sum of squares between treatments requires the following steps:

1. Find the difference between each treatment mean and the grand mean.
2. Square each difference.
3. Multiply each squared difference by the sample size of each treatment.
4. Sum the treatment products.

We shall postpone discussing the meaning of the sum of squares between treatments until after we illustrate computation of the within-treatment sum of squares. This variation is defined as

(20.4) $$SS_w = \sum_{j=1}^{k} \sum_{i=1}^{r} (X_{ij} - \bar{X}_j)^2$$

where SS_w = within-treatment sum of squares.
X_{ij} = observed value in the ith row and jth column (treatment)
$\bar{X}_j$ = mean of the jth column (treatment)

The meaning of double summation signs has been already explained in formula (20.2).

Example 20.4

Calculation of SS_w for our problem is conveniently summarized in Table 20.2. From the observed values in each treatment of Table 20.1 we subtract its treatment mean, square each difference, and sum the squared differences. For example, the sum of the squared differences for treatment (advertising method) 1 is

$$\Sigma (X_{i1} - \bar{X}_1) = (20 - 21)^2 + (24 - 21)^2 + (18 - 21)^2 + (22 - 21)^2$$
$$= 1 + 9 + 9 + 1$$
$$= 20$$

as shown under column 1, Table 20.2.

Table 20.2.
Calculation of the Within-Treatment Sum of Squares for Donaldson Associates Problem

$(X_{i1} - \bar{X}_1)^2$ (1)	$(X_{i2} - \bar{X}_2)^2$ (2)	$(X_{i3} - \bar{X}_3)^2$ (3)
1	1	1
9	4	1
9	4	1
1	1	1
20	10	4

$$SS_w = \sum_j \sum_i (X_{ij} - \bar{X}_j)^2 = 20 + 10 + 4 = 34$$

Section 20 Analysis of Variance

The same calculations are repeated for the observed X_{i2} and X_{i3} values of Table 20.1. The squared differences are summed to 10 and 4 in columns 2 and 3, respectively. Finally, the column sums are added to yield a value of 34 for SS_w.

In general, calculation of the sum of squares within treatments involves the following steps:

1. Find the difference of each observed value from its treatment mean.
2. Square each difference.
3. Sum the squared differences of each column (treatment).
4. Add all column (treatment) totals.

What is the meaning of the variations between and within treatments? Suppose the null hypothesis were true, that is, the samples are drawn from populations having identical means and variances. Then both SS_b and SS_w would have reflected the same kind of chance or sampling error. In fact, the values of SS_b and SS_w adjusted as explained later, may not differ significantly; they would have been based on samples drawn from populations with identical means and variances. On the other hand, if the null hypothesis were false, the between-treatment sum of squares would have reflected variation of differences between treatments which may be attributed to or explained by the experimental factor in addition to sampling error. For this reason, between-treatment variation is also called *explained variation*. By contrast, the within-treatment variation reflects differences which can be attributed only to sampling error. Since such differences cannot be explained by the experimental factor, the within-treatment variation is also called *unexplained variation*. Thus, testing with analysis of variance rests on the comparison of the variation between and within treatments.

The F Statistic

The two sums of squares cannot be compared directly because they are based on a different number of observations, SS_b on 3 sample means and SS_w on 12 sample observations. We must divide each sum of squares by the corresponding degrees of freedom in order to obtain the variances. The ratio of the variance between treatments to the variance within treatments, called the F statistic, is the basis for testing the null hypothesis.

We already know that the variance of a sample of n observations is the sum of the squared deviations of each observation from the sample mean divided by $n - 1$. Symbolically,

$$(20.5) \qquad s^2 = \frac{\Sigma (x - \bar{x})^2}{n - 1}$$

Within the context of the present analysis the numerator in (20.5) is referred to as sum of squares SS_b and the denominator as degrees of freedom $k - 1$. Hence, by analogy to formula (20.5) the variance between treatments is

$$(20.6) \qquad \boxed{MS_b = \frac{SS_b}{k - 1}}$$

This variance is also referred to as the *mean square* between treatments. The $k-1$ degrees of freedom are explained by the fact that computation of the sum of squares is based on k column (treatment) means. We lose 1 degree of freedom because we use the grand mean to estimate the population mean. Hence, we are left with $k-1$ degrees of freedom. Alternatively, if we are given the value of $k-1$ sample means, the value of the kth mean can be determined residually.

Example 20.5   Consider the data in Table 20.1. Any one of the three column means can be found as the difference between the sum of the three necessary to determine the value of the grand mean less the sum of the other two column (treatment) means. Once the sum of the three means is given, there is no freedom left for varying one of the three means. Its value is fixed by the other two means. Since k is 3, there are $3-1$ or 2 degrees of freedom.

Earlier we found that the sum of squares between treatments is 72. By formula (20.6) the corresponding mean square is

$$MS_b = \frac{72}{2} = 36$$

Since the within-treatment sum of squares SS_w is based on k columns and r rows of observations, there are $k(r-1)$ degrees of freedom and the corresponding mean square is

(20.7)
$$\boxed{MS_w = \frac{SS_w}{k(r-1)}}$$

The $k(r-1)$ degrees of freedom may be explained in a similar manner. There are kr degrees of freedom which correspond to the total number of observations in a problem. We lose k degrees of freedom because we use k column means as estimates of the corresponding population means and for determining the sum of squares within treatments. Hence, the remaining degrees of freedom are $kr - k = k(r-1)$.

Example 20.6   Consider again the data in Table 20.1. There are three columns and four rows. Therefore, $k(r-1) = 3(4-1) = 9$.

We have already found in Table 20.2 that the within-treatment sum of squares is 34. By formula (20.7) the corresponding mean square is

$$MS_w = \frac{34}{9} \simeq 3.78$$

The total variance is the sum of the variances between and within treatments. Alternatively, it can be obtained if the total sum of squares defined in (20.2) is divided by $rk - 1$ degrees of freedom. Although computation of total variance is not necessary for testing, it may be desirable to explain the degrees of freedom. As already explained, there are rk degrees of freedom in a problem. We lose 1 degree of freedom because we use the grand mean $\bar{X}$ as an estimate of the population mean assumed in a true null hypothesis from which we determine total

Section 20 Analysis of Variance

variation. Hence, total sum of squares has $rk - 1$ degrees of freedom. Alternatively, the degrees of freedom in total sum of squares is the sum of the degrees of freedom in the other two variations. In symbols,

$$rk - 1 = (k - 1) + (rk - k)$$

Since the F statistic is the ratio of the explained variance over the unexplained variance, it is defined by

(20.8)
$$F = \frac{MS_b}{MS_w}$$

That is,

$$\frac{\text{Explained variance between treatments}}{\text{Unexplained variance within treatments}} = \frac{SS_b/(k-1)}{SS_w/k(r-1)}$$

Example 20.7

We have already found that MS_b in our illustration is 36 and MS_w is 3.78. By formula (20.8),

$$F_o = \frac{36}{3.78} \simeq 9.52$$

where F_o denotes the *observed value* of the F statistic. The major computational results of our problem are shown in Table 20.3. Note that the total sum of squares and its degrees of freedom may be used to check the computations for the explained and unexplained variances.

Table 20.3.
Analysis of Variance for Donaldson Associates Problem

Source of Variation	Sum of Squares	Degrees of Freedom	Mean Square
Between-treatments or *explained*	72	2	36
Within-treatments or *unexplained*	34	9	3.78
Totals:	106 ✓	11 ✓	

$$F_0 = \frac{36}{3.78} \simeq 9.52$$

The F Distribution

What does the value of the F statistic mean? How can the F statistic become the basis for testing our null hypothesis? These related questions lead into the heart of the testing procedure.

The meaning of the F statistic is directly related to our earlier discussion about variations. If our null hypothesis were true, the involved population distributions would have, by assumption, identical means and variances. Then the explained variance, as well as the unexplained variance, would be an unbiased estimate of a single population variance. Their ratio, which is the F statistic, would be one except for random or chance errors due to sampling. However, if our hypothesis were false, the F statistic would be greater than one because the numerator variance would reflect the influence of the experimental factor in addition to the presence of random errors.

The larger the value of F_o, the greater our doubts that the difference between the explained and unexplained variances can be attributed to random errors only. The question is: How large should the F statistic be before we conclude that such a difference is significant and therefore reject our null hypothesis?

We can get the answer to this question by referring the observed F_o value to the F distribution. As in the case of the chi-square statistic, the sampling distribution of the F statistic in (20.8) can be approximated with a probability model named F distribution in honor of its discoverer, R. A. Fisher. The F distribution, unlike the chi-square, has two parameters, the df (degrees of freedom) in the numerator and the df in the denominator of the F ratio. Two parameters are necessary because the F statistic is the ratio of two random variables, the sample variance between and the sample variance within treatments.

Again the F probability model represents a family of distributions, one for each combination of df values. The graphs of three such distributions are shown in Fig. 20.1. Note that for df (2, 12), that is, 2 for the numerator and 12 for the denominator, the F distribution is skewed to the right so that large F values correspond to a 5 percent or 1 percent probability. For the same probabilities the value of F gets closer to the mean ratio 1 as the degrees of freedom increase. At the same time the curve becomes symmetrical around the mean.

For convenience, the 5 percent and 1 percent values of F distributions for a select combination of df values are shown in Appendix H. The degrees of freedom in the numerator of the F statistic, df $= k - 1$, are across the top of the table. The leftmost column of the table shows the degree of freedom in the denominator of the F statistic, df $= k(r - 1)$. For each set of df values, lightface figures correspond to the 5 percent and boldface to 1 percent of the specified F distribution.

Figure 20.1.
Graph of three F distributions.

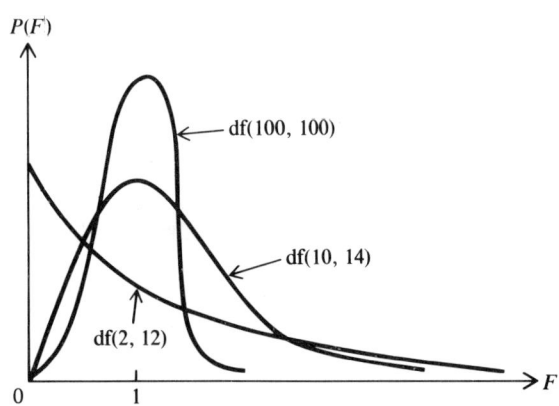

Example 20.8

The null hypothesis in our problem was that the advertising displays are ineffective, that is, they have not affected sales significantly. Suppose we wish to test this hypothesis at 5 percent level of significance. According to Table 20.3, the numerator df is 2 and the denominator df is 9. Hence, the critical F value is

$$F_{05}(2, 9) = 4.26$$

read at the intersection of the 2nd column and 9th row of Appendix H. The decision rule is

If $F_o \leq 4.26$, accept H_0 (displays do not affect sales)
If $F_o > 4.26$, reject H_0 (displays affect sales)

We reject the null hypothesis because we have already found that the observed F_o value is 9.52. We conclude that the advertising displays may have affected sales significantly.

In sum, the entire testing procedure requires the following steps:

1. Formulate the null and the alternative hypotheses, assuming that the involved populations are normally distributed with identical means and variances.
2. Specify the level of significance and determine the critical value of F_α.
3. Specify the decision rule.
4. Compute the treatment means and the grand mean.
5. Calculate the sum of squares between and within treatments and, if desirable, check results by computing the total sum of squares.
6. Divide each sum of squares by the corresponding degrees of freedom to find the between-treatment variance MS_b and the within-treatment variance MS_w.
7. Divide the between-treatment variance MS_b by the within-treatment variance MS_w to find the observed F_o value.
8. Test your null hypothesis by comparing the observed and critical values of the F statistic and draw your conclusion.

A Few Important Comments

As pointed out repeatedly, we should guard against mechanistic application of statistical techniques. We should be well aware that statistical results are frequently subject to more than one interpretation. In the Donaldson Associates problem we reached the conclusion that the advertising method may have affected sales significantly. But the conclusion should be considered tentative and not without qualification. Other factors may have also affected sales. Although the participating retail outlets were randomly assigned to each treatment, *one-factor analysis* of variance presupposes that all experimental stores are identical or homogeneous in their responsiveness to the treatments. Yet such stores may differ significantly with respect to type of retail outlet, size, quality of merchandise, the type of neighborhood they serve, and other factors. The effects of advertising method and, for example, neighborhood socioeconomic characteristics may be *confounded*. This means that the two factors act together to produce the observed differences between sample means. To the extent that the two factors are confounded, attributing sales effectiveness to advertising method without qualification would be an erroneous conclusion. Further analysis may be necessary. However, more sophisticated methods such as a *two-factor analysis* of variance lie outside the scope of this text.

Analysis of variance raises a number of important points. They relate to the appropriate application of ANOVA as well as to the interpretation of test results.

1. The F distribution model assumes that the parent populations are *normally distributed* with *identical* means and variances and that the sample observations are *independent*. The F test is, however, relatively insensitive to violations of the normality and equal-variance assumptions. Usually, we need not be too concerned about the validity of these assumptions if each treatment contains an equal number of 25 or more observations.

2. As with the chi-square test, we are able to control only the α risk for rejecting a true null hypothesis since the sample size is fixed in advance. The F test is suitable for testing a true null hypothesis. The β risk for accepting a false null hypothesis may be large. Greater protection against β risk can be obtained by increasing the sample size.

3. Analysis of variance is a method which tests *simultaneously all* possible pairs of sample means. It fails to provide information about the magnitude of the difference *between a given pair of means*. This point raises the question: Which method or treatment of the experimental factor is most effective? In our illustration, an obvious answer to this question is to select the advertising method 2, which has the largest mean sales. But this choice does not safeguard us against the possibility that the difference between method 2 and the next most effective method 1 may not be significant. Neither is testing the difference of sample means pairwise an appropriate method. Such tests between two sample means would be really dependent because they would be based on common unexplained variance.

4. In rejecting the null hypothesis we concluded that treatments and effects are related. We found that advertising method is related to sales volume. But, as in the case of chi-square testing, the association is qualitative in nature since treatments may represent a categorical variable. Unlike regression analysis, which we take up in the next chapter, analysis of variance is not designed to estimate the values of one variable from the known values of another variable or variables

5. Analysis of variance is also an integral part of regression analysis we consider in the next chapter. More sophisticated applications of ANOVA can be found in statistical literature.

PROBLEMS

Group One

20.1. Find the critical value F_c for each set of degrees of freedom and specified level of significance.
 *(a) df (1, 8), α = .01   (c) df (1, 25), α = .01
  (b) df (5, 10), α = .05   (d) df (2, 48), α = .05

Answers to asterisked (*) problems are appended.

Section 20 Analysis of Variance

20.2. Sarah Messing is a chemical engineer with Positex Company. A leading product of the company is Curifix, used extensively for manufacturing Tecron, a synthetic fiber. Sarah is studying three different processes of preparing Curifix in order to determine whether type of preparation affects Tecron's yield. The null hypothesis is that the process of preparing Curifix has no effect on Tecron yield. Each process is used in five batches of Tecron. The basic summary measures are as follows:

Source of Variation	Sum of Squares
Explained (between-treatments)	150
Unexplained (within-treatments)	600
Total:	750

*(a) Determine the degrees of freedom and find the critical value F_c at 5 percent significance level.
(b) Specify the decision rule.
(c) Determine the observed F_o value. Should the null hypothesis be accepted or rejected? Explain.

20.3. Suppose the three processes for preparing Curifix in Problem 20.2 are tried in manufacturing four other synthetic fibers X, Y, Z, and W. The null hypothesis is the same for each fiber but each process of Curifix preparation is used in a sample of 10 batches of each fiber. For each synthetic fiber, test the null hypothesis at the indicated level of significance.
*(a) Fiber X: $F_o = 12.36$ and $\alpha = .01$
(b) Fiber Y: $F_o = 1.69$ and $\alpha = .05$
(c) Fiber Z: $F_o = 6.24$ and $\alpha = .05$
(d) Fiber W: $F_o = 2.76$ and $\alpha = .01$

20.4. Donald Facey is in charge of State Bank's credit card department. Under Donald's supervision are four employees who are responsible for collecting overdue credit from delinquent accounts. Each week an equal number of delinquent accounts is randomly assigned to the four collection employees. Donald wants to know whether variations in the number of accounts successfully removed from the list of delinquent accounts can be attributed to the collectors of delinquent debtors. Analysis of variance of the number of removed delinquent accounts during the last 4 weeks yields the following summary measures ("treatments"-collectors):

Source of Variation	Sum of Squares
Explained (between-treatments)	90
Unexplained (within-treatments)	24
Total:	114

254 Chapter 7 Chi-Square Tests and Analysis of Variance

*(a) Determine the degrees of freedom and find the critical value F_c at 1 percent level of significance.
(b) Specify the decision rule.
(c) Determine the observed F_o value. Should the null hypothesis be accepted or rejected? Explain.

20.5. Identify and explain the following terms:
(a) Explained variance
(b) Unexplained variance
(c) Total variance
(d) Sum of squares
(e) Degrees of freedom
(f) F distribution
(g) One-factor analysis of variance
(h) Mean square
(i) Two-factor analysis of variance

Group Two

20.6 Robert Hunter, the production manager of Acmetronics Inc., receives four machines to meet increased demand for the company's major product. The supplier claims that the machines have the same output capabilities. Sixteen random samples yield the following hourly output in hundreds of units:

Samples from Each Machine	Machine			
	A	B	C	D
1	4	2	4	6
2	4	3	5	6
3	3	4	6	7
4	5	3	5	5

(a) Formulate the null and the alternative hypotheses.
(b) Find the critical value F_c at 1 percent level of significance.
(c) Specify the decision rule.
(d) Find the sum of squares between and within treatments.
(e) Find the observed value F_o.
*(f) Is the claim of the supplier about the machines justified?

20.7. The Consumer Protection Agency wishes to determine whether there is a significant difference in the lifetime of automobile batteries manufactured in three factories of a company. Six batteries are selected at random from each factory. The data representing the lifetime of batteries in hundreds of hours are as follows:

Sampled Batteries from Each Factory	Factory		
	A	B	C
1	10	9	11
2	13	10	12
3	10	10	8
4	12	8	9
5	10	9	10
6	11	8	10

Section 20 Analysis of Variance

*(a) Are battery lifetimes significantly different? The agency carried out the test at 1 percent level of significance.

(b) Consumer Advocates, a watchdog group, objected that the agency's test level should be raised to 5 percent in order to reduce the risk of permitting the marketing of batteries with significant differences. Do you agree with their argument? Explain why or why not.

20.8. Students attending a multisection course wanted to know whether or not the grading of three instructors was significantly different. From the displayed grade sheet of each instructor they select at random the grades of five students. The selected grades based on a 100-point scale are:

Sample Students from Each Instructor	Instructor		
	A	B	C
1	82	66	91
2	94	88	62
3	72	75	70
4	60	90	80
5	77	81	67

*(a) Test at 1 percent level of significance.

(b) The test results are proudly shown to a statistics instructor; he points out that if all randomization rules were observed and if all the students in each grade sheet were included, test results might be different. Explain why you may agree or disagree with this remark.

20.9. A coffee manufacturer claims that the decaffeinated coffee of the company, called Yamka, unlike the competing regular and instant coffee brands, does not increase significantly the pulse rate (heart beats per minute) of a consumer. To demonstrate this point, 15 noncoffee drinkers were randomly assigned to three groups. The pulse of each person was measured before and after drinking a given type of coffee. The difference in the pulse rate of each individual is as follows:

Individuals for Each Type of Coffee	Type of Coffee		
	Regular	Instant	Yamka
1	7	3	3
2	6	6	2
3	4	3	2
4	5	4	1
5	6	5	3

*(a) Is the claim of the manufacturer justified? Test at 1 percent level of significance.

(b) Are there any other factors which may "explain" some of the variation? Indicate at least two factors.

(c) Is there any way by which the basis of comparison among types of coffee may be improved?

20.10. A feed dealer considers the importation of foreign feedstuffs. Five tropical feedstuffs are each fed to a lot of four baby chicks. When the chickens reached marketable age, the gains in weight (ounces) were as follows:

Sampled Chicks for Each Feedstuff	Feedstuff				
	A	B	C	D	E
1	50	48	53	58	68
2	55	52	40	62	62
3	60	58	41	65	71
4	43	42	54	55	63

(a) What is the probability value of F_o? Do the feedstuff populations have different μ? Test at 1 percent significance level.
(b) If differences among feedstuffs are significant, which feedstuff would you recommend for importation?
(c) What qualifications may you incorporate in your recommendation?

20.11. An electronics manufacturer receives microelectronic components from five subcontractors. The normal weekly shipment from each supplier consists of four batches each containing 1000 components. Each week the receiving clerk records the average number of defective components found in the batches of each shipment and computes the standard deviation. This week's information is as follows:

Measurement	Subcontractor				
	A	B	C	D	E
Mean	21	22	25	19	28
Standard deviation	5	3	4	3	6

Are the shipments from the suppliers uniform with respect to defective components? Test at 5 percent level of significance. (*Hint:* Assume that each standard deviation was computed using $n - 1$ in the denominator.)

Chapter 8
REGRESSION AND CORRELATION ANALYSIS

We have seen that both chi-square tests and analysis of variance may establish a qualitative association between variables. Neither technique handles an association in terms of a numerical variable; nor do these techniques tell us anything about *how* the two variables may be associated and what the *degree* of such an association may be.

This information can be obtained with regression and correlation analysis. *Regression analysis** provides a mathematical expression, an equation, for estimating or predicting the values of one variable from the known values of one or more other variables. For example, with analysis of variance we were able to determine whether or not unit sales depend on different *methods* of advertising: regression analysis provides the basis for predicting unit sales from different *amounts* of advertising dollars. This technique is called *simple regression* because we use a single variable, advertising expenditure, to estimate or predict another variable, unit sales. Regression analysis is called *linear* if the equation of the method represents a straight line and *curvilinear* if it represents a curve. In addition to advertising expenditures, we may introduce other variables such as population, income, and family size to predict unit sales. Then the method is called *multiple regression*. Regression analysis is not only the basis for predicting the values of a variable; it also describes the nature as well as the importance of the relationship between two or more variables.

Correlation analysis is a method designed to measure the *degree* of association between variables. For example, correlation may express the degree of association between verbal and mathematical scores of students entering college, cash flow requirements and sales, or smoking and the incidence of lung cancer. We shall see that correlation is useful for understanding regression. Simple and multiple correlation models are studied in conjunction with the corresponding simple and multiple regression models.

---

*Around the turn of the century Sir Francis Galton compared the heights of individuals to the heights of their parents. He concluded that successive generations of offspring from tall individuals "regress" down toward the mean height of the population. In other words, children of unusually tall parents tend to be shorter than their parents. The reverse was true for children of very short parents. Since then the term *regression* has been accepted to describe the general method of predicting the value of one variable from the value of another variable.

Chapter 8 Regression and Correlation Analysis

Regression and correlation are the most complex and the most widely applied of all statistical techniques we have encountered so far. For these reasons, we devote a whole chapter to cover just the basics of the subject. First, we introduce the basic concepts and the computational method of the simple regression and correlation models. Next, we deal with testing and estimating procedures of simple regression and correlation. We close the subject with multiple regression and correlation.

We concentrate on linear simple regression and multiple regression, which represent the basis of the analysis. Curvilinear regression is studied as an extension of this base. To the extent possible, we use a single motivating example throughout the chapter. This approach reduces numerical effort to a minimum and allows us to concentrate on discussing methodology, interpretation of results, and limitations of the models. The problems at the end of each section offer an opportunity to apply the technique to a variety of situations.

SECTION 21 / INTRODUCTION TO REGRESSION AND CORRELATION

Since this entire chapter is on regression and correlation, this section is devoted exclusively to introducing some basic elements of the subject. First, we discuss the nature of the relationship between two variables in graphic terms. Then we concentrate on four important topics: deviations from a regression equation, the computational method of deriving a linear equation, the regression model, and the correlation model.

Relationships Between Variables

Predicting the unknown values of a variable is one of the most important needs for both profit and nonprofit organizations. Business firms need to forecast a number of key variables such as sales, cash requirements, and raw materials for planning and control. Public utilities must forecast the demand for services several years in advance in order to plan expansion of production capacity. Town officials need to forecast changes in the town's population for expanding or curtailing educational and other facilities. Scientists wish to predict disastrous earthquakes. Forecasting unemployment and economic conditions in general is a well-known recurring event.

But forecasting is not the only practical result of regression and correlation analysis. For example, the method may enable us to determine the relative contribution that each salesperson is expected to make to the dollar sales of a company. We may obtain an estimate of the average costs in hospitals or find out whether such costs are associated with hospital size. We may find the amount of money consumers may spend collectively for every additional dollar increase in their earnings. The list of practical applications is long and covers a wide range of situations.

Section 21 Introduction to Regression and Correlation

Of course, most studies may require multiple regression and other more sophisticated techniques. Our immediate purpose is much simpler, namely, to use *simple regression* in order to predict the unknown value of one variable from the known value of another variable. The variable whose value is known is called the *independent variable*, while the variable whose value is to be predicted is called the *dependent variable*. By convention, the independent variable is denoted by X and the dependent variable is denoted by Y.

Example 21.1

Colleges and universities use admission tests and other criteria for evaluating applicants seeking formal education beyond high school. How may regression and correlation analysis help us establish a comprehensive admission policy for a master's program in business administration (M.B.A.)? At best, we hope that such an analysis may yield a regression equation which may predict, subject to sampling error, the academic performance of applicants to the program. At least, we hope that with such an analysis we may be able to identify critical variables which may be used as criteria for admission.

We may begin our study with simple regression and correlation analysis. We may consider that the cumulative college grade point average (college GPA) and the graduate grade point average (graduate GPA) are acceptable measures of academic performance for students who have successfully completed their college and M.B.A. degree programs, respectively. For illustrating simple regression, let us consider the statistical population of 30 graduates. The basic data are shown in Table 21.1. The independent variable X represents the college GPA and the dependent variable Y the graduate GPA. We wish to derive a regression equation from randomly sampled observations of 10 students. The circled student numbers represent

Table 21.1. College GPA and Graduate GPA Population of 30 M.B.A. Graduates (Data Hypothetical)

Student Number	Grade Point Average Graduate Y	Grade Point Average College X	Student Number	Grade Point Average Graduate Y	Grade Point Average College X	Student Number	Grade Point Average Graduate Y	Grade Point Average College X
1	3.9	4.0	11	3.4	3.3	21	3.6	3.4
2	2.9	2.6	12	3.7	3.4	㉒	2.7	2.5
③	3.3	3.7	13	3.3	3.2	23	3.5	3.7
4	3.5	3.2	⑭	2.6	2.9	㉔	3.0	3.3
⑤	2.8	3.1	15	3.9	3.8	25	3.0	2.7
⑥	3.1	3.0	16	2.8	3.0	㉖	2.9	2.9
7	3.8	4.0	17	3.4	3.8	27	3.9	3.6
⑧	3.7	3.7	⑱	3.2	3.5	28	3.4	3.6
9	3.3	3.4	19	3.6	4.0	㉙	2.9	3.2
10	3.8	3.5	20	3.0	3.5	30	3.2	2.9

our sample. If the equation is proven statistically reliable, we can use it to predict a new student's Y value (graduate GPA) if we know the student's X value (college GPA).

Both the population and sample sizes in our illustration are deliberately kept small in order to reduce computational work. In reality, the statistical population of the example is considered to be infinite because we wish to study the admission *process*, the population characteristics are unknown, and the sample would be larger than 10 observations.

Our immediate purpose is to evaluate the academic performance of future students entering the graduate program as measured by their graduate GPA on the basis of the GPA they received while attending college. As a first step, we may examine *how* the two variables may be related. In other words, is the relationship linear or curvilinear?

Example 21.2

The sample data are plotted on a graph shown in Fig. 21.1. This graph is called a *scatter diagram*. By convention the independent variable is plotted along the X axis and the dependent variable along the Y axis. A pair of X and Y values *determine one point* on the scatter diagram.* For instance, the point for student number 3 corresponds to X equal to 3.7 and Y equal to 3.3 shown in Table 21.1; the point for student number 5 corresponds to X equal to 3.1 and Y equal to 2.8; and so on. At the present time, the straight line through the points may be ignored.

Figure 21.1.
Scatter diagram of college GPA and graduate GPA of a sample of ten M.B.A. graduates.

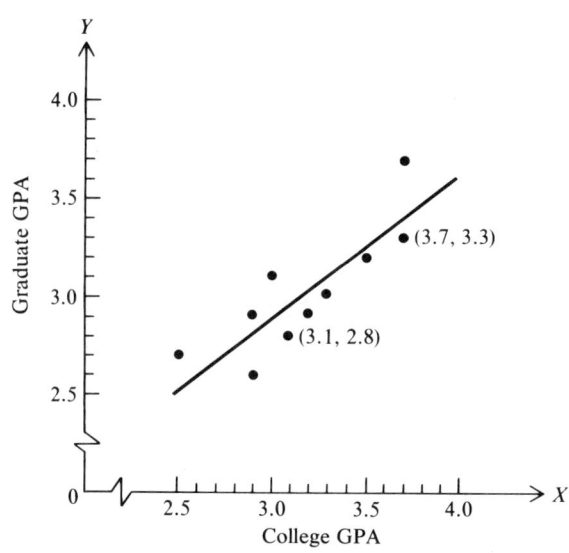

*Following tradition and contrary to earlier sample notation, we shall use throughout this chapter capital letters to denote sample observations.

Scatter diagrams such as the ones shown in Fig. 21.2, give some indication of the nature and strength of the relationship between two variables.

1. The scatter of the points can tell us whether a straight line may adequately describe the average relationship between two variables. Since a straight line through the points in Fig. 21.2(a) appears to describe the data adequately, the relationship between X and Y is assumed to be *linear*. If a curve other than a straight line, like the one in Fig. 21.2(b), better describes a relationship between two variables, such a relationship is called *curvilinear*.

2. The points of a scatter diagram may also indicate whether the relationship between X and Y variables is positive or negative. If the points have the

Figure 21.2.
Scatter diagrams illustrating different relationships between an independent variable X and a dependent variable Y: (a) inverse linear, (b) direct curvilinear, (c) perfect linear, (d) inverse curvilinear, (e) no correlation, (f) low correlation.

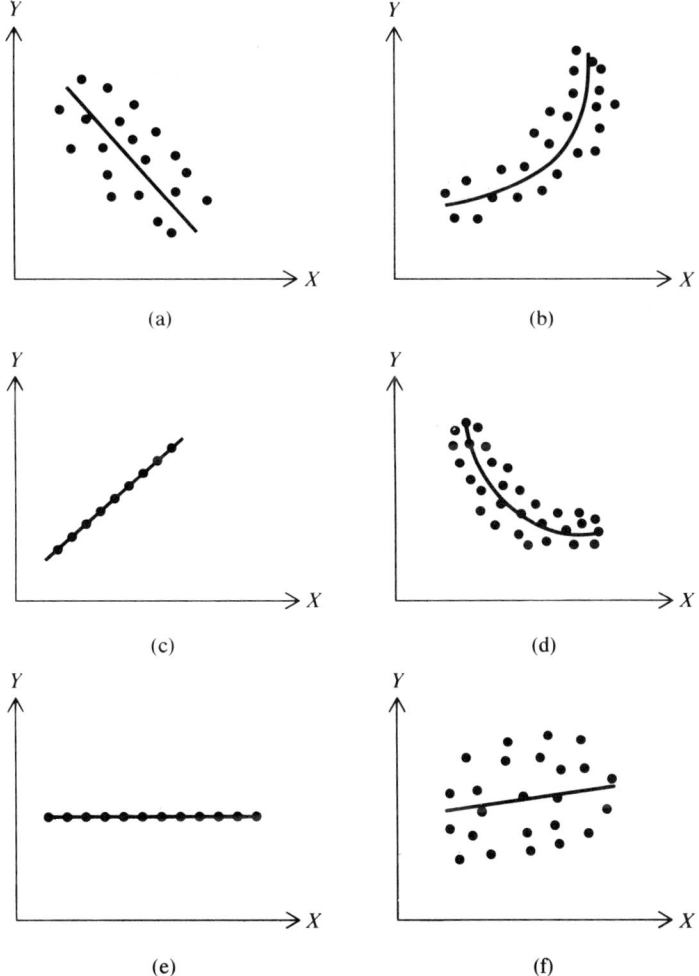

general tendency to run from the lower left to the upper right-hand side of the graph, the relationship is *direct* or *positive*. Figure 21.1 shows a positive relationship where the value of the dependent variable Y tends to increase as the value of the independent variable X increases. So does Fig. 21.2(b). Conversely, the relationship is *inverse* or *negative*, as in Figs. 21.2(a) and (d), if the points of a scatter diagram are running from the upper left to the lower right-hand side of the graph. Then the value of the dependent variable Y tends to decrease as the value of the independent variable X increases.

3. Also, the scatter of data points around the regression line or curve is an indication of the correlation or degree to which the two variables are related. The scatter diagrams in Figs. 21.2(a), (b), and (d) show that there is a fairly strong relationship between X and Y since most data points cluster close to the regression line. The wider the scatter of the points, the weaker is the relationship even if the regression line or curve slopes steeply upward or downward. For example, Fig. 21.2(f) shows a weak or low correlation between X and Y. Of course, the correlation between two variables is perfect, as in Fig. 21.2(c), in the unusual situation where all data points are on the regression line or curve. We can imagine such a case if we assume that all students who successfully completed the graduate program in Example 21.1 were given a graduate GPA equal to the GPA each received in college.

4. Finally, there is no relationship between the two variables if the regression line is horizontal, that is, parallel to the X axis, as in Fig. 21.2(e), even when all points are on the regression line. In such a case we can assume that all students who successfully completed the graduate program in Example 21.1 were given the same graduate GPA irrespective of the score they received while in college.

The important thing to remember in studying the relationship between two variables is that we often do not know in advance how they are related. The scatter diagram is a means of studying the nature and to some extent the strength of that relationship.

Deviations from a Regression Equation

Our next step is to derive a linear equation which describes the observed relationship. This procedure is called *fitting a line*; our objective is to derive an equation which minimizes the deviations of the Y observations from the fitted line. This topic requires a review of the basics about linear equations and an understanding of the difference between deviations and sampling error before introducing the computational method of fitting a straight line.

Our immediate objective is to derive a linear equation of the form

(21.1) $$\boxed{Y_c = a + bX}$$

where a is called the *intercept* (Y intercept); it is the computed value of Y when $X = 0$. Letter b, the slope of the line, is called the *regression coefficient*. Symbol Y_c denotes a *computed* value, while Y, without the subscript, denotes an *observed* value of the dependent variable. The importance of this distinction will become evident soon. In the meantime, let us take a closer look at Eq. (21.1).

Example 21.3

Consider a regression equation such as

$$Y_c = 1 + .5X$$

The graph of the equation is shown in Fig. 21.3. Each point on the graph represents a pair of X and Y_c values which can be obtained from the equation. To sketch the graph of this equation we need only to know the coordinates of two points. For convenience, one of the two points can be the intercept. Letting X equal 0, Y_c equals 1 as follows:

$$Y_c = 1 + .5(0) = 1$$

You see immediately that $a = 1$. Coordinates (0, 1) represent the point where the graph of the equation intersects the Y axis. We may arbitrarily select the coordinates of a second point. For example, if X is 8, then

$$Y_c = 1 + .5(8) = 5$$

The graph of the equation is obtained by connecting points (0, 1) and (8, 5) with a straight line. The slope b of the line is .5. This means that for each unit increase of the independent variable X the value of the dependent variable Y increases by .5 unit. For example, we found that Y_c is 5 when X is 8. Suppose X increases from 8 to 9. Then

$$Y_c = 1 + .5(9) = 5.5$$

an increase of Y_c by .5 unit.

What about the deviations of the Y observations from the fitted line?

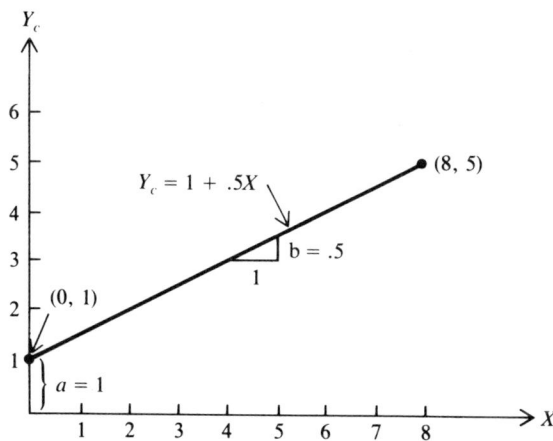

Figure 21.3. Graph of linear equation $Y_c = 1 + .5X$.

Example 21.4

Suppose the equation given in the previous example best fits a sample of 10 pairs of X and Y observations. Deviations from the regression line are illustrated in Fig. 21.4. Although we could have plotted all 10 data points, 2 of them, say A and B, illustrate deviations sufficiently. The deviation for point

Figure 21.4.
Graphic representation of deviations from a best-fit regression line.

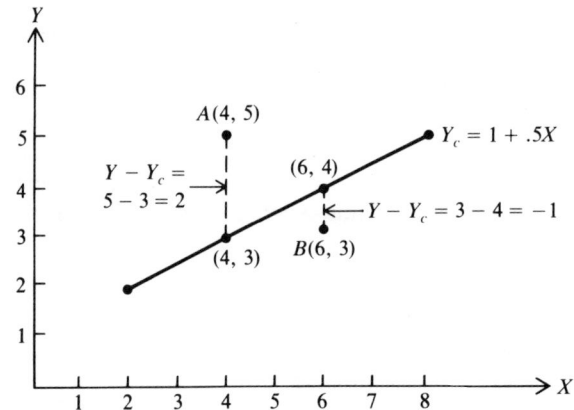

A is 2; it represents the difference between the observed value $Y = 5$ and the corresponding computed value Y_c. Letting $X = 4$ and solving the given equation for Y_c, we have

$$Y_c = 1 + .5(4) = 3$$

Hence, the deviation is

$$Y - Y_c = 5 - 3 = 2$$

The deviation for point B is -1. Since $X = 6$, the Y_c value is

$$Y_c = 1 + .5(6) = 4$$

The observed value Y at point B is 3; so the deviation is

$$Y - Y_c = 3 - 4 = -1$$

In general, data points, such as point A, lying above the fitted line have positive deviations while data points, such as point B, lying below the fitted line have negative deviations. Since our sample in Fig. 21.1 consists of 10 paired observations, there is an equal number of deviations. They are called *residuals*. Deviations from a regression line should not be confused with the sampling errors of a sampling distribution. Sampling errors are deviations of a statistic from its parameter.

The Least-Squares Method

Now we are ready to discuss the question of fitting a line to observed data. The objective is to fit a line that minimizes the deviations or residuals. First, we may consider fitting a freehand line to the data. Then the equation of the line can be derived by reading the intercept and the slope of the line from the graph. This method, however, has two major drawbacks. Different people may fit different freehand lines to the same data. Moreover, such a line cannot be used for estimation because it lacks the properties necessary for measuring statistical precision.

Section 21 Introduction to Regression and Correlation

Second, we may consider fitting a line so that the positive deviations just offset the negative deviations. In other words, the algebraic sum of all deviations is equal to zero, $\Sigma (Y - Y_c) = 0$. This criterion also has serious flaws. Any line passing through point $(\bar{X}, \bar{Y})$, representing the means of X and Y observations, satisfies this criterion. For example, we can fit a line perpendicular to the line in Fig. 21.1 which satisfies this criterion. So the criterion fails to distinguish between good and bad fits.

Third, we can overcome the sign problem by fitting a line which minimizes the sum of the absolute values of deviations, $\Sigma |Y - Y_c|$. This criterion rules out some bad fits because large positive deviations are not allowed to offset large negative deviations. Yet, we can fit a line to observed data which satisfies the minimizing criterion but may fail to take into account all data points.*

Fourth, another way for overcoming the sign problem is to fit a line which minimizes the sum of the squared deviations:

(21.2) $$\Sigma (Y - Y_c)^2$$

Squaring deviations overcomes the sign problem since all deviations become positive. Also, squaring emphasizes the large deviations; at the same time, in attempting to satisfy the minimizing criterion, large deviations are avoided as much as possible. This is the well-known *least-squares* criterion. The mathematics of least squares is very manageable. Furthermore, the method yields a regression equation which, we shall see, has many desirable properties.

The procedure for minimizing the sum in (21.2) requires calculus and lies outside the scope of this text.* The method leads to the following solution for determining the values of b and a of Eq. (21.1):

(21.3) $$\boxed{b = \frac{\Sigma XY - n\bar{X}\bar{Y}}{\Sigma X^2 - n\bar{X}^2}}$$

(21.4) $$\boxed{a = \bar{Y} - b\bar{X}}$$

---

*For example, consider a straight line fitted to three data points with deviations $-1, -1$, and $+2$ so that $\Sigma |Y - Y_c| = 4$. Also, consider another line fitted to the same data points with deviations $0, 0,$ and $+3$ so that $\Sigma |Y - Y_c| = 3$. Although the second line satisfies the minimizing criterion, it fails to take into account the third point with $+3$ deviation.

*The sum in (21.2) is expressed as a function of the regression coefficients a and b by substituting the right-hand side of Eq. (21.1) as follows:

$$F(a, b) = \Sigma [(Y) - (a + bX)]^2$$

Then partial differentiation of this function and equating derivatives to zero yield two normal equations:

$$\Sigma Y = na + b\Sigma X$$
$$\Sigma XY = a\Sigma X + b\Sigma X^2$$

with values a and b representing the minimum of the sum in (21.2). Formulas (21.3) and (21.4) are obtained by solving these normal equations for a and b.

Chapter 8 Regression and Correlation Analysis

where $\bar{X}$ and $\bar{Y}$ denote the arithmetic means of the independent and dependent variables, respectively.

Example 21.5

Now we are ready to fit a regression line to the sample data of our problem shown in Table 21.1. The initial data, together with the required basic calculations for computing the values of a and b, are shown in Table 21.2. The arithmetic means of X and Y variables are

$$\bar{X} = \frac{\Sigma X}{n} = \frac{31.8}{10} = 3.18$$

and

$$\bar{Y} = \frac{\Sigma Y}{n} = \frac{30.2}{10} = 3.02$$

Also, from Table 21.2 we have

$$\Sigma XY = 96.96, \qquad \Sigma X^2 = 102.44$$

Substituting these values in expressions (21.3) and (21.4), we obtain

$$b = \frac{96.96 - 10(3.18)(3.02)}{102.44 - 10(3.18)^2} = \frac{.924}{1.316} \simeq .70213$$

and

$$a = 3.02 - .70213(3.18) \simeq .78723$$

So the regression equation is

$$Y_c = .787 + .702X \qquad (n = 10)$$

with the values of coefficients rounded to the nearest third decimal. The graph of this equation is shown in Fig. 21.1.

Table 21.2. Basic Calculations for Regression and Correlation Analysis for the Sample Data of M.B.A. Graduates

Student Number	Graduate GPA Y	College GPA X	XY	Y²	X²
3	3.3	3.7	12.21	10.89	13.69
5	2.8	3.1	8.68	7.84	9.61
6	3.1	3.0	9.30	9.61	9.00
8	3.7	3.7	13.69	13.69	13.69
14	2.6	2.9	7.54	6.76	8.41
18	3.2	3.5	11.20	10.24	12.25
22	2.7	2.5	6.75	7.29	6.25
24	3.0	3.3	9.90	9.00	10.89
26	2.9	2.9	8.41	8.41	8.41
29	2.9	3.2	9.28	8.41	10.24
	30.2	31.8	96.96	92.14	102.44

Section 21 Introduction to Regression and Correlation

What is the usefulness and meaning of this equation? Full use and interpretation of it must wait until we carry out significance tests. In the meantime, we may be satisfied with the following illustration.

Example 21.6

Provisionally, let us assume that tests show a significant association between X and Y. Now

$$Y_c = .787 + .702X \qquad (n = 10)$$

may be used to help us evaluate the academic performance of a student entering the graduate program as measured by the graduate GPA. For instance, an entering student with a 3.5 college GPA is expected to get a graduate GPA of

$$Y_c = .787 + .702(3.5) = 3.24$$

The intercept value of .787 is obtained if X is zero; it has no empirical meaning because no student is admitted to the program with less than say, 2.5 college GPA.* However, in many situations to be found among the problems in this chapter the intercept may have an important and meaningful empirical interpretation. At any rate, for a 2.5 score, the student's graduate GPA is expected to be

$$Y_c = .787 + .702(2.5) = 2.54$$

Note that, for a unit change in the college GPA, the graduate GPA changes by .702 unit, the value of the regression coefficient b.

It is important to realize that predictions obtained from a regression equation represent values of the dependent variable which are expected to occur on the average.

At this point we shall summarize important properties of a regression equation fitted by the least-squares method:

1. The graph of the equation passes through the point $(\bar{X}, \bar{Y})$ whose coordinates are the means of the independent and dependent variables.
2. The sum of the positive deviations equals the sum of the negative deviations. Symbolically, $\Sigma(Y - Y_c) = 0$, that is, the algebraic sum of the deviations about the regression line equals zero.
3. The sum of the squared deviations, expressed by formula (21.2), is a minimum.
4. If the nature of the relationship justifies it, the least-squares method can be used also to derive a curvilinear regression equation.

*GPA scores correspond to the following letter grades:

GPA	4.0	3.7	3.3	3.0	2.7	2.3	2.0
Grade	A	A−	B+	B	B−	C+	C

268 Chapter 8 Regression and Correlation Analysis

5. The least-squares regression equation is the *best linear unbiased estimator* of the corresponding unknown population regression equation.

The Regression Model

A sample equation, such as the one we have already derived by the method of least squares, is one of all possible sample equations. Like any other statistic, the intercept and the slope (regression coefficient) of all possible equations derived from a given sample size each form a sampling distribution. And on the basis of these sampling distributions and their properties, we draw inferences about the true but unknown corresponding parameters of the population regression equation.

Drawing valid inferences, however, is based on a regression model. The model consists of a set of assumptions about the dependent variable Y in relation to the independent variable X. Statistical inference is further complicated because regression analysis requires inferring simultaneously both parameters of the population equation. Thus, we need to pay attention to the regression model, the sampling distribution of the intercept and the slope, and the related measures of sampling error. These elements of regression theory are necessary for understanding the potentialities as well as the limitations of regression analysis.

In the regression model, the independent variable X is fixed and predetermined at specific values, while the dependent variable Y is a random variable. In our example, the college GPA, the value of the independent variable X of each student, is determined prior to entering the graduate program. For a given college GPA, however, the value of the graduate GPA, the dependent variable Y, varies at random. This means that for every value of X there is a conditional distribution of Y, as illustrated in Fig. 21.5. Note that for a given value of X such as X_1 there is a conditional distribution of Y. For example, 100 college graduates may have identical college GPA X_1, say 3.0. But their graduate GPA Y may range from 2.5 to 4.0. A frequency distribution of these 100 graduate GPAs represents a conditional distribution at $X_1 = 3.0$. The mean μ_{X_1} (read "mu sub-X-sub-1") denotes the true conditional population mean of Y at X_1. And we have one conditional distribution of Y for each value of X such as at X_1, X_2, X_3, and so on.

Figure 21.5. The linear regression model and conditional population distributions of dependent variable Y at X_1, X_2, and X_3 values of the independent variable.

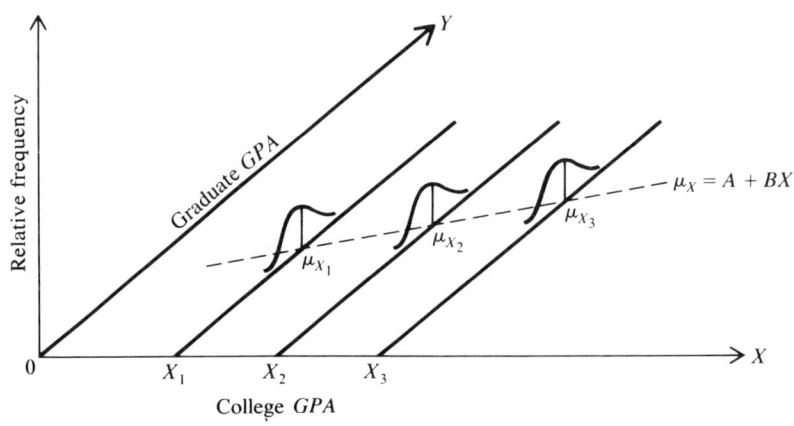

Section 21 Introduction to Regression and Correlation

Statistical inference requires that the conditional distributions of Y observations meet the following conditions:

1. All the means μ_X lie on a straight line having an equation

$$\mu_X = A + BX \tag{21.5}$$

as shown in Fig. 21.5. This is the *true* (population) regression equation which is specified by the population parameters A and B; they are to be estimated from sample information.

2. The standard deviation $\sigma_{Y|X}$, read "sigma sub-Y-given-X," of Y values about their mean is the same for every conditional distribution of Y. Note that $\sigma_{Y|X}$ is a *conditional standard deviation* of Y values for a given value of X. For example, $\sigma_{Y|X_1}$ corresponds to the conditional distribution of Y at X_1, $\sigma_{Y|X_2}$ corresponds to the conditional distribution of Y at X_2, and so on. The data points in Fig. 21.5 have the same amount of variability around the regression line so that $\sigma_{Y|X_1} = \sigma_{Y|X_2} = \sigma_{Y|X_3}$ and so on for every conditional distribution of Y. This is known as the *homoscedasticity* assumption.

3. Another underlying condition of the regression model is the assumption of *independence*. Deviations are independent of one another. In other words, the deviation of one data point about the regression line is not affected by or related to the deviation of any other data point.*

4. The deviations of Y values about the regression line are *normally distributed*. This means that each conditional distribution of Y has approximately the shape of a normal distribution as illustrated in Fig. 21.5 for three such distributions. As in the case of drawing inferences about a population mean, the *normality* assumption is important for regression analysis based on a small sample. It requires application of the t distribution. The normal distribution is used as a reasonable approximation to the t distribution when the regression equation is obtained from a large sample. Hence, for most estimation procedures, the normality assumption may be ignored if the sample is sufficiently large.

A point estimate of $\sigma_{Y|X}$ is $s_{Y|X}$, called the *standard error of estimate*; it is obtained from a sample and defined as

$$s_{Y|X} = \sqrt{\frac{\Sigma (Y - Y_c)^2}{n - 2}} \tag{21.6}$$

Note that the standard error of estimate measures the deviations of each observed Y value in a sample from its corresponding Y_c computed by the regression equation. We can calculate more easily $s_{Y|X}$ by the equivalent formula

$$s_{Y|X} = \sqrt{\frac{\Sigma Y^2 - a \Sigma Y - b \Sigma XY}{n - 2}} \tag{21.7}$$

---

*The theorem which proves that the least-squares regression equation is the best linear unbiased estimator follows from these three assumptions. They are referred to as the "weak set," since the proof does not require the more restrictive normality assumption.

Chapter 8 Regression and Correlation Analysis

Note that the divisor in (21.7) is $n - 2$ rather than n and the summation signs are over the range $i = 1, 2, \ldots, n$. Subtracting 2 from n is a correction which makes $s_{Y|X}$ a better estimator of $\sigma_{Y|X}$. We subtract 2 rather than 1 from n because the deviations of Y observations are computed from the regression equation which estimates two parameters, A and B.

Example 21.7

In Example 21.5 we found that

$$\Sigma Y^2 = 92.14, \quad \Sigma Y = 30.2, \quad \Sigma XY = 96.96$$
$$a = .78723, \quad b = .70213$$

Substituting these values in formula (21.7) we obtain

$$s_{Y|X} = \sqrt{\frac{92.14 - .78723(30.2) - .70213(96.96)}{10 - 2}} \simeq .189$$

Simple linear regression analysis involves the sampling distributions of three statistics: one for each statistic a and b of the sample regression equation and one for the standard error of estimate $s_{Y|X}$. We can easily illustrate this point.

Example 21.8

As mentioned earlier, the statistical population for evaluating the academic performance of graduate students is considered infinite since we wish to study the admission process. However, for the sake of illustrating regression theory we assumed that the population consists of only the 30 pairs of X and Y observations shown in Table 21.1. Using the least-squares method, we can obtain the regression equation of this statistical population of form (21.5)

$$\mu_X = A + BX = .851 + .733X \qquad (N = 30)$$

with a conditional standard deviation $\sigma_{Y|X} = .246$. The values of these parameters are shown in the bottom row of Table 21.3. Point estimates of these parameters from our sample are shown in the first row of Table 21.3. Then we obtained 9 sets of point estimates from 9 additional random samples of 10 observations each from our population as shown in the table. Each column of point estimates represents part of a sampling distribution. Note that each mean of the 10 point estimates is close to the corresponding parameter.

Consequently, each Y_c value we can obtain from the sample equation is a point estimate of the corresponding μ_X value. In Example 21.6, we found that $Y_c = 3.24$ when $X = 3.5$ and $Y_c = 2.54$ when $X = 2.5$. These values are point estimates of

$$\mu_{3.5} = .851 + .733(3.5) \simeq 3.42$$

and

$$\mu_{2.5} = .851 + .733(2.5) \simeq 2.68$$

respectively.

Table 21.3.
An Illustration of Sampling Distributions of Intercept a, Slope b, and Standard Error $s_{Y|X}$

		"Sampling" Distributions		
	Sample Number	Intercept a	Regression Coefficient b	Standard Error $s_{Y\|X}$
	1	.787	.702	.189
	2	.793	.742	.278
	3	.512	.848	.262
	4	.924	.694	.264
	5	.248	.905	.325
	6	1.416	.515	.197
	7	.802	.733	.223
	8	.420	.844	.274
	9	.700	.787	.265
	10	.748	.787	.296
Means:		.735	.756	.257
		A	B	$\sigma_{Y\|X}$
Parameters:		.851	.733	.246

Now we are in a position to understand why the sample regression equation of form (21.1) computed by the least-squares method is a linear unbiased estimator of the population regression equation of form (21.5). In earlier estimation procedures, a *single statistic* represents a point estimate. In regression analysis, however, a point estimate represents an *equation* in the sense that each value of Y_c for a given value of X lies on the regression line. Such a Y_c value is a point estimate of the *corresponding value of parameter* μ_X. This is so because the expected values of intercept a and slope b obtained from all possible samples of size n equal their corresponding parameters. In other words, the statistics a and b are unbiased estimators of parameters A and B, respectively. Symbolically,

(21.8) $$E(a) = A \quad \text{and} \quad E(b) = B$$

In addition, these least-squares estimators are the best because their sampling distributions have minimum variance. The variances of a and b will be introduced later.

The Correlation Model

Simple regression shows *how* two variables may be related with a mathematical function, an equation. Correlation measures the *degree* of linear association between two variables. The two techniques are very closely related mathematically, so we need to explain the basic elements of the correlation model in order to better interpret the results of regression analysis.

The regression model is applied to situations where the independent variable X is fixed and predetermined; it is not a random variable. The college GPA of a student is computed before admission to a graduate program. Therefore, it is a fixed and predetermined quantity. Only the graduate GPA is a random variable. By contrast, correlation is appropriate for situations where both variables are considered random.

Example 21.9

Consider again the statistical population of 30 students shown in Table 21.1. The quantitative and verbal GMAT (Graduate Management Admission Test) scores of the same students are shown in Table 21.4.* Correlation analysis is applicable here because both scores X and Y are determined simultaneously as part of the admission procedure. Both variables are considered random. We are not interested in the potential cause-and-effect relationship; in fact, such a notion is inconceivable because we do not know which variable precedes the other; we are interested in measuring the degree to which the two variables vary together, regardless of whether one may affect the other, each affects the other, or both are influenced by some other, third variable.

Table 21.4.
Quantitative and Verbal GMAT Scores of a Population of 30 M.B.A. Graduates (Data Hypothetical)

Student Number	GMAT Scores Quant. Y	GMAT Scores Verbal X	Student Number	GMAT Scores Quant. Y	GMAT Scores Verbal X	Student Number	GMAT Scores Quant. Y	GMAT Scores Verbal X
1	600	580	11	630	650	21	670	650
2	680	670	12	750	760	(22)	470	500
(3)	600	660	13	690	730	23	570	650
4	700	750	(14)	400	450	(24)	370	500
(5)	330	450	15	730	650	25	480	460
(6)	620	650	16	540	560	(26)	500	480
7	770	700	17	460	450	27	790	700
(8)	570	550	(18)	550	580	28	580	680
9	530	580	19	500	490	(29)	390	520
10	650	600	20	560	580	30	440	430

The correlation model has a *bivariate normal distribution.* You can imagine such a three-dimensional distribution as a pitcher's mound or a Mexican hat located on the floor near the corner of a room. The lines where the two walls of the corner meet the floor represent the Y and X variables, and the vertical line where the two walls meet represents the probability with which pairs of Y and X values occur. Such a bivariate population is based on the same conditions of the regression model enumerated earlier. In fact, it is mathematically possible to derive two regression equations from such a bivariate distribution, one with X as the independent and Y as the dependent variable and another with Y as the independent and X as the dependent variable. Although such regression analysis is technically possible, it is not likely to be empirically meaningful because it ignores the two-random-variable assumption of the correlation model.

The net of the matter is that the correlation model has *one* index measuring the degree of the association between the two variables for either regression equa-

---

*This is the former Admission Test for Graduate Study in Business, or ATGSB, administered to applicants for graduate work in management since 1954. The verbal and quantitative scales of the test range from 0 to 60, while the total scale ranges from 200 to 800 points. For the purpose of serving the present analysis, quantitative and verbal scores are expressed in terms of the scale for the total score.

tion. This index is called the *correlation coefficient* and is denoted by ρ (Greek letter *rho*). This measure is the unknown parameter of the correlation model. A point estimate of ρ is the statistic correlation coefficient, denoted by r, which we can calculate from a sample. For example, from a simple random sample of 10 students whose numbers are circled in Table 21.4 we can calculate a positive correlation coefficient r of about $+.826$. (How to calculate r and what it means will be discussed shortly.) This statistic is a point estimate of the unknown ρ of the statistical population of 30 students. And we can easily illustrate the relationship between the sampling distribution of statistic r and its parameter ρ by preparing a table similar to Table 21.3. The theory of statistical inference is applicable to the correlation coefficient in the same way it was shown to be applicable to the coefficients of the regression model. Moreover, testing and estimating ρ in correlation analysis can be obtained directly from regression analysis.

Technically, statistic r should not be used to test or estimate parameter ρ unless both variables are random. However, the correlation coefficient r *can* be calculated even when the independent variable is not random but predetermined as in our study of graduate and college GPA scores. This measure can be used to better understand regression analysis. Statistic r^* is defined as

$$(21.9) \qquad r = \frac{\Sigma XY - n\overline{X}\overline{Y}}{\sqrt{(\Sigma X^2 - n\overline{X}^2)(\Sigma Y^2 - n\overline{Y}^2)}}$$

Example 21.10

Let us go back to the basic calculations in Table 21.2 for our initial sample of 10 students. We found that

$$\Sigma XY = 96.96, \qquad \overline{X} = \frac{31.8}{10} = 3.18, \qquad \overline{Y} = \frac{30.2}{10} = 3.02$$

$$\Sigma X^2 = 102.44, \qquad \Sigma Y^2 = 92.14$$

Substitution of these values in (21.9) yields the unadjusted correlation coefficient

$$r = \frac{96.96 - 10(3.18)(3.02)}{\sqrt{[102.44 - 10(3.18)^2][92.14 - 10(3.02)^2]}}$$

$$= \frac{96.96 - 96.036}{1.109854}$$

$$= +.833$$

A close look at formula (21.9) explains why coefficient correlation r has been selected as a measure of association between X and Y. The denominator in (21.9) will always be positive because it involves squares of numbers. The numerator on the other hand is identical to the numerator in formula (21.3) for calculating the regression coefficient b, the slope of the regression line. Hence, the correlation coefficient will always have the same sign as the slope b. And r will be zero when

---

*This correlation coefficient is unadjusted for degrees of freedom. The adjusted correlation coefficient will be discussed shortly.

Chapter 8 Regression and Correlation Analysis

b is zero, indicating no correlation. The value of correlation coefficient r varies from $+1$ for perfectly positive correlation to -1 for perfectly negative correlation. A positive value for r like $+.833$ calculated in Example 21.10 means the regression line slopes upward to the right. A negative value for r means the regression line slopes downward. Such relationships have already been discussed in general terms in connection with scatter diagrams (Fig. 21.2).

Another important measure in correlation analysis is r^2, called the *coefficient of determination*. We can find r^2 by squaring r obtained from formula (21.9) after adjusting its value for degrees of freedom. In order to relate correlation to regression analysis, however, we shall calculate the adjusted r^2 from the following equivalent formula:*

(21.10) $$r^2 = 1 - \frac{s^2_{Y|X}}{s^2_Y} \quad \left(1 - \frac{\text{unexplained variance}}{\text{total variance}}\right)$$

where $s^2_{X|Y}$ is given in (21.7) and s^2_Y is defined as

(21.11) $$s^2_Y = \frac{\Sigma Y^2 - \bar{Y}\Sigma Y}{n-1}$$

Example 21.11

Consider the basic calculations in Table 21.2 for our initial sample of 10 students. We found that

$$\Sigma Y^2 = 92.14, \quad \Sigma Y = 30.2, \quad \bar{Y} = \frac{\Sigma Y}{n} = \frac{30.2}{10} = 3.02$$

Substituting these values in (21.11), the variance of the dependent variable is

$$s^2_Y = \frac{92.14 - (3.02)(30.2)}{10 - 1} = .104$$

In Example 21.7, we found that $s_{Y|X}$ is approximately $.189$ so that $s^2_{Y|X}$ is about $.0357 = (.189)^2$. Substitution in (21.10) yields

$$r^2 = 1 - \frac{s^2_{Y|X}}{s^2_Y} = 1 - \frac{.0357}{.104} \simeq .657$$

What does this value of r^2 mean? A close look at formula (21.10) may help us understand this measure. Note that $s^2_{X|Y}$ is the square of the standard error of

---

*This coefficient is adjusted for degrees of freedom. Henceforth, we shall follow the rule to quote the adjusted value of a coefficient if it is the result of direct calculations in the text. Otherwise, we shall quote the unadjusted value of a coefficient obtained from computer printouts. The relationship between adjusted and unadjusted r^2 values is given by formula (22.15). For sufficiently large samples the difference between adjusted and unadjusted values may be ignored.

estimate as defined in (21.7); it measures the variation of the dependent variable Y which is *unexplained* by the regression equation. This variance is divided by the total variance s_Y^2 of the dependent variable Y; the resulting percentage is subtracted from 1. Thus, r^2 measures the proportion of the variation in the dependent variable Y which is reduced by the regression equation. According to Example 21.11, the regression equation of the independent variable X, college GPA scores, on the dependent variable Y, graduate GPA, has reduced the total variation in Y by 65.7 percent. In order to facilitate communication we shall express such a reduction with the statement that "65.7 percent of the variation in Y can be *explained by* or *attributed to* the independent variable X."

In sum, the correlation coefficient r is an index which may vary between -1 and $+1$, with the sign indicating the direction of the association; the correlation coefficient r in Example 21.11 is about $+.811$* or the positive square root of .657. The coefficient of determination tells us how important index r is by expressing the degree of the association between X and Y in terms of the percentage reduction in the variation of the dependent variable Y. This is important because r alone may give us an exaggerated impression about the extent of the association between X and Y. For example, a correlation coefficient r close to .5 implies that using X to estimate Y reduces the total variation in Y by only $r^2 = .25$ or 25 percent. Finally, we should keep in mind that the coefficient of correlation r is a measure of *linear correlation*; this means that X and Y can be highly related by a nonlinear equation even when the observed value of r is close or equal to zero.

PROBLEMS

Group One

21.1. For each study indicate which is the independent and which the dependent variable:
  *(a) On the basis of train reservations, a railroad manager wishes to determine the number of meals to be served on a train between New York and Chicago.
  (b) A hospital administrator studies the daily number of blood transfusions in order to find the need for blood donations.
  (c) An investment research analyst wishes to forecast changes in bond prices which are attributed to changes in interest rates.
  (d) A publisher wishes to find out the relationship between number of pages in books and printing errors.

21.2. Prepare a scatter diagram by plotting the following data on coordinate paper. Use a ruler to draw a "freehand" straight line which summarizes the underlying relationship between the independent and dependent variables. On the basis of this straight line, derive a regression equation by determining graphically the intercept a and the coefficient b of the equation.

---

*As already explained, this adjusted r is slightly less than its unadjusted value $+.833$ found in Example 21.10.
Answers to asterisked (*) problems are appended.

Typed Pages (Number) X	Typing Errors (Number) Y	Typed Pages (Number) X	Typed Errors (Number) Y
14	8	34	17
16	11	40	18
26	13	44	18
34	13	20	10
52	20	20	13

21.3. For each regression equation:
   (i) Sketch its graph.
   (ii) Explain the slope.
   (iii) Indicate whether the relationship between X and Y is positive or negative.
   *(a) $Y_c = 5 + 2X$
   (b) $Y_c = -6 + 5X$
   (c) $Y_c = 50 - 4X$
   (d) $Y_c = 100 - (0)X$

21.4. Consider the data given in Table 21.1.
   (a) Prepare a scatter diagram of 30 observations. Then on the same diagram sketch the graph of the regression equation for the population and for samples 1, 3, 5, and 10 whose coefficients are given in Table 21.3.
   *(b) Explain the differences between the graphs of the population and the sample equations.
   (c) According to formula (21.8) the expected value of statistics a and b must equal the corresponding parameters A and B. Explain this property.

21.5. The additional nine samples whose regression coefficients are listed in Table 21.3 represent the following student numbers in Table 21.1:

n_2	n_3	n_4	n_5	n_6	n_7	n_8	n_9	n_{10}
06	15	28	19	17	28	11	07	25
25	13	21	10	26	07	14	03	29
23	03	18	06	19	02	05	26	23
24	30	25	16	22	20	21	01	19
09	02	03	25	29	06	17	27	17
27	16	26	11	14	23	30	29	10
14	26	27	15	09	16	09	18	05
01	11	05	01	20	24	08	02	30
20	14	19	09	02	02	20	10	27
02	12	16	14	30	21	02	08	08

In cooperation with eight other classmates, do the following: each of you select one of the nine samples and compute the regression equation of your sample. Verify your computations with the answers given in Table 21.3.

21.6. Suppose the coefficient of determination ρ^2 of the statistical population in Table 21.4 is about .777 and its correlation coefficient ρ is .882.

Section 21 Introduction to Regression and Correlation

    *(a) In cooperation with eight other classmates, do the following: each select one of the nine samples whose student numbers are given in the previous problem and compute the corresponding statistics from your sample.
    *(b) Collectively prepare a table such as Table 21.3, listing the parameter values and all 10 sample statistics.
    (c) Explain what such a table illustrates.

21.7. Distinguish between:
    (a) Simple and multiple regression
    (b) Regression and correlation model
    (c) The standard error of estimate and conditional standard deviation
    (d) Linear and curvilinear regression
    (e) The regression coefficient and the correlation coefficient
    (f) Sampling errors and residuals
    (g) Dependent and independent variable with respect to regression analysis
    (h) Conditional and bivariate normal distributions

21.8. Explain:
    (a) The coefficient of determination   (e) Intercept
    (b) Scatter diagram   (f) Homoscedasticity
    (c) The least-squares method   (g) Linearity
    (d) Normality   (h) Independence

Group Two

21.9. Consider the data given in Problem 21.2.
    (a) Prepare a table such as Table 21.2 of basic calculations for fitting a regression equation to the data by the method of least-squares.
    *(b) Derive the regression equation.
    (c) Interpret the meaning of the regression coefficient.
    (d) Calculate the coefficient of determination using formula (21.10) and explain the meaning of this measure.

21.10. Algonquin Electric, a utility company, has issued several long-term bonds. In the past, the monthly average prime interest rate and the monthly average price of these bonds were as follows:

Interest (Percentage) X	Bond Prices (Hundreds of Dollars) Y	Interest (Percentage) X	Bond Prices (Hundreds of Dollars) Y
10	104	17	85
13	95	11	101
20	79	16	89
15	96	10	103

    (a) Prepare a table such as Table 21.2 of basic calculations for fitting a regression equation to the data by the method of least-squares.
    (b) Derive the regression equation.
    (c) Interpret the meaning of the regression coefficient.
    (d) Calculate the coefficient of determination using formula (21.10) and explain the meaning of this measure.

Chapter 8 Regression and Correlation Analysis

21.11. Regression analysis of corn yields in bushels per acre and seasonal rainfall over a period of years showed a total variance of 36 (squared) bushels. Of this total variance, a variance of 11 cannot be attributed to variations in rainfall.
  *(a) Compute the coefficients of determination and correlation.
  (b) Explain the meaning of these measurements.

21.12. Consider the regression equation

$$Y_c = 120 + .30X$$

where X represents fertilizer in pounds and Y_c wheat yield in bushels per acre.
  (a) Explain the meaning of this equation in terms of wheat yield and fertilizer.
  (b) If a bushel of wheat sells for $4 and fertilizer costs $1 per pound, would it be economical to use fertilizer?
  (c) How much should the cost of fertilizer be in order to make fertilizer application profitable?

21.13. Icecream Land Company operates a chain of retail stores. In addition to dairy products, each store operates a candy counter. In order to evaluate the contribution of the counter to overhead, a study is carried out of the relationship between average daily net revenue (sales less direct costs) and square feet of candy shelf space for all 50 stores over the past 6 months. A scatter diagram shows that the relationship is linear with data points uniformly distributed about the line. The basic data are as follows: $n = 50$; $\Sigma Y = 420$; $\Sigma X = 1200$; $\Sigma XY = 10{,}480$; $\Sigma Y^2 = 3656$; and $\Sigma X^2 = 30{,}800$.
  (a) Derive the regression equation.
  (b) Interpret the meaning of this equation in terms of the variables involved.
  (c) Calculate the standard error of estimate.
  (d) Suppose a store uses 20 square feet of shelf space and averages a $7.00 daily net revenue. How do you rate the performance of this store in comparison to all other stores? Answer in terms of the standard error of estimate.

21.14. Home Oil Company is a distributor of heating oil to residential properties. Last winter the service manager collected data on average daily temperature and daily consumption of oil in gallons per single home with three bedrooms and one thermostat. A sample of 10 such observations is shown below (sample is deliberately kept small in order to reduce computations):

Day	Oil Consumed (Gallons) Y	Temperature (°F) X	Day	Oil Consumed (Gallons) Y	Temperature (°F) X
1	36	−20	6	23	20
2	2	60	7	16	30
3	27	0	8	20	10
4	30	−14	9	10	50
5	15	40	10	11	34

  (a) Plot the data on a scatter diagram. Would a straight line be a reasonable fit?

(b) Change the scale of the independent variable so that X is 0 for $-20°F$ temperature and 80 for $60°F$ temperature. Then use the least-squares method to derive a regression equation. Sketch the graph of this equation on the scatter diagram.

(c) What is the meaning of this equation in terms of temperature and oil consumption?

(d) The company has the policy of making oil deliveries to homes before 80 percent of the oil in a 250-gallon oil tank is consumed. Since last delivery, daily temperatures averaged $-20, -10, 0, 5, -10, -20,$ and $0°F$. During which day should the next oil delivery be made?

SECTION 22 / SIMPLE REGRESSION AND CORRELATION

Now that we know the basic theory and concepts of regression and correlation analysis, we are ready to answer two important questions. Is the computed regression equation reliable for evaluating the academic performance of M.B.A. students as measured by the graduate GPA? We have hypothesized that a relationship exists between college and graduate GPAs. Now we want to test that hypothesis. We focus on two tests: the t test and the F test for analysis of variance. The second question is how and under what qualifications is a regression equation utilized? In particular, how may we use the results of regression and correlation as a basis for establishing admission standards for M.B.A. education? This question requires statistical estimation focused on interval estimation of the individual and the average value of the dependent variable, graduate GPA.

We simplify matters by placing the computational steps for analysis of variance and a computer printout of simple regression in section appendices. In order to introduce the basics of the subject with minimum effort, we selected a sample of 10 from a population of 30 M.B.A. graduates. Now we consider *all 30 observations shown in Table 21.1 as a random sample*. Since we wish to study the admission *process, the statistical population is infinite*. Initially, we concentrate on large samples; later we introduce some refinements related to small samples.

The t Test

We have seen that slope b is a random variable subject to sampling error: b may be other than zero, indicating that X and Y are correlated, while in reality the unknown parameter B may be zero, indicating no correlation. This raises the familiar problem of statistical inference. Earlier hypothesis-testing techniques can be employed to test whether or not the observed slope b is significantly different from zero. If the test result is statistically significant, the sample equation may be employed to estimate Y, the graduate GPA of an M.B.A. applicant, for a given value of X, the applicant's college GPA.

Furthermore, we already know that slope b is an unbiased estimator of parameter B. The sampling distribution of b has a standard deviation called the

Chapter 8 Regression and Correlation Analysis

standard error of the regression coefficient defined as

(22.1) $$s_b = \frac{s_{Y|X}}{\sqrt{\Sigma (X - \bar{X})^2}}$$

Note that $s_{Y|X}$ is the standard error of estimate explained earlier. The denominator $\Sigma (X - \bar{X})^2$ is the total variation of X from its mean $\bar{X}$. Thus s_b is a function of residuals, that is, the deviations of data points around the regression line, and the dispersion of the X values around their mean.

Example 22.1

The regression equation of our problem is

$$Y_c = .851 + .733X \qquad (n = 30)$$

with $s_{Y|X} = .246$. It is copied from Example 21.8. Symbols μ_X and $\sigma_{Y|X}$ are changed to Y_c and $s_{Y|X}$, respectively, in order to indicate that now this is a sample equation representing 30 M.B.A. graduates from a continuous admission process. Computation of $\Sigma (X - \bar{X})^2$ is illustrated in Table 22.1, where the three dots represent the missing rows, 3 through 29. First, we total the thirty X values of the sample; this total divided by the sample size yields the mean as follows:

$$\bar{X} = \frac{\Sigma X}{n} = \frac{100.4}{30} \simeq 3.347$$

Second, we subtract this mean from each X value to obtain the column of deviations. For example, the deviation for the first observation from the mean is

$$X - \bar{X} = 4.0 - 3.347 = +.653$$

Except for discrepancies due to rounding, the algebraic sum of deviations $\Sigma (X - \bar{X})$ must be equal to zero, a good check on calculations.

Finally, each deviation is squared in the last column of the table; so, total variation $\Sigma (X - \bar{X})^2$ is about 4.912.

Table 22.1. Calculation of $\Sigma (X - \bar{X})^2$ for the M.B.A. Problem ($n = 30$)

Student Number[a]	College GPA[a] X	Deviations from Mean $X - \bar{X}$	Deviations Squared $(X - \bar{X})^2$
1	4.0	+.653	.426
2	2.6	−.747	.558
.	.	.	.
.	.	.	.
.	.	.	.
30	2.9	−.447	.200
	100.4	= 0	4.912

[a]From Table 21.1.

Section 22 Simple Regression and Correlation

Substituting the appropriate values in (22.1), we have

$$s_b = \frac{.246}{\sqrt{4.912}} \simeq .111$$

the standard error of the regression coefficient.
On the basis of formula (15.3), the t statistic in this case is defined as

(22.2) $$t = \frac{b - B}{s_b}$$

It is important to remember that the t distribution is the appropriate distribution for such a test for any sample size n. However, we can use the normal distribution as an approximation to the t distribution for sufficiently large samples. We may illustrate this point with our problem.

Example 22.2

Our hypothesis is that the parameter slope B is zero: college GPA scores X have no effect on graduate GPA scores Y. The null and the alternative hypotheses are

$H_0: B = 0$ (college GPA does not affect graduate GPA)
$H_1: B \neq 0$ (college GPA affects graduate GPA)

This is a two-sided test because we are not certain that college performance would affect graduate work favorably. Otherwise, a one-sided test might have been appropriate. We may consider that a sample of 30 observations requires the use of the t distribution. Suppose we wish to test our hypothesis at 1 percent significance level. For an area of $.005 = .01/2$ and for $28 = 30 - 2$ degrees of freedom the critical t_c value is 2.763, obtained from Appendix E. The decision rule is

If $-2.763 \leq t_o \leq +2.763$, accept H_0 (college GPA does not affect graduate GPA)
If $t_o > +2.763$ or $t_o < -2.763$, reject H_0 (college GPA affects graduate GPA)

We have assumed that B is zero and we have found that $b = .733$ and $s_b = .111$. Substituting these values in (22.2), we have

$$t_o = \frac{b - B}{s_b} = \frac{.733 - 0}{.111} \simeq 6.603$$

Since the observed t_o value is larger than the critical value, we reject the null hypothesis. The test result is statistically significant; college GPA may affect graduate GPA scores.

Also, we may consider a sample of 30 observations sufficiently large to justify the use of the normal distribution as an approximation to the t distribution. For the same 1 percent significance level, that is, for an area of .005, the critical z_c value, from Appendix D, is 2.58. Again, we reject the null hypothesis and arrive at the same conclusion since the observed $t_o = 6.603$ is larger than the critical $z_c = 2.58$. Therefore, the sample equation may be used for evaluating the academic performance of students.

At this point a few summarizing comments may help us view the testing procedure in a wider perspective.

1. Remember that the appropriate distribution for testing the slope of an equation is always the t distribution. For this reason it is called the t test. The normal distribution is a reasonable approximation to the t distribution when the sample size is sufficiently large.

2. The testing procedure controls only the risk of erroneously rejecting the null hypothesis of no correlation between X and Y. In our example, we assumed a 1 percent risk of erroneously concluding that the regression equation may be reliable for evaluating academic performance, when in reality there may be no correlation between the two variables. Hypothesis testing carries also the risk of erroneously accepting a false null hypothesis; in other words, we may conclude that there is no correlation, although in reality the two variables are correlated. Such a risk is not fixed at specified levels. Of course, both risks can be reduced by increasing the sample size.

3. A one-sided t test is appropriate if we are fairly certain that the relationship between an independent variable and the dependent variable is positive or negative. Since such knowledge is not usually available from other sources prior to regression analysis, testing is usually two-sided. Thus, all tests in regression analysis in this text are two-sided unless otherwise specified.

4. Testing may also be carried out in terms of confidence intervals. We may test for assumed values of B other than zero.

5. The regression and correlation coefficients are related with the expression

(22.3) $$b = r \left(\frac{s_Y}{s_X} \right)$$

where r = correlation coefficient
s_Y = standard deviation of Y observations
s_X = standard deviation of X observations

This means that if either b or r is zero, the other will also be zero. Thus we can perform a test equivalent to the above test, assuming that ρ rather than B is zero.

6. A test may show statistically significant results even when the degree of correlation is of little practical importance. For example, with a sufficiently large sample, even a low correlation coefficient may be found significantly different from zero. But with low correlation we may not be willing to employ the regression equation for decision making.

The F test

For simple regression analysis this test is equivalent to the t test. Within the context of regression analysis the value of the F statistic is the ratio of the explained

Section 22 Simple Regression and Correlation

to the unexplained variance defined by

(22.4) $$F = \frac{\Sigma(Y_c - \bar{Y})^2/(k-1)}{\Sigma(Y - Y_c)^2/(n-k)} \quad \left(\frac{\text{explained variance}}{\text{unexplained variance}}\right)$$

where k is the number of constants in the regression equation. The computational steps for finding the F statistic are appended to this section. At this point, it may be necessary to explain conceptually total, explained, and unexplained variance.

Example 22.3

Consider the first pair of observations in our problem for an M.B.A. program (Table 21.1), where $X = 4.0$ and $Y = 3.9$. This data point and the graph of our regression equation are shown in Fig. 22.1. For $X = 4.0$, the computed value of the dependent variable is

$$Y_c = .851 - .733(4.0) = 3.783 \qquad (n = 30)$$

The unconditional mean $\bar{Y}$ is about 3.303 as calculated in Appendix 22.I.

Note that the total deviation is the vertical distance between the observed value and the unconditional mean of the dependent variable:

Total deviation: $\quad Y - \bar{Y} = 3.90 - 3.303 = .597$

Figure 22.1.
Illustration of total, explained, and unexplained deviation in Y (graduate GPA).

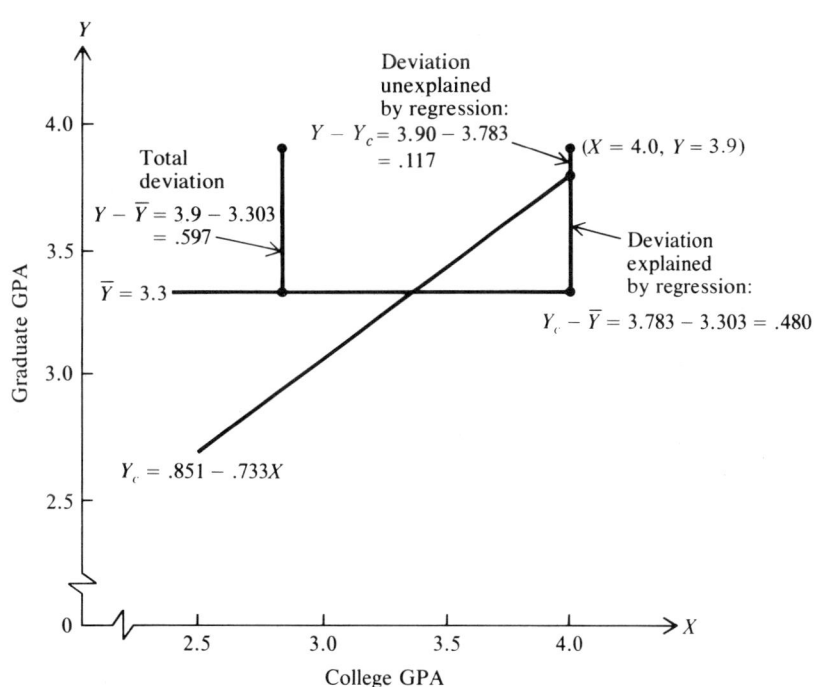

The deviation explained by or attributed to the regression equation is the vertical distance between the conditional or computed value and the unconditional mean of the dependent variable:

Explained deviation: $Y_c - \bar{Y} = 3.783 - 3.303 = .480$

Finally, the deviation which cannot be explained by or attributed to the regression equation is the vertical distance between the observed and the computed value of the dependent variable:

Unexplained deviation: $Y - Y_c = 3.90 - 3.783 = .117$

Thus total deviation (.597) is composed of two types of deviations: explained (.480) and unexplained (.117). It is important to recall that the unexplained deviation represents the residuals which we illustrated earlier.

In general, for any X value of the independent variable, the regression equation decomposes total deviation of the dependent variable Y so that

(22.5) $$(Y - \bar{Y}) = (Y_c - \bar{Y}) + (Y - Y_c)$$

Total deviation = explained + unexplained

Squaring each deviation and summing the products for all sample observations, we obtain the corresponding variations:

(22.6) $$\Sigma (Y - \bar{Y})^2 = \Sigma (Y_c - \bar{Y})^2 + \Sigma (Y - Y_c)^2$$

Total variation = explained + unexplained

Each of these variations is called a *sum of squares*.

Dividing the explained and the unexplained sums of squares by the corresponding degrees of freedom, we obtain their variances or mean squares. It is important to realize that the unexplained or residual variance is the square of the standard error of estimate $s_{Y|X}$, introduced in the previous section. And it can be seen that the F statistic, formula (22.4), is the ratio of the explained to the unexplained variance.

Example 22.3 (continued)

From the computations in Appendix 22-I we have found that the explained and the unexplained variations in our problem are about 2.649 and 1.701, respectively.

The value k in (22.4) denotes the number of constants in the regression equation. Since a simple regression equation has two constants, the intercept and the slope, k is 2. So the degrees of freedom in the numerator of the F statistic are

$$k - 1 = 2 - 1 = 1$$

Then the degrees of freedom in the denominator of F are

$$n - k = 30 - 2 = 28$$

Table 22.2.
Analysis of Variance Applied to the Regression Problem of M.B.A. Graduates ($n = 30$)

Source of Variation	Variation or Sum of Squares	Degrees of Freedom	Variance or Mean Squares	
Attributable to regression (explained)	2.649	1	2.649	$F_o = \dfrac{2.649}{.06075} \simeq 43.605$
Deviation from regression (unexplained or residual)	1.701	28	.06075	
Totals:	4.350	29		

This is so because 2 degrees of freedom are used to calculate each Y_c value from the regression equation in order to determine the 30 deviations or residuals.

These numerical results are conveniently summarized in Table 22.2. Note that the sum of the explained and unexplained variations is equal to the total variation 4.350. Also, the sum of the number of degrees of freedom in the numerator and in the denominator equals

$$n - 1 = 30 - 1 = 29$$

This is so because 1 degree of freedom is used to calculate the unconditional mean $\overline{Y}$ from which the 30 total deviations are obtained.

Substitution of the appropriate values in formula (22.4) yields the observed $F_o = 43.605$.

Is this observed F_o value significant at 1 percent level? The critical value $F_{01}(1, 28)$ can be obtained from the F distribution given in Appendix H. It is 7.64, which appears under column 1 in row 28 of the table. Since the observed F_o is greater than the critical $F_{01}(1, 28)$, the null hypothesis that B is zero is rejected by the F test as it was with the t test. Again, we conclude that the sample equation may be employed to evaluate the academic performance of M.B.A. applicants.

Prediction and Confidence Intervals

With the t and F tests we are able to establish whether or not X and Y are associated. We can now show estimation procedures. We first concentrate on the construction of estimation intervals from large samples which may justify the use of the normal distribution as an approximation to the t distribution. For illustrative purposes, we shall consider the 30 observations in our sample to be sufficiently large to construct estimation intervals with the Z deviate and with *approximate* formulas. Refinements using the t distribution and the *exact* formulas for constructing estimation intervals are discussed in the next subsection.

A regression equation is the basis for constructing two types of estimation intervals. One type estimates an *individual value* of the dependent variable Y. For example, we may be interested in estimating the graduate GPA for a *particular applicant* whose college GPA is 2.7. The interval is usually referred to as a *prediction interval*. The second type estimates the *conditional mean* μ_X of the dependent variable Y. For example, for establishing an admission policy we may also need to estimate the *average* graduate GPA for applicants whose college GPA is 2.7. An interval estimate for this conditional average is called a *confidence interval*.

The standard error of estimate is important for both types of estimation intervals. Introduced in the previous section, it is repeated here for convenience.

(22.7)
$$s_{Y|X} = \sqrt{\frac{\Sigma Y^2 - a\Sigma Y - b\Sigma XY}{n-2}}$$

On the basis of this measure we can construct an *approximate* prediction interval with the following expression:

(22.8)
$$Y_c \pm z s_{Y|X}$$

where all symbols have been introduced earlier.

Example 22.4

Let us again consider the regression equation of our problem.

$$Y_c = .851 + .733X \qquad (n = 30)$$

with $s_{Y|X} = .246$. We may recall (Example 22.1) that this is the sample equation for all 30 M.B.A. graduates. Suppose a student applying for admission to the graduate program has a college GPA of 2.7. In letter grades, this score is equivalent to a B− average. We wish to predict the student's graduate GPA with 95 percent degree of confidence.

Substituting for $X = 2.7$ in the above regression equation, we obtain a point estimate of the student's graduate GPA equal to

$$Y_c = .851 + .733(2.7) = 2.83$$

The value of z is 1.96, obtained from Appendix D. Substituting these z and Y_c values in (22.8), we have the approximate prediction interval

$$2.83 \pm 1.96(.246) = 2.35 \text{ to } 3.31$$

In letter grades, this interval means that this particular student with a B− average from college may get a graduate GPA score representing an overall grade from as low as a C+ to as high as a B+ with 95 percent confidence.

In discussing this result, let us assume that an applicant must have at least a 2.7 GPA to be admitted as well as to graduate from the program. On its face value, the computed interval appears to be of little practical use. The standard error of .246 makes the interval too wide. We can easily find from the normal distribution that the applicant has about 30 percent chance of failing the program.*

We may get additional insight into this analysis by examining the confidence interval for the conditional mean of the dependent variable Y. This is an interval estimate of a point on the regression line. For large samples, the standard error for this estimate reduces to the standard error of intercept a, denoted by s_{Y_c} and defined as

(22.9) $$s_{Y_c} = \frac{s_{Y|X}}{\sqrt{n}} \qquad (n \geqslant 30)$$

So an *approximate* confidence interval for the conditional mean μ_X is

(22.10) $$\boxed{Y_c \pm z \frac{s_{Y|X}}{\sqrt{n}}}$$

Note that for such an interval the standard error of estimate $s_{Y|X}$ is divided by the square root of sample size n.

Example 22.5

For applicants with a college GPA of 2.7, a point estimate of the conditional mean μ_X is 2.83, (Example 22.4). For a 95 percent confidence and by (22.10), we have the approximate confidence interval

$$2.83 \pm 1.96 \frac{.246}{\sqrt{30}} = 2.83 \pm 1.96(.045)$$
$$= 2.74 \text{ to } 2.92$$

We are 95 percent confident that the graduate GPA of many applicants each with a B− overall grade from college may *average* from 2.74 to 2.92 or from B− to B.

This information may be of little use in formulating admissions policy. If we wish to virtually eliminate the possibility of admitting students who are likely to fail, individual value indicates that the minimum college GPA for admission be raised to 3.53 or at least a B+.* Of course, this policy would result in the rejection of some students who in fact would be capable of completing the M.B.A. program.

The wisdom of such a policy may be further questioned with the confidence interval of the conditional mean. The lower limit of the average graduate GPA

---

*Assuming that $\mu_X = 2.83$ and that an applicant must obtain at least a 2.7 graduate GPA in order to complete the M.B.A. program,

$$P\left(z \leqslant \frac{2.70 - 2.83}{.246}\right) = P(z \leqslant -.528) = .5000 - .201 \simeq .30$$

*For $P(z \geqslant 3) = .5000 - .49865 = .00135$ and the lower limit would be $.851 + .733(3.53) - 3(.246) = 2.7$.

Chapter 8 Regression and Correlation Analysis

would be 2.74, above the failing point. Since we do not know *which* students are likely to fall below this lower limit, we may give applicants the benefit of the doubt by recommending that the admission cutoff point be maintained at 2.7 college GPA. In this way we let the graduate program identify failing students.

In fact, the confidence interval for the conditional mean could be used as a control device. Students with graduate GPA below the lower limit of the interval could be identified. Such cases can be examined in order to find assignable causes for poor performance.

If college GPA were the only admission criterion, either policy may be of some merit. Obviously, this is not likely to be the case; this criterion alone does not appear to be reliable. A wiser course of action may be to suspend judgment and continue the search for additional criteria for evaluating applicants. This may be accomplished with multiple regression, to be introduced in the next section.

Refinements on Estimation Intervals*

In the meantime, let us turn our attention to some refinements we deliberately left behind. The standard error of estimate, formula (22.7), may be used for constructing prediction intervals from large samples as in our illustration. It may be considered an approximation to the *exact* formula

$$(22.11) \qquad s'_{Y|X} = s_{Y|X} \sqrt{1 + \frac{1}{n} + \frac{(X - \bar{X})^2}{\Sigma (X - \bar{X})^2}}$$

which should be used for samples of any size. The expression under the square root sign represents the variance of the total sampling error which is a combination of the variances involved in constructing prediction intervals. Total variance can be easily understood if we square both sides of (22.11) and change it into form

$$(22.12) \qquad s'^2_{Y|X} = s^2_{Y|X} + \frac{s^2_{Y|X}}{n} + \frac{s^2_{Y|X}(X - \bar{X})^2}{\Sigma (X - \bar{X})^2}$$

Actually, expression (22.12) can be viewed as the algebraic sum of three terms:

1. The variance of residuals, $s^2_{Y|X}$, formula (22.7)

2. The variance of intercept a, $s^2_{Y_c}$, formula (22.9)

3. The variance of slope b, s^2_b, formula (22.1) weighted by the squared deviation $(X - \bar{X})^2$ of the predicting X value from its mean

For increasingly large samples, the expression under the square root sign in (22.11) approaches 1 so that $s_{X|Y}$ in (22.7) may be considered an approximation to $s'_{Y|Y}$ in (22.11).

---

*This topic may be omitted if construction of intervals with the exact formulas is not desired.

Section 22 Simple Regression and Correlation

Example 22.6

Consider an applicant for an M.B.A. program where X is 2.7. From Table 22.1 we can easily find that

$$\bar{X} = \frac{\Sigma X}{n} = \frac{100.4}{30} = 3.347 \quad \text{and} \quad \Sigma(X - \bar{X})^2 = 4.912$$

Substituting these values in formula (22.11), we obtain

$$s'_{Y|X} = .246 \sqrt{1 + \frac{1}{30} + \frac{(2.7 - 3.347)^2}{4.912}}$$
$$= .260$$

This exact standard error of estimate is only .014 or 5.8 percent larger than the approximate value .246. The difference gets increasingly smaller and may be ignored for samples larger than 30 observations.

Analogously, the standard error for the conditional mean given in (22.9) may be considered an approximation to the *exact* formula

(22.13) $$s'_{Y_c} = s_{Y|X} \sqrt{\frac{1}{n} + \frac{(X - \bar{X})^2}{\Sigma(X_i - \bar{X})^2}}$$

This formula should be used for samples of any size. The expression under the square root sign has been already explained. The variance of residuals is excluded since (22.13) measures the sampling errors of the regression line.

Again, for increasingly large samples, the expression under the square root sign approaches 1, so that s_{Y_c} in (22.9) may be considered an approximation to s'_{Y_c} in (22.13).

Example 22.7

Consider the values given in the previous example. Substituting in (22.13), we obtain

$$s'_{Y_c} = .246 \sqrt{\frac{1}{30} + \frac{(2.7 - 3.347)^2}{4.912}}$$
$$= .085$$

This is a substantial difference from the approximate value .045, (Example 22.5). But again, such a difference may be ignored for large samples.

What is the practical significance of the exact formulas (22.11) and (22.13)? These formulas reinforce our decision to suspend judgment, especially if we used the exact t for $n - 2$ degrees of freedom rather than the approximate z values. More importantly, our case points out the importance of estimation intervals. With approximate formulas (22.7) and (22.9), the upper and lower limits of such intervals will represent parallel lines above and below the regression line. Of course, for a given degree of confidence, a prediction interval for individual value will represent a wider band than the band for a confidence interval of the condi-

Figure 22.2.
Exact estimation intervals for an individual value and the conditional mean.

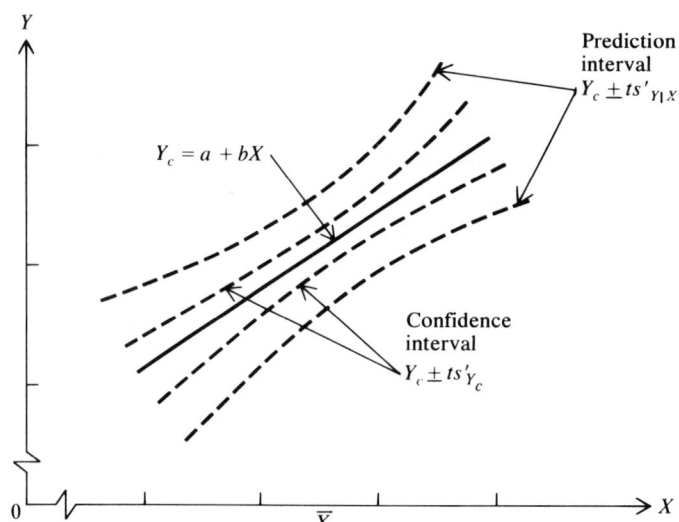

tional mean. But each interval band will be of the same width throughout the range of observed data. This will not be the case if the same estimation intervals were constructed with the exact formulas (22.11) and (22.13).

A general diagram of such intervals is portrayed in Fig. 22.2. It can be seen that for a given sample size, the width of both intervals widens as we move away in either direction from the mean value of the independent variable X. This is due to the numerator of the weighting term

$$(22.14) \qquad \frac{(X - \bar{X})^2}{\Sigma (X - \bar{X})^2}$$

under the square root sign of formulas (22.11) and (22.13). If the predicting value of X, for which intervals are constructed, is equal to $\bar{X}$, the numerator is zero, so term (22.14) is zero. Since all other terms of the exact formulas are constants, the width of both intervals is at the narrowest point when $X = \bar{X}$. The larger the deviation of the predicting value of X from its mean, the wider both intervals are. This explains the differences between approximate and exact standard error formulas, especially in Example 22.7. The practical significance of the widening intervals is obvious: other things being equal, estimation becomes less reliable the further the predicting value of X is from its mean.

In sum, two refinements are important in constructing estimation intervals:

1. For small samples, usually less than 30 observations, we should use the t distribution and the exact standard error formulas of this subsection for constructing estimation intervals. For large samples, we may construct approximate estimation intervals as illustrated earlier.
2. Another qualification relates to the normality assumption of the regression model. In constructing estimation intervals with large samples, the normality

Section 22 Simple Regression and Correlation

condition may be relaxed for estimating the conditional mean but not for predicting an individual value.

Appendix 22-I Computational Steps for Calculating the Explained and Unexplained Variation of F Statistic in Formula (22.4)

For the regression equation

$$Y_c = .851 + .733X \qquad (n = 30)$$

of our problem the basic computational steps for calculating the F statistic are summarized in Table 22.3.

Step 1. We total the 30 Y values of the sample, yielding a sum of 99.1; this total divided by the sample size yields the mean

$$\bar{Y} = \frac{\Sigma Y}{n} = \frac{99.1}{30} = 3.303$$

Step 2. We subtract this mean from each observed Y value to obtain the total deviation and square each deviation. For example, the first squared total deviation is calculated as follows:

$$(Y - \bar{Y})^2 = (3.9 - 3.303)^2 = .356$$

Thus the sum of squares for the total variation is

$$\Sigma (Y - \bar{Y})^2 = 4.350$$

Step 3. For each X value we calculate Y_c and subtract the mean $\bar{Y}$ to obtain the explained deviation. Then we square each deviation and sum the squares to obtain the explained variation. For example, the first squared explained deviation .230 is calculated as follows: From Table 22.1, we see that X is 4.0, so

$$Y_c = .851 + .733(4) = 3.783$$

Table 22.3. Determining Explained and Unexplained Variation for the M.B.A. Problem

		Variation		
Student Number[a]	Graduate GPA[a] Y	Total $(Y - \bar{Y})^2$	Explained by Regression $(Y_c - \bar{Y})^2$	Unexplained or Residual $(Y - Y_c)^2$
1	3.9	.356	.230	.014
2	2.9	.162	.298	.020
.	.	.	.	.
.	.	.	.	.
.	.	.	.	.
30	3.2	.011	.106	.050
	99.1	4.350	2.649	1.701

[a]From Table 21.1.

and the explained deviation squared is about

$$(Y_c - \bar{Y})^2 = (3.783 - 3.303)^2 = .230$$

Hence, the sum of squares for the explained variation is about

$$\Sigma (Y_c - \bar{Y})^2 = 2.649$$

Step 4. We subtract each Y_c from the corresponding observed value Y to obtain the unexplained deviation. Then we square each deviation and sum the squares to obtain the unexplained variation. For example, from the previous step we already know that Y_c is 3.783. So the unexplained deviation squared is

$$(Y - Y_c)^2 = (3.9 - 3.783)^2 = .014$$

and the sum of squares for the unexplained variation is

$$\Sigma (Y - Y_c)^2 = 1.701$$

Note that total variation 4.350 is equal to the sum of the explained 2.649 and the unexplained 1.701 variations as it should be.

Appendix 22-II Computer Printout*

Regression and correlation analysis requires considerable computation, particularly with sizable problems requiring multiple regression. Computers have eliminated tedious calculations so that we can concentrate on results which are of practical importance. Therefore, increasing availability of computers makes it desirable to get acquainted with some of their output.

At this point, we introduce and explain a computer printout for simple regression of the data (Table 21.1) of our M.B.A. problem, which is shown in Table 22.4.

Table 22.4. Computer Printout for Simple Regression for the M.B.A. Problem ($n = 30$)

1. Since the INTERCEPT is .85145 and the REGRESSION COEFFICIENT is .73264, the linear regression equation is

$$Y_c = .851 + .733X \qquad (n = 30)$$

INTERCEPT	0.85145	$Y_c = .851 + .733X$
REGRESSION COEFFICIENT	0.73264	
STD. ERROR OF REG. COEF.	0.111	
COMPUTED T-VALUE	6.603	
CORRELATION COEFFICIENT	0.780	
STANDARD ERROR OF ESTIMATE	0.246	

ANALYSIS OF VARIANCE FOR THE REGRESSION

SOURCE OF VARIATION	DF	SUM OF SQ.	MEAN SQ.	F VALUE
ATTRIBUTABLE TO REGRESSION	1	2.649	2.649	43.603
DEVIATION FROM REGRESSION	28	1.701	.061	
TOTAL	29	4.350		

*If no computer facilities are available, this topic may be omitted without loss of continuity on subject matter.

It is written in boldface print on the table and it was used throughout this section.

2. The STANDARD ERROR OF ESTIMATE $s_{Y|X}$ is .246 as used earlier.

3. The STANDARD ERROR OF REGRESSION COEFFICIENT is .111 as calculated by hand in Example 22.1.

4. The COMPUTED T VALUE is 6.603, the same as the one we calculated by hand in Example 22.2 except for a slight difference due to rounding.

5. Computer printouts in this text show the unadjusted CORRELATION COEFFICIENT r_u which in this case is .780. We can obtain the adjusted coefficient r_a with formula

(22.15) $$r_a^2 = 1 - (1 - r_u^2)\left(\frac{n-1}{n-k}\right)$$

Since $n = 30$ in our case,

$$r_a^2 = 1 - [1 - (.780)^2]\left(\frac{29}{28}\right) \simeq .594$$

so $r_a = \sqrt{.594} = .771$. Note that the unadjusted r_u^2 is the ratio of the explained to the total variation, shown in Table 22.3. Thus

$$r_u^2 = \frac{\Sigma(Y_c - \overline{Y})^2}{\Sigma(Y - \overline{Y})^2} = \frac{2.649}{4.350} \simeq .609$$

so $r_u = \sqrt{.609} = .780$.

As pointed out earlier, the adjustment term $(n - 1)/(n - k)$ may be ignored for increasingly large samples.

6. The basic measurements for ANALYSIS OF VARIANCE FOR THE REGRESSION are shown in Table 22.2.

PROBLEMS

Group One

22.1. For each case perform the required t test:
*(a) $b = 52$, $s_b = 20$, $n = 25$, $\alpha = .01$, two-sided
 (b) $b = -.825$, $s_b = .375$, $n = 100$, $\alpha = .05$, two-sided
 (c) $b = -2012$, $s_b = 970$, $n = 16$, $\alpha = .05$, one-sided
 (d) $b = 563$, $s_b = 275$, $n = 225$, $\alpha = .01$, one-sided

22.2. For each case perform an F test.
*(a) $F_o = 8.07$, df (1, 9), $\alpha = .01$
 (b) $F_o = 7.56$, df (1, 30), $\alpha = .05$
 (c) $F_o = 4.60$, df (1, 14), $\alpha = .01$
 (d) $F_o = 4.08$, df (1, 40), $\alpha = .05$

22.3. For each case:
 (i) Find the value of Y for a given value of X.
 (ii) Construct a prediction interval for individual value.
 (iii) Construct a confidence interval for the conditional mean.
*(a) $Y_c = 27 + 5X$, $s_{Y|X} = 3$, $n = 100$, 99 percent, $X = 10$
 (b) $Y_c = 13 - .2X$, $s_{Y|X} = 1$, $n = 49$, 95 percent, $X = 20$

Answers to asterisked (*) problems are appended.

Chapter 8 Regression and Correlation Analysis

*(c) $Y_c = 113 + 11X$, $s_{Y|x} = 5$, $(X - \bar{X})^2/\Sigma(X - \bar{X})^2 = .50$, $n = 25$, 99 percent, $X = 6$

(d) $Y_c = 278 - 3X$, $s_{Y|x} = 9$, $(X - \bar{X})^2/\Sigma(X - \bar{X})^2 = 2$, $n = 16$, 95 percent, $X = 4$

22.4. Consider the testing procedure in Example 22.2. An interval estimate of the slope B of the regression equation is defined as

$$b \pm ts_b$$

Using the t distribution:

(a) Construct a 99 percent confidence interval for the slope B of the problem. Should the null hypothesis that $B = 0$ be rejected? Explain.

*(b) What is the smallest value of b for which parameter slope B may be larger than zero? Use a 95 percent confidence interval.

22.5. We have found that the *exact* formulas (22.11) and (22.13) yield standard errors larger than the corresponding *approximate* formulas (22.7) and (22.9).

*(a) Use the data given in Examples 22.4, 22.5, 22.6, and 22.7 to construct exact estimation intervals with 95 percent confidence for individual value and the conditional mean with the t distribution.

(b) Compare these exact with the approximate intervals of the text. How do the exact intervals affect the decision to suspend judgment and search for additional admissions criteria?

22.6. Explain why estimation becomes increasingly unreliable the further the predicting value of the independent variable is from its mean.

*22.7. The regression coefficient and the adjusted correlation coefficient in the test case are .733 and .771, respectively. On the basis of the data given in Tables 22.1 and 22.2, verify expression (22.3) that

$$b = r\left(\frac{s_Y}{s_X}\right)$$

*22.8. The statistic for testing the slope of a simple regression equation by assuming that ρ rather than B is zero is defined as

$$t = \frac{r - \rho}{\sqrt{(1 - r^2)/(n - 2)}}$$

Given that in our case r is .771, use this formula to test the null and the alternative hypotheses formulated in Example 22.2 and compare results.

22.9. Distinguish between:

(a) Sum of squares and mean squares
(b) Explained, unexplained, and total variation
(c) Mean squares and standard deviation
(d) Deviation and variation

(e) Standard error of regression coefficient and standard error of estimate
(f) Individual value and conditional mean
(g) Approximate and exact estimation intervals

22.10. Explain:

(a) Scatter diagram of residuals
(b) F test for regression analysis
(c) Test t for regression analysis
(d) Standard deviation of residuals

Group Two

22.11. Consider the general graph of estimation intervals shown in Fig. 22.2.

*(a) Construct 99 percent confidence intervals for the conditional mean when the college GPA is 2.5, 3.0, 3.347, and 4.0, using formulas (22.10) and (22.13) and the t distribution.

Section 22 Simple Regression and Correlation

(b) Sketch the graph of such exact confidence intervals.

(c) Explain how such a graph may be used as a device for further studying the academic performance of students.

22.12. Consider again the regression equation

$$Y_c = 120 + .30X$$

given in Problem 21.12, where X denotes fertilizer in pounds and Y_c wheat yield in bushels per acre. The equation is derived from data of 16 experimental plots. The standard error of estimate is 1.49; the explained variation of Y is 18.82 and the unexplained variation is 28.84. The mean of X is 90 pounds with total variation 330.58.

*(a) Is the relationship between fertilizer and wheat yield significant? Formulate the null and the alternative hypotheses and test with both the t and F statistics at 1 percent significance level. Explain the meaning of the tests.

(b) A farmer applies 100 pounds of the tested fertilizer per acre in a farm. Construct estimation intervals of individual value and the conditional mean with 99 percent degree of confidence. Interpret the meaning of these intervals.

(c) What kind of risk has the farmer assumed in applying the new fertilizer? Explain.

22.13. The regression equation for 50 stores in problem 21.13 is

$$Y_c = 3.60 + .20X$$

where X represents shelf space ranging from 10 to 30 square feet and Y_c daily net revenue in dollars. The standard error of estimate is $1 and the total variation of X is 100. Explained variation and unexplained variation of Y are 6.52 and 48, respectively.

*(a) Is the relationship between shelf space and revenue significant? Carry out a one-sided t test and an F test at 5 percent significance level.

*(b) Friendly Corner, one of the retail stores, has 20 square feet of shelf space. Estimate the net earnings of this store with a 95 percent prediction interval. Explain the meaning of the forecast.

(c) Construct a 95 percent confidence interval for the conditional mean and sketch the interval band. Suppose Friendly Corner realizes $7.00 net revenue. Evaluate the store's performance in terms of this control chart.

22.14. The computer printout for regression of Problem 21.14, where X represents temperature and Y consumption oil in gallons, is as follows:

INTERCEPT	34.24930
REGRESSION COEFFICIENT	−0.37193
STD. ERROR OF REG. COEF.	0.034
COMPUTED T-VALUE	−11.007
CORRELATION COEFFICIENT	−0.969
STANDARD ERROR OF ESTIMATE	2.712

ANALYSIS OF VARIANCE FOR THE REGRESSION

SOURCE OF VARIATION	DF	SUM OF SQ.	MEAN SQ.	F VALUE
ATTRIBUTABLE TO REGRESSION	1	891.154	891.154	121.151
DEVIATION FROM REGRESSION	8	58.846	7.356	
TOTAL	9	950.000		

(a) Write the regression equation.
(b) Carry out the t and F tests at 1 percent significance level.
(c) Explain the meaning of the coefficients of correlation and determination.
*(d) Construct a chart such as the one shown in Fig. 22.2 of the text for the conditional mean with 99 percent degree of confidence. For sketching the interval band, let X equal zero, the mean 41, and 80. Total variation of X is 7122. For the appropriate X scale see Problem 21.14(b).
(e) A random sample of 5 days' oil consumption of a particular home yields the following data: (20°F, 26), (60°F, 11), (40°F, 17), (0°F, 36), and (−20°F, 42). Plot the data on the control chart you constructed in part (d). Discuss your findings with respect to saving energy.
*(f) The management of Home Oil Company has the inventory policy of reordering for oil before half of the 400,000 gallons of oil inventory is depleted. Suppose daily temperatures averaged −20, −10, 0, 5, −10, −20 and 0°F and the company serves 1000 homes. Use the upper limit of the interval band you constructed in part (d) to determine how soon the company should reorder. What is the probability of underestimating total oil consumption?

22.15. A sample of 10 common stocks selected at random from the stocks listed in Capital Stock Exchange have shown the following price earnings relationship at the closing of a given year:

Stock Number	Stock Price Y	Earnings per Share X	Stock Number	Stock Price Y	Earnings per Share X
1	$15	$ .90	6	$38	$4.00
2	9	1.00	7	25	1.50
3	16	1.40	8	33	2.70
4	38	3.20	9	35	3.70
5	18	2.10	10	23	2.50

(a) Plot the data on a scatter diagram in order to verify whether a linear relationship exists between two variables.
*(b) Derive a regression equation by the least-squares method.
(c) Sketch the graph of this regression equation on the scatter diagram and interpret it.
*(d) Is the relationship between earnings and price significant? Apply both the t and the F tests at 1 percent significance level.
*(e) Compute estimation intervals with 99 percent degree of confidence for individual value, the conditional mean, and the regression coefficient B when earnings of a stock are $2.00 per share. Interpret the meaning of each interval and discuss its practical use.
(f) Compute the coefficients of determination and correlation and interpret their meaning. Compare these measurements with your discussion about prediction intervals.

SECTION 23 / MULTIPLE REGRESSION AND CORRELATION

Frequently, simple regression may not serve satisfactorily the purpose of a statistical investigation. This was the conclusion we reached with a simple regression and correlation analysis of our example: college GPA scores alone may not be an adequate criterion for admission purposes. We decided to continue the search for additional criteria by which to evaluate M.B.A. applicants. Multiple regression and correlation enable us to study the relationship between a dependent variable and two or more independent variables. In addition to college GPA, we can consider the GMAT scores of applicants. Furthermore, multiple regression allows the introduction of categorical variables. In our case we consider the quality of the undergraduate college attended. Our purpose is to identify several variables which may increase our ability to evaluate the academic performance of M.B.A. applicants.

Multiple regression and correlation are extensions of the corresponding two-variable analysis in several respects. The basic assumptions of these bivariate models and the principles of statistical inference apply to multivariate analysis. Likewise, procedures for testing the significance of the relationship as well as for constructing estimation intervals are similar. In short, multivariable analysis is built on the foundation of two-variable analysis.

Let us focus, then, on differences. First, we illustrate the method of least squares for fitting a linear equation with three variables and discuss the multiple regression model in general. The basic measurements of standard error and correlation coefficients precede testing and estimation procedures. Further analysis deals with the introduction of additional independent variables and a brief discussion of qualifications and limitations of regression and correlation analysis. We close with two computer printouts which summarize our numerical analysis and interpretation.

The Multiple Regression Equation

The method of least squares is appropriate for deriving a regression equation with two or more independent variables. We illustrate the technique with two independent variables in order to keep computation to a minimum. This illustration leads easily to the general discussion of the multiple regression model.

In addition to college grade point average (GPA), let us assume the quantitative Graduate Management Admission Test (GMAT) scores are chosen as the second independent variable. These scores were given earlier (Table 21.4). The general form of a linear regression equation with two independent variables is

(23.1) $$Y_c = a + b_1 X_1 + b_2 X_2$$

where Y_c = computed graduate GPA
X_1 = college GPA
X_2 = quantitative GMAT score

Note that the two independent variables are distinguished by subscripts 1 and 2.

The graph of Eq. (23.1) can be sketched by plotting the coordinates of each point in three dimensions along the X_1, X_2, and Y axes as shown in Fig. 23.1. Solid dots represent observed Y values for a given set of X_1 and X_2 values. For example, the coordinates of student number 25 are $X_1 = 2.7$, $X_2 = 480$, and $Y = 3.0$ from Tables 21.1 and 21.4. The corresponding computed Y_c values are shown in hollow dots. The Y_c value for the observed point Y can be computed after we obtain the coefficients a, b_1, and b_2 of Eq. (23.1). The computed Y_c values form a plane which is the graph of Eq. (23.1). Some observed Y values lie above and some below the linear regression plane exactly as in the two-variable equation, where some observed Y values lie above and some below the regression line. The vertical distance of each observed Y value from the corresponding computed Y_c value on the plane represents a residual or unexplained deviation.

We can use the least-squares method to obtain the best-fitting three-variable linear regression equation. Its properties are identical to the properties of a two-variable equation already explained. The only difference is that now the computational procedure requires solving simultaneously a system of three equations:

$$(23.2) \quad \begin{aligned} \Sigma Y &= na + b_1 \Sigma X_1 + b_2 \Sigma X_2 \\ \Sigma X_1 Y &= a \Sigma X_1 + b_1 \Sigma X_1^2 + b_2 \Sigma X_1 X_2 \\ \Sigma X_2 Y &= a \Sigma X_2 + b_1 \Sigma X_1 X_2 + b_2 \Sigma X_2^2 \end{aligned}$$

for the coefficients a, b_1, and b_2 in (23.1).

As an initial step we must calculate the sums of (23.2) from a given set of data.

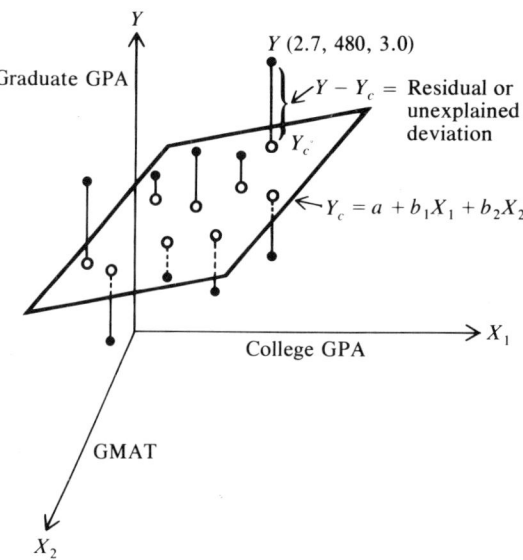

Figure 23.1. Scatter diagram illustrating a three-variable regression equation.

Example 23.1

The basic calculations for obtaining these sums from the data of our case are shown in Table 23.1. Substituting into system (23.2), we have

$$99.10 = 30.0a + 100.40b_1 + 17,120b_2$$
$$335.27 = 100.4a + 340.94b_1 + 57,898b_2$$
$$57,587.00 = 17,120.0a + 57,898.00b_1 + 10,202,800b_2$$

Solving this system of equations simultaneously, we obtain the coefficients of the regression equation (23.2)

$$a \simeq .585$$
$$b_1 \simeq .531$$
$$b_2 \simeq .00165$$

Table 23.1. Basic Calculations for Deriving a Three-Variable Regression Equation for the M.B.A. Problem ($n = 30$)

(a)

Student Number	Graduate GPA[a] Y	College GPA[a] X_1	Quantitative GMAT[a] X_2
1	2.9	2.6	600
2	3.9	4.0	680
.	.	.	.
.	.	.	.
.	.	.	.
30	3.2	2.9	440
Totals:	$\Sigma Y = 99.1$	$\Sigma X_1 = 100.4$	$\Sigma X_2 = 17,120$
Means:	$\bar{Y} = 3.3033$	$\bar{X}_1 = 3.347$	$\bar{X}_2 = 570.667$

(b)

Student Number	$X_1 Y$	$X_2 Y$	$X_1 X_2$
1	7.54	1,740	1,560
2	15.60	2,652	2,720
.	.	.	.
.	.	.	.
.	.	.	.
30	9.28	1,408	1,276
Totals:	$\Sigma X_1 Y = 335.27$	$\Sigma X_2 Y = 57,587$	$\Sigma X_1 X_2 = 57,898$

(c)

Student Number	Y^2	X_1^2	X_2^2
1	8.41	6.76	360,000
2	15.21	16.00	462,400
.	.	.	.
.	.	.	.
.	.	.	.
30	10.24	8.41	193,600
Totals:	$\Sigma Y^2 = 331.71$	$\Sigma X_1^2 = 340.94$	$\Sigma X_2^2 = 10,202,800$

[a]From Tables 21.1 and 21.4.

Computation for finding these regression coefficients as well as for subsequent measurements may be simplified if we transform the original data into deviations of each variable from its mean. Letting $y = Y - \bar{Y}$, $x_1 = X_1 - \bar{X}_1$, and $x_2 = X_2 - \bar{X}_2$ the second and third equations in (23.2) may be transformed into

(23.3)
$$\Sigma x_1 y = b_1 \Sigma x_1^2 + b_2 \Sigma x_1 x_2$$
$$\Sigma x_2 y = b_1 \Sigma x_1 x_2 + b_2 \Sigma x_2^2$$

We can find the coefficients of a three-variable equation by solving (23.3) simultaneously for b_1 and b_2 and substituting their values in

(23.4)
$$a = \bar{Y} - b_1 \bar{X}_1 - b_2 \bar{X}_2$$

to find intercept a.

Example 23.1 (continued)

Finding the regression equation of our problem by (23.3) and (23.4) requires computation of sums of deviations. These basic calculations are conveniently summarized in Table 23.2. Substituting these results into (23.3), we obtain

$$3.5823 = 4.9012 b_1 + 597.36 b_2$$
$$1033.9010 = 597.3600 b_1 + 432,981.00 b_2$$

Table 23.2. Intermediate Calculations for Deriving a Three-Variable Regression Equation for the M.B.A. Problem ($n = 30$)

$\Sigma y^2 = \Sigma Y^2 - (\bar{Y})(\Sigma Y)$	=	$331.71 - (3.303)(99.1)$	$= 4.3827$
$\Sigma x_1^2 = \Sigma X_1^2 - (\bar{X}_1)(\Sigma X_1)$	=	$340.94 - (3.347)(100.4)$	$= 4.9012$
$\Sigma x_2^2 = \Sigma X_2^2 - (\bar{X}_2)(\Sigma X_2)$	=	$10,202,800.00 - (570.667)(17,120.00)$	$= 432,981$
$\Sigma x_1 y = \Sigma X_1 Y - (\bar{X}_1)(\Sigma Y)$	=	$335.27 - (3.347)(99.1)$	$= 3.5823$
$\Sigma x_2 y = \Sigma X_2 Y - (\bar{X}_2)(\Sigma Y)$	=	$57,587.00 - (570.667)(99.1)$	$= 1033.901$
$\Sigma x_1 x_2 = \Sigma X_1 X_2 - (\bar{X}_1)(\Sigma X_2) =$		$57,898.00 - (3.347)(17,120)$	$= 597.36$

Solving this system of two equations simultaneously, we again find

$$b_1 \simeq .531$$
$$b_2 \simeq .00165$$

Substitution of these values and the values for $\bar{Y}$, $\bar{X}_1$, and $\bar{X}_2$ from Table 23.1 in (23.4) yields

$$a = 3.3033 - (.531)(3.347) - (.00165)(570.667)$$
$$\simeq .585$$

For real-world problems either method may require the use of computers. Two printouts from computer programs handling multiple regression problems are appended to this section (Appendix 23-I).

Example 23.1 (continued)

Either computational method yields the following regression equation for our problem:

$$Y_c = .585 + .531 X_1 + .00165 X_2 \qquad (n = 30)$$

Section 23 Multiple Regression and Correlation

Now we may be able to estimate the expected academic performance as measured by the graduate GPA based on the applicant's college GPA and quantitative GMAT. Consider an applicant with 2.7 and 480 scores for X_1 and X_2 respectively. Then

$$Y_c = .585 + .531(2.7) + .00165(480)$$
$$\simeq 2.81$$

or a grade slightly better than B−.

Incidentally, this is the computed value of the observed $Y = 3.0$, shown in Fig. 23.1; it represents a point estimate of the conditional mean, a single point on the estimated regression plane; the value of the deviation for this point is

$$Y - Y_c = 3.0 - 2.8 = .2$$

as portrayed in Fig. 23.1.

The Multiple Regression Model

In simple regression analysis, we discussed the interpretation of constants a and b in equations of form

$$Y_c = a + bX$$

The analogous interpretation of constants a, b_1, and b_2 in equations of form

$$Y_c = a + b_1 X_1 + b_2 X_2$$

is different in two important respects.

First, in multiple regression the b_i values are called *net regression coefficients*. The b_1 coefficient measures change in Y_c per unit of change in X_1 when X_2 is unchanged. Consider two applicants in Example 23.1 with identical quantitative GMATs, so that X_2 is held fixed, while their college GPA values X_1 differ by 1 unit. The expected graduate GPA Y_c of the applicant with a larger X_1 value is greater than the applicant with the smaller X_1 value by .531 unit. In other words, the net effect of one unit GPA differential at the college level results in one-half unit GPA differential at the graduate level if the value of X_2 is the same. The interpretation of net regression coefficient b_2 is similar to b_1. For applicants having the same college GPA so that X_1 is fixed, their graduate GPAs differ by .00165 unit for every unit change in their GMAT score. This incremental effect of each independent variable on the dependent variable is based on the linear relationship which Eq. (23.1) depicts.

The difference in the coefficient values between simple and multiple regression analyses is worth discussing. In the simple regression equation

$$Y_c = .851 + .733X$$

the value of coefficient b is .733 when college GPA is the only independent variable. In the multiple regression equation

$$Y_c = .585 + .531X_1 + .00165X_2$$

the value of the net regression coefficient is .531 for college GPA when the quantitative GMAT is included as a second independent variable. The simple regression coefficient .733 does not explicitly take into account the effect of the second independent variable. The net regression coefficient .531 has been isolated from the effect of the quantitative GMAT. However, it is not isolated from the effect of other independent variables which happen to be correlated with college GPA but are not explicitly included in the analysis.

Second, closely related to net regression coefficients is another measure of multiple regression, the *beta coefficients*. Frequently, independent variables are stated in different units. This makes a comparison between net regression coefficients difficult and potentially misleading. According to our multiple regression equation, the dependent variable changes by .531 unit per unit change in X_1 and by .00165 unit per unit change in X_2. Are we to infer that the relative influence of X_1 on Y is 322 (.531/.00165) times greater than the influence of X_2? Such an inference fails to take into consideration that X_1 is stated in units while X_2 in hundreds of units. A meaningful comparison is achieved with the beta coefficients defined as:

(23.5)
$$\beta_1 = b_1 \left(\frac{s_{X_1}}{s_Y}\right) = b_1 \sqrt{\frac{\Sigma x_1^2}{\Sigma y^2}}$$

$$\beta_2 = b_2 \left(\frac{s_{X_2}}{s_Y}\right) = b_2 \sqrt{\frac{\Sigma x_2^2}{\Sigma y^2}}$$

Note that the beta coefficients transform the net regression coefficients into standard deviation units of Y.

Example 23.2

Beta coefficients can be calculated from the second expressions in (23.5) since the numerical values under the square root signs are given in Table 23.2. Substitution yields

$$\beta_1 = .531 \sqrt{\frac{4.9012}{4.3827}} \simeq .562$$

and

$$\beta_2 = .00165 \sqrt{\frac{432{,}981}{4.3827}} \simeq .519$$

These values mean that for each increase of one standard deviation unit in X_1, Y increases by about .562 standard deviation unit; and for each increase of one standard deviation unit in X_2, Y increases by .519 standard deviation unit. Thus, the relative influence of college GPA and quantitative GMAT on graduate GPA is approximately the same.

So far our discussion has been limited to a multiple regression equation with two independent variables. This can be generalized to cases with $k - 1$ independent variables, where k denotes the number of constants in the regression equation. The general form of such a linear regression equation is

(23.6)
$$Y_c = a + b_1 X_1 + b_2 X_2 + \cdots + b_{k-1} X_{k-1}$$

Section 23 Multiple Regression and Correlation

This equation is an estimate of the unknown parameter regression equation

(23.7) $$\mu_c = A + B_1 X_1 + B_2 X_2 + \cdots + B_{k-1} X_{k-1}$$

Statistics $a, b_1, b_2, \ldots, b_{k-1}$ in (23.6) are unbiased estimators of parameters $A, B_1, B_2, \ldots, B_{k-1}$ in (23.7). The graph of a multiple regression equation derived by the least-squares method is a *hyperplane* in k-dimensional space with linear properties analogous to the properties of the simple regression model. The multiple regression model (23.7) is based on the assumptions of linearity, homoscedasticity, independence, and normality of the simple regression model.

Basic Measurements

The interpretation of the standard error of estimate, the standard error of net regression coefficients, and the correlation coefficient for multiple regression is similar to the corresponding measurements for simple regression. Calculations, however, are more complex; so it is necessary to carry out this task before testing the reliability of the multiple regression equation.

The standard error of estimate around a regression hyperplane with $k - 1$ independent variables is

(23.8) $$s_{Y|12\ldots(k-1)} = \sqrt{\frac{\Sigma (Y - Y_c)^2}{n - k}}$$

where n is the sample size and k the number of constants in the regression equation. Number $n - k$ represents the number of degrees of freedom; it is an adjustment for making the standard error a better estimator of the parameter standard deviation. The subscripts to the standard error denote the dependent variable Y given the independent variables $X_1, X_2, \ldots, X_{k-1}$. The value of (23.8) for the regression equation of two independent variables can be conveniently computed from

(23.9) $$s_{Y|12} = \sqrt{\frac{\Sigma y^2 - b_1 \Sigma x_1 y - b_2 \Sigma x_2 y}{n - 3}}$$

Example 23.3

In Example 23.1 we found that

$$\Sigma y^2 = 4.3827, \quad \Sigma x_1 y = 3.5823, \quad \Sigma x_2 y = 1033.9$$
$$b_1 = .531, \quad b_2 = .00165, \quad n = 30$$

Substitution of these values in formula (23.9) yields

$$s_{Y|12} = \sqrt{\frac{4.3827 - (.531)(3.5823) - (.00165)(1033.9)}{30 - 3}}$$
$$\simeq .164*$$

The introduction of a second independent variable may change the standard error of estimate of simple regression analysis. In our case, the simple regression error has decreased from .246 (Example 22.1) to .164. The introduction of quantitative

*Computed value .169 has been changed to .164 in order to be consistent with computer calculations.

Chapter 8 Regression and Correlation Analysis

GMAT has increased statistical precision and consequently the reliability of the regression equation.

Let us now concentrate on the *multiple correlation coefficient* and the *coefficient of multiple determination*. For a three-variable analysis, the formula of the latter measurement, adjusted for degrees of freedom, is defined as

(23.10)
$$R^2_{Y|12} = 1 - \frac{s^2_{Y|12}}{s^2_Y}$$

Except for notational differences already explained, formula (23.10) is analogous to the formula for the simple coefficient of determination. So are the characteristics of the multiple correlation model.

Example 23.4

The unconditional variance of the dependent variable Y was defined earlier (Eq. 21.11) as

$$s^2_Y = \frac{\Sigma Y^2 - \bar{Y}\Sigma Y}{n - 1}$$

From Table 23.1, we have

$\Sigma Y^2 = 331.71,$ $\Sigma \bar{Y} = 3.303,$ $\Sigma Y = 99.1$ $n = 30$

Substituting these values in the above equation, we obtain

$$s^2_Y = \frac{331.71 - (3.303)(99.1)}{30 - 1}$$
$$\simeq .151$$

In Example 23.3, we have already found that $s_{Y|12}$ is about .164 so $s^2_{Y|12}$ is about .0269. Substitution of these values in (23.10) yields an adjusted coefficient of determination

$$R^2_{Y|12} = 1 - \frac{.0269}{.151}$$
$$\simeq .822$$

This means that about 82.2 percent of the variation in graduate GPA can be attributed to the variation in college GPA *and* the variation in quantitatitive GMAT.

The introduction of a second independent variable may increase the value of the correlation coefficient. In our case, the correlation coefficient has increased from .771 in simple correlation to .907 ($= \sqrt{.822}$). Commensurately, the coefficient of determination has increased from about .594 to .822, a difference of .228. This means that, given college GPA is already in the regression, 22.8 percent of the variation in graduate GPA can be attributed to the introduction of the second independent variable, quantitative GMAT. This increase, together with the reduction in the standard error of estimate, is a clear sign that this second independent variable should be included in the regression equation.

Section 23 Multiple Regression and Correlation

The standard error of the net regression coefficient for the ith independent variable in a regression equation with two independent variables is

$$(23.11) \quad s_{b_i} = \frac{s_{Y|12}}{\sqrt{\sum x_i^2 (1 - r_{12}^2)}} \quad (i = 1, 2)$$

They are estimators of the corresponding parameters just as in the case of the simple regression model. Unlike simple regression, however, formula (23.11) differs in one important respect—the presence of term $(1 - r_{12}^2)$. Observe that r_{12}^2 is the coefficient of determination of the two independent variables. If the independent variables are highly correlated, r_{12}^2 will be close to one, term $(1 - r_{12}^2)$ close to zero, and s_{b_1} very large. In such a case, the net regression coefficient itself becomes unreliable; a test may not be statistically significant. And this in spite of the fact that simple regression of the dependent variable with each independent variable may show statistically significant results. This makes sense; if X_1 and X_2 vary together, it is very difficult to separate their individual effects on Y. In short, the standard errors s_{b_i} are sensitive to the correlation between X_1 and X_2. This is the so-called problem of *multicollinearity*.

Ignoring the correction for sample bias, r_{12}^2 is defined as

$$(23.12) \quad r_{12}^2 = \frac{(\sum x_1 x_2)^2}{(\sum x_1^2)(\sum x_2^2)}$$

Example 23.5.

In Table 23.2 we found that

$$\sum x_1 x_2 = 597.36, \quad \sum x_1^2 = 4.9012, \quad \sum x_2^2 = 432{,}981$$

Substituting these values in formula (23.12), we obtain

$$r_{12}^2 = \frac{(597.36)^2}{(4.9012)(432{,}981)} \simeq .168$$

Now we are ready to calculate s_{b_1} and s_{b_2} of our M.B.A. problem. Since $s_{Y|12}$ is .164 and the other measures are already given, substitution in formula (23.11) yields

$$s_{b_1} = \frac{.164}{\sqrt{(4.9012)(1 - .168)}} \simeq .081$$

and

$$s_{b_2} = \frac{.164}{\sqrt{(432{,}981)(1 - .168)}} \simeq .00027$$

Testing; Estimation Intervals

We have already seen clear indications for including the second independent variable in the regression equation. Inclusion may be finally determined with the t and F tests which are analogous to those employed in simple regression.

The t statistic for multiple regression is

(23.13) $$t_i = \frac{b_i - B_i}{s_{b_i}}$$

where i is any independent variable. Again, the degrees of freedom for the t statistic are $n - k$, where n is the sample size and k the number of constants in the equation. For reasons already explained in simple regression, we concentrate on testing and estimating from large samples using the Z deviate of the normal distribution as an approximation to the t distribution.

Example 23.6

For our multiple regression the null and the alternative hypotheses are

$$H_0: B_1 = 0$$
$$H_1: B_1 \neq 0$$

and

$$H_0: B_2 = 0$$
$$H_1: B_2 \neq 0$$

Our null hypotheses state that neither college GPA nor quantitative GMAT has any effect on graduate GPA. Although we expect both independent variables to positively affect graduate work, it is always wise to use a two-sided test in multiple regression.

Suppose we wish to test again at 1 percent level of significance so that the critical z_c value is 2.58. We have already found that

$$b_1 = .531, \quad b_2 = .00165 \quad \text{(Example 23.1)}$$
$$s_{b_1} = .081, \quad s_{b_2} = .00027 \quad \text{(Example 23.5)}$$

Substitution in formula (23.13) yields

$$z_1 = \frac{.531 - 0}{.081} \simeq 6.56 \qquad (n = 30)$$

and

$$z_2 = \frac{.00165 - 0}{.00027} \simeq 6.11 \qquad (n = 30)$$

The critical z_c is 2.58. Since the observed z_1 is 6.56, we reject the null hypothesis for the college GPA variable x_1. We also reject the null hypothesis for the quantitative GMAT variable x_2 since the observed z_2 is 6.11. College GPA and quantitative GMAT may be considered to be reliable variables for formulating an admission policy.

For convenience, formula (22.4) for the F test is reproduced here:

(23.14) $$F = \frac{(Y_c - \bar{Y})^2/(k - 1)}{(Y - Y_c)^2/(n - k)} \qquad \left(\frac{\text{explained variance}}{\text{unexplained variance}}\right)$$

Section 23 Multiple Regression and Correlation

Example 23.6 (continued)

For our case the null and the alternative hypotheses for the F test are

$$H_0: B_1 = B_2 = 0$$
$$H_1: \text{at least one coefficient is not zero}$$

Again, our null hypothesis states that neither college GPA nor quantitative GMAT has any effect on graduate GPA. The alternative hypothesis states that at least one independent variable has an effect on graduate GPA.

The sum of squares is about 3.625 for the numerator in formula (23.14) and .725 for the denominator. Computation of these values is analogous to the one illustrated in Table 22.3. Note that the sum of the two figures equals 4.350, the total variation. The degrees of freedom in the numerator are 2 since k equals 3, the number of constants in the regression equation. The degrees of freedom in the denominator are 27 since our sample size is 30 and 3 degrees of freedom are used to compute each Y_c value from the regression equation in order to determine the residuals.

Substitution of these numerical values in (23.14) yields an observed value of

$$F_o = \frac{3.625/2}{.725/27} \simeq 67.500$$

Suppose we wish to test again at 1 percent significance level. The test result is statistically significant since the critical F_{01} (2, 27) value, read from Appendix H, is only 5.49. Note that introduction of quantitative GMAT in the equation has increased the observed F_o value from 43.603 in simple regression to 67.500.

Construction of estimation intervals with exact standard error formulas is too technical and requires laborious computations. Therefore, we limit presentation to illustrating construction of intervals with the *approximate* formulas. Estimation intervals are defined as follows:

(23.15) $\quad\boxed{Y_c \pm z s_{Y|12\ldots(k-1)}}$

for an individual value Y and

(23.16) $\quad\boxed{Y_c \pm z \dfrac{s_{Y|12\ldots(k-1)}}{\sqrt{n}}}$

for the conditional mean μ_c where k denotes the number of constants in the regression equation and $s_{Y|12\ldots(k-1)}$ is given in formula (23.8).

Example 23.7

Since the test results were found to be statistically significant, we may construct approximate estimation intervals based on the multiple regression equation

$$Y_c = .585 + .531 X_1 + .00165 X_2 \qquad (n = 30)$$

Suppose an applicant has a 2.7 college GPA and a 480 quantitative GMAT. In Example 23.1 we found that Y_c is 2.81. This is a point estimate of the applicant's academic performance as measured by the graduate GPA. Also, we have found that $s_{Y|12}$ is about .164. For a 95 percent degree of confidence and by (23.15) we obtain the approximate prediction interval

$$2.81 \pm 1.96(.164) \simeq 2.49 \text{ to } 3.13$$

In words, we are 95 percent confident that an applicant with a 2.7 college GPA and a 480 quantitative GMAT may earn a graduate GPA between a 2.5 (halfway between C+ and B−) and a 3.13 (halfway between B and B+).

For a 95 percent degree of confidence and by (23.16) we get the approximate confidence interval

$$2.81 \pm 1.96 \left(\frac{.164}{\sqrt{30}} \right) \simeq 2.75 \text{ to } 2.87$$

On the *average,* applicants with the same X_1 and X_2 scores may complete the graduate program with a little better than a B−.

With simple regression analysis we considered two admissions policies:

1. Raise the minimum college GPA to 3.53, or B+, in order to virtually eliminate admission of students who are likely to fail; or
2. Keep the college GPA at 2.7 or B−, and let the graduate program identify failing students.

Assuming that a graduate student must maintain a minimum graduate GPA of 2.7 to complete the program, the second admission criterion, quantitative GMAT, appears to have somewhat improved implementation of either policy. Now we need to set college GPA at 3.0, or B, and a quantitative GMAT at 520 in order to practically eliminate potentially failing applicants. Or we can keep minimum admissions standards of 2.7 for college GPA and 480 for the quantitative GMAT. Then the probability that students with such a record will fail the program is about .25,* slightly less than .30 found in simple regression. If college GPA and quantitative GMAT were the only admission criteria, either policy may be of greater merit than a policy based on a single criterion. Again, it may be wiser to continue our search for additional admission criteria.

Introducing Additional Variables

Our quest for a better fit of the regression equation to the data continues with the introduction of one numerical variable and one categorical variable. The former will give us the opportunity to discuss the problem of multicollinearity, while the latter deals with *dummy variables.*

---

*Again, assuming that $\mu_c = 2.81$ and an applicant must obtain at least 2.7 graduate GPA in order to complete the M.B.A. program,

$$P\left(z \leqslant \frac{2.70 - 2.81}{.164} \right) = P(z \leqslant -.67) = .5000 - .2486 \simeq .25$$

Example 23.8

Continuing our problem, we may consider introducing the verbal GMAT scores as a third independent variable X_3 into the regression equation. The data are taken from Table 21.4. The least-squares method yields the linear equation

$$Y_c = 3.779 + .539X_1 + .00249X_2 - .00119X_3 \qquad (n = 30)$$

The information for testing the reliability of the regression equation appears below:

$$s_{Y|123} = .157 \quad s_{b_1} = .0776 \quad s_{b_2} = .00052 \quad s_{b_3} = .00064$$
$$F_o = 50.28 \quad z_1 = 6.94 \quad z_2 = 4.78 \quad z_3 = -1.87$$

It can be seen that the tests for X_1 and X_2 variables are statistically significant; observed values z_1 and z_2 are larger than the critical z_c value of 2.58 for a two-sided test at 1 percent significance level. But introduction of X_3, verbal GMAT, leads to odd results. While the net regression coefficient has a negative value of $-.00119$, it can be found that the simple correlation coefficient between the dependent variable Y and X_3 has a positive value of .615. Furthermore, the test results are not statistically significant for X_3; z_3 is $|-1.87|$, less than the critical z_c value of 2.58. Also, note that the values of z_2 and F_o, although still significant, are lower than the corresponding values prior to the introduction of X_3, the verbal GMAT scores. The source of the problem is high correlation between X_2 and X_3; it can be easily found that an unadjusted r_{23} is .886.

In general, a positive regression coefficient of the independent variable in simple regression may change to a negative net regression coefficient if the same variable is highly correlated with other independent variables of the multiple regression equation. The reverse may occur for a negative regression coefficient. Because of multicollinearity the t test becomes unreliable. The usual procedure is to drop one of the correlated independent variables. This may be the case if the F test is also statistically insignificant and there are no substantive reasons to contradict the test results with our prior knowledge of the field of application.

In our case, retaining the verbal GMAT variable may be justified for several reasons. In the first place, the negative coefficient b_3 is contrary to our prior belief that X_3 and Y are likely to be positively related; this belief is verified with an unadjusted .615 positive correlation coefficient. For this reason the t test is not statistically significant. On the other hand, the F test, although lowered in value from 67.480 to 50.28, is still statistically significant because of the strong influence exerted by X_1 and X_2. Furthermore, applicants vary with respect to aptitude and educational background; some of them may get high quantitative and low verbal GMAT scores; other applicants may demonstrate a reverse performance. No less important is the fact that the orientation of the program may require that verbal skills be given equal if not greater emphasis than quantitative skills. So the question may not be whether or not to include X_3 but how inclusion may cope with the multicollinearity problem. One way which appears as an exercise among the problems of this section is to replace the quantitative GMAT with the average of the quantitative and verbal GMAT scores. Another way would be to use the sum of the two scores. For illustrative purposes, which will become evident later, we drop the verbal GMAT scores from our regression equation.

In addition to numerical variables, multiple regression analysis may include qualitative information in the form of a *dummy variable* which takes on the value of either zero or one.

Example 23.9

Quality of undergraduate college may be an important admission criterion. The undergraduate college of the sampled students may be classified into two categories: selective and most selective. A dummy variable may be included in our regression equation which assigns a zero to denote a selective college and a one to denote a most selective college. The dummy variable assigned to the 30 students of our problem is shown in Table 23.3.

The multiple linear equation is

$$Y_c = 1.197 + .309X_1 + .00163X_2 + .284X_3 \qquad (n = 30)$$

where X_3 is the dummy variable and all other variables remain the same. The information for testing the reliability of the regression equation is given below:

$$S_{y|123} = .119 \quad S_{b_1} = .074 \quad S_{b_2} = .0002 \quad S_{b_3} = .0567$$
$$F_o = 93.51 \quad z_1 = 4.19 \quad z_2 = 8.20 \quad z_3 = 5.01$$

Note that all t tests are statistically significant at 1 percent level of significance since the observed z_o values are larger than the critical z_c value of 2.58. Also, the F test is statistically significant. The degrees of freedom in the numerator of the F ratio are $k - 1 = 4 - 1 = 3$ and in the denominator $n - k = 30 - 4 = 26$. For 1 percent level of significance F_{01} (3, 26) is 4.64, read from Appendix H, far below the observed F_o value of 93.51. Furthermore, the introduction of the dummy variable increases the observed F_o value from 67.48 to 93.51. The adjusted coefficient of multiple determination has increased from .822, (Example 23.4), to .906; it indicates that

Table 23.3. Dummy Variable Denoting Selectivity of Undergraduate College for the M.B.A. Problem ($n = 30$)[a]

Student Number	Dummy Variable	Student Number	Dummy Variable	Student Number	Dummy Variable
1	0	11	0	21	1
2	1	12	1	22	0
3	0	13	0	23	1
4	0	14	0	24	1
5	0	15	1	25	0
6	0	16	0	26	0
7	1	17	1	27	1
8	1	18	0	28	1
9	1	19	1	29	0
10	1	20	0	30	1

[a]Hypothetical data

8.4 percent $(= .906 - .822)$ of the variation in graduate GPA can be attributed to the introduction of the dummy variable after the influence of X_1 and X_2 is accounted for. Last but not least, the standard error of estimate has fallen from .164, computed in Example 23.3, to .119. All indicators point out that this equation is more reliable in evaluating academic performance than the equation found in Example 23.1 without the dummy variable.

The introduction of a dummy variable explicitly isolates the effect of a qualitative factor in the regression analysis. This can be illustrated when we use the regression equation for estimation.

Example 23.9 (continued)

Letting X_3 be zero or one, the initial equation is equivalent to the following two equations:

$Y_c = 1.197 + .309X_1 + .00163X_2 \quad X_3 = 0:$ for selective schools
$Y_c = 1.481 + .309X_1 + .00163X_2 \quad X_3 = 1:$ for most selective schools

Intercept a in the first equation remains unchanged since

$$1.197 + .284(0) = 1.197.$$

On the other hand, intercept a in the second equation is increased since

$$1.197 + .284(1) = 1.481.$$

For minimal requirements of 2.7 college GPA and 480 for quantitative GMAT, the approximate prediction intervals with 95 percent degree of confidence for individual values are

For selective schools:

$$Y_c = 1.197 + .309(2.7) + .00163(480)$$
$$\simeq 2.81$$

and by formula (23.15),

$$2.81 \pm 1.96(.119) \simeq 2.58 \text{ to } 3.04$$

For most selective schools:

$$Y_c = 1.481 + .309(2.7) + .00163(480)$$
$$\simeq 3.10$$

and by formula (23.15),

$$3.10 \pm 1.96(.119) \simeq 2.87 \text{ to } 3.33$$

Again, we are 95 percent confident that the graduate GPA of an applicant with 2.7 college GPA, a 480 quantitative GMAT, and from a selective school may be between 2.58 (halfway between C+ and B−) and 3.04 (a B). On the other hand, we are practically certain that applicants with identical scores but from most selective schools can complete the program with at least B− graduate GPA.

Chapter 8 Regression and Correlation Analysis

It can be seen that the dummy variable has introduced an important admissions criterion. For applicants from most selective schools, doubts about which of the two admissions policies should be adopted have been eliminated: we no longer need to raise the minimum admissions standards to virtually eliminate applicants who may fail the program. Furthermore, the procedure for evaluating applicants from selective schools has been also improved. Now we need to set college GPA at 3.0, or B, and a quantitative GMAT at 500 in order to practically eliminate the admission of potentially failing applicants. Or we can keep the above minimum admissions standards. Then the probability that an applicant may fail the program is reduced from .25 to .18* with the introduction of the dummy variable.

Dummy variables introduce great flexibility in applying regression and correlation analysis to real-world problems. Suppose applicants to the graduate program are classified into three categories of undergraduate schools. A three-way classification may be introduced with two dummy variables (always one less than the number of classes) as follows:†

	Dummy Variable	
School Category	First	Second
Selective	0	0
Very selective	0	1
Most selective	1	0

Dummy variables can be applied to a wide variety of cross-section problems such as our case where data represent one point in time. They can also be applied to time series problems where data are reported periodically on a yearly, quarterly, or other basis. For instance, we may be able to study how aggregate consumption is related to national income over time using a dummy variable to isolate the effect of a few war or recession years. In problems of this nature, dummy variables serve a double purpose. First, they allow regression analysis with categorical independent variables. Second, they make regression analysis more reliable by combining a limited number of observations from each class of a categorical variable into a larger sample.

Obviously, we can consider a fairly large number of variables for inclusion into a regression equation. Special computer programs are available which make it possible to systematically search for independent variables which may increase the reliability of the regression equation.‡ However, there are limits to this process. First, although computers have greatly decreased the cost of data processing,

---

*Assuming that μ_c for selective colleges is 2.81 and an applicant must obtain at least 2.7 graduate GPA in order to complete the M.B.A. program,

$$P\left(z \leqslant \frac{2.70 - 2.81}{.119}\right) = P(z \leqslant -.90) = .5000 - .3159 \simeq .18$$

†Of course, instead of two we can also use three dummy variables, one for each classification.
‡See Appendix 23-I for a simplified version of a technique called stepwise regression.

the cost of data collection and difficulties in implementing and monitoring the model place a limit on the number of independent variables to be considered. Second, final inclusion into the regression equation is limited by the fact that the coefficient of multiple determination cannot be larger than one; so each additional independent variable is likely to contribute less and less to the explained variance; diminishing returns set in quickly. As a result, a multiple regression equation is likely to include no more than a few independent variables. Thus, in applying regression and correlation as well as any other statistical technique, we must constantly strive to reach an optimal point where the cost of obtaining additional information does not exceed the value of such information.

A Few General Considerations

So far we have concentrated on explaining the regression and correlation models and interpreting numerical results. We now consider a number of general points relevant to meaningful application of these important statistical tools. Whenever appropriate, we shall take the opportunity to look at our admissions policy case in a broader context than previously discussed.

First, we should guard against mechanical acceptance or rejection of a null hypothesis. Accepting a null hypothesis does not prove that there is no relationship between an independent and the dependent variable. We have illustrated this point with the introduction of verbal GMAT scores into the regression equation. We should examine the test results for consistency with other measurements and in the light of prior knowledge about the particular situation. The decision whether or not to include an independent variable into the regression equation should not be based solely on statistical evidence.

Second, in many applications construction of estimation intervals of dependent variable Y is the objective of regression analysis. In estimating corn yields on the basis of rainfall and fertilizer, heating oil consumption on the basis of weather temperature and other variables, or changes in the gross national product on the basis of changes in the money supply and government spending, such intervals may become the basis for decision making. In other problems, however, testing and estimating may be used merely as a guide to identifying critical variables rather than obtaining numerical answers. The minimal ultimate objective in our case was to identify variables which can be used as criteria for evaluating applicants; testing and estimating were means to that end. Admissions policies are usually based on a broader spectrum of criteria than the variables which can be identified with regression and correlation analysis.

Third, the relevance of past data to estimation is another important consideration. Estimation is based on the assumption that past data will be relevant in the future. In other words, we assume that the same basic conditions reflected in the data will prevail at the time estimation is being made. Important changes in the graduate program requirements, for instance, might significantly alter the observed relationship between graduate GPA and the independent variables. In studying the effect of fertilizer and rainfall on wheat yields some extremely low yields may be attributed to an assignable cause such as a hailstorm. Failure to update or refine the data so that they reflect current and anticipated conditions may lead to misleading estimation.

Fourth, closely related to the relevance of past data are difficulties related to measurements. In our case, we assumed that GMAT scores accurately measure academic potential. Some educators may question whether such scores accurately measure the academic potential of culturally disadvantaged applicants. Assuming that graduate GPA adequately measures academic performance, the same index does not necessarily measure the degree of success in business. Such issues of measurement may partly explain the wide diversity of admissions standards employed by educational institutions.

Fifth, estimating beyond the range of observed data may be extremely hazardous. We have already explained why estimation intervals are wider at both limits of the range of observed data. Additional uncertainties may be present in multiple regression. To the extent that certain combinations of independent variables are excluded from the sample of observations, no valid estimates of the dependent variable can be made for these missing combinations of values. And these difficulties are compounded when, for example, we attempt to estimate wheat yields beyond the observed values of fertilizer and rainfall. We have no assurance that the apparent linear relationship will still be linear for more or less rainfall than the range of observed data. To the extent that such a relationship may not be linear, extrapolations become questionable and misleading.

Last but not least, correlation does not necessarily mean a cause-and-effect relationship between the dependent and independent variables. The following well-known fallacy is pertinent at this point. We may argue that if we observe factors X and A, X and B, or X and C to vary with Y, then we may infer that the common factor X causes Y. Thereupon, three individuals drink water and whisky, water and rum, and water and gin. In each instance, they all get drunk; consequently, they decide to refrain from drinking water! Correlation between smoking and lung cancer has long been established. Yet the dispute whether smoking *causes* cancer may continue. The major argument is that such correlation may be spurious and attributable to smog, tensions, food, and scores of other factors related to living in a highly industrialized society. The fact remains that the initially observed correlation led to large-scale studies and experimentation. Although this evidence may not support causation in a deterministic sense, it does demonstrate causation in a probabilistic sense.

In sum, simple and, in particular, multiple regression and correlation analysis are extremely useful statistical tools with wide applications. However, their application requires a good background in the theory of the models, knowledge of the situation under study, judgment, and constant awareness that we deal with a complex and ever-changing real world.

Appendix 23-I Computer Printouts*

Continuing our effort in this direction we discuss the computer printouts of two programs: multiple regression and a simplified version of a technique called stepwise regression. They summarize the most important measurements of multiple regression and correlation of our case and demonstrate systematic selection of independent variables.

---

*If no computer facilities are available, this topic may be omitted.

Section 23 Multiple Regression and Correlation

Multiple Regression. The measurements for multiple regression with the three independent variables of our M.B.A. case are shown in Table 23.4. There is one important change in subscript notation. In this as well as the following computer printouts the dependent variable Y is denoted by X_1. Hence, the subscripts of the independent variables are increased by one so that

$$X_2 = \text{college GPA}$$
$$X_3 = \text{quantitative GMAT}$$
$$X_4 = \text{selectivity of undergraduate college}$$

Except for this change in notation and differences due to rounding, most measurements shown in Table 23.4 have been discussed in Example 23.9 with equation

$$X_1 = 1.197 + .309X_2 + .00163X_3 + .248X_4 \qquad (n = 30)$$

Table 23.4. Multiple Regression for the M.B.A. Problem ($n = 30$)

$X_1 = 1.197 + .309X_2 + .00163X_3 + .284X_4$

VARIABLE	REG. COEF.	STD. ERROR COEF.	COMPUTED T	BETA COEF.
2	0.30905	0.07370	4.19307	0.32918
3	0.00163	0.00020	8.19796	0.51412
4	0.28399	0.05669	5.00990	0.37291
INTERCEPT	1.19714			
MULTIPLE CORRELATION	.95665			
STD. ERROR OF ESTIMATE	.11912			

ANALYSIS OF VARIANCE FOR THE REGRESSION

SOURCE OF VARIATION	DF	SUM OF SQ.	MEAN SQ.	F VALUE
ATTRIBUTABLE TO REGRESSION	3	3.981	1.327	93.506
DEVIATION FROM REGRESSION	26	0.369	0.014	
TOTAL	29	4.350		

Simplified Stepwise Regression. One important problem in multiple regression is the search for independent variables which collectively explain the largest portion of the variance of the dependent variable. The search for independent variables can be done systematically with a special computer program. We illustrate this procedure with all five variables discussed in our case, where

$$X_1 = \text{graduate GPA (the dependent variable)}$$
$$X_2 = \text{college GPA}$$
$$X_3 = \text{quantitative GMAT}$$
$$X_4 = \text{verbal GMAT}$$
$$X_5 = \text{selectivity of undergraduate college}$$

This systematic search for fitting a multiple regression equation to a set of data is a simplified version of a technique called *stepwise regression;* it may yield a regression equation with a reasonably good set of independent variables from those considered in the analysis. A computer printout for our case is shown in Table 23.5.

Table 23.5.
Stepwise regression for the M.B.A. problem ($n = 30$)

STEP 1
VARIABLE SELECTED.....2....... $X_1 = .851 + .733X_2$
SUM OF SQUARES REDUCED IN THIS STEP 2.649
PROPORTION OF VARIANCE OF Y REDUCED..... 0.609
F FOR THIS VARIABLE (DF = 1, 28) 43.603
CUMULATIVE SUM OF SQUARES REDUCED...... 2.649
CUMULATIVE PROPORTION REDUCED .... 0.609 OF 4.350
MULTIPLE CORRELATION COEFFICIENT 0.780
F FOR ANALYSIS OF VARI. (DF = 1, 28) 43.603
STANDARD ERROR OF ESTIMATE 0.246

VARIABLE	REG. COEF.	STD. ERROR COEF.	COMPUTED T	BETA COEF.
2	0.73264	0.11095	6.603	0.78035
INTERCEPT	0.85145			

STEP 2
VARIABLE SELECTED......3...... $X_1 = .585 + .531X_2 + .00165X_3$
SUM OF SQUARES REDUCED IN THIS STEP 0.976
PROPORTION OF VARIANCE OF Y REDUCED..... 0.224
F FOR THIS VARIABLE (DF = 1, 27) 36.334
CUMULATIVE SUM OF SQUARES REDUCED...... 3.635
CUMULATIVE PROPORTION REDUCED .... 0.833 OF 4.350
MULTIPLE CORRELATION COEFFICIENT 0.913
F FOR ANALYSIS OF VARI. (DF = 2, 27) 67.480
STANDARD ERROR OF ESTIMATE 0.164

VARIABLE	REG. COEF.	STD. ERROR COEF.	COMPUTED T	BETA COEF.
2	0.53124	0.08099	6.560	0.56584
3	0.00165	0.00027	6.028	0.51996
INTERCEPT	0.58500			

STEP 3
VARIABLE SELECTED.....5....... $X_1 = 1.197 + .309X_2 + .00163X_3 + .284X_5$
SUM OF SQUARES REDUCED IN THIS STEP 0.356
PROPORTION OF VARIANCE OF Y REDUCED..... 0.082
F FOR THIS VARIABLE (DF = 1, 26) 25.099
CUMULATIVE SUM OF SQUARES REDUCED...... 3.981
CUMULATIVE PROPORTION REDUCED .... 0.915 OF 4.350
MULTIPLE CORRELATION COEFFICIENT 0.957
F FOR ANALYSIS OF VARI. (DF = 3, 26) 93.506
STANDARD ERROR OF ESTIMATE 0.119

VARIABLE	REG. COEF.	STD. ERROR COEF.	COMPUTED	BETA COEF.
2	0.30905	0.07370	4.193	0.32918
3	0.00163	0.00020	8.198	0.51412
5	0.28399	0.05669	5.010	0.37291
INTERCEPT	1.19714			

Section 23 Multiple Regression and Correlation

STEP 4
VARIABLE SELECTED. . 4. . $X_1 = 1.246 + .327X_2 + .002X_3 + .266X_5 - .0005X_4$
SUM OF SQUARES REDUCED IN THIS STEP 0.016
PROPORTION OF VARIANCE OF Y REDUCED..... 0.004
F FOR THIS VARIABLE (DF = 1, 25) 1.145
CUMULATIVE SUM OF SQUARES REDUCED...... 3.997
CUMULATIVE PROPORTION REDUCED   0.919 OF   4.350
MULTIPLE CORRELATION COEFFICIENT 0.959
F FOR ANALYSIS OF VARI. (DF = 4, 25) 70.807
STANDARD ERROR OF ESTIMATE 0.119

VARIABLE	REG. COEF.	STD. ERROR COEF.	COMPUTED T	BETA COEF.
2	0.32659	0.07531	4.337	0.34787
3	0.00201	0.00041	4.929	0.63453
5	0.26592	0.05900	4.507	0.34918
4	−0.00054	0.00050	−1.070	−0.13722
INTERCEPT	1.24626			

Each step of the analysis contains measurements for each entering independent variable and cumulative measurements of all independent variables, including the entering variable.

In *step 1,* the SUM OF SQUARES REDUCED IN THIS STEP, 2.649, is the variation in X_1 which can be explained by the entering variable X_2. This sum divided by the total variation 4.350 of X_1 equals .609 which is the PROPORTION OF VARIANCE OF Y REDUCED. (See calculation of these two sums of squares in Table 22.3.) In this initial step, ratio .609 represents the simple regression coefficient of determination. Thus, 60.9 percent of the total variation in X_1 can be explained by variable X_2. The COMPUTED T value of 6.603 was found to be statistically significant (Example 22.2). The F FOR THIS VARIABLE, 43.603, was also found to be statistically significant (Example 22.3).

The cumulative part of step 1 contains measurements for the simple regression analysis between X_1, graduate GPA, and X_2, college GPA, shown in Table 22.3. Except for different symbols, the equation is

$$X_1 = .851 + .733X_3 \qquad (n = 30)$$

with a STANDARD ERROR OF ESTIMATE of .246, the same as found earlier. So we conclude that independent variable X_2, college GPA, may be related to the dependent variable X_1, graduate GPA.

Should the other independent variables be introduced into the equation? Analysis of subsequent steps is focused on answering this question. The decision whether or not each entering independent variable should be retained depends on four key measurements:

1. PROPORTION OF VARIANCE OF Y REDUCED
2. COMPUTED T
3. F FOR THIS VARIABLE
4. STANDARD ERROR OF ESTIMATE

In *step 2* the independent variable X_3, quantitative GMAT, is entered into the equation. This variable should be retained because it explains 22.4 percent of the variation in the dependent variable X_1 given that X_2 is accounted for. Both the COMPUTED T value of 6.028 and the partial F_3 value of 36.334 for this variable are statistically significant (Example 23.6). Note that now we are using the partial F value for X_3 only rather than the F value for X_2 and X_3 used in the text. Finally the standard error of estimate is reduced from .246 to .164. The measurements of the cumulative part of this step correspond to the measurements already illustrated (Example 23.6) except for discrepancies due to different computational and rounding procedures. The equation is

$$X_1 = .585 + .531X_2 + .00165X_3 \qquad (n = 30)$$

as found earlier.

On similar grounds, the independent dummy variable X_5, selectivity of undergraduate college, entered in *step 3*, should be retained in the regression equation. This variable explains 8.2 percent of the variation in the dependent variable given that X_2 and X_3 are accounted for. Both the COMPUTED T value of 5.01 and the F_5 value of 25.099 are statistically significant for critical value $z_c = 2.58$ and $F_{01}(1, 26) = 7.72$ at 1 percent significance level. Additionally, the standard error of estimate is further reduced from .164 to .119. Except for differences in format, most of the cumulative part of this step is shown in Table 23.4 with equation

$$X_1 = 1.197 + .309X_2 + .00163X_3 + .284X_5 \qquad (n = 30)$$

and a discussion in Example 23.9.

But independent variable X_4, verbal GMAT, entered in *step 4*, should be dropped from the equation. It explains only .4 percent of the variation in X_1 after all the previously introduced independent variables are accounted for. Both the COMPUTED T value of -1.070 and the F_4 value of 1.145 are not statistically significant for critical values $z_c = 2.58$ and $F_{01}(1, 25) = 7.77$ at 1 percent significance level. Also, note that the introduction of X_4 into the equation has not reduced the standard error of estimate which remained at .119. We conclude that previous step 3 includes the equation which should be used as a basis of analysis.

Computer programs vary in format and type of information they supply. Furthermore, different computer packages may lead to slightly different results because of variations in the procedures for rounding computer output. This may be particularily important in multiple regression where some independent variables may be highly correlated. Errors due to rounding may be a source of difficulty. In order to overcome such a difficulty, the output of a test problem from a new computer program may be compared against results of known accuracy.

This is a small sample of what computer programs can accomplish. Several nonlinear models can be transformed into a linear regression equation; a large number of independent variables can be tested; the reliability of the regression equation can be increased with the systematic selection of the most important independent variables. This plethora of numerical information may demand a greater effort on our part to guard against cost, misuse of techniques, and routine acceptance of computer output.

Section 23 Multiple Regression and Correlation

PROBLEMS

Group One

23.1. Consider the equation

$$Y_c = .585 + .531X_1 + .00165X_2$$

found in Example 23.1 and calculate the unexplained deviation for each given set of values of the variables (data from Tables 21.1 and 21.4):
*(a) $Y = 3.3$, $X_1 = 3.7$, $X_2 = 600$ (student number 3)
(b) $Y = 2.6$, $X_1 = 2.9$, $X_2 = 400$ (student number 14)
(c) $Y = 3.9$, $X_1 = 3.6$, $X_2 = 790$ (student number 27)

23.2. A study of 50 three-bedroom single homes yields the following equation:

$$Y_c = .\quad 60 \quad + \quad 1.054X_1 \quad + \quad .467X_2 \quad - \quad .0256X_3$$
$$(s_{Y|123} = .654) \quad (s_{b_1} = .325) \quad (s_{b_2} = .112) \quad (s_{b_3} = .006)$$

where Y = price in thousands of dollars
X_1 = area in thousands of square feet, range 10 to 30
X_2 = location, scale from 1 to 15
X_3 = index of housing starts, base 100

(a) Test the reliability of the equation with both the t and F tests at 1 percent significance level. Assume that F_o is 15.23.
*(b) Construct 95 percent estimation intervals for individual value and the conditional mean when $X_1 = 20$, $X_2 = 5$, and $X_3 = 120$, and interpret their meaning.
(c) Suppose you are a real estate broker. How would you use the above results in evaluating the market value of a given house? Explain in both quantitative and nonquantitative terms.

23.3. Consider the equation given in Problem 23.2. Discuss briefly why you agree or disagree with each of the following statements:
(a) The coefficient of determination .90 is equal to the sum of the simple coefficients of determination of each independent variable with the dependent variable.
(b) Since R^2 is .90, approximately 10 percent of the variance in price must be attributed to variables other than area X_1, location X_2, and index of housing starts X_3.
(c) Other things being equal, the price of a house increases by $1054.00 for every 1000 square feet increase in the area.
(d) Since b_1 is more than twice as large as b_2, the effect of area on price is likely to be about twice as great as the effect of location.
(e) The base price of a three-bedroom house without the land or other considerations is $60,000.
(f) The index of housing starts X_3 does not have a significant effect on price both in statistical and in numerical terms.

23.4. According to formula (23.6) the general form of a linear equation with three independent variables is

$$Y_c = a + b_1X_1 + b_2X_2 + b_3X_3$$

Answers to asterisked (*) problems are appended. Problems which may require a computer are marked with a dagger (†).

Suppose R is .99. Discuss briefly why you agree or disagree with each of the following statements:
 (a) The coefficients b_1, b_2, and b_3 are likely to be significantly different from zero.
 (b) Variables X_1, X_2, and X_3 explain 99 percent of the variation in Y.
 (c) The linear equation is the best fit to the data.
 (d) The value of R^2 would not decline very much if we dropped from the equation either X_1, X_2, or X_3 and recomputed the regression equation with the remaining variables.
 (e) The observed Y values are very close to the computed Y_c values.

23.5. Explain:
 (a) Beta coefficients
 (b) Multicollinearity
 (c) Dummy variables
 (d) Net regression coefficients
 (e) Regression hyperplane

23.6. Discuss the qualifications for a proper and meaningful application of regression and correlation models to real-world problems.

Group Two

23.7 Basic calculations for the relationship between dollar income of 23 dairy farms (Y), farm size (X_1) in acres, and number of dairy cows (X_2) yields the following averages and sums of deviations:

$\bar{Y} = 2000$,	$\Sigma y^2 = 244{,}400$,	$\Sigma x_1 y = -2400$
$\bar{X}_1 = 125$,	$\Sigma x_1^2 = 900$,	$\Sigma x_2 y = 8200$
$\bar{X}_2 = 10$,	$\Sigma x_2^2 = 300$,	$\Sigma x_1 x_2 = -200$

 *(a) Derive the regression equation and interpret the meaning of the regression coefficients.
 (b) Find the coefficient of multiple determination. What does it mean?
 *(c) Test whether the b_i coefficients are significantly different from zero at 1 percent significance level.
 (d) Suppose the explained and unexplained variations of Y are 102,250 and 142,150, respectively. Test at 1 percent level of significance.
 (e) What is the relative importance of farm size and cow herd on income? Do the necessary calculations and explain.
 (f) Construct estimation intervals for individual value and the conditional mean for a 100-acre farm and 20 cows. Use the approximate formulas of the text and interpret the meaning of each interval.

23.8. The marketing department of Quality Stores, a chain, has studied the relationship between weekly dollar sales (Y) in thousands, inventory (X_1) in thousands of dollars, and the number of customers on welfare (X_2). The basic calculations from the data of 53 stores yield the following sums:

$\Sigma Y = 1{,}060$,	$\Sigma X_1 Y = 11{,}000$,	$\Sigma Y^2 = 21{,}850$
$\Sigma X_1 = 530$,	$\Sigma X_2 Y = 12{,}920$,	$\Sigma X_1^2 = 5{,}600$
$\Sigma X_2 = 636$,	$\Sigma X_1 X_2 = 6{,}560$,	$\Sigma X_2^2 = 8{,}032$

*(a) Derive the regression equation and interpret the meaning of the regression coefficients.
(b) Find the coefficient of multiple determination and explain its meaning.
*(c) Are the regression coefficients significantly different from zero? Carry out t tests at 1 percent significance level.
*(d) Suppose $\Sigma (Y_c - \bar{Y})^2$ is 8,325 and $\Sigma (Y - Y_c)^2$ is 13,525. Carry out an F test at 1 percent level of significance.
*(e) A particular store has an inventory of about $10,000 and 20 customers on welfare. Construct 95 percent estimation intervals for individual value and the conditional mean. Interpret the meaning of each interval.
(f) For the past few months weekly sales of the store in part (e) have averaged $21,000. Can such performance be explained as a random phenomenon? Explain how management can use this information.

23.9. In Problem 22.15 we studied the relationship between price and earnings per share of 10 common stocks in Capital Stock Exchange. Suppose we wish to consider whether or not stock prices are also related to the labor force employed by each of the 10 companies in the sample. The data for this three-variable analysis are:

Stock Price Y	Earnings per Share X_1	Labor Force Size (Thousands) X_2
$15	$ .90	20
9	1.00	15
16	1.40	25
38	3.20	40
18	2.10	12
38	4.00	46
25	1.50	50
33	2.70	22
35	3.70	31
23	2.50	35

*(a) Derive a linear regression equation by the method of least squares.
(b) Explain the meaning of the net regression coefficients.
(c) Compute the coefficient of multiple determination and explain the meaning of this measurement.
*(d) Carry out the appropriate t and F tests at 1 percent significance level. Are the two test results consistent? Explain.
†(e) Perform stepwise regression and compare the t and F tests with those you found in part (d). Discuss why or why not you should drop from the equation any of the independent variables.
*(f) Assuming that both independent variables should be included in the regression equation, construct 95 percent estimation intervals for individual value and the conditional mean. From the viewpoint of estimating the price of a stock, are any of the intervals of practical use?

23.10. The marketing manager of a company wanted to establish a systematic and fair method of compensating the travel expenses of salespersons. One approach was to study whether or not travel expenses are related to miles traveled and length of trip in days. The following data on 10 trips formed the basis of this study:

Travel Expense Y	Miles Traveled X_1	Days in Trip X_2
$205	300	4
102	50	1
50	40	2
70	150	3
126	100	4
182	200	5
50	40	4
95	90	3
267	176	8
156	92	5

*(a) Use the least-squares method to fit a linear equation to the data.

*(b) Are the net regression coefficients significantly different from zero at 1 percent level? Carry out both the t and the F tests and explain results.

†(c) Perform stepwise regression and discuss why or why not you should drop from the equation any of the independent variables. If your decision is to drop one of the independent variables, form the simple regression equation for the variable which should be retained.

(d) Assuming that both independent variables should be included in the regression equation, show how you can use the net regression coefficients to establish a policy for compensating travel expenses.

(e) Suppose a salesperson submits a bill of $230 for a trip of 250 miles which lasted 4 days. Do you think such a travel expense is out of line with what is expected on the average?

23.11. In addition to average daily temperature, the management of Home Oil Company wishes to consider whether or not home insulation is related to daily oil consumption. The data for this analysis are shown below, where 1 indicates a noninsulated home.

Oil Consumption (Gallons) Y	Temperature X_1[a]	Whether Home Insulated X_2
36	0	1
2	80	0
27	20	0
30	6	0
15	60	1
23	40	1
16	50	1
20	30	0
10	70	1
11	54	0

[a] Scale adjusted according to requirements specified in Problem 21.14(b).

Section 23 Multiple Regression and Correlation

    *(a)   Fit a linear equation to data by the method of least squares.

    (b)   Interpret the meaning of the regression coefficients of the equation you found in part (a). On the average, how much warmer is an insulated compared to a noninsulated home likely to be?

    *(c)   Are the net regression coefficients significantly different from zero? Carry out both the t and F tests at the 1 percent significance level.

    †(d)   Verify the test results with stepwise regression.

†23.12. One way of coping with the problem of multicollinearity between two independent variables is to replace them with their average value. This suggestion was made in connection with our discussion of the findings in Example 23.8. Let X_1 denote the dependent variable, graduate GPA, and X_2 the independent variable, college GPA. Their values for the 30 students in the sample are given in Table 21.1. Let X_3 denote the average of quantitative and verbal GMAT scores whose values can be computed from Table 21.4. Finally, let X_4 denote selectivity of undergraduate college whose values are given in Table 23.3.

    (a)   Carry out stepwise regression and determine which independent variables should be kept in the equation. Explain your position in terms of proportion of variance of Y reduced, t values, F values, and standard error of estimate.

    (b)   Form the regression equation and construct 95 percent intervals for both types of undergraduate schools. Are these intervals substantially different from the intervals computed in the text? In what important respects may averaging of the two GMAT scores have improved the results of regression analysis?

Chapter 9
NONPARAMETRIC STATISTICS

The hypothesis-testing procedures we have introduced thus far are based on inferences about one or more population parameters, such as the mean μ or the parameter π. Since testing involves parameters, these tests are commonly referred to as *parametric* and the test statistics as *parametric statistics*. In this chapter we introduce another family of hypothesis-testing methods called *nonparametric;* the term is justified on the ground that most of these methods are concerned with testing the form, without specifying the parameter values, of the population to be sampled.

In addition, many parametric tests are based on assumptions restricting the form of the population to be sampled. Particularly restrictive is the normality assumption for testing with small samples. For example, both the t test and the F test for analysis of variance assume that the parent populations are normal. In many cases we cannot be certain that this assumption is true; in other cases, we may hesitate to make this assumption or we may know that the population is far from being normal. Then for small sample sizes use of parametric tests is inappropriate. Instead we can apply nonparametric tests because they are free of such restrictive assumptions concerning the population to be sampled. Hence, nonparametric methods are also called *distribution-free* although the two terms are not considered strictly synonymous.

A third characteristic of nonparametric or distribution-free methods is their applicability to problems with data which are difficult to quantify. Responses can be only ordered or ranked in an arbitrary scale. For example, a consumer panel may be employed to rate the palatability of a new food product; industrial psychologists may subjectively rank employees in terms of certain performance characteristics; scales of satisfaction or dissatisfaction may be used to measure responses to working conditions or social issues. Such response measurements cannot be easily handled with parametric tests; they are usually analyzed with nonparametric techniques.

In addition, nonparametric statistics are easy to calculate. Often their sampling distributions can be easily explained by simple probability laws. The fact that they are based on few restrictive assumptions is important for studies where sample sizes cannot be large. Thus nonparametric tests are particularly useful to biological and behavioral sciences where only small samples may be physically or economically possible.

Nonparametric methods, on the other hand, are just as dependent on random sampling as are parametric tests. Therefore, while free of some restrictive assumptions about the sampled populations, nonparametric tests are not free of the assumptions about the form of the underlying sampling distribution. Like the sampling distribution of a parametric test, the sampling distribution of a nonparametric test can take any form, including the student t, the normal, the chi-square, or other suitable probability distribution.

Furthermore, the null and the alternative hypotheses for a nonparametric test are less clearly defined than in a parametric test. For example, in testing the difference between the means of two feed products A and B the null hypothesis for a two-tailed parametric test would be that $\mu_A = \mu_B$. The corresponding null hypothesis for a comparable nonparametric test would be that the two population distributions are identical.

Nonparametric tests are less powerful than their corresponding parametric methods. This is the primary drawback of nonparametric statistics. Since nonparametric techniques are based on ranking or ordering of responses, they use less sample information than corresponding parametric tests based on numerical values. Thus for a given sample size and α probability risk, the β probability risk would be greater for a nonparametric than for a corresponding parametric test; in order to obtain a comparable level of statistical precision a nonparametric requires a larger sample than a parametric test.

In sum, nonparametric tests are applicable to situations where the following conditions prevail. First, the population(s) to be sampled do not conform to the restrictive assumptions, such as normality, required by parametric tests. Second, the nature of response measurements make application of a parametric test inappropriate. Third, the loss of statistical precision is not crucial while the test results are needed quickly. In situations in which both parametric and nonparametric tests are applicable we must carefully weigh the advantages and disadvantages of each test. If both types are desirable, we should remember that only one test should be applied to any given set of data.

In this chapter we introduce four nonparametric tests. They are a few of the many nonparametric statistical measures available. The reader is referred to the literature for extensive coverage of the subject (see, for example, the entries in the Selected Bibliography at the end of this volume). These four tests correspond to parametric tests covered earlier. The rank-sum test for two independent samples is the counterpart of the earlier parametric t test for two independent samples. The signed-rank test for matched samples is analogous to the earlier parametric test for matched samples. For the parametric one-factor analysis of variance we introduce the corresponding nonparametric one-factor analysis of variance by ranks. Finally, in regression and correlation analysis we discussed the parametric correlation coefficient r; here, we introduce a corresponding rank correlation coefficient. Since each test may be considered a subject in itself, each occupies a separate section.

SECTION 24/ RANK-SUM TEST FOR TWO INDEPENDENT SAMPLES

Earlier (Section 18), we introduced a procedure for testing whether two small independent samples have been drawn from populations with identical means. That parametric t test for the difference between two sample means, however, is adequate only when the sampled populations are normally distributed or nearly so. This assumption of normality may be frequently invalid. The testing procedure referred to as the *Wilcoxon* rank-sum test* is free of the normality assumption. Furthermore, this nonparametric test is based on the assumption that the two samples are selected from identical populations; the t test assumes that the two populations have only equal means and variances. Except for these differences, the rank-sum test may be viewed as an alternative to the parametric small-sample t test as well as to the large-sample normal distribution test for the difference between two sample means.

The Wilcoxon test compares a control sample and an experimental sample. The null hypothesis is that the two independent samples came from the same population. If the null hypothesis is true, then the observations from the two samples can be combined and their values ranked from smallest to largest. In order to illustrate this ranking procedure let us consider the situation used to introduce the earlier parametric t test. The experiment was a cooperative venture between McDonald Brothers, a manufacturer of animal feed, and Hope Enterprises, a feedlot operator. The test was based on an experimental random sample of 10 steers given a new C2 feed and a control sample of 15 steers fattened with ordinary feed. The test result led to the conclusion that the new C2 feed is superior to the ordinary feed.

Example 24.1

In order to double-check this conclusion, McDonald Brothers conducts another experiment for a rank-sum test. In cooperation with Kaplowitz Farms, another feedlot, two samples of 11 steers each are selected at random. During the cattle-fattening period, the steers of sample A are given C2 feed and those of sample B ordinary feed. All other feeding and living conditions are kept the same for both samples. At the end of the fattening period the weight each steer gained is listed in Table 24.1.

The null hypothesis is that the population of steers which gained weight on C2 feed is identical to the population of steers which gained weight on ordinary feed. The alternative hypothesis is that the two populations are not identical. Formally,

H_0: The two feed products are equally effective
H_1: The two feed products are not equally effective

---

*After the statistician Frank Wilcoxon, who proposed it in 1945.

Table 24.1.
Two Samples of Steers Fattened with Different Animal Feed (Weight in Pounds)

Sample A C2 Animal Feed	Sample B Ordinary Feed
710	660
695	600
790	550
660	620
880	800
845	630
750	695
740	730
690	660
820	570
710	608

The alternative hypothesis may be true if C2 feed is better than ordinary feed; it may also be true if ordinary feed is better than C2 feed. Thus, the experiment may be considered to involve a *two-tailed test*.

Since the null hypothesis assumes a single population, we can combine the two samples and rank their observations. This is done in Table 24.2. Note that ties occurred in ranking the combined observations. Three steers, two from sample *B* and one from sample *A*, gained the same weight of 660 pounds. Since the three observations occupy ranks, 7, 8, and 9, we assign 8, the average of the three rank values, to each observation. Also, we assign rank 11.5, the average ranks of 11 and 12, to the same weight of 695 pounds gained by one steer from sample *B* and one from sample *A*. In general, when ties occur between samples, we assign to each observation the average of the rank values. If, on the other hand, a tie occurs within the same sample, we assign arbitrarily successive rank values to the tied observations. This occurs with two steers from sample *A* each gaining 710 pounds. These observations are assigned ranks 13 and 14.

Table 24.2.
Ranking of Steers Fed Two Kinds of Animal Feed by Weight Gained (Weight in Pounds)

Sample	Weight	Rank	Sample	Weight	Rank
B	550	1	A	695	11.5
B	570	2	A	710	13
B	600	3	A	710	14
B	608	4	B	730	15
B	620	5	A	740	16
B	630	6	A	750	17
B	660	8	A	790	18
A	660	8	B	800	19
B	660	8	A	820	20
A	690	10	A	845	21
B	695	11.5	A	880	22

Section 24 Rank-Sum Test for Two Independent Samples

If the two feed products were equally effective, we would expect observations from sample A to be ranked low or high as frequently as observations from sample B. In other words, the first rank value as well as any other rank value is no more likely to be assigned to observations from sample A than to observations from sample B. The sum of the ranks from either sample may be the test statistic. We may calculate the sum of the ranks for sample A from Table 24.2. This value, denoted by W_A, is

$$W_A = 8 + 10 + 11.5 + 13 + 14 + 16 + 17 + 18 + 20 + 21 + 22 = 170.5$$

Value 170.5 of statistic W_A measures the difference between the ranked observations of the two samples. Statistic W_A can take on as many values as the number of possible ways we can select 11 ranks from a total of 22 ranks. All these possible values form a sampling distribution of W_A. Very large or very small W_A values give evidence that the two samples may not have originated from the same population. How large or how small a W_A value must be in order to refute our null hypothesis is determined with a test of significance based on the sampling distribution W_A.

The distribution of W_A has a mean

(24.1) $$\mu_W = \frac{n_A(n_A + n_B + 1)}{2}$$

where n_A = size of sample A
n_B = size of sample B

and a standard deviation

(24.2) $$\sigma_W = \sqrt{\frac{n_A n_B(n_A + n_B + 1)}{12}}$$

When ties occur a correction may be used for calculating σ_W. For large samples, however, this correction is negligible and may be ignored.

Example 24.1 (continued)

Since the sizes of samples n_A and n_B are 11, substitution in formulas (24.1) and (24.2) yields

$$\mu_W = \frac{11(11 + 11 + 1)}{2} = 126.5$$

and

$$\sigma_W = \sqrt{\frac{(11)(11)(11 + 11 + 1)}{12}} \simeq 15.23$$

If n_A and n_B are both less than 10, special tables are required for determining the significance of statistic W_A. If n_A and n_B are both greater than 10, the sampling distribution of W_A may be considered approximately normal. Then the normal deviate is defined as

$$(24.3) \qquad z_o = \frac{W - \mu_W}{\sigma_W}$$

Example 24.1 (continued)

Suppose MacDonald Brothers wishes to test the null hypothesis of the two feed products having identical effectiveness at 5 percent significance level; this is the same level used for carrying out the earlier parametric t test. Since the present experiment is considered to involve a two-tailed test, the critical z_c value of the normal deviate, from Appendix D, is ± 1.96. The decision rule is

If $-1.96 \leq z_o \leq +1.96$, accept H_0 (the two feed products are equally effective)

If $z_o > +1.96$ or $z_o < -1.96$, reject H_0 (the two feed products are not equally effective)

In order to apply this rule, we must calculate the observed z_o value of the normal deviate. Substitution of $W_A = 170.5$, $\mu_W = 126.5$, and $\sigma_W = 15.23$ in (24.3) yields

$$z_o = \frac{170.5 - 126.5}{15.23} = +2.89$$

The null hypothesis is rejected because the observed $z_o = +2.89$ falls in the rejection right-hand tail of the normal curve. A large W_A value and therefore a positive z_o value indicate that high ranks have been assigned to the sample of steers given C2 feed. Hence, C2 feed may be superior to ordinary feed.

The test result is the same if we use the sum of ranks W_B for sample B. Then a low W_B value would result in a negative z_o value of -2.89. This indicates that low ranks have been assigned to the sample of steers fattened with ordinary feed. The conclusion is the same: ordinary feed is less effective than C2 feed and therefore C2 feed may be superior.

Also, the same experiment can be formulated as an *upper-tailed test* as in the case with the earlier parametric t test.

Example 24.1 (continued)

For our nonparametric test, the null and the alternative hypotheses may be changed to

H_0: The effectiveness of C2 feed is equal to or less than the effectiveness of ordinary feed
H_1: Feed C2 is superior to ordinary feed

The observed z_o value is 2.89, the same as with the two-sided test. The critical z_c value, however, changes to 1.64 since the 5 percent risk, read from

Section 24 Rank-Sum Test for Two Independent Samples

Appendix D, corresponds to area .4495. Again, the test result is to reject the null hypothesis and conclude that C2 feed may be superior to the ordinary feed.

The summary formula of the Wilcoxon rank-sum test is

(24.4)
$$z_o = \frac{W - \dfrac{n_A(n_A + n_B + 1)}{2}}{\sqrt{n_A n_B(n_A + n_B + 1)/12}}$$

How does this test compare with the earlier parametric t test for the difference between two sample means? We have seen that the two tests yield similar results. We should keep in mind, however, that the two tests are not substitutes without qualifications. Here are a number of important points to remember:

1. Each test would normally be chosen before sampling and only one test would ordinarily be applied to any given set of data. The two experiments for MacDonald Brothers illustrate this point.
2. The t test requires that the two populations be normally distributed. No such assumption is necessary for the Wilcoxon rank-sum test.
3. Unlike the t test, the Wilcoxon test can handle observations measured on a ranking scale. Thus, the Wilcoxon test can be more widely used, especially in the study of personnel management and consumer preference.
4. On the other hand, the Wilcoxon test is less powerful than the t test; for a given set of data, we need a larger sample with the Wilcoxon than with the t test in order to obtain a comparable level of statistical precision.

PROBLEMS

Group One

24.1. For each Wilcoxon rank-sum test:
  (i) Formulate the null and the alternative hypotheses.
  (ii) Specify the decision rule at the stated α significance level.
  (iii) Apply the decision rule and interpret result.
  *(a) $n_A = 11$, $n_B = 11$, $W_B = 82.5$; n_A represents steers given C2 feed, and n_B steers fattened with ordinary feed; use $\alpha = .05$ for a two-tail test.
  (b) $n_A = 10$, $n_B = 15$, $W_A = 185$; n_A represents a wage incentive plan, and n_B a straight-hours wage plan; use $\alpha = .01$ for an upper-tailed test.
  (c) $n_A = 50$, $n_B = 70$, $W_A = 2776$; n_A represents repair costs of 3-year-old compact cars manufactured by company A, and n_B of cars manufactured by company B; use $\alpha = .05$ for a lower-tailed test.
  (d) $n_A = 20$, $n_B = 20$, $W_A = 425$; n_A is the dollar sales of salespersons in the Atlantic coastal states, and n_B the dollar sales of salespersons in the Pacific coastal states; use $\alpha = .01$ for a two-tailed test.

Answers to asterisked (*) problems are appended.

Group Two

*24.2. Grand Lieto is told that there is no significant difference in profits between dealers trading in dollars and those trading in gold. Grand wants to verify this statement because he is interested in getting a job in this field. He records the profits realized by 25 traders during the last 3 years and ranks them as follows:

Dollar traders: 1, 3, 4, 5, 6, 8, 9, 10, 13, 14, 16, 19
Gold traders: 2, 7, 11, 12, 15, 17, 18, 20, 21, 22, 23, 24, 25

(a) Is this a one-sided or two-sided test?
(b) Is what Grand was told correct? Test at 5 percent significance level.

24.3. In addition to parametric test for proportions (Example 18.3), Pettina Sacks, the agronomist of Tree Farms wants to have a quick check of the earlier test result. She selects at random 22 orange trees, 11 protected with ladybugs and 11 with palathion against aphid infestation. Company records show that the following pounds of marketable oranges were collected from each tree:

Ladybugs (A):   129, 122, 130, 127, 118, 131, 99, 117, 125, 106, 102
Palathion (B):   102, 97, 99, 101, 89, 115, 95, 100, 90, 110, 99

Pettina's hypothesis is that ladybugs offer no better protection than palathion.
(a) Formulate the null and the alternative hypotheses. Is this a one-sided or two-sided test?
(b) Prepare a table ranking the observations from the smallest to the largest.
(c) Test at .001 level of significance and interpret the test result.

24.4. The management of Natural Foods Inc. wants to evaluate the palatability of a new food product H. Individuals are randomly assigned to two samples of 50 persons each, half male and half female. Each person in sample A is asked to taste product H in liquid form and rate the product on a 100-point scale ranging from 1 to 100. The persons in sample B are asked to taste and rate a competing product C on the same scale. Ranking of the rating from the two samples yields a rank sum $W_A = 2986$. Management's hypothesis is that product H is no better than the competing product C.
(a) Is this an upper-tailed or a lower-tailed test?
(b) Should management introduce product H? For a situation describing an analogous parametric test with large samples see Problem 18.9 or its *source:* L. Street and M. B. Carroll, "Preliminary Evaluation of a New Food Product," in J. M. Tanur, F. Mosteller, et al., eds., *Statistics: A Guide to the Unknown* (San Francisco: Holden-Day, 1972), pp. 220–28.

SECTION 25 / SIGNED-RANK TEST FOR MATCHED SAMPLES

The signed-rank test for matched samples is a nonparametric test analogous to the parametric t test for matched samples discussed earlier (Section 18). In both tests the test statistic is the difference d between two measurements, x_1 and x_2. In matched-pairs sampling, d is the difference between x_1 and x_2 measurements obtained from two paired elementary units; x_1 is the measurement from an elementary unit of the control sample, and x_2 is the measurement from the matched

Section 25 Signed-Rank Test for Matched Samples

elementary unit of the experimental sample. In matched-observations sampling, d is the difference between x_1 and x_2 measurements obtained from a single elementary unit; x_1 is the measurement before and x_2 the measurement after the introduction of the experimental stimulus. The parametric t test, however, requires the assumption that the underlying population of differences is normally distributed. No such assumption is necessary for the Wilcoxon test.

In order to maintain logical continuity, we illustrate the *Wilcoxon signed-rank test* with an earlier situation involving matched-observations sampling; applications of the test to matched-pairs sampling appear among the problems. Richard Maytag, the production manager of General Autos Company, wanted to find out whether X1-CC (X1 catalytic converter) reduces significantly the sulfur dioxide emissions level of engines. The t test was applied to a random sample of 10 engines whose emissions level was measured before and after the installation of X1-CC. The test result led to the conclusion that X1-CC may effectively lower the sulfur dioxide emissions level of the tested engines.

Example 25.1

Although Richard was encouraged with the result of the parametric test, he wanted to do some additional experimenting. Another sample of 10 engines is selected at random for an independent Wilcoxon signed-rank test. The emission of each engine in ppm (parts per million) before and after the installation of X1-CC is shown in Table 25.1, columns 2 and 3.

As in the case of the parametric test, the signed differences d between the paired measurements are obtained as shown in column 4. Then the *absolute values* of the differences $|d|$ are ranked from 1 to n, where the smallest difference is assigned the rank of 1. If two or more d values are identical, each is assigned the average of the tied ranks. For example, the d values for engines 1 and 6 are tied, representing ranks 8 and 9; then each

Table 25.1. Basic Calculations for the Wilcoxon Signed-Rank Test for Matched Samples: Emission Level Experiment with 10 Automobile Engines

	Emissions Level (ppm)				Signed Rank	
Engine Number (1)	Before x_1 (2)	After x_2 (3)	Difference $d = x_2 - x_1$ (4)	Rank of $\lvert d \rvert$ (5)	Rank (+) (6)	Rank (−) (7)
1	60	51	−9	8.5		8.5
2	56	58	+2	2	2	
3	63	63	0	—		
4	52	49	−3	3		3
5	61	55	−6	6		6
6	65	56	−9	8.5		8.5
7	58	59	+1	1	1	
8	62	57	−5	5		5
9	64	60	−4	4		4
10	65	58	−7	7		7
					Σ rank (+) = 3	Σ rank (−) = 42

d value is assigned the average 8.5 of the two ranks. If the difference d is zero, then the elementary unit is dropped and the sample size is reduced accordingly. For example, engine 3 has a d value of zero. Then the sample size is reduced to $n = 10 - 1 = 9$ engines. Finally, the ranking values are separated into positive and negative ranked differences, as shown in columns 6 and 7, and each column summed.

In general, calculations of the rank sums requires three steps:

1. Find the signed difference d between each paired measurement.
2. Rank the absolute values $|d|$ of these differences.
3. List the positive and negative ranks in separate columns and sum each column.

The null hypothesis is that the differences between the paired measurements are symmetrically distributed around a mean of zero; this means that, if the null hypothesis is true, the sum of the positive ranks equals the sum of the negative ranks. In symbols, the null and the alternative hypotheses are

$$H_0: \Sigma \text{ rank }(+) = \Sigma \text{ rank }(-)$$
$$H_1: \Sigma \text{ rank }(+) \neq \Sigma \text{ rank }(-)$$

This is a *two-sided test* where the null hypotheses will be refuted if either rank sum is significantly smaller than the other. The test statistic, recognized as Wilcoxon's T statistic, is the smaller of the two rank sums. In our case, it is the positive rank sum $\Sigma \text{ rank }(+) = 3$, shown in Table 25.1. As the name of the test indicates, the T statistic considers both the sign as well as the ranked absolute value of each difference.

For large samples ($n \geq 25$), the sampling distribution of statistic T is approximately normally distributed with mean*

(25.1) $$\mu_T = \frac{n(n+1)}{4}$$

and standard deviation

(25.2) $$\sigma_T = \sqrt{\frac{n(n+1)(2n+1)}{24}}$$

Accordingly, the normal deviate is defined as

(25.3) $$z_o = \frac{T - \mu_T}{\sigma_T}$$

---

*Sample sizes smaller than 25 require a special table of critical T values. For a given sample size, the null hypothesis is rejected when the computed T value is smaller than the critical value. Here, we use z values instead because the test results were found to be nearly identical to those obtainable from a special table.

Section 25 Signed-Rank Test for Matched Samples

Example 25.1 (continued)

Richard Maytag's null and alternative hypotheses are

H_0: Σ rank $(+)$ = Σ rank $(-)$ (sulfur dioxide emission levels before and after the installation of X1-CC are the same; do not install X1-CC)

H_1: Σ rank $(+)$ $\neq$ Σ rank $(-)$ (sulfur dioxide emission levels are not the same; install X1-CC, if emission level is reduced)

Suppose Richard wants to establish a .05 significance level for installing an effective X1-CC on all automobile engines next year. Since this is a two-tailed test, the critical z_c value is 1.96, corresponding to .025 or half the test level (see Appendix D). The decision rule is

If $-1.96 \leq z_o \leq +1.96$, accept H_0 (do not install X1-CC)
If $z_o > +1.96$ or $z_o < -1.96$, reject H_0 (install X1-CC)

Substituting for $n = 9$, the nonzero differences, in the above formulas, we obtain

$$\mu_T = \frac{(9)(9+1)}{4} = 22.5$$

$$\sigma_T = \sqrt{\frac{(9)(9+1)[2(9)+1]}{24}} \simeq 8.44$$

and since T is equal to 3,

$$z_o = \frac{3 - 22.5}{8.44} \simeq -2.31$$

The null hypothesis is rejected because the observed value z_o falls in the rejection region of the normal curve. The positive rank sum indicates that the emission level is lower than the expected average level after the installation of X1-CC. The converter may be installed on all automobile engines next year.

The same experiment can be formulated as a *lower-tailed test* like the earlier parametric test.

Example 25.1 (continued)

For our nonparametric test the null and the alternative hypotheses may be changed to

H_0: Σ rank $(+)$ $\geq$ Σ rank $(-)$ (sulfur-dioxide emission level before the installation of X1-CC is greater than or equal to the level after the installation; do not install X1-CC)

H_1: Σ rank $(+)$ $<$ Σ rank $(-)$ (sulfur-dioxide emission level before the installation of X1-CC is smaller than the level after the installation; install X1-CC)

Chapter 9 Nonparametric Statistics

The critical value z_c changes from 1.96 to 1.64 since 5 percent risk, read from Appendix D, corresponds to area .4495. The decision rule is

If $z_o \geq -1.64$, accept H_0 (do not install X1-CC)
If $z_o < -1.64$, reject H_0 (install X1-CC)

The observed z_o value -2.31, however, remains unchanged. The observed z_o value always has a negative sign because Wilcoxon's T statistic represents the smaller of the two rank sums. We again reject the null hypothesis. We reach the same conclusion that X1-CC may be installed on all automobile engines next year.

In conclusion, testing may be carried out with the z deviate summarized as follows:

(25.4)
$$z_o = \frac{T - \frac{n(n+1)}{4}}{\sqrt{n(n+1)(2n+1)/24}}$$

In applying the Wilcoxon signed-ranked test we should keep in mind the following important points:

1. The parametric for matched samples and the nonparametric Wilcoxon signed-ranks tests should not be considered substitutes without qualifications. If it is desirable to apply both tests, separate samples should be used for each testing procedure. Maytag's experiments illustrate this point.
2. The parametric test requires the assumption that the underlying population of differences is normally distributed. The Wilcoxon test does not require such an assumption.
3. The Wilcoxon test requires adjustment when there are many ties between differences of opposite signs.
4. The Wilcoxon signed-rank test is less powerful than the analogous parametric test for matched samples. Thus, in order to obtain a comparable level of statistical precision we need a larger sample with the Wilcoxon than with the parametric test. Again, Maytag's experiments illustrate this point.

PROBLEMS

Group One

25.1. For a given n nonzero difference, T value, and significance level:
   (i) Indicate whether the Wilcoxon signed-rank test is two-sided or one-sided.
   (ii) Test at the specified α significance level.
   *(a) H_0: Σ rank $(+) \geq \Sigma$ rank $(-)$, $n = 15$, $T = 16$, $\alpha = .01$
   (b) H_0: Σ rank $(+) = \Sigma$ rank $(-)$, $n = 45$, $T = 365$, $\alpha = .05$

Answers to asterisked (*) problems are appended.

Section 25 Signed-Rank Test for Matched Samples

(c) $H_0: \Sigma$ rank $(+) \geq \Sigma$ rank $(-)$, $n = 8$, $T = 2$, $\alpha = .05$
*(d) $H_0: \Sigma$ rank $(+) \geq \Sigma$ rank $(-)$, $n = 39$, $T = 272$, $\alpha = .05$
(e) $H_0: \Sigma$ rank $(+) = \Sigma$ rank $(-)$, $n = 31$, $T = 143$, $\alpha = .10$

25.2. Is mileage with unleaded gasoline as good as mileage with leaded gasoline? Mary Fishbone of Consumer Advocates Inc., a private organization, wants to find an answer to this question. A sample of 30 compact cars of a given make is randomly assigned to two equal groups. For a period of time and under controlled conditions one group of cars is run with unleaded and the other with leaded gasoline. Then the type of gasoline used for each group is reversed. The 30 nonzero differences (mileage per gallon with unleaded minus with leaded gasoline) yield a Wilcoxon statistic $T = \Sigma$ rank $(-) = 148.5$.
*(a) Is this a two-tailed or one-tailed test?
(b) Formulate the null and the alternative hypotheses.
(c) Specify the decision rule at .01 significance level.
(d) Apply the decision rule using the normal curve approximation and interpret result.

25.3. Ten pairs of newly hired salespersons are matched with respect to sex, age, and other personality characteristics. One salesperson from each pair receives special training and the other does not. Then each pair is assigned to roughly comparable sales districts. Philip Sablosky, the director of educational programs at International Business Computers (IBC), wants to test the effectiveness of the training program. In other words, the null hypothesis is that there are no significant differences in sales between the two samples of salespersons. After a year's experience, monthly sales averaged as follows:

Salesperson	Monthly Sales (Thousands of Dollars)		Salesperson	Monthly Sales (Thousands of Dollars)	
	Untrained	Trained		Untrained	Trained
1	32	35	6	82	88
2	35	34	7	57	62
3	46	48	8	48	60
4	75	79	9	54	61
5	63	65	10	69	66

*(a) Is this a two-tailed or one-tailed (upper or lower) test?
(b) Formulate the null and the alternative hypotheses.
(c) Specify the decision rule at .05 significance level.
(d) Prepare a table such as Table 25.1 and calculate the T value for a Wilcoxon signed-rank test.
(e) Is the training program effective? Test.

25.4. In order to control unnecessary surgery, the Medicaid recipients in a state are required to have a second medical opinion prior to surgery. Five types of surgeries are included in this "second opinion" program. The following data are assembled for the eight state districts:

	Monthly Average of Surgeries			Monthly Average of Surgeries	
District	Before	After	District	Before	After
1	60	55	5	58	52
2	72	70	6	75	60
3	81	80	7	93	85
4	67	70	8	85	75

Each pair of numbers represents the average monthly surgeries performed during 1 year prior and 1 year after the initiation of the "second opinion" program. Has the program reduced the number of surgeries significantly? Assuming normal approximation, use a .05 significance level in a one-sided test.

SECTION 26/ ONE-FACTOR ANALYSIS OF VARIANCE BY RANKS

One-factor analysis of variance by ranks, a nonparametric technique also called the *Kruskal-Wallis test*,* is a generalization of the Wilcoxon rank-sum test we have already introduced. Then we ranked the combined observations from two independent samples; now we rank the pooled observations from more than two independent samples. In this respect, the Kruskal-Wallis test is analogous to the one-factor parametric analysis of variance, except for two important differences. First, differences between sample means are the basis for the F test while sample rank sums are the basis for the Kruskal-Wallis test. Second, the parametric F test is based on the assumption that the sampled populations are normally distributed; no such requirement is necessary for applying the Kruskal-Wallis test.

As with the Wilcoxon rank-sum test, the null hypothesis is that the k independent simple random samples, where $k > 2$, were drawn from k identically distributed populations. If the null hypothesis is true, then the observations from all the k sample groups can be combined and their values ranked from the smallest to the largest. In order to establish continuity with the parametric F test, we shall illustrate ranking for the Kruskal-Wallis test with an earlier case (from Section 20). Donaldson Associates, an advertising agency, wanted to test the sales effectiveness of 2 advertising displays with different campaign themes. Each of the 2 displays was assigned to a randomly selected sample of 4 stores. A third random sample of 4 stores used "ordinary" advertising with no special display or promotion; it provided the basis for comparing the other 2 advertising methods. The experiment lasted 4 weeks. An F test on the sales from the 12 participating stores led to the conclusion that the advertising displays may have increased sales significantly.

*After W. H. Kruskal and W. A. Wallis, who proposed it in 1952.

Section 26 One-Factor Analysis of Variance by Ranks

Example 26.1

In order to collect data for a Kruskal-Wallis test, the same experiment is conducted with another set of 12 retail stores for 4 weeks. The new set of data together with the basic calculations for the test are shown in Table 26.1. (Although sample sizes could vary, they were kept to 4 stores each in this experiment.)

Table 26.1. Basic Calculations for the Kruskal-Wallis One-Factor Analysis of Variance by Ranks: Donaldson Associates Problem

Display 1		Display 2		"Ordinary" Advertising	
Sales[a]	Rank	Sales[a]	Rank	Sales[a]	Rank
20	6.5	23	9.0	17	1.5
24	10.0	26	12.0	19	4.5
20	6.5	19	4.5	17	1.5
22	8.0	25	11.0	18	3.0
	$R_1 = 31.0$		$R_2 = 36.5$		$R_3 = 10.5$
	$n_1 = 4$		$n_2 = 4$		$n_3 = 4$

[a]In units per 1000 customers.

The null hypothesis is that the three samples were selected from identical populations. Thus, the null and the alternative hypotheses are

H_0: Sales between samples are not different, displays are not effective

H_1: Sales between samples are different; displays are effective

Since the null hypothesis assumes a single population, we can combine the three sample groups and rank their observations as shown in Table 26.1. The smallest observation value is given the rank of 1 and the largest a rank of 12. As usual, ties are assigned the average of the tied ranks. Then the ranks of each sample are added. Thus, on the basis of the null hypothesis, each sales value has the same prior probability of being assigned any rank from 1 to 12.

The test statistic K is based on the variation of rank sums between samples. It is defined as

(26.1) $$K_o = \frac{12}{n(n+1)} \left(\sum \frac{R_j^2}{n_j} \right) - 3(n+1)$$

where R_j = sum of the ranks in the jth sample group
n_j = number of observations in the jth sample group
n = total number of observations in the k sample groups, that is,
$n = n_1 + n_2 + \cdots + n_k$

Chapter 9 Nonparametric Statistics

If all sample groups contain at least 3 observations each, the sampling distribution of statistic K is approximately the same as the χ^2 (chi-square) distribution with $k - 1$ degrees of freedom, where k is the number of sample groups. So testing can be carried out using the χ^2 distribution.

Example 26.1 (continued)

Suppose that Donaldson Associates wishes to test the null hypothesis again at 5 percent significance level as with the F test. Since our problem involves three sample groups, k is 3 and the number of degrees of freedom is $k - 1 = 3 - 1 = 2$. For 5 percent significance level and two degrees of freedom we find, from Appendix G, that the critical χ_c^2 is 5.99. The decision rule for the observed value K_o of the test statistic is

If $K_o \leq 5.99$, accept H_0 (displays are not effective)
If $K_o > 5.99$, reject H_0 (displays are effective)

We can apply this rule now by calculating the observed K_o from formula (26.1). Substitution of the appropriate values from Table 26.1 yields

$$K_o = \frac{12}{12(12+1)} \left(\frac{31^2}{4} + \frac{36.5^2}{4} + \frac{10.5^2}{4} \right) - 3(12+1)$$
$$\simeq 7.22$$

We reject the null hypothesis since the observed value $K_o = 7.22$ is larger than the critical value $\chi_c^2 = 5.99$. We conclude that the differences in sales between sample groups are significant. Looking at Table 26.1, we observe that sales for displays 1 and 2 are larger than sales from the stores with no promotion. We conclude that the advertising displays may be effective.

If ties occur, the observed K_o value must be corrected to K_c as follows:

(26.2) $$K_c = \frac{K_o}{1 - \frac{\Sigma (t_j^3 - t_j)}{n^3 - n}}$$

where t_j represents the number of ties in the jth sample group.

Example 26.1 (continued)

From Table 26.1 we observe that $t_1 = 2$, $t_2 = 1$, and $t_3 = 3$ ties. Hence by (26.2) we have

$$K_c = \frac{7.22}{1 - [(2^3 - 2) + (1^3 - 1) + (3^3 - 3)]/(12^3 - 12)}$$
$$\simeq 7.35$$

Note that the corrected K_c is always larger than the unadjusted K_o; so the correction is unnecessary if K_o is significant, as in this example.

In applying the Kruskal-Wallis test we should keep in mind the following important points:

1. This nonparametric test is analogous to one-factor parametric analysis of variance. Application of each test, however, to the same problem would require a separate set of data.

Section 26 One-Factor Analysis of Variance by Ranks

2. While the parametric F test requires that the sampled populations are normally distributed, the Kruskal-Wallis test is free of this requirement.
3. Correction of the test statistic K_o for ties in ranks is necessary only if the test is not significant and we accept the null hypothesis.

PROBLEMS

Group One

26.1. For a given set of basic calculations:
  (i) Formulate the decision rule at the specified α significance level.
  (ii) Calculate the Kruskal-Wallis test statistic K_o and K_c, if necessary, and apply the rule.
  *(a) $R_1 = 57$, $R_2 = 54.5$, $R_3 = 59.5$, $\alpha = .01$;
      $n_1 = 5$, $n_2 = 7$, $n_3 = 6$;
      $t_1 = 0$, $t_2 = 0$, $t_3 = 0$
  (b) $R_1 = 71.5$, $R_2 = 56$, $R_3 = 83$, $R_4 = 42.5$, $\alpha = .01$;
      $n_1 = 5$, $n_2 = 6$, $n_3 = 4$, $n_4 = 7$;
      $t_1 = 1$, $t_2 = 1$, $t_3 = 1$, $t_4 = 1$
  (c) $R_1 = 120.5$, $R_2 = 115.5$, $R_3 = 89$, $\alpha = .05$;
      $n_1 = 7$, $n_2 = 8$, $n_3 = 10$;
      $t_1 = 5$, $t_2 = 7$, $t_3 = 8$

Group Two

26.2. Robin Goldfischer represents the U.S. Chamber of Industry before a congressional Committee on Taxation. Robin argues that there are no significant differences between the profits realized by manufacturing firms of different sizes. To support his argument he presents the following data obtained from three random samples:

	Size of Firm	
Large	Medium	Small
10%	11%	7%
12	13	15
20	17	9
15	14	8
21	16	
	18	

Figures represent 3-year average profits before taxes as a percent of dollar sales. Firms classified as large employ more than 10,000 employees; medium, between 1000 and 10,000 employees; and small, less than 1000 employees.
  (a) Formulate the null and the alternative hypotheses.
  (b) Establish a decision rule at .025 significance level.
  *(c) Do the data support Robin's argument?

Answers to asterisked (*) problems are appended.

Chapter 9 Nonparametric Statistics

26.3. Are the earnings of alumni from different schools at Harrison University significantly different? Bjorn Kapstad, the director of placement, believes that the differences are not significant even 5 years after graduation. Mona Peet, the director of alumni giving, argues that the differences are significant. Random samples of alumni with 5 years of employment report the following 5-year average earnings in thousands of dollars:

Engineers	Liberal Arts	Management	Science
$18.2	$17.6	$18.5	$18.0
20.6	15.4	19.3	15.5
19.5	16.7	21.1	18.3
20.1		18.9	19.4
		23.1	17.3
		20.8	

(a) Formulate the null and the alternative hypotheses.
(b) Establish a decision rule at .05 significance level.
(c) Who is correct, Bjorn or Mona?

26.4. Robert Hunter, the production manager of Acmetronics Inc., receives four machines to meet increased demand for the company's major product. The supplier claims that the machines have the same output capabilities. Sixteen random samples yield the following hourly output in hundreds of units:

	Machine		
A	B	C	D
4	2	4	6
4	3	5	6
3	4	6	7
5	3	5	5

Is the supplier's claim justified? Test at .01 significance level.

SECTION 27 / RANK CORRELATION

A parametric correlation coefficient r was introduced as part of regression and correlation analysis (Section 21). As explained then, r is an index which measures the degree of linear association between two variables. An analogous nonparametric measure of association between two variables is the *Spearman rank correlation coefficient* r_s. The two measures, however, differ in two important

Section 27 Rank Correlation

respects. First, calculation of the parametric correlation coefficient is based on the values of the two variables; calculation of Spearman's r_s is based on the ranks of the values of the two variables. Second, the parametric r is based on the assumption of linearity; the nonparametric correlation coefficient r_s requires only that there is ever-increasing or ever-decreasing, but not necessarily linear, relation between the two ranked variables.

Again, for continuity's sake we introduce the basic calculations for the nonparametric r_s using the data for illustrating calculation of the parametric r. Then variable Y represented the graduate GPA (grade point average) and variable X the college GPA of a random sample of 10 M.B.A. graduates. We raised the question: Is there an association between the GPA scores a person receives as a college student and as an M.B.A. student? In other words, are high (low) college GPA scores associated with high (low) graduate GPA scores? We found (Example 21.10) that the parametric correlation coefficient r is $+.833$. Here, we can raise the same question in terms of ranks. Are high (low) ranks of college GPA scores associated with high (low) ranks of graduate GPA scores? Spearman's r_s answers this question; the coefficient requires calculation of $\Sigma\, d^2$, the sum of squared rank differences between pairs of Y and X observations.

Example 27.1

The basic calculations for finding $\Sigma\, d^2$ are shown in Table 27.1. The first three columns of this table are copied from Table 21.2. First, we rank the values of each variable, beginning with rank 1 for the smallest, as shown under columns R_Y and R_X. For tied values we take the average of the tied ranks. For example, students number 26 and 29 have the same Y value, 2.9 graduate GPA. They represent ranks 4 and 5. The average $4.5 = (4 + 5)/2$ is assigned to each Y value. Second, we calculate the difference, $d = R_Y - R_X$, between the two ranks for each pair of observations. Third, these differences are squared. Finally, the squared rank differences are added so $\Sigma\, d^2 = 24$.

Table 27.1.
Basic Calculations for Spearman's Rank Correlation Coefficient: College GPA and Graduate GPA Scores of 10 M.B.A. Graduates

Student Number in Sample[a]	Graduate GPA[a] Y	College GPA[a] X	R_y	R_x	$d = R_y - R_x$	$d^2 = (R_y - R_x)^2$
3	3.3	3.7	9.0	9.5	$-.5$	.25
5	2.8	3.1	3.0	5.0	-2.0	4.00
6	3.1	3.0	7.0	4.0	$+3.0$	9.00
8	3.7	3.7	10.0	9.5	$+.5$	.25
14	2.6	2.9	1.0	2.5	-1.5	2.25
18	3.2	3.5	8.0	8.0	0.0	0.00
22	2.7	2.5	2.0	1.0	$+1.0$	1.00
24	3.0	3.3	6.0	7.0	-1.0	1.00
26	2.9	2.9	4.5	2.5	$+2.0$	4.00
29	2.9	3.2	4.5	6.0	-1.5	2.25
					$\Sigma\, d^2 =$	24.00

[a] From Table 21.2.

Chapter 9 Nonparametric Statistics

A simple formula for calculating the Spearman rank correlation coefficient r_s is

(27.1)
$$r_s = 1 - \frac{6 \Sigma d^2}{n^3 - n}$$

where d = difference between the ranks of two paired observations
n = number of paired observations

As in the case with the parametric r correlation coefficient, the value of r_s can range from $+1$, indicating perfect positive correlation, to -1, indicating perfect negative correlation. Formula (27.1) is an approximation if there are ties in either Y or X observations.* But the approximation is good if the number of ties is small in relation to the number of paired observations.

Example 27.1 (continued)

In our case n is 10 and d^2 was found to be 24. Substitution of these values in formula (27.1) yields

$$r_s = 1 - \frac{6(24)}{10^3 - 10}$$
$$= +.855$$

Is the correlation between Y and X variables statistically significant? The null hypothesis is that the parameter rank correlation coefficient ρ_s (where ρ is Greek letter *rho*) is zero and the alternative hypothesis is that ρ_s is not zero. In symbols,

$$H_0: \rho_s = 0$$
$$H_1: \rho_s \neq 0$$

If we expect that the rank correlation coefficient is positive, we can restate the alternative hypothesis that $\rho_s > 0$ for an upper-tailed test; if we expect a negative rank correlation, we can state that $\rho_s < 0$ for a lower-tailed test.

For large or infinite populations and a sample size of no more than 10 paired observations, testing the above hypothesis requires special tables of the probability distribution of r_s. For more than 10 paired observations, the normal distribution may be used as a close approximation for testing the above hypothesis. Then the observed values of r_s are approximately normally distributed about a mean equal to zero with standard deviation

(27.2)
$$s_{r_s} = \frac{1}{\sqrt{n-1}}$$

and a test statistic defined as

(27.3)
$$z_o = \frac{r_s - \rho_s}{1/\sqrt{n-1}}$$

---
*The exact value of r_s can be obtained from formula (21.9) for calculating parameter r using ranks rather than values of the paired observations.

Section 27 Rank Correlation

Since $\rho_s = 0$ according to the null hypothesis, formula (27.3) can be simplified to

(27.4) $$z_o = r_s \sqrt{n - 1}$$

Example 27.1 (continued)

For our illustration let us assume that formula (27.4) is applicable although n is exactly 10 paired observations.

We expect that the ranked pairs of college and graduate GPA scores are positively correlated. So we can formulate the alternative null hypothesis for an upper-tailed test as follows:

H_0: $\rho_s = 0$ (there is zero correlation between the ranked pairs of college and graduate GPA scores)
H_1: $\rho_s > 0$ (the correlation between the ranked pairs is positive)

Suppose we wish to test our null hypothesis at 1 percent significance level. For $\alpha = .01$, the critical z_c value from Appendix D is 2.33. The decision rule is

If $z_o \leq 2.33$, accept H_0 (there is no correlation)
If $z_o > 2.33$, reject H_0 (there is positive correlation)

We have already found that $r_s = +.855$ and n is 10. Substitution of these values in formula (27.4) yields

$$z_o = +.855 \sqrt{10 - 1}$$
$$= 2.57$$

We reject the null hypothesis because the observed z_o value is larger than the critical value 2.33. We conclude that there may be positive correlation between the ranked college and graduate GPA scores.

We have seen that the Spearman rank correlation coefficient like other nonparametric statistics can be easily calculated. Unlike the parametric r, Spearman's r_s works *when one or both variables can be expressed only on a ranking scale*. Furthermore, parametric r is based on the assumption that the underlying relationship between two variables is linear; that is not the case with Spearman's r_s because this nonparametric measure requires only an ever-increasing or ever-decreasing relationship between the two ranked variables which need not be linear.

PROBLEMS

Group One

27.1. For a given n, Σd^2, and α significance level:
    (i) Formulate the null and the alternative hypotheses.
    (ii) Specify the decision rule at the stated significance level.

(iii) Calculate Spearman's r_s.
(iv) Apply the decision rule and interpret the result.
*(a) $n = 20$, $\Sigma d^2 = 91$, $\alpha = .002$; age of principle wage earner and family income
(b) $n = 16$, $\Sigma d^2 = 1221$, $\alpha = .05$; a negative association between years of exposure to noxious chemicals and breathing ability
(c) $n = 18$, $\Sigma d^2 = 736$, $\alpha = .05$; a positive correlation between age and number of days absent from work
(d) $n = 101$, $\Sigma d^2 = 116{,}162$, $\alpha = .01$; dollar size of accounts receivable and length of time before payment

Group Two

27.2. At congressional hearings the shoe industry is criticized for lack of competition. One of the arguments advanced by consumer groups is that there is very little association between the quality of footwear and the prices which consumers pay. As part of the investigation a panel of experts is asked to rank regular men's shoes from 16 manufacturers. These ranks, with 1 representing shoes of the poorest quality, and the corresponding retail prices are shown below:

Shoe Company	Panel's Ranking	Retail Price	Shoe Company	Panel's Ranking	Retail Price
A	2	$10.50	I	12	$27.50
B	6	12.95	J	7.5	14.00
C	1	9.95	K	4	13.95
D	16	30.00	L	11	55.95
E	5	13.00	M	15	32.92
F	7.5	15.95	N	9	16.75
G	3	14.00	O	13	15.25
H	14	29.95	P	10	14.95

(a) Formulate the null and the alternative hypotheses. Is this a two-sided or a one-sided (upper or lower) test?
(b) Specify the decision rule at .005 significance level.
*(c) Does the evidence refute the criticism? Explain.

27.3. Gordon Freling is the marketing manager of Discount Stores Inc. Gordon feels that this year buyers are more sensitive to prices for appliances. To check on this possibility as well as on other matters, Gordon studies periodically the response of a carefully selected panel of regular customers. Last time the panel's response showed an $r_s = -.675$ between the preferences and prices of 15 different types of dryers. Correlation was significant at 1 percent level. This year the panel's response yielded a Σd^2 equal to 1056 on the 15 dryers.
(a) Calculate r_s and test at .01 level of significance.
(b) Other things being equal, does the test result support Gordon's hunch?

27.4. Do factors such as closeness of recent elections, registration procedures, age, race, and education affect voter registration rates? Three scholars set out to study this

Answers to asterisked (*) problems are appended.

Section 27   Rank Correlation

and other questions. As a first step they carried out a simple regression and correlation analysis of registration and voting turnout rates as a percent of the voting age population in 104 of the largest cities in the United States. A random sample of paired observations for 15 cities is shown below:

Registration Rate	Turnout Rate	Registration Rate	Turnout Rate
92.6	71.6	74.0	63.3
90.4	80.3	71.2	50.5
87.7	76.5	70.7	46.6
84.9	73.1	67.7	60.2
81.9	69.3	59.0	32.4
81.7	71.1	46.5	31.2
78.8	68.3	33.8	25.6
77.1	67.0		

Calculate r_s and test at .001 significance level. For the results of the study see E. R. Tufte, "Registration and Voting," in J. M. Tanur, F. Mosteller, et al., eds., *Statistics: A Guide to the Unknown* (San Francisco: Holden-Day, 1972), pp. 153–61.

Chapter 10

TIME SERIES ANALYSIS AND INDEX NUMBERS

All the techniques we have introduced so far dealt with cross-sectional data, that is, data where observations are recorded at one point of time. Now we turn to the study of time series, that is, values of a variable which are recorded over several time periods. Both categories of statistical information are helpful in making managerial decisions in the private as well as in the public sector of our economy. For example, a firm manufacturing building supplies may conduct a survey to assess the demand for energy-saving insulation material (cross section); the same firm may relate the collected data to housing starts (time series) for forecasting future demand for such material.

Depending on type of economic activity and usage, the observations of time series are reported on the basis of a variety of time periods. Stock prices, for example, are usually quoted daily; car loadings are recorded weekly. Many time series in employment, wages, production, finance, and sales are reported monthly. National time series, on the other hand, such as the gross national product (GNP) and the balance of payments account are quoted on a quarterly or on an annual basis.

Although both cross-sectional data and time series are valuable for making decisions, the time-dependence nature of time series makes such series particularly important for forecasting. And peering into the future is essential for planning and control of business as well as nonbusiness operations. For example, a garment manufacturer may decide when and what quantities of merchandise to manufacture by projecting past times series of sales into next season. An electric company may determine the need to increase its generating capacity several years into the future on the basis of past growth rates for power. Economists may use sophisticated mathematical models in order to predict the future state of our economy.

Scholars have studied historical time series intensively in an attempt to unravel the factors which may explain the ups and downs of economic activity. This intensive effort has yielded a wide variety of forecasting methods ranging from pure subjective to computer-based mathematical or econometric models. The set of such procedures which use data arranged in chronological order is called *time series analysis*. Our primary subject of discussion is the so-called *clas-*

sical time series model. This type of analysis does not focus on identifying the factors which may explain changes in economic activity. Time series may be affected by a multitude of domestic and international factors such as changes in weather, population composition and size, capital formation, technology, energy, customs, consumer preferences, government policies, and many others.

The task of identifying and measuring such determinants of change and then relating them mathematically to time series would have been formidable and impractical. Instead, classical time series analysis is basically a descriptive method; it attempts to decompose a time series into the following four time series components of variation:

$$T = \text{secular trend}$$
$$C = \text{cyclical fluctuations}$$
$$S = \text{seasonal variations}$$
$$I = \text{irregular movements}$$

The classical time series model combines four components into a simple equation of the form

(I) $$\boxed{Y = T \times C \times S \times I}$$

where Y denotes the values of the original time series.

This is a *multiplicative model;* it assumes that the numerous explanatory factors associated with each time series component can be multiplied to provide the value of the dependent variable Y.

Secular trend or simply *trend* is a gradual growth or decline of a time series over a long period of time. For describing the trend of a time series it may be necessary to consider a minimum of 15 to 20 years. Trends are thought to be attributable to long-run changes in factors such as population, technology, energy, or consumer preferences. For example, Fig. I(a)* shows the original time series of monthly housing starts from 1960 through 1978 with a linear trend fitted to the original data. Note that in the graph of a time series the horizontal axis represents time and the vertical axis represents the variable of interest. The trend indicates that during this period of 19 years, housing starts increased by a moderate annual increment. Later, we shall find out that this increase has averaged about 29,000 housing starts per year. Other time series may display a long-run declining trend. For example, relatively less expensive labor supply in the southern states as well as other factors such as synthetic fibers brought about a long-run decline of cotton manufacturing in New England. During 1921–25, cotton spindles in place averaged 18.7 million per year; 30 years later, during 1951–55, New England claimed an average of only 3.7 million cotton spindles in place.

Cyclical fluctuations or *business cycles* are characterized by wide swings above and below a trend. Such business cycle movements vary in duration from as few as 2 years to as many as 15 years or more. Furthermore, a host of factors may affect not only the duration of a cycle but also its amplitude, that is, the

*Unless otherwise stated, this time series and all others in this chapter are from *Business Statistics* and the *Survey of Current Business*. U.S. Department of Commerce.

percentage rise and fall over the trend line. Figure I(b) shows the cyclical fluctuations of housing starts as a percent from the trend line (=100) for 1960–78. From the lowest to the next lowest point, the first cycle begins during the first half of 1961 and ends during the second half of 1966, a duration of about 5 1/2 years. A second cycle lasts only about 3 1/2 years, from the second half of 1966 to the first half of 1970. Finally, a third cycle covers about 4 1/2 years, from the first half of 1970 to the second half of 1975. In addition, we may recognize a cycle of

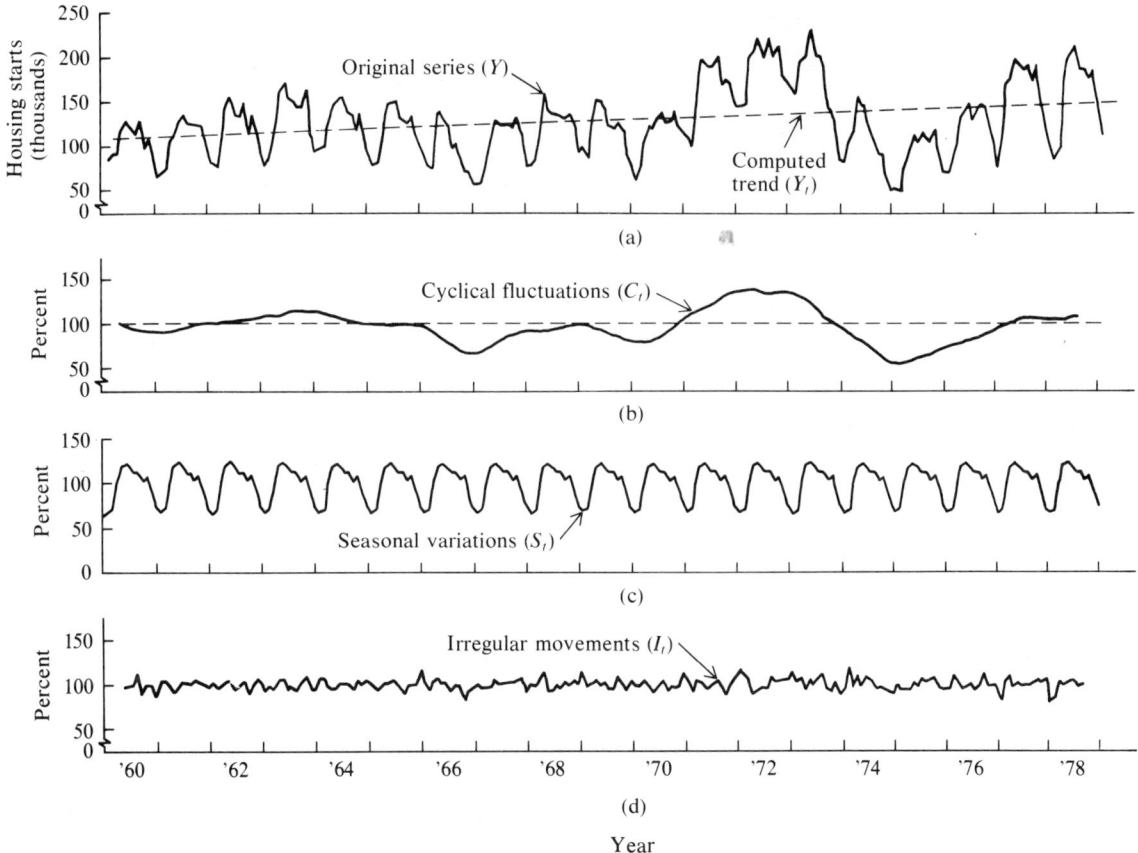

Figure 1.
Time series components of monthly housing starts in the United States, 1960–1978 (number of starts for privately owned houses in thousands).

9 years' duration, from the highest point in 1963 to the next highest point in 1972 or from the lowest point in 1966 to the next lowest point in 1975. Note that prior to 1970 the intensity of cyclical fluctuations is less than after that year.

Seasonal variations are upward and downward movements of a time series which usually recur in an annual pattern. Weather, holidays, and customs in general are considered the major factors for such annual patterns. The seasonal variations of housing starts for 1960–78 are shown in Fig. I(c). Note that for each year, peak activity coincides with the months of April, May, and June in anticipation of summer sales; the lowest volume occurs during December, January, and

February. Other time series display distinct seasonal fluctuations. For example, monthly motor fuel consumption has a pronounced seasonal pattern with the highest volume during the vacation summer months and the lowest during the winter. Department store sales show a moderate peak before Easter and a dramatic increase during the preholiday Christmas season. Although seasonal variations display fairly stable patterns, they are not immune to change over long periods of time.

After the trend, cyclical, and seasonal variations of a time series have been eliminated, the remaining or residual variations are called *irregular movements*. Such changes in time series are short in duration, erratic in nature, and display no discernible pattern. The irregular movements of monthly housing starts for 1960–78 are shown in Fig. I(d). Note that irregular movements appear to be short, jerky, and without a pattern. This is unlike the trend, cyclical, and seasonal variations which according to the classical time series model are considered the collective result of *systematic influences*. In general, irregular movements are attributed to sudden and sporadic occurences such as storms, accidents, strikes, important national and international political events, and erratic changes in consumer behavior.

In contrast to secular trend, cyclical fluctuations, seasonal variations, and irregular movements are frequently called the *fluctuating components* of time series. The classical time series model has a number of limitations which we shall discuss later. Despite these shortcomings, however, the model has been proven a valuable statistical tool. It has been used extensively for the analysis of historical time series. Such analysis has led to a better understanding of the complex nature and underlying probable causes of economic activity, especially cyclical fluctuations. Furthermore, the model can be a useful forecasting device if its descriptive features are supplemented with sound judgment and applied judiciously.

In this chapter we focus primarily on the classical model of time series analysis. In the first section we discuss secular trend and cyclical fluctuations. Then we focus on seasonal variations which together with a brief discussion of forecasting methods occupy the second section. The last section of the chapter deals with the construction and interpretation of index numbers. In its simplest form, an *index number* is a percentage which expresses the *relative* change in a variable compared with some 100 percent base. A sequence of index numbers of the same variable with the same base, such as the annual index numbers of milk prices from 1970 (100) through 1979, forms an *index time series*. Thus time series analysis is largely applicable to index time series as well.

SECTION 28/ SECULAR TREND AND CYCLICAL FLUCTUATIONS

After a brief introduction, we illustrate fitting three types of curves by the method of least squares: linear, parabolic, and exponential. The section ends with a discussion of the importance of trend and cyclical fluctuations to forecasting.

Section 28 Secular Trend and Cyclical Fluctuations

Introduction

Analysis under the classical model involves a separate statistical treatment of the four components of a time series. The first step in this analysis is the procedure for fitting a secular trend to the data of a particular time series. It is important to realize that this procedure requires a systematic and critical examination of the time series under study. In this connection, we should keep in mind four general points: the *purpose of fitting trend lines,* the need for *adjusting the original data,* the *different types of trend movements,* and the *various methods of fitting a trend.*

First, the *purpose* of our analysis is important in the selection of the appropriate period and trend line. Is trend fitting for a historical study, for forecasting, or for studying other components of a time series?

Second, before determining the type of trend we should fit to a time series, it may be necessary to evaluate the original data critically and, if necessary, *adjust the observations.* Are the reported figures consistent with respect to method of data collection, definition of statistical units, geographical area covered, and inflation? Adjustments for calendar variation of monthly or weekly series may be particularly important.

Third, *trend movements* vary for different periods of time within a particular time series. In fact, most time series do not change by an equal *amount* over time; they increase or decrease at a *rate* which itself changes.

The growth of total federal government receipts, mainly from taxes, in current dollars, is similar to the trend line shown in Fig. 28.1(a). For the last several years, receipts have increased at an increasing rate. This means that the absolute annual increase in a given year represents a larger percentage of the total receipts compared to the percentage of the previous year. Figure 28.1(b) shows a time series whose trend values decrease at a decreasing rate. Examples of such a trend are the decline in the number of cotton spindles in place in New England during 1921–55 and of railroad passengers carried in the United States during the 1950s and 1960s. At the start of the period the decline is rapid but it slows with time. Curves of the type shown in Figs. 28.1(a) and (b) are called *exponential.*

Some analysts of time series have adopted biological *growth curves* to describe long-run changes in the output of a firm or industry. Two of the best-known growth curves in statistics are the *logistic* and the *Gompertz.* The general feature of these growth curves is that they are S-shaped like the one shown in Fig. 28.1(c). Output is slow at first, during the period of experimentation, and then increases at an increasing rate. The *inflection point* of the curve indicates a change in the growth pattern. This point signals the beginning of a maturing period for the firm or industry where output increases at a decreasing rate.

The final point in the trend-fitting procedure refers to the *method of isolating a trend.* We may fit a *freehand* trend by inspection. Although in many instances the graphic method of fitting a trend may be satisfactory, the method has a serious disadvantage. For the same time series, different analysts are likely to obtain a different trend. Even the same analyst may not be able to derive exactly the same trend values in different trials. This predominantly subjective derivation of trend may create difficulties for further analysis of the time series.

Also, a trend may be fitted to a time series by the method of a *moving average.* The most widely used moving average method will be introduced in the next section in connection with the analysis of seasonal variations.

Figure 28.1
Three representative types of nonlinear trend movements in time series: (a) Y increases at an increasing rate; (b) Y decreases at a decreasing rate; (c) firm or industry growth curve.

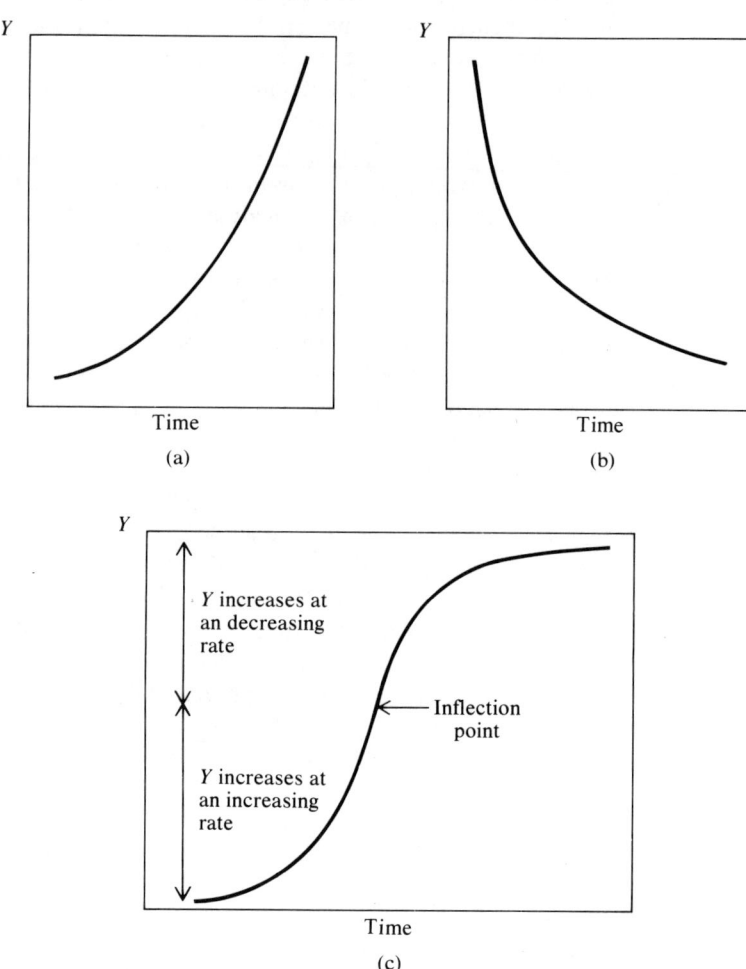

At this point, we concentrate on the mathematical measurement of a trend by the method of *least squares*. The method was used earlier in deriving a regression equation. As in the case of regression, the least-squares trend minimizes the sum of the vertical distances of data points from the trend line. In trend fitting, however, the probabilistic assumptions of the regression model are not met. For example, in fitting a trend to the housing starts series we used the least-squares method. Later, we illustrate the procedure for fitting a trend to the annual data of the series. It is not reasonable to assume that the deviations of actual housing starts from the housing starts computed from the trend equation are random errors. Neither is it reasonable to assume that the number of housing starts for a given year are independent of the housing starts of the preceding year. Because these assumptions as well as the assumptions of equal variance and normality of random errors are not met, we cannot construct interval estimates about the val-

Section 28 Secular Trend and Cyclical Fluctuations

ues of the dependent variable. In trend fitting, the least-squares method is used for its good-fit characteristics.

In the next three subsections, we use the least-squares method to fit a linear, parabolic, and exponential trend to time series.

Fitting a Linear Trend

In regression analysis we used the least-squares method to derive the linear equation of the form

(28.1) $$Y_c = a + bX$$

where X is the independent variable and Y_c is the computed value of the dependent variable Y for a given value of X (see formula 21.1). In time series analysis, we can simplify the computations by transforming the independent variable X, time units, as the deviation x from the middle time unit or mean $\bar{X}$ so that $x = X - \bar{X}$. Therefore, for time series analysis the straight-line equation may be defined as

(28.2) $$Y_t = a + bx$$

where Y_t stands for the *computed* trend value at a given x deviation value from the mean time period. Note that we denote the computed trend value with a t subscript in order to distinguish it from the original series Y and its true trend component T. We shall use this subscript notation in order to distinguish the computed values of the other three components of a series from their true counterpart values as well.

Example 28.1

This transformation of X to x for fitting a linear trend to the annual housing starts series for 1960–78 is illustrated in Table 28.1. The 19 years of the period are numbered successively from 0 for 1960 to 18 for 1978 with a

Table 28.1. Least-Squares Linear Trend Fit to Annual Housing Starts, 1960–78

Year (1)	Year from Center of Period $x = X - 9$ (2)	Housing Starts (Thousands) Y (3)	xY (4)	x^2 (5)	Trend Y_t (6)	Percent of Trend [(3) ÷ (6)] × 100 (7)
1960	−9	1,252	−11,268	81	1,318	95.0
⋮	⋮	⋮	⋮	⋮	⋮	⋮
1968	−1	1,509	−1,509	1	1,550	97.3
1969	0	1,467	0	0	1,579	92.9
1970	1	1,433	1,433	1	1,608	89.1
⋮	⋮	⋮	⋮	⋮	⋮	⋮
1978	9	2,022	18,198	81	1,840	109.9
	0	29,997	16,543	570		

Note: Dots denote intermediate years of the period omitted here for convenience.

Chapter 10 Time Series Analysis and Index Numbers

middle year or mean $\bar{X}$ equal to 9. Then we subtract the mean $\bar{X}$ from every successive time unit number. For instance, for 1960 x is -9 since $0 - 9 = -9$, for 1969 x is 0 since $9 - 9 = 0$, and for 1978 x is 9 since $18 - 9 = 9$. The resulting x deviations are shown under column 2 of the table.

In regression analysis, the formulas for fitting a straight-line equation, (21.3) and (21.4), are given as

(28.3) $$b = \frac{\Sigma xY - n\bar{x}\bar{Y}}{\Sigma x^2 - n\bar{x}^2}$$

and

(28.4) $$a = \bar{Y} - b\bar{x}$$

where deviation x replaces X because of the transformation. We know that the sum of the deviations of all observed values from their mean equals zero. Hence, Σx is zero; therefore $\bar{x}$ is zero because $\bar{x} = \Sigma x/n = 0/n = 0$. So formulas (28.3) and (28.4) can be simplified to

(28.5) $$\boxed{b = \frac{\Sigma xY}{\Sigma x^2}}$$

and

(28.6) $$\boxed{a = \bar{Y} = \frac{\Sigma Y}{n}}$$

where n is the number of time units in the trend period. Note that slope b of (28.5) is the ratio of two sums which can be computed very easily; intercept a is simply the mean of the original Y values of a time series.

Example 28.1 (continued)

The original series for 1960–78 housing starts and the basic computations for finding b and a are shown in Table 28.1, columns 3 through 5. The sums under these columns are as follows:

$$\Sigma Y = 29{,}997, \quad \Sigma xY = 16{,}543, \quad \Sigma x^2 = 570$$

Substitution of these sums and $n = 19$ in formulas (28.5) and (28.6) yields

$$b = \frac{16{,}543}{570} = 29$$

and

$$a = \frac{29{,}997}{19} = 1578.8$$

The straight-line trend equation of form (28.2) is

$$Y_t = 1578.8 + 29x$$

Section 28 Secular Trend and Cyclical Fluctuations

where $x = 0$; origin: July 1, 1969
x = deviations in 1-year intervals
Y_t = housing starts in thousands

We may compute the trend values for any year of the 1960–78 period by substituting in the trend equation the appropriate value for x. For example, for 1960, x is -9 and

$$Y_t = 1578.8 + 29(-9)$$
$$\simeq 1318 \ (\times 1000) \text{ housing starts}$$

For 1969, x is zero and

$$Y_t = 1578.8 + 29(0)$$
$$\simeq 1579 \ (\times 1000) \text{ housing starts}$$

In this manner we can obtain the trend values of housing starts for all 19 years of the period as shown under column 6 in Table 28.1. The values shown under column 7 will be explained later.

The original time series of annual housing starts and their trend values are graphed in Fig. 28.2. The trend is sketched by drawing a straight line through two points representing the values of any two years for the 1960–78 period. For example, we found that $Y_t = 1318$ for 1960 and $Y_t = 1579$ for 1969. We plot the two points on the graph and draw the broken trend line shown in the diagram.

The x deviations with origin at 1969 can be easily transformed back to the original X year values with origin at 1960. We found that $Y_t = 1318$ when $x = -9$. But this is the intercept when $X = x + \bar{X} = 0 = -9 + 9$. So the trend equation shown in Fig. 28.2 is

$$Y_t = 1318 + 29X$$

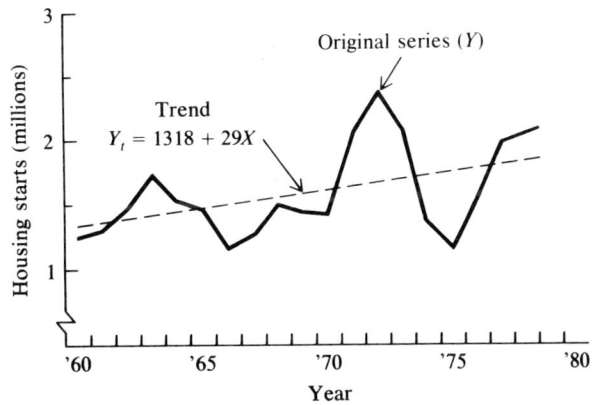

Figure 28.2. Original series and linear trend for annual housing starts, 1960–1978 (number of housing starts for privately owned houses in millions). (Original series and trend values from Table 28.1, columns 3 and 6, respectively.)

where $X = 0$; origin: July 1, 1960
X = deviations in 1-year intervals
Y_t = housing starts in thousands

Since X equals 0 at 1960, the intercept of this equation indicates that housing starts at the beginning of the 1960–78 period stood at 1,318,000 units per year; the slope shows that housing starts during 1960–78 have increased at a constant amount of 29,000 units per year. This least-squares trend is the best fit to the original annual time series. This means that the sum of the squared deviations of the original data from the computed trend is less than from any other straight line, that is, Σx^2 is a minimum sum. And the sum of the deviations is equal to zero, that is, $\Sigma x = 0$; in other words, the total of the deviations above the trend line equals the total deviations below the line.

In general, the trend-fitting procedure raises an important technical point: computing a trend from an even number of time units. In Example 28.1, the trend period contained an odd number of years (19). The average time unit was centered on July 1, 1969, the middle of the year, so successive years were assigned integer x deviations $-1, -2, -3, \ldots$ before and $1, 2, 3, \ldots$ after the 1969 origin. This facilitated the computations shown in Table 28.1. A problem would have arisen, however, if the trend period had contained an even number of years.

Example 28.2

Suppose the trend period for the housing starts series is 1961–78. Then the trend period will contain 18 time units. The origin $x = 0$ will be at 1969 1/2 years or on December 31, 1969. The middle points for 1969 and 1970 will deviate from the new origin by $-1/2$ and $1/2$ year, respectively. And successive years would be assigned fractional x values $-1/2, -3/2, -5/2, \ldots$ before and $1/2, 3/2, 5/2, \ldots$ after the new origin. In order to avoid computations with fractions, we may state the x deviations in terms of half-year intervals. Thus, successive years may be assigned $-1, -3, -5, \ldots$ before and $1, 3, 5, \ldots$ after the origin. Except for this adjustment to x deviations, computation of a straight line trend is the same as shown in Table 28.1. The linear trend equation of housing starts for the 18 years 1961–78 is

$$Y_t = 1597 + 14x$$

where $x = 0$; origin: December 31, 1969
x = deviations in half-year intervals
Y_t = housing starts in thousands

Both intercept and slope values of this equation can be adjusted in order to express the trend equation on an annual basis on July 1, 1969, the middle rather than the end of 1969. The intercept value is reduced by the slope value 14, the half-year incremental change, and the slope value is multiplied by 2. Thus the trend is

$$Y_t = 1583 + 28x$$

Section 28 Secular Trend and Cyclical Fluctuations

where $x = 0$; origin: July 1, 1969
x = deviations in 1-year intervals
Y_t = housing starts in thousands

Trend projections will be discussed later.

Deriving a Parabolic Trend

A straight-line equation describes a situation where a trend increases or decreases by a constant amount per time unit. In the real world, very few time series are likely to change linearly over a long period of time. For example, we fit a linear trend to the series for housing starts largely for illustrative purposes; looking at Fig. I of the introduction to this chapter, it is apparent that a nonlinear curve might have been a better fit. In fact, most time series require fitting a nonlinear curve.

The second-degree equation or *parabola* is one such curve. In this type of equation, the amount of change in the dependent variable Y_t does not remain constant over time; it may increase or decrease per time unit. For this reason, a parabola can be an appropriate fit to many time series whose values *change by increasing or decreasing amounts*.

The general form for the parabolic trend curve is

(28.7)*
$$Y_t = a + bx + cx^2$$

where a, b, c are constants, x represents deviations from the origin, and Y_t is the computed trend value. The formula for determining constant b is

(28.8)
$$b = \frac{\Sigma\, xY}{\Sigma\, x^2}$$

the same as formula (28.5) for determining the slope of a linear equation; constants a and c are determined by the following system of equations:

(28.9)
$$\Sigma\, Y = na + c\, \Sigma\, x^2$$
$$\Sigma\, x^2 Y = a\, \Sigma\, x^2 + c\, \Sigma\, x^4$$

Example 28.3

Suppose we decide that the most appropriate trend to the annual gross national product (GNP) series for 1960–78 is a parabola. The series is shown in Table 28.2, columns 1 and 3. The values of GNP are kept in current billions of dollars although trend fitting for forecasting purposes would have required deflating current into constant dollars.

The basic computations for fitting a parabola to the GNP series by the least-squares method are shown in the same table. Again the independent

---

*In a straight-line equation, the independent variable x is raised to the first power, while in a parabola, x is raised to the second power. For this reason, such equations are called first- and second-degree, respectively. These two types of equations as well as others whose variable x is raised to powers higher than the second belong to the family of so-called polynomial functions. They can be easily fit to time series by the least-squares method.

Table 28.2.
Least-Squares Parabolic Trend Fit to Annual Gross National Product, 1960–78

Year (1)	Year from Center of Period $x = X - 9$ (2)	Gross National Product (Billions)[a] Y (3)	xY (4)	x^2 (5)	x^2Y (6)	x^4 (7)	Trend Y_t (8)
1960	−9	506	−4,554	81	40,986	6,561	544
⋮	⋮	⋮	⋮	⋮	⋮	⋮	⋮
1968	−1	869	−869	1	869	1	838
1969	0	936	0	0	0	0	916
1970	1	982	982	1	982	1	1,003
⋮	⋮	⋮	⋮	⋮	⋮	⋮	⋮
1978	9	2,108	18,972	81	170,748	6,561	2,033
	0	20,026	47,148	570	663,118	30,666	

[a] Billions of current dollars.
Note: Dots denote intermediate years of the period omitted here for convenience.

variable, years, is expressed as deviation x from the origin or mean value $\bar{X} = 9$ at 1969 under column 2. The original GNP data and the required products appear under columns 3 through 7 with sums as follows:

$$\Sigma Y = 20{,}026, \quad \Sigma xY = 47{,}148, \quad \Sigma x^2 = 570,$$
$$\Sigma x^2 Y = 663{,}118, \quad \Sigma x^4 = 30{,}666$$

Substitution of the appropriate sums in (28.8) yields

$$b = \frac{47{,}148}{570} \simeq 82.7$$

and in (28.9) with $n = 19$ yields the following system of equations:

$$20{,}026 = 19a + 570c$$
$$663{,}118 = 570a + 30{,}666c$$

Solving this system of equations simultaneously, we find that

$$a \simeq 916 \quad \text{and} \quad c \simeq 4.6$$

Substitution of these constants in (28.7) yields the parabolic trend

$$Y_t = 916 + 82.7x + 4.6x^2$$

where $x = 0$; origin: July 1, 1969
x = deviations in 1-year intervals
Y_t = GNP in billions of current dollars

The computed trend values are shown in column 8 of Table 28.2. Any trend value can be obtained from the parabolic trend by substituting an appropriate value for x. For example, for the base year 1969, x is zero, so

$$Y_t = 916 + 82.7(0) + 4.6(0)$$
$$= 916 \text{ billions of current dollars}$$

For year 1960, x is -9 and

$$Y_t = 916 + 82.7(-9) + 4.6(-9)^2$$
$$\simeq 544 \text{ billions of current dollars}$$

The original time series and their trend values are graphed in Fig. 28.3. Note that, at the origin year 1969, constant $a = 916$ is the trend value; constant $b = 82.7$ is the slope of the parabola; constant $c = 4.6$ is the amount by which trend values decelerate per unit of time before and accelerate after that origin.

The parabola in Fig. 28.3 appears to provide a good fit to the gross national product series. However, we should always guard against mechanically extending the series into the future. Projecting the trend line is only justified if an analysis of all the underlying factors which determine the trend do not signal a change in the direction of the series. Trend projecting will be further discussed after we show fitting a third type of trend.

Deriving an Exponential Trend Curve

Earlier, we pointed out that trend fitting requires a systematic and critical examination of a particular time series. And we have seen that each trend assumes a particular type of long-run behavior. A straight-line trend assumes that a time series increases or decreases by a constant amount over time. The underlying assumption of a parabolic trend is that a time series increases or decreases by an amount which changes per time unit. For many time series neither a straight-line trend nor a parabolic trend provides a good fit to the data. For example, some time series increase or decrease exponentially, that is, by a constant percentage over time, and the best fit is an *exponential* trend.

Example 28.4

A time series which during the past several years has increased exponentially is the total of federal government receipts, mainly taxes. The graph of the series for 1960–78 and its exponential trend are shown in Fig. 28.4. For

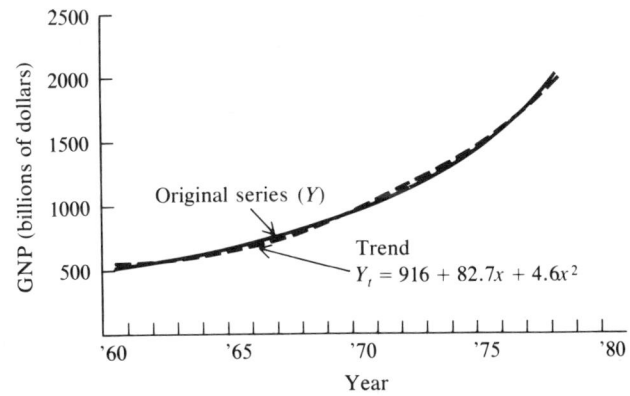

Figure 28.3. Original series and parabolic trend for gross national product, 1960–1978 (billions of 1978 dollars).

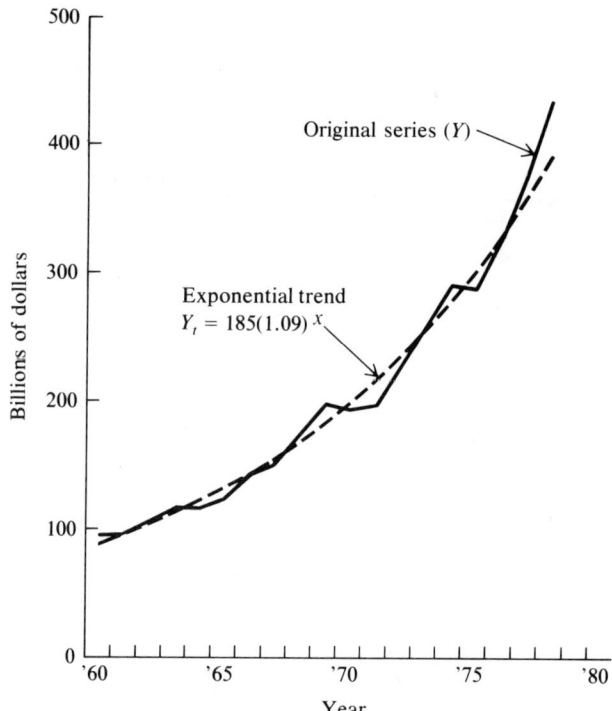

Figure 28.4.
Exponential trend fitted to total federal government receipts, 1960–1978 (billions of 1978 dollars).

illustrating the method of fitting an exponential trend the series is kept in current billions of dollars instead of being deflated into constant dollars.

The general form of such an increasing exponential curve is

(28.10) $$Y_t = ab^x$$

where a is the intercept at $x = 0$, b is called the base and is always positive, and x is the deviations from the origin. By contrast, the volume of railroad passengers declined exponentially during the 1950s and 1960s. The general form of an exponentially declining series such as railroad passengers is the same as in (28.10) with the only difference that x has a negative sign.

Fitting an exponential trend to a series is facilitated by expressing (28.10) in logarithmic terms as

(28.11) $$\boxed{\log Y_t = \log a + x \log b}$$

Note that (28.11) is a linear equation where $\log a$ is the intercept and $\log b$ the slope. This means that an exponential curve of form (28.10) is a straight line if graphed on semilogarithmic paper.

Section 28 Secular Trend and Cyclical Fluctuations

Example 28.4 (continued)

According to Fig. 28.4, the exponential trend function is

$$Y_t = 185(1.09)^x$$

According to formula (28.11), this trend function can be converted to a logarithmic function

$$\log Y_t = \log 185 + x \log 1.09$$

From Appendix I we find that

$$\log Y_t = 2.6272 + .03607x$$

How this logarithmic trend and the trend values are obtained is explained next.

The formulas for fitting a logarithmic trend (28.11) to a series are given as

(28.12)
$$\log b = \frac{\Sigma \, x \log Y}{\Sigma \, x^2}$$

and

(28.13)
$$\log a = \frac{\Sigma \log Y}{n}$$

Note that these formulas are analogous to formulas (28.5) and (28.6) we used earlier to compute an arithmetic straight line. The only difference is that we must find the logarithms of slope b and intercept a. For that, logarithms have replaced the values of variable Y.

Example 28.4 (continued)

The original time series of federal government receipts for 1960–78 and the deviations from the origin year 1969 are shown in Table 28.3, columns 1 through 3. The logarithms for the Y values under column 4 were obtained from Appendix I. The basic computation under columns 4 through 6 yield the following sums:

$$\Sigma \log Y = 43.077, \qquad \Sigma \, x \log Y = 20.5607, \qquad \Sigma \, x^2 = 570$$

Substitution in formulas (28.12) and (28.13) yields

$$\log b = \frac{20.5607}{570} = .03607$$

and for $n = 19$

$$\log \alpha = \frac{43.077}{19} = 2.2672$$

Therefore, the logarithmic trend equation is

$$\log Y_t = 2.2672 + .03607x$$

Table 28.3: Logarithmic Trend Curve Fit to Total Federal Government Receipts, 1960–1978	Year (1)	Year from Center of Period $x = X - 9$ (2)	Government Receipts (Billions)^a Y (3)	log Y (4)	x log Y (5)	x^2 (6)	Trend Y_t (7)
	1960	−9	96.1	1.9827	−17.84 43	81	87.6
	⋮	⋮	⋮	⋮	⋮	⋮	⋮
	1968	−1	174.7	2.2422	−2.2422	1	170.3
	1969	0	197.0	2.2945	0	0	185.0
	1970	1	192.1	2.2835	2.2835	1	201.0
	⋮	⋮	⋮	⋮	⋮	⋮	⋮
	1978	9	431.4	2.6349	23.7141	81	390.9
		0		43.0770	20.5607	570	

^{a}Billions of current dollars.
Note: Dots denote intermediate years of the period omitted here for convenience.

where $x = 0$; origin: July 1, 1969
x = deviations in 1-year intervals
$\log Y_t$ = logarithm of receipts

From this equation we can obtain the trend values shown under column 7 in Table 28.3. For example, for 1960, $x = -9$, so

$$\log Y_t = 2.2672 + .03607(-9)$$
$$\simeq 1.9426$$

and

$$Y_t = \text{antilog }(1.9426) \simeq 87.6 \text{ billions of current dollars*}$$

A logarithmic straight line avoids the troublesome problem of curvature. However, for very long periods of time the growth curve becomes too optimistic. This is so because the line increases indefinitely at a geometric rate. The reverse may be true with a decreasing logarithmic curve. It tends to be too pessimistic.

In the search for finding the best fit to a time series, it may be helpful to plot the data on both arithmetic and semilogarithmic paper. Scatter diagrams of this type may be useful guides for finding the best fit. Also, fitting a trend curve of

*We can obtain the exponential function sketched in Fig. 28.4 from the computed logarithmic function

$$\log Y_t = 2.672 + .03607x$$

Since $\log a = 2.2672$,

$$a = \text{antilog }(2.2672) = 185$$

and since $\log b = .03607$,

$$b = \text{antilog }(.03607) = 1.0867 \simeq 1.09$$

Therefore,

$$Y_t = 185(1.09)^x$$

Section 28 Secular Trend and Cyclical Fluctuations

third or higher degree is feasible. However, such curves may obscure attempts to separate trend and cyclical fluctuations; they may follow too closely the cyclical swings of a series by permitting too many changes in direction.

Cyclical Fluctuations and Trend Projecting

As mentioned earlier, seasonal variations repeat their pattern within each year. Therefore, deviations of annual time series from the trend line are attributable to the other two fluctuating components of the series: cyclical fluctuations and irregular movements. In other words, for annual time series the classical multiplicative model reduces to

(28.14) $$Y = T \times C \times I$$

where Y = original time series
T = trend values
C = cyclical fluctuations
I = irregular movements

Seasonal variations are absent because this fluctuating component of the series occurs within a year. The nonseasonal fluctuating components can be isolated by dividing the annual data of each year by the corresponding computed trend value. Thus

(28.15) $$\frac{Y}{Y_t} \times 100 = \frac{T \times C \times I}{T} = C \times I$$

By convention these deviations are multiplied by 100 in order to express the result of this division as a percentage of trend. Cyclical fluctuations, however, represent the dominant component. Hence, a study of deviations from trend essentially amounts to an analysis of cyclical fluctuations. Note that the leftmost term of expression (28.15) represents what is actually done to eliminate the computed trend values from the original series. The other two terms of the expression are idealizations of this operation in terms of the classical time series model.

Example 28.5

The deviation of annual housing starts as a percent of the linear trend value, which we computed earlier, is shown in Fig. 28.5. These percentage devia-

Figure 28.5. Housing starts as percent of trend; 1960–1978. (Data from Table 28.1, column 7)

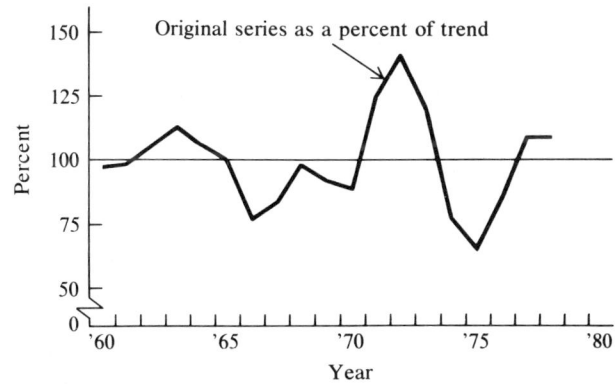

tions appear in column 7, Table 28.1. They were obtained by dividing the housing starts of each year under column 3 by the corresponding trend value under column 6 and multiplying by 100. Thus, the original time series are expressed as percentages above or below the trend curve representing 100 percent. As noted earlier, the cyclical swings of the series are more pronounced since 1970 than in earlier years. This development may be attributed partially to the antiinflation policies of the Federal Reserve System which changed mortgage interest rates, thus affecting the number of housing starts.

The same procedure is used to express nonseasonal fluctuating components as a percent of trend values obtained from exponential, logarithmic, or other equations. Sometimes the nonseasonal fluctuating components are expressed in terms of *relative cyclical residuals* defined as

(28.16) $$\frac{Y - Y_t}{Y_t} \times 100$$

This means that, instead of dividing the original data by the corresponding trend value, we first subtract the trend value from the corresponding original data; then we divide this difference by the trend value and multiply by 100. For 1960, for example, housing starts and trend value were 1252 and 1318, respectively. The deviation is 95 percent of trend shown in Table 28.1, column 7. By formula (28.16) the corresponding relative cyclical residual is

$$\frac{1252 - 1318}{1318} \times 100 = -5 \text{ percent}$$

A graph of relative cyclical residuals will be identical to the one shown in Fig. 28.5. The only difference would be that the fluctuations will be around a zero baseline, with pluses above and minuses below the line.

Both deviations from trend and relative cyclical residuals measure the sensitivity of the fluctuating components of an annual time series. Sensitivity depends on the amplitude, that is, the height, as well as frequency of the swings above or below the trend or zero line. The larger the amplitude and the more frequent the swings are, the more sensitive a series.

The question is: How do the nonseasonal fluctuating components of a time series relate to trend projections? Generally speaking, projecting these fluctuating components of a time series with some degree of reliability is a difficult task. Yet this limitation is not serious for reliable long-run trend projecting, if we keep in mind a number of important considerations.

First, reliable trend projecting depends on the selection of an appropriate *trend period* as well as the *type of trend curve*. This selection is important because a reliable projection assumes that the factors which affected the series in the past will continue to operate in the future.

Example 28.6

Suppose the management of Mayflower Lumber Corporation wishes to estimate the long-run demand for lumber. Trend projections of housing starts may be one of the bases for estimating such a demand. We may project the trend of housing starts by the graphic method. We can simply extend the straight-line trend in Fig. 28.2 beyond the year 1978. If the trend is plotted on detailed coordinate paper, we may be able to read the approximate projected value from the charts.

Exact projections can be obtained by substituting the appropriate value of X years into the trend equation. Earlier, we found that the trend equation for the housing starts series is

$$Y_t = 1318 + 29X$$

where $X = 0$; origin: July 1, 1960
X = deviations in 1-year intervals
Y_t = housing starts in thousands

Suppose management wishes to predict the trend level of housing starts for 1985. Since $X = 25$ (1985 − 1960), substitution of this X value in the equation yields

$$Y_t = 1318 + 29(25)$$
$$= 2043 \ (\times 1000) \text{ housing starts}$$

Bear in mind, however, that this figure is an extrapolation; its reliability depends on the extent to which the series will exhibit a linear growth pattern for 7 years beyond 1978 similar to the one experienced in the past; the further the projection is into the future, the less reliable it is likely to be. Furthermore, this projection is an estimate of only the trend level in 1985; it is not an annual forecast of actual housing starts. If such a forecast is desired, it would be necessary to combine the trend projections with estimates of the nontrend factors. And we have seen that cyclical and irregular factors contribute to the sensitivity of the series.

Second, trend fitting is *usually applied to series representing physical volume* such as housing starts, telephones in service, and so forth. This limitation is justified on grounds that a trend is considered to describe growth in physical quantities.

Many series, however—on sales, production, and other economic activities such as GNP and government receipts—are available only in current dollars. And dollar value series are affected by the physical quantities of goods and services involved as well as by the prices of these quantities. For forecasting and other purposes, it is necessary to know how much of the change in dollar value may be attributed to a real change in physical quantities and how much to price changes. In order to eliminate the effect of price changes, the dollar values of a time series are divided by an appropriate index which measures changes in the prices of goods and services the series represents. The procedure is called *price deflation;* it expresses current dollar values of a series in terms of dollars with constant purchasing power over a specified base period.

In fitting parabolic and exponential trends, we used time series of GNP and government receipts in current dollars. This was done because our principal objective was to illustrate methods of trend fitting. For trend projecting we need to deflate the current dollar values of these series before fitting a trend. Then after obtaining trend projections we need to adjust the deflated values back to current dollars; we multiply the deflated values by the anticipated change in the deflator price index.

Third, trend analysis is a useful tool for long-run planning for management concerned with a projection of the *trend level* of a series. Consider again that the management of Mayflower Lumber Corporation is interested in estimating the long-run demand for lumber used in building private homes. A trend estimate of housing starts without considering fluctuating components may be an adequate basis for forecasting the long-run demand for lumber.

Fourth, the reliability of trend projections may also depend on the *sensitivity* of the fluctuating components in a time series. We have seen, for example, that the annual series of housing starts is quite sensitive; Figure 28.5 shows that fluctuations of the series from trend are considerable, especially since 1970. Thus, graphing the deviations or the relative cyclical residuals from trend is a valuable aid to trend projecting. Other things being equal, a trend projection of housing starts is not likely to be as reliable as projections with other, less sensitive series. Time series such as the number of electricity or gas customers and number of telephones in service exhibit a trendlike behavior with very small variations attributable to nontrend factors. Some companies use a computer to fit several types of trend curves to a time series; for each trend projection the computer prints out an error band based on the deviations or relative cyclical residuals from trend; then these projections are compared, evaluated subjectively, and modified if necessary.

In the next section, we shall illustrate how trend projecting may be combined with seasonal variations for short-run forecasting.

PROBLEMS

Group One

28.1. Use the appropriate trend equation to compute the trend values shown in:
   (a) Table 28.1, for housing starts
   (b) Table 28.2, for GNP
   (c) Table 28.3, for federal government receipts (taxes)

28.2. Find the projected trend value for 1985 using the appropriate trend equation for:
   *(a) GNP in Example 28.3
   *(b) Federal government receipts (taxes) in Example 28.4
   (c) What kind of adjusting do each of these monetary series need before being used for trend projecting?

28.3. For each time series:
   (i) Compute the relative cyclical residuals using formula (28.16).
   (ii) Prepare a diagram like the one shown in Fig. 28.5; change the vertical scale by subtracting 100 and then plot the residuals.
   *(iii) In terms of amplitude and frequency of swings above and below the zero line, is the particular series more or less sensitive than housing starts?

Answers to asterisked (*) problems are appended. Unless otherwise stated, the sources of all time series are *Business Statistics* and the *Survey of Current Business*, U.S. Department of Commerce.

Section 28 Secular Trend and Cyclical Fluctuations

*(a) Original data for GNP and trend values for the intermediate years not shown in Table 28.2 are as follows:

Year	GNP (Billions) Y	Trend (Billions) Y_t	Year	GNP (Billions) Y	Trend (Billions) Y_t
1961	523	549	1971	1063	1100
1962	564	563	1972	1171	1206
1963	595	585	1973	1307	1320
1964	636	618	1974	1413	1445
1965	688	659	1975	1529	1578
1966	753	709	1976	1700	1720
1967	796	769	1977	1887	1872

*(b) Original data for federal government receipts and trend values for the intermediate years not shown in Table 28.3 are as follows:

Year	Government Receipts (Billions) Y	Trend (Billions) Y_t	Year	Government Receipts (Billions) Y	Trend (Billions) Y_t
1961	98.1	95.2	1971	198.6	218.5
1962	106.2	104.6	1972	227.5	237.5
1963	114.4	113.7	1973	258.3	258.0
1964	114.9	122.1	1974	288.6	280.3
1965	124.3	132.7	1975	286.9	305.3
1966	141.8	144.1	1976	332.3	331.1
1967	150.5	157.4	1977	374.5	359.7

28.4. Discuss briefly the following:
   (a) Trend fitting requires a systematic and critical examination of the time series under study.
   (b) Under what considerations may trend projecting give us reliable forecasts?

28.5. Explain the following terms:
   (a) Fluctuating components of a time series
   (b) Parabolic trend
   (c) Inflection point
   (d) Cyclical fluctuations
   (e) Gompertz curve
   (f) Linear trend
   (g) Classical time series model
   (h) Business cycles
   (i) Least-squares method
   (j) Irregular movements
   (k) Relative cyclical residuals

Chapter 10 Time Series Analysis and Index Numbers

(l) Exponential trend
(m) Seasonal variations
(n) Secular trend
(o) Logistic curve
(p) Logarithmic trend
(q) Price deflation

Group Two

28.6. For 1960–78, the deflated gross national product in 1972 constant dollars is as follows:

Year	GNP (Billions)	Year	GNP (Billions)	Year	GNP (Billions)
1960	737	1967	1008	1973	1235
1961	755	1968	1052	1974	1218
1962	799	1969	1079	1975	1202
1963	831	1970	1075	1976	1275
1964	874	1971	1108	1977	1333
1965	926	1972	1171	1978	1386
1966	981				

(a) Plot this deflated series on the graph shown in Fig. 28.3. What type of trend curve fits best to the series?
*(b) Compute a straight-line trend equation by the method of least squares with origin July 1, 1969. What is the incremental real increase in the gross national product?

28.7. The following annual times series represents millions of telephones in service in the United States for 1970–78:

Year	Telephones (Millions)	Year	Telephones (Millions)
1970	104	1975	132
1971	112	1976	139
1972	117	1977	150
1973	123	1978	150
1974	128		

(a) Sketch the series on ordinary coordinate paper.
*(b) Fit a straight-line by the method of least squares with origin July 1, 1974.
(c) Sketch the trend on the same graph.
(d) Assuming the trend period is sufficiently long, find the trend value for 1988.
(e) Elizabeth Gensay, an analyst for TEL & TEL Corporation, believes that this trend projection is a fairly reliable long-run forecast of the actual number of telephones in service. Do you agree? Discuss in terms of sensitivity of the series and other considerations.

Section 28 Secular Trend and Cyclical Fluctuations 371

28.8. During 1970–78, air cargo in billion of ton-miles carried by airlines in international operations was as follows:

Year	Ton-Miles (Billions)	Year	Ton-Miles (Billions)
1970	1299	1975	2048
1971	1518	1976	2187
1972	1738	1977	2302
1973	1916	1978	2314
1974	2083		

(a) Sketch the series on ordinary coordinate paper.
*(b) Fit a straight-line to the data with origin July 1, 1974.
(c) Sketch the trend on the same graph.
(d) Assuming the trend period is sufficiently long, find the trend value for 1988.
(e) Sharon Landis is a statistician with the U.S. Department of Transportation. What reservations may Sharon have about the reliability of such a projection as a forecast to actual air cargo volume?

28.9. Factory sales of new passenger automobiles from plants in the United States were as follows:

Years	Automobiles (Millions)
1973	9.7
1974	7.3
1975	6.7
1976	8.5
1977	9.2

(a) Plot the series on ordinary coordinate paper allowing space for including later the year 1978.
(b) What type of trend curve does the graph suggest as a best fit to the 1973–77 series?
*(c) Find the trend equation suggested in part (b) by the method of least squares with origin July 1, 1975 and sketch the trend curve on the same graph.
(d) Auto sales in 1978 were about 9 million. Would the trend equation you computed in part (c) fit fairly well if the 1978 data were included? Explain why or why not.
(e) Joe Spivack is an economist working for the National Automobile Workers of America. Among other criteria, Joe uses auto sales projections for estimating employment opportunities for production workers in the automobile industry. Such projections are especially important for preparing

strategies in negotiating a new labor contract. Cite reasons why the equation computed in part (c) would or would not give reliable trend projections.

28.10. During 1975–78, annual demand for gasoline in the United States in millions of barrels (each barrel contains 42 gallons) was as follows:

Year	Gasoline (Million Barrels)
1975	2452
1976	2569
1977	2632
1978	2722

*(a) Fit a straight line by method of least squares with origin July 1, 1975.
(b) Compute the relative cyclical residuals. Do the residuals indicate that the straight-line trend is a good fit?
(c) George MacLeod, the vice-president of Ponoco Oil Company, observes that during the past several years the demand for gasoline has increased by a constant of 87 million barrels per year. Therefore, he concludes that the straight-line equation may be used for reliable long-run trend projections. What important assumption did the vice-president make which supports his conclusion?

28.11. During 1966–78, expenditures of the federal government in billions of current dollars were as follows:

Year	Expenditures (Billions)	Year	Expenditures (Billions)	Year	Expenditures (Billions)
1966	144	1971	221	1975	357
1967	164	1972	245	1976	386
1968	181	1973	265	1977	423
1969	188	1974	299	1978	461
1970	204				

(a) Plot the series on ordinary coordinate paper.
(b) Do the same on semilogarithmic paper.
(c) What type of trend curve do the two graphs suggest as a better fit to the series? Explain.
*(d) Use the series for the years 1974–78 to fit a logarithmic straight line with origin July 1, 1976.
(e) Convert the logarithmic equation into an exponential equation. What is the percentage rate with which government expenditures have grown during 1974–78?
(f) What kind of adjusting does the series need before using it for trend projecting?

SECTION 29/ SEASONAL VARIATIONS

Seasonal peaks and troughs of economic activity recur in a pattern which repeats itself over a period of a year or less duration. We have already seen that housing starts have a distinct annual seasonal pattern. By comparison, payment of dividends and corporate taxes are characterized by quarterly seasonal movements. Payroll departments operate with cash inflow-outflow cycles of a month or less. Most public eating places exhibit two distinct rhythms of economic activity, a daily cycle and a weekday-weekend cycle.

Besides duration, seasonal variations may vary in intensity depending on the stage of a "production" process. For example, in many product lines, such as cotton textiles, seasonal movements are more pronounced at the origin (cotton crops) and the point of consumption (fashion of cotton goods) than at the intermediate manufacturing stages. Supply of grain, such as wheat, is markedly seasonal, while consumption, such as bread, is fairly steady over a year. In general, production and sales time series exhibit less seasonal variation than inventory series and more seasonal variation than price time series. Few business as well as nonbusiness organizations are free of seasonal variations in their activities.

As in the case of secular trend, construction of seasonal indices serves two major objectives: forecasting and further analysis of a time series. While trend projecting is the basis for long-run forecasting, measuring seasonal variations provides the basis for short-run planning. In addition, construction of seasonal indices may serve a second purpose. Seasonal indices may be used for deseasonalizing the original data. Removing the seasonal effect from a time series facilitates studying the other fluctuating components, cyclical as well as irregular.

In this section, we focus our attention on the analysis of monthly seasonal variations whose cycle has 1 year duration. The analysis, however, is equally applicable to quarterly time series. Quarterly series appear among the problems of the section. First, we introduce the ratio-to-moving-average method for isolating seasonal variations and constructing an index. Then we show how seasonal indices may be used for short-run forecasting and for further analysis of a time series.

Ratio-to-Moving-Average Method

Several methods, ranging from a graphic approach to computer-based programs, exist for computing seasonal indices. Regardless of method, however, we may first have to adjust our series for inconsistencies, especially for calendar variation, as pointed out earlier. Then we plot the series on a chart in order to study the general nature of the seasonal fluctuations. Seasonal measurement may not be worthwhile unless our series exhibit a stable seasonal pattern where the peaks and troughs generally occur during the same months each 12-month period. For example, the graph of our monthly housing starts series for 1960–78, shown in Fig. I(a) at the beginning of this chapter, exhibits a stable seasonal pattern. In general, peak activity coincides with the summer months, especially May through July, and troughs occur during the December-February winter months. The full cycle repeats itself within a 12-month period. For series having a stable pattern, the period for seasonal analysis should be at least 6 to 7 years. A longer period may be necessary for averaging out pronounced irregular movements. This was one of the reasons for choosing a 19-year period for analyzing the housing starts series. A change in the seasonal pattern requires special handling.

In trend analysis, we expressed the original annual series as percent of trend. Then these percentage deviations were considered to measure the cyclical and, to some extent, the irregular movements of a series. By analogy, for isolating seasonal variation it would have been desirable to express the original monthly series as a percent of some baseline which would contain the trend, cyclical, and irregular components of the series. But this ideal approach is not feasible. Most refined methods express the original data for a given month as percent of a trend-cycle base in several years; then they average these percentage deviations by months in order to eliminate the irregular movements and isolate the seasonal component of the series.

One such technique is the *ratio-to-moving-average method,* which we illustrate here. It consists of two phases. In the *first phase,* the original monthly series are expressed as a percentage of a 12-month moving average. This is an annual average of the original monthly data successively advanced 1 month at a time. In terms of the components of the classical time series model (trend T, cyclical C, seasonal S, and irregular I), the procedure may be expressed in symbols as follows:

$$(29.1) \qquad \frac{Y}{M_t} \times 100 = \frac{T \times C \times S \times I}{T \times C} = S \times I$$

where Y = original monthly data
M_t = 12-month moving average

Since the moving average M_t is of 12 months' duration, seasonal variations are excluded. Also, irregular movements tend to cancel out when they are averaged over a year's period. Hence, a 12-month moving average tends to include only the trend and the cyclical components, that is, $M_t \simeq T \times C$. Dividing the original monthly data by the moving average M_t eliminates the trend and cyclical fluctuations from the original data. The result represents the seasonal and irregular components of the monthly series, that is, $S \times I$, expressed as a percentage of the moving average.

Example 29.1

The computational steps for the first phase of the method for our housing starts series with 1960–78 base period are shown in Table 29.1.

First, we obtain a 12-month moving total shown in column 3. The first total, 1252, is the sum of the 12 monthly data for 1960 shown in column 2. Then the January 1960 original figure is subtracted and the January 1961 figure is added to the first total in order to obtain the second total, 1236. Thus the 12-month total is successively advanced 1 month at a time until the last 12-month moving total 2022 is obtained for 1978. The three dots in each column represent the missing figures; they reduce the table to a convenient size. Of course, moving totals cannot be calculated for the first 6 and the last 6 months of the base period.

Table 29.1.
Basic Calculations for Seasonal Indices for New Housing Starts, 1960–78 (Data in Thousands)

Month (1)	Original Data: Housing Starts Y (2)	12-Month Moving Total (3)	Sum of Two Successive 12-Month Totals (4)	Monthly Moving Average M_t $\left(\dfrac{\text{column 4}}{24}\right)$ (5)	Original Data as a Percentage of Moving Average $\dfrac{Y}{M_t} \times 100$ $\left(\dfrac{\text{column 2}}{\text{column 5}} \times 100\right)$ (6)
1960:					
Jan.	86				
Feb.	91				
March	91				
April	123				
May	130				
June	123				
		1252			
July	114		2488	103.7	109.9
		1236			
Aug.	130		2455	102.3	127.1
		1219			
Sept.	97		2451	102.1	95.0
		1232			
Oct.	110		2454	102.3	107.5
		1222			
Nov.	93		2442	101.8	91.4
		1220			
Dec.	64		2452	102.2	62.6
⋮	⋮	⋮	⋮	⋮	⋮
1978:					
		2026			
Jan.	89		4054	168.9	52.7
		2028			
Feb.	101		4053	168.9	59.8
		2025			
March	172		4053	168.9	101.8
		2028			
April	198		4055	169.0	117.2
		2027			
May	211		4058	169.1	124.8
		2031			
June	216		4053	168.9	127.9
		2022			
July	192				
Aug.	191				
Sept.	181				
Oct.	192				
Nov.	159				
Dec.	120				

Note: Dots denote intermediate years of the period omitted here for convenience.

Second, the 12-month moving totals are centered in the middle of each year, that is, the end of June 30. They must be adjusted so that each monthly moving average is centered on the 15th of each month. For this adjustment we obtain the sum of two successive 12-month totals as shown in column 4. For example, the first sum, 2488, is obtained by adding the two first 12-month totals from column 3, 1252 and 1236. The second sum, 2455, is the result of adding the second (1236) and the third (1219) 12-month totals.

Third, we divide each sum under column 4 by 24, the number of included monthly figures, to obtain a monthly average as shown under column 5. This procedure centers each average on the 15th of each month. For example, the first monthly moving average of 103.7 ($\times 1000$) housing starts is centered on July 15, 1960.

Fourth, we express the original monthly data as a percentage of the 12-month moving average as shown under column 6. For example, the original monthly 114 ($\times 1000$) housing starts for July 15, 1960 under column 2 is divided by the corresponding average 103.7 under column 5 and multiplied by 100 to yield 109.9 percent shown under column 6. The last figure means that housing starts in July 15, 1960 were 9.9 percent above the trend-cycle level.

What does this first computational phase for measuring seasonal variations accomplish? We may assess results visually by sketching on a graph the major steps of the procedure. The original monthly series of housing starts and the monthly moving average (columns 2 and 5 in Table 29.1, respectively) are sketched in Fig. 29.1(a). As explained earlier, the original series exhibit a stable seasonal pattern. The smooth, snakelike curve through the graph of the original series is the monthly moving average; it is the baseline which contains a slow-growing trend and cyclical fluctuations. As pointed out earlier, business cycles are especially pronounced during the second half of the 1960–78 base period. The graph of the original monthly series as a percentage of this trend-cycle base line (column 6 in Table 29.1) is shown in Fig. 29.1(b). Note that the trend and cycle components of the original series are no longer present. The graph exhibits only the presence of $S \times I$, the seasonal and irregular components of the series. These residual values are referred to as *percentage of moving averages*.

Figure 29.1
Original series, moving average, and percentage of moving average for monthly housing starts, 1960–78 (number of starts for privately owned houses in thousands).

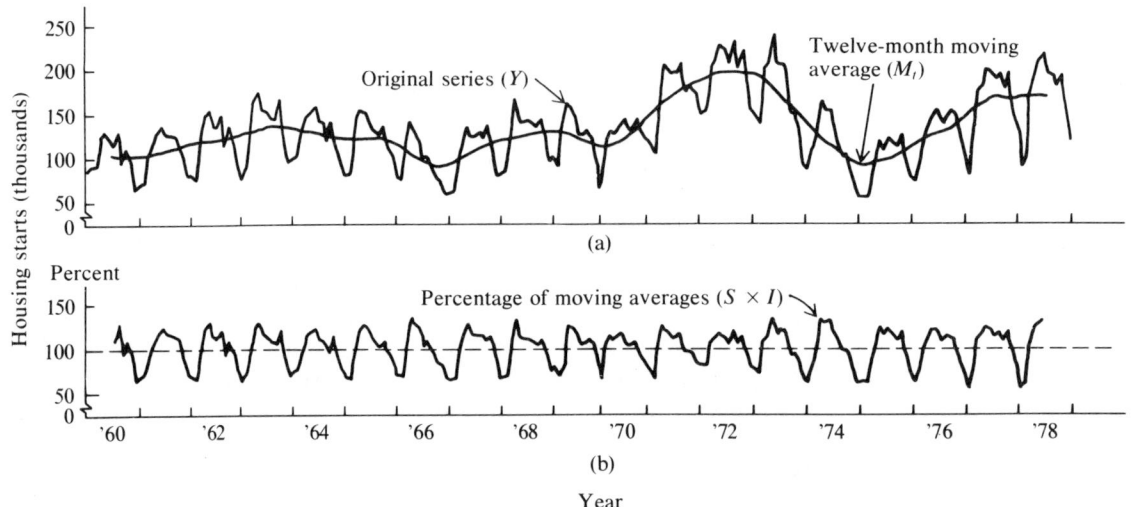

Section 29 Seasonal Variations

Removing the effect of irregular movements from the percentage of moving averages is the *second phase* of the procedure for constructing seasonal indices. The classical model assumes that the value of the particular month is raised or lowered by short-term random disturbances from the level at which it would have otherwise been. For a particular month, these disturbances will have a positive effect in some years and a negative one in other years. Over a period of several years, however, their net effect will be zero. Assuming a constant seasonal level for the same month from one year to the next, variations in the percentage of moving averages must be attributed to the irregular component. Therefore, we may be able to remove the irregular movements and identify the seasonal component of a series as the average of the percentage of moving averages for each month.

The procedure of averaging out irregular movements may be accomplished either by selecting the median or calculating a modified mean from all percentages of moving averages for each month. We shall use the modified mean approach in our illustration.

Example 29.1 (continued)

The second phase for constructing seasonal indices for our housing starts series is shown in Table 29.2.

First, we group the percentage moving average of each month for all 18 years of the base period under a separate column.

Second, we omit the largest and smallest percentage moving averages from each monthly column. According to the classical time series model, these extreme averages are dominated by irregular factors and therefore are excluded. For example, consider the percentage moving averages 92.5 and 114.3 for September 1962 and 1976, respectively, shown in Table 29.2. They are omitted with a slash because they represent the smallest and the largest percentage moving averages for September.

Third, we divide the total of the remaining percentages of moving averages under each monthly column by 16. The result is the modified means (because of the exclusion of the two extreme averages), shown in a separate row.

Fourth, these modified means are preliminary indices adding up to 1196.2. Since this total is less than 1200, the 12 preliminary indices need to be adjusted so they can average 100 percent. To accomplish this we multiply each modified mean by the adjustment factor $1200/1196.2 = 1.0032$. This adjustment raises each modified mean by the same .32 percentage point, thus forcing their values to total 1200. The seasonal indices S_t for our housing starts series appear at the last row of the table.

The graph of seasonal variation S_t for the housing starts is shown in Fig. I(c) at the beginning of this chapter.

The above ratio-to-moving-average method is equally applicable to quarterly time series for the construction of quarterly seasonal indices:

1. Obtain the 4-quarter moving totals.
2. Find the sum of two successive 4-quarter moving totals.

Table 29.2:
Calculation of Monthly Seasonal Indices From Percentage of Moving Average for New Housing Starts, 1960–78 (Data in Thousands)

Year	Percentage of Monthly Moving Averages											
	J	F	M	A	M	J	J	A	S	O	N	D
1960							109.9	~~127.1~~	95.0	107.5	91.4	62.6
1961	67.8	71.4	99.3	106.1	119.1	124.2	115.6	114.9	112.9	110.6	89.1	70.2
1962	69.1	64.9	97.5	128.7	129.0	112.9	112.5	121.0	~~92.5~~	108.6	96.3	74.0
⋮	⋮	⋮	⋮	⋮	⋮	⋮	⋮	⋮	⋮	⋮	⋮	⋮
1976	63.8	77.3	98.9	112.3	119.1	121.5	106.7	112.6	~~114.3~~	107.9	89.9	73.6
1977	54.2	73.6	111.0	114.0	123.5	120.1	114.5	117.0	107.7	116.4	92.9	76.7
1978	~~52.7~~	~~59.8~~	101.8	117.2	124.8	127.9						
Modified means:	66.9	69.9	100.1	118.7	123.0	118.9	112.2	112.3	102.5	108.3	90.9	72.5

Total of modified means: 1196.2
Adjustment factor: $1200/1196.2 \simeq 1.0032$

| Seasonal Indices S_i: | 67.1 | 70.1 | 100.4 | 119.1 | 123.4 | 119.3 | 112.6 | 112.7 | 102.8 | 108.6 | 91.2 | 72.7 |

^aDots denote intermediate years of the period omitted here for convenience.
Source: Table 29.1, column 6.

Section 29 Seasonal Variations

3. Divide each sum by 8, the number of included quarterly figures, to find a quarterly moving average centered in the middle of each quarter.
4. Divide the original quarterly series by the corresponding quarterly moving average to find the percentage of moving averages.
5. Group the percentage of moving averages of each quarter for all the years of the base period under a separate column.
6. Omit the largest and the smallest percentage of moving averages from each quarterly column.
7. Find the modified means or preliminary seasonal indices by dividing the remaining percentage of moving averages for each quarter by the number of years.
8. Find the seasonal quarterly indices by adjusting the modified means so they can add up to 400 or a 100 percent average.

Before discussing the use of seasonal indices for forecasting and time series analysis, it is desirable to make a few general remarks about the above procedure. Although the ratio-to-moving-average method is the most frequently used technique for constructing seasonal indices, it yields rough and approximate results. Usually, the moving average contains the trend and *most* of the cyclical fluctuations. Consequently, the percentage of moving averages may contain some of the cyclical fluctuations in addition to the seasonal and irregular components of a series. Furthermore, the modified means (or the medians for that matter) may not completely eliminate irregular movements from the percentage of moving averages. In spite of these reservations, however, the ratio-to-moving-average method yields reasonable results for a series exhibiting a stable seasonal pattern. Unlike seasonal variations, which have a fixed duration and a fairly regular amplitude, cyclical fluctuations vary in both respects. As a result, the seasonal rhythm of a time series can be measured and projected with a greater degree of accuracy than cyclical fluctuations.

Seasonal Forecasting

In the previous section we have shown how and discussed when trend projecting may be a reliable data base for long-run planning. Here, we concentrate on seasonal forecasting. For a series which is not too sensitive to cyclical and irregular influences, seasonal forecasting is an important part in short-run business planning. It requires two steps: projecting monthly trend values for a year and then adjusting these trend values to reflect the influence of seasonal variations.

Usually, a trend equation is derived from the annual data of a time series. This is desirable in order to eliminate the influence of seasonal variations and irregular movements which are considered to occur in less than 1-year periods. For seasonal forecasting, on the other hand, we need to project monthly trend values. To find these values we need to convert the initially derived trend equation from an annual to a monthly basis.

Example 29.2

Real Estate Associates (REA) is a real estate brokerage firm with branch offices in many cities throughout the United States. At the end of each year research focuses on estimating the monthly supply of private houses. And seasonal forecasts of new housing starts for 1979 is part of this research effort.

In Example 28.1, we found that the annual trend equation for our housing starts series was

$$Y_t = 1318 + 29X$$

where $X = 0$; origin: July 1, 1960
X = deviations in 1-year intervals
Y_t = housing starts in thousands

Conversion of this equation to monthly values involves the following steps:

First, we divide both the intercept 1318 and the slope 29 by 12. Since the new intercept is 109.8 = 1318/12 and the slope is 2.4167 = 29/12, the new equation is

$$Y_t = 109.8 + 2.4167X$$

Second, the new slope refers to an *annual* change in monthly housing starts. In other words, slope 2.4167 is the amount of change in housing starts which would occur between a given month and the same month *next year*. This slope value must be divided again by 12 so that it will reflect the change between a given month and the next month of the *same year*. Thus the appropriate value of the slope is .201 = 2.4167/12 and the previous equation is adjusted to

$$Y_t = 109.8 + .201X$$

Third, the origin of this equation is July 1, 1960. We wish to move this origin to December 15, 1978 in order to obtain monthly projections for 1979. Between July 1, 1960 and December 15, 1978 there are 221.5 months, 5.5 months to December 15, 1960 and 216 months to December 15, 1978. Hence, intercept 109.8 must be increased by 44.5 = 221.5 × .201 to 154.3, and the finally adjusted equation is

$$Y_t = 154.3 + .201X$$

where $X = 0$; origin: December 15, 1978
X = deviations in 1-month intervals
Y_t = housing starts in thousands

The slope of this equation needs careful interpretation. The slope value is the monthly incremental change; housing starts increase by 201 units from one month to the next within the same year.

We can easily obtain monthly projections from the adjusted equation by letting X be equal to 1 for January, 2 for February, and so on for each month number in 1979. For example, X is 3 for March; therefore,

$$Y_t = 154.3 + .201(3)$$
$$= 154.9 \ (\times 1000) \text{ housing starts}$$

Table 29.3.
Monthly Forecasts for 1979 Housing Starts Based on $Y_t = 154.3 + .201X$ Trend and Seasonal Indices (Housing Starts in Thousands)

Month (1)	Month Number (2)	Monthly Trend Level Y_t (3)	Seasonal Indices S_t (4)	Monthly Forecasts $\left(\dfrac{\text{col. 3} \times \text{col. 4}}{100}\right)$ (5)
January	1	154.5	67.1	103.7
February	2	154.7	70.1	108.4
March	3	154.9	100.4	155.5
April	4	155.1	119.1	184.7
May	5	155.3	123.4	191.6
June	6	155.5	119.3	185.5
July	7	155.7	112.6	175.3
August	8	155.9	112.7	175.7
September	9	156.1	102.8	160.5
October	10	156.3	108.6	169.7
November	11	156.5	91.2	142.7
December	12	156.7	72.7	113.9
Totals:		1867.2	1200.0	1867.2

The month numbers and the monthly trend projections appear in Table 29.3, columns 2 and 3, respectively.

The graph of this monthly linear trend for 1960–78 housing starts is shown in Fig. I(a) of the introduction to this chapter.

Conversion of an annual equation to quarterly values is analogous to the above procedure. The only difference is that the unit divisor is 4 instead of 12 per year.

This is a short digression. Our main course is to illustrate how monthly trend projections are adjusted so they can reflect the influence of seasonal variations.

Example 29.2 (continued)

For this adjustment, we first record the seasonal indices S_t as shown in Table 29.3, column 4; they are copied from Table 29.2. Then we multiply each monthly trend projection by the corresponding seasonal index. Finally, each product is divided by 100 to yield the seasonal forecasts which appear under column 5.

It is important to realize that seasonal or short-term forecasts can be fairly accurate if a series exhibits a stable seasonal pattern and is insensitive to short-run cyclical and irregular influences. Unfortunately, this is not the case with our housing starts series. We used this series only to illustrate the arithmetic steps of the method for seasonal forecasting. We have seen that housing starts exhibit a stable seasonal pattern. Our seasonal forecasts, however, are not likely to be accurate. Our series is strongly influenced by cyclical and irregular factors. This is especially true since 1970. For example, the graph of the 12-month moving average of the series in Fig. 29.1(a) shows that the trend-cycle component may begin its

Seasonal Indices and Time Series Analysis

downward swing. Furthermore, antiinflation monetary policies of the Federal Reserve System may bring about a sudden change in mortgage interest rates which can have a significant short-run effect on the volume of housing starts. More accurate seasonal forecasts would require that monthly trend projections take into consideration the influence of these nonseasonal fluctuating components of the series.

How do we cope with the uncertainties related to projecting the influence of cyclical and irregular factors? Seasonal indices are utilized for long-run forecasting in two important respects. First, we can remove the seasonal effect from a time series in order to analyze the long-term movements of the other components. Second, we can use the seasonal indices and trend values to isolate the cyclical and irregular components of a time series. After illustrating this dual use of seasonal indices, we point out some of the difficulties in forecasting with time series in general.

Removing the seasonal influence from a series is accomplished by dividing the original monthly time series by the seasonal index of the corresponding month. In terms of the components of the multiplicative classical model, this operation may be expressed by

$$(29.2) \qquad D_t = \frac{Y}{S_t} \times 100 = \frac{T \times C \times S \times I}{S} = T \times C \times I$$

where D_t represents a time series which is *adjusted for seasonal variation* or *deseasonalized*. Term Y/S_t indicates the actual division of the original Y series by the computed seasonal indices S_t. The remaining two terms of the expression are idealizations of the procedure where elimination of the seasonal index S results in a series representing the trend (T), cyclical fluctuations (C) and irregular movements (I).

Example 29.3

The housing starts Y for May 1960 amounted to 130 ($\times 1000$) and the seasonal index S_t for the same month is 123.4. Dividing Y by S_t and multiplying by 100 we find, according to expression (29.2), that

$$D_t = \frac{Y}{S_t} \times 100 = \frac{130}{123.4} \times 100 = 105.3 \ (\times 1000) \text{ housing starts}$$

This figure represents the level of housing starts for May 1960, when the influence of seasonal variations is eliminated. Repeating the procedure for each month yields a deseasonalized series of housing starts for 1960–78.

How important is a deseasonalized time series? Elimination of seasonal variations makes it easier to compare changes from month to month between years and to identify nonseasonal components, especially the cyclical turns, of a series. For example, the deseasonalized series of gross national product (GNP) is frequently used as the basis for determining the state of our economy. The Consumer Price Index (CPI) measures the percentage change in current prices in relation to a base period representing 100. A slowing down in the increase of the deseasonalized CPI may signal a weakening of inflationary pressures in our economy. Fre-

Section 29 Seasonal Variations

quently, the current rate of inflation is stated in annual terms. For example, if the deseasonalized CPI has increased by 1 percent over the previous month, we multiply this percent by 12 to arrive at an annualized 12 percent rate of inflation.

Seasonal indices and the trend values are the basis for isolating the other two components of a time series. In symbolic terms the deseasonalized time series D_t is divided by the corresponding computed monthly trend values (Y_t) in order to isolate the cyclical (C) and irregular (I) movements:

(29.3) $$\frac{D_t}{Y_t} \times 100 = \frac{T \times C \times I}{T} = C \times I$$

The computational steps indicated by expressions (29.2) and (29.3) eliminate the $S \times T$ components of a time series. Then we can isolate the cyclical component of a series from the residual product $C \times I$ with a moving average.

Example 29.4

In Example 29.3, we found that the deseasonalized value D_t for May 1960 is 105.3 ($\times 1000$) housing starts. This figure is divided by the trend value 109.5 ($\times 1000$) housing starts and multiplied by 100 to yield the cyclical irregular component of the series expressed as a percentage of trend:

$$\frac{D_t}{Y_t} \times 100 = \frac{105.3}{109.5} \times 100 = 96.2 \text{ percent}$$

This means that the deseasonalized series, representing the cyclical-irregular component, constitutes 96.2 percent of the trend value for May 1960. Since irregular movements are assumed to be of short duration (less than 1 year), they may be eliminated with a moving average. Various moving averages may be used to isolate the cyclical component from the residual product $C \times I$. For our housing starts series we used a 9-month moving average. Such a method tends to smooth or average out the irregular movements in the residual product $C \times I$. The cyclical value C_t for May 1960 was found to represent 98.6 percent of trend. The graph of the cyclical component of our series is shown in Fig. I(b) of the introduction to this chapter.

The final component of irregular movements is isolated if we divide the original time series Y by the product of the computed trend Y_t, the cyclical fluctuations C_t, and the seasonal variations S_t and multiply by 100. In symbols the computed irregular component is

(29.4) $$I_t = \frac{Y}{Y_t \times C_t/100 \times S_t/100} \times 100 = \frac{T \times C \times S \times I}{T \times C \times S}$$

Example 29.5

For May 1960 we have already found that $Y_t = 109.5$, $C_t = 98.6$, and $S_t = 123.4$. For the value $Y = 130$ of the original series,

$$I_t = \frac{130}{109.5 \times 98.6/100 \times 123.4/100} \times 100 = 97.6 \text{ percent}$$

This means that the trend, cyclical, and seasonal components represent 97.6 percent of 130 ($\times 1000$) housing starts. Irregular movements account for

2.4 percent (100 − 97.6) or 3120 housing starts. The graph of the irregular component of our series is shown in Fig. I(d) at the beginning of this chapter.

The above computational procedures for isolating the time series components of the classical model present no difficulties. The difficulties lie elsewhere.

First, it is questionable whether these procedures achieve a true separation of the components. Trend fitting is largely judgmental depending on the purpose of the analysis and the selected time period. Furthermore, we cannot be certain that the fitted trend line completely separates the trend component from the non-seasonal fluctuating components. Also, we have already pointed out that seasonal indices may contain some of the cyclical fluctuations and irregular movements. Finally, cycles are so erratic and so interwoven with irregular movements that it is impossible to separate them completely.

Second, the accuracy of a forecast depends, to a considerable degree, on how sensitive a time series is to cyclical and irregular forces. Time series in agricultural production, retail trade, and personal services offer better opportunities for a satisfactory level of forecast accuracy than do series in heavy industrial production and finance. The former series are less sensitive to cyclical fluctuations and irregular movements than the latter. Cyclical fluctuations vary in duration and in amplitude. Some irregular movements such as weather, strikes, and government policies induce or alter business cyclical fluctuations. Other irregular forces influence the behavior of a time series in numerous small ways. Thus, the cyclical-irregular components are more difficult to forecast than trend and seasonal variations. Yet the stakes are so high that efforts to improve the level of forecasting accuracy continue unabated.

A wide variety of techniques exist for forecasting economic activity. They range from naive and subjective to the mathematically most sophisticated forecasting methods called econometric models. All lie outside the scope of this text. At any rate, management may choose not to rely on a single forecasting method for predicting the future. Greater reliance should be placed on a consensus of a number of forecasts obtained from independent forecasting techniques. Such a consensus may make a valuable contribution to decision making by helping management to narrow the range of the initially available options for action. Then managerial judgment may determine the course of action which best serves the planning, operational, and control functions of the enterprise.

PROBLEMS

Group One

29.1. The original monthly housing starts series for 1961 are as follows (data in thousands):

Jan.	70	April	113	July	127	Oct.	125
Feb.	74	May	128	Aug.	127	Nov.	103
March	104	June	135	Sept.	125	Dec.	82

Section 29 Seasonal Variations

(a) Continue the basic calculations shown under columns 3 through 6 of Table 29.1.
(b) Check your answers under column 6 with those given in Table 29.2.

29.2. Suppose computation of seasonal indices for our housing starts series involved only the years 1963–68 and the percentage of monthly moving averages were as follows:

Year	\multicolumn{12}{c}{Month}
	J	F	M	A	M	J	J	A	S	O	N	D
1963							112.4	106.2	105.6	121.6	88.7	71.2
1964	73.6	72.2	98.2	113.7	119.6	123.1	111.2	110.1	96.8	113.9	89.7	75.2
1965	66.5	66.0	97.9	121.6	125.2	124.1	113.3	104.6	102.4	109.3	92.2	85.5
1966	68.6	67.6	107.5	133.0	127.3	122.5	102.8	107.6	95.6	84.7	81.3	66.6
1967	64.6	65.2	95.9	114.3	126.9	117.2	115.3	115.1	108.2	116.1	99.5	66.9
1978	67.1	69.8	103.5	131.3	113.7	110.3						

*(a) Calculate the seasonal indices following the procedure illustrated in Table 29.2.
(b) Plot the seasonal patterns of indices for 1960–78 given in Table 29.2 and for 1963–68 that you calculated in part (a) on the same diagram. Are the two patterns similar?

29.3. The annual trend equation for our housing starts series was given as

$$Y_t = 1318 + 29X$$

where $X = 0$; origin: July 1, 1960
X = deviations in 1-year intervals
Y_t = housing starts in thousands

*(a) Convert this annual equation into a quarterly equation with origin November 15, 1978.
(b) Find the quarterly projections for 1979.
(c) Calculate the quarterly forecasts for 1979 assuming the following quarterly seasonal indices:

Winter	Spring	Summer	Fall
78.3	117.4	112.1	92.2

and show all results in a table such as Table 29.3.
(d) Do you think the management of Real Estate Associates can rely on these quarterly forecasts? Explain why or why not.

Answers to asterisked (*) problems are appended. Unless otherwise stated, the sources of all time series are *Business Statistics* and the *Survey of Current Business*, U.S. Department of Commerce.

Chapter 10 Time Series Analysis and Index Numbers

29.4. The monthly housing starts series for 1974–78 in thousands is as follows:

						Month						
Year	J	F	M	A	M	J	J	A	S	O	N	D
1974	85	109	125	160	149	148	127	111	98	97	75	55
1975	56	55	80	98	116	110	119	117	112	124	97	76
1976	73	90	118	137	148	154	137	146	152	148	127	107
1977	81	113	174	182	201	198	190	194	178	193	155	129
1978	89	101	172	198	211	216	192	191	181	192	159	120

(a) Use the seasonal indices given in Table 29.2 to deseasonalize the above data.

(b) Plot the deseasonalized series on a graph and compare results with the graph of the original data given in Fig. I(a) of the introduction to this chapter.

(c) Explain why it is easier to use deseasonalized rather than the original series in order to compare changes from month to month between years. Illustrate your point by comparing the deseasonalized housing starts for December 1977 and 1978.

29.5. The multiplicative classical time series model implies that the product of the component for a given month must equal the value of the original series for that month. In symbols,

$$Y_t \times \frac{C_t}{100} \times \frac{S_t}{100} \times \frac{I_t}{100} = Y$$

In Example 29.5, the May 1960 value for the trend Y_t is 109.5 ($\times$1000) housing starts, the cyclical C_t is 98.6, the seasonal S_t is 123.4, and the irregular I_t is 97.6 percent.

(a) Multiply these values of the components to verify that the Y value of the original series is indeed 130 ($\times$1000) housing starts.

(b) Does this verification mean that the computational procedures isolate completely the components of a time series? Explain in detail.

29.6. Consider the trend equation

$$Y_t = 480{,}000 + 14{,}400X$$

where $X = 0$; origin: July 1, 1980
X = deviations in 1-year intervals
Y_t = the number of production workers in the steel industry

*(a) Convert the equation to monthly basis with origin January 15, 1980 and explain the meaning of the slope.

(b) Find the quarterly equation with origin February 15, 1980 and explain the meaning of the slope.

29.7. Describe briefly the computational steps for:

(a) Constructing seasonal indices by the ratio-to-moving-average method

(b) Making a seasonal forecast

Section 29 Seasonal Variations

(c) Calculating cyclical fluctuations and irregular movements from a deseasonalized series

29.8. Explain why the computational procedures introduced in the text fail to isolate completely the four components of the classical model time series.

Group Two

29.9. Linda Tober is the manager in charge of buying for Vanity Fair Department Stores. For determining the volume of purchases for men's shirts as well as other merchandise for the winter holiday season, Linda uses the following procedure. First, she obtains a forecast of sales volume for the holidays quarter—October, November, December. Second, she allocates the forecast volume according to size using a relative frequency distribution of past sales by size—perimeter of neck and length of sleeves. Finally, she uses her judgment to place orders by color and style for each size.

For the fourth quarter of 1980, trend projection is for 8500 shirts and the quarterly index is 122.
(a) Explain the meaning of the trend value.
(b) What is the meaning of the quarterly index?
*(c) Determine the forecast volume.
(d) What does Linda assume about the influence of cyclical and irregular factors for a reliable forecast?

29.10. Andy Spencer manages Prometheus Inc., a distributor of home heating oil. Andy forecasts the winter months sales on the basis of monthly trend projections and seasonal indices, then adds the monthly forecasts to arrive at his winter forecast. For monthly trend projections Andy uses the equation

$$Y_t = 450 + 5X$$

where $X = 0$; origin: July 15, 1980
X = deviations in 1-month intervals
Y_t = heating oil in thousands of gallons

The seasonal indices for the winter months, November through March, are 135, 172, 215, 196, and 142, respectively.
(a) Explain the meaning of the trend equation.
(b) What does the 215 index for January mean?
*(c) Find the forecast for the winter 1980–81.
(d) What irregular factors may render Andy's winter forecast unreliable?

29.11. Thomas Fishbone manages Texafo Gas Station. Storage capacity for gasoline is limited, requiring frequent deliveries, especially during the summer months. Recently, gasoline shortages have created ill feelings among regular customers. In addition, two-digit interest rates for short-term borrowing for gasoline purchases increased significantly. Thomas's accountant, a recent college graduate working for Pratt CPA Associates, suggests an increase in the gasoline storage capacity of the station equal to the monthly average demand. Benefits would more than offset construction costs. Such an increase in capacity would reduce interest charges and delivery costs by allowing Thomas to borrow at least two-thirds of the yearly gasoline sales at lower interest rates and insure a steadier gasoline supply to customers. Expensive short-term financing would be limited to the summer months of peak sales.

A time series analysis of gasoline sales would help to determine the needed storage capacity and the extent of short-term financing. The accountant finds that the seasonal indices for January, May, and June are 93, 105, and 108, respectively.

*(a) Sales increased from 60,450 gallons in January to 65,100 in May. Find the percentage change in the deseasonalized gasoline sales between January and May.

(b) The forecast of gasoline sales for the next 12 months is 720,000 gallons. The trend-cycle component for June is estimated at 3 percent above average monthly sales. Assuming irregular factors are negligible, find the forecast for June.

29.12. During 1975–78, monthly demand for gasoline in the United States in millions of barrels (1 barrel = 42 gallons) was as follows:

	Year			
Month	1975	1976	1977	1978
January	193	199	201	208
February	172	183	194	194
March	197	215	215	226
April	203	216	222	217
May	214	214	219	241
June	214	226	229	239
July	220	228	232	236
August	219	224	231	246
September	203	214	221	224
October	212	216	222	233
November	193	212	217	226
December	212	222	229	232

(a) Show the basic calculations of the ratio-to-moving-average method in a table such as Table 29.1.

*(b) Show the calculation of monthly seasonal indices in a table such as Table 29.2. Average *all* three percentages of moving averages for each month.

(c) Plot the original series and the 12-month moving average on the same diagram.

(d) Sketch the percentage of moving averages on a separate diagram.

(e) Present graphically the seasonal pattern of the series for the 1975–78 period.

29.13. The monthly average of housing starts by quarters is given below in thousands of units:

	Year				
Quarter	1974	1975	1976	1977	1978
Winter	106.2	63.7	93.6	122.5	120.7
Spring	152.1	108.1	146.4	193.7	208.2
Summer	112.0	116.2	144.8	187.2	187.9
Fall	75.6	98.9	127.6	159.0	156.7

(a) Show the basic calculations of the ratio-to-moving-average method in a table such as Table 29.1.

*(b) Show the calculation of quarterly seasonal indices in a table such as Table 29.2.

SECTION 30/ INDEX NUMBERS

The prices of commodities and services which a family purchases increase or decrease at different rates in the same city as well as between cities. How can we express such a diversity of price changes with a single figure which can be used for meaningful comparisons? Index numbers are designed to accomplish this task. In its simplest form, an *index number* is a percentage which expresses a *relative* change in a variable compared with some base as 100. For example, suppose the price of a quart of milk was 36¢ in 1970 and 57¢ in 1979. Dividing 57¢ by 36¢ and multiplying by 100 we obtain 158.3. It means that the price of a quart of milk in 1979 is 158.3 percent of the price in 1970. Such an index number is called a *percentage price relative*.

Usually, we are interested in measuring price changes of several items rather than of a single item. We may be interested, for example, in an index of food prices, industrial production output, or value of building contracts. These summary measures are referred to as *composite* index numbers because they involve several items. In this section we focus on the construction and interpretation of composite index numbers. Therefore, we shall use the term *index numbers* to mean *composite index numbers*.

Index numbers have wide and varied applications in the private as well as the public sector of our economy. We have already seen that index numbers measure the seasonal variations of a time series and are used as a basis for short-run forecasting. Also, index numbers measure the level of economic activity in a company, industry, geographic area, or the entire economy. Price indices are used as escalators in wage and other business contracts against loss of purchasing power through inflation and as deflators of a time series. No less important is the fact that indices are used as guides or "triggers" for action in business as well as in government.

Index numbers are conveniently classified into three categories: *price, quantity,* or *value indices*. The Consumer Price Index, the wholesale Price Index, and the Dow-Jones stock price averages are widely used price indices. Quantity indices measure the physical volume of industrial production, construction, or employment in manufacturing in general, in specific industries, or in specific stages of production and distribution. The Index of Industrial Production and the Business Week Index are two widely used quantity indices. Two commonly used value indices are the Manufacturing Production Worker Payrolls and the Construction Contracts Awarded.

Chapter 10 Time Series Analysis and Index Numbers

In this section, we first focus on the construction of price indices. They enable us to illustrate most problems of construction, interpretation, and usage of quantity and value indices as well. In order to simplify matters we use a simple example for illustrating construction of various price indices and for discussing the advantages and limitations of each method. But the exposition provides for a sufficient conceptual base to introduce two important indices, the Consumer Price Index and the Index of Industrial Production. Finally, we deal with some general problems of index number construction.

Unweighted Aggregate Price Indices

One method for constructing a price index is to follow roughly the approach of a television commentator.

Example 30.1

Let us consider a typical wage earner's family with wife and two children living in a city. The family's "market basket" includes expenses on several goods and services representing necessities of life. For convenience, however, we may assume that the family's market basket consists of only four food commodities: milk, bread, hamburger, and canned tuna. In reality, even this spartan market basket must be very carefully defined in terms of grade or quality each commodity price represents. But these as well as other details are put aside in order to concentrate on the essential aspects of index construction.

Calculation of the price index for 1979 with a base 1970 taken as 100 percent is shown in Table 30.1.* For convenience we use calendar years as subscripts. Thus, symbol P_{70} denotes the price for 1970 and P_{79} the price for 1979. First, we add the unit prices of the four commodities for the base year 1970 and the nonbase year 1979 so that $\Sigma P_{70} = \$2.28$ and $\Sigma P_{79} = \$4.75$.

Table 30.1. Unweighted Aggregates Price Index for Four Food Items for 1979 (1979 = 100)

Item	Unit Price 1970 P_{70}	1979 P_{79}
Milk (quart)	$ .36	$ .57
Bread (loaf)	.59	.89
Hamburger (pound)	.98	2.30
Canned tuna (7 ounces)	.35	.99
	$2.28	$4.75

$$\frac{\Sigma P_{79}}{\Sigma P_{70}} \times 100 = \frac{\$4.75}{\$2.28} \times 100 = 208.3$$

*Unless otherwise stated, all data in this section are hypothetical.

Section 30 Index Numbers

Thus the family's market basket costs $2.28 in 1970 and $4.75 in 1979. Second, we divide the sum of prices for 1979 by the sum of prices for 1970 and multiply by 100; the index for 1979 is

$$\frac{\Sigma P_{79}}{\Sigma P_{70}} \times 100 = \frac{\$4.75}{\$2.28} \times 100 = 208.3$$

This index means that the cost of the market basket in 1979 is 208.3 percent of the cost in 1970, which is taken as 100 percent. If such a market basket included all the necessities of life, the family's cost of living has more than doubled between 1970 and 1979. We could have used the same computational procedure to calculate the index for 1978 or earlier years if the appropriate data were given.

The point of time to which all prices of later points of time are compared is called *base period* and is equal to 100 percent. All other points of time are called *nonbase periods*. In our example, the base period is the year 1970 = 100, while year 1979 is a nonbase period. Since we used sums or aggregates of unweighted prices, the index in Table 30.1 is called *unweighted aggregate price index*. In general terms, such an index may be expressed by

(30.1)
$$\frac{\Sigma P_n}{\Sigma P_0} \times 100$$

where P_0 = unit price of a commodity or service in a base period
P_n = unit price of a commodity or service in a nonbase period

An unweighted aggregate price index has an important limitation. One difficulty arises from the fact that the units for which the prices are quoted may be selected arbitrarily. For example, the value of the index would change if the price of milk were stated in gallons rather than quarts. Furthermore, we cannot overcome this difficulty if we state the prices of all commodities in the "market basket" in a common unit, say pounds. Suppose the market basket includes coffee, which has a high price per pound. The index would be dominated by a commodity with a high price. Such an effect would be particularly important if the high-priced commodity is consumed infrequently because it is expensive.

Second, regardless of unit selection, such an index is unduly influenced by a high-priced item. In Table 30.1 we found that the price totals for 1970 and 1979 are $2.28 and $4.75, respectively. Suppose the market basket includes shoes, having a price per pair decline from $30 in 1970 to $24 in 1979 because of competition from imports. Then the price totals for 1970 and 1979 would be $32.28 and $28.75, respectively. These aggregate prices yield an index of 89.1 = 28.75/32.28 × 100. Now the family's market basket in 1979 is only 89.1 percent of the cost in 1970. The cost of living declined by 10.9 percent. In short, this supposedly unweighted aggregate price index in expression (30.1) has a system of implicit equal weights.

Weighted Aggregate Price Indices

For a meaningful price index we need to apply explicitly stated weights. Traditionally, the weights used in constructing price indices are *quantity weights* in proportion to the importance or usage of the items in the index. For example, a consumer price index would use quantities of the consumed commodities and services, an index of import prices would use the imported quantities, and a stock price index would use the volume of negotiated stocks. With respect to the weight period, we consider three possibilities.

In the first place, we may use the *weights of the base period*.

Example 30.2

The initial family's "market basket" with unit prices for 1970 and 1979 is reproduced in Table 30.2. In addition, we introduce quantity weights for the 1970 base year. These weights may represent the average number of units for each item consumed per week during 1970. So the family's weekly consumption has been 2 quarts of milk, 1 loaf of bread, 3 pounds of hamburger, and 1 can of tuna.

The weighted aggregate price index is calculated as follows. First, we multiply each unit price by the corresponding weight and add the products to find the sums of $4.60 for 1970 and $9.92 for 1979. These sums represent the average weekly expenditures of the family for purchasing the market basket for 1970 and 1979. Second, we divide the total expenditures of the 1979 nonbase year by the total expenditures of the 1970 base year and multiply by 100. The index is

$$\frac{\Sigma P_{79}Q_{70}}{\Sigma P_{70}Q_{70}} \times 100 = \frac{\$9.92}{\$4.60} \times 100 = 215.7$$

According to this index, the cost of the market basket in 1979 is 215.7 percent of the cost in 1970 taken as 100 percent. Note that this weighted index has a value of 215.7, which is higher than the value of 208.3 we obtained earlier. This is principally attributed to the greater weight given to hamburger, which experienced a greater price increase than did milk and bread during the 1970–79 period.

Table 30.2. Weighted Aggregates Price Index for Four Food Items for 1979—Laspeyres Method (1970 = 100)

Item	Unit Price 1970 P_{70}	Unit Price 1979 P_{79}	Quantity (Units), 1970 Q_{70}	Total Value $P_{70}Q_{70}$	Total Value $P_{79}Q_{70}$
Milk (quart)	$ .36	$ .57	2	$ .72	$1.14
Bread (loaf)	.59	.89	1	.59	.89
Hamburger (pound)	.98	2.30	3	2.94	6.90
Canned tuna (7 ounces)	.35	.99	1	.35	.99
				$4.60	$9.92

$$\frac{\Sigma P_{79}Q_{70}}{\Sigma P_{70}Q_{70}} \times 100 = \frac{\$9.92}{\$4.60} \times 100 = 215.7$$

Section 30 Index Numbers

This weighted aggregate price index, using base period weights, is known as the *Laspeyres index;* its general expression is

$$(30.2) \qquad \frac{\Sigma P_n Q_0}{\Sigma P_0 Q_0} \times 100$$

where Q_0 denotes the quantity weights of the base period with the other symbols already defined.

The use of base period weights is an important advantage of the Laspeyres index. Calculation of the index for successive nonbase periods avoids the time-consuming and costly effect of obtaining new weights and recomputing the base period with such weights. Base period weights provide the basis for a meaningful comparison of price changes over a base period. Such weights express the relative importance of each item in the index. Since weights are not allowed to vary, the Laspeyres index reflects changes attributable to price movements. Furthermore, shifting the base period can be accomplished without having to recompute the index for all periods.

With the passage of time, however, the advantage of the Laspeyres index may become a serious handicap. With fixed weights the index assumes a frozen consumption pattern. In a dynamic economy such as ours a fixed consumption pattern becomes increasingly unrealistic as time goes on; it fails to reflect significant shifts in consumption patterns brought about by changes in consumer taste and earnings.

From the economic standpoint, it would be more realistic to consider a second possibility: *current* (nonbase) *period weights*. The weighted aggregate price index using period weights is known as the *Paasche index;* its general formula is

$$(30.3) \qquad \frac{\Sigma P_n Q_n}{\Sigma P_0 Q_n} \times 100$$

where Q_n denotes current period weights with the other symbols defined earlier.

Example 30.3

Since 1970 physicians and dieticians representing private as well as government institutions have been emphasizing the importance of diet in our health. Among other matters, these experts recommended that we eat more fish and poultry than red meat and red meat products. This dietary information and other developments such as higher earnings have influenced the family's "market basket." The average weekly consumption pattern of the family for 1979 is for 2½ rather than 3 pounds of hamburger and 1½ rather than 1 can of tuna. The weekly quantities of milk and bread remained the same as in 1970, 2 and 1 units respectively. What is the Paasche index for the family in 1979?

The weighted price aggregates are, for 1979,

$$\Sigma P_{79} Q_{79} = .57(2) + .89(1) + 2.30(2.5) + .99(1.5) = \$9.265$$

and for 1970,

$$\Sigma P_{70} Q_{79} = .36(2) + .59(1) + .98(2.5) + .35(1.5) = \$4.285$$

The Paasche index for 1979 by formula (30.3) is

$$\frac{\Sigma P_{79}Q_{79}}{\Sigma P_{70}Q_{79}} \times 100 = \frac{\$9.265}{\$4.285} \times 100 = 216.2$$

Note that the Paasche index for 1979 is higher than the Laspeyres index of 215.7 found earlier. The difference is due to the shift toward consumption of more fish, which experienced a greater price increase than meat during the 1970–79 period. Unlike the Laspeyres index, the Paasche index reflects changes in prices as well as changes in the consumption pattern of the family.

While the Paasche index may make sense from the economic standpoint, the use of current period weights has certain important disadvantages. Current period weights make it impossible to compare year-to-year price changes; we cannot isolate the effect of price changes from the effect of changing consumption patterns. In addition, calculating the Paasche index requires a new set of weights each year. The Paasche indices for our case in Example 30.3 would be, for 1971,

$$\frac{\Sigma P_{71}Q_{71}}{\Sigma P_{70}Q_{71}} \times 100$$

and for 1972,

$$\frac{\Sigma P_{72}Q_{72}}{\Sigma P_{70}Q_{72}} \times 100$$

and so on. For a real price index such as the Consumer Price Index, obtaining an appropriate set of weights each period (even yearly rather than monthly) is a very costly undertaking. Furthermore, shifting the base period would require recomputing the index for all periods; the reason is that the value of the weighted price aggregate of the base period changes every year. For these reasons, the Paasche method based on current base weights is not used in constructing any of the well-known index time series.

A third possibility in constructing a weighted aggregate price index is to use *fixed weights*. A *fixed-weight aggregate price* index is defined by

(30.4)
$$\boxed{\frac{\Sigma P_n Q_f}{\Sigma P_0 Q_f} \times 100}$$

where Q_f denotes a fixed set of quantity weights with the other symbols already defined. The Laspeyres index may be considered a special case of formula (30.4) if the period of fixed weights coincides with the base period, that is, if $Q_f = Q_0$.

The fixed-weight aggregate price index provides for a workable solution of the dilemma of weights posed by the Laspeyres and Paasche indices. The period of fixed weights called *weight base* may not be the same with the so-called *reference base,* set at 100, from which price changes are measured. For example, the weight base for the Consumer Price Index has been revised in the past every 10 to 15 years, with the most recent revision in 1972–73. But the reference base years have not coincided with the weight base years. The reference base year for the

Section 30 Index Numbers

present Consumer Price Index is 1967 = 100. Thus with fixed weights we are able to isolate the effect of price changes while with updating the weight base we are able to incorporate into the index changes in consumption patterns. This is a distinct advantage of the fixed-weight aggregate price index.

Unweighted Price Relatives Index

We have seen that the first step for constructing an aggregate price index is to sum the prices (unweighted or weighted) of each period. Then we calculate an index by dividing the sum of a nonbase period by the sum of the base period. Another approach to constructing a price index would be to divide first the price of each commodity in a nonbase period by its price in the base period. For example, suppose a pound of hamburger was selling for $.98 in 1970 and for $2.30 in 1979. Then the price of hamburger in 1979 would be $2.30/$.98 × 100 = 234.7 percent of the price of hamburger in 1970. As stated earlier, this measurement is called *percentage price relative*. In general, such a measurement may be expressed as

(30.5) $$\frac{P_n}{P_0} \times 100$$

with the symbols already defined.

A percentage of price relative can be the basis for meaningful comparisons. For example, we may calculate the price relatives of a pound of hamburger for several years with base year 1970 for two locations, such as two metropolitan areas. The two time series would show the relative increase in the price of hamburger over the years between the two locations. But the usefulness of price relatives for a single community is limited. Certainly, we cannot use the price relatives of a pound of hamburger or any other commodity as an index measuring the general movement in prices. On the other hand, we can obtain such a measure by combining the price relatives of several representative commodities into a composite price index.

One method is to calculate the arithmetic mean of the sum of price relatives of several commodities. This approach gives rise to the *unweighted price relatives index* defined by

(30.6) $$\frac{\Sigma \left(\frac{P_n}{P_0} \times 100 \right)}{n}$$

where $\frac{P_n}{P_0} \times 100$ = price relative of a commodity or service
n = number of commodities and services

Example 30.4

Calculation of such a composite price index for the family's "market basket" is shown in Table 30.3. The unit prices of the four commodities for 1970 and 1979 are reproduced from Table 30.2. First, we calculate the percentage price relatives by applying formula (30.5) to the prices of each commodity. For example, the price of a quart of milk for 1970 is P_{70} = $.36 and for 1979 is P_{79} = $.57. By formula (30.5) we have

$$\frac{P_{79}}{P_{70}} \times 100 = \frac{\$.57}{\$.36} \times 100 = 158.3$$

Table 30.3.
Unweighted Price Relatives Index for Four Food Items for 1979 (1970 = 100)

Item	Unit Price 1970 P_{70}	Unit Price 1979 P_{79}	Percentage Price Relative $\frac{P_{79}}{P_{70}} \times 100$
Milk (quart)	$ .36	$ .57	158.3
Bread (loaf)	.59	.89	150.8
Hamburger (pound)	.98	2.30	234.7
Canned tuna (7 ounces)	.35	.99	282.9
			826.7

$$\frac{\Sigma \left(\frac{P_{79}}{P_{70}} \times 100 \right)}{n} = \frac{826.7}{4} = 206.7$$

Second, we add these price relatives to find the sum

$$\Sigma \left(\frac{P_{79}}{P_{70}} \times 100 \right) = 826.7$$

Finally, we divide this sum by 4, the number of commodities in the market basket. The unweighted price relatives index for 1979 is 206.7

Simplicity is an obvious feature of the unweighted price index. Besides, the index is independent of the units in which prices are quoted. Whether the price of milk, for example, is quoted by the gallon or by the quart, the price relative of milk remains unchanged. Like the unweighted aggregate price index, however, the unweighted price relatives index is in fact weighted implicitly; all items are given equal weight irrespective of their importance or frequency of use. Consequently, percentage increases are balanced off against equal percentage decreases irrespective of the absolute price of the involved items. For example, suppose the price of a pound of chicken increased from 60¢ in 1970 to 72¢ in 1979, an increase of 20 percent; also suppose the price of a pair of shoes decreased from $30 in 1970 to $24 in 1979, a decline of 20 percent. The unweighted price relatives index for the two items would be 100 in 1979; this indicates that, on the average, the level of prices has remained unchanged. For this reason practically none of the important price indices compiled by government agencies or private organizations use the method of unweighted price relatives.

Weighted Price Relatives Index

The need to use explicit weights for expressing the importance of each item in an index is widely recognized.* By convention the weights used for constructing weighted price relatives indices are *value weights,* that is, total values of items produced, sold, or consumed. For a consumer price index, value weights would

---

*Theoretically, several averages can be used to calculate an index of price relatives. In practice, which we follow here, the weighted arithmetic mean is used almost universally because it is easier to calculate and easier to understand than other averages.

Section 30 Index Numbers

represent the amounts spent on each item in the index. Such an amount is determined by price times the quantity consumed. In our illustration, the price of a quart of milk in 1970 was 36¢ and our typical family consumed an average of 2 quarts per week. Then the value weight for milk is 72¢ (36 × 2). As in the case of weighted aggregate price indices, there can be several value weights depending on whether prices and quantities represent the base period or a nonbase period.

The general expression of *weighted average of price relatives index* is

(30.7)
$$\boxed{\frac{\Sigma\left(\frac{P_n}{P_0} \times 100\right)W}{\Sigma W}}$$

where W denotes value weights, with the other symbols defined earlier.

Example 30.5   Calculation of the weighted price relatives index (30.7) with base period value weights $W = P_0 Q_0$ for our illustration is shown in Table 30.4. The basic unit price data and the percentages from Table 30.3 are recorded under columns 1 through 3. The quantities consumed (quantity weights Q_{70}) from Table 30.2 are recorded under column 4. Multiplying the base period price by quantity ($P_{70} Q_{70}$) for each commodity, we obtain the value weights under column 5. The weighted price relatives shown under column 6 are the products of price relatives, column 3, and value weights, column 5. Finally, the sum of the weighted price relatives, $992.0, divided by the sum of value weights, $4.60, yields the weighted price relatives index of 215.7 for 1979.

Note that this index number is identical to the Laspeyres index number found in Table 30.2. This is not surprising since the two indices are algebraically identical. If value weights W represent *base period value weights* $P_0 Q_0$, expression (30.7) gives rise to the following weighted price relatives index.

(30.8)
$$\frac{\Sigma\left(\frac{P_n}{P_0}\right)P_0 Q_0}{\Sigma P_0 Q_0} \times 100 = \frac{\Sigma P_n Q_0}{\Sigma P_0 Q_0} \times 100$$

where constant 100 has been factored out of the sum of relatives. The base period prices P_0 in the numerator of the weighted price relative index in expression (30.8) cancel to yield the Laspeyres index (30.2) shown on the right-hand side.

We can obtain other weighted price relatives indices from expression (30.7) by replacing W with different value weight systems. If W represents *current period value weights* $P_0 Q_n$, expression (30.7) yields an index which is algebraically equivalent to the Paasche index (30.3); if W represents *fixed-value weights* $P_0 Q_f$, expression (30.7) yields an index algebraically equivalent to the fixed-weight aggregate price index (30.4). Other values of W yield weight price relatives indices which would not be as meaningful as the above.

In general, the weighted average relatives and aggregative methods frequently yield identical results, as already shown. The question remains: Which is

Table 30.4.
Weighted Price Relatives Index for Four Food Items for 1979 (1970 = 100)

Item	Unit Price 1970 (1)	Unit Price 1979 (2)	Percentage Price Relatives $\frac{P_{79}}{P_{70}} \times 100$ (3)	Quantity Weights, 1970 Q_{70} (4)	Value Weights $P_{70}Q_{70}$ (5)	Weighted Price Relatives $\left(\frac{P_{79}}{P_{70}} \times 100\right)(P_{70}Q_{70})$ (6)
Milk (quart)	$.36	$.57	158.3	2	$.72	$114.0
Bread (loaf)	.59	.89	150.8	1	.59	89.0
Hamburger (pound)	.98	2.30	234.7	3	2.94	690.0
Canned tuna (7 ounces)	.35	.99	282.9	1	.35	99.0
					$4.60	$992.0

$$\frac{\Sigma \left(\frac{P_{79}}{P_{70}} \times 100\right)(P_{70}Q_{70})}{\Sigma P_{70}Q_{70}} = \frac{\$992.0}{\$4.60} = 215.7$$

the better method to use? The method of aggregates may be preferred when appropriate quantity weights are available and when we are interested in the composite index as a whole rather than in comparing its components. On the other hand, data availability and other considerations favor the use of the average of relatives method. First, it may be easier to obtain value weights than quantity weights. For example, manufacturers find it easier to provide data on value of production weights (sales less cost of raw materials) than data on produced quantities necessary for constructing the Index of Industrial Production. Second, we may be interested in comparing the components of a composite index such as the Wholesale Price Index; price relatives enable us to make such comparisons. Third, frequently data are easily obtainable in the form of relatives rather than in the form of absolute values. For example, the use of price relatives facilitates computation of the Consumer Price Index because of the need to substitute items.

The Consumer Price Index

Interested students are referred to the statistical literature which describes hundreds of business indices. Here, we discuss briefly some important features, uses, and limitations of the Consumer Price Index (CPI) compiled by the U.S. Bureau of Labor Statistics.

The index is a measure of the average change in prices over time in a fixed "market basket" of goods and services. Since 1978 the index is published for two population groups. The *Consumer Price Index for All Urban Consumers* (CPI-U) covers approximately 80 percent of the total noninstitutionalized civilian population. A revised *Consumer Price Index for Urban Wage Earners and Clerical Workers* (CPI-W) covers about half the population covered by the CPI-U. In addition to wage earners and clerical workers, the new CPI-U covers groups initially excluded from coverage such as professional, managerial, and technical workers, the self-employed, short-term workers, the unemployed, retirees, and others not in the labor force. The two indices are published for the nation as a whole and for 28 cities on a monthly or bimonthly basis; regional indices are available for urban areas of different population sizes; component indices are published for goods, services, and commodities other than food.

The CPI is computed by the weighted arithmetic mean of relatives method with fixed weights (modified Laspeyres). As mentioned earlier, 1967 = 100 is the most recent reference base, while 1972–73 is the most recent weight base. Every 10 to 15 years a nationwide Consumer Expenditures Survey is carried out for the selection and weighting of items in the market basket. The most recent survey was conducted in 1972–73; it classified expenditures into 68 classes which included a total of 382 lower-level or *entry-level* items; it assigned the following weights to five major groups of items for CPI-U: food and alcoholic beverages 18.8 percent, housing 42.9 percent, apparel 7 percent, transportation 17.7 percent, health–recreation–other 13.6 percent. These weights differ somewhat for CPI-W. For example, weights for food and transportation are higher and for housing lower than the weights for CPI-U.

Data on price changes are collected with surveys too elaborate to describe in detail here. The most recent revision of the index involved a point-of-purchase survey of 23,000 families for determining the specific retail stores in which these families shop. This survey as well as other auxiliary sources were used as the basis of selecting a full probability sample of retail stores and other outlets. The sample consists of over 60,000 reporting outlets located in 85 urban areas. Price quotations for food, fuels, and a few other items are obtained monthly while prices for other items are collected bimonthly.

The Consumer Price Index is used as an aid for adjusting wages and salaries for changes in consumer prices. Many labor contracts contain an escalator clause which provides for an automatic adjustment of hourly wages. In simple terms, an escalator clause works as follows: if the index increases by 10 percent over the previous year, hourly wages are increased accordingly to offset the loss of purchasing power. Escalator clauses based on the index are also used to adjust rents, pensions, alimony, fiduciary payments, and payments in many business contracts.

The CPI is used as a deflator of other economic time series. Deflating adjusts such series to price changes by expressing current dollars in inflation-free dollars of constant purchasing power of the base year. Deflated time series such as retail sales, hourly and weekly earnings, some personal consumption expenditures, and the gross national product are important for measuring the performance of our economy and for formulating national policy.

The reciprocal of the CPI may be conceptually considered to represent a purchasing power index. For example, suppose the CPI increases to 116 percent this year over the previous year taken as 100 percent. Taking the reciprocal of 116 and multiplying by 100, we obtain $86.2 = 1/116 \times 100$, which is the corresponding purchasing power index number for this year. This means that a dollar of average weekly wages last year is worth only 86.2¢ this year.

In using the Consumer Price Index we should keep in mind that this important measurement has a number of limitations:

1. Although the sampling procedures are reasonably well under control, the index is still subject to a small sampling error and respondent bias.
2. The index measures price changes only as related to a fixed market basket of goods and services; it does not measure changes in the standard or manner of living.
3. Although efforts are being made to account for changes in product quality, the index does not always reflect quality gains or losses. It may be claimed that the index overstates the rate of inflation by reflecting price increases due to stricter environment controls while failing to reflect gains in the quality of the environment. On the other hand, during wartime the index may understate the rate of inflation by failing to reflect the full inflationary impact of black market prices and deterioration of product quality.
4. The index measures changes in consumer prices from time to time. Changes in consumer prices between different locations at a single point in time cannot be measured by the index itself; they may be measured by comparing individual prices compiled for the index.
5. The index measures average changes in consumer prices only for the two statistical populations defined earlier. It does not measure price changes for any individual family, for families in nonurban areas, or for other income groups.

Quantity Indices; Index of Industrial Production

As explained earlier, quantity indices measure changes in the physical volume of industrial production, construction, employment in manufacturing, and other activities. The computational procedures employed in the construction of price indices are also employed in the construction of quantity indices.

The Index of Industrial Production (IP), issued monthly by the Federal Reserve Board, is one of the most widely used quantity indices in the nation. It has measured changes in the physical volume of factories, mines, and gas and electric utilities since 1919. In addition to the Index of Industrial Production as a whole, component indices are published in six major groupings: materials, manufacturing, business equipment, utilities–mining, consumer goods, and construction supplies. Following the Standard Industrial Classification System of the U.S. Bureau of the Budget, separate indices are compiled for hundreds of individual industrial groups and subgroups.

The Index of Industrial Production is one of the important coincident time series for forecasting economic conditions both at the national and industry levels. Also, the index is compared with unemployment figures, inventories, new orders, manufacturers' shipments, and retail sales in order to establish significant associations for forecasting; components of the index are used for comparing growth rates between sectors of the economy; and individual industry indices comprise the basis for studying the production performance of single companies. Thus, the index is a valuable tool for making decisions for a company, individual industry, and the economy as a whole.

Yet the Index of Industrial Production is not free of limitations. The index cannot serve as a measure of total production because agriculture, construction, transportation, communications, and other important service industries are excluded. These excluded industries represent more than 60 percent of the employed labor force of the United States. Equally important is the fact that changes in electric power consumption, man-hours, and other times series sometimes fail to estimate accurately changes in the corresponding physical volume of production. Such a failure may be especially serious during times of peace-to-war and war-to-peace conversion of the economy. Similar difficulties may arise from the recent conversion from oil to coal as a source of electric power production.

Revision and Evaluation of Index Numbers

Construction and use of index numbers give rise to numerous problems. We discuss a few related to two technical points about index time series: how we may *shift* the reference base period and how we may combine two index time series covering different periods of time into a single continuous series by *splicing*. We conclude with a brief account of a number of points we should keep in mind in evaluating index numbers.

Sometimes, it may be necessary to change the reference base of an index time series from one time period to another time period. This procedure, commonly referred to as *shifting* the base, is necessary for two major reasons. First, with the passage of time the reference base of an index may become difficult to relate to current circumstances. For example, the U.S. Bureau of Labor statistics in 1971 shifted the reference period of the Consumer Price Index from 1959 to 1967 in order to make inflationary comparisons more meaningful. For the same reason, a new shifting of the reference base may occur in the near future. Second, shifting the base may be desirable in order to facilitate comparisons with the time series of another index. The reference base of the index measuring base prices paid by farmers was shifted from 1910–14 to 1967 for easy comparison with the Consumer Price Index (1967 = 100).

Shifting the base is a simple procedure which does not require returning to the original data and recomputing the entire index time series.

Example 30.6

Suppose a price index for electrical appliances shown in Table 30.5, column 1, has 1971 as a reference base and we wish to shift the base to the year 1974. The original price index numbers must be transformed so that the index number 126.5 for 1974, the new reference base, is equal to 100. We can accomplish this by dividing each index number in the original series by 126.5 and multiplying by 100. Thus, the original index number for 1970 shifted to the new base 1974 is $99.2/126.5 \times 100 = 78.4$, for 1971 it is $100.0/126.5 \times 100 = 79.1$, and so on. The new price index time series with shifted reference base to 1974 is shown in column 2.

Table 30.5.
Shifting in Index Time Series for Electrical Appliances to a New Reference Base

Year	Original Price Index (1971 = 100) (1)	Price Index with Shifted Base (1974 = 100) (2)
1970	99.2	78.4
1971	100.0	79.1
1972	111.8	88.4
1973	118.3	93.5
1974	126.5	100.0
1975	133.6	105.6
1976	139.1	110.0

Shifting the base raises two important questions: Do the original and the shifted index time series provide the same year-to-year percentage price increases? The answer is yes. For example, the percentage increase of the index from 1970 to 1971 is the same in both index series, since $100.0/99.2 = 1.008$ and $79.1/78.4 = 1.008$. The same holds true throughout the two index series. The new index series may be considered to reflect the purchasing power of 1974 dollars for electrical appliances. For example, in 1970 we would have spent only 78.4¢ to buy the same quantity of electrical appliances costing $1.00 in 1974.

What are the implications of a shifted base to the weighting system? Suppose the original index time series was constructed using the Laspeyres weighted aggregate prices method. Then the year 1971 would represent both the reference base and the weight base periods. Shifting the base changed the reference base to 1974 while the weight base 1971 is the same. We can easily show this result with symbols. Consider the indices for 1972 and 1974 in the original series. Shifting

Section 30 Index Numbers

the base required dividing 111.8 by 126.5 (multiplication by 100 is ignored in order to simplify matters). By the Laspeyres formula (30.2) this operation yields

$$\frac{\Sigma P_{72}Q_{71}}{\Sigma P_{71}Q_{71}} \div \frac{\Sigma P_{74}Q_{71}}{\Sigma P_{71}Q_{71}} = \frac{\Sigma P_{72}Q_{71}}{\Sigma P_{71}Q_{71}} \times \frac{\Sigma P_{71}Q_{71}}{\Sigma P_{74}Q_{71}} = \frac{\Sigma P_{72}Q_{71}}{\Sigma P_{74}Q_{71}}$$

which is the index number 88.4 in column 2. Note that, while the reference base changed to 1974, the weight base Q_{71} remained the same. The new index is no longer a Laspeyres index. This development is not considered serious and the procedure of shifting the base is widely practiced.

Sometimes an index may undergo a substantial revision. Such a revision may involve a new method of calculation, the inclusion of a new commodity, but more importantly, a major change in quantity weights. Revision of the weight base may coincide with a new reference base. Yet it may be desirable to obtain a continuous index series with the old unrevised index of earlier years. This is accomplished by a procedure referred to as *splicing*.

Example 30.7

In 1974 the original price index for electrical appliances underwent a major revision of quantity weights. The revision was necessary in order to include newly invented products such as pocket calculators, video recording and playback machines, and home minicomputers. The revised index is shown in Table 30.6, column 2. The year 1974 is a new reference as well as a new weight base. The old index time series prior to this revision is shown in column 1. In reality, the base year would be much earlier than 1971, before the time the new commodities were invented and marketed; the longer time period was shortened to minimize calculations. Also, note that for 1974 the two index series are overlapping in order to provide the basis for splicing.

Splicing of the two index series is carried out in order to obtain a continuous series with a new base in 1974; it is accomplished by dividing each index number of the old series by 126.5 and multiplying by 100. For example, for 1970 the revised old index is 99.2/126.5 × 100 = 78.4, for 1971 it is 100.0/126.5 × 100 = 79.1, and so on. The results appear in column 3. The procedure shifts the reference base to 1974. The resulting spliced

Table 30.6.
Splicing of Two Index Number Series for Electrical Appliances

Year	Old Price Index (1971 = 100) (1)	Revised Price Index (1974 = 100) (2)	Old Index Shifted to Base 1974 (3)	Spliced Price Index (1974 = 100) (4)
1970	99.2		78.4	78.4
1971	100.0		79.1	79.1
1972	111.8		88.4	88.4
1973	118.3		93.5	93.5
1974	126.5	100.0	100.0	100.0
1975		105.6		105.6
1976		110.0		110.0

index series is the combination of the revised series in column 2 and the old index with a shifted base in column 3; it appears in column 4.

Suppose we wish to state the spliced index series on the 1971 reference base rather than on the 1974 base. We can accomplish this by multiplying each index number of the revised index in column 2 by 126.5 and dividing by 100. For example, for 1974 the revised index would be (100 × 126.5) ÷ 100 = 126.5, for 1975 (105.6 × 126.5) ÷ 100 = 133.6, and so on.

Note that shifting the base in Table 30.5, column 2, and splicing in Table 30.6, column 4, yield identical numerical results. The difference is substantive. Shifting involves changing the reference base only while the weight base remains unchanged. Splicing, on the other hand, involves a new weight base or an important revision which may or may not coincide with changing the reference base. Splicing makes interpretation of the resulting continuous index series difficult. This may be particularly true in cases, as in our illustration, where the base of the revised index contains new products and the old index does not contain these commodities. Yet splicing frequently offers the only practical approach to establishing some degree of comparability with the past.

Shifting and splicing are only two of the technical points which we should consider in order to determine whether an index is suitable for serving our needs. In addition, we should keep in mind the following:

1. We should clearly understand the exact purpose for which an index is intended.
2. It is important that the data-collecting sampling procedures for constructing an index conform to the sampling principles explained earlier in the text. Otherwise, we have no basis for drawing valid generalizations from the results.
3. It is desirable for the base period of an index to meet a number of criteria such as normality of the period, reliability of the data in the period, comparability with existing indices, inclusion of census years, and a base not too distant from the present.
4. We have already discussed some important aspects related to the selection of appropriate weights.
5. Use of index time series for economic analysis and forecasting requires numerous statistical adjustments. Some of these adjustment procedures, such as deseasonalizing, have already been covered in the two preceding sections.

PROBLEMS

Group One

30.1. Last year the average price of heating oil was 74¢ per gallon. This year's price is expected to average 129.50¢ per gallon.
    *(a) Calculate a price relatives index based on last year's price.
    (b) Last year a family received a $300 heating oil allowance from a federal

Answers to asterisked (*) problems are appended.

Section 30 Index Numbers

agency. Assuming that adjustments of oil allowances are directly proportional to price increases, what should the family's oil allowance be this year?

*30.2. Suppose average weekly wages in a metropolitan area and the area's Consumer Price Index were as follows:

Year	Wages	CPI (1967 = 100)
1970	$185	116.3
1975	267	161.2

Between the two years, have real wages increased or decreased? How much?

30.3. In Example 30.3 we found that the Paasche index number for our hypothetical family is 216.2 in 1979.
   (a) Verify this answer using the equivalent weighted price relatives index with current quantity weights.
   (b) Under what conditions would calculations of the Paasche index be preferred to the equivalent of price relatives index?

30.4. Discuss the advantages and limitations of the following indices:
   (a) Unweighted aggregate price index
   (b) Laspeyres index
   (c) Paasche index
   (d) A fixed-weight aggregate price index
   (e) An unweighted price relatives index

30.5. Give reasons why weighted price indices are preferable to unweighted ones.

30.6. Discuss the merits of the following methods of constructing weighted price indices:
   (a) Aggregate of prices
   (b) Average of price relatives

30.7. Discuss some uses and limitations of the following indices:
   (a) Consumer Price Index
   (b) Index of Industrial Production

30.8. What points should we keep in mind in order to determine whether an index is suitable for serving our needs?

30.9. Explain the following terms:
   (a) Quantity indices
   (b) Aggregate price indices
   (c) Composite index numbers
   (d) Value indices
   (e) Price relatives indices
   (f) Price indices

30.10. Distinguish between:
   (a) Shifting and splicing
   (b) Reference base and weight base
   (c) Quantity weights and value weights
   (d) Price relatives and quantity relatives
   (e) Base period and nonbase period

Group Two

30.11. Gabot and Gabot Corporation owns a large apartment complex. Water, heating oil, and electricity are included in the rent. Among other considerations, management uses a utility index to adjust rents for the following year. For the base year 1977 and for 1979 unit prices of the three utilities and the quantities consumed were as follows:

	Unit Price		Quantities Consumed (Thousands of Units[a])	
Item	1977	1979	1977	1979
Water	$1.20	$1.35	18.2	19.2
Heating oil	.52	.98	60.2	50.1
Electricity	.38	.86	52.3	49.7

[a]Cubic feet, gallons, and kilowatt-hours, respectively.

*(a) Calculate the Laspeyres index for 1979.
*(b) Calculate the Paasche index for 1979.
(c) Which of the two indices do you consider more suitable for the stated purpose? Explain why.

30.12. Consider the data given in Problem 30.11.
*(a) Calculate the unweighted aggregate price index for 1979.
*(b) Calculate the unweighted price relatives index for 1979.
(c) Why do these two index numbers differ? Explain.
(d) Discuss the advantages and limitations of each method.

30.13. Wheat and corn prices and quantities sold during 1972 and 1979 were as follows:

	Unit Price		Quantities Sold (Billions of Bushels)	
Item	1972	1979	1977	1979
Wheat	$1.80	$3.20	1.52	1.92
Corn	1.40	2.80	5.65	6.23

*(a) Calculate the Laspeyres index for 1979 with base year 1972.
(b) Calculate the weighted price relatives index with 1972 weights and base year.
(c) Interpret the meaning of the indices.
(d) Compare the merits of the indices in this case and in general.

30.14. Consider the data given in Problem 30.13.
*(a) Compute the Laspeyres index for 1979 with the base year 1972.

Section 30 Index Numbers

*(b) Suppose grain quantities represent production. Calculate an index of grain production for 1979 with 1972 price weights and base.

(c) Interpret the meaning of the two indices.

30.15. Presently the index of prices farmers pay for family living items has 1967 as a base year in order to facilitate comparisons with the Consumer Price Index (1967 = 100). The price index time series for farmers for the last few years is as follows:

Year	Index	Year	Index
1975	152	1978	187
1976	160	1979	195
1977	175	1980	208

(a) Suppose 1980 is established as the new reference base for the Consumer Price Index. Shift the base of the price index for the farmers to the new reference base in 1980 in order to maintain comparability with CPI. Show work in a table such as Table 30.5.

(b) What are the advantages and limitations of shifting the base of an index?

30.16. Karen Fisher is a free-lance reporter specializing on financial issues of interest to the general public. Karen is currently working on an article about the growing role of the federal government in the U.S. economy. Among other data, she considers the following information about the gross national product and federal expenditures:

Year	GNP[a]	Federal Expenditures[a]	Deflator Index
1972	$1171.1	$245	100.0
1978	2107.6	461	152.1

[a]In billions of current dollars.

*(a) Use the deflator index to express the 1978 current dollars for GNP and for federal expenditures in terms of 1972 constant dollars.

(b) Find the percentage relatives for real GNP and federal expenditures in 1978 over 1972.

(c) What conclusion may Karen include in her article?

30.17. Frank Yandel is responsible for compiling a state price index for ski equipment. Since 1962, the base year, the index has been used by the merchants of the state for making pricing and inventory decisions for the following season. The index, however, has increasingly become less representative of the current products used in skiing. New varieties of old products have seriously altered the old product mix on the basis of which weights were determined. In addition, growing demand for cross-country skiing has introduced new products which were not included in the index. These developments necessitated a revision of the index with a new weight and reference base in 1976. The old and the new indices were initially published as shown below:

Year	Old Price Index (1962 = 100)	Revised Price Index (1976 = 100)
1974	253.5	
1975	261.7	
1976	272.3	100.0
1977		112.3
1978		121.5

This discontinuous reporting created such a confusion among the users of the index, so splicing of the two indices was necessary.
(a) Splice the two indices and show work in a table such as Table 30.6.
(b) Why does splicing make interpretation of the resulting continuous index difficult?

Chapter 11
DECISION ANALYSIS

In this last chapter of our text, we deal with another set of techniques which have come to be known as *statistical decision theory*. Decision making is central to this body of statistical methods. They provide for systematic and rational selection among alternative courses of action on the basis of their explicitly stated consequences and under conditions of uncertainty. Furthermore, the new techniques provide for combining subjective and objective probabilities. The subjective probabilities based on the prior belief of the decision maker or other usually nonsampling information about the likelihood of various alternatives are revised with sample evidence by means of Bayes's formula. Since Bayes's theorem is central to this approach, the subject matter is alternatively called *Bayesian decision theory*.

Essentially, the material of this chapter revolves around three ultimate questions: What is the optimal course of action among alternatives of a decision problem? What is the value of collecting additional information by sampling or experimenting? Finally, what is the data collection strategy which optimizes the value of this additional information? The three sections of the chapter deal in turn with the basic concepts of the subject, analysis with decision trees, and procedures for determining an optimal course of action in the light of additional information.

SECTION 31 / BASIC CONCEPTS

Our immediate task is to discuss the following questions: What is the structure of a decision problem under uncertainty? What is the most appropriate decision criterion? What is the value of information which eliminates uncertainty? And, finally, how do we handle a decision maker who is risk-averse (that is, reluctant to take large losses)? Such a task will give us the opportunity to introduce the basic concepts of the subject.

The Structure of a Decision Problem

Obviously, no decision problem can exist unless the situation at hand involves at least two courses of action from which only one can be chosen. But the existence of alternative courses of action is not a sufficient characteristic for a decision prob-

Chapter 11 Decision Analysis

lem under uncertainty. A linear programming problem, for example, is a decision problem. It contains a large number of feasible solutions which can be considered alternative courses of action. This is a decision problem under certainty because choosing an optimal solution is carried out under perfect information.

By comparison, consider the following simple but illustrative decision problem.

Example 31.1

Jerome Poulos has been working as a waiter in a summer resort. Earnings were heavily dependent on weather conditions because of great variations in income from tipping. According to his own experience, as well as the experience of others, a waiter is expected to make about $3000 in excellent weather, $2000 in good weather, but only $1000 if summer weather is poor. These earnings are sufficient only to partially finance his college education.

So Jerome is looking for other, more rewarding employment alternatives. For the next summer season, he seriously considers the possibility of managing the concession on a hamburger stand. Two locations are available. According to past records, net earnings after deducting all operating costs were about $30,000 for the season from location A and $35,000 from location B, if excellent weather prevailed. In good weather, net earnings fell to $20,000 and $10,000, respectively. Poor weather, on the other hand, brought losses of $5000 for stand A and $2000 for stand B. This information is shown in Table 31.1 with pluses denoting gains and minuses losses.

This simple case contains all the major structural elements of a decision problem under uncertainty.

1. *The decision maker.* This is a person or persons who are responsible for making the decision. The decision maker can be an individual, as in the above case, or a committee representing a corporation or a government agency.
2. *Alternative courses of action.* In the example, the student manager has three choices: manage the stand at location A or at location B or work as a waiter. These courses of action are denoted in Table 31.1 as a_1, a_2, and a_3, respectively; they are also called *acts* and they depend on the decision maker's will. Acts are *mutually exclusive*. For example, Jerome's three acts would not have

Table 31.1.
Payoffs for Poulos's Decision Problem (Thousands of Dollars)

Event (Weather)	Act		
	Stand A a_1	Stand B a_2	Waiter a_3
Excellent	+$30	+$35	+$3.0
Good	+ 20	+ 10	+ 2.0
Poor	− 5	− 2	+ 1.0

Section 31 Basic Concepts

been mutually exclusive if we thought he could manage stand A and at the same time work as a waiter at night elsewhere.
3. *Events.* These are related to each act. Events are mutually exclusive, so that one and only one can occur. In our case, summer weather can be classified only under one of the three categories. Events are also collectively exhaustive. The three types of weather exhaust all possible weather conditions. Events are also called *states of the world* or *states of nature.* They are beyond the control of the decision maker.
4. *Payoffs.* Each payoff represents the net benefit to the decision maker for a chosen act and an occurring event. Each payoff specifies one and only one event-act combination, and hence it is uniquely determined. Table 31.1 contains nine uniquely determined payoffs. Payoffs may represent monetary as well as nonmonetary benefits to the decision maker. Furthermore, two or more payoffs may have identical values. A set of payoffs such as the one shown in Table 31.1 is called a *payoff table.*
5. *Uncertainty.* It is uncertain which event may occur. It is the element of uncertainty which separates deterministic problems such as linear programming and decision analysis problems.

In short, a decision problem under uncertainty has a structure which consists of five components: a decision maker, acts, events, payoffs, and uncertainty about which event may occur. A great number of managerial situations may be formulated and effectively analyzed as decision problems under uncertainty regardless of type of decision.

Expected Value as a Decision Criterion

What criterion should a decision maker employ for selecting the optimal act? At this point we should realize that we are concerned with *decision theory* and not *game theory.* Decision theory may be considered a branch of game theory. However, there is a difference between these two subjects which is important for determining the most appropriate decision criterion. In game theory, our opponent may be another human being. Here, we are concerned with problems where the decision maker's opponent is nature; and nature does not think and plot against its opponent. Therefore, a decision criterion which may be considered quite appropriate against a thinking opponent may be less suitable in a game against nature; we are looking for a decision criterion which is most appropriate when our opponent is nature.

Although mathematical statisticians and others have suggested several criteria, *expected value** is considered to be the most appropriate criterion for this type of analysis. Under this criterion the decision maker assigns *nonzero* probabilities to *all* states of nature or events of the problem. These probabilities may represent relative frequencies of historical data or hunches of the decision maker or a combination of the two sources. Then we calculate the expected value of each act and select the act with the largest expected payoff as optimal.

*At this point, you may wish to have a quick review of expected value in Section 8.

Example 31.1 (continued)

Jerome Poulos consulted the local weather bureau and found that on the basis of next summer's forecast, weather conditions are likely to occur with probabilities shown in Table 31.2. These probabilities also reflected his own belief about next season's weather. Accordingly, he decides to choose act a_1, manage the hamburger stand on location A, with the largest expected payoff

$$E(a_1)^* = .30(+30) + .40(+20) + .30(-5) = \$15.5 \, (\times 1000)$$

Table 31.2. Expected Values for Poulos's Decision Problem (Thousands of Dollars)

Event (Weather)	Probability	Act Stand A a_1	Act Stand B a_2	Act Waiter a_3
Excellent	.30	+$30	+$35	+$3.0
Good	.40	+ 20	+ 10	+ 2.0
Poor	.30	− 5	− 2	+ 1.0
Expected value: $E(a_j)$ =		+$15.5 ↑ Optimal	+$13.9	+$2.0

The expected value criterion can be interpreted as a process which selects as the optimal act, marked with an asterisk, that act which yields the largest long-run average payoff. Suppose Jerome Poulos has repeatedly made the same decision of choosing act a_1 under identical environmental conditions; as the number of such decisions becomes large, average net earnings would approach the expected value of $15,500 per season. Insurance companies determine premiums, to a large extent, on the basis of expected losses. The solvency of a retirement system such as Social Security is estimated on the basis of expected receipts and expected payable benefits.

Expected value is intuitively consistent with what most decision makers are likely to consider an appropriate guide to action. In addition, expected value possesses a number of desirable properties for making decisions under uncertainty. Discussion of these properties, however, lies outside the scope of this text.

We should keep in mind that the task of formulating a situation into a decision problem is not an easy one. We may use a discrete or a continuous probability distribution as long as such a distribution reflects our belief about the uncertainty of states of nature; comparability of acts requires a common measuring unit for all payoffs, whether such a unit be dollars, days, or a physical or social index; magnitudes of payoffs should be determined with care; finally, acts should be carefully selected and illegal or inadmissible acts should be eliminated.

Expected Value of Perfect Information

Suppose a decision maker can obtain information which will eliminate the uncertainty in a decision problem. How much is this information worth? This cost for eliminating uncertainty is called *expected value of perfect information (EVPI)*; it

Section 31 Basic Concepts

can be a useful guide for deciding whether or not to collect additional information for a problem.

We shall introduce EVPI with a case which illustrates managerial problems centered on the decision to stock, manufacture, or lease goods or services in anticipation of uncertain demand.

Example 31.2

Bill Quint, a retailer, handles a perishable commodity which costs $3 and sells for $8 a unit. Since the merchandise is worthless if not sold by the end of the day it is stocked, the retailer is forced to place an order for the item daily. This situation creates a problem, however; if daily demand is greater than the ordered stock, foregone gross profit is $5 per unit of unsatisfied demand (possible loss of customer goodwill is excluded). If daily demand is less than the ordered stock, he loses $3 per overstocked unit. For the past 40 days, demand for the commodity has been as follows:

Demand (units)	1	2	3	4
Sales days	8	12	12	8

How many units should Bill stock in order to maximize his daily gross profit? Analysis is conveniently summarized in Table 31.3. Number of demanded units is considered to represent a random variable with the relative frequencies as probabilities. For example, since demand for 1 unit occurred in 8 out of 40 sales days, the probability is 8/40 or .20. Entries in the payoff table are determined as follows: We realize a $5 profit if we stock 1 unit, act a_1, since this is the only unit which can be sold whether demand is 1 or more units. If we stock 2 units, act a_2, and 1 unit is demanded, profit will be $2 since we earn $8 for selling 1 unit and pay $6 for stocking 2 units. If 2 units are demanded, we net $10 since we earn $16 and pay $6. Also, we realize $10 whether demand is 3 or 4 units since we can sell no more

Table 31.3.
Expected Values for Quint's Decision Problem

Event (Units Demanded)	Probability	Act (Units Stocked)			
		a_1 1	a_2 2	a_3 3	a_4 4
1	.20	+$5*	+$2	−$1	−$4
2	.30	+ 5	+10*	+ 7	+ 4
3	.30	+ 5	+10	+15*	+12
4	.20	+ 5	+10	+15	+20*
Expected value: $E(a_j) =$		+$5	+$8.40	+$9.40 ↑ Optimal	+$8.00

*Payoffs under certainty.

Chapter 11 Decision Analysis

than the 2 units we have stocked. The remaining payoffs are determined in a similar manner. Bill Quint should stock 3 units with a largest expected profit obtained as follows:

$$E(a_3)^* = .20(-1) + .30(+7) + .30(+15) + .20(+15) = +\$9.40$$

The expected profit of other acts is calculated the same way.

In order to eliminate uncertainty Bill Quint is thinking of selling the commodity on a subscription basis. According to his estimates, the cost of keeping subscriber records amounts to $2.00 per day. Should Bill switch to subscription? The answer would be yes if the cost of uncertainty, that is, EVPI is larger than $2.00. In order to calculate EVPI we need to find the expected value of the problem under certainty.

Example 31.2 (continued)

If the commodity were to be sold on subscription, the demand, although varying, will be known with certainty. Each day we will always stock the correct number of units to be demanded and realize the maximum gross profit. For instance, if demand is for 1 unit, we stock 1 unit and realize $5 gross profit; if demand is for 2 units, we stock 2 units and realize $10 gross profit; and so forth. Note that the payoffs under certainty represent the largest payoffs for each event-row. The payoffs under certainty, marked with an asterisk, are shown in Table 31.3. The expected gross profit under certainty is

$$EVC = .20(+5) + .30(+10) + .30(+15) + .20(+20) = +\$12.50$$

where EVC stands for expected value under certainty. Then EVPI is the difference between expected value under certainty and expected value of the optimal act (under uncertainty):

$$EVPI = EVC - E(a_1)^* = 12.50 - 9.40 = \$3.10$$

Therefore, it pays for Quint to switch to subscription.

The EVPI of a problem is also equivalent to the *expected opportunity loss* (EOL) of the optimal act. An *opportunity loss* is the gain which we would have realized or the cost which we could have avoided with perfect information.

Example 31.2 (continued)

Consider the payoffs in Table 31.3. Suppose demand is for 2 units; if we stock 1 unit, our opportunity loss is $5, the profit which we would have realized had we stocked the second unit; if we stock 2 units, our opportunity loss is zero since we have made the maximum profit of $10; if we stock 3 units, our opportunity loss is $3, the cost of stocking the third unsold unit; if we stock 4 units, our opportunity loss is $6, the cost of stocking the 2 unsold units. Thus, when demand is for 2 units the opportunity losses are $5, 0, $3, and $6, as shown in the second row of Table 31.4. In general, we obtain the opportunity losses for each row by subtracting algebraically each payoff in that row from the asterisked payoff in the corresponding row of

Table 31.4.
Expected Opportunity Losses for Quint's Decision Problem

		Act (Units Stocked)			
Event (Units Demanded)	Probability	a_1 1	a_2 2	a_3 3	a_4 4
1	.20	$0	$3	$6	$9
2	.30	5	0	3	6
3	.30	10	5	0	3
4	.20	15	10	5	0
Expected opportunity loss: EOL (a_j) =		$7.50	$4.10	$3.10 ↑ Optimal	$4.50

Table 31.3. For example, when demand is for 1 unit, the opportunity losses are

$$5^* - (5) = 0, \quad 5^* - (2) = 3, \quad 5^* - (-1) = 6, \quad 5^* - (-4) = 9$$

as shown in the first row of Table 31.4. Note that opportunity losses are always positive values.

Now, instead of wishing to maximize profit, we wish to minimize opportunity loss. The optimal act, indicated in Table 31.4, is again a_3 (stock 3 units) with the smallest expected opportunity loss

$$EOL(a_3)^* = .20(6) + .30(3) + .30(0) + .20(5) = \$3.10$$

This is also the EVPI of the problem found earlier.

In sum, we have introduced two alternative methods for computing the cost of uncertainty:

EVPI = expected value under certainty less expected value of the optimal act (under uncertainty); in symbols, EVPI = EVC − $E(a_j)^*$

EVPI = expected opportunity loss of the optimal act; in symbols, EVPI = EOL$(a_j)^*$

In calculating EVPI by either method it is useful to remember the following relationship: the sum of expected value and expected opportunity loss of *each* act is always equal to the expected value under certainty. Consider, for example, act a_1; $E(a_1)$ = \$5 from Table 31.3 plus EOL(a_1) = \$7.50 from Table 31.4 equals \$12.50, the EVC of the problem.

In obtaining an optimal solution to our problem we used a probability model where demand is conceived as a random variable. But randomness implies that the occurrence of future daily demand, like the outcome in rolling a die, is the result of an independent trial. So we assume that the demand of a particular day does not depend on the demand of the preceding or following days. Furthermore, the demand for the commodity in question neither affects nor is affected by the sale of other items.

In spite of these limitations, the model can be advantageously applied as a first approximation to a great number of real-world situations. Most common cases involve commodities such as newspapers, highly seasonal items, and the services of leased equipment. The salvage value, if any, of such "perishable" commodities and the value of good will can be easily incorporated into the model.

Expected Utility

We have already explained that expected value is a long-run average which assumes that the optimal decision is repeated a large number of times. Many important personal and business decisions, however, are made once under unique conditions. In addition, such one-time decisions may involve large gains as well as large losses, so that a decision maker may not be willing to take the risk of a large loss. How do we cope with one-time decision problems involving the risk of large losses?

The magnitude of the risk that a person is willing to assume is a matter of personal preference. Consider the following game: We win $10 if we correctly guess the outcome of tossing a fair coin *once;* but we lose $5 if we guess wrong. A hungry person with only $5 in his pocket will likely refuse to play the game, although the expected value is

$$.50(+10) + .50(-5) = +\$2.50$$

The 50–50 chance that he may lose the only means of partially satisfying his pressing need may be overwhelming. But many people would be willing to bet since the stakes are small and they expect to win twice as much as they may lose. Next, suppose the stakes are raised to win $1000 and lose $500. Now the expected value is

$$.50(+1000) + .50(-500) = +\$250$$

or 100 times larger than previously. Yet for many persons the 50 percent chance of losing $500 may be so important that they would rather refuse to play the game than bet. In fact, if the stakes are raised sufficiently high, even a millionaire may refuse to gamble.

This simple illustration suggests that for a given person the importance attached to the use of money, that is, the *utility* of money, is numerically equal to monetary value up to a given sum. Of course, such a sum may vary from one time to another for a certain individual as well as from one individual to another. For problems involving smaller amounts than such a sum, a decision maker is risk-neutral; then expected monetary value is the appropriate criterion for determining the optimal act. For problems with amounts greater than the given sum, a decision maker is not risk-neutral; then utility rather than monetary value becomes an appropriate measure of an individual's attitude toward risk; then expected utility is the appropriate criterion for determining the optimal act.

Techniques are available which enable us to determine whether or not a decision maker is risk-neutral and, if not, to derive a utility curve reflecting his attitude toward risk. These techniques are too elaborate to be included here. We assume that a utility curve is properly derived and illustrate application of expected utility with a concrete case.

Section 31 Basic Concepts

Example 31.3

Using expected value we found that the best act for Jerome Poulos is to manage stand A (Table 31.2). Jerome felt uneasy about the fact that, if next season's weather turned out to be poor, he would be losing $5000. He could ill afford such a large loss. A special test disclosed that Jerome was not risk-neutral; in fact, he was risk-averse in accordance with a utility curve shown in Fig. 31.1. The vertical scale of this graph consists of units, called *utiles,* which reflect Poulos's utility towards the earnings from his venture.

Figure 31.1.
Jerome Poulos's utility curve.

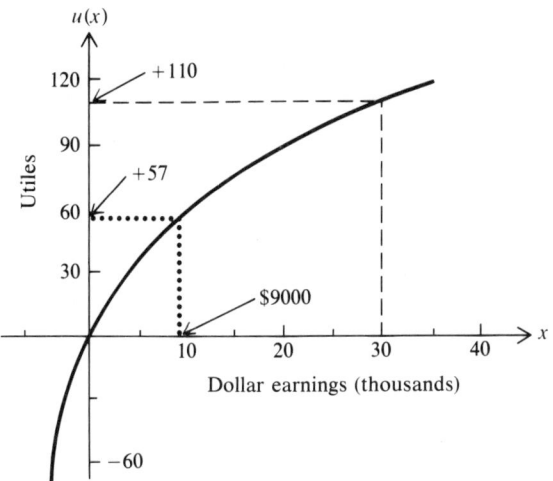

From this curve we can obtain the utiles which Jerome would like to assign to all the consequences of his problem and determine the optimal act using expected utility as a criterion. For instance, suppose we wish to find the utility value for payoff $30,000 (Table 31.2, act a_1, first row); we start at point 30 on the horizontal axis in Fig. 31.1 following the broken line upward and to the left. At the point where the line meets the vertical axis we read +110 utiles. This is Jerome's utility value for +$30,000. At this point, we may ignore the dotted line. Table 31.5 shows the utiles which in

Table 31.5.
Expected Utility Values for Poulous's Decision Problem[a]

Event (Weather)	Probability	Stand A a_1	Stand B a_2	Waiter a_3
Excellent	.30	+110	+120	+27
Good	.40	+ 90	+ 60	+15
Poor	.30	− 70	− 10	+ 8
Expected utility $EXU(a_j)$ =		+ 48	+ 57	+16.5
			↑ Optimal	

[a]Payoff table and expected values represent utiles.

this manner can be assigned to each initial payoff of earnings. Now the optimal act is a_2, manage stand B, with the largest expected utility

$$\text{EXU}(a_2)^* = .30(+120) + .40(+60) + .30(-10) = +57 \text{ utiles}$$

We can determine the dollar equivalent of the best act from Fig. 31.1. We locate the point on the vertical axis representing $+57$ utiles; then from that point we follow the dotted line parallel to the horizontal axis until the line intersects the utility curve; from that point we follow the dotted line parallel to the vertical axis; at the point this line meets the horizontal axis we read approximately $9000. This is the dollar equivalent of the best act.

Derivation of utility curves is based on the assumption that people act rationally and in accordance with certain rules of consistent behavior. But this, it is argued, is contrary to the way people may *actually behave* in real-world situations. Advocates of decision analysis, on the other hand, point out that utility theory prescribes how people *should behave*. This *normative* approach to action must be followed if our acts are to be consistent with our probabilistic assessment of events and choices among payoffs.

In further developing the subject of decision analysis, we shall assume that the decision maker is risk-neutral, that is, his utility curve is linear. And we shall use expected monetary value as our only decision criterion.

PROBLEMS

Group One

31.1. Jerome Poulos's problem in Table 31.2 was simplified in order to focus on essentials. For each qualification, determine what Jerome's decision should be.
  *(a) He forgot to subtract from the payoffs of acts a_1 and a_2 the wages which he would have earned if he were employed as a waiter.
  (b) Personal income taxes would have changed his payoff table as follows (data in thousands of dollars):

Weather	a_1	a_2	a_3
Excellent	+$21.0	+$24.0	+$2.8
Good	+ 15.0	+ 7.0	+ 1.7
Poor	− 4.0	− 1.5	+ .9

  (c) Probabilities of the initial problem have changed to .05 for excellent, .20 for good, and .75 for poor weather.
31.2. Consider Jerome Poulos's problem in Table 31.2.
  *(a) Construct an opportunity loss table and calculate the expected opportunity loss of the optimal act or EVPI.

Answers to asterisked (*) problems are appended.

Section 31 Basic Concepts

(b) Verify that EVPI is the expected value under certainty less the expected value of the optimal act (under uncertainty).

(c) Interpret the value of EVPI.

31.3. Grand River Nursery contemplates stocking Christmas trees for the forthcoming season. On the average, each tree costs $4 to stock and sells for $5. Any unsold trees at the end of the season are worthless. The past sales record is:

Sales (hundreds)	4	5	6	7	8	9	10
Relative frequency	.05	.10	.10	.20	.25	.20	.10

(a) Construct a profit payoff table.
*(b) Find the expected value of the optimal act.
(c) Construct an opportunity loss table and find EVPI or the expected opportunity loss of the optimal act.
(d) Verify that EVPI is the expected value under certainty less the expected value of the optimal act (under uncertainty).
(e) What is the meaning of EVPI?

31.4. Cindy Wacks runs a florist shop. In order to satisfy the needs of a number of regular and sophisticated customers, Cindy stocks a highly perishable flower. A dozen flowers cost $30 and sell for $100. Any flowers not sold the day they are stocked are worthless. Demand in dozens of flowers has been as follows:

Demand	0	1	2	3	4	5
Relative frequency	.10	.20	.30	.20	.10	.10

(a) Construct a profit payoff table.
*(b) Find the expected value of the optimal act.
(c) Construct an opportunity loss table and find EVPI.
(d) What alternative solutions do you recommend for eliminating uncertainty about demand?

31.5. W. J. Morgan Enterprises will realize a profit of $2 million during the first 3 years after a new product is introduced. However, if the introduced product fails, losses during the 3-year period are expected to be $900,000.
*(a) What is the probability of success which may allow the firm to break even?
(b) Formulate a simple decision rule in terms of the range of probabilities for which management would introduce the new product.

31.6. Consider the data in Tables 31.3 and 31.4.
(a) Plot the expected profit and expected opportunity loss of each act on coordinate paper, where the x axis represents stock level Q and the y axis expected profit and expected opportunity loss.
(b) Connect each set of points with a line.
(c) Discuss the relationship that may exist between these two sets of measures and expected profit under certainty.

Chapter 11 Decision Analysis

31.7. Explain the following:
   (a) Payoff table
   (b) Statistical decision theory
   (c) Acts
   (d) Decision maker
   (e) States of the world
   (f) Events
   (g) Bayesian decision theory
   (h) Uncertainty

31.8. Distinguish between:
   (a) Expected value (under uncertainty) and expected value under certainty
   (b) Expected opportunity loss and expected value of perfect information
   (c) Expected monetary value and expected utility
   (d) Decision theory and game theory

Group Two

*31.9. George Moore is in charge of production planning at Wright Toys Manufacturing Co. Two machines are considered for manufacturing the springs for the action mechanism of a space robot. Machine A costs $100,000 and machine B $200,000. During the life of machines total sales are expected to be 200,000, 400,000, and 500,000 units with probabilities .20, .30, and .50, respectively. Machine B has the capacity to handle the maximum sales volume without an increase in machine unit costs. Machine A, on the other hand, has limited capacity so that unit cost increases by $.30 at a 400,000-unit production level and by $.60 at a 500,000-unit production level. If expected machine unit cost is the appropriate decision criterion, which machine should George choose?

31.10. Under current wheat prices, farmer McCoy figures out that he will receive a $22,000 government subsidy if he keeps his farmland idle, a $10,000 subsidy for partial planting, and no subsidy for full planting. After full costing calculations, he expects the following net earnings without the subsidies (data in thousands of dollars):

Crop Outcome	Probability	Full Planting a_1	Partial Planting a_2	No Planting a_3
Poor	.20	−$10	−$4	−$2
Average	.50	+ 40	+ 25	− 2
Bumper	.30	+ 60	+ 40	− 2

   (a) Prepare a profit payoff table which incorporates the subsidies.
   *(b) Find the expected value of the optimal act.
   (c) Discuss some important assumptions on which farmer McCoy bases his payoff table.

31.11. Mohawk Paper Company buys paper pulp from another mill at $100 per ton for manufacturing newsprint. Management considers the possibility of buying the required machinery for producing their own pulp. Type A machinery costs $200,000, type B $400,000, and type C $600,000; this machinery would reduce the cost of producing pulp to $98, $96, and $94 per ton, respectively. For the

Answers to asterisked (*) problems are appended.

Section 31 Basic Concepts

next 5 years, the normal life period of the new machinery, Mohawk's needs are expected to average 16,000 tons per year with probability .40; 20,000 tons with probability .30; 24,000 tons with probability .20; and 30,000 tons with probability .10.

(a) Prepare a payoff table of net cost savings for each machine.
(b) Find the expected value of the optimal act.
(c) Discuss possible limitations of payoffs.

31.12. Frederick Levey, the new sales manager of Grand River Nursery (Problem 31.3), finds that, after subtracting overhead charges, the cost of stocking is only $2.50 per tree. Each tree sells for $5.00 but, during the last few hours before closing for Christmas, the remaining trees are sold for $1.00 apiece. Furthermore, Frederick observes that, on the average, the company loses $.50 profit for every natural tree sold because customers do not buy a substitute artificial tree. Assuming that demand for Christmas trees remains the same as shown in Problem 31.3:

(a) Construct a profit payoff table.
(b) Find the expected value of the optimal act.

31.13. Friendly Corner is a small general store located in a busy summer resort. Jeff Mertz has supplied the store's summer customers with Sunday issues of a daily newspaper. Each copy costs $.50 and sells for $.80. Jeff has been informed that henceforth no unsold papers will be returnable. His past sales are:

Newspaper (number)	32	33	34	35	36
Relative frequency	.10	.20	.20	.30	.20

(a) Construct a profit payoff table and find the expected profit of the optimal act.
(b) Since the manager is afraid that he may lose regular summer customers if they find him an unreliable source, he decides to order 36 copies each week. What is the cost of preserving his customers' goodwill?
(c) If he has regular customers, what alternative solution do you recommend?

31.14. Consider the following profit payoff table and the utility curves X, Y, and Z (data in thousands of dollars):

Probability	a_1	a_2	a_3
.30	+$30	+$20	+$35
.40	+ 10	+ 30	0
.30	− 5	− 20	− 10

For each of the following three entrepreneurs:
(i) Indicate whether the person is risk-neutral, a risk avoider, or a risk taker and select the appropriate utility curve.
(ii) Construct a payoff table of utiles, find the expected utility of the optimal act, and determine the act's dollar equivalent.

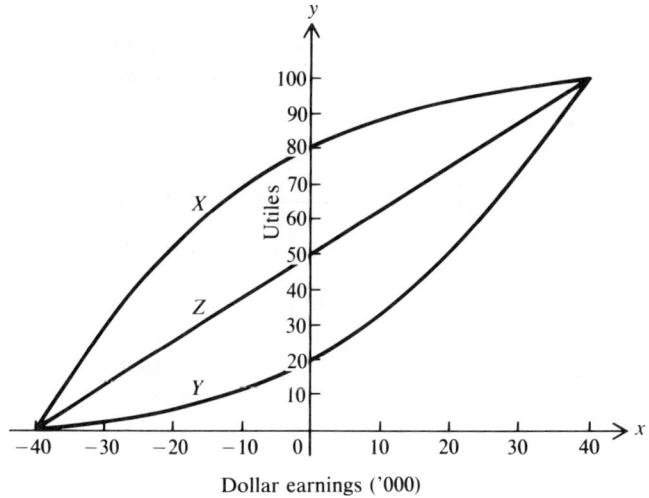

*(a) Mr. Gernes is supplied with sufficient working capital for his large operation. He believes that moderate risks should be self-insured.
(b) Ms. Black is in such a tight financial position that a loss of $20,000 makes her feel very cautious and conservative.
(c) Mr. White is a confirmed optimist.

SECTION 32/ DECISION TREE ANALYSIS

So far we have analyzed decision problems under uncertainty by means of a payoff table. These simple problems had two distinct characteristics: there is only one decision and each act of this decision relates to the same set of events. More frequently than not, real-world problems are too complex and lack these two characteristics. Decisions must be made sequentially at two or more points in time where uncertain events may occur between decisions. Furthermore, each act may relate to a different set of events and probabilities. Sometimes, analysis can be carried out in terms of payoff tables. Tabular analysis, however, is cumbersome at best. Systematic and effective analysis of such complex managerial problems requires special tree diagrams called *decision trees*.

We carry out decision tree analysis with an illustrative case. First, we introduce the structural components of a decision tree by portraying the acts and events of the problem. Second, we assign probabilities and determine payoffs. Third, we calculate expected payoffs in order to determine the optimal course of action. Finally, we discuss in general decision trees as tools of analysis.

Section 32 Decision Tree Analysis

Identifying Acts and Events

It is important to realize that all problems, whether they involve a single decision or a sequence of decisions, can be portrayed with decision tree diagrams. Displaying, however, elements of a single decision problem, namely, acts, events, probabilities, and payoffs, is trivial; decision tree analysis is not significantly more than a visual representation of tabular analysis. By contrast, construction of a decision tree diagram for a sequential decision problem must be carried out with care. Our first task consists of drawing the skeleton of a decision tree by identifying the problem's acts and events and their sequence.

Example 32.1

In the past, oil wildcatter Thomas Drucker did not use to take seismic tests before drilling; he relied heavily on his personal experience in deciding whether to drill or to sell his option before the lease expired; and he was frequently successful in striking oil instead of drilling a dry hole. This time, however, Drucker is not confident about the underlying structure of the present drilling site; as an alternative, he seriously considers taking seismic tests before drilling. Seismic tests could tell whether the underlying geophysical structure of the site is favorable or unfavorable for striking oil.

The structure of the decision tree diagram for Drucker's problem is shown in Fig. 32.1. Note that decisions are to be made at two separate stages or points of time. The immediate choice requires selecting one of two acts: "Do not test," that is, do not take seismic tests, or "Test," that is, take seismic tests. The choice of the two acts is displayed with a *decision fork,* having one branch for each act. For convenience, we use a square to denote the starting point of a decision fork and number it to facilitate identification.

If the choice is "Do not test," such an act leads to another decision fork, at

Figure 32.1.
Structure of the decision tree for Drucker's problem.

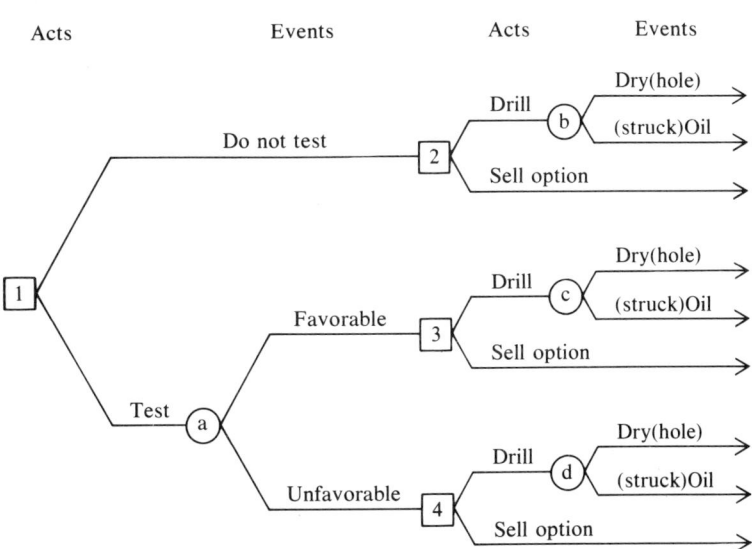

point 2, with two acts: "Drill" or "Sell option." The branch leading to point 2 is long enough to align with acts of decision forks 3 and 4, which occur at the same decision-making stage of the problem. The decision to drill leads to the *chance fork,* at point *b*; events "Dry (hole)" and "(struck) Oil" are shown in separate branches. Note that we use a circle and assign a letter to this as well as other chance forks of the problem. Unlike the "Drill" act, the "Sell option" act does not lead to a chance fork; it is a "dummy" branch lengthened in order to align with act-events of decision fork 2.

If the choice is "Test," this act leads to chance fork at point *a* because the outcome of the test is uncertain; the two branches of the chance fork represent favorable and unfavorable test results. Regardless of which event occurs, each branch leads to a new decision fork at points 3 and 4; then the branching of acts and events for each test result is identical to that at decision fork 2.

Observe that the flow of acts and events in a decision tree diagram such as the one shown in Fig. 32.1 follows a chronological sequence from left to right; the starting point on the left is a decision fork because a decision must be made before an event occurs; each arrow end on the right portrays a *path,* that is an act-event sequence, which leads to a unique outcome of the problem; for example, the fourth path from the top of the diagram depicts the following act-event sequence; test, favorable, drill, dry (hole). A path should not be confused with a decision rule which selects one act for each possible event of a chance fork; for example, one such decision rule is: Test; if test is favorable, drill; if test is unfavorable, sell option. Such a rule is referred to as a *strategy.* A rule which selects the optimal act for each possible event is called the *optimal decision rule* or the *optimal strategy.*

Structurally, a decision tree diagram is like the probability tree diagram we introduced earlier, with one significant difference. A probability tree diagram consists of only chance forks in order to accommodate the two elements of a random experiment, events and their probabilities; each chance fork portrays all possible event-probabilities of a trial in a series of successive trials. A decision tree diagram, on the other hand, consists of decision forks and chance forks; each decision fork portrays the acts which are relevant to that decision; each act may be followed by a chance fork which portrays all possible events relevant to that act. Thus, a decision tree diagram is designed to accommodate four elements of a decision problem: acts, events, probabilities, and payoffs. Discussion of the last two elements will be our next topic.

As in the case of single-decision problems, construction of decision trees for sequential-decision problems must meet two important requirements. First, both the acts of each decision fork and the events of each chance fork must be *mutually exclusive.* For example, not taking seismic tests entirely excludes taking such tests; drilling entirely excludes selling the option to drill. The same can be said about the events of the case: seismic tests can be either favorable or unfavorable but not both; drilling can result in either a dry hole or striking oil but not both. Second, the events of each chance fork must be *collectively exhaustive.* For example, the favorable and unfavorable seismic tests exhaust all possible test results; a dry hole and striking oil exhaust all possible drilling results. Of course, a more realistic

Section 32 Decision Tree Analysis

approach to Drucker's problem may include more than two acts in each decision fork. Regardless of the number of acts or events, however, these two requirements must be met.

Drucker's case purposely describes a highly simplified situation. Identifying the alternative acts of a complex real-world problem requires careful analysis of the situation, and the question arises: What guidelines should we employ in determining the acts of a problem? We may be faced with the dilemma of determining which of the possible acts are relevant to our problem. The suggestion that a problem should include every act which a decision maker wishes to consider may not be satisfactory; for instance, we may not be aware of certain technological aspects of our problem. Soliciting the advice of experts is frequently important, if not necessary. In addition, we should have a clear understanding of the goal of our analysis: Is our goal, as decision makers, to achieve a high level of sales, maximize profits, minimize costs, economize time, maximize reliability of a product, or maintain managerial control? Whatever our goal is, we should make a realistic appraisal of available resources and determine a time horizon consistent with probable changes in the state of technology.

Assigning Probabilities and Determining Payoffs

Identifying acts and events delineates the skeleton of a decision tree diagram. Assigning probabilities to events and determining payoffs for each path mark the first stage in decision tree analysis. We may continue with Drucker's decision problem.

Example 32.2

After studying the present drilling site carefully, Thomas Drucker believes that the probability of striking oil without taking seismic tests is 40 percent. Using seismic tests, however, would change significantly this probability: if the tests are favorable, the chances of striking oil would increase to 75 percent; these chances would decrease to 8 percent if the seismic tests are unfavorable. In the past and under similar geophysical formations, seismic tests showed favorable results 48 percent of the time.

The relevant probabilities for each event of our decision problem are shown in Fig. 32.2. Probabilities are shown in parentheses. At this point of time, we may ignore the dollar net payoffs which appear at the end point of each path. The probability of drilling a dry hole without seismic tests is .60 since $1 - .40 = .60$, that is, this is the complementary probability for striking oil without seismic tests. On the same basis, the probability for unfavorable seismic tests is .52 since $1 - .48 = .52$; if tests are favorable, the probability of drilling a dry hole is .25 since $1 - .75 = .25$; and if tests are unfavorable, the probability of drilling a dry hole is .92 since $1 - .08 = .92$.

Note that the probabilities at chance forks c and d are conditional; they occur on the condition that the result of seismic tests is known to be favorable or unfavorable. These conditional probabilities will be the center of our discussion in the next section.

In the meantime, let us consider determination of payoffs for Drucker's problem.

Figure 32.2.
Drucker's decision tree showing probabilities and payoffs.

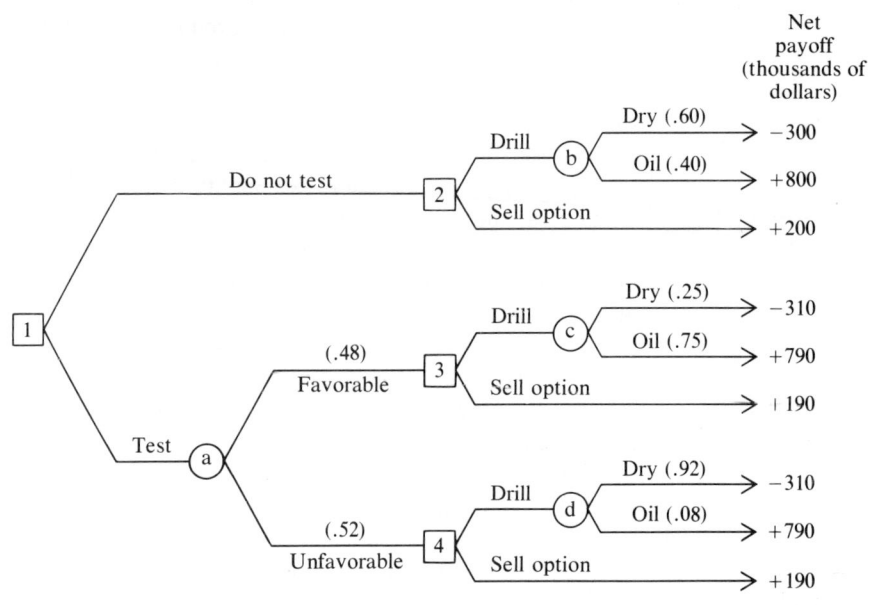

Example 32.3

Again, relying on personal experience Thomas Drucker figures out that he can sell his option to drill for $200,000; this was his best estimate under going market conditions for drilling options. If Thomas decides to drill, the drilling cost would be $300,000; this sum would be a total loss if no oil is found; striking oil, on the other hand, would bring in $1,100,000; these drilling payoffs would be realized with as well as without taking seismic tests. Seismic tests, however, cost $10,000.

The net payoffs in thousands of dollars are shown at the end of each path of the decision tree diagram in Fig. 32.2. Minus signs means losses and plus signs gains. The loss of $300,000 for drilling a dry hole and the gain of $200,000 for selling the drilling option without seismic tests are net payoffs as stated initially. The net payoff for striking oil without seismic tests would be the revenue of $1,100,000 less the drilling costs of $300,000 or $800,000. These net payoffs without seismic tests would be changed by $10,000 if seismic tests are taken. Whether seismic tests are favorable or unfavorable, the drilling losses for a dry hole would increase to $310,000; gains for striking oil or selling the option would decrease to $790,000 and $190,000 respectively.

In the previous section we pointed out that formulating a situation into a decision problem is not an easy task. This is true with the formulation of single-decision problems; the difficulties are more challenging in decision tree analysis. A few additional points may be helpful for both assigning probabilities to events and determining payoffs.

First, with respect to events and their probabilities in a real-life problem each chance fork may represent a probability distribution. Such a distribution may be discrete, representing demand for a product with hundreds or even thousands of events, that is, number of units demanded; it may also be a probability model such as the binomial, Poisson, or normal distribution. Which probability distribution we choose will depend on the nature of the problem and the type of analysis we, as decision makers, wish to carry out or consider appropriate to the case.

In the second place, the probability distribution of a decision problem may reflect the interactive effect of a nearly infinite array of future events. Consider for example, a decision problem whether to test-market or not to test-market a new product before the product is distributed nationally. The demand distribution of such a product may reflect the combined effect of customer response, competition, technology, resource scarcity, population growth, government regulations, and so forth. Although these future events are beyond our control, we believe that their net result is reflected by the chosen demand distribution for the product.

Third, frequently the distinction is made between *risk* and *uncertainty*. According to this distinction, the term *risk* applies only to events, such as events from tossing coins or rolling dice, which justify the assignment of objective probabilities; the term *uncertainty* applies only to events, such as demand for a product or an economic recession, to which subjective probabilities can be assigned. Recent developments tend to make this distinction between risk and uncertainty one of degree of belief, and to refer to the entire range of possible events as one of uncertainty. Hence, consistent with these developments, we use the term *uncertainty* in its broadest sense and regardless of whether the initial probabilities of a problem are determined objectively or subjectively.

For determining the net payoffs of a decision problem we should keep in mind two important points. The first point has to do with the *measuring unit* of the payoffs; such a unit could be dollars or time; it could also be an index measuring reliability of engineering systems, productivity, product acceptability, administrative effectiveness, pollution control, social welfare, national defense capabilities, and so forth, depending on what we intend to optimize. Whatever our objective may be, all payoffs of a decision problem must be expressed in the same measuring unit; otherwise, the alternative acts of the problem cannot be comparable.

The second point has to do with the *magnitude* of the payoffs. Each payoff must represent the *net* cash inflow of future receipts and expenditures. For example, receiving $1,100,000 from striking oil is not a net payoff in Drucker's problem; we must subtract from that sum the $300,000 drilling costs. Past revenues and costs are irrelevant; so are revenues or costs which occur irrespective of which act is chosen. Finally, if the cash flows occur over different and long time periods, payoffs must represent the present value of discounted cash flows.

The Rollback Method of Evaluation

Our problem has been organized in the chronological order of the decisions to be made and the chances to be taken. The decision tree diagram is like a roadmap which indicates the penalties and rewards associated with each act-event sequence. Now we are ready to analyze our problem.

Of course, we would wish to select an immediate act at decision point 1 in Fig. 32.2. Selection requires that we calculate the expected payoffs of the two

428 Chapter 11 Decision Analysis

acts, not taking or taking seismic tests, and then choose the one with the largest expected payoff. But this is impossible unless first we evaluate all later decisions which result from choosing the immediate act. For example, in order to find the expected payoff for the act of taking seismic tests, we must first specify which acts are chosen at decision points 3 and 4. In other words, we must determine whether drilling or selling the option is the preferred act if seismic tests are favorable and determine the same thing if seismic tests are unfavorable; then and only then shall we be able to calculate the expected payoff of the act to take seismic tests. In short, evaluation of decision points must be made in reverse chronological sequence; from the right (end) to the left (start) of the decision tree diagram. This evaluation procedure is a unique characteristic of analyzing sequential decision problems. Since such a procedure is carried out backward, it is called *backward induction* or *rollback method*.

Example 32.4

Backward induction for Drucker's problem is illustrated in Fig. 32.3. We can imagine ourselves traveling into the future and standing at the right end points of the diagram. Then we work our way backward by calculating expected payoffs at each chance fork and selecting the act which yields the largest expected payoff at each decision point.

If we were in a position to choose the acts at decision point 2, what course of action would we have taken? If we decided to drill, there is a .60 probability of finding a dry hole for a $-\$300,000$ payoff; however, there is

Figure 32.3.
Drucker's decision tree illustrating backward induction.

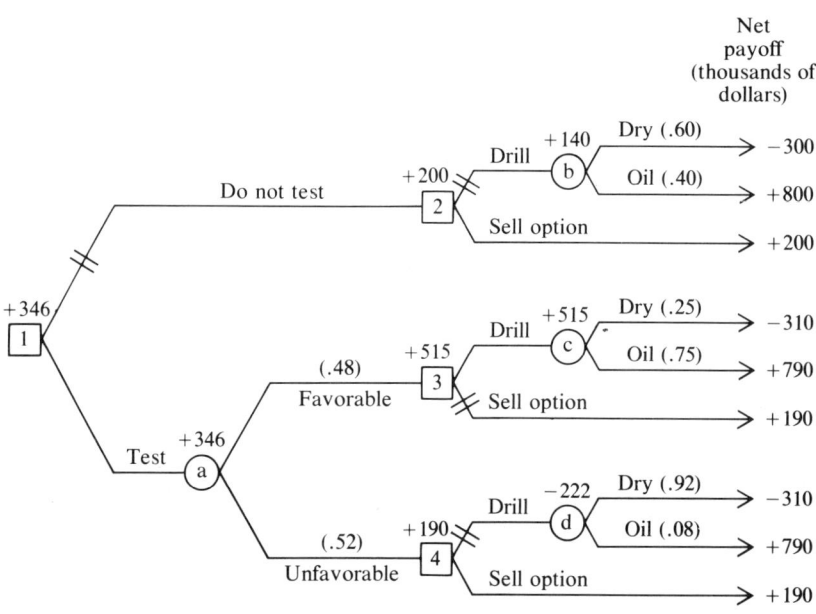

a .40 probability of striking oil for a $800,000 payoff. The expected payoff of chance fork *b* is

$$.60(-300) + .40(+800) = +\$140 \, (\times 1000)$$

We enter this sum above chance point *b*; it is the expected payoff for the decision to drill. The act to sell option, at decision point 2, brings in a certain payoff of $200,000. Since the payoff to sell option is larger than the $140,000 expected payoff of drilling, we should choose the act of selling the option for decision point 2. This future choice is shown by "pruning" the drilling act with a double slash mark; this act is no longer taken into consideration. In other words, had Drucker decided not to take seismic tests, he would choose to sell his option as his optimal act. Thus, we enter "+200" ($\times \$1000$) above decision point 2. However, evaluation at decision point 1 must wait until we find the expected payoff at chance fork *a*.

This requires first finding the expected payoffs at decision points 3 and 4. Consider decision point 3. The expected payoff to drill is

$$.25(-310) + .75(+790) = +\$515 \, (\times 1000)$$

This expected payoff is larger than the certain payoff of $190,000 for selling the option; the optimal act is to drill; we prune the branch for the act to sell the option and enter "+515" ($\times \$1000$) above decision point 3.

For decision point 4, the expected payoff to drill is

$$.92(-310) + .08(+790) = -\$222 \, (\times 1000)$$

This expected payoff is smaller than the certain payoff of $190,000 for the act to sell the option; so the latter act is optimal; we prune the branch for the act to drill and enter "+190" ($\times \$1000$) above decision point 4.

Now we are ready to calculate the expected payoff at chance point *a*. The branch representing favorable seismic tests leads to the portion of the decision tree with $515,000 expected payoff; the unfavorable seismic tests event leads to the portion of the tree with $190,000 expected payoff; the two events occur with probabilities .48 and .52, respectively. The expected payoff at chance fork *a* is:

$$.48(+515) + .52(+190) = +\$346 \, (\times 1000)$$

which is entered above chance point *a*.

Finally, we are able to choose between the two immediate acts at decision point 1: not test or test. The act of taking seismic tests leads to an expected payoff of $346,000; this sum is larger than the expected payoff of $200,000 for not testing. Drucker should take seismic tests before drilling; the sum of $346,000 is brought back and entered above decision point 1; the branch representing the "Do not test" act is pruned. This completes our backward induction.

What is Drucker's optimal strategy? Take seismic tests; if tests favorable, drill; if tests unfavorable, sell option. Suppose Thomas Drucker has repeatedly followed the decision rule under similar conditions at other drilling sites; as a number of these decisions become large, average net earnings would approach the expected payoff of $346,000 per drilling site.

In carrying out decision tree analysis, we should keep in mind the following general points:

1. Expected payoffs are calculated at chance forks only, never at decision forks.
2. Pruning of branches takes place at decision forks only, never at chance forks.
3. In averaging and folding back, we choose the best single payoff among all payoffs at a given decision fork and bring this payoff back to the decision point of that fork. The procedure leads to the optimal strategy for the problem.

Decision Trees as Analytical Tools

We may close this section with a few comments on the potentialities as well as the limitations of decision tree analysis.

Decision tree analysis simulates the course of action which a decision maker should take under the currently available information. Backward induction, therefore, is the beginning rather than the end of such an analysis.

In the first place, we can perform sensitivity analysis. For example, Drucker may wish to know the probability of favorable seismic tests which will make him indifferent between taking or not taking seismic tests. Let p represent the probability of favorable tests in Fig. 32.3. Then $(1 - p)$ will be the probability of unfavorable seismic tests; and the expected payoff for testing must be equal to $200,000, the expected payoff for not testing. The equation is

$$p(+515) + (1 - p)(+190) = +\$200 \ (\times 1000)$$

Solving this equation, we find that the probability p for making Drucker indifferent between testing and not testing is about .03. Suppose Drucker feels that testing is not worthwhile unless the expected payoff at decision point 1 is $400,000. What should the probability of favorable tests then be to earn the desired expected payoff? The equation is

$$p(+515) + (1 - p)(+190) = +\$400 \ (\times 1000)$$

Solving this equation, we find that p should be about .65.

Sensitivity analysis can also be performed on the net payoffs of the problem. For example, how much should the net payoff for striking oil without seismic tests be increased in order to make Drucker indifferent between drilling or selling the option? Let x be the unknown net payoff for striking oil without seismic tests. Then the equation is

$$.60(-300) + .40x = +\$200 \ (\times 1000)$$

that is, the expected payoff at chance fork b must equal the net payoff for selling the option. Solving this equation we find that $x = \$950,000$. Sensitivity analysis may help Drucker strengthen his belief about the initial probabilities and payoffs or revise their values before the optimal strategy is carried out.

Second, decision tree diagrams can be used as the basis for computer simulation. A decision tree is converted into a *stochastic decision tree*. This is accomplished by providing several outcomes for each act and assigning probabilities to these outcomes. For example, instead of a $10,000 cost, we can provide for a probability distribution of testing costs before chance fork a in Fig. 32.3; the act "Do not test" may be replaced with a probability distribution of several choices; also, the act to drill or sell option may be replaced with appropriate probability distributions. Real-life problems represented with stochastic decision trees become so complex that a computer is utilized to perform several thousand trials of all strategies of the problem. The results are expressed in terms of a probability distribution for each strategy rather than single expected payoff for further analysis of the problem.

Third, selection of the initial act of the optimal strategy does not render selection of later acts irrevocable. After Drucker decides to take seismic tests, he can still revise the remaining part of the tree if new information dictates such a revision. For example, an increase in the price of oil since the initial analysis may require a upward revision of earnings; drilling costs may have gone up; or the probabilities may need revising. Real-world problems may represent a complicated chain of decisions and intervening uncertain events. The decision to test-market or not test-market a new product, for example, may be followed by other decisions on the method of production, location to produce, level and method of advertising, and channels of product distribution, to mention a few. Each of these decisions is subject to uncertainties. Furthermore, the chain of these decisions may span a period of years. Decision tree analysis permits us to continually revise the remaining tree diagram before the next decision is made in the light of new information.

A decision tree diagram allows us to arrange the elements of a complex decision problem in a meaningful and orderly manner; it forces us to quantify our informal thinking, hunches, judgments, and uncertainties; it makes clear the logical implications and consequences of each decision; and it provides an effective means for communicating the reasoning which underlies a recommended strategy. In short, a decision tree diagram serves as a marvelous communication and decision-making tool. This is particularly important when the decision maker is a committee rather than a single person. Then a tree serves as a means of identifying differences and reconciling these differences for arriving at an acceptable strategy.

Decision tree analysis is not restricted only to marketing, investment, and other business decisions. It has become increasingly applied in the analysis of problems in medicine, engineering, national defense, foreign policy, and other government activities.

A common obstacle to the use of decision tree analysis is the difficulties a decision maker may encounter in quantifying uncertainties and measuring risk aversion. Analysis seems to be more successful when the analyst works intimately with and reports directly to the decision maker; it is likely to be least successful when the analytical tasks are performed by a group which is organizationally distant from the decision maker.

432 Chapter 11 Decision Analysis

PROBLEMS

Group One

32.1. Construct a decision tree diagram and evaluate Jerome Poulos' problem whose tabular analysis is given in Table 31.2.

32.2. Instead of pruning acts with double slash marks, we may truncate (that is, erase) the segments of a decision tree diagram which do not represent the best act at each decision fork. Show the decision tree analysis given in Fig. 32.3 with a truncated decision tree diagram. What are the advantages of the truncating technique in decision tree analysis?

32.3. Consider Drucker's decision tree analysis shown in Fig. 32.3. Find the probability of drilling a dry hole which will make Drucker indifferent between drilling or selling the option at:
  *(a) Decison fork 2
  (b) Decision fork 3
  (c) Decision fork 4

32.4. Consider the following decision tree diagram whose dollar net payoffs represent profit.

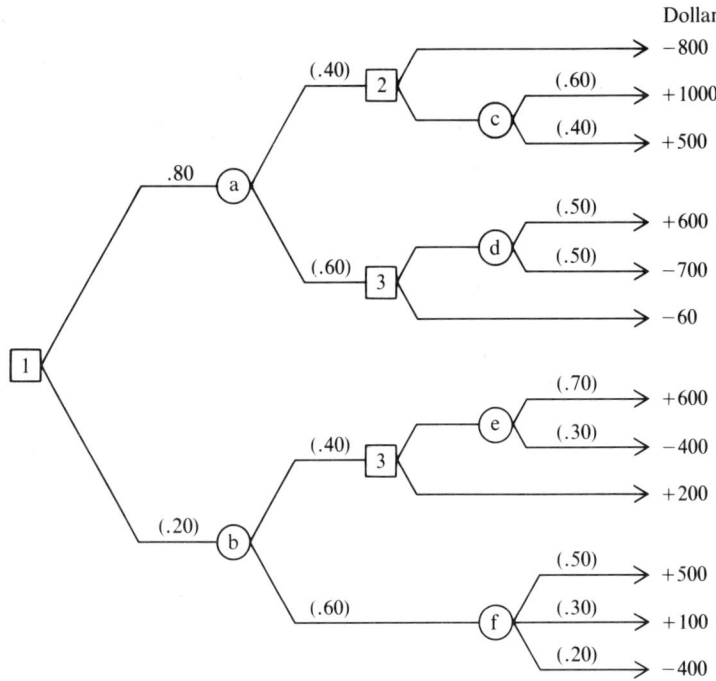

*(a) Find the expected payoff of the optimal strategy using backward induction.

Answers to asterisked (*) problems are appended.

Section 32 Decision Tree Analysis

(b) Show this optimal strategy with a truncated decision tree diagram, that is, by eliminating the segments of the tree which do not represent the best act at each decision fork.

32.5. Find the net payoff for striking oil with seismic tests in order to make Drucker in Fig. 32.3 indifferent between drilling or selling the option when seismic tests are:

*(a) Favorable
(b) Unfavorable

32.6. Another aspect of sensitivity analysis is focused on determining the influence which net payoff changes may have on the strategies of a decision problem. For each set of net payoffs for Drucker's problem in Fig. 32.3, as altered below, what is the optimal strategy? Construct a decision tree diagram and use backward induction.

(a) Receipts from selling the option to drill increase from $300,000 to $500,000, and the cost of seismic tests rises from $10,000 to $50,000. Drilling costs and net payoff from striking oil remain unchanged.

(b) In addition to the changes in part (a), the net payoff from striking oil increases from $800,000 to $10,000,000.

32.7. Ruth Dobbins is vice-president of marketing at Universal Foods, Inc. She must decide whether or not to introduce a new can of soup which meets all current dietary restrictions of the federal government. Ruth prepared the decision tree diagram of her problem shown below. She feels that the probability of success for introducing the product nationally and without a market test is .20; however, the probability of this event increases to .80 when the product is introduced through a food chain. The probability for a favorable market test is .30; if the market test is favorable and the product is introduced nationally, the probability of success is .60; the probability of such an event is reduced to .20 if the market test is unfavorable.

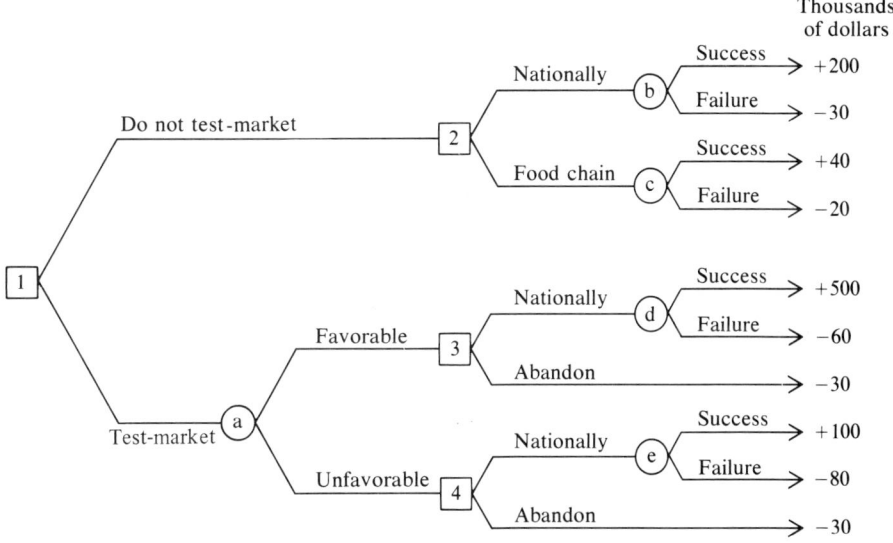

(a) Assign the approximate probability to each event on the given decision tree diagram.
*(b) Find the expected payoff of the optimal strategy using the rollback method.
(c) State this optimal strategy.

32.8. Explain why backward induction or rollback method is a unique characteristic of analyzing sequential decision problems.

32.9. Explain the following terms:
(a) Backward induction
(b) Mutually exhaustive acts and events
(c) Collectively exhaustive events
(d) Sensitivity analysis
(e) Rollback method

32.10. Distinguish between:
(a) Path and strategy
(b) Risk and uncertainty
(c) Decision fork and chance fork
(d) Probability tree and decision tree
(e) Single-decision and multiple-decision problem
(f) Decision tree and stochastic decision tree

Group Two

32.11. Victor Murphy of Golden Coach Realtors drew up the following agreement with a client. Victor can offer exclusively for sale two properties of a client, one in Lexington for $150,000 and one in Bedford for $100,000. He can offer for sale either the Lexington or the Bedford property first but not both at the same time. If he offers either property first and sells it within a month, then he can offer the second property for sale; if he fails to sell the first property, he would not be allowed to sell the second property. Of course, Victor can also refuse to offer for sale both properties or either remaining property after selling the first property.

Whichever property is sold first, brokerage commissions will amount to 6 percent of sales price; commissions will be only 4 percent for whichever property is sold second. The cost directly related to selling each property amounts to 1 percent of sales price.

The probability of selling the Lexington property first is .60 and the Bedford property first is .80; however, there is a .50 probability of selling either property second.

(a) Prepare a decision tree diagram.
*(b) Find the expected net commission of the optimal strategy using backward induction.
(c) State the optimal strategy.

32.12. William Snyder, president and principal stockholder of Petro Enterprises, must decide whether he should exercise an option to drill for oil or allow the option to expire within 2 weeks. Two recent dry holes have reduced his liquid assets to $130,000. If Snyder does not let the option expire, he can drill immediately for a cost of $100,000 or take seismic tests prior to drilling for a cost of $30,000. If oil is discovered, Petro can sell the oil rights for $400,000. According to the company geologists, there is .55 probability for striking oil without seismic tests. However, if the seismic tests are favorable, this probability increases to .85, and if the tests are unfavorable, such probability falls to .10. According to past experience, test results are favorable 60 percent of the time.
(a) What strategy should Snyder follow in order to maximize his liquid assets?
(b) What is the minimum sum for selling his option to drill?
(c) Snyder's utility curve is shown below.

Section 32   Decision Tree Analysis   435

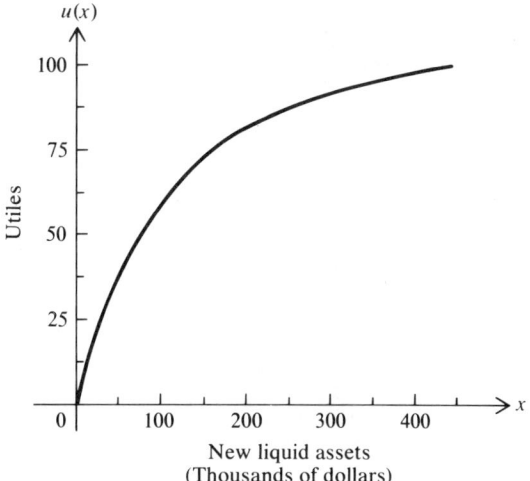

What is Snyder's strategy now in terms of expected utility? And what is the minimum dollar equivalent sum for selling his option to drill? (For details, read J. S. Hammond, III, "Better Decisions with Preference Theory." *Harvard Business Review*, November–December, 1967, 123–141.

32.13. The management of MTV Enterprises contemplates the introduction of Discovision, or DV for short, a new device which records television shows on a disc and plays them back instantly. Management considers introducing the new product either internationally or domestically.

If DV is introduced internationally, demand probabilities and net earnings in millions are:

Demand	Probability	Net Earnings
Heavy	.40	+$8.5
Moderate	.30	+ 3.0
Light	.30	− 4.0

If DV is introduced domestically, the probability for initial large demand is .70 and for small demand .30; if demand is small and continues to be small, net earnings will amount to only $2 million. If initial domestic demand is large, management considers the option to distribute later the product internationally or limit distribution to the domestic market. The demand probabilities and net earnings in millions for either acts are:

	International			Domestic		
Demand	Probability	Earnings	Demand	Probability	Earnings
---	---	---	---	---	---
Large	.57	+$5.0	Large	.57	+$2.0
Small	.43	− 1.0	Small	.43	+ 1.0

(a) Construct a decision tree diagram and find the expected net earnings of the optimal strategy.
(b) State the optimal strategy.

SECTION 33 / THE VALUE OF ADDITIONAL INFORMATION

So far we have been able to determine two important points in decision analysis: first, whether it pays to collect additional information; second, if it does pay, what the optimal strategy is in the light of this information. For example, in Drucker's case we found that it pays to collect additional information by taking seismic tests; and the optimal strategy is to drill if the tests are favorable and to sell the option if the tests are unfavorable.

However, our presentation failed to explain two crucial aspects of decision analysis intimately related to the value of additional information. In the first place, we did not explain how we incorporate additional information into our analysis. This is done by revising the initial probabilities of the problem. We use Drucker's problem to illustrate revision of probabilities; then we repeat the decision analysis of the problem in a slightly modified form in order to introduce important terminology. In the second place, we failed to compare optimal strategies under different methods of information collection. For example, we failed to compare optimal strategies in Drucker's problem under different types of exploratory costs. We introduce a new case which illustrates how we determine the best among alternative "sampling" methods. The same case summarizes systematically the essentials of the decision analysis procedure.

Revision of Probabilities

In the preceding two sections, we have shown how expected value can be used as a criterion for making decisions under uncertainty. This is one of the two critical elements of decision analysis. The other element is revision of probabilities. We first show how we can revise the initial probabilities of a problem in order to incorporate additional information.

Example 33.1

In discussing the assignment of probabilities in Drucker's case (Fig. 32.2), we pointed out the importance of the conditional probabilities at chance forks c and d. How did we obtain these probabilities?

We know that Drucker's probability of drilling a dry hole without taking seismic tests is .60; this probability reflects his personal experience about past failures to find oil prior to collecting additional information. What we

Section 33 The Value of Additional Information

did not disclose at that time is the fact that Drucker collected information about the predictive performance of past seismic tests; he looked into the historical record of seismic tests taken at sites with geophysical formation similar to that of the present site; he found that favorable seismic tests ended up in drilling a dry hole 20 percent of the time and in striking oil 90 percent of the time.

The procedure for obtaining the probabilities at chance forks c and d of the problem (Fig. 32.2) is shown in Table 33.1. They are called *posterior* because they represent the state of knowledge *after* the new information has been incorporated.

Let us take a closer look at this procedure. The initial marginal probabilities of the problem, namely .60 for a dry hole and .40 for striking oil, are called *prior;* the term comes from the fact that these probabilities represent the past *before* any new information is collected. The second column of probabilities, called *conditional,* represents new information; *when,* or on the *condition,* a dry hole was drilled, seismic tests indicated a favorable rock formation with probability .20 and an unfavorable one with probability .80 since $1 - .20 = .80$; when, or on the *condition,* oil was found, seismic tests indicated a favorable rock formation with probability .90 and an unfavorable one with probability .10 since $1 - .90 = .10$.

Then we multiply each prior by its corresponding conditional probability to find the *joint* probabilities. For example, the probability of drilling a dry hole *and* favorable seismic tests is $(.60)(.20) = .12$. This is application of our familiar multiplication rule; it is repeatedly applied for finding the remaining three joint probabilities of the problem. Summing each set of joint probabilities, we find that the probability of favorable seismic tests is .48 and of unfavorable tests is .52; they are a new set of marginal probabilities. Dividing each joint probability by its corresponding marginal, we obtain the posterior probabilities. For example, dividing .12 by .48 we get the posterior probability .25; this means that if the seismic tests are favorable, there is .25 probability of drilling a dry hole and .75 probability of striking oil; the other two posterior probabilities can be interpreted in a similar manner.

Table 33.1. Revision of Probabilities for Drucker's Problem

Event	Probabilities			
	Prior	Conditional	Joint	Posterior
Dry hole	.60	.20	.12	.25
Struck oil	.40	.90	.36	.75
Probability of favorable tests →			.48	1.00
Dry hole	.60	.80	.48	.92
Struck oil	.40	.10	.04	.08
Probability of unfavorable tests →			.52	1.00

Bayes's Formula

Revision of probabilities is based on Bayes's formula*

(33.1) $$P(B_1|A) = \frac{P(B_1)\ P(A|B_1)}{\sum_{i=1}^{n} P(B_i)\ P(A|B_i)}$$

where $P(B_1)$ = prior probability of the first event
$P(A|B_1)$ = conditional probability of the relevant prior probability
$\sum_{i=1}^{n} P(B_i)\ (A|B_i)$ = sum of the joint probabilities from i equals 1 to i equals n

For example, application of the formula for finding the first-row posterior probability shown in Table 33.1 is as follows:

$$P(B_1|A) = \frac{(.60)(.20)}{(.60)(.20) + (.40)(.90)} = \frac{.12}{.48} = .25$$

where $P(B_1) = .60$
$P(A|B_1) = .20$
$\sum_{i=1}^{2} P(B_i)\ (P(A|B_i)) = (.60)(.20) + (.40)(.90)$

Repeated application of Bayes's formula yields the remaining three posterior probabilities.

This example illustrates what can be accomplished with Bayes's formula. In general, we begin with a set of hypotheses. They are expressed in terms of prior probabilities reflecting the "intensity of belief" in each hypothesis. In the example, prior probabilities represent Drucker's personal experience in oil explorations. In other cases, they may represent past sales records or the decision maker's hunches or a combination of both. With the new evidence becoming available in the form of conditional probabilities, we revise our priors and obtain the posterior probabilities. With this process, objective evidence revises our belief, strengthening the intensity of our belief in some hypotheses and weakening it in others.

Prior, Posterior, and Preposterior Analysis

The result of revised probabilities has already been shown in the previous section. We repeat such a decision tree analysis here in order to emphasize the value of additional information and introduce the relevant terminology.

Example 33.1 (continued)

Drucker's decision tree analysis (Fig. 32.3) is shown again in Fig. 33.1. Payoffs are net, except for the $10,000 cost of seismic tests. This cost is not added to or subtracted from the appropriate payoffs as it was done earlier; instead, it appears as a toll at a gate ━━ which Drucker must pay in case he decides to take seismic tests.

*Named after Thomas Bayes, who first used it in a paper published in 1763.

Figure 33.1.
Drucker's decision tree analysis.

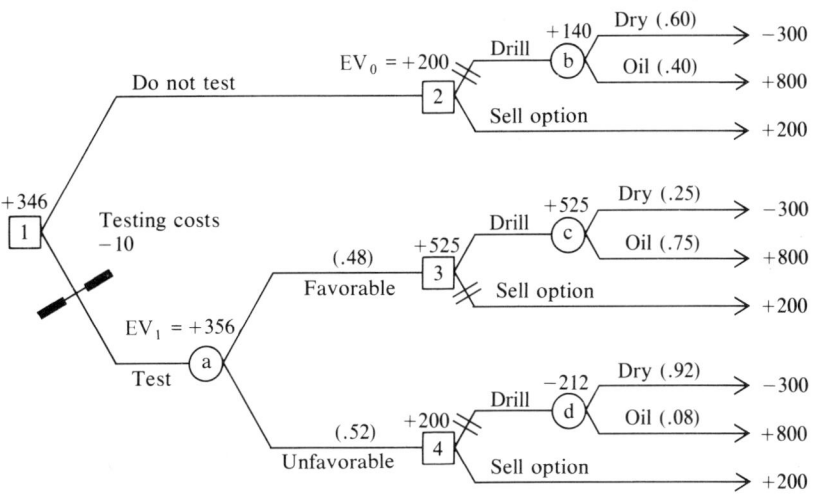

What is the value of additional information? This is the difference between the expected payoff without the additional information (EV_0) and the expected payoff with the additional information (EV_1); it is generally called the *expected value of sample information* (EVSI). It consists of two elements, the *cost of sample information* (CSI) and the *expected net gain of sample information* (ENGS).

Example 33.1 (continued)

For Drucker's case these terms have the following values:

$$EVSI = EV_1 - EV_0$$
$$= 356 - 200$$
$$= \$156 \ (\times 1000)$$

Since CSI is $10,000,

$$ENGS = EVSI - CSI$$
$$= 156 - 10$$
$$= \$146 \ (\times 1000)$$

Note the term *sample* is used in a very general sense; it represents any research effort for collecting information, such as experimental, measuring, or other methods like taking seismic tests, in addition to sampling.

If analysis is carried out without collecting additional information, it is called *prior analysis*. The upper segment of the decision tree diagram in Fig. 33.1, leading to decision point 2 with $EV_0 = \$200{,}000$, portrays the prior analysis of the problem. If the evaluation of a problem is carried out after additional information is collected, it is called *posterior analysis*. For example, suppose Drucker actually took seismic tests and the tests were favorable; then the segment of the tree at decision point 3 would have portrayed his posterior analysis. An unfavorable outcome of seismic tests would have portrayed another posterior analysis at decision point 4. Thus posterior analysis evaluates a single "sample" outcome *after* the fact, that is, after additional information has been obtained. If all feasible sample outcomes are considered prior to actually collecting information, such an evaluation is called *preposterior analysis*. Drucker's tree leading to chance fork *a* portrays the preposterior analysis of the problem. Note that the expected payoff of each posterior analysis is weighted by the frequency with which it may occur to yield $EV_1 = \$356,000$. In other words, preposterior analyses *simulates* posterior analyses of all possible sample outcomes.

A complete preposterior analysis of Drucker's problem could be carried out with the evaluation of data from different types of exploratory tests. Then the optimal "sampling" strategy would have been the one which maximizes ENGS. But this task is more systematically illustrated with a case requiring different sample sizes rather than different methods of data collection.

Metal Products, Inc.

Decision analysis with sampling follows the general procedural steps already described. Yet analysis of this type of problem deserves special attention. Revision of probabilities are based on conditional probabilities derived from a probability model, and the optimal strategy is related to a sample of specified size.

Example 33.2

Metal Products, Inc., uses an automatic machine to produce a certain part requiring a considerable amount of processing in order to meet assembly specifications. Each production run contains 500 parts. Defective parts in each run require special hand-fitting which costs $4 per part.

In setting up the machine for each run an operator must make two delicate adjustments. If both adjustments are made properly, the average fraction defective of the *process* π is .01. The machine is then in state A, which cannot be improved because of mechanical limitations. If one of the delicate adjustments is not properly made by the operator, the machine is in state B with π equal to .10; and if both adjustments are improperly made, the machine is in state C with π equal to .20. A master mechanic, however, can always make both adjustments properly so that the machine is certain to be in state A before a production run. The fee for the mechanic's services is $72, which would be a complete loss had the machine operator made both adjustments properly.

John Dalton, the production manager, believes that the machine performs as a Bernoulli process. From past records and long experience, John believes that the operator is likely to set up the machine 70 percent of the time in state A, 20 percent in state B, and 10 percent in state C.

Prior Analysis. Such analysis answers the question: Should the manager accept the operator's setup or invite the mechanic to readjust the machine? Note that

Section 33 The Value of Additional Information

payoffs in this problem represent costs. Therefore, the optimal act would be the one with the smallest expected payoff.

Example 33.3

The prior probabilities and the cost payoffs of the problem are shown in Table 33.2. Since each defective costs $4, the cost of defectives in each production run will be $\$4 \times 500\pi = \$2000\pi$ if the manager *accepts* the operator's setup: cost payoffs will be $\$2000(.01) = \$20$ if the machine is in state A, $\$2000(.10) = \$200$ if the machine is in state B; and $\$2000(.20) = \$400$ if in state C, as shown under the acceptance act a_1. If Dalton *rejects* the operator's setup, then the expected number of defectives will always be $500(.01) = 5$ parts. This is so because no matter what the state of the machine happens to be when adjusted by the operator, it is certain that the invited mechanic will adjust the machine to state A. Hence, cost payoffs will be $\$4 \times 5 = \$20$ plus the mechanics fee of $72, a total of $92, as shown under the rejection act a_2. Expected payoffs are $94 for accepting and $92 for rejecting the operator's setup. Accordingly, the optimal act is for the manager *always* to reject the operator's setup, thus saving $2 per run, on the average.

Table 33.2.
Prior Probabilities and Cost Payoffs for Metal Products, Inc.

State of Machine	Fraction Defective π	Prior Probabilities $P(\pi)$	Accept a_1	Reject a_2
A	.01	.70	+$ 20*	+$92
B	.10	.20	+ 200	+ 92*
C	.20	.10	+ 400	+ 92*
		$E(a_j) =$	+ $94	+$92
				↑ Optimal

As part of this prior analysis we may wish to calculate EVPI, which may be a useful guide to further analysis. The payoffs under certainty are marked with an asterisk in Table 33.2. They represent the smallest cost under each state of the machine. The expected value under certainty is

$$\text{EVC} = .70(+20) + .20(+92) + .10(+92) = +\$41.60$$

and

$$\begin{aligned}\text{EVPI} &= E(a_2)^* - \text{EVC} \\ &= 92 - 41.60 \\ &= \$50.40\end{aligned}$$

This is the maximum sum that John Dalton should spend for collecting sample information.

Chapter 11 Decision Analysis

Posterior Analysis. Of course, we cannot obtain perfect information before a production run is completed. But we can certainly obtain some additional information about the fraction defective π of the process by taking a sample run; we can revise the manager's prior probabilities with this sample information; and then we can determine the optimal act by calculating posterior expected payoffs. Therefore, posterior analysis focuses on the question: Does it pay to take a sample before a terminal decision is made?

Example 33.4

Suppose we arbitrarily choose to take a sample run of one part and find that the part is not defective. It costs $3 to test a part in order to determine whether it is defective or not. Did it pay to sample?

The manager believes that defective parts are binomially distributed. So we can use the sample evidence to obtain additional information about the value of fraction defective π from the appropriate binomial distribution. In particular, we need to find the conditional probability of obtaining a nondefective part for each of the three states π of the machine. These probabilities are obtained from Appendix B. For example, the conditional probability for a nondefective part, that is for $X = 0$, when $\pi = .01$, is

$$P(X = 0 | n = 1, \pi = .01) = 1.00 - .01 = .99$$

This conditional probability together with the other two for $\pi = .10$ and for $\pi = .20$ are shown in column 3, Table 33.3. At this time we carry out posterior analysis for a single sample outcome of a nondefective part when $n = 1$. Therefore, we should pay attention to revising probabilities when $X = 0$. On the basis of prior probabilities in column 2 and conditional probabilities in column 3 and repeated application of Bayes's formula, we obtain the joint probabilities in column 5 and the posterior probabilities in column 7. Multiplying these posterior probabilities times the cost payoffs for each act given in Table 33.2, we obtain the posterior expected payoffs for accepting (a_1) and rejecting (a_2) the operator's setup:

$$E(a_1)^* = .727(+20) + .189(+200) + .084(+400) = +\$85.94$$
$$E(a_2) = .727(+92) + .189(+92) + .084(92) = +\$92$$

Table 33.3. Determining Posterior Probabilities of Fraction Defective Parts, Metal Products, Inc.

Fraction Defective π (1)	Prior P (π) (2)	Conditional P(X = x | n = 1, π)		Joint P(π and X)		Posterior P(π|X)	
		X = 0 (3)	X = 1 (4)	X = 0 (5)	X = 1 (6)	X = 0 (7)	X = 1 (8)
.01	.70	.99	.01	.693	.007	.727	.149
.10	.20	.90	.10	.180	.020	.189	.426
.20	.10	.80	.20	.080	.020	.084	.425
				.953	.047	1.000	1.000

In the light of *this* sample outcome, the optimal act is now to *accept* rather than reject the operator's setup with expected cost of $85.94 per run. Since the prior expected payoff of the optimal act EV_0 is equal to $92 and the posterior EV_1 is equal to $85.94, the value of additional sample information is

$$EVSI = EV_0 = EV_1$$
$$= 92 - 85.94$$
$$= \$6.06$$

and since the cost of sample information is $3,

$$ENGS = EVSI - CSI$$
$$= 6.06 - 3$$
$$= \$3.06$$

Therefore, it may pay to sample before making a terminal decision. John Dalton would save $3.06 per run, on the average, by accepting the operator's setup *if* the sampled part turns out to be good.

In situations such as this, however, posterior analysis may be of little practical value to a decision maker. We may find, *after the fact,* that ENGS is negative. Posterior analysis may not have important economic consequences if the cost of obtaining sample information is small. However, in most decision problems this cost may represent a substantial sum of money. Even an ENGS of $3.06 per run in the Metal Products case may accumulate into sizable savings if several production runs are made each day. In problems requiring a one-shot survey such costs may run into thousands of dollars. Furthermore, sample information may be costly because the sampling process itself may be destructive. For example, missile testing is the most spectacular and perhaps the costliest self-destructive sampling process. Last but not least, posterior analysis, even if profitable after the fact, fails to go about finding the optimal sampling strategy. In short, posterior analysis is an intermediate step, a single analytical phase of the problem. In fact, both prior and posterior analyses of this case were introduced here for the sake of conceptual continuity and for summarizing the entire decision analysis procedure.

Preposterior Analysis. The appropriate question to be raised about the kind of problem we consider here is not whether it pays to sample, but *what is the sample size and strategy which maximizes ENGS?* This question requires preposterior analysis.

Example 33.5

Part of this analysis for Metal Products, Inc. is shown in Fig. 33.2. Prior probabilities and cost payoffs are copied from Table 33.2. The posterior probabilities for sample size 1 for *both* sample outcomes, that is, when defective parts X can be 0 or 1, are copied from Table 33.3, columns 7 and 8. Note that for a sample of 2 parts there are three sample outcomes since the number of defective parts X can be 0, 1, or 2. The posterior probabilities

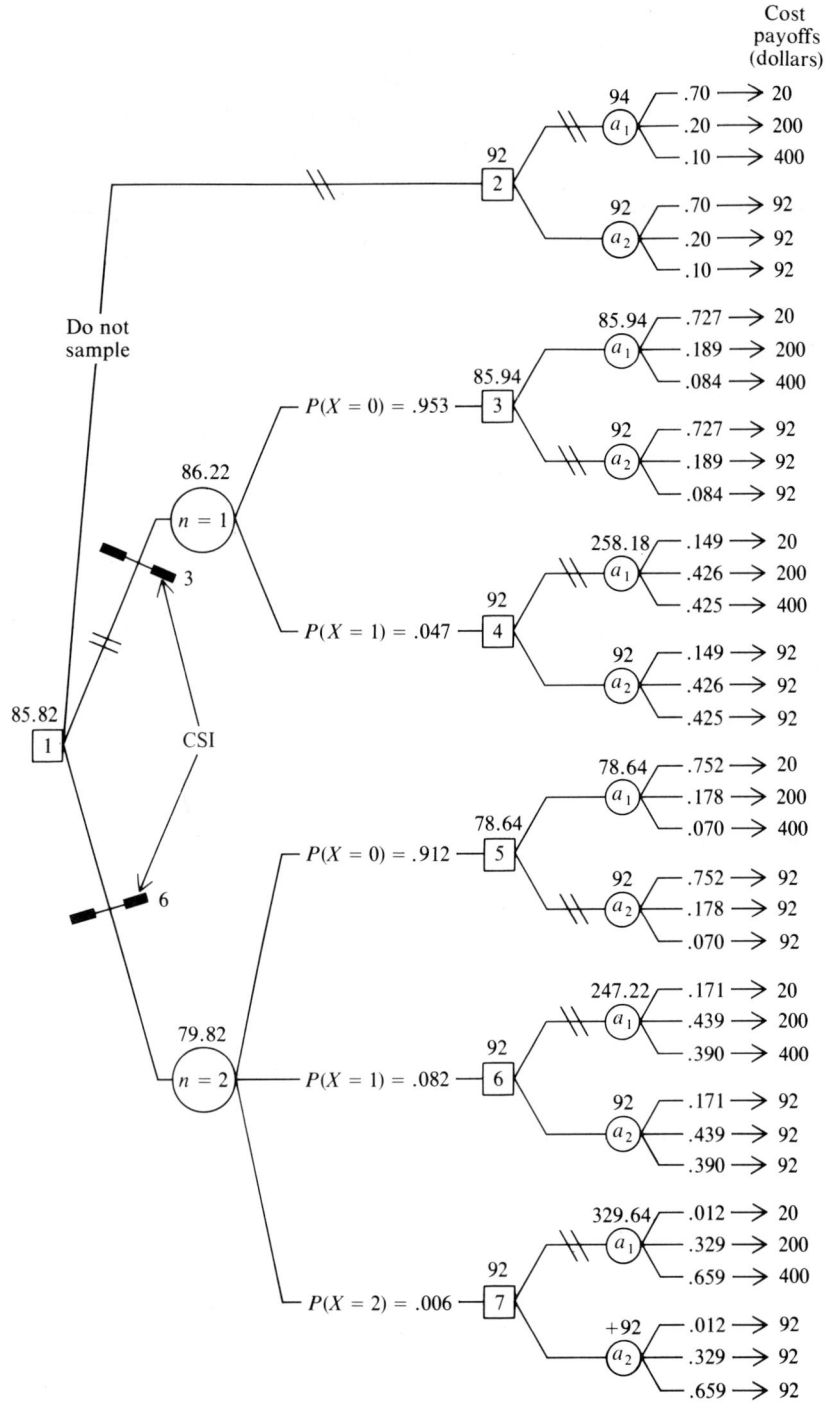

Figure 33.2.
Decision tree analysis, Metal Products, Inc.
(a_1 = Accept
a_2 = Reject)

Section 33 The Value of Additional Information

for each sample outcome shown in the appropriate branches are obtained from the binomial distribution, as already illustrated.

Backward induction leads to an optimal sampling strategy for taking a sample of 2 parts. The position values for each sample outcome are weighted by their respective marginal probabilities to yield a preposterior expected payoff

$$EV_1\,(n = 2) = .912(+78.64) + .082(+92) + .006(+92) = +\$79.82$$

The value of additional information is

$$\begin{aligned}EVSI &= EV_0 - EV_1\,(n = 2)\\ &= 92 - 79.82\\ &= \$12.18\end{aligned}$$

But at the toll gate for $n = 2$ we pay \$6 for the cost of sampling, which in turn increases the total cost of the optimal strategy to \$85.82 and thus

$$\begin{aligned}ENGS &= EVSI - CSI\\ &= 12.18 - 6\\ &= \$6.18\end{aligned}$$

If John Dalton were to stop preposterior analysis at this point, his optimal strategy would be: Take a sample of two parts and *accept* (a_1) the operator's setup if the sample contains no defective parts; otherwise, *reject* (a_2) the operator's setup and invite the mechanic to adjust the machine. Of course, preposterior analysis must consider larger samples until the sample which maximizes ENGS is found. This is left as an exercise.

Note that preposterior analysis changes a prior *optimal act* into an *optimal strategy*. Sample information introduces flexibility into the decision process. In the prior analysis the decision maker must choose one of two acts unconditionally. Now the choice *depends* on the sample outcome.

In standard statistical terminology the optimal strategy of the example is called the (2, 1) decision rule. In general, the strategy is called the *(n, c) decision rule,* where *n* denotes sample size and *c* the least number of defectives for which a process must be rejected; the rule which is optimal is called *Bayes's decision rule.*

The value of EVPI places an upper limit on the sum a decision maker may be willing to spend for additional information. So the sample size of an optimal strategy must be finite. The largest sample size for the Metal Products, Inc. case is 16 parts since the EVPI of \$50.40 divided by unit sampling cost of \$3 yields a sample size of 16. Even samples of moderate size, however, require heavy computational work. A sample size of 8 parts in our case would require a decision tree diagram with 54 end branches (9 sample outcomes times 2 acts times 3 states of nature). So preposterior analysis of real-world problems may require the use of computers.

PROBLEMS

Group One

*33.1. Present the joint probabilities in Table 33.1 in a 2 × 2 table, where column totals represent the marginal probabilities for favorable and unfavorable seismic tests.
  (a) What is the probability that Drucker strikes oil (O), given that the seismic tests are favorable (F)?
  (b) What is the probability that Drucker drills a dry hole (H) if he knows that the tests are unfavorable (U)?

33.2. Use two probability tree diagrams to portray application of Bayes's formula for obtaining the posterior probabilities shown in Table 33.1.
  (a) In the first diagram begin by using the given priors as marginal probabilities and the conditionals to calculate the joint probabilities.
  (b) In the second diagram begin by using the new set of marginal probabilities on test results and the obtained joint probabilities from the first diagram to calculate the revised probabilities.

33.3. A manufacturer receives 60 percent of special transistors for assembling radios from company A and 40 percent from company B. Experience has shown that 1 percent of the transistors produced by company A are defective, while the fraction defective for company B is 2 percent.
  *(a) Present in a tabular form like Table 33.1 the calculation of posterior probabilities.
  (b) Explain in words the given conditional probabilities and the obtained posterior probabilities.

33.4. A 12-member congressional subcommittee considers financial aid to New York City in order to prevent default. Nine members vote for aid, six members are from the East, and three members who are not from the East vote against aid. Assuming that the committee members vote independently of one another:
  (a) Prepare a 2 × 2 table of joint events.
  (b) What is the probability that a congressman is not from the East if we know that this congressman voted for aid?
  *(c) What is the probability that a congressman has voted for aid if we know that this congressman is from the East?

33.5. A manufacturing operation is known to produce 20 percent defective parts. A test has been devised to detect defective parts which shows the following experience: a part known to be good will test good 70 percent of the time; a part known to be defective will test defective 80 percent of the time. If the test shows that a randomly chosen part is good, what is the probability that this part is actually defective?

*33.6. In blending whiskey, a panel of taste experts is often used to determine whether a given batch is distinguishable from previous batches. An expert is presented with two pairs of samples, a pair of "matched" samples from the same batch and a pair of "odd" samples from two different batches. One of the two pairs is selected at random, and the expert is asked whether the pair is the matched or the odd. Past experience has shown that experts are right in picking a matched sample 70 percent of the time and in picking an odd sample 80 percent of the

Answers to asterisked (*) problems are appended.

Section 33 The Value of Additional Information

time. If an expert guesses right, what is the probability that the pair of samples is odd?

33.7. As a tourist in Las Vegas you are attracted to a well-known "two-urn" game. Urn I contains two black balls and urn II one black and one red ball.
*(a) An urn is randomly selected and a ball is randomly drawn from the selected urn. If the ball is black, what is the probability that the black ball comes from urn I?
(b) Instead of selecting one ball, two balls are randomly drawn with replacement from the selected urn. If both balls are black, what is the probability that the black balls came from urn I?
(c) If you guess correctly that the ball(s) came from urn I, you win $2 for every $1 you bet; otherwise, you lose your bet. Which of the two games, (a) or (b), would you prefer to play?

33.8. Verify the posterior probabilities for $n = 2$ shown in Fig. 33.2 by preparing a table such as Table 33.3.

33.9. Explain the following terms:
(a) Prior probabilities   (e) Conditional probabilities
(b) Bayes's formula   (f) Posterior probabilities
(c) Joint probabilities   (g) Bayes's decision rule
(d) (n, c) Decision rule   (h) "Sample" information

33.10. Distinguish between:
(a) Expected value of sample information and expected net gain from sampling
(b) Posterior and preposterior analysis
(c) Prior and posterior analysis
(d) Optimal act and optimal strategy

Group Two

33.11. Before making a terminal decision, Thomas Drucker got in touch with Explorers Associates, an oil consulting outfit. Gloria Henderson, a geologist of the firm, informed Drucker that her company was using the latest seismic test instruments. According to available data unfavorable seismic tests with the new instruments correctly indicated a dry hole 90 percent of the time and incorrectly indicated the presence of oil only 5 percent of the time. The fee for these new tests is $20,000. What should Drucker do?
*(a) Revise the prior probabilities of the problem with this information. Show your work in a tabular form as in Table 33.1.
(b) Use this new information to carry out preposterior analysis of the problem with a decision tree diagram.
(c) Should Drucker prefer the new seismic tests? Find ENGS and indicate optimal strategy.

33.12. Continue the preposterior analysis shown in Fig. 33.2 for sample sizes 3, 4, 5, 6, and 7 parts in order to determine the sample size which maximizes ENGS.
(a) For each sample size, find the posterior probabilities for $X = 0, 1$, and at least 2 defective parts.
(b) Calculate the preposterior expected payoff for each sample size.
*(c) Summarize your calculations from part (b) in a table and find ENGS for each sample.
(d) Formulate the (n, c) rule for the optimal sampling strategy.
(e) Sketch the graphs representing the EVSI and CSI values for each sample size and indicate with a vertical line the magnitude of ENGS at the opti-

mal sample size. Extrapolate the EVSI and CSI curves in order to estimate the sample size where EVSI equals CSI.

33.13. A physician believes it very likely that a 49-year-old patient has essential hypertension (EH) with a 1 in 20 chance of functional renal artery stenosis (FRAS). If a patient indeed has this condition, tests successfully diagnose it (a true positive) with .90 probability. On the other hand, if such hypertension is not a symptom of FRAS, tests falsely diagnose FRAS (a false positive) with .02 probability. What is the probability that the patient indeed has FRAS if the test is positive? (For a decision tree analysis illustrating how this probability has been used see W. B. Schwartz, G. A. Gorry and J. P. Kassirer, "Decision Analysis and Clinical Judgment," *American Journal of Medicine,* October 1973, pp. 459–72.

33.14. Genesis Enterprises has developed a new electronic component for deep-sea exploration devices. On the basis of prior experience, management believes that demand for the new product will be high (for 200,000 units) with probability .30, moderate (for 80,000 units) with probability .30, and low (for 20,000 units) with probability .40.

Unit price of the new product will be $10. In-plant manufacturing will provide a low fixed cost of $80,000 but a high variable cost of $8 per unit. Because of scheduling and other problems, management considers the possibility of manufacturing the new product abroad in order to take advantage of low hourly wages. Variable cost will be only $6 per unit, and fixed costs will be $250,000. Management also considers the possibility of selling the patent rights of the new product to another manufacturer. Then royalties for each unit sold will be $2 for the first 20,000 units, $1 for the next 60,000 units, and $.50 cents for any additional sales volume.

Stuart Benton, the president of the company, considers commissioning a research firm for a marketing survey costing $50,000. Stuart feels that there is a 70 percent chance for the survey to show favorable results, that is, high demand when demand is indeed high. However, a survey may erroneously show favorable results 20 percent of the time when actual demand is moderate and 30 percent of the time when actual demand is low.

(a) Prepare a payoff table of net revenues.
(b) Find the posterior probabilities.
(c) Carry out prior and preposterior analysis with a decision tree diagram.
(d) Find ENGS.
(e) What is the optimal strategy?

SELECTED BIBLIOGRAPHY

The Role of Statistics

Campbell, S. K. *Flaws and Fallacies in Statistical Thinking.* Englewood Cliffs, N.J.: Prentice-Hall, 1974.

Huff, D. *How to Lie with Statistics.* New York: W. W. Norton, 1954.

Moroney, M. J., ed. *Facts from Figures.* Baltimore: Penquin Books, 1965.

Tanur, J. M., F. Mosteller, W. H. Kruskal, R. F. Link, R. S. Pieters, and G. R. Rising, eds. *Statistics: A Guide to the Unknown.* San Francisco: Holden-Day, 1972.

Selected Bibliography

Probability

Feller, W. *An Introduction to Probability Theory and Its Applications,* vol. 1, 3rd ed. New York: John Wiley & Sons, 1968.

Goldberg, S. *Probability: An Introduction.* Englewood Cliffs, N.J.: Prentice-Hall, 1960.

Kemeny, J. G., A. Schliefer, J. L. Snell, and G. L. Thompson. *Finite Mathematics with Business Applications.* Englewood Cliffs, N.J.: Prentice-Hall, 1962.

Mosteller, F. R., R. E. K. Bourke, and G. B. Thomas. *Probability with Statistical Applications.* Reading, Mass.: Addison-Wesley, 1961.

General Statistics

Ezekiel, M., and K. Fox. *Methods of Correlation and Regression Analysis,* 3rd ed. New York: John Wiley & Sons, 1959.

Hamburg, M. *Statistical Analysis for Decision Making,* 2nd ed. New York: Harcourt Brace Jovanovich, 1977.

Lapin, L. *Statistics for Modern Business Decisions,* 2nd ed. New York: Harcourt Brace Jovanovich, 1978.

Mendenhall, W., and J. E. Reinmuth. *Statistics for Management and Economics,* 3rd ed. North Scituate, Mass.: Duxbury Press, 1978.

Neter, J. S., W. Wasserman, and G. A. Whitmore. *Fundamental Statistics for Business and Economics,* 4th ed. Boston: Allyn and Bacon, 1973.

Snedecor, G. W., and W. G. Cochran. *Statistical Methods,* 5th ed. Ames: Iowa State College Press, 1956.

Spurr, W. A., and C. P. Bonini. *Statistical Analysis for Business Decisions,* rev. ed. Homewood, Ill.: Richard D. Irwin, 1973.

Wonnacott, T. H., and R. J. Wonnacott. *Introductory Statistics for Business and Economics.* New York: John Wiley & Sons, 1972.

Zeisel, H. *Say It with Figures,* 4th ed. New York: Harper & Brothers, 1957.

Survey Sampling Methods

Cochran, W. G. *Sampling Techniques,* 2nd ed. New York: John Wiley & Sons, 1963.

Deming, W. E. *Sample Designs in Business Research.* New York: John Wiley & Sons, 1960.

Hansen, M. H., W. N. Hurwitz, and W. G. Madow. *Sample Survey Methods and Theory,* 2 vols. New York: John Wiley & Sons, 1953.

Kish, L. *Survey Sampling.* New York: John Wiley & Sons, 1965.

Nonparametric Statistics

Bradley, J. V. *Distribution-Free Statistical Tests.* Englewood Cliffs, N.J.: Prentice-Hall, 1968.

Gibbons, J. D. *Nonparametric Statistical Inference.* New York: McGraw-Hill, 1971.

Mosteller, F. R., and R. E. K. Bourke. *Sturdy Statistics: Nonparametric and Order Statistics.* Reading Mass.: Addison-Wesley, 1973.

Noether, G. E. *Elements of Nonparametric Statistics.* New York: John Wiley & Sons, 1967.

Time Series and Index Numbers

Mudgett, B. D. *Index Numbers.* New York: John Wiley & Sons, 1951.

U.S. Department of Labor, Bureau of Labor Statistics, *The Consumer Price Index: Concepts and Content over the Years.* Report 517 (revised). Washington, D.C., May 1978.

U.S. Department of Labor, Bureau of Labor Statistics, *The Consumer Price Index Revision—1978.* Washington, D.C., March 1978.

Board of Governors of the Federal Reserve System. *Industrial Production (Index): 1976 Revision.* Washington D.C., December 1977.

Decision Theory and Utility

Bass, F. M. "Marketing Research Expenditures: A Decision Model." *Journal of Business,* January 1966, pp. 77–90.

Hammond, J. S., III. "Better Decisions with Preference Theory." *Harvard Business Review,* November–December 1967, pp. 123–41.

Raiffa, H. *Decision Analysis: Introductory Lectures on Choices under Uncertainty.* Reading, Mass.: Addison-Wesley, 1968.

Schlaifer, R. *Probability and Statistics for Business Decisions.* New York: McGraw-Hill, 1959.

Schwartz, W. B., G. A. Gorry, and J. P. Kassirer. "Decision Analysis and Clinical Judgment." *American Journal of Medicine,* October 1973, pp. 459–72.

Swalm, R. O. "Utility Theory: Insights into Risk Taking." *Harvard Business Review,* November–December 1966, pp. 123–36.

Statistical Tables

Fisher, R. A., and F. Yates. *Statistical Tables for Biological, Agricultural, and Medical Research,* 6th ed. London: Longman Group, 1974.

National Bureau of Standards. *Tables of the Binomial Distribution.* Washington, D.C.: U.S. Government Printing Office, 1950.

Rand Corporation, *A Million Random Digits with 100,000 Normal Deviates.* New York: Free Press, 1955.

Standard Mathematical Tables, 17th ed. Cleveland: Chemical Rubber Publishing Co., 1969.

APPENDIXES: STATISTICAL TABLES

APPENDIX A / 2500 RANDOM DIGITS

Line No.	1-5	6-10	11-15	16-20	21-25	26-30	31-35	36-40	41-45	46-50
0	10097	32533	76520	13586	34673	54876	80959	09117	39292	74945
1	37542	04805	64894	74296	24805	24037	20636	10402	00822	91665
2	08422	68953	19645	09303	23209	02560	15953	34764	35080	33606
3	99019	02529	09376	70715	38311	31165	88676	74397	04436	27659
4	12807	99970	80157	36147	64032	36653	98951	16877	12171	76833
5	66065	74717	34072	76850	36697	36170	65813	39885	11199	29170
6	31060	10805	45571	82406	35303	42614	86799	07439	23403	09732
7	85269	77602	02051	65692	68665	74818	73053	85247	18623	88579
8	63573	32135	05325	47048	90553	57548	28468	28709	83491	25624
9	73796	45753	03529	64778	35808	34282	60935	20344	35273	88435
10	98520	17767	14905	68607	22109	40558	60970	93433	50500	73998
11	11805	05431	39808	27732	50725	68248	29405	24201	52775	67851
12	83452	99634	06288	98083	13746	70078	18475	40610	68711	77817
13	88685	40200	86507	58401	36766	67951	90364	76493	29609	11062
14	99594	67348	87517	64969	91826	08928	93785	61368	23478	34113
15	65481	17674	17468	50950	58047	76974	73039	57186	40218	16544
16	80124	35635	17727	08015	45318	22374	21115	78253	14385	53763
17	74350	99817	77402	77214	43236	10210	45521	64237	96286	02655
18	69916	26803	66252	29148	36936	87203	76621	13990	94400	56418
19	09893	20505	14225	68514	46427	56788	96297	78822	54382	14598
20	91499	14523	68479	27686	46162	83554	94750	89923	37089	20048
21	80336	94598	26940	36858	70297	34135	53140	33340	42050	82341
22	44104	81949	85157	47954	32979	26575	57600	40881	22222	06413
23	12550	73742	11100	02040	12860	74697	96644	89439	28707	25815
24	63606	49329	16505	34484	40219	52563	43651	77082	07207	31790
25	61196	90446	26457	47774	51924	33729	65394	59593	42582	60527
26	15474	45266	95270	79953	59367	83848	82396	10118	33211	59466
27	94557	28573	67897	54387	54622	44431	91190	42592	92927	45973
28	42481	16213	97344	08721	16868	48767	03071	12059	25701	46670
29	23523	78317	73208	89837	68935	91416	26252	29663	05522	82562
30	04493	52494	75246	33824	45862	51025	61962	79335	65337	12472
31	00549	97654	64051	88159	96119	63896	54692	82391	23287	29529
32	35963	15307	26898	09354	33351	35462	77974	50024	90103	39333
33	59808	08391	45427	26842	83609	49700	13021	24892	78565	20106
34	46058	85236	01390	92286	77281	44077	93910	83647	70617	42941
35	32179	00597	87379	25241	05567	07007	86743	17157	85394	11838
36	69234	61406	20117	45204	15956	60000	18743	92423	97118	96338
37	19565	41430	01758	75379	40419	21585	66674	36806	84962	85207
38	45155	14938	19476	07246	43667	94543	59047	90033	20826	69541
39	94864	31994	36168	10851	34888	81553	01540	35456	05014	51176
40	98086	24826	45240	28404	44999	08896	39094	73407	35441	31880
41	33185	16232	41941	50949	89435	48581	88695	41994	37548	73043
42	80951	00406	96382	70774	20151	23387	25016	25298	94624	61171
43	79752	49140	71961	28296	69861	02591	74852	20539	00387	59579
44	18633	32537	98145	06571	31010	24674	05455	61427	77938	91936
45	74029	43902	77557	32270	97790	17119	52527	58021	80814	51748
46	54178	45611	80993	37143	05335	12969	56127	19255	36040	90324
47	11664	49883	52079	84827	59381	71539	09973	33440	88461	23356
48	48324	77928	31249	64710	02295	36870	32307	57546	15020	09994
49	69074	94138	87637	91976	35584	04401	10518	21615	01848	76938

Source: Rand Corporation, *A Million Random Digits* with 100,000 Normal Deviates (New York: Free Press, 1955). Reprinted by permission.

APPENDIX B / CUMULATIVE PROBABILITIES OF THE BINOMIAL DISTRIBUTION

$$P(X \geq x \mid n, \pi)$$

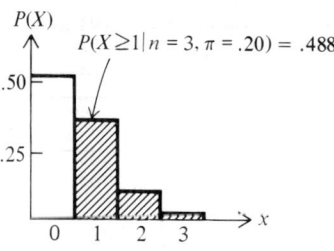

$P(X \geq 1 \mid n = 3, \pi = .20) = .488$

n = 1

π \ x	.01	.02	.03	.04	.05	.06	.07	.10	.11	.12
1	.0100	.0200	.0300	.0400	.0500	.0600	.0700	.1000	.1100	.1200

π \ x	.13	.15	.20	.25	.30	.33	.35	.40	.45	.50
1	.1300	.1500	.2000	.2500	.3000	.3300	.3500	.4000	.4500	.5000

n = 2

π \ x	.01	.02	.03	.04	.05	.06	.07	.10	.11	.12
1	.0199	.0396	.0591	.0784	.0975	.1164	.1351	.1900	.2079	.2256
2	.0001	.0004	.0009	.0016	.0025	.0036	.0049	.0100	.0121	.0144

π \ x	.13	.15	.20	.25	.30	.33	.35	.40	.45	.50
1	.2431	.2775	.3600	.4375	.5100	.5511	.5775	.6400	.6975	.7500
2	.0169	.0225	.0400	.0625	.0900	.1089	.1225	.1600	.2025	.2500

n = 3

π \ x	.01	.02	.03	.04	.05	.06	.07	.10	.11	.12
1	.0297	.0588	.0873	.1153	.1426	.1694	.1956	.2710	.2950	.3185
2	.0003	.0012	.0026	.0047	.0073	.0104	.0140	.0280	.0336	.0397
3				.0001	.0001	.0001	.0002	.0003	.0010	.0013	.0017

π \ x	.13	.15	.20	.25	.30	.33	.35	.40	.45	.50
1	.3415	.3859	.4880	.5781	.6370	.6992	.7254	.7840	.8336	.8750
2	.0463	.0608	.1040	.1563	.2160	.2548	.2818	.3520	.4253	.5000
3	.0022	.0034	.0080	.0156	.0270	.0359	.0429	.0640	.0911	.1250

n = 4

π / x	.01	.02	.03	.04	.05	.06	.07	.10	.11	.12
1	.0394	.0776	.1147	.1507	.1855	.2193	.2519	.3439	.3726	.4003
2	.0006	.0023	.0052	.0091	.0140	.0199	.0267	.0523	.0624	.0732
3			.0001	.0002	.0005	.0008	.0013	.0037	.0049	.0063
4								.0001	.0001	.0002

π / x	.13	.15	.20	.25	.30	.33	.35	.40	.45	.50
1	.4271	.4780	.5904	.6836	.7599	.7985	.8215	.8704	.9085	.9375
2	.0847	.1095	.1808	.2617	.3483	.4015	.4370	.3248	.6090	.6875
3	.0079	.0120	.0272	.0508	.0837	.1082	.1265	.1792	.2415	.3125
4	.0003	.0005	.0016	.0039	.0081	.0119	.0150	.0256	.0410	.0635

n = 5

π / x	.01	.02	.03	.04	.05	.06	.07	.10	.11	.12
1	.0490	.0961	.1413	.1846	.2262	.2661	.3043	.4095	.4416	.4723
2	.0010	.0038	.0085	.0148	.0226	.0319	.0425	.0815	.0965	.1125
3		.0001	.0003	.0006	.0012	.0020	.0031	.0086	.0112	.0143
4						.0001	.0001	.0005	.0007	.0009

π / x	.13	.15	.20	.25	.30	.33	.35	.40	.45	.50
1	.5016	.5563	.6723	.7627	.8319	.8650	.8840	.9222	.9497	.9688
2	.1292	.1648	.2627	.3672	.4718	.5325	.5716	.6630	.7438	.8125
3	.0179	.0266	.0579	.1035	.1631	.2050	.2352	.3174	.4069	.5000
4	.0013	.0022	.0067	.0156	.0308	.0436	.0540	.0870	.1312	.1875
5		.0001	.0003	.0010	.0024	.0039	.0053	.0102	.0185	.0313

n = 6

π / x	.01	.02	.03	.04	.05	.06	.07	.10	.11	.12
1	.0585	.1142	.1670	.2172	.2649	.3101	.3530	.4686	.5030	.5356
2	.0015	.0057	.0125	.0216	.0328	.0459	.0608	.1143	.1345	.1556
3		.0002	.0005	.0012	.0022	.0038	.0058	.0159	.0206	.0261
4					.0001	.0002	.0003	.0013	.0018	.0025
5								.0001	.0001	.0001

π / x	.13	.15	.20	.25	.30	.33	.35	.40	.45	.50
1	.5664	.6229	.7379	.8220	.8824	.9095	.9246	.9533	.9723	.9844
2	.1776	.2235	3446	.4661	.5798	.6422	.6809	.7667	.8364	.8909
3	.0324	.0473	.0989	.1694	.2557	.3130	.3529	.4557	.5585	.6563
4	.0034	.0059	.0170	.0376	.0705	.0969	.1174	.1792	.2553	.3438
5	.0002	.0004	.0016	.0046	.0109	.0170	.0223	.0410	.0692	.1094
6			.0001	.0002	.0007	.0013	.0018	.0041	.0083	.0156

n = 7

x \ π	.01	.02	.03	.04	.05	.06	.07	.10	.11	.12
1	.0679	.1319	.1920	.2486	.3017	.3513	.3983	.5217	.5577	.5913
2	.0020	.0079	.0171	.0294	.0444	.0618	.0813	.1497	.1750	.2012
3		.0003	.0009	.0020	.0038	.0063	.0097	.0257	.0331	.0416
4				.0001	.0002	.0004	.0007	.0027	.0039	.0054
5								.0002	.0003	.0004

x \ π	.13	.15	.20	.25	.30	.33	.35	.40	.45	.50
1	.6227	.6794	.7903	.8665	.9176	.9394	.9510	.9720	.9848	.9922
2	.2281	.2834	.4233	.5551	.6706	.7304	.7662	.8414	.8976	.9375
3	.0513	.0738	.1480	.2436	.3529	.4217	.4677	.5801	.6836	.7734
4	.0072	.0121	.0333	.0706	.1260	.1682	.1998	.2898	.3917	.5000
5	.0006	.0012	.0047	.0129	.0288	.0434	.0556	.0963	.1529	.2266
6		.0001	.0004	.0013	.0038	.0065	.0090	.0188	.0357	.0625
7				.0001	.0002	.0004	.0006	.0016	.0037	.0078

n = 8

x \ π	.01	.02	.03	.04	.05	.06	.07	.10	.11	.12
1	.0773	.1492	.2163	.2786	.3366	.3904	.4404	.5695	.6063	.6404
2	.0027	.0103	.0223	.0381	.0572	.0792	.1035	.1869	.2171	.2480
3	.0001	.0004	.0013	.0031	.0058	.0096	.0147	.0381	.0487	.0608
4			.0001	.0002	.0004	.0007	.0013	.0050	.0071	.0097
5							.0001	.0004	.0007	.0010
6										.0001

x \ π	.13	.15	.20	.25	.30	.33	.35	.40	.45	.50
1	.6718	.7275	.8322	.8999	.9484	.9594	.9681	.9832	.9916	.9961
2	.2794	.3428	.4967	.6329	.7447	.7994	.8309	.8936	.9368	.9648
3	.0743	.1052	.2031	.3215	.4482	.5236	.5722	.6846	.7799	.8555
4	.0129	.0214	.0563	.1138	.1941	.2519	.2936	.4059	.5230	.6367
5	.0015	.0029	.0104	.0273	.0580	.0846	.1061	.1737	.2604	.3633
6	.0001	.0002	.0012	.0042	.0113	.0187	.0253	.0498	.0885	.1445
7			.0001	.0004	.0013	.0024	.0036	.0085	.0181	.0352
8					.0001	.0001	.0002	.0007	.0017	.0039

$n = 9$

x \ π	.01	.02	.03	.04	.05	.06	.07	.10	.11	.12
1	.0865	.1663	.2398	.3075	.3698	.4270	.4796	.6126	.6496	.6835
2	.0034	.0131	.0282	.0478	.0712	.0978	.1271	.2252	.2599	.2951
3	.0001	.0006	.0020	.0045	.0084	.0138	.0209	.0530	.0672	.0833
4			.0001	.0003	.0006	.0013	.0023	.0083	.0117	.0158
5						.0001	.0002	.0009	.0014	.0021
6								.0001	.0001	.0002

x \ π	.13	.15	.20	.25	.30	.33	.35	.40	.45	.50
1	.7145	.7684	.8658	.9249	.9596	.9728	.9793	.9899	.9954	.9980
2	.3304	.4005	.5638	.6997	.8040	.8522	.8789	.9295	.9615	.9805
3	.1009	.1409	.2618	.3993	.5372	.6146	.6627	.7682	.8505	.9102
4	.0209	.0339	.0856	.1657	.2703	.3415	.3911	.5174	.6386	.7461
5	.0030	.0056	.0196	.0489	.0988	.1398	.1717	.2666	.3786	.5000
6	.0003	.0006	.0031	.0100	.0253	.0404	.0536	.0994	.1658	.2539
7			.0003	.0013	.0043	.0078	.0112	.0250	.0498	.0898
8				.0001	.0004	.0009	.0014	.0038	.0091	.0195
9							.0001	.0003	.0008	.0020

$n = 10$

x \ π	.01	.02	.03	.04	.05	.06	.07	.10	.11	.12
1	.0956	.1829	.2626	.3352	.4013	.4614	.5160	.6513	.6882	.7215
2	.0043	.0162	.0345	.0582	.0861	.1176	.1517	.2639	.3028	.3417
3	.0001	.0009	.0028	.0062	.0115	.0188	.0283	.0702	.0884	.1087
4			.0001	.0004	.0010	.0020	.0036	.0128	.0178	.0239
5					.0001	.0002	.0003	.0016	.0025	.0037
6								.0001	.0003	.0004

x \ π	.13	.15	.20	.25	.30	.33	.35	.40	.45	.50
1	.7516	.8031	.8926	.9437	.9718	.9818	.9865	.9940	.9975	.9990
2	.3804	.4557	.6242	.7560	.8507	.8920	.9140	.9536	.9767	.9893
3	.1308	.1798	.3222	.4744	.6172	.6930	.7384	.8327	.9004	.9453
4	.0313	.0500	.1209	.2241	.3504	.4316	.4862	.6177	.7340	.8281
5	.0053	.0099	.0328	.0781	.1503	.2064	.2485	.3669	.4956	.6230

x \ π	.13	.15	.20	.25	.30	.33	.35	.40	.45	.50
6	.0006	.0014	.0064	.0197	.0473	.0732	.0949	.1662	.2616	.3770
7	.0001	.0001	.0009	.0035	.0106	.0185	.0260	.0548	.1020	.1719
8			.0001	.0004	.0016	.0032	.0048	.0123	.0274	.0547
9					.0001	.0003	.0005	.0017	.0045	.0107
10								.0001	.0003	.0010

n = 11

x \ π	.01	.02	.03	.04	.05	.06	.07	.10	.11	.12
1	.1047	.1993	.2847	.3618	.4312	.4937	.5499	.6862	.7225	.7549
2	.0052	.0195	.0413	.0692	.1019	.1382	.1772	.3026	.3452	.3873
3	.0002	.0012	.0037	.0083	.0152	.0248	.0370	.0896	.1120	.1366
4			.0002	.0007	.0016	.0030	.0053	.0185	.0256	.0341
5					.0001	.0003	.0005	.0028	.0042	.0061
6								.0003	.0005	.0008
7										.0001

x \ π	.13	.15	.20	.25	.30	.33	.35	.40	.45	.50
1	.7839	.8327	.9141	.9578	.9802	.9878	.9912	.9964	.9986	.9995
2	.4286	.5078	.6779	.8029	.8870	.9216	.9394	.9698	.9861	.9941
3	.1632	.2212	.3826	.5448	.6873	.7587	.7999	.8811	.9348	.9673
4	.0442	.0694	.1611	.2867	.4304	.5179	.5744	.7037	.8089	.8867
5	.0087	.0159	.0504	.1146	.2103	.2807	.3317	.4672	.6029	.7256
6	.0012	.0027	.0117	.0343	.0782	.1171	.1487	.2465	.3669	.5000
7	.0001	.0003	.0020	.0076	.0216	.0366	.0501	.0994	.1738	.2744
8			.0002	.0012	.0043	.0082	.0122	.0293	.0610	.1133
9				.0001	.0006	.0013	.0020	.0059	.0148	.0327
10						.0001	.0002	.0007	.0022	.0059
11									.0002	.0005

n = 20

x \ π	.01	.02	.03	.04	.05	.06	.07	.10	.11	.12
1	.1821	.3324	.4562	.5580	.6415	.7099	.7658	.8784	.9028	.9224
2	.0169	.0599	.1198	.1897	.2642	.3395	.4131	.6083	.6624	.7109
3	.0010	.0071	.0210	.0439	.0755	.1150	.1610	.3231	.3802	.4369
4		.0006	.0027	.0074	.0159	.0290	.0471	.1330	.1710	.2127
5			.0003	.0010	.0026	.0056	.0107	.0432	.0610	.0827
6				.0001	.0003	.0009	.0019	.0113	.0175	.0260
7						.0001	.0003	.0024	.0041	.0067
8								.0004	.0008	.0014
9								.0001	.0001	.0002

x \ π	.13	.15	.20	.25	.30	.33	.35	.40	.45	.50
6	.9383	.9612	.9885	.9968	.9992	.9997	.9998	1.0000	1.0000	1.0000
7	.7539	.8244	.9308	.9757	.9924	.9964	.9979	.9995	.9999	1.0000
8	.4920	.5951	.7939	.9087	.9645	.9811	.9879	.9964	.9991	.9998
9	.2573	.3523	.5886	.7748	.8929	.9356	9556	.9840	.9951	.9987
10	.1083	.1702	.3704	.5852	.7625	.8411	.8818	.9490	.9811	.9941
11	.0370	.0673	.1958	.3828	.3836	.6917	.7546	.8744	.9447	.9793
12	.0103	.0219	.0867	.2142	.3920	.5079	.5834	.7500	.8701	.9423
13	.0024	.0059	.0321	.1018	.2277	.3268	.3990	.5841	.7480	.8684
14	.0005	.0013	.0100	.0409	.1133	.1818	.2376	.4044	.5857	.7483
15	.0001	.0002	.0026	.0139	.0480	.0866	.1218	.2447	.4086	.5881
16			.0006	.0039	.0171	.0350	.0532	.1275	.2493	.4119
17			.0001	.0009	.0051	.0119	.0196	.0563	.1308	.2517
18				.0002	.0013	.0034	.0060	.0210	.0580	.1316
					.0003	.0008	.0015	.0065	.0214	.0577
						.0001	.0003	.0016	.0064	.0207
								.0003	.0015	.0059
									.0003	.0013
										.0002

$n = 30$

x \ π	.01	.02	.03	.04	.05	.06	.07	.10	.11	.12
1	.2603	.4545	.5990	.7061	.7854	.8437	.8866	.9576	.9697	.9784
2	.0361	.1205	.2269	.3388	.4465	.5445	.6306	.8163	.8573	.8900
3	.0033	.0217	.0601	.1169	.1878	.2676	.3513	.5886	.6558	.7153
4	.0002	.0029	.0119	.0306	.0608	.1026	.1550	.3526	.4234	.4929
5		.0003	.0019	.0063	.0156	.0315	.0553	.1755	.2295	.2882
6			.0002	.0011	.0033	.0079	.0162	.0732	.1049	.1431
7				.0001	.0006	.0017	.0040	.0258	.0407	.0606
8					.0001	.0003	.0008	.0078	.0136	.0221
9							.0002	.0020	.0039	.0069
10								.0005	.0010	.0019
11								.0001	.0002	.0005
12										.0001

x \ π	.13	.15	.20	.25	.30	.33	.35	.40	.45	.50
1	.9847	.9924	.9988	.9998	1.0000	1.0000	1.0000	1.0000	1.0000	1.0000
2	.9159	.9520	.9895	.9980	.9997	.9999	1.0000	1.0000	1.0000	1.0000
3	.7670	.8486	.9558	.9894	.9979	.9993	.9997	1.0000	1.0000	1.0000
4	.5594	.6783	.8773	.9626	.9907	.9963	.9981	.9997	1.0000	1.0000
5	.3499	.4755	.7448	.9021	.9698	.9866	.9925	.9985	.9998	1.0000

x \ π	.13	.15	.20	.25	.30	.33	.35	.40	.45	.50
6	.1872	.2894	.5725	.7974	.9234	.9615	.9767	.9943	.9989	.9998
7	.0858	.1526	.3930	.6519	.8405	.9102	.9414	.9828	.9960	.9993
8	.0339	.0698	.2392	.4857	.7186	.8235	.8762	.9565	.9879	.9974
9	.0116	.0278	.1287	.3264	.5685	.7007	.7753	.9060	.9688	.9919
10	.0035	.0097	.0611	.1966	.4112	.5529	.6425	.8237	.9306	.9786
11	.0009	.0029	.0256	.1057	.2696	.4000	.4922	.7085	.8650	.9506
12	.0002	.0008	.0095	.0507	.1593	.2631	.3452	.5689	.7673	.8998
13		.0002	.0031	.0216	.0845	.1563	.2198	.4215	.6408	.8192
14			.0009	.0082	.0401	.0835	.1263	.2855	.4975	.7077
15			.0002	.0028	.0169	.0399	.0652	.1754	.3552	.5722
16			.0001	.0008	.0064	.0170	.0301	.0971	.2309	.4278
17				.0002	.0021	.0065	.0124	.0481	.1356	.2923
18				.0001	.0006	.0022	.0045	.0212	.0714	.1808
19					.0002	.0006	.0015	.0083	.0334	.1002
20						.0002	.0004	.0029	.0138	.0494
21							.0001	.0009	.0050	.0214
22								.0002	.0016	.0081
23								.0001	.0004	.0026
24									.0001	.0007
25										.0002

$n = 50$

x \ π	.01	.02	.03	.04	.05	.06	.07	.10	.11	.12
1	.3950	.6358	.7819	.8701	.9231	.9547	.9734	.9948	.9971	.9983
2	.0894	.2642	.4447	.5995	.7206	.8100	.8735	.9662	.9788	.9869
3	.0138	.0784	.1892	.3233	.4595	.5838	.6892	.8883	.9237	.9487
4	.0016	.0178	.0628	.1391	.2396	.3527	.4673	.7497	.8146	.8655
5	.0001	.0032	.0168	.0490	.1036	.1794	.2710	.5688	.6562	.7320
6		.0005	.0037	.0144	.0378	.0776	.1350	.3839	.4760	.5647
7		.0001	.0007	.0036	.0118	.0289	.0583	.2298	.3091	.3935
8			.0001	.0008	.0032	.0094	.0220	.1221	.1793	.2467
9				.0001	.0008	.0027	.0073	.0579	.0932	.1392
10					.0002	.0007	.0022	.0245	.0435	.0708
11						.0002	.0006	.0094	.0183	.0325
12							.0001	.0032	.0069	.0135
13								.0010	.0024	.0051
14								.0003	.0008	.0018
15								.0001	.0002	.0006
16									.0001	.0002

x \ π	.13	.15	.20	.25	.30	.33	.35	.40	.45	.50
1	.9991	.9997	1.0000	1.0000	1.0000	1.0000	1.0000	1.0000	1.0000	1.0000
2	.9920	.9971	.9998	1.0000	1.0000	1.0000	1.0000	1.0000	1.0000	1.0000
3	.9661	.9858	.9987	.9999	1.0000	1.0000	1.0000	1.0000	1.0000	1.0000
4	.9042	.9540	.9943	.9995	1.0000	1.0000	1.0000	1.0000	1.0000	1.0000
5	.7956	.8879	.9815	.9979	.9998	1.0000	1.0000	1.0000	1.0000	1.0000
6	.6463	.7806	.9520	.9930	.9993	.9998	.9999	1.0000	1.0000	1.0000
7	.4789	.6387	.8966	.9806	.9975	.9994	.9998	1.0000	1.0000	1.0000
8	.3217	.4812	.8096	.9547	.9927	.9980	.9992	.9999	1.0000	1.0000
9	.1955	.3319	.6927	.9084	.9817	.9942	.9975	.9998	1.0000	1.0000
10	.1074	.2089	.5563	.8363	.9598	.9856	.9933	.9992	.9999	1.0000
11	.0535	.1199	.4164	.7378	.9211	.9683	.9840	.9978	.9998	1.0000
12	.0242	.0628	.2893	.6184	.8610	.9371	.9658	.9943	.9994	1.0000
13	.0100	.0301	.1861	.4890	.7771	.8873	.9339	.9867	.9982	.9998
14	.0037	.0132	.1106	.3630	.6721	.8157	.8837	.9720	.9955	.9995
15	.0013	.0053	.0607	.2519	.5532	.7223	.8122	.9460	.9896	.9987
16	.0004	.0019	.0308	.1631	.4308	.6120	.7199	.9045	.9780	.9967
17	.0001	.0007	.0144	.0983	.3161	.4931	.6111	.8439	.9573	.9923
18		.0002	.0063	.0551	.2178	.3760	.4940	.7631	.9235	.9836
19		.0001	.0025	.0287	.1406	.2703	.3784	.6644	.8727	.9675
20			.0009	.0139	.0848	.1826	.2736	.5535	.8026	.9405
21			.0003	.0063	.0478	.1156	.1861	.4390	.7138	.8987
22			.0001	.0026	.0251	.0685	.1187	.3299	.6100	.8389
23				.0010	.0123	.0379	.0710	.2340	.4981	.7601
24				.0004	.0056	.0196	.0396	.1562	.3866	.6641
25				.0001	.0024	.0094	.0207	.0978	.2840	.5561
26					.0009	.0042	.0100	.0573	.1966	.4439
27					.0003	.0018	.0045	.0314	.1279	.3359
28					.0001	.0007	.0019	.0160	.0780	.2399
29						.0002	.0007	.0076	.0444	.1611
30						.0001	.0003	.0034	.0235	.1013
31							.0001	.0014	.0116	.0595
32								.0005	.0053	.0325
33								.0002	.0022	.0164
34								.0001	.0009	.0077
35									.0003	.0033
36									.0001	.0013
37										.0005
38										.0002

APPENDIX C / CUMULATIVE PROBABILITIES OF THE POISSON DISTRIBUTION

$$P(X \geq x \mid m)$$

Example: $P(X \geq 3 \mid m = .70) = .034$

x \ m	.001	.002	.003	.004	.005	.006	.007	.008	.009	.010
1	.001	.002	.003	.004	.005	.006	.007	.008	.009	.010
2										
3										

x \ m	.20	.25	.30	.40	.50	.60	.70	.80	.90	1.0
1	.181	.221	.259	.330	.393	.451	.503	.551	.593	.632
2	.018	.026	.037	.062	.090	.122	.156	.191	.228	.264
3	.001	.002	.004	.008	.014	.023	.034	.047	.063	.080
4				.001	.002	.003	.006	.009	.013	.019
5							.001	.001	.002	.004
6										.001
7										
8										

x \ m	2.1	2.2	2.3	2.4	2.5	2.6	2.7	2.8	2.9	3.0
1	.878	.889	.900	.909	.918	.926	.933	.939	.945	.950
2	.620	.645	.669	.692	.713	.733	.751	.769	.785	.801
3	.350	.377	.404	.430	.456	.482	.506	.531	.554	.577
4	.161	.181	.201	.221	.242	.264	.286	.308	.330	.353
5	.062	.072	.084	.096	.109	.123	.137	.152	.168	.185
6	.020	.025	.030	.036	.042	.049	.057	.065	.074	.084
7	.006	.007	.009	.012	.014	.017	.021	.024	.029	.034
8	.001	.002	.003	.003	.004	.005	.007	.008	.010	.012
9			.001	.001	.001	.001	.002	.002	.003	.004
10							.001	.001	.001	.001
11										
12										

x \ m	4.1	4.2	4.3	4.4	4.5	4.6	4.7	4.8	4.9	5.0
1	.983	.985	.986	.988	.989	.990	.991	.992	.993	.993
2	.915	.922	.928	.934	.939	.944	.948	.952	.956	.960
3	.776	.790	.803	.815	.826	.837	.848	.857	.867	.875
4	.586	.605	.623	.641	.658	.674	.690	.706	.721	.735
5	.391	.410	.430	.449	.468	.487	.505	.524	.542	.560

Appendixes: Statistical Tables

.02	.03	.04	.05	.06	.07	.08	.09	.10	.15	m / x
.020	.030	.039	.049	.058	.068	.077	.086	.095	.139	1
		.001	.001	.002	.002	.003	.004	.005	.010	2
									.001	3

1.1	1.2	1.3	1.4	1.5	1.6	1.7	1.8	1.9	2.0	m / x
.667	.699	.727	.753	.777	.798	.817	.835	.850	.865	1
.301	.337	.373	.408	.442	.475	.507	.537	.566	.594	2
.100	.121	.143	.167	.191	.217	.243	.269	.296	.323	3
.026	.034	.043	.054	.066	.079	.093	.109	.125	.143	4
.005	.008	.011	.014	.019	.024	.030	.036	.044	.053	5
.001	.002	.002	.003	.004	.006	.008	.010	.013	.017	6
			.001	.001	.001	.002	.003	.003	.005	7
							.001	.001	.001	8

3.1	3.2	3.3	3.4	3.5	3.6	3.7	3.8	3.9	4.0	m / x
.955	.959	.963	.967	.970	.973	.975	.978	.980	.982	1
.815	.829	.841	.853	.864	.874	.884	.893	.901	.908	2
.599	.620	.641	.660	.679	.697	.715	.731	.747	.762	3
.375	.397	.420	.442	.463	.485	.506	.527	.547	.567	4
.202	.219	.237	.256	.275	.294	.313	.332	.352	.371	5
.094	.105	.117	.129	.142	.156	.170	.184	.199	.215	6
.039	.045	.051	.058	.065	.073	.082	.091	.101	.111	7
.014	.017	.020	.023	.027	.031	.035	.040	.045	.051	8
.005	.006	.007	.008	.010	.012	.014	.016	.019	.021	9
.001	.002	.002	.003	.003	.004	.005	.006	.007	.008	10
		.001	.001	.001	.001	.002	.002	.002	.003	11
							.001	.001	.001	12

5.1	5.2	5.3	5.4	5.5	5.6	5.7	5.8	5.9	6.0	m / x
.994	.994	.995	.995	.996	.997	.997	.997	.997	.998	1
.963	.966	.969	.971	.973	.976	.978	.979	.981	.983	2
.884	.891	.898	.905	.912	.918	.923	.928	.933	.938	3
.749	.762	.775	.787	.798	.809	.820	.830	.840	.849	4
.577	.594	.610	.627	.642	.658	.673	.687	.701	.715	5

m\x	4.1	4.2	4.3	4.4	4.5	4.6	4.7	4.8	4.9	5.0
6	.231	.247	.263	.280	.297	.314	.332	.349	.366	.384
7	.121	.133	.144	.156	.169	.182	.195	.209	.223	.238
8	.057	.064	.071	.079	.087	.095	.104	.113	.123	.133
9	.024	.028	.032	.036	.040	.045	.050	.056	.062	.068
10	.010	.011	.013	.015	.017	.020	.022	.025	.028	.032
11	.003	.004	.005	.006	.007	.008	.009	.010	.012	.014
12	.001	.001	.002	.002	.002	.003	.003	.004	.005	.005
13			.001	.001	.001	.001	.001	.001	.002	.002
14									.001	.001
15										
16										

m\x	6.1	6.2	6.3	6.4	6.5	6.6	6.7	6.8	6.9	7.0
1	.998	.998	.998	.998	.998	.999	.999	.999	.999	.999
2	.984	.985	.987	.988	.989	.990	.991	.991	.992	.993
3	.942	.946	.950	.954	.957	.960	.963	.966	.968	.970
4	.857	.866	.874	.881	.888	.895	.901	.907	.913	.918
5	.728	.741	.753	.765	.776	.787	.798	.808	.818	.827
6	.570	.586	.601	.616	.631	.645	.659	.673	.686	.699
7	.410	.426	.442	.458	.473	.489	.505	.520	.535	.550
8	.270	.284	.298	.313	.327	.342	.357	.372	.386	.401
9	.163	.174	.185	.197	.208	.220	.233	.245	.258	.271
10	.091	.098	.106	.114	.123	.131	.140	.150	.151	.170
11	.047	.051	.056	.061	.067	.073	.079	.085	.092	.099
12	.022	.025	.028	.031	.034	.037	.041	.045	.049	.053
13	.010	.011	.013	.014	.016	.018	.020	.022	.024	.027
14	.004	.005	.005	.006	.007	.008	.009	.010	.011	.013
15	.002	.002	.002	.003	.003	.003	.004	.004	.005	.006
16	.001	.001	.001	.001	.001	.001	.002	.002	.002	.002
17						.001	.001	.001	.001	.001
18										
19										
20										
21										
22										

Appendixes: Statistical Tables

5.1	5.2	5.3	5.4	5.5	5.6	5.7	5.8	5.9	6.0	m/x
.402	.419	.437	.454	.471	.488	.505	.522	.538	.554	6
.253	.268	.283	.298	.314	.330	.346	.362	.378	.394	7
.144	.155	.167	.178	.191	.203	.216	.229	.242	.256	8
.075	.082	.089	.097	.106	.114	.123	.133	.143	.153	9
.036	.040	.044	.049	.054	.059	.065	.071	.077	.084	10
.016	.018	.020	.023	.025	.028	.031	.035	.039	.042	11
.006	.007	.008	.010	.011	.012	.014	.016	.018	.020	12
.002	.003	.003	.004	.004	.005	.006	.007	.008	.009	13
.001	.001	.001	.001	.002	.002	.002	.003	.003	.004	14
				.001	.001	.001	.001	.001	.001	15
									.001	16

7.1	7.2	7.3	7.4	7.5	8.0	8.5	9.0	9.5	10.0	m/x
.999	.999	.999	.999	.999	1.000	1.000	1.000	1.000	1.000	1
.993	.994	.994	.995	.995	.997	.998	.999	.999	1.000	2
.973	.975	.976	.978	.980	.986	.991	.994	.996	.997	3
.923	.928	.933	.937	.941	.958	.970	.979	.985	.990	4
.836	.844	.853	.860	.868	.900	.926	.945	.960	.971	5
.712	.724	.736	.747	.759	.809	.850	.884	.911	.933	6
.565	.580	.594	.608	.622	.687	.744	.793	.835	.870	7
.416	.431	.446	.461	.475	.547	.614	.676	.731	.780	8
.284	.297	.311	.324	.338	.407	.477	.544	.608	.667	9
.180	.190	.201	.212	.224	.283	.347	.413	.478	.542	10
.106	.113	.121	.129	.138	.184	.237	.294	.355	.417	11
.058	.063	.068	.074	.079	.112	.151	.197	.248	.303	12
.030	.033	.036	.039	.043	.064	.091	.124	.164	.208	13
.014	.016	.018	.020	.022	.034	.051	.074	.102	.136	14
.006	.007	.008	.009	.010	.017	.027	.041	.060	.083	15
.003	.003	.004	.004	.005	.008	.014	.022	.033	.049	16
.001	.001	.001	.002	.002	.004	.007	.011	.018	.027	17
	.001	.001	.001	.001	.002	.003	.005	.009	.014	18
					.001	.001	.002	.004	.007	19
						.001	.001	.002	.003	20
								.001	.002	21
									.001	22

APPENDIX D / AREAS FOR STANDARD NORMAL DISTRIBUTION

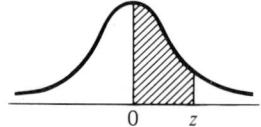

Example: For $z = 2.0$, the shaded area is .4772.

z	.00	.01	.02	.03	.04	.05	.06	.07	.08	.09
0.0	.0000	.0040	.0080	.0120	.0160	.0199	.0239	.0279	.0319	.0359
0.1	.0398	.0438	.0478	.0517	.0557	.0596	.0636	.0675	.0714	.0753
0.2	.0793	.0832	.0871	.0910	.0948	.0987	.1026	.1064	.1103	.1141
0.3	.1179	.1217	.1255	.1293	.1331	.1368	.1406	.1443	.1480	.1517
0.4	.1554	.1591	.1628	.1664	.1700	.1736	.1772	.1808	.1844	.1879
0.5	.1915	.1950	.1985	.2019	.2054	.2088	.2123	.2157	.2190	.2224
0.6	.2257	.2291	.2324	.2357	.2389	.2422	.2454	.2486	.2518	.2549
0.7	.2580	.2612	.2642	.2673	.2704	.2734	.2764	.2794	.2823	.2852
0.8	.2881	.2910	.2939	.2967	.2995	.3023	.3051	.3078	.3106	.3133
0.9	.3159	.3186	.3212	.3238	.3264	.3289	.3315	.3340	.3365	.3389
1.0	.3413	.3438	.3461	.3485	.3508	.3531	.3554	.3577	.3599	.3621
1.1	.3643	.3665	.3686	.3708	.3729	.3749	.3770	.3790	.3810	.3830
1.2	.3849	.3869	.3888	.3907	.3925	.3944	.3962	.3980	.3997	.4015
1.3	.4032	.4049	.4066	.4082	.4099	.4115	.4131	.4147	.4162	.4177
1.4	.4192	.4207	.4222	.4236	.4251	.4265	.4279	.4292	.4306	.4319
1.5	.4332	.4345	.4357	.4370	.4382	.4394	.4406	.4418	.4429	.4441
1.6	.4452	.4463	.4474	.4484	.4495	.4505	.4515	.4525	.4535	4545
1.7	.4554	.4564	.4573	.4582	.4591	.4599	.4608	.4616	.4625	.4633
1.8	.4641	.4649	.4656	.4664	.4671	.4678	.4686	.4693	.4699	.4706
1.9	.4713	.4719	.4726	.4732	.4738	.4744	.4750	.4756	.4761	.4767
2.0	.4772	.4778	.4783	.4788	.4793	.4798	.4803	.4808	.4812	.4817
2.1	.4821	.4826	.4830	.4834	.4838	.4842	.4846	.4850	.4854	.4857
2.2	.4861	.4864	.4868	.4871	.4875	.4878	.4881	.4884	.4887	.4890
2.3	.4893	.4896	.4898	.4901	.4904	.4906	.4909	.4911	.4913	.4916
2.4	.4918	.4920	.4922	.4925	.4927	.4929	.4931	.4932	.4934	.4936
2.5	.4938	.4940	.4941	.4943	.4945	.4946	.4948	.4949	.4951	.4952
2.6	.4953	.4955	.4956	.4957	.4959	.4960	.4961	.4962	.4963	.4964
2.7	.4965	.4966	.4967	.4968	.4969	.4970	.4971	.4972	.4973	.4974
2.8	.4974	.4975	.4976	.4977	.4977	.4978	.4979	.4979	.4980	.4981
2.9	.4981	.4982	.4982	.4983	.4984	.4984	.4985	.4985	.4986	.4986
3.0	.49865	.4987	.4987	.4988	.4988	.4989	.4989	.4989	.4990	.4990
4.0	.4999683									

APPENDIX E / t DISTRIBUTION

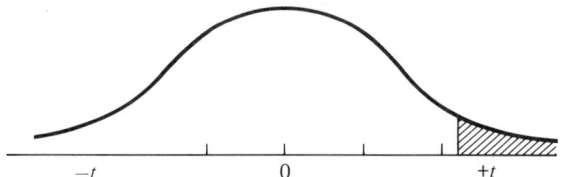

Example: For the *t* distribution with 10 degrees of freedom, .01 of the area in the right tail of the curve, shaded area, falls beyond the value of *t* = + 2.764.

					Upper-Tail Probability							
df	.45	.40	.35	.30	.25	.20	.15	.10	.05	.025	.01	.005	df
1	.158	.325	.510	.727	1.000	1.376	1.963	3.078	6.314	12.706	31.821	63.657	1
2	.142	.289	.445	.617	.816	1.061	1.386	1.886	2.920	4.303	6.965	9.925	2
3	.137	.277	.424	.584	.765	.978	1.250	1.638	2.353	3.182	4.541	5.841	3
4	.134	.271	.414	.569	.741	.941	1.190	1.533	2.132	2.776	3.747	4.604	4
5	.132	.267	.408	.559	.727	.920	1.156	1.476	2.015	2.571	3.365	4.032	5
6	.131	.265	.404	.553	.718	.906	1.134	1.440	1.943	2.447	3.143	3.707	6
7	.130	.263	.402	.549	.711	.896	1.119	1.415	1.895	2.365	2.998	3.499	7
8	.130	.262	.399	.546	.706	.889	1.108	1.397	1.860	2.306	2.896	3.355	8
9	.129	.261	.398	.543	.703	.883	1.100	1.383	1.833	2.262	2.821	3.250	9
10	.129	.260	.397	.542	.700	.879	1.093	1.372	1.812	2.228	2.764	3.169	10
11	.129	.260	.396	.540	.697	.876	1.088	1.363	1.796	2.201	2.718	3.106	11
12	.128	.259	.395	.539	.695	.873	1.083	1.356	1.782	2.179	2.681	3.055	12
13	.128	.259	.394	.538	.694	.870	1.079	1.350	1.771	2.160	2.650	3.012	13
14	.128	.258	.393	.537	.692	.868	1.076	1.345	1.761	2.145	2.624	2.977	14
15	.128	.258	.393	.536	.691	.866	1.074	1.341	1.753	2.131	2.602	2.947	15
16	.128	.258	.392	.535	.690	.865	1.071	1.337	1.746	2.120	2.583	2.921	16
17	.128	.257	.392	.534	.689	.863	1.069	1.333	1.740	2.110	2.567	2.898	17
18	.127	.257	.392	.534	.688	.862	1.067	1.330	1.734	2.101	2.552	2.878	18
19	.127	.257	.391	.533	.688	.861	1.066	1.328	1.729	2.093	2.539	2.861	19
20	.127	.257	.391	.533	.687	.860	1.064	1.325	1.725	2.086	2.528	2.845	20
21	.127	.257	.391	.532	.686	.859	1.063	1.323	1.721	2.080	2.518	2.831	21
22	.127	.256	.390	.532	.686	.858	1.061	1.321	1.717	2.074	2.508	2.819	22
23	.127	.256	.390	.532	.685	.858	1.060	1.319	1.714	2.069	2.500	2.807	23
24	.127	.256	.390	.531	.685	.857	1.059	1.318	1.711	2.064	2.492	2.797	24
25	.127	.256	.390	.531	.684	.856	1.058	1.316	1.708	2.060	2.485	2.787	25
26	.127	.256	.390	.531	.684	.856	1.058	1.315	1.706	2.056	2.479	2.779	26
27	.127	.256	.389	.531	.684	.855	1.057	1.314	1.703	2.052	2.473	2.771	27
28	.127	.256	.389	.530	.683	.855	1.056	1.313	1.701	2.048	2.467	2.763	28
29	.127	.256	.389	.530	.683	.854	1.055	1.311	1.699	2.045	2.462	2.756	29
30	.127	.256	.389	.530	.683	.854	1.055	1.310	1.697	2.042	2.457	2.750	30
∞	.12566	.25335	.38532	.52440	.67449	.84162	1.03643	1.28155	1.64485	1.95996	2.32634	2.57582	∞

Source: R. A. Fisher and F. Yates: *Statistical Tables for Biological, Agricultural, and Medical Research* (Edinburgh: Oliver and Boyd Ltd., 1974), Table III. Reprinted by permission of the authors and the publishers.

APPENDIX F / PERCENT OF ERROR e FOR A GIVEN STATISTIC p AND SAMPLE SIZE n WITH 95 PERCENT CONFIDENCE

$$e = (1.96)\sqrt{\frac{p(1-p)}{n}}(100)$$

(e in percentages)

n \ p	.05	.10	.15	.20	.25	.30	.35	.40	.45	.50
30									18.1	18.2
50	Normal approximation poor						13.4	13.7	13.9	14.0
100						9.0	9.3	9.6	9.8	9.8
150					6.9	7.3	7.6	7.8	8.0	8.0
200				5.5	6.0	6.4	6.6	6.8	6.9	6.9
250				5.0	5.4	5.7	5.9	6.1	6.2	6.2
300				4.5	4.9	5.2	5.4	5.5	5.6	5.7
350				4.2	4.5	4.8	5.0	5.1	5.2	5.2
400			3.5	3.9	4.2	4.5	4.7	4.8	4.9	4.9
450			3.3	3.7	4.0	4.2	4.4	4.5	4.6	4.6
500			3.1	3.5	3.8	4.0	4.2	4.3	4.4	4.4
550			3.0	3.3	3.6	3.8	4.0	4.1	4.2	4.2
600		2.4	2.9	3.2	3.5	3.7	3.8	3.9	4.0	4.0
650		2.3	2.7	3.1	3.3	3.5	3.7	3.8	3.8	3.8
700		2.2	2.6	3.0	3.2	3.4	3.5	3.6	3.7	3.7
750		2.1	2.6	2.9	3.1	3.3	3.4	3.5	3.6	3.6
800		2.1	2.5	2.8	3.0	3.2	3.3	3.4	3.4	3.5
850		2.0	2.4	2.7	2.9	3.1	3.2	3.3	3.3	3.4
900		2.0	2.3	2.6	2.8	3.0	3.1	3.2	3.3	3.3
950		1.9	2.3	2.5	2.8	2.9	3.0	3.1	3.2	3.2
1000		1.9	2.2	2.5	2.7	2.8	3.0	3.0	3.1	3.1
2000	1.0	1.3	1.6	1.8	1.9	2.0	2.1	2.1	2.2	2.2
3000	.8	1.1	1.3	1.4	1.5	1.6	1.7	1.8	1.8	1.8
4000	.7	.9	1.1	1.2	1.3	1.4	1.5	1.6	1.5	1.5

APPENDIX G / CHI-SQUARE DISTRIBUTION

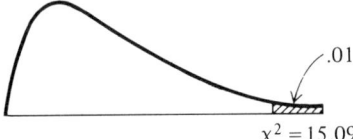

Example: For the chi-square distribution with 5 degrees of freedom, the area to the right of the chi-square value of 15.09 is .01.

	Shaded Area in Right Tail								
df	.900	.750	.500	.250	.100	.050	.025	.010	.005
1	0.02	0.10	0.45	1.32	2.71	3.84	5.02	6.64	7.88
2	0.21	0.58	1.39	2.77	4.61	5.99	7.38	9.21	10.60
3	0.58	1.21	2.37	4.11	6.25	7.81	9.35	11.35	12.84
4	1.06	1.92	3.36	5.39	7.78	9.49	11.14	13.28	14.86
5	1.61	2.67	4.35	6.63	9.24	11.07	12.83	15.09	16.75
6	2.20	3.45	5.35	7.84	10.64	12.59	14.45	16.81	18.55
7	2.83	4.25	6.35	9.04	12.02	14.07	16.01	18.48	20.28
8	3.49	5.07	7.34	10.22	13.36	15.51	17.53	20.09	21.96
9	4.17	5.90	8.34	11.39	14.68	16.92	19.02	21.67	23.59
10	4.87	6.74	9.34	12.55	15.99	18.31	20.48	23.21	25.19
11	5.58	7.58	10.34	13.70	17.28	19.68	21.92	24.73	26.76
12	6.30	8.44	11.34	14.85	18.55	21.03	23.34	26.22	28.30
13	7.04	9.30	12.34	15.98	19.81	22.36	24.74	27.69	29.82
14	7.79	10.17	13.34	17.12	21.06	23.68	26.12	29.14	31.32
15	8.55	11.04	14.34	18.25	22.31	25.00	27.49	30.58	32.80
16	9.31	11.91	15.34	19.37	23.54	26.30	28.85	32.00	34.27
17	10.00	12.79	16.34	20.49	24.77	27.59	30.19	33.41	35.72
18	10.86	13.68	17.34	21.60	25.99	28.87	31.53	34.81	37.16
19	11.65	14.56	18.34	22.72	27.20	30.14	32.85	36.19	38.58
20	12.44	15.45	19.34	23.83	28.41	31.41	34.17	37.57	40.00
21	13.24	16.34	20.34	24.93	29.62	32.67	35.48	38.93	41.40
22	14.04	17.24	21.34	26.04	30.81	33.92	36.78	40.29	42.80
23	14.85	18.14	22.34	27.14	32.01	35.17	38.08	41.64	44.18
24	15.66	19.04	23.34	28.24	33.20	36.42	39.36	42.98	45.56
25	16.47	19.94	24.34	29.34	34.38	37.65	40.65	44.31	46.93
26	17.29	20.84	25.34	30.43	35.56	38.89	41.92	45.64	48.29
27	18.11	21.75	26.34	31.53	36.74	40.11	43.19	46.96	49.64
28	18.94	22.66	27.34	32.62	37.92	41.34	44.46	48.28	50.99
29	19.77	23.57	28.34	33.71	39.09	42.56	45.72	49.59	52.34
30	20.60	24.48	29.34	34.80	40.26	43.77	46.98	50.89	53.67

Source: R. A. Fisher and F. Yates: *Statistical Tables for Biological, Agricultural, and Medical Research*, (Edinburgh: Oliver and Boyd Ltd., 1974), Table IV. Reprinted by permission of the authors and the publishers.

APPENDIX H / F DISTRIBUTION (COMPUTER-GENERATED)

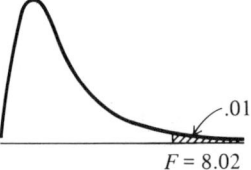

$F = 8.02$

Example: For the F distribution with 2 degrees of freedom in the numerator and 9 degrees of freedom in the denominator, the area to the right of F value of 8.02 is .01 in boldface type. Lightface type numbers represent .05 areas.

Degrees of Freedom in Denominator	Degrees of Freedom in Numerator											
	1	2	3	4	5	6	7	8	9	10	11	12
1	161	200	216	225	230	234	237	239	241	242	243	244
	4052	**4999**	**5403**	**5625**	**5764**	**5859**	**5928**	**5981**	**6022**	**6056**	**6082**	**6106**
2	18.51	19.00	19.16	19.25	19.30	19.33	19.36	19.37	19.38	10.39	19.40	19.41
	93.49	**99.00**	**99.17**	**99.25**	**99.30**	**99.33**	**99.34**	**99.36**	**99.38**	**99.40**	**99.41**	**99.42**
3	10.13	9.55	9.28	9.12	9.01	8.94	8.88	8.84	8.81	8.78	8.76	8.74
	34.12	**30.82**	**29.46**	**28.71**	**28.24**	**27.91**	**27.67**	**27.49**	**27.34**	**27.23**	**27.13**	**27.05**
4	7.71	6.94	6.59	6.39	6.26	6.16	6.09	6.04	6.00	5.96	5.93	5.91
	21.20	**18.00**	**16.69**	**15.98**	**15.52**	**15.21**	**14.98**	**14.80**	**14.66**	**14.54**	**14.45**	**14.37**
5	6.61	5.79	5.41	5.19	5.05	4.95	4.88	4.82	4.78	4.74	4.70	4.68
	16.26	**13.27**	**12.06**	**11.39**	**10.97**	**10.67**	**10.45**	**10.27**	**10.15**	**10.05**	**9.96**	**9.89**
6	5.99	5.14	4.76	4.53	4.39	4.28	4.21	4.15	4.10	4.06	4.03	4.00
	13.74	**10.92**	**9.78**	**9.15**	**8.75**	**8.47**	**8.26**	**8.10**	**7.98**	**7.87**	**7.79**	**7.72**
7	5.59	4.74	4.35	4.12	3.97	3.87	3.79	3.73	3.68	3.63	3.60	3.57
	12.25	**9.55**	**8.45**	**7.85**	**7.46**	**7.19**	**7.00**	**6.84**	**6.71**	**6.62**	**6.54**	**6.47**
8	5.32	4.46	4.07	3.84	3.69	3.58	3.50	3.44	3.39	3.34	3.31	3.28
	11.26	**8.65**	**7.59**	**7.01**	**6.63**	**6.37**	**6.19**	**6.03**	**5.91**	**5.82**	**5.74**	**5.67**
9	5.12	4.26	3.86	3.63	3.48	3.37	3.29	3.23	3.18	3.13	3.10	3.07
	10.56	**8.02**	**6.99**	**6.42**	**6.06**	**5.80**	**5.62**	**5.47**	**5.35**	**5.26**	**5.18**	**5.11**
10	4.06	4.10	3.71	3.48	3.33	3.22	3.14	3.07	3.02	2.97	2.94	2.91
	10.04	**7.56**	**6.55**	**5.99**	**5.64**	**5.39**	**5.21**	**5.06**	**4.95**	**4.85**	**4.78**	**4.71**
11	4.84	3.98	3.59	3.36	3.20	3.09	3.01	2.95	2.90	2.86	2.82	2.79
	9.65	**7.20**	**6.22**	**5.67**	**5.32**	**5.07**	**4.88**	**4.74**	**4.63**	**4.54**	**4.46**	**4.40**
12	4.75	3.88	3.49	3.26	3.11	3.00	2.92	2.85	2.80	2.76	2.72	2.69
	9.33	**6.93**	**5.95**	**5.41**	**5.06**	**4.82**	**4.65**	**4.50**	**4.39**	**4.30**	**4.22**	**4.16**
13	4.67	3.80	3.41	3.18	3.02	2.92	2.84	2.77	2.72	2.67	2.63	2.60
	9.07	**6.70**	**5.74**	**5.20**	**4.86**	**4.62**	**4.44**	**4.30**	**4.19**	**4.10**	**4.02**	**3.96**

Degrees of Freedom in Denominator	Degrees of Freedom in Numerator											
	1	2	3	4	5	6	7	8	9	10	11	12
14	4.60 8.86	3.74 6.51	3.34 5.56	3.11 5.03	2.96 4.69	2.85 4.46	2.77 4.28	2.70 4.14	2.65 4.03	2.60 3.94	2.56 3.86	2.53 3.80
15	4.54 8.68	3.68 6.36	3.29 5.42	3.06 4.89	2.90 4.56	2.79 4.32	2.70 4.14	2.64 4.00	2.59 3.89	2.55 3.80	2.51 3.73	2.48 3.67
16	4.49 8.53	3.63 6.23	3.24 5.29	3.01 4.77	2.85 4.44	2.74 4.20	2.66 4.03	2.59 3.89	2.54 3.78	2.49 3.69	2.45 3.61	2.42 3.55
17	4.45 8.40	3.59 6.11	3.20 5.18	2.96 4.67	2.81 4.34	2.70 4.10	2.62 3.93	2.55 3.79	2.50 3.68	2.45 3.59	2.41 3.52	2.38 3.45
18	4.41 8.28	3.55 6.01	3.16 5.09	2.93 4.58	2.77 4.25	2.66 4.01	2.58 3.85	2.51 3.71	2.46 3.60	2.41 3.51	2.37 3.44	2.34 3.37
19	4.38 8.18	3.52 5.93	3.13 5.01	2.90 4.50	2.74 4.17	2.63 3.94	2.55 3.77	2.48 3.63	2.43 3.52	2.38 3.43	2.34 3.36	2.31 3.30
20	4.35 8.10	3.49 5.85	3.10 4.94	2.87 4.43	2.71 4.10	2.60 3.87	2.52 3.71	2.45 3.56	2.40 3.45	2.35 3.37	2.31 3.30	2.28 3.23
21	4.32 8.02	3.47 5.78	3.07 4.87	2.84 4.37	2.68 4.04	2.57 3.81	2.49 3.65	2.42 3.51	2.37 3.40	2.32 3.31	2.28 3.24	2.25 3.17
22	4.30 7.94	3.44 5.72	3.05 4.82	2.82 4.31	2.66 3.99	2.55 3.76	2.47 3.59	2.40 3.45	2.35 3.35	2.30 3.26	2.26 3.18	2.23 3.12
23	4.28 7.88	3.42 5.66	3.03 4.76	2.80 4.26	2.64 3.94	2.53 3.71	2.45 3.54	2.38 3.41	2.32 3.30	2.28 3.21	2.24<>3.14	2.20 3.07
24	4.26 7.82	3.40 5.61	3.01 4.72	2.78 4.22	2.62 3.90	2.51 3.67	2.43 3.50	2.36 3.36	2.30 3.25	2.26 3.17	2.22 3.09	2.18 3.03
25	4.24 7.77	3.38 5.57	2.99 4.68	2.76 4.18	2.60 3.86	2.49 3.63	2.41 3.46	2.34 3.32	2.28 3.21	2.24 3.13	2.20 3.05	2.16 2.99
26	4.22 7.72	3.37 5.53	2.98 4.64	2.74 4.14	2.59 3.82	2.47 3.59	2.39 3.42	2.32 3.29	2.27 3.17	2.22 3.09	2.18 3.02	2.15 2.96
27	4.21 7.68	3.35 5.49	2.96 4.60	2.73 4.11	2.57 3.79	2.46 3.56	2.37 3.39	2.30 3.26	2.25 3.14	2.20 3.06	2.16 2.98	2.13 2.93
28	4.20 7.64	3.34 5.45	2.95 4.57	2.71 4.07	2.56 3.76	2.44 3.53	2.36 3.36	2.29 3.23	2.24 3.11	2.19 3.03	2.15 2.95	2.12 2.90
29	4.18 7.60	3.33 5.42	2.93 4.54	2.70 4.04	2.54 3.73	2.43 3.50	2.35 3.33	2.28 3.20	2.22 3.08	2.18 3.00	2.14 2.92	2.10 2.87
30	4.17 7.56	3.32 5.39	2.92 4.51	2.69 4.02	2.53 3.70	2.42 3.47	2.34 3.30	2.27 3.17	2.21 3.06	2.16 2.98	2.12 2.90	2.09 2.84
32	4.15 7.50	3.30 5.34	2.90 4.46	2.67 3.97	2.51 3.66	2.40 3.42	2.32 3.25	2.25 3.12	2.19 3.01	2.14 2.94	2.10 2.86	2.07 2.80
34	4.13 7.44	3.28 5.29	2.88 4.42	2.65 3.93	2.49 3.61	2.38 3.38	2.30 3.21	2.23 3.08	2.17 2.97	2.12 2.89	2.08 2.82	2.05 2.76
36	4.11 7.39	3.26 5.25	2.86 4.38	2.63 3.89	2.48 3.58	2.36 3.35	2.28 3.18	2.21 3.04	2.15 2.94	2.10 2.86	2.06 2.78	2.03 2.72

Degrees of Freedom in Denominator	Degrees of Freedom in Numerator											
	1	2	3	4	5	6	7	8	9	10	11	12
38	4.10	3.25	2.85	2.62	2.46	2.35	2.26	2.19	2.14	2.09	2.05	2.02
	7.35	**5.21**	**4.34**	**3.86**	**3.54**	**3.32**	**3.15**	**3.02**	**2.91**	**2.82**	**2.75**	**2.69**
40	4.08	3.23	2.84	2.61	2.45	2.34	2.25	2.18	2.12	2.07	2.04	2.00
	7.31	**5.18**	**4.31**	**3.83**	**3.51**	**3.29**	**3.12**	**2.99**	**2.88**	**2.80**	**2.73**	**2.66**
42	4.07	3.22	2.83	2.59	2.44	2.32	2.24	2.17	2.11	2.06	2.02	1.99
	7.27	**5.15**	**4.29**	**3.80**	**3.49**	**3.26**	**3.10**	**2.96**	**2.86**	**2.77**	**2.70**	**2.64**
44	4.06	3.21	2.82	2.58	2.43	2.31	2.23	2.16	2.10	2.05	2.01	1.98
	7.24	**5.12**	**4.26**	**3.78**	**3.46**	**3.24**	**3.07**	**2.94**	**2.84**	**2.75**	**2.68**	**2.62**
46	4.05	3.20	2.81	2.57	2.42	2.30	2.22	2.14	2.09	2.04	2.00	1.97
	7.21	**5.10**	**4.24**	**3.76**	**3.44**	**3.22**	**3.05**	**2.92**	**2.82**	**2.73**	**2.66**	**2.60**
48	4.04	3.19	2.80	2.56	2.41	2.30	2.21	2.14	2.08	2.03	1.99	1.96
	7.19	**5.08**	**4.22**	**3.74**	**3.42**	**3.20**	**3.04**	**2.90**	**2.80**	**2.71**	**2.64**	**2.58**
50	4.03	3.18	2.79	2.56	2.40	2.29	2.20	2.13	2.07	2.02	1.98	1.95
	7.17	**5.06**	**4.20**	**3.72**	**3.41**	**3.18**	**3.02**	**2.88**	**2.78**	**2.70**	**2.62**	**2.56**

APPENDIX I/ FOUR-PLACE COMMON LOGARITHMS

We can use the attached table of common logarithms to find: (a) the logarithm of a given number and (b) the number of a given logarithm.

Logarithms consist of two parts: an integer called the *characteristic* and a fraction called the *mantissa*. To find the logarithm of a number we first determine the characteristic and then read the mantissa from the attached table. For example, the characteristic of number 96.1 is 1 which is equal to the two nondecimal digits less 1. The mantissa is .9827 read from row 96 under column N and column 1 of the attached table. Therefore, the logarithm is

$$\log 96.1 = 1.9827$$

as shown in Table 28.3, column 4.

Suppose we wish to find the logarithm of 106.2. Since this number has three nondecimal digits, the characteristic is 2, that is, 3 less 1. We locate the mantissa under row 10 and column 6 which is .0253. The logarithm for 106 is 2.0253. To this number we add .0008 which represents the logarithm of the proportional part .2 of number 106.2. So

$$\log 106.2 = 2.0253 + .0008 = 2.0261$$

The number of a given logarithm called the *antilogarithm* can be found by reversing the procedure. To find the antilogarithm of logarithh 1.9426 we locate the mantissa .9425 which corresponds to number 876. The difference, .9426 − .9425 = .0001, corresponds to the proportional part .02. So the number is 87.62, as shown in Example 28.4.

										Proportional Parts								
N	0	1	2	3	4	5	6	7	8	9	1	2	3	4	5	6	7	8	9
10	0000	0043	0086	0128	0170	0212	0253	0294	0334	0374	4	8	12	17	21	25	29	33	37
11	0414	0453	0492	0531	0569	0607	0645	0682	0719	0755	4	8	11	15	19	23	26	30	34
12	0792	0828	0864	0899	0934	0969	1004	1038	1072	1106	3	7	10	14	17	21	24	28	31
13	1139	1173	1206	1239	1271	1303	1335	1367	1399	1430	3	6	10	13	16	19	23	26	29
14	1461	1492	1523	1553	1584	1614	1644	1673	1703	1732	3	6	9	12	15	18	21	24	27
15	1761	1790	1818	1847	1875	1903	1931	1959	1987	2014	3	6	8	11	14	17	20	22	25
16	2041	2068	2095	2122	2148	2175	2201	2227	2253	2279	3	5	8	11	13	16	18	21	24
17	2304	2330	2355	2380	2405	2430	2455	2480	2504	2529	2	5	7	10	12	15	17	20	22
18	2553	2577	2601	2625	2648	2672	2695	2718	2742	2765	2	5	7	9	12	14	16	19	21
19	2788	2810	2833	2856	2878	2900	2923	2945	2967	2989	2	4	7	9	11	13	16	18	20
20	3010	3032	3054	3075	3096	3118	3139	3160	3181	3201	2	4	6	8	11	13	15	17	19
21	3222	3243	3263	3284	3304	3324	3345	3365	3885	3404	2	4	6	8	10	12	14	16	18
22	3424	3444	3464	3483	3502	3522	3541	3560	3579	3598	2	4	6	8	10	12	14	15	17
23	3617	3636	3655	3674	3692	3711	3729	3747	3766	3784	2	4	6	7	9	11	13	15	17
24	3802	3820	3838	3856	3874	3892	3909	3927	3945	3962	2	4	5	7	9	11	12	14	16
N	0	1	2	3	4	5	6	7	8	9	1	2	3	4	5	6	7	8	9

N	0	1	2	3	4	5	6	7	8	9	\multicolumn{9}{c}{Proportional Parts}
											1	2	3	4	5	6	7	8	9
25	3979	3997	4014	4031	4048	4065	4082	4099	4116	4133	2	3	5	7	9	10	12	14	15
26	4150	4166	4183	4200	4216	4232	4249	4265	4281	4298	2	3	5	7	8	10	11	13	15
27	4314	4330	4346	4362	4378	4393	4409	4425	4440	4456	2	3	5	6	8	9	11	13	14
28	4472	4487	4502	4518	4533	4548	4564	4579	4594	4609	2	3	5	6	8	9	11	12	14
29	4624	4639	4654	4669	4683	4698	4713	4728	4742	4757	1	3	4	6	7	9	10	12	13
30	4771	4786	4800	4814	4829	4843	4857	4871	4886	4900	1	3	4	6	7	9	10	11	13
31	4914	4928	4942	4955	4969	4983	4997	5011	5024	5038	1	3	4	6	7	8	10	11	12
32	5051	5065	5079	5092	5105	5119	5132	5145	5159	5172	1	3	4	5	7	8	9	11	12
33	5185	5198	5211	5224	5237	5250	5263	5276	5289	5302	1	3	4	5	6	8	9	10	12
34	5315	5328	5340	5353	5366	5378	5391	5403	5416	5428	1	3	4	5	6	8	9	10	11
35	5441	5453	5465	5478	5490	5502	5514	5527	5539	5551	1	2	4	5	6	7	9	10	11
36	5563	5575	5587	5599	5611	5623	5635	5647	5658	5670	1	2	4	5	6	7	8	10	11
37	5682	5694	5705	5717	5729	5740	5752	5763	5775	5786	1	2	3	5	6	7	8	9	10
38	5798	5809	5821	5832	5843	5855	5866	5877	5888	5899	1	2	3	5	6	7	8	9	10
39	5911	5922	5933	5944	5955	5966	5977	5988	5999	6010	1	2	3	4	5	7	8	9	10
40	6021	6031	6042	6053	6064	6075	6085	6096	6107	6117	1	2	3	4	5	6	8	9	10
41	6128	6138	6149	6160	6170	6180	6191	6201	6212	6222	1	2	3	4	5	6	7	8	9
42	6232	6243	6253	6263	6274	6284	6294	6304	6314	6325	1	2	3	4	5	6	7	8	9
43	6335	6345	6355	6365	6375	6385	6395	6405	6415	6425	1	2	3	4	5	6	7	8	9
44	6435	6444	6454	6464	6474	6484	6493	6503	6513	6522	1	2	3	4	5	6	7	8	9
45	6532	6542	6551	6561	6571	6580	6590	6599	6609	6618	1	2	3	4	5	6	7	8	9
46	6628	6637	6646	6656	6665	6675	6684	6693	6702	6712	1	2	3	4	5	6	7	7	8
47	6721	6730	6739	6749	6758	6767	6776	6785	6794	6803	1	2	3	4	5	5	6	7	8
48	6812	6821	6830	6839	6848	6857	6866	6875	6884	6893	1	2	3	4	4	5	6	7	8
49	6902	6911	6920	6928	6937	6946	6955	6964	6972	6981	1	2	3	4	4	5	6	7	8
50	6990	6998	7007	7016	7024	7033	7042	7050	7059	7067	1	2	3	3	4	5	6	7	8
51	7076	7084	7093	7101	7110	7118	7126	7135	7143	7152	1	2	3	3	4	5	6	7	8
52	7160	7168	7177	7185	7193	7202	7210	7218	7226	7235	1	2	2	3	4	5	6	7	7
53	7243	7251	7259	7267	7275	7284	7292	7300	7308	7316	1	2	2	3	4	5	6	6	7
54	7324	7332	7340	7348	7356	7364	7372	7380	7388	7396	1	2	2	3	4	5	6	6	7
55	7404	7412	7419	7427	7435	7443	7451	7459	7466	7474	1	2	2	3	4	5	5	6	7
56	7482	7490	7497	7505	7513	7520	7528	7536	7543	7551	1	2	2	3	4	5	5	6	7
57	7559	7566	7574	7582	7589	7597	7604	7612	7619	7627	1	2	2	3	4	5	5	6	7
58	7634	7642	7649	7657	7664	7672	7679	7686	7694	7701	1	1	2	3	4	4	5	6	7
59	7709	7716	7723	7731	7738	7745	7752	7760	7767	7774	1	1	2	3	4	4	5	6	7
60	7782	7789	7796	7803	7810	7818	7825	7832	7839	7846	1	1	2	3	4	4	5	6	6
61	7853	7860	7868	7875	7882	7889	7896	7903	7910	7917	1	1	2	3	4	4	5	6	6
62	7924	7931	7938	7945	7952	7959	7966	7973	7980	7987	1	1	2	3	3	4	5	6	6
63	7993	8000	8007	8014	8021	8028	8035	8041	8048	8055	1	1	2	3	3	4	5	5	6
64	8062	8069	8075	8082	8089	8096	8102	8109	8116	8122	1	1	2	3	3	4	5	5	6
N	0	1	2	3	4	5	6	7	8	9	1	2	3	4	5	6	7	8	9

Appendixes: Statistical Tables

N	0	1	2	3	4	5	6	7	8	9	Proportional Parts								
											1	2	3	4	5	6	7	8	9
65	8129	8136	8142	8149	8156	8162	8169	8176	8182	8189	1	1	2	3	3	4	5	5	6
66	8195	8202	8209	8215	8222	8228	8235	8241	8248	8254	1	1	2	3	3	4	5	5	6
67	8261	8267	8274	8280	8287	8293	8299	8306	8312	8319	1	1	2	3	3	4	5	5	6
68	8325	8331	8338	8344	8351	8357	8363	8370	8376	8382	1	1	2	3	3	4	4	5	6
69	8388	8395	8401	8407	8414	8420	8426	8432	8439	8445	1	1	2	2	3	4	4	5	6
70	8451	8457	8463	8470	8476	8482	8488	8494	8500	8506	1	1	2	2	3	4	4	5	6
71	8513	8519	8525	8531	8537	8543	8549	8555	8561	8567	1	1	2	2	3	4	4	5	5
72	8573	8579	8585	8591	8597	8603	8609	8615	8621	8627	1	1	2	2	3	4	4	5	5
73	8633	8639	8645	8651	8657	8663	8669	8675	8681	8686	1	1	2	2	3	4	4	5	5
74	8692	8698	8704	8710	8716	8722	8727	8733	8739	8745	1	1	2	2	3	4	4	5	5
75	8751	8756	8762	8768	8774	8779	8785	8791	8797	8802	1	1	2	2	3	3	4	5	5
76	8808	8814	8820	8825	8831	8837	8842	8848	8854	8859	1	1	2	2	3	3	4	5	5
77	8865	8871	8876	8882	8887	8893	8899	8904	8910	8915	1	1	2	2	3	3	4	4	5
78	8921	8927	8932	8938	8943	8949	8954	8960	8965	8971	1	1	2	2	3	3	4	4	5
79	8976	8982	8987	8993	8998	9004	9009	9015	9020	9025	1	1	2	2	3	3	4	4	5
80	9031	9036	9042	9047	9053	9058	9063	9069	9074	9079	1	1	2	2	3	3	4	4	5
81	9085	9090	9096	9101	9106	9112	9117	9122	9128	9133	1	1	2	2	3	3	4	4	5
82	9138	9143	9149	9154	9159	9165	9170	9175	9180	9186	1	1	2	2	3	3	4	4	5
83	9191	9196	9201	9206	9212	9217	9222	9227	9232	9238	1	1	2	2	3	3	4	4	5
84	9243	9248	9253	9258	9263	9269	9274	9279	9284	9289	1	1	2	2	3	3	4	4	5
85	9294	9299	9304	9309	9315	9320	9325	9330	9335	9340	1	1	2	2	3	3	4	4	5
86	9345	9350	9355	9360	9365	9370	9375	9380	9385	9390	1	1	2	2	3	3	4	4	5
87	9395	9400	9405	9410	9415	9420	9425	9430	9435	9440	0	1	1	2	2	3	3	4	4
88	9445	9450	9455	9460	9465	9469	9474	9479	9484	9489	0	1	1	2	2	3	3	4	4
89	9494	9499	9504	9509	9513	9518	9523	9528	9533	9538	0	1	1	2	2	3	3	4	4
90	9542	9547	9552	9557	9562	9566	9571	9576	9581	9586	0	1	1	2	2	3	3	4	4
91	9590	9595	9600	9605	9609	9614	9619	9624	9628	9633	0	1	1	2	2	3	3	4	4
92	9638	9643	9647	9652	9657	9661	9666	9671	9675	9680	0	1	1	2	2	3	3	4	4
93	9685	9689	9694	9699	9703	9708	9713	9717	9722	9727	0	1	1	2	2	3	3	4	4
94	9731	9736	9741	9745	9750	9754	9759	9763	9768	9773	0	1	1	2	2	3	3	4	4
95	9777	9782	9786	9791	9795	9800	9805	9809	9814	9818	0	1	1	2	2	3	3	4	4
96	9823	9827	9832	9836	9841	9845	9850	9854	9859	9863	0	1	1	2	2	3	3	4	4
97	9868	9872	9877	9881	9886	9890	9894	9899	9903	9908	0	1	1	2	2	3	3	4	4
98	9912	9917	9921	9926	9930	9934	9939	9943	9948	9952	0	1	1	2	2	3	3	4	4
99	9956	9961	9965	9969	9974	9978	9983	9987	9991	9996	0	1	1	2	2	3	3	3	4
N	0	1	2	3	4	5	6	7	8	9	1	2	3	4	5	6	7	8	9

ANSWERS TO PROBLEMS MARKED WITH AN ASTERISK

SECTION 1

1.1. (a) Age, years
1.2. (a) Party affiliation: Democrat, Republican, Independent
1.3. (b)

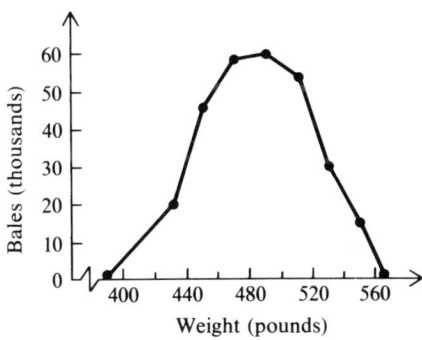

1.4. (a)

Sales (Dollars)	Frequency (Numbers)
20 and under 30	2
30 and under 40	4
40 and under 50	7
50 and under 60	9
60 and under 70	3
Total:	25

1.6. (a)

Miles per Gallon	Taxi Cabs
18.0 and under 19.0	2
19.0 and under 20.0	4
20.0 and under 21.0	6
21.0 and under 22.0	5
22.0 and under 23.0	3
Total:	20

1.9. (a) (i) Good-defective ball bearings in a shipment. (ii) Good-defective ball bearings in the manufacturing process.
1.10. (a) (i) Production workers. (ii) Years old. (iii) Absent-present.
1.12. (a)

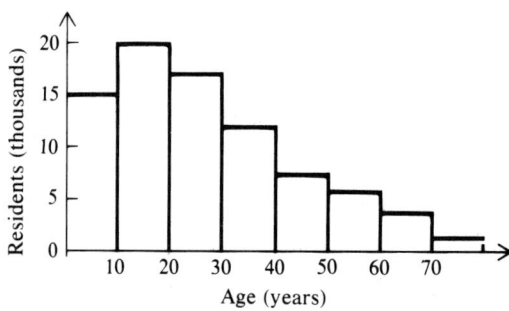

SECTION 2

2.1. $\mu = 14$; Md $= 14.5$; Mo $= 15$
2.2. $\mu_W = \$21,667$
2.4. Right-set; $\mu_R = 75$; $\mu_Q = 100$
2.5. (a) $\mu = \$172.58$; Md $= \$157.06$; Mo $= \$138.46$
2.7. (a) 11.67%; (b) 9.22%
2.11. (a) $\mu = \$48.34$; Md $= \$48.86$
2.13. (a) 17%, 18%, 14%, 15%, 19%
2.14. (a) None of the measures in this section

SECTION 3

3.1. (a) 16, 7; (b) $\mu = 23.67$, $\sigma = 4.86$ proposals
3.2. (a) $\mu = 579$; Md $= 554.48$; Mo $= 536.30$ hours
3.3. (a) $\mu = 632$; Md $\simeq 651$; Mo $\simeq 677$ GMAT
3.4. (a) $\sigma^2 = 14,919$; $\sigma \simeq 122.14$ hours
3.5. (a) CRV $= 21.09\%$
3.9. (b) Md $\simeq 550$; Md $= 554.48$ hours

Answers to Problems Marked With an Asterisk

3.10. (b) Md $\simeq$ 650; Md = 651 GMAT
3.11. (a) μ = 146.18; Md = 149.81 pounds

SECTION 4

4.1. (a) Infinite
4.2. (a) Without replacement
4.3. (a) $S = \{(2, 4), (2, 6), (4, 2), (4, 6), (6, 2), (6, 4)\}$
4.4. (a) $S = \{(6, 6), (6, 12), (6, 24), (12, 6), (12, 12), (12, 24), (24, 6), (24, 12),$
       $(24, 24)\}$;
       $E = \{(6, 24), (24, 6)\}$
4.5. (a) not-$E = \{5, 6\}$
4.8. (a) $\{(X, Y, Z), (X, Y, W), (X, Z, W)\}$
4.9. (a) Infinite
4.11. (a) 10 billion

SECTION 5

5.1. (c) No
5.2. (a) 6/16
5.3. (a) 6/24
5.4. (a) 1/2
5.5. (a) 1 to 1; (b) 1 to 9
5.6. (a) $P(A$ and $C) = 0$
5.7. (a) .55
5.8. (a) Yes
5.9. (a) 2/9
5.10. (a) 2/6
5.11. (a) 2/16

SECTION 6

6.1. (c) Two marginal, two conditional, one joint
6.2. (c) Events are dependent.
6.3. (a) 250/1100
6.4. (a) .000125
6.5. (a) No
6.7. (a) .025
6.9. (a) 9/35
6.11. (a) .50
6.14. (a) 2/5

SECTION 7

7.1. (a) 720
7.2. (a) 120
7.4. (a) 1/720
7.6. (a) 3,276,000

7.7. LS, LH, SH
7.8. (a) (1, 1), (1, 2), (1, 3), (2, 1), (2, 2), (2, 3), (3, 1), (3, 2), (3, 3)
7.9. (a) 720
7.10. (a) 120
7.11. (a) 1200

SECTION 8

8.1. $2.60
8.2. No
8.4. (a) $4600
8.5. (a)

x	$P(X = x)$
0	.81
1	.18
2	.01

8.7. (a) $E(X) = 7$, $V(X) = 2$; (b) $E(Y) = 7$, $V(Y) = 1.6$
8.9. (a)

$\bar{x}$	$P(\bar{X} = \bar{x})$
$9,000	1/3
15,000	1/3
18,000	1/3
	1.00

8.10. (a)

x	$P(X = x)$
0	.512
1	.384
2	.096
3	.008
	1.000

SECTION 9

9.1. (a) .961; (b) .114; (c) .678; (d) .730; (e) .014; (f) .188
9.2. (a)

$X = x$	0	1	2	3	≥ 4
$P(X = x)$	.531	.355	.098	.015	.001

Answers to Problems Marked With an Asterisk

9.3. .168
9.4. (a) .088
9.5. (a) .005
9.6. (a) .134; (b) .436; (c) .302
9.9. (a) 250 customers; (b) 208 to 292 customers; (c) .164
9.11. (b)

$X = x$	0	1	2	3	4
$P(X = x)$	.397	.429	.152	.021	.001

9.13. (a) 40 loans; (b) 250 loans

SECTION 10

10.1. (a) .150; (b) .267; (c) .706; (d) .895; (e) .258; (f) .221; (g) .955; (h) .744
10.2. (a)

$X = x$	0	1	2	3	4	5	6	7	≥ 8
$P(X = x)$	.135	.271	.271	.180	.090	.036	.012	.004	.001

10.3. (a) .090
10.4. (a) .228
10.5. (a) .827
10.6.   .083
10.7. (a) .001
10.9. (a) .011
10.11. (a) .143

SECTION 11

11.1. (a) Economy and timeliness
11.4. (a) 09, 34, 33, 07, 39, 11, 31, 32, 48, 29, 40, 42, 01, 45, 06, 28, 13
11.5.   None of the statements
11.6. (a) $4
11.7. (a) $\bar{x} = \$205$
11.9. (a) $\bar{x} = 1.8$ blemishes
11.12. (a) 3,125,000 readers
11.14. (a) $\mu = 450$, $\bar{x} = 454$, random error 4 pounds

SECTION 12

12.1. (b)

$\bar{X} = \bar{x}$	70	75	80	85	90	95	100	105	120
$P(\bar{X} = \bar{x})$	1/16	2/16	3/16	2/16	1/16	2/16	2/16	2/16	1/16

12.2. (b)

$P = p$	0	1/2	1
$P(P = p)$	9/16	6/16	1/16

12.3. (a) $\mu = 1, \sigma \simeq .82$
12.4. (a) $\pi = 2/3$
12.5. (a)

$P = p$	0	.20	.40	.60	.80	1.00
$P(P = p)$	.3277	.4096	.2048	.0512	.0064	.0003

12.11. (a) $n = 1$:

$\overline{X} = \overline{x}$	4	5	6
$P(\overline{X} = \overline{x})$	.40	.20	.40

$n = 2$:

$\overline{X} = \overline{x}$	4	4.5	5	5.5	6
$P(\overline{X} = \overline{x})$	.16	.16	.36	.16	.16

$n = 3$:

$\overline{X} = \overline{x}$	4	4 1/3	4 2/3	5	5 1/3	5 2/3	6
$P(\overline{X} = \overline{x})$	.064	.096	.240	.200	.240	.096	.064

$n = 4$:

$\overline{X} = \overline{x}$	4	4 1/4	4 2/4	4 3/4	5	5 1/4	5 1/2	5 3/4	6
$P(\overline{X} = \overline{x})$	.026	.050	.141	.179	.207	.179	.141	.050	.026

12.12. (b)
$n = 1: E(\overline{X}) = 75, \sigma_{\overline{x}} \simeq 6.7$
$n = 2: E(\overline{X}) = 75, \sigma_{\overline{x}} \simeq 4.7$
$n = 3: E(\overline{X}) = 75, \sigma_{\overline{x}} \simeq 3.9$
$n = 4: E(\overline{X}) = 75, \sigma_{\overline{x}} \simeq 3.35$
12.13. (b) $n = 10: E(P) = .20, \sigma_p \simeq .126$
$n = 20: E(P) = .20, \sigma_p \simeq .089$
$n = 30: E(P) = .20, \sigma_p \simeq .073$

Answers to Problems Marked With an Asterisk

SECTION 13

13.1. (a)

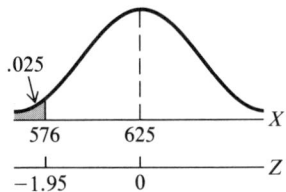

13.2. (a) Same as Problem 13.1(a)
13.4.   82.95 inches
13.7. (a) .0228
13.8. (a) .0848
13.11. (a) .5532
13.13. (a) .0228

SECTION 14

14.1. (a) Proportion; (b) mean
14.3. (a) $105,000; (b) $19,368; (c) $p = .50$
14.5.   Increase sample size or decrease degree of confidence.
14.6. (a) Stratified sample
14.7.   No, statistical precision depends on the sample size, not on the population size; the fpc adjusts, does not determine, sample size.
14.11.   576
14.12. (a) 1498
14.13. (a) 1076

SECTION 15

15.1. (a) 007, 017, 027, 037, ..., 097; (b) 007, 018, 023, 035, 045, 054, 069, 074, 087, 095
15.2. (a) 40/3
15.3.   50, 58, 66, 74, 82, 08, 16, 24, 32, and 40
15.4. (a) 2.228
15.5. (a) .01
15.12. (a) 7.84 to 8.16 servings
15.13. (a) 15.42 to 15.58 inches

SECTION 16

16.1. (a) .165 to .235; (b) .272 to .328
16.2. (a) 250
16.3. (a) symmetrical: .09 to .31; nonsymmetrical: .10 to .34

Answers to Problems Marked With an Asterisk

16.4. 0 to .035
16.7. .02 to .57
16.8. .68 to .72
16.9. .043 to .057

SECTION 17

17.4. (a) Agree
17.5. (a) (1) Type II; (2) and (3) correct; (4) Type I
17.6. (a) Lower-tailed test; accept H_o

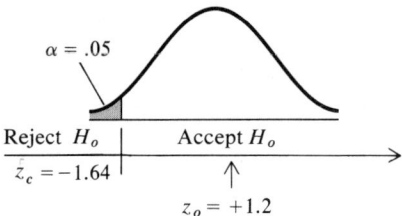

17.7. (a) Upper-tailed test; reject H_o

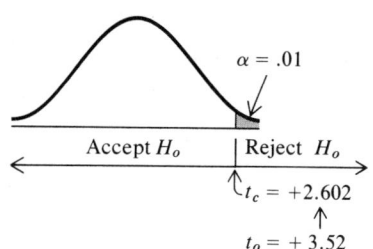

17.10. (a) (i) Two-tailed test
(ii) 48.7; 51.29
(iii) Reject H_0
(iv) $z_o = -3 < z_c = -2.58$

17.11. (a) (i) Upper-tailed test
(ii) .3427
(iii) Reject H_0
(iv) $z_o = +2.73 > +2.33$

17.12. (a) Hypotheses: $H_0: \pi \leq .25$
                            $H_1: \pi > .25$
       Decision rule: If $z_o \leq +2.33$, accept H_o (place special adds)
                                 If $z_o > +2.33$, reject H_o (do not place special adds)

17.13. (a) Hypotheses: $H_0: \pi \geq .30$
                            $H_1: \pi < .30$
       Decision rule: If $z_o \geq -1.65$, accept H_o (association is correct)
                                 If $z_o < -1.65$, reject H_o (association is not correct)

Answers to Problems Marked With an Asterisk

SECTION 18

18.1. (a) Accept H_0

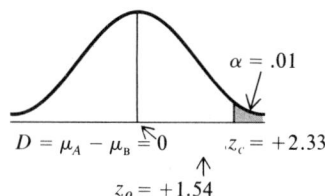

$D = \mu_A - \mu_B = 0 \quad z_c = +2.33$

$z_0 = +1.54$

falls in acceptance region

18.2. (a) (i) $d^* = +15.17$ pounds
(ii) If $d \leq +15.17$, accept H_0 (keep old method B)
If $d > +15.17$, reject H_0 (introduce new method A)
(iii) Accept H_0 since $d = +10$ pounds

18.5. (a) $H_0: \mu_A \leq \mu_B$
$H_1: \mu_A > \mu_B$

18.6. (a) $H_0: \mu_B - \mu_S = .0015$ inch
$H_1: \mu_B - \mu_S \neq .0015$ inch

18.7. (a) $\bar{d} = +60; s_d = 29.05$

18.8. (a) $H_0: \pi_A = \pi_B$
$H_1: \pi_A \neq \pi_B$

18.9. (a) $H_0: \mu_H \leq \mu_C$
$H_1: \mu_H > \mu_C$

18.10. (a) $H_0: \pi_A \geq \pi_B$
$H_1: \pi_A < \pi_B$

SECTION 19

19.1. (a) 15.09

19.2. Comparison B only, since $\chi_o^2 > \chi_c^2$

19.3. (a) (i) H_0: Magazine readership is independent of compliance trait
H_1: Magazine readership is not independent of compliance trait
(ii) 2
(iii) If $\chi_o^2 \leq 9.21$, accept H_0;
if $\chi_o^2 > 9.21$, reject H_0
(iv) Accept H_0 since $\chi_o^2 = 5.36$

19.4. (a) (i) 6
(ii) $\chi_c^2 = 16.81$
(iii) Accept H_0: Medical practice and knowledge-use of formula Y may not be related

19.5. (a) $\chi_o^2 = 38.6$; yes, since $\chi_c^2 = 3.84$

19.6. (a) $\chi_o^2 = 16.48$; reject H_0: The binomial distribution for $n = 5$ and $\pi = .45$ may not be a good fit

19.8. For $\pi = .10$, $\chi_o^2 = 26.11$; the manager's claim may not be justified.
For $\pi = .12$ $\chi_o^2 = 5.25$; the engineer's claim may be justified.
19.9. (b) $\chi_o^2 = 9.04$
19.10. (c) Accept H_0: Type of store may be unrelated to reasons customers prefer each store

SECTION 20

20.1. (a) 11.26
20.2. (a) $F_{05}(2, 12) = 3.88$
20.3. (a) Reject H_0, since $F_{01}(2, 27) = 5.49$: Curifix may affect yield of fiber X
20.4. (a) $F_{01}(3, 12) = 5.95$
20.6. (f) Reject H_0: The claim that machines have the same output capabilities may not be justified
20.7. (a) $F_o = 4.08$
20.8. (a) $F_o = .35$
20.9. (a) $F_o = 11.84$

SECTION 21

21.1. (a) X = reservations; Y = meals
21.3. (a) (ii) For every increase (decrease) of 1 unit in X, Y_c increases (decreases) by 2 units.
(iii) Positive, linear
21.4. (b) Differences portray graphically sampling errors with respect to both slope B and intercept A parameters.
21.6. (a), (b)

Sample Number	Distribution of Coefficient of:	
	Determination r^2	Correlation r
1[a] (Example 21.10)	.657	.833
2	.772	.879
3	.863	.929
4	.703	.839
5	.817	.904
6	.466	.683
7	.811	.900
8	.859	.927
9	.740	.860
10	.688	.829
Averages:	.740	.858
Parameters:	.777	.882

[a]Sample of 10 students whose numbers are circled in Table 21.4.

Answers to Problems Marked With an Asterisk

21.9. (b) $Y_c = 5.43 + .289X$
21.11. (a) $r^2 = .694; r \simeq .833$

SECTION 22

22.1. (a) Accept H_0, since $t_o = 2.60 < t_c = 2.807$
22.2. (a) Accept H_0, since $F_{01}(1, 9) = 10.56$
22.3. (a) (i) $Y_c = 77$
   (ii) Ind.: 69.26 to 84.74
   (iii) Mean: 76.226 to 77.774
   (c) (i) $Y_c = 179$
   (ii) Ind.: 161.6 to 196.4
   (iii) Mean: 168.7 to 189.3
22.4. (b) .189
22.5. (a) Ind.: 2.30 to 3.36;
   Mean: 2.66 to 3.00
22.7. $s_X \simeq .41$ from Table 22.1; $s_y \simeq .387$ from Table 22.2
22.8. 6.425
22.11. (a) $X = 2.5$: 2.40 to 2.97
   $X = 3.0$: 2.89 to 3.21
   $X = 3.347$: 3.18 to 3.42
   $X = 4.0$: 3.54 to 4.01
22.12. (a) $t_o = 3.66; F_o \simeq 9.14$
22.13. (a) $z_o = 2; F_o = 6.52$
   (b) Ind.: $5.64 to $9.56
22.14. (d) $X = 0$: 29.0 to 39.6 gallons
   $X = 41$: 16.1 to 21.9 gallons
   $X = 80$: $-.6$ to 9.6 gallons

			Consumption (Gallons)	
Day	Temp. (°F)	X	Daily	Cumulative
1	-20	0	39,500	39,500
2	-10	10	35,000	74,500
3	0	20	31,000	105,500
4	5	25	26,500	132,000
5	-10	10	35,000	167,000 ←
6	-20	0	39,500	206,500
7	0	20	31,000	237,500

22.14. (f) Reorder during the fifth day; probability is .005.
22.15. (b) $Y_c = 5.16 + 8.63X$
   (d) $t_o = 4.90; F_o \simeq 37.85$
   (e) Ind.: $1.79 to $43.05
   Mean: $15.98 to $28.86
   Slope: $2.73 to $14.53

SECTION 23

23.1. (a) $Y_c = 3.5397$; deviation $= -.2397$
23.2. (b) Ind.: $79,061 to $81,625
Mean: $80,162 to $80,524
23.7. (a) $Y_c = 1200 + 4X_1 + 30X_2$
(c) $t_1 \simeq 5.55$; $t_2 \simeq 24$
23.8. (a) $Y_c = 8 + 1.5X_1 - .25X_2$
(c) $z_1 \simeq 15$; $z_2 \simeq -2.87$
(d) $F_o = 15.39$
(e) Ind.: $15,229 to $20,771
Mean: $17,619 to $18,381
23.9. (a) $Y_c = 1.464 + 7.414X_1 + .219X_2$
(d) $t_1 \simeq 5.322$; $t_2 \simeq 1.840$; $F_o \simeq 26.294$
(f) Ind.: $20.63 to $39.93
Mean: $27.23 to $33.33
23.10. (a) $Y_c = -2.611 + .395X_1 + 21.535X_2$
(b) $t_1 \simeq 2.31$; $t_2 \simeq 2.895$; $F_o \simeq 12.472$
23.11. (a) $Y_c = 32.513 - .382X_1 + 4.292X_2$
(c) $t_1 \simeq -22.081$; $t_2 \simeq 4.894$; $F_o \simeq 243.997$

SECTION 24

24.1 (a) (i), (ii) Same as in Example 24.1
(iii) $z_o = -2.89$; reject H_0
24.2. (a) Two-tailed test
(b) $z_o = -2.61$; reject H_0

SECTION 25

25.1. (a) (i) Lower-tailed test
(ii) $z_o = -2.50$; reject H_0
(d) (i) Lower-tailed test
(ii) $z_o = -1.64$; hold judgment
25.2. (a) Two-tailed test
25.3. (a) Two-tailed test

SECTION 26

26.1. (a) (i) If $K_o \leq 9.21$, accept H_0
If $K_o > 9.21$, reject H_0
(ii) $K_o = 1.39$; $K_o = K_c$; accept H_0
26.2. (c) $K_o = 4.66$; accept H_0 since $\chi_c^2 = 7.38$

SECTION 27

27.1. (a) (i) H_0: $\rho_s = 0$
H_1: $\rho_s \neq 0$

Answers to Problems Marked With an Asterisk 489

        (ii) If $-3.08 \le z_o \le +3.08$; accept H_0
            If $z_o < -3.08$ or $z_o > +3.08$; reject H_0
        (iii) $r_s = +.932$
        (iv) $z_o = 4.06$; reject H_0
27.2. (c) $r_s = +.876$; $z_o = 3.39$; reject H_0

SECTION 28

28.2. (a) $Y_t = \$3425.04$ billion (current dollars)
     (b) $Y_t = \$698.7$ billion (current dollars)
28.3. (a) (iii) The GNP series is much less sensitive than housing starts series.
     (b) (iii) The government receipts series is as sensitive as housing starts with respect to frequency of swings above and below the zero line; it is much less sensitive than housing starts with respect to amplitude.
28.6. (b) $Y_t = 1055 + 34.7x$; $\$34.7$ billion (1972 dollars) per year
28.7. (b) $Y_t = 128 + 6x$
28.8. (b) $Y_t = 1934 + 124x$
28.9. (c) $Y_t = 7.052 + .02x + .614x^2$
28.10. (a) $Y_t = 2463 + 87x$
28.11. (d) $Y_t = 2.5772 + .04876x$

SECTION 29

29.2. (a)

J	F	M	A	M	J	J	A	S	O	N	D
67.4	67.8	101.2	122.4	123.9	121.0	112.3	108.0	101.6	113.1	90.2	71.1

29.3. (a) $Y_t = 462.7 + 1.8125X$
29.6. (a) $Y_t = 39{,}450 + 100X$
29.9. (c) 10,370 shirts
29.10. (c) 4,129,900 gallons of oil
29.11. (a) 4.6 percent decline
29.12. (b)

J	F	M	A	M	J	J	A	S	O	N	D
93.6	87.7	100.4	100.1	102.4	105.2	106.4	105.4	99.3	100.9	96.3	102.3

29.13. (b)

I	II	III	IV
76.3	119.7	112.6	91.4

SECTION 30

30.1. (a) 175.0
30.2.   By $\$6.56$ (1967 = 100)

Answers to Problems Marked With an Asterisk

30.11. (a) 176.0; (b) 173.2
30.12. (a) 151.9; (b) 175.8
30.13. (a) 194.3
30.14. (a) 194.3; (b) 114.4
30.16. (a) GNP: $1385.7 billion; federal expenditures: $303.1 billion

SECTION 31

31.1. (a) $E(a_1) = \$13.5$ ($\times 1000$)
31.2. (a) $EOL(a_1) = \$3.3$ ($\times 1000$)
31.3. (b) $E(a_6) = \$5$
31.4. (b) $E(a_3) = \$110$
31.5. (a) $p \simeq .31$
31.9. $E(B) = \$.55$
31.10. (b) $E(a_1) = +\$36$ ($\times 1000$)
31.14. (a) (i) Curve Z
(ii) $EXU(a_2) = \$12,000$

SECTION 32

32.3. (a) $p \simeq .545$
32.4. (a) $+\$265$
32.5. (a) $x \simeq \$356,667$
32.7. (b) $+\$61.8$ ($\times 1000$)
32.11. (b) $+\$5$ ($\times 1000$)

SECTION 33

33.1. (a) $P(O|F) = .75$
(b) $P(H|U) = .92$
33.3. (a) $P(A|G) = .602$; $P(A|D) = .429$
33.4. (c) $P(A|E) = 1$
33.6. $P(O|R) = .467$
33.7. (a) $P(I|B) = 2/3$
33.11. (a) $P(H|F) = .14$; $P(H|U) = .96$
33.12. (c)

n	EMV_1	EVSI	CSI	ENGS
1	$86.22	$ 5.78	$ 3	$2.78
2	79.82	12.18	6	6.18
3	74.57	17.43	9	8.43
4	70.50	21.50	12	9.50
5*	67.04	24.96	15	9.96*
6	64.05	27.95	18	9.95
7	61.79	30.21	21	9.21

INDEX

Absolute difference (value), 25, 333
Accept vs. reject H_0, 190, 194. *See also* Hypothesis testing
Acts, 410
Addition rule, 58
After-only experiment, 213
Aggregate, 18. *See also* Mean
Aggregate price indices, 390–94
   unweighted, 390–91
   weighted, 392–94
Alpha (α) risk, 190, 201. *See also* Errors
Alternative courses of action, 410
Alternative hypothesis, 190. *See also* Hypothesis testing
Analysis of variance, 243–52
   assumptions–limitations, 252
   decision rule, 251
   decomposition of total variation, 245–47. *See also* Variation
   degrees of freedom, 248–49
   F test, 249–50
   hypotheses, 244
   nonparametric test by ranks, 338
   notation, 244
   regression in, 282–85, 307
   summary of procedure, 251–52
   two-factor, 251–52
Arithmetic mean. *See* Mean
Attribute, 4. *See also* Variable
Average dispersion, 30. *See also* Standard deviation
Average fraction defective, 70, 95
Averages. *See also* Mean; Expected value
   ratio-to-moving average, 374–76
   unweighted, 21
   weighted, 20

Backward induction, 428. *See also* Decision tree analysis
Base period, 393. *See also* Index numbers
Bayesian decision theory, 409. *See also* Decision analysis
Bayes's decision rule, 445
Bayes's formula, 438
Bayes, Thomas, 438

Before-and-after experiment, 218
Bernoulli, James, 94
Bernoulli, process, 94
Bernoulli, trials, 94
Beta (β) risk. *See also* Errors
   calculation, 201–202
   definition, 190
Between-columns variation. *See* Between-treatments variation
Bias, procedural, 123
Bimodal frequency distribution, 32
Binomial distribution, 94–101
   Bernoulli process, 94
   characteristics of, 98
   chi-square test and, 232
   decision analysis and, 442
   finding probabilities, 96–97, 99–100
   formula of, 96
   mean of, 100
   normal approximation to, 150
   parameters of, 98
   table of probabilities, 454–61
   variance and standard deviation of, 101
Bivariate normal distribution, 272
Business cycles, 350

Categorical variable, 4. *See also* Variable
Causal relation (correlation), 313–14
Census:
   definition of, 113
   limitations, 114–16
Central limit theorem (CLT), 135–37
Central tendency, measures of, 16. *See also* Mean; Median; Mode
Chance. *See* Probability
Chance fork, 424
Chi-square distribution, 228–31. *See also* Chi-square tests
   formula, 229
   graph of, 230
   table of values, 469
Chi-square tests, 227–39. *See also* Contingency tests; Goodness-of-fit tests
   definitions, 227
   formulas, 229, 237

(Chi-square tests *continued*)
   general procedure of, 228–31
   limitations, 238–39
   summary, 238
Class frequency distribution, 2. *See also* Frequency distribution
Class intervals, 7–8
   limits of, 7
   midpoint of, 7
   number of, 7
   open-ended, 8
   width of, 7
Classical time series model, 350
Clusters, 116
Cluster sampling, 167
Cochran, William G., 161, 182
Coefficient:
   of correlation (adjusted), 274, 293
   of correlation (unadjusted), 273, 293
   of determination, 274
   of multiple correlation, 304
   of multiple determination, 304
   of relative variation, 38
Collectively exhaustive:
   acts, 410, 424
   elements of a sample space, 45
   events, 45, 411, 424
Combinations, 78
   Compared to permutations, 80
Comparative experiments, 209
Complement of an event, 48
Composite hypothesis, 201
Composite index numbers, 389
Compound event, 48
Computer printouts:
   of multiple regression, 315
   of simple aggression, 292, 295
   of step-wise regression, 316–17
Conditional standard deviation, 269. *See also* Standard deviation
Confidence intervals:
   conditional mean, 286
   definition, 155, 159, 178
   difference of two means, 211
   interpretation, 158, 178
   mean:
      large samples, 173
      small samples, 177
   proportion:
      nonsymmetrical, 183–85
      symmetrical, 181–83, 468
   upper and lower limits of, 178

Confidence level. *See* Degree of confidence
Consistency, 156
Consumer Price Index (CPI), 399–401
Consumer's risk, 196. *See also* Type I error
Contingency tests or tests of independence, 234–38. *See also* Chi-square tests
   contingency table, 236
   definition, 227, 234
   degree of freedom, 237
   formula, 237
   hypothesis, 235
Continuity correction:
   chi-square tests for, 237
   normal approximation for, 150
Control sample, 213
Correlation, 257. *See also* Coefficient of correlation
   assumptions of, 271–72, 275
   direct or positive, 262
   inverse or negative, 262
   limitations of, 313–14
Correlation coefficient. *See* Coefficient of correlation
Cost of sample information (CSI), 439
Critical values, 192. *See also* Hypothesis testing
Cross-sectional data, 1
Cyclical fluctuation, 350

Decision analysis, 409–45
   decision trees, 423–27. *See also* Decision tree analysis
   expected utility, 416–18
   expected value, 411–12
   expected value of perfect information, (EVPI), 412–16
   prior, posterior, and preposterior analysis, 438–45
   revision of probabilities, 436–38
   rollback method or backward induction, 427–30
   sensitivity analysis, 430
   structure of problem, 409–11
Decision fork, 423. *See also* Decision analysis; Decision tree analysis
Decision maker, 410
Decision parameters, 129
Decision rule, 191. *See also* Hypothesis testing
Decision theory, 411
Decision tree analysis, 422–31
   acts and events, 423–25
   probabilities and payoffs, 425–27
   rollback method, 427–30
   sensitivity analysis, 430
   stochastic decision tree, 431
Decision trees, 422. *See also* Decision analysis; Decision tree analysis

Degree of confidence, 159, 178
   risk levels, 160
Degrees of freedom for:
   contingency tests, 237
   F distribution, 247–49
   goodness-of-fit tests, 233
   regression analysis, 284–85, 307
   student t distribution, 176
Dependent events, 68
Dependent variable, 259. *See also* Variable
Descriptive statistics, xi
Deseasonalized data, 382
Deviation, 34, 264
Direct or positive relationship between variables, 262. *See also* Correlation
Discrete probability distributions. *See* Binomial distribution; Poisson distribution; Probability distribution
Disjoint events, 51
Dispersion, measures of, 29. *See also* Interquartile range; Range; Standard deviation
Distance measures of dispersion, 30. *See also* Interquartile range; Range; Standard deviation
Distribution-free statistics, 325
Distributions. *See also* Frequency distribution and under individual listings
   bimodal, 32
   exponential, 32
   frequency, 2
   negatively skewed, 31
   normal, 30, 140
   population, 1, 5
   positively skewed, 31
   rectangular (uniform), 31
   symmetrical, 30
   unimodal, 31
Dummy variables, 308, 310, 312

Efficiency, 157
Elementary event, 48
Elementary unit, 2
Elements of a sample space, 43
Equally likely or equiprobable outcomes, 56
Error probabilities, 190. *See also* Errors
Errors:
   deviations from regression and, 264
   procedural bias and, 123
   random sampling, 123
   tolerable, 159, 468
   Type I, 190
   Type II, 190
Estimation, 170–85
   criteria for good estimators, 156–157
   interval estimate, 155. *See also* Confidence intervals
   point estimate, 133
Estimator, 133
   consistent, 156
   efficient, 157
   unbiased, 156
Events:
   collectively exhaustive, 45, 411, 424
   complement, 48
   compound, 48
   dependent, 68
   elementary, 48
   independent, 69
   intersection, 49
   joint, 51
   mutually exclusive, 45, 51, 411, 424
   simultaneous, 63
   successive, 63
   union, 50
Expected net gain of sample information (ENGS), 439
Expected opportunity loss (EOL), 414
Expected utility, 417
Expected value. *See also* Random variable; Probability distribution
   certainty under (EVC), 414
   compared to mean, 88
   as a decision criterion, 411–12
   definition of, 88
   posterior, 443
   preposterior, 445
   prior, 443
   sample mean of, 130
   sample proportion of, 131
   sample variance of, 156
   uncertainty under, 415
Expected value of perfect information (EVPI), 412, 415
Expected value under certainty (EVC), 414
Expected value of sample information (EVSI), 439
Experimental sample, 213
Explained variation:
   in analysis of variance, 247, 249
   in regression analysis, 275
Exponential:
   deriving equation, 361–65
   frequency distribution, 32
   function, 364
   trend curve, 353–54

Factorials, 76, 96
F distribution, 247–51
   degrees of freedom, 247–49
   graph of, 250
   table of F test, 249
   table of values, 470
Fisher, R. A., 250
Fluctuating components, 352
Finite population, 3
Finite population correction (fpc), 163
Fitting a line, 262. *See also* Least squares method; Regression analysis; Trend fitting
Forecasting. *See* Time series analysis
Fractiles, 34
Frame, 116. *See also* Population (universe)
Frequency curve:
   construction of, 10
   ogive, 33. *See also* Distributions
Frequency distributions. *See also* Distributions
   absolute, 11
   construction of, 5–7
   cumulative, 12
   definition of, 2
   graphic presentation of, 9–11
   population, 6
   relative, 11
   sample, 119
Frequency per unit width, 8. *See also* Class intervals
Frequency polygon, 9
F statistic, 247. *See also* F distribution; Analysis of variance
F test. *See* Analysis of variance

Galton, Sir Francis, 257
Game theory, 411
Gompertz curve, 353
Goodness-of-fit tests, 231–34. *See also* Chi-square tests
   definition, 227, 231
   degrees of freedom, 233
   determination of expected frequencies, 232
   formula, 229
   hypotheses, 234
   size of frequencies, 232
Gossett, W. S., 176
Growth curves, 353–54

Histogram, 9
Homoscedasticity, 269. *See also* Regression analysis
Hyperplane, 303. *See also* Multiple regression
Hypotheses, 189. *See also* Hypothesis testing
Hypothesis testing, 189–221

   basic concepts, 190–91
   definition of, 189
   lower- and upper-tailed procedures, 195–97
   summary, 199–201
   two-sided procedure, 191–95
   using confidence intervals, 192–93, 197
   using t statistic, 200, 213–14, 220–21, 281

Independence:
   multiplication law and, 69
   relevant to regression, 269
   sampling with replacement, 46
   testing for, 227, 234
Independent variable, 259. *See also* Variable
Index numbers, 389–404. *See also* Aggregate price indices; Consumer Price Index; Price relatives indices; Quantity indices
   definitions, 389
   limitations of, 391, 393–94, 396, 399–401
   quantity weights:
      base period, 393
      current period, 393
      fixed, 394
   summarizing points, 404
   value weights, 397
Index time series, 352
Inferential statistics, xi, 113. *See also* Hypothesis testing; Confidence intervals
Infinite population, 3, 114
Inflection point, 353
Intercept, 262
Interquartile range, 33
Intersection of two events, 49
Interval estimate. *See* Confidence intervals
Inverse or negative relationship between variables, 262. *See also* Correlation
Irregular movements, 352

Joint events, 51
Joint probability, 63, 437
   independence and, 71
   multiplication law and, 66
   table of, 64
Judgmental probability. *See* subjective probability

Kruskal, W. H., 338
Kruskal-Wallis test, 338–41

Laspeyres price index, 393, 397
Least squares method, 264–68. *See also* Time series analysis
   calculations of, 266
   desirable features of, 267

(Least squares method *continued*)
   determining regression equation, 266
   fitting a trend:
      exponential, 363–64
      linear, 355–57
      parabolic, 359–60
Level of significance, 194. *See also* Errors
Logarithmic trend, 363
Logistic curve, 353
Lower limit. *See* Confidence intervals
Lower-tailed test, 196

Marginal probability, 63. *See also* probability
Mathematical expectation, 88. *See also* Expected value
Matched samples, 217–21
   compared to independent samples, 221
   matched observations, 218
   matched pairs, 218
   testing procedure, 218–21
Mean, 17–21, 120. *See also* Expected value
   definition of, 17
   grouped data, 19–20
   parameter, 19–20, 128
   properties of, 24–25
   sample, 120
   symbolism, 18
   ungrouped data, 17–19
   unweighted, 21
   weighted, 20
Mean square, 248. *See also* Analysis of variance
Median, 21–22
   calculation of, 21–22
   characteristic of, 21
   compared to mean, 24
   used to calculate seasonal indices, 377
Midpoint value, 8, 19–20
Mode:
   calculation of, 23
   characteristics of, 23
   compared to mean, 26
Moving averages. *See* Ratio-to-moving average method
Multicollinearity, 305
Multiple-(sequential) decision problem, 423
Multiple regression analysis, 297–318
   beta coefficients, 302
   calculation of equation, 298, 301
   coefficient of correlation, 304
   coefficient of determination, 304
   confidence intervals, 307–308
   dummy variables, 308, 310, 312
   equations, 297, 302
   F test, 307
   hyperplane, 303
   multiple regression computer printout, 315
   net regression coefficients, 301–302
   prediction intervals, 307–308, 311
   scatter diagram, 298
   standard error of estimate, 303
   standard error of net regression coefficient, 305
   stepwise regression computer printout, 316–17
   t tests, 306
Multiplication principle, 75. *See also* Combinations; Permutations
Multiplication rule, 66
Multiplicative model, 350
Mutually exclusive:
   acts, 410, 424
   addition rule and, 58
   compared to independent events, 71
   elements of a sample space, 45
   events, 45, 51, 411, 424

(n,c) decision rule, 445
Negative skewed distribution, 31
n-factorial, 96
Nonparametric statistics, 325–45
   advantages and disadvantages of, 325–26
   definition of, 325
Nonsampling bias, 123
Normal curve, 145. *See also* Normal distribution
Normal distribution, 30, 140–51
   approximation to binomial, 150
   approximation to sampling distributions, 148–51
   areas under the normal curve, 142
   characteristics of, 143
   compared to student t distribution, 175–76
   finding areas (probabilities), 146–47
   formula, 140
   parameters of, 140, 143
   standard normal deviate Z, 144–51
   table of areas, 466
   z transformation, 144
Normality assumption:
   regression analysis and, 269
   t distribution and, 175
   testing difference of two means and, 213
Normally distributed, 30, 123, 140, 213, 252, 269. *See also* Normal distribution
Normative approach to action, 418
Null hypothesis, 190. *See also* Hypothesis testing

Objective probability, 54. *See also* Probability

Observed value, 194. *See also* **Hypothesis testing**
Odds, 56
Ogive, 33
One-factor analysis of variance by ranks, 338–41
One-tailed (one-sided) test, 195. *See also* **Hypothesis testing**
   difference between means, 212
   difference between proportions, 216
   lower-tailed vs. upper-tailed, 196
   mean, 195–97
   proportion, 197–99
Operating characteristics or OC curve, 203
Opportunity loss, 414
Optimal decision rule (optimal strategy), 424, 445. *See also* **Decision tree analysis**
Optimal sample designs, 165–68
Outcome, in a random experiment, 43, 45

Paasche price index, 393
Parameter:
   definition of, 16
   compared to statistic, 122
   relation to procedural bias, 123
Parametric statistics, 325. *See also* **Statistics**
Path vs. strategy, 424
Payoff (table), 411
Percentage of moving averages, 376
Percentage of price relatives, 389
Percentile, 34
Permutations, 77
   compared to combinations, 80
Point estimate, 133, 155
Poisson distribution, 103–109
   approximation to binomial, 108–109
   characteristics of, 106
   conditions of Poisson process, 104
   finding probabilities, 106–107
   formula of, 105
   mean of, 106
   parameter of, 105–106
   table of probabilities, 462
Poisson process, 104
Poisson, Simeon Denis, 104
Population (universe), 1–42
   definition of, xi, 1, 5
   elementary units of, 2
   finite, 3
   infinite, 3, 114, 279
   models, 11
   qualitative, 4
   quantitative, 3
   sampling frame, 116
   skewed, 31
Positively skewed distribution, 31
Posterior analysis, 440, 442–43. *See also* **Decision tree analysis**
Posterior probability, 437
Power curve (function), 201–05
   definition of, 202
   controlling Type I and Type II errors, 203–204
   graph of, 202
Power of a test, 203
Precision, of estimate, 134–35
Prediction interval in:
   multiple regression, 307–308, 311. *See also* **Multiple regression analysis; Regression analysis**
   simple regression, 286
Preposterior analysis, 440, 443–45. *See also* **Decision tree analysis**
Price deflation, 367
Price relatives indices, 395–99
   unweighted, 395–96
   weighted, 396–99
Prior analysis, 439, 440–41. *See also* **Decision tree analysis**
Probability:
   characteristics, 55–56
   complementary, 60
   conditional, 63, 65, 437
   joint, 63, 437
   marginal, 63
   objective, 54
   posterior, 437
   prior, 437
   subjective, 55
Probability distribution (of a discrete random variable), 83–91. *See also* **Binomial distribution; Poisson distribution, sampling distributions**
   characteristics of, 87
   definition of, 83
   discrete, 84
   graph of, 85
   standard deviation of, 91
   variance of, 90
Probability rules:
   addition, 58
   multiplication, 66
Probability sample, 118
Probability trees compared to decision trees, 424
Procedural bias, 123
Producer's risk, 196
Proportion:

definition of, 16, 122
parameter, 3, 16
statistic, 3, 122
Qualitative population, 4. *See also* Population (universe)
Quantitative population, 3. *See also* Population (universe)
Quantity indices, 389, 401
Quartiles, 33–34

Random digits, table of, 453
Random error. *See* Random sampling error
Random experiment, 44
Random process, 94–95, 104
Random samples. *See also* Sampling
  cluster, 167
  independent, 210
  matched, 217-18
  simple, 117-18
  stratified, 167
  systematic, 172
Random sampling error:
  definition of, 123
  compared to procedural bias, 123
  illustration of, 119–20
Random selection, 117
Random variable. *See also* Expected value
  continuous, 143, 176, 229, 232, 250
  definition of, 83
  discrete, 87
  expected value of, 88
  probability distribution of a discrete random variable, 83–91
  standard deviation of, 91
  variance of, 90
Range, 33. *See also* Interquartile range
Rank correlation, 324–45
Rank sum test for two independent samples, 327, 331
Ratio-to-moving average method, 374–76
Raw data, 5
Reduction factor, 165
Rectangular (uniform) distribution, 31
Regression analysis, simple, 257–93
  assumptions of, 269
  confidence intervals, 287
  compared to correlation, 271
  curvilinear, 257, 261
  deviations from regression line, 264
  exact estimation intervals, 290
  F test, 282–85
  interpretation of regression equation, 267
  least squares method, 264–68
  limitations of, 313–14
  linear, 257, 261
  multiple, 257. *See also* Multiple regression analysis
  prediction intervals, 286
  scatter diagrams, 260–62
  t test, 281-82
Regression coefficient (slope), 262
Reject vs. accept H_0, 190, 194. *See also* Hypothesis testing
Relative cyclical residuals, 366
Revised probability. *See* Posterior probability
Residuals, 264. *See also* Unexplained variation
Relative frequency distribution, 11. *See also* Frequency distribution
Risk levels. *See* Degree of confidence
Risk vs. uncertainty, 427

Sample design, 155
Sample fraction, 165
Sample outcome, 43, 45
Sample vs. population, xi
Sample selection, 117–18, 171–72
Sample size:
  controlling α and β risks:
    for mean, 203
    for proportion, 204
  estimating mean, 160, 164
  estimating proportion, 162, 164
Sample space, 43, 45
Sample standard deviation, 121. *See also* Standard deviation
  sample outcome, 43, 45
Sampling. *See also* Random samples
  cluster, 167
  random, 117–18
  with replacement, 46, 71
  without replacement, 47, 71
  simple random, 118
  stratified random, 167
  systematic, 171
  systematic random, 172
Sampling bias, 123
Sampling distributions, 127–37
  characteristics of, 131–32
  definition of, 127–28
  difference between two means, 210
  difference between two proportions, 216
  mean of, 130
  normal approximation to, 148–51
  properties of, 132–34
  proportion of, 131
  regression analysis and, 271
Sampling error. *See* Random sampling error

Sampling with replacement, 46
Sampling without replacement, 47
Scatter diagrams, 260–62
Seasonal index. *See also* Time series analysis
   calculation of, 374–78
   forecasting with, 379–81
Seasonal variations, 351
Secular trend, 350. *See also* Time series analysis
Semilogarithmic paper, 362, 364
Sensitivity analysis, 430
Set, 45
Shifting base of index numbers, 401–402
Sigma (σ) for standard deviation, 35
Signed-rank test for matched samples, 332–36
Significance level, 194. *See also* Errors
Significance test, 189. *See also* Hypothesis testing
Significant difference. *See* Statistically significant test result
Simple random sample, 117–18
Simple regression analysis. *See* Regression analysis
Single decision problem, 423
Skewness, 31
Slope of line, 263
Snedecor, George W., 161
Spearman rank correlation coefficient, 342
Splicing index numbers, 403–404
Standard deviation:
   binomial distribution of, 101
   calculation of, 34–37
   conditional, 269
   meaning of, 37
   parameter, 37, 128
   probability distribution, 91
   sample, 121
Standard error of estimate, 131
   difference $\bar{d}$, 220
   difference between two means, 211
   difference between two proportions, 216
   mean, 133
   multiple regression:
      equation, 303
      net regression coefficient, 305
   proportion, 134
   relation to sample size, 135
   simple regression:
      approximate, 269, 286
      exact, 288–89
      regression coefficient, 280
Standard error of the regression coefficient, 280
Standard normal deviate, 144–51. *See also* Normal distribution

Standard normal distribution, 145. *See also* Normal distribution
States of nature or states of the world, 411
Statistical Abstract of the United States, x
Statistical decision theory, xiv, 409. *See also* Decision analysis
Statistical independence. *See* Independence
Statistical inference, xi, 113. *See also* Confidence intervals; Estimation; Hypothesis testing
Statistically dependent events, 68
Statistically independent events, 69
Statistically significant test result, 194. *See also* Hypothesis testing
Statistical population, xi. *See also* Population (universe)
Statistics:
   definition of, x, 120
   importance of, x
   parametric vs. nonparametric, 325
   scope of, xi
Stepwise regression, 316–17
Strata, 167
Strategy, 424. *See also* Decision tree analysis
Stratified random sampling, 167
Student t distribution, 175–77
   compared to normal, 175–76
   degrees of freedom, 176
   estimation with, 177
   hypothesis testing with, 200, 213–14, 220–21, 281
   nature of, 176
   table of values, 467
   t statistic, 175
Subjective probability, 55. *See also* Probability
Summation sign (Σ), 18
Sum of squares, 245
Symmetrical distribution, 30
Systematic influences, 352
Systematic sampling, 171–72. *See also* Random samples; Sampling

Tally, 6
t distribution. *See* Student t distribution
Time series analysis, 349–404. *See also* Index numbers and under individual listings
   classical model, 350
   constructing a seasonal index:
      calculations, 377–78
      ratio-to-moving average method, 374–76
      summary steps, 377–79
   seasonal forecasting, 379–81

(Time series analysis *continued*)
  trend fitting:
    exponential, 363–64
    limitations, 384
    linear, 355–57
    parabolic, 359–60. *See also* Least squares method
  trend projecting:
    calculations, 367
    limitations, 365–68
Time series components, 350
Tolerable error, 159
Total sum of squares, 245
Total variation, 245. *See also* Analysis of variance
Treatments, 243. *See also* Analysis of variance
Tree diagrams, 46, 47, 67
Trend, 350. *See also* Time series analysis
Trial, 44
True population:
  regression equation of, 269, 271
  relevant to procedural bias, 123
t statistic, 175
Two-tailed or two-sided test, 192. *See also* Hypothesis testing
  difference between means, 212
  difference between proportions, 216
  mean, 191–95
  proportion, 197
Type I error, 190. *See also* Errors
Type II error, 190. *See also* Errors

Unbiased estimator, 133, 156, 210, 271
Unbiasedness, 156
Uncertainty, 411, 427
Unexplained variation in:
  analysis of variance, 247, 249
  regression analysis, 275
Unimodal distribution, 31
Union of two events, 50
Universe. *See* Population
Upper limit. *See* Confidence intervals
Upper-tailed test, 196
U.S. Business Statistics, 350
U.S. Survey of Current Business, 350
Utiles, 417
Utility, 416
Utility curve, 417

Value indices, 389
Value weights for index numbers, 397. *See also* Index numbers
Variable:
  categorical, 4
  continuous, 4
  dependent, 259
  discrete, 4
  dummy, 308, 310, 312
  independent, 259
  numerical, 3
  random, 83. *See also* Random variable
Variation. *See also* Analysis of variance
  between treatments, 245–46, 249
  total, 245, 249
  within treatments, 246–47, 249
Variance. *See* Standard deviation

Wallis, W. A., 338
Wilcoxon, Frank, 327
Wilcoxon rank sum tests for two independent samples, 327–31
Wilcoxon signed-rank test for matched samples, 332–36